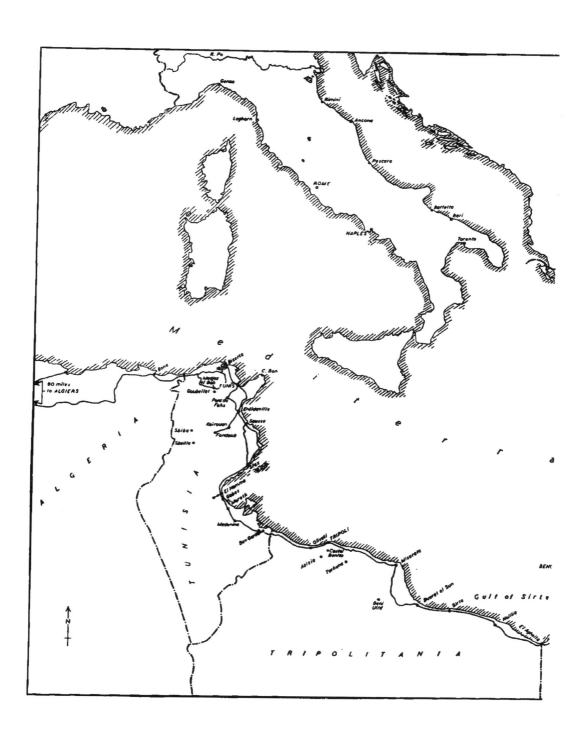

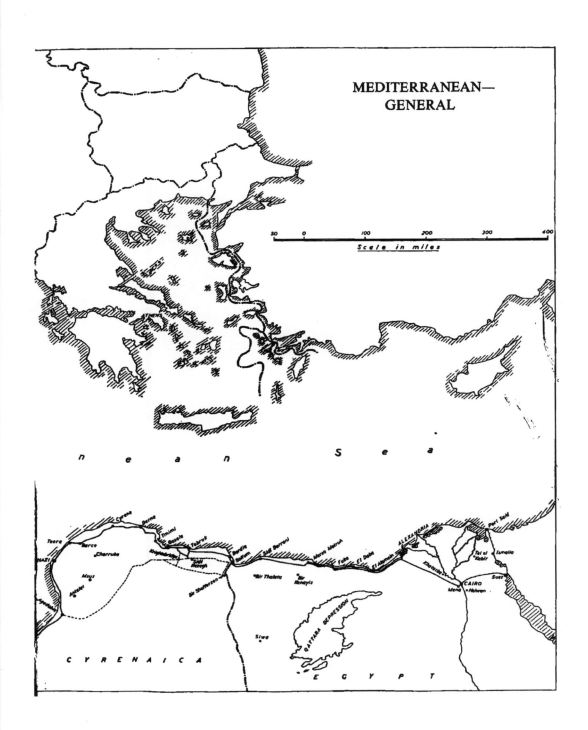

MEDITERRANEAN—
GENERAL

50   0   100   200   300   400
Scale in miles

THE NINTH QUEEN'S ROYAL LANCERS
1936-1945

APPROACH TO ALAMEIN: NIGHT 23rd/24th OCTOBER, 1942

THE NINTH QUEEN'S ROYAL LANCERS

1936—1945

THE STORY OF AN ARMOURED
REGIMENT IN BATTLE

Edited by
Joan Bright, O.B.E.

The Naval & Military Press Ltd

Published by

The Naval & Military Press Ltd

Unit 5 Riverside, Brambleside
Bellbrook Industrial Estate
Uckfield, East Sussex
TN22 1QQ England

Tel: +44 (0)1825 749494

www.naval-military-press.com
www.nmarchive.com

This book is dedicated
to all those gallant members of the Regiment
who have given their lives for our Country
and our Cause.

Our Regiment has held a proud place in
the History of England and of the Army for
more than two hundred years, and this has
been achieved by the unfailing and selfless
courage of all ranks and particularly of
those who have met their death in its
service.

9th QUEEN'S ROYAL LANCERS

"Peninsula," "Punniar,"

"Sobraon,"

"Chillianwallah," "Goojerat,"

"Punjaub," "Delhi, 1857,"

"Lucknow," "Charasiah," "Kabul, 1879,"

"Kandahar, 1880,"

"Afghanistan, 1878-80," "Modder River,"

"Relief of Kimberley," "Paardeberg,"

"South Africa, 1899-1902."

The Great War.—"Mons," "Le Cateau," **"Retreat from Mons,"** **"Marne, 1914," "Aisne, 1914,"** "La Bassée, 1914," **"Messines, 1914,"** "Armentières, 1914," **"Ypres, 1914, '15,"** "Gravenstafel," "St. Julien," "Frezenberg," "Bellewaarde," **"Somme, 1916, '18,"** "Pozières," "Flers-Courcelette," **"Arras, 1917,"** "Scarpe, 1917," **"Cambrai, 1917, '18,"** "St. Quentin," **"Rosières,"** "Avre," "Amiens," "Albert, 1918," "Hindenburg Line," **"Pursuit to Mons,"** "France and Flanders, 1914-18."

CONTENTS

ILLUSTRATIONS

MAPS

This was the basis of the Regimental Christmas Card for 1945 and was drawn by Captain H. A. P. Stephens, 9th Lancers. The initials at the bottom of each volume are those of the Commanding Officer. The book-ends represent the "Rhino," the sign of 1st Armoured Division.

FOREWORD

By General Sir Richard L. McCreery,
K.C.B., K.B.E., D.S.O., M.C.

It is a real pleasure, and indeed a privilege, to write a foreword to the History of the 9th Lancers, 1936-1945.

I had a very long and close friendship with the Regiment in the 2nd Armoured Brigade of the 1st Armoured Division, first whilst I commanded the 2nd Armoured Brigade in 1940, and later in the Middle East, in the Western Desert and throughout the Italian campaign.

No regiment had a longer record of battle service, and there can be no finer tribute to the splendid fighting qualities and *esprit de corps* of the Regiment than the enterprising and dashing part which was played during the last great battle in Italy, in the break through the narrow defile between Lake Comacchio and a vast flooded area when every difficulty of terrain was overcome. This led to the destruction of the German armies south of the River Po. This decisive success was due above all to good junior leadership and training. To have retained this high standard through five and half years of war, and through heavy casualties, is a great tribute to all ranks, but particularly to a succession of good Commanding Officers who were real leaders of men.

The 9th Lancers took part in many other decisive battles, none more so perhaps than the long withdrawal from Knightsbridge, south of Gazala, to El Alamein. Many think that Egypt was saved when the Eighth Army defeated Rommel's last big attack in the Western Desert at the end of August, 1942. Actually, Egypt was saved earlier during those first few critical days of July when Rommel drove his tanks and self-propelled guns and trucks forward along the Ruweisat Ridge in close formations, to be stopped by the 25-pounders and the remnants of the 2nd Armoured Brigade with their "thin-skinned" Crusader tanks. In this critical action the 9th Lancers took the principal part. Throughout that long withdrawal from Knightsbridge, when the fluctuating Battle of Gazala had finally swung against the Eighth Army, past Sollum and Matruh to the Ruweisat Ridge, only seventy miles from Alexandria, the 2nd Armoured Brigade with the 9th Lancers always there but often reduced to only a handful of tanks, fought on skilfully and with gallant endurance and determination. Egypt was then saved indeed and with the arrival of the 9th Australian Division from Syria about the 6th of July, the tide of the whole war was turned.

Many other exploits of the 9th Lancers were more spectacular, such as the famous "left hook" with General Freyberg's New Zealanders, which enabled the Eighth Army to break through the Mareth Line, or the final battle in Italy already mentioned, but none was more decisive than the hard defensive fighting during that summer of 1942.

The morale and fighting spirit of tank crews during those difficult days showed how good well-trained veterans can be. Remember that these veterans were then badly out-tanked by the Germans. Our tanks were drilled and set alight only too easily and we still had only a small proportion of 6-pounder guns to hit back with. To add to the troubles of our tank crews at this time the Crusaders frequently fell by the wayside owing to mechanical faults.

After the front was stabilized on the El Alamein position came a period of three months' intensive training, particularly with the new Sherman tanks which were now arriving in a steady stream, "the gift of President Roosevelt." It is well to recall the enthusiasm and personal interest of the Prime Minister in this new equipment. Every day Mr. Churchill received a telegram telling him how many new tanks and self-propelled guns had passed through ordnance work-shops into the hands of the fighting troops. Inspired by the Prime Minister's dynamic personality and attention to detail, the supply services had never worked harder! Few realize the amount of work necessary on a new tank after a long sea voyage before it is fit for battle.

Right well did the intensive training of the 9th Lancers with the Sherman bear fruit in the great battle which followed. As the world knows, the break-through at El Alamein did not come quickly. Rommel had had two months to build up defences and minefields in depth. However, in the ten days' "dog-fight" tank crews with their new 75-mm. guns were knocking out far more enemy tanks than our infantry appreciated at the time.

During this strenuous, prolonged fighting the veterans of the 2nd Armoured Brigade played a big part, one indeed which was not fully appreciated at the time. The wearing-down process wasted Rommel's armour and conditions for a successful break-out were achieved.

After the Germans were turned out of Africa it was some time before the 9th Lancers were again in the thick of the battle. It is during these prolonged intervals which are part of the make-up of modern war that the commanding officer has one of his most difficult tasks, to keep up enthusiasm and morale. Right well was this done with the Regiment. Italy was no ideal battleground for tanks, but the old Cavalry soldier showed all his traditional resource and enterprise, and the Regiment was right up at the kill in May, 1945.

Many lessons had to be learnt since May-June, 1940, when the Vickers light tank Mark VI-C was still the chief equipment of the Regiment, but the Cavalry spirit was always there.

I was proud to have the Regiment under my command for so long, and I shall recall many friends, and many days of comradeship together, when reading this History.

Richard L. McCreery

PREFACE

I FEEL that the History of the 9th Lancers, covering the period 1936 to 1945, would not be complete without a few words in preface about the fine work which has been done for the Regiment by its Colonel, Major-General Charles Norman, C.B.E. As I was his predecessor as Colonel of the Regiment, I am only too glad to write them.

Charles Norman commanded the Regiment from March, 1936, to October, 1938, with outstanding ability. During this period he had to face the difficult task of changing over from horses to mechanization. The readiness with which the Regiment then carried out its new duties and accepted this unpopular decision was very largely due to the tact and personality of its Commanding Officer.

In 1938 he was promoted colonel and G.S.O.1 at the War Office and in the following year Inspector, Royal Armoured Corps, as brigadier. In 1940 he was appointed to form and command the 1st Armoured Reconnaissance Brigade, consisting of divisional cavalry regiments in France. After operations extending from the River Dendre to Cassel and Bergues, the Brigade was evacuated from the beaches on the 30th and 31st of May. In October, 1941, he received command of the 8th Armoured Division as major-general, but soon after reaching Egypt the Division was broken up and its units distributed as reinforcements to other formations. Charles himself was appointed Major-General, A.F.V., at G.H.Q., M.E.F.

In 1944 he returned home and took over the Aldershot District. Among his predecessors at the Aldershot Headquarters had been such famous 9th Lancers as Sir Hope Grant and Sir David Campbell.

Since his retirement in 1946, having been appointed Colonel of the Regiment in 1940, he has been indefatigable in his work for the Regiment, including the raising of the Memorial Fund and the production of the History.

As a very old 9th Lancer I am proud to pay this tribute to Charles Norman for all that he has done for the Regiment.

Desmond. J. E. Beale-Browne

Brigadier-General.

INTRODUCTION

By Major-General C. W. Norman, C.B.E.

It is with great pride that I set out to write an introduction to this volume. There is a gap to be filled between the first volume, which appropriately ended with the coming of mechanization, and the story of the Second World War. These pages are an attempt to fill it. Also there are things to be said about some of those gallant people who for nearly six years of active service carried on the splendid traditions of the past and set such a wonderful standard for the future, and I shall try—if inadequately—to say them.

However long the 9th Lancers may survive, there was one event during my period of command which can never happen to them again—the change from horse to machine, from a mount which Nature had standardized to one which changes its characteristics almost year by year. This unique event gave back to the Cavalry its place on the battlefield, a place from which it had almost been ousted by the bullet and the shell. Up to 1914 reconnaissance, mobile fire power and shock action had been accepted as its normal and permanent functions. Even during mobilization in August, 1914, the 2nd Cavalry Brigade completed its training with a series of charges on a brigade scale. Real war put an end to these tactics, and the 9th Lancers' only genuine mounted combat was the affair of Moncel on the 7th of September, 1914. Henceforward, in Europe at any rate, horses were to give mobility to fire power only, though in the Middle East more favourable ground and an inferior opponent still gave some opportunities for mounted action.

In the twenties and early thirties we continued to train on the old lines, though all of us who had seen war knew that we were acting in a farce. The armoured vehicle was to give back to us with interest our traditional role, and the 9th Lancers proved in battle after battle that they were masters of mounted warfare, whatever the mount.

When Joseph Kingstone handed over his command he left a very fine regiment. The inspection report of the Major-General in charge of Administration, Southern Command, in April, 1936, ran: "This is a splendidly administered unit. I find it very hard to fault their administration in any way. The discipline is excellent. The physical appearance of all ranks is very good. The men look fit and happy and proud of their Regiment."

The General Officer Commanding-in-Chief added: "I have been full of admiration at the spirit in which the Regiment has accepted its new role, and at the thoroughness with which all ranks have set about the business of mastering it. The Regiment is admirably commanded, administered and trained, and only requires the equipment to which it is entitled to be fit for any task."

Indeed it is true to say that all ranks were highly trained in both mounted and dismounted work and that the officers and non-commissioned officers were well versed in the tactics of the other branches of the Service and in the co-operation of all arms. Such was the material which I had the good fortune to take over when I was appointed to the command in the spring of 1936.

Our armoured training began forthwith and was accompanied by the departure of the horses, of which some were sent away for sale and some were posted to other and still horsed regiments. It was a depressing business, but the new work in hand left us little time for sentiment. We were allowed to retain the officers' chargers and until the autumn about forty of our best troop horses, which enabled us to compete with success in the Tidworth Horse Show and to give a final display in full-dress uniform at the Tattoo. After his final inspection of the horses "Priest" Alexander, the Director of Remounts, wrote a most glowing report, which unfortunately has not been preserved.

I want here to pay a tribute to the loyalty with which all ranks took to their new role and to the enthusiasm which they displayed in learning it. For the younger soldiers it was no hardship: it was an adventure; and they were at the same time equipping themselves for civilian life. But an older dog does not easily learn new tricks, and some of the senior non-commissioned officers naturally found it hard work not only to learn the new techniques but to become instructors in them. They were magnificent, however, and I shall always remember with gratitude their loyal support.

The officers, too, were splendid. They had joined the Army and the Regiment in the expectation of having horses to ride all their service, and this prospect was wiped out at a stroke, although the War Office, as mentioned, let us down gently by allowing chargers to be retained as a temporary measure. I was fortunate in having a few officers who owned aeroplanes as well as animals and had always been interested in mechanical things. The brothers Prior-Palmer were invaluable in this category. All round, a most admirable spirit was shown, and the result was a successful achievement which was fully recognized by our commanders.

Officers, non-commissioned officers and men went off on technical courses to Bovington, and local courses were arranged through the good offices of Lieutenant-Colonel Clifton and the 1st Battalion Royal Tank Corps, our neighbours at Perham Down. Officers of the Royal Tank Corps came to assist at our exercises and give us advice on armoured tactics. We found it difficult entirely to accept the theories about the employment of armoured troops which held sway at this period, since they seemed to us to put too high a value on armour in comparison with the other arms.

Our instincts in these matters proved to be sound, for the experience of the war soon showed that the tank alone cannot perform all the tactical roles and that the co-operation of all arms in the right proportions is as necessary as ever

Major-General C. W. NORMAN, C.B.E.

for success in battle. We also believed that all ranks should continue to be trained in the use of ground weapons and in dismounted action, since there would certainly be periods when, for one reason or another, tank crews would find themselves "unhorsed" and obliged to defend themselves like any other troops. This belief too was borne out by experience. Indeed, the new organization for cavalry was for some time in the melting pot, and at one period our squadrons contained dismountable riflemen borne in tracked carriers as well as the tank troops. At the time we believed this to be a sound organization, provided that the carriers for the riflemen could be armoured, but it did not find favour with the armoured experts of the day. It is interesting to note that at the end of the war the Kangaroo, an armoured infantry carrier, was adapted from a tank and used with great success in close co-operation with armour. Even then, however, there was considerable opposition and it was only through the persistence of another 9th Lancer Commanding Officer, Jack Price, that the "Corps de Chasse" based on this combination was allowed to remain in being under his command with such startling results in the final break-through in Italy. At the time the decision went against the mixed squadron, and a complete tank organization was adopted.

We were first issued with worn-out Carden Lloyd carriers, small, open, weaponless armoured vehicles whose over-heating Ford engines scalded the occupants with super-heated steam from their cooling systems. After every exercise the plain round Tidworth was dotted for miles with our mechanized casualties, which were recovered during the next thirty-six hours by the devoted labours of the Regimental and Ordnance Corps fitters. A special mobile meals service was arranged by the Quartermaster's department to feed the stranded crews.

For the training season of 1937 the Carden Lloyds were replaced by ancient light tanks mainly of the earliest marks, though a small number of Mark V were issued. These actually carried machine guns and wireless sets, and we began to feel that we were getting somewhere. True, the tanks had been returned as unserviceable from Egypt; their turrets still had desert sand upon the floors; the engines, transmission and tracks were in a sad state. The same routine of recovery and feeding of crews after an exercise had therefore to be maintained, but at least they were real tanks.

The early wireless sets, Nos. 1 and 7, gave plenty of scope for the display of humour and the practice of self-control—not always achieved! It was said on one occasion that the tail of the column half a mile away could hear the Commanding Officer over the air but not over the ether! The War Office felt obliged to send out a letter (of which I regret I have no copy) to the effect that civilians were complaining about the language which their receivers were picking up and asking that messages should contain military nouns only, unqualified by superfluous military adjectives. On one happy occasion two civilian gentlemen appeared at our orderly room with their credentials, saying that they were respectively the designer and the manufacturer of the new No. 11 wireless set, and had come to see at first hand the conditions under which the sets would be required to work. Their arrival was perfectly timed, as we were about to start on an exercise, and each was installed with his set in the hold of a Mark V tank. Long before we reached the Avon both gentlemen had emerged bruised, shaken and sea-sick, saying that they had learnt all that was required, and would like to be sent back to the railway station as quickly and as smoothly as possible!

We contrived not to live too hard on these outings. There is a convention (which to some extent is observed in war also) that active operations cease at dusk, and the evening is given to maintenance and refreshment. This we gladly and fully observed. The lorries came up and in the light of their headlamps all ranks enjoyed a properly cooked evening meal. Having carefully observed anti-air precautions by day, we took for granted immunity by night! Our Brigadier, Cecil Heydeman, was often our guest on these occasions and his presence usually resulted in a convivial party which did not disperse to its bivouacs and beds until a late hour. Our civilian mess cook, Pilgrim, deserves a special mention for his efforts on these occasions.

One evening just before dusk, Headquarters, 9th Lancers, happened to be near the civilian airfield at High Post, and Otho Prior-Palmer suggested that he should hire an air-taxi and reconnoitre the enemy's bivouacs. There was some discussion about the morality of this, but I let him go, with good results for our plans for action at first light. These exercises usually ended fairly soon after dawn, and the Regiment assembled for the march home across the plain, stopping for an excellent breakfast in the Hare Field at Netheravon whither the cooks' lorries had already withdrawn to prepare it.

The training season of 1938 was somewhat of an anti-climax. It was considered that the 9th had had their share of the training vehicles which were available and all but a handful of the tanks were withdrawn for the use of other regiments. We therefore had to make do to a great extent with trucks, pretending to be tanks. Apart from this, however, we continued to make progress, especially in wireless. For gunnery there were few facilities and none at all for teaching the larger tank weapons, but we did let off our machine guns, heavy and light, on the field-firing range at Bourne Bottom and on the triangular "run" on the Downs above Warminster.

In the spring of 1938 the 1st Mobile Division, later to become the 1st Armoured Division, was formed, with its headquarters at Andover, under the command of Major-General Alan Brooke, afterwards Chief of the Imperial General Staff. It consisted at first of the 1st Armoured Brigade (the old 1st Cavalry Brigade) at Aldershot, and the 2nd Armoured Brigade (the old 2nd Cavalry Brigade) at Tidworth. The 2nd Armoured Brigade comprised the Queen's Bays, 9th Lancers and 10th Hussars, and remained unchanged throughout the war. The formation of the Division with its other components of artillery, engineers and signals, brought fresh interest as well as new problems to our training.

The following story is perhaps worth telling!

A very agreeable young German officer was attached for some weeks to the 12th Lancers. He was permitted to see such training as was considered good for him, but he was always accompanied by an officer. On one occasion a bridging demonstration had been laid on at a site on the Avon usually employed for such training. It was being run by the Divisional Engineers, who, like the rest of us, were exceedingly short of men and of modern equipment. The morning was wet and, while the Royal Engineers began to "do their stuff" with one or two out-moded pontoons on the sodden banks of the sluggish stream, the spectators stood about in chilled and dripping groups grasping the damp programmes which had been distributed. Altogether, it was a dispiriting spectacle.

Presently the young German arrived, very smart in his grey coat, went up to the Brigadier, clicked heels and saluted smartly. The Brigadier acknowledged his salute and handed him a programme, with the words: "Good morning, old boy; here's a piece of bumph. Damn poor show, I'm afraid; don't tell Adolf!" The German took the paper, clicked heels again and retired without any change of expression.

The young man's letters were, of course, censored, and a few days later he wrote: "Here in Tidworth there are few troops and still less modern material, and I am permitted to see such training as goes on during the week. But on Friday afternoons all ranks disappear. Practically no one is left except myself and the orderly officer, who looks after me. I can only conclude that there is some secret training area where they spend their week-ends doing up-to-date training with the latest equipment."

The season ended with a War Office skeleton exercise in and around Bedford-shire, which coincided with the Munich crisis. It fell rather flat because many of the senior directing staff were retained in London, but as things turned out the war was postponed for another year. Slit trenches were dug round the barracks at Tidworth and other passive defence measures were taken, but rearmament still tarried, and the crisis produced few visible results from the Regiment's point of view.

The man-power problem in the Regular Army at home was always acute during the inter-war period, just as it is today, and when Mr. Hore-Belisha became Secretary of State for War in 1937 he set himself to tackle this problem. One morning I was rung up by Command Headquarters and told that the Commander-in-Chief, Sir "Jock" Burnett-Stuart, would be visiting me shortly and bringing the Secretary of State with him. I was to be prepared to inform him on our man-power difficulties. I quickly assembled the necessary facts and figures—indeed, they were mostly in my head—and before long the visitors arrived. Sir "Jock" came in first and said: "Norman, you can have the Secretary of State to yourself for fifteen minutes. Be kind to him, because he doesn't know anything about the Army and asked me just now if there were eleven divisions in Tidworth. Mind you make his flesh creep." Mr. Hore-Belisha was charming and most sympathetic and promised to do his best, but remarked on leaving that even if satisfactory recruiting could start at once it would take twenty years to put the situation right if one took into consideration the provision of adequate Regular reserves! I thought this was unduly pessimistic, and would have been more than satisfied with a hundred recruits on the spot and a promise that we should not have to find a draft of eighty for India in a few months' time. However, nothing happened.

In October, 1938, the command changed. Christopher Peto took my place and continued with training under much the same conditions. There were, however, two important matters with which he had to deal, the first an act of the Government and the second the result of his own initiative.

In the early summer, Parliament approved conscription for a period of six months' training, and the conscripts, who were called "militiamen," began to join the Regiment. At about the same time a large number of Regular reservists were called up for training. To deal with this situation a special squadron had to be formed, and the regimental training staffs were fully extended in imparting instruction to the newcomers.

The Commanding Officer's private contribution to these preparations for war was the issue of an invitation to several old 9th Lancer officers, some of whom had long left the Regiment, suggesting that they should come to Tidworth and undergo a refresher course. Several agreed to this admirable arrangement which was to put them into touch with the modern Army. Certainly in some cases it was the means of their being given important employment when war broke out for which otherwise they would not have been selected. Among others who came were Majors G. H. Phipps-Hornby and J. F. Colvin, M.C., Captains The Hon. E. R. Joicey, M.C., G. C. Bishop, C. C. Lomax, W. T. Pott, M.C., E. C. Radcliffe and W. G. Gisborne, M.C., and Lieutenant F. Flower. They stayed for varying periods and studied the art of mechanized warfare. In addition, several officers of the Supplementary Reserve joined the Regiment for an attachment.

The spring and summer of 1939, however, were not all work. Tidworth found time for sport as well as for training and the 9th Lancers took their share. Among other achievements they pulled off some notable successes in boxing, winning the Salisbury Plain Area Championship for the fourth year in succession, a record performance. Corporal A. E. Loveless (later promoted sergeant and killed in action) twice reached the final of the Army Championships, and the 9th Lancers' novices were Salisbury Plain Area champions and the only unit to win this cup for two years in succession since its inauguration. At polo, in the Inter-Regimental Tournament, the 9th Lancers were beaten by only one goal by the 10th Hussars, who were the eventual winners of the cup. Altogether, it had been a happy and prosperous year for the Regiment, as had been the previous five years since its arrival in Tidworth in 1933.

By the end of August the Regiment had completed three and a half years of mechanized training and was as fit and ready for war as was possible in the circumstances, the chief limiting factor still being, as always hitherto, lack of modern equipment. Few doubted that it was only a question of time before the explosion would occur and they would be required to put the results of so much preparation to the decisive test. They had not long to wait.

So much, then, for the narrative of events from 1936 until the storm burst. From that date the story will be taken up by others, but this seems an appropriate point at which to record my own great pride at the honour which came to me in August, 1940, in being appointed Colonel of the Regiment, surely the most coveted position which an officer can hold. The names of his predecessors, while they fill him with humility, are at the same time an inspiration and a spur to give of the best that is in him.

As I was a serving soldier and liable at any time to be prevented by circumstances from carrying out my full duties, I asked Brigadier-General Beale-Browne to carry on with the administrative business of the Regimental Association, which he kindly and most efficiently did until I was able to assume it myself. The officers' list was kept by a committee of which Geoff Phipps-Hornby, Geoffrey Bishop and William Pott were the nucleus, and the quality of our war-time officers bears witness to the excellence of their work. I took every opportunity of visiting the Regiment when near enough to do so, and spent some happy hours with them at Warminster in July, 1940, after their return from France, on an exercise in the spring of 1941 and at Ogbourne in the autumn just before they sailed to Egypt. Later I saw them again in the line on the Ruweisat Ridge, training for Alamein at Khatatba, and later in a rest period at Tmimi. I saw them leave Khatatba camp at full strength in their new Shermans for one of the pre-Alamein exercises, an inspiring sight.

Those visits, and others since their return to England in December, 1947, have filled me with pride and admiration. I can assure all 9th Lancers, past and present, that their wonderful heritage still stands as high as it has always stood, and I would ask those who come after to preserve that heritage in the future, remembering the signal from the Army Commander during the darkest days in the desert: "Send up your best team; suggest 9th Lancers."

My next task, and a most pleasant one, is to write a little about some of the people whose courage, energy and devotion brought the 9th Lancers through the next six years with such a record of glorious achievements.

No regiment was ever more fortunate in its war-time commanding officers. Five of them, all Regular 9th Lancers, covered the period from 1938 to 1945. Each was outstanding in his own way and each was awarded the D.S.O.

Chris Peto took over the regular command in October, 1938. His task was to carry on the mechanized training through the last months of so-called peace, to mobilize the Regiment when war came, and to take it to France in May, 1940. He almost alone of the officers had seen active service in the 1914-18 war. His was the responsibility of showing all ranks how to behave under fire, and so much depends upon leadership the first time men go into battle. His calm and fearless example was an inspiration to all, and laid the foundation of the enthusiasm, fortitude and steadiness which the Regiment so consistently displayed throughout the war. He commanded with conspicuous ability in the fantastic operations south of the Somme until a severe wound obliged him to be evacuated. He earned the D.S.O. for his services in France in 1940, though this was not known until Major-General Victor Fortune, Commander of the 51st (Highland) Division, was able to make his recommendations on his return from captivity in Germany. These he backed up by a personal visit to the War Office. Those who did not take part can have little idea of a commanding officer's difficulties during those two years. Many were caused by failure in higher places to foresee more accurately the type of equipment which would be required, to provide it in time, and to settle with less vacillation the organization of the troops who would use it. Luckily for the Regiment, Chris Peto had, and has, an inexhaustible fund of humour and an irrepressible spirit. These, he would be the first to admit, have sometimes got him into trouble, but they were invaluable assets through those years of exasperating trial. He did not come back after his recovery, but was promoted to the command of an armoured brigade. The Regiment owes him a deep debt.

Ronald Macdonell, the Second-in-Command, took over the Regiment when Peto left, and brought it back from France. He commanded from June, 1940, to September, 1942, when he was promoted to colonel and went as second-in-command to an armoured brigade. He alone of the five did not survive the war and the circumstances of his death in action are described later in this book. He too came in for a grim period of frustration in the first year of his command. The campaign in France brought a realization of our need for more armoured troops and vast schemes of expansion were quickly put in hand. The formation of new units means the milking of the old ones, and a heart-breaking process of bleeding began which deprived the Regiment during the next months of many, if not most, of the commanders and instructors which it had been at such pains to train. Commanding a regiment is like the game of snakes and ladders—no sooner do you climb a few painful rungs than you tread on a snake and slide back to the bottom. His letters to me during this period show the anxieties that he went through. But somehow "J. R. M." competed, and it must have been with thankfulness that he got his orders for overseas in the autumn of 1941. Once abroad, the Regiment was due to become the recipient of reinforcements and new equipment rather than a source of supply.

The story of the desert war is told elsewhere. Under "J. R. M.'s" inspired command the Regiment fought with unrivalled tenacity and brilliance, and was the means of saving Egypt on that July evening on the Ruweisat Ridge in 1942. Nothing could shake the patient courage and calm determination which flowed from him to everyone else. He was one of the best-loved 9th Lancers of all time, and I can only repeat here what I wrote about him in *The Times*: "Ronald was a rare combination of soldier and saint. As a subordinate, as an equal, and as a superior, he had the confidence and affection of everyone with whom he came in contact. As a commanding officer he loved his regiment and was loved and trusted by every individual in it.

"He was utterly unselfish and single-minded in the pursuit of what he knew to be right. If he had a fault it was an excessive modesty and dislike of thrusting himself forward. He was a tactician of unerring judgment and an artist in the command of a regimental or brigade group of all arms. In the bad days of the desert retreat in 1942 he was quite unmoved by events, and a tower of strength to everybody. Yet he hated war and most of the things connected with it. In private life he was a charming companion with a shrewdly humorous outlook and unfailing sympathy, patience and good nature.

"Though he is no longer with us, he will not be forgotten. The healthy and happy stream of his influence will flow on in the life of his regiment and in the lives of his friends for many years to come."

He was awarded the D.S.O. for his services in the desert. Later this proved to have been a bar to an earlier D.S.O. which he had won in France in 1940, again on the recommendation of Major-General Victor Fortune. Ronald therefore never knew of his first decoration.

When, in September, 1942, Ronald Macdonell was promoted colonel and went as Second-in-Command to the 23rd Armoured Brigade, the Regiment was fortunate in having Gerald Grosvenor to take his place.

Grosvenor was Adjutant of the Regiment from the 13th of November, 1935, to November, 1938, when he left us to become Adjutant of the Notts Yeomanry and went to Palestine with the Yeomanry Division in the winter of 1939-40. During the next two and a half years he was on the staff of the 7th Armoured Division in the desert campaign of September, 1940, to February, 1941, went to the Staff College at Haifa, and became Brigade Major in turn of the 1st and 22nd Armoured Brigades, returning to the 9th Lancers in August, 1942, as Second-in-Command. On assuming command he carried on Macdonell's tradition and led the Regiment with outstanding ability through the period which began with the Battle of Alamein, included the famous "left hook" to Gabes, and ended with the surrender at Tunis. He received the D.S.O. for his splendid work in the Alamein fighting. He thus commanded in three of the major operations in which the Regiment took part. He was then sent back to England to command and train the 22nd Dragoons and took them to the invasion of Normandy, where he was so grievously wounded that he was never able to return to soldiering.

On Grosvenor's departure the Regiment was fortunate in finding Stanley Perry available. Perry also was a yeomanry adjutant in 1939 and he too went to Palestine with his regiment and the Yeomanry Division, and was on the staff of the 7th Armoured Division in Wavell's campaign of the winter of 1940-41.

He returned to the 9th in June, 1941, to command a squadron and was wounded in the course of the Knightsbridge battle in May, 1942, returning as Second-in-Command in September, 1942, in time for Alamein. In April, 1943, he was lent by the 9th for temporary command of the Lothians and Border Horse, and led them in their memorable attack along the beach and through the sea at Hammamet, which broke the last resistance of the Germans in the Cap Bon Peninsula, and for which he received the D.S.O. He was offered the continuation of this command, but knowing the needs of the 9th he chose rather to return to them as Second-in-Command. On Grosvenor's departure he succeeded to the command, and after a period of inactivity in North Africa took the Regiment to Italy. There in the fighting for the Gothic Line, during the subsequent slog northwards and during the two months of infantry work in January and February, 1945, he maintained the splendid tradition established by his predecessors. He was wounded for the second time in September, 1944, but was able to return to his command in a fortnight. Diphtheria obliged him to go into hospital for a period and finally to return to England in June, 1945, where he received command of the Royal Armoured Corps O.C.T.U. at Bovington.

Jack Price replaced him as fifth and last Commanding Officer of the war period. He had served with the Regiment continuously, succeeding Grosvenor as Adjutant in 1938, and had been with it through the campaign in France. He was a brilliant commander of the Crusader Squadron in the desert, and won his M.C. commanding it in a tank charge at Hagfet El Haiad. The miracle of his survival when his tank was blown up is recorded later.

To him fell the good fortune of playing a leading part in the final victory in Italy for which he too was awarded the D.S.O. In the last weeks he commanded what he named a "Corps de Chasse" of all arms, including the 9th, which was launched through the gaps made by other troops and brought about the final rout and destruction of the enemy. Such a command and such a role are the dream of every cavalry officer and this unique opportunity happily fell to a brilliant leader in command of brilliant troops. The achievements of those final days if ever equalled can never be surpassed, and the fame of the 9th Lancers was spread through the whole British Army in Italy.

Such were our five Commanding Officers of the war—one had been my Second-in-Command, one had been one of my Squadron Leaders, and three had been my Adjutants or acting Adjutants during the strenuous conversion period of 1936, 1937 and 1938. May I be forgiven if in pride in their performances I make the boast borrowed from another trade—"Winners trained by Norman"?

It is difficult within a reasonable space to say all that should be said about individuals, and impossible to include all of those who should be mentioned. For their gallant leadership of squadrons and of echelons the names of Derek Allhusen, David Steel, David Laurie, George Meyrick, Cecil Lomax and Tony Cooke stand out, but this leadership could not have availed without the loyal following of every junior officer, warrant officer, non-commissioned officer and man in the Regiment. The list of honours and awards is the testimony of their work, but much bravery and endurance goes without recorded recognition and is known only to those who bravely endured. The Roll of Honour bears witness to some of these.

All soldiers know the worth of a good Adjutant and this exacting office was admirably filled in turn by Jack Price, Cecil Lomax, Guy Gardner and Francis Pym. The last two each gained the Military Cross while serving as Adjutant, a very rare occurrence. They have earned the warmest thanks of all 9th Lancers for having written the most important portions of this History, as also Miss Joan Bright for editing their work and writing the remainder.

John Reid was an invaluable Signals Officer, a vital post when communications depend upon the efficient operation and maintenance of nearly a hundred wireless sets.

The same can be said of "Jock" Henderson of the Royal Electrical and Mechanical Engineers, who with his Light Aid Detachment did such sterling work in recovering our damaged machines and keeping our host of tanks and wheeled vehicles on the road.

The Regiment was most fortunate in its Quartermasters, Will Tully and Edward Donnley. A quartermaster's work is largely behind the scenes. It does not attract much notice while things go right. Both of these merit the warmest recognition for their unfailing and efficient service. Mention too must be made of the Regimental Sergeant-Majors of the period, Percy Oxley, who was commissioned into the Regiment in 1941, A. Blandford and finally T. Hardwidge. The last served as Regimental Sergeant-Major from 1943 to 1947 and was a tower of strength, resource and reliability. Space forbids the naming of all the sergeant-majors, quartermaster-sergeants, non-commissioned officers and men who made up our splendid team. In an armoured regiment there are no passengers; everyone is a key man, be he tank commander, driver, gunner or wireless operator, or driver with the transport, the lifeline without which none of the others can live. All did their part, all had their share in the achievements of the whole.

Nor must our Medical Officers be forgotten, to whose bravery and devotion so many 9th Lancers owe their lives, particularly Captains J. Dougan, G. Dison and J. W. R. Kemp, who all earned Military Crosses during their service with the Regiment; nor our Chaplains, with their ever-ready spiritual service and material help in matters of welfare.

Apart from those who served mainly with the Regiment itself there is a long list of 9th Lancers who brought honour to the Regiment for their work with other units or in other spheres: Joseph Kingstone, who commanded the Regiment from 1932 to 1936, Christopher Peto, Otho Prior-Palmer, Errol Prior-Palmer and George Todd all commanded brigades, while Wyndham Diggle organized and commanded a brigade named "Digforce" in the Beauman Division, improvised from line-of-communication troops south of the Somme in 1940. Before receiving his brigade command Errol Prior-Palmer was given the task of reorganizing Sandhurst as the Royal Armoured Corps O.C.T.U. and made a brilliant success of this task.

Mention must also be made of Peter Farquhar, who came to the Regiment from the 16th/5th Lancers at a critical time in 1941 when there was an acute shortage of older officers. He did great work as Second-in-Command to Ronald Macdonell, and was severely wounded in the Ruweisat fighting. Later he went to command the 3rd Hussars and won the D.S.O. for his services at El Alamein.

Geoffrey Roberts did outstanding work on the staffs of fighting formations, ending as a brigadier with the appointment of D.A. and Q.M.G. to General Dempsey's army. In the early days in the desert he was taken prisoner with the ill-fated 2nd Armoured Division, but with his brother managed to escape by night and drove in a lorry to safety.

Mike Aird and Archie Little commanded armoured regiments, Wyndham Diggle and Jack Colvin pioneer groups, and Derek Bryant an infantry battalion. Geoff Phipps-Hornby commanded a training regiment and later held a colonel's staff appointment with the British Liberation Army.

Osbert Vesey served throughout the war in the M.S. Branch at the War Office; Rex Benson went out to France in 1939 as liaison officer with the First French Army, and in 1941 was appointed Military Attaché in Washington with the rank of colonel; Tony Cook, John Scott, Fordham Flower and Donald Erskine, after regimental service, filled first-grade staff appointments as lieutenant-colonels, the last spending a year in Australia organizing the training of armoured troops. William Pott and Christopher Beckett did invaluable work as adjutants of training regiments.

George Vere-Laurie ended in command of the Depot of the Military Police in Egypt. Cecil Lomax filled a staff appointment at General Headquarters, Cairo, after excellent work in command of the Regiment's "B" Echelon.

Teddy Pettit was killed in an air crash in India, where he was serving as a lieutenant-colonel.

Tony Phillimore went to France in the early days from the War Office to a staff appointment at General Headquarters, B.E.F., and was killed while gallantly attempting the evacuation of reserve tanks at Arras. He was one of our most grievous losses.

Edward Radcliffe went to France with the Regiment and Geoffrey Bishop commanded the Headquarter Squadron of the 2nd Armoured Brigade, a good effort seeing that he had been permanently lamed by a wound in the 1914-18 war. Both served later as instructors at Sandhurst. Pat Kelly was A.D.C. to General Lumsden when commanding the 1st Armoured Division; and in this capacity he was killed in the desert.

These were the achievements of only some of the 9th. A fuller list is given in the appendix. Surely this is a record of which any regiment could be proud.

Lastly, I come to our Roll of Honour, the list of gallant dead which must be the sad accompaniment of war, however victoriously ended. We must not allow the names of those who died in the service of their country and of their regiment to be forgotten. On their sacrifice was built the memorable success which we others have lived to see achieved. This book is dedicated to them and is a part of their memorial. May their bodies rest in tranquillity, where they lie in France, in Madagascar, in Africa, and in Italy and may their spirits know that peace which this world cannot give.

"Their name liveth for evermore."

Brigadier C. H. M. PETO, D.S.O.

Photo: Vandyk

CHAPTER I

WAR AND BATTLE

At 11 o'clock on the morning of the 3rd of September, 1939, the Commanding Officer, Lieutenant-Colonel Peto, was walking with R.S.M. Oxley across the square of Mooltan Barracks, Tidworth, when they were surprised to see the normally stately figure of the Bandmaster, Mr. Allen, coming towards them at a run. He told them that the Prime Minister, Mr. Neville Chamberlain, had just announced over the wireless that we were at war with Germany.

Hectic weeks followed. Reservists began to arrive in large numbers, some of whom were absorbed into the Regiment, while others were posted elsewhere. The other-rank reservists numbered about six hundred men, and it was a fine sight to see these highly trained cavalry soldiers on parade in the new tank park between the stables and the football ground. Nearly all of these men had gone on the reserve before mechanization had taken place and, as the Regiment was due to go to France, it was decided by those in authority that there would not be time to retrain them in mechanical work. As events turned out, however, there would have been plenty of time, and the fifty or so reservists that the Regiment was allowed to keep soon picked up their duties and became highly proficient.

The rest of the reservists would have been invaluable to the yeomanry—a whole division still being mounted as cavalry units at that time—or even to the infantry. Instead they were sent off to labour in the docks at Southampton and in the French ports. It was sad to say good-bye to them, as, under the command of Major J. C. Colvin, they steamed out of Tidworth station to the strains of "Auld Lang Syne" played by the Regimental Band. It is pleasing to be able to record that eventually many of them were transferred to yeomanry regiments, and that later on in the Middle East the older members of the Regiment frequently met their old comrades-in-arms, most of whom by then were sergeants or warrant officers in new regiments.

A training regiment was formed in Mooltan Barracks—the 53rd Training Regiment, Royal Armoured Corps—and staffed by several officers and non-commissioned officers of the 9th Lancers, while other non-commissioned officers went to the Royal Armoured Corps Depot at Catterick : so when the Regiment left Tidworth it contained a very small proportion of the old and bold, and a high proportion of young and untrained soldiers.

The sequel to mobilization, however, was much less dramatic now than it had been twenty-five years earlier. In August, 1914, the Regiment had marched out of Mooltan Barracks to entrain at Amesbury and go straight to France. This

C

1

war began with a "phoney period," and the 1st Armoured Division was not among the formations selected for early transfer overseas. Instead, during the autumn, to counter a possible invasion of the East Coast, the Division was moved to Suffolk and the surrounding counties.

The Regiment, except for "C" Squadron, which was accommodated near by, was billeted in the village of Clare, and seldom can soldiers have been treated with more kindness than we were by the hospitable inhabitants, who did everything they could to make our stay a pleasant one. We did much good and useful training despite the demands made on us in our operational role.

During the winter the 1st Armoured Division was relieved and moved to a training area round Wimborne, in Dorset, in preparation for the part it was to play with the British Expeditionary Force in France in the spring. We were to go in May and, on arrival there, were due to complete our training near Pacy-sur-Eux, in Normandy. Various changes took place: the 1st Armoured Brigade (the old 1st Cavalry Brigade) was replaced by the 3rd Armoured Brigade (the old Tank Brigade). After the production of cruiser tanks it was decided that armour no longer needed artillery support, and so the 2nd Royal Horse Artillery left the Division to go in support of the 3rd Infantry Division in France. We were to fight with this fine regiment in the Middle East later, when it rejoined the 1st Armoured Division and remained with it for the rest of the war.

In April Brigadier McCreery, late of the 12th Lancers, whom most of the officers knew well from the Tidworth days, took over the Brigade. He had recently been a G.S.O.1 in General Alexander's 1st Division of the B.E.F. and was well qualified to command the Brigade on the next stage of its travels. A few of the new cruiser tanks arrived during the last few weeks we were at Wimborne, but not much else. We were to get the new equipment in France, but, in fact, much of it did not yet exist.

The Regiment remained in camp at Warminster and Tilshead doing squadron training until the 6th of May, when we were told to be ready to move overseas at ten days' notice. We struck camp and returned to Wimborne.

For the next ten days frantic efforts were made to bring the Regiment up to strength in men and equipment. New vehicles and tanks kept arriving, while others were withdrawn or transferred to other units. Stores and equipment were being issued daily, and peace equipment withdrawn from squadrons and returned to the Royal Army Ordnance Corps. About fifty men came in in drafts from various training regiments: they had done very little tank training, few having driven a tank for more than one hour, others not at all. The tasks of the Quartermaster's and Technical Officer's staffs were not made easier by the fact that, for every single item, the peace-time procedure of issue-and-receipt accountancy was supposed to be maintained. This was, of course, quite impossible. Moreover, no G1098 (list of war equipment) had been issued for the Regiment, so no one knew the correct scale. We eventually received all our "B" vehicles, but the tanks—a good proportion of them transfers from other units and in very bad condition—continued to arrive in driblets up to the last moment. A certain number of A9 and A10 cruisers and some close-support tanks were received, but no one in the Regiment had driven or maintained this type before; we hoped we should have a chance to train with them in France.

At this point Major O. L. Prior-Palmer, the Second-in-Command, left us on posting to take command of the second-line regiment of the Northamptonshire Yeomanry. Major J. R. Macdonell became Second-in-Command in his place.

After many changes, definite orders were at last received that vehicles and drivers were to proceed to Southampton by road on the 17th of May, and that the remainder of the Regiment were to move to the same port by rail on the 20th of May. Tanks, machine guns, spare parts, equipment and stores were still arriving, and as there was no time to break bulk they were loaded just as they arrived. Anything which came after the vehicles had left was carried to the port by train with the dismounted party. The picture of "C" Squadron Leader driving down the Southampton road in his private car handing out machine guns, belt boxes and telescopes to his tanks was a grim reminder of our appalling lack of readiness. Before we left, the Regiment had the honour of being inspected by His Majesty The King—a fitting send-off, much appreciated by all ranks.

On the 10th of May, 1940—the day on which the divisional billeting parties set off for France—the Germans attacked Holland, and the French and British forces moved into Belgium. It looked as though the Division would not be able to continue training in France but would be needed for battle almost at once.

The billeting parties arrived in the Arras area on the 15th of May there to await the divisional concentration. The road from Le Havre to Arras had been crowded with French and Belgian refugees, both civilian and military, motoring through at top speed, and French liaison officers, who joined the billeting parties at Arras, told them that the Germans were over the River Meuse at Sedan.

The 1st Armoured Division began to cross the Channel on the 17th of May, and the 9th Lancers sailed from Southampton on the 20th of May. The crossing was uneventful, and the feelings of anxious expectancy among those who were going on active service for the first time were lulled by the singing of soldiers' songs until "Lights Out." In the Quartermaster's department particularly there was a sense of relief—relief that we had at last freed ourselves from the red tape of soldiering in England and that at any rate for a time we could forget the endless stream of Army forms and returns which had been dealt with during the past nine months.

In the meantime the situation in France was deteriorating rapidly. The Germans had pushed on from the Meuse, breaking through the French Seventh Army, and capturing in rapid succession Cambrai, Amiens and, on the 21st of May, Abbeville. By the 24th of May the French and British forces north of the Somme were completely cut off, not only from the rest of the French Army but also from their bases. It was at this point that the withdrawal to Dunkirk began.

The leading elements of the 1st Armoured Division were the only troops to land at Le Havre before that port became unusable. The remainder of the Division was diverted to Cherbourg and landed on the 21st of May at 5 a.m. The 9th Lancers spent the night in Cherbourg, sending as many men and vehicles as possible to harbour in the outskirts because air raids were expected. The next day was spent in maintenance and fitting guns into tanks, and that night two trains left for Pacy-sur-Eux, later proceeding to Blaru, where they joined Captain Scott and the advance party. Soon afterwards the first tank train arrived and was unloaded.

Lieutenant-Colonel Peto was met by Lieutenant-Colonel Charles Keightley, Assistant Adjutant and Quartermaster-General of the 1st Armoured Division, who was able to give information and orders. The Germans were on the Somme with parties south of the river. Brigade Headquarters and the Queen's Bays, at that moment in the Forêt de Lyons, had been ordered to advance and secure a crossing over the Somme. The 9th Lancers were to be prepared at short notice to reinforce the Bays. The orders arrived later on a grubby bit of paper, one paragraph of which read: "Frequencies and code names as for last brigade exercise in Wimborne." Luckily somebody had a copy of the code.

*   *   *   *

At this point it would be well to state briefly the general situation south of the Somme. From Abbeville the German forces had moved north along the coast towards Boulogne, Calais and Dunkirk. Boulogne was occupied on the 23rd; Calais fell on the night of the 26th after a superb resistance which contributed to the miracle of the Dunkirk evacuation. By the 23rd of May the I and II Corps of the B.E.F. had been withdrawn from Belgium and were back on the frontier defences north and east of Lille. To the south of the B.E.F. lay the First French Army under attack from the Germans, while the Belgian Army was being driven back from the Lys Canal. On the 25th the Commander-in-Chief, Lord Gort, had to come to the decision that the Weygand plan for a southerly attack towards Cambrai would have to be abandoned and he ordered the 5th and 50th Divisions (now an independent force under the command of Major-General Franklyn) to join II Corps and fill the widening Belgian gap. The 1st French Army Group withdrew on the 26th to a line behind the Lys Canal west of Lille with the object of forming a bridgehead round Dunkirk. In conjunction with the French and Belgian forces the B.E.F. began to draw in towards the Dunkirk beach-head, where the large and small rescue ships were so soon to make their great contribution. The surrender of the Belgian Army on the 28th brought fresh dangers. The fate of the B.E.F. hung by a thread. But the thread was strong: by magnificent and tenacious fighting the corridor was kept open for the withdrawal, and on the 30th of May G.H.Q. were able to report that all British divisions had come into the Dunkirk perimeter.

Meanwhile, it had become obvious by the 23rd of May that the 1st Armoured Division would not be able to join up with the B.E.F. and its immediate role

FRANCE, 1940

Leaving Southampton

The Regimental Altar

The same tank later in the day

The Commanding Officer and Adjutant (Lieut.-Colonel C. H. M. Peto, in the tank, and Captain K. J. Price)

FRANCE, 1940

Captain G. E. Prior-Palmer during the withdrawal to the Seine

Crossing the Pont de l'Arche over the River Seine on 8th June, 1940. The French sentry is guarding the demolition charge

Lieut.-Colonel
J. R. Macdonell

Some cruiser tanks of "C" Squadron (on the right an A9, the other two A13's)

could only be in support of the French forces south of the River Somme. The commander, Major-General Evans, had on that date received orders to seize and hold the crossings over the Somme between Picquigny and Pont Remy and afterwards to advance northwards to the St. Pol area to come to the rescue of the B.E.F. This was the first of many conflicting and confusing orders. "Unfortunately," he wrote, "the lack of effective communication with G.H.Q. made it physically impossible to put the correct situation to the C.-in-C. and it was morally impossible to hesitate to comply with what I thought to be his orders.

"In view of the urgency of the order I decided not to wait to concentrate the 2nd Armoured Brigade before moving, but to get something forward towards the Somme at once.

"At this point Beauman came forward with a generous offer to lend me one of his L. of C. battalions—which he himself could ill spare. I was able, therefore, to improvise a 'shadow' support group, under the command of my C.R.E. . . ."

The available strength of the 1st Armoured Division at that moment was the 2nd Armoured Brigade, of which two regiments were in process of detraining at Pacy, thirty miles away; the 101st Light Anti-Aircraft and Anti-Tank Regiment, R.A., dispersed to cover certain crossings over the Seine; and one or two units of ancillary services. "It was with this travesty of an armoured division," continued Major-General Evans, "a formation with less than half its proper armoured strength, without any field guns or a proper complement of anti-tank and anti-aircraft guns, without bridging equipment, without infantry, without air support, without the bulk of its ancillary services, and with part of its headquarters in a three-ply wooden 'armoured' command vehicle—that I was ordered to force a crossing over a defended, unfordable river, and afterwards to advance some sixty miles, through four *real* armoured divisions, to the help of the British Expeditionary Force."

* * * *

The narrative which follows can only give an incoherent account of the part played by the 9th Lancers in the confusing events of the last few weeks of the Battle of France. It is difficult enough to follow the despatches of those in command; to give a clear picture of the actions of a regiment is well-nigh impossible.

As far as the 9th Lancers were concerned, the state of "A" Squadron (in theory mounted in cruiser tanks with the new 2-pounder gun) gives a picture of the general state of the armament and equipment of the Regiment. There were only enough tanks at the outset—and before there were any casualties—to mount two of the four troops in the squadron. The squadron's second-in-command, Captain Scott, was mounted in a fine new tank, an A9, which had a powerful 3.7-inch howitzer. Unfortunately, there was not one round of ammunition for this useful weapon. There was plenty of ammunition, however, for the secondary armament—a Vickers machine gun. The method of aiming this machine gun required a telescopic sight, but there was no such sight and, if there had been, it would have been of little use, as there was no hole pierced in the front of the turret into which it could be fitted. This supposedly powerful tank therefore set off to meet the Germans with a rifle as its only effective weapon. Second-Lieutenant Close was mounted in a new light tank, but instead of armoured plating its turret was made of three-ply wood and there was no weapon other than this officer's revolver and rifle.

Lieutenant-Colonel Peto's diary describes the movements of the Regiment during the next two or three days after they had all arrived at Blaru on the 23rd of May:

"Before giving out orders most officers had to find the correct maps which were packed up in their kit, and fit them back on to their map boards. I gave out orders and finished them by saying that the Regiment would be prepared to move in support of the Bays that afternoon. Owing to the guides from the Military Police not meeting the second train which arrived at Breval at about 11 a.m., a considerable amount of time was wasted by 'B' Squadron trying to find their billeting area. Eventually they arrived at 1.30 p.m.

"It was difficult to get the transport loaded correctly for war and ready to move within a few hours; most of the vehicles had been loaded at Wimborne, together with additional spare parts and other Ordnance stores which had arrived at the last moment.

"There was, too, the difficulty of having new tanks, some of which had never been run or even seen before.

"I attended a conference at 2 p.m. at Divisional Headquarters and received orders to move up in the shortest possible time with a view to reinforcing the Bays the next day.

"I agreed to move at 5 o'clock that afternoon, and the 10th Hussars were to follow us an hour later. The move up was much impeded by countless refugees and their vehicles, and also by what appeared to be thousands of French soldiers of the Ninth Army going the wrong way. When I called to them and suggested that they should go the other way, and asked them what was the matter, all they could say, as they hurried along in retreat, was: 'Oh, c'est fini, tout est perdu, et c'est tout la faute de Léon Blum!'"

"At 8 p.m. the Regiment arrived at Gisors, where there was a considerable delay, because the Bois de Gisors was found to be full of French ambulances which were blocking the entrances. During the march into Gisors Lieutenant T. M. P. Tew was accidentally run down and killed by a tank whilst directing it into harbour, a tragic loss of a most promising young officer.

"At about midnight on the 23rd/24th the following signal was received from Major-General Evans:

" 'I am informed by the Commander-in-Chief that a crisis in operations makes it imperative to call upon us all to the utmost endeavour of which we are capable. The result of the war may depend upon the speediness of our action. Consequently you will not halt tonight, but will continue your march to complete concentration of 2nd Armoured Brigade and to engage the enemy tomorrow.' "

At 2 a.m. on the 24th of May the 9th Lancers, followed by the 10th Hussars, left Gisors. All ranks were extremely tired, having spent the previous night in the train and the night before in extreme discomfort at Cherbourg. After what seemed an interminable march in the dark, and without lights, they arrived at Hornoy at 7 a.m. Squadrons took cover in the woods north of Selincourt and Regimental Headquarters was established. Having been out of touch with Brigade Headquarters since arrival in France, Lieutenant-Colonel Peto went off in a scout car to find it, but, in his absence, contact was made and orders came from Brigade Headquarters to refuel at Lincheux. The petrol dump was found with difficulty, and filling up was a long process, as all tanks were practically empty; there were no funnels and the Regiment could not concentrate owing to danger of air attack. At 1.15 p.m. the Colonel returned with fresh orders, and the Regiment moved to take up a position of observation at Forêt d'Ailly and Ferrière. During the morning patrols from the Bays and Brigade Headquarters with a detachment of Borderers had attempted to cross the Somme between Amiens and Ailly, but had found the bridges blown and only one platoon of Borderers succeeded in crossing. They were driven back almost immediately.

"On the afternoon of this day at about half-past five," continues Lieutenant-Colonel Peto in his diary, "we were in the Forêt d'Ailly. There were three patrols out, one towards Amiens under Lieutenant Meyrick, one towards Ailly under Second-Lieutenant Steel, and one watching the far end of the wood under Second-Lieutenant Mostyn. No news had come in from any of them until Sergeant Allen arrived in his tank to say that Steel's troop to which he belonged had been attacked, and that Steel and his tank were in difficulties and under fire at close range.

"I ordered Major Vere-Laurie to collect the rest of 'B' Squadron, which consisted of two weak troops, and go out and get him back if possible. A minute afterwards a message was brought to me that Mostyn's troop had disappeared and could not be found, nor was it in communication on the wireless.

"I was then sent for to Brigade Headquarters in Ferrière to receive orders for the night—the Regiment was to hold the Bois d'Ailly, which would entail not less than four patrols of a troop each being out on the alert all night. As part of the wood was, in my opinion, already in German hands, and as to the best of my knowledge one, if not two, of my patrols had already been captured, but mainly on account of our forced march with no proper rest and having been in action all day, I said that I did not think the wood was a suitable place for my Regiment to stay in that night, and that I could not count on them remaining sufficiently alert to avoid being overrun in a night attack.

"The Brigadier agreed and said that in view of what I had put forward we should withdraw to harbour at Lincheux. I was much relieved.

"He accompanied me back to the wood and was very nearly killed by a shell which synchronized its arrival with his, and did, I think, rub in my argument as to the suitability of that locality as a resting place.

"I found that the Meyrick patrol had come in safely, although it had been shot-up by anti-tank guns. One tank, I think, was holed. Major Vere-Laurie reported that he had not been able to get Steel and feared he was dead. He said he had located the tank with two Germans standing on it. Later we found that this sad news was true. Second-Lieutenant R. O. P. Steel had been killed, and his crew—Trooper Dolton and Lance-Corporal Hipple—captured.

"Here let me quote the account given subsequently by Lieutenant G. Meyrick:

" 'In the late afternoon of the 24th of May 1st Troop, "C" Squadron, was ordered to carry out a patrol to discover if the enemy was holding Amiens, and if so in what strength.

" 'Orders were given out near the water tower in the Forêt d'Ailly, and a short ground reconnaissance was made. About half a mile from the edge of the Forêt we descended into a small valley, and gained cover near a small, square fir wood just under the crest of the ridge, where the troop leader received a message that the Bays had lost a tank by anti-tank fire from a largish wood five hundred yards to our right. After moving three hundred yards north we crossed the ridge and a small sunken road. This was a nasty tank obstacle, as was the railway farther on which ran on an embankment. We were lucky to find a level place in this and then proceeded up a long slope to the crest six hundred yards farther on.

" 'On reaching this second ridge we were fired on from the front (east) and so again turned left (north), where we saw two men running back up a ridge eight hundred yards away. Corporal C. H. Riley opened fire and knocked them over before they reached their anti-tank rifle on the ridge. Rifle fire from this ridge and from some bushes on it was then silenced by machine-gun fire from all three tanks. We went on another two hundred yards from where we could see a large column of enemy lorries approaching Amiens from the north along a straight main road. A bombing attack was in progress on these and shells now began to fall on the north-eastern edge of the Forêt d'Ailly. We then saw about a hundred Germans lying prone on a small ridge on the outskirts of Amiens about six hundred yards from us to the south-east. A good view of the cathedral was obtained and it was intact, although houses quite close to it were in ruins and on fire.

" 'While we were in observation from this point, which was rather exposed, fire was again opened on us from the front and also from the ridge where we had knocked over the two Germans. This fire was returned by all the three tanks.'

"A minute later, Lieutenant Meyrick saw two anti-tank bullets plough up the ground between the two rear tanks and realized that the troop was being fired on from the rear left flank. He now decided to return. On reaching headquarters he found that it was leaving, as the forest was being shelled from a position east of Saveuse and enemy reconnaissance planes were active overhead. Rejoining the squadron, the patrol proceeded back to Lincheux for the night.

"There was still no news of either of the other two patrols. The only available tanks near me consisted of two light tanks and Major Aird's cruiser, apart from my own. I took these and went out to look for Mostyn. After a search I found him and his troop near a tin shed east of the wood.

"Just after giving him orders to go back I saw what I took to be a German tank coming up from the direction of the Somme. On approaching I found that it belonged to the Bays, and was the remains of a troop who had suffered heavily, and who were trying to get back to join their own regiment. I took them under my wing and escorted them back.

"On arriving at Lincheux at about 8 p.m. I found the Regiment already in harbour awaiting the arrival of 'B' Echelon. This arrived just before dark, and we were pleased to find that it had brought a hot meal, tea and a free issue of cigarettes.

"The next morning (the 25th), at about 10 o'clock, the Brigadier came to Lincheux and gave me orders. He informed me that the Forêt d'Ailly and Ferrière were both held by the Germans, who had attacked strongly during the night and had, luckily for the Regiment, found both unheld.

"We spent the day in support of the French on their left flank, which remained stationary throughout the day. The right flank of the French on this front was supposed to be carrying out a powerful counter-attack on the bridgehead at Amiens.

"Two French batteries of howitzers in the rear of my headquarters opened fire on Ferrière village for twenty minutes at about 2 p.m.

"I ordered 'B' Squadron to send a patrol into Ferrière to see whether it was held or not. This patrol under Mostyn went right through and found no Germans. They also found that the French batteries had failed to hit the village —the whole fire effect had gone just beyond it.

"That evening at about 5 o'clock I visited the forward squadrons—'C' on the right and 'B' on the left—and met Mostyn's troop, which had just come in from Ferrière.

"I had a message from the Brigadier that he wanted to know whether Ailly village was still held by the Germans or not. Mostyn's troop was then within three miles of it, so I sent him off, to save time, with orders to reconnoitre the village and the ground overlooking the Somme from the far bank.

"In due course he reported that Ailly was not held, but that he had seen a good deal of activity on the far side of the river which looked as if the enemy were withdrawing.

"On my way round I had given orders for holding our present positions throughout the night, and returned to my headquarters just as it was getting dark.

"On arrival there I found that fresh orders had just come in cancelling the previous ones, and ordering us to move that night through Vidame and Hornoy to Villiers Campsart, which would entail a night march of about thirty miles. Owing to German jamming I did not get orders to the forward squadrons until 9 p.m."

The sudden change of orders came from General Altmeyer, the French general in command of Groupement "A," Seventh Army—later Tenth Army. His new intention was to clear the Germans off the south bank of the Somme from Longpré to the sea as a preliminary to an offensive north of the river.

It was somewhat naturally difficult for General Altmeyer to realize that the English armoured division was not, in fact, the powerful force (incorporating heavy tanks, supporting artillery, infantry, etc.) that he conceived it to be. The 2nd Armoured Brigade was ordered in consequence to move to the area Fresnoy —Oisement—Maisinières to support operations of the 2nd Division Legère Mechanisée, and the 3rd Armoured Brigade, now detraining in the Forêt du Hellet, was to move up on the left to support the 5th Division Legère Mechanisée. Had the formations taking part been at full strength and equipment the plan might have been sound and the role allotted to the 2nd Armoured Brigade reasonable; as it was, the plan was no more than a "projet," an academic scheme which bore little relation to such practical details as the lack of troops, guns and essential equipment.

During the whole of these three days the air was completely dominated by German aircraft, except for a spectacular battle on the 25th, when the Regiment was in its defensive position and six British fighters appeared and engaged a very large number of German bombers.

On the evening of the 26th orders were issued for an attack the next morning against the Abbeville bridgehead. The 2nd Armoured Brigade, which was to be supported by French infantry and artillery, was to capture the escarpment over-looking the River Somme from Bray to Mareuil. The attack was to go in at 5 a.m. with the Bays on the right, the 10th Hussars on the left, and the 9th Lancers in reserve. The intermediate objective was the line Bailleul—Huppy, the latter place known to be strongly held. This attack, against prepared enemy positions, seems in retrospect to have had little chance of success. Apart from the fact that most of the tanks taking part were light tanks, barely bullet-proof, and equipped only with machine guns, there was no tie-up between the 2nd Armoured Brigade and the French troops supporting the attack, nor were even the regimental commanders and squadron leaders enabled to make any sort of reconnaissance.

The attack was timed to start at 5 o'clock on the 27th of May and the 9th Lancers moved forward at 4 a.m. The French artillery was not ready, and the attack was put off until 6 a.m. Eventually it went in without any artillery support at all. As was to be expected, it was a total failure with heavy losses. The Bays on the right suffered badly from well-sited and dug-in German anti-tank guns, while the 10th Hussars fared even worse in their most gallant efforts to capture Huppy. The 9th Lancers were not engaged.

It was fortunate that the Germans lacked temporarily the means to counter-attack, and were holding the Somme mainly with infantry and anti-tank guns. Their main forces were at this time trying to destroy the British and French armies up north, where by now Boulogne had fallen, Calais was cut off, and the Belgian Army and British Expeditionary Force completely encircled.

That evening (the 27th) the Regiment moved into the area Ramburelle (Regimental Headquarters and "B" Squadron) and Biencourt ("A" and "C" Squadrons), where it remained in a temporarily defensive role. The Bays and 10th Hussars were withdrawn to refit. Biencourt was a pleasant country house whose owner had departed. It was a most comfortable billet, and had a double avenue of trees in which the transport could be hidden from the hordes of German aircraft which monopolized the sky.

The next morning the 9th Lancers (as the only portion of the Brigade at the time fit to fight) were placed in support of General de Gaulle, who had arrived and was in command of a French division. This division comprised several battalions of motorized infantry and a battalion (about thirty-five tanks) of "Chars 'B'," heavily armoured French tanks, which mounted a 75-mm. gun, at that time the best tanks on either side. This tank was very similar to the American General Grant with which we were to be partially equipped in the summer of 1942.

Their attack, which was properly staged and supported, had a considerable degree of success, and after two days' fighting they captured the Bailleul—Limeux position, but failed to reach the Somme. From our reserve position north of Hochincourt on the second day of the attack, the 29th of May, we had a grandstand view of the French troops advancing behind artillery concentrations. We afterwards returned to Ramburelle and Biencourt, and some of the officers and non-commissioned officers had a look round the captured German positions at Huppy and Bailleul. We were much impressed by their beautifully laid-out positions, and their guns were well sited, dug in and concealed.

An extract from the Regimental War Diary of this date says: "The Regiment was ordered back to its harbour area at 1500 hours. Lieutenant-Colonel Peto personally conducted a tour of the battlefield." He felt that, as the Regiment had sat in reserve and had had only a few patrols out throughout the day, it would be good for morale if the squadron leaders and some other officers had a closer acquaintance with the scene of action. (The battlefield was over the same ground as that on which the Bays and the 10th Hussars had lost fairly heavily on the 27th of May.) The diary goes on to say: "This nearly ended in disaster twice; first by nearly driving straight into Germany; second, by exposing themselves so much whilst examining Bays' tank casualties as to draw a good-sized shoot from German field guns. Salvage of Bays' and 10th Hussars' tanks was carried out and many of their men were buried."

On the 31st of May a special Brigade Order of the Day was issued by Brigadier R. L. McCreery, over the signature of Captain Sir Douglas Scott, acting Brigade Major, 2nd Armoured Brigade, and later to succeed to the command of the Regiment. It read as follows:

"The Brigade Commander has received the following letter from the G.O.C. 1st Armoured Division. He wishes the contents brought to the notice of all ranks.

'I could not find words yesterday to express what I felt for you over the losses the 2nd Armoured Brigade has sustained. It was so inadequate to say "I am sorry," and it is so hard for us British to say more convincingly. What the Brigade has done is magnificent, and I could not have believed that such endurance and such an uncomplaining acceptance of an impossible task could have been shown. Last evening General Weygand sent an officer to see me to give a personal message to the effect that he attached so much importance to depriving the Germans of the Abbeville bridgehead, that he felt that he must be prepared to pay any price for it; the attempt to cross the Somme previously was represented to me by the C.I.G.S. and the Prime Minister as vital to the B.E.F. I do want you to realize that the sacrifices that your troops have made were not idly called for.

'Believe me, I appreciate to the full what the Brigade has done in the past seven days. From the point of view of endurance alone it is what one would expect of the old Cavalry spirit, and I cannot say more than that.'

"(Signed) D. W. Scott, *Captain,*

"Staff Captain, Acting Brigade Major, 2nd Armoured Brigade."

CHAPTER II

BATTLE AND EVACUATION

ON the 30th of May the 51st (Highland) Division, which had been in the Maginot Line when the Germans invaded Holland, began to arrive. As the 1st Armoured Division was to come under its command, Major-General Evans visited Major-General Fortune and explained that his battle casualties and losses through mechanical wear and tear amounted to sixty-nine cruisers and fifty-one light tanks, a total of one hundred and twenty; and that, apart from these, many tanks, particularly in the 3rd Armoured Brigade, were lacking important equipment such as telescopes, shoulder-pieces, wireless sets and, in some cases, full complement of weapons. Before the regiments could continue operations, therefore, the deficiencies had to be made good. Until they were, the best course was to organize into a composite armoured regiment the remaining "runners" of the 2nd Armoured Brigade. This regiment would consist of Regimental Headquarters and "A" and "C" Squadrons from the 9th Lancers, and "B" Squadrons from the Bays and 10th Hussars, the whole under the command of Lieutenant-Colonel Peto, and would be placed at the disposal of the 51st Division pending a reconstitution of General Evans's forces. General Fortune agreed and further accepted the proposal that he should also have the available troops of the Support Group (Brigadier Morgan) and the Divisional Engineers. Colonel Broomhall, G.S.O.1 of the 1st Armoured Division, remained to advise on the tactical employment of the Armoured Composite Regiment, while General Evans and the remainder of his headquarters proceeded to supervise the reorganization and repair of the bulk of the Division.

On the 1st of June the Composite Regiment was ordered to move to St. Leger-aux-Bois. The squadrons moved off and were all in St. Leger by midnight, where they found "B" Echelon of the Composite Regiment under Major Radcliffe, 9th Lancers, awaiting them with a hot meal.

The next day the Regiment came under the command of the 51st Division as mobile reserve, and was brought up to strength in scout cars and tanks, some of the latter coming from the 3rd Armoured Brigade. Major Vere-Laurie was appointed Liaison Officer, 51st Division, and Captain Wynne took over the adjutancy of the Regiment when Captain Price was evacuated with pleurisy and pneumonia. On the 3rd of June Trooper Tron was accidentally killed by an unidentified French soldier shooting stray dogs.

While we were at St. Leger a French cavalry regiment passed through. This was the 11th Cuirassiers, the nearest French equivalent to our Household

Cavalry. Captain Scott and Lieutenant Allhusen paid them a visit. The squadron leader on whom they called was delighted to see them, and showed them his horses. His own charger had won several steeplechases, and he had four good polo ponies in the ranks. The morale of these cavalrymen was quite different from that of the other French troops we encountered: they had knocked out several tanks with their horse-drawn anti-tank guns, and as befitted the mounted arm they were imbued with a fine fighting spirit. The two 9th Lancers watched them riding off into the dusk and felt thoroughly homesick for the familiar sights and sounds of happier days.

*   *   *   *

The Dunkirk evacuation was completed by the night of the 2nd / 3rd of June. In France on the 4th of June were the 51st Division, the remains of the 1st Armoured Division and "Beauman Force," which, it will be recalled, had been made up from the bases and line-of-communication troops: it was armed mainly with rifles and a very few anti-tank weapons and had neither transport nor signals. The 52nd Division was on its way from England as reinforcement. With the Tenth French Army these meagre forces were trying to hold the line of the Somme.

On the 4th of June the 51st Division, with a French division and French tanks, attacked unsuccessfully the German bridgehead at Abbeville.

On the 5th of June, free to turn the whole of their strength upon the Somme front, the Germans attacked the British positions in force, the beginning of a series of operations which was to end for the 51st Division at St. Valery-en-Caux.

North of the River Bresle, which divides Normandy from Picardy, the 51st Division was soon hard pressed, and the Composite Regiment was ordered up through the Haute Forêt d'Eu. "A" and "C" Squadrons were placed in support of the 153rd Infantry Brigade on the right ("A" at Le Translat and "C" at Tours), while "B" Squadron remained in reserve at Beauchamp on the river. Lieutenant-Colonel Peto and Regimental Headquarters joined Headquarters, 154th Brigade, at Belloy.

Shortly after this the 154th Brigade was forced to give ground and "B" Squadron moved up to block the approaches to Woincourt from the north-east. The Germans were pressing round the Brigade's left flank as well as attacking frontally, and at 5 p.m. "A" Squadron of the Composite Regiment was ordered to the area Le Tréport—Eu to block this German movement. Two miles west of Beauchamp the squadron met serious opposition, for the Germans had already reached the River Bresle. The leading troops came into action with two German armoured cars just east of Eu; both tanks were stopped by anti-tank fire and there were several casualties which included the troop leader, Second-Lieutenant Mostyn. Moving up in support, Lieutenant Allhusen's troop engaged the enemy in buildings at Pont et Marais, but met the same fate at the hands of German tanks. In this engagement Corporal Parker was killed, Lance-Corporal Peters taken prisoner, and Lieutenants Mostyn and Allhusen, Lance-Corporal Taylor and Troopers Hall and Morris were wounded. Captain Scott, second-in-command of "A" Squadron, walked forward and found dismounted Germans moving around north of these two troops. He sent for a scout car and superintended the evacuation of the wounded, seven men being held on the scout car by Sergeant Brown. With the Germans working round to its right, "A" Squadron was ordered to fall back on Beauchamp, delaying the enemy until dark. This operation was most successfully carried out by T.S.M. Pope's troop of light tanks, covered by the Second-in-Command's A9 tank, firing smoke from the 3.7-inch howitzer. (When we first landed in France it will be remembered that there was no ammunition for these guns: some smoke ammunition eventually made its appearance, but we never had any high explosive.) At 9.30 that night the Composite Regiment (less "C" Squadron) was ordered to withdraw south of the River Bresle and harbour in the south edge of the Forêt d'Eu, leaving two troops north of the river to guard the approaches to Beauchamp. "C" Squadron harboured at Point 152 on the north bank of the river, where they were refuelled with difficulty. Colonel Broomhall (G.S.O.1 of the 1st Armoured Division) personally led the petrol lorries to the squadron. This was a wonderful officer who never spared himself, and, all the time, until he was captured, he did all he could to get supplies of petrol to our tanks.

The next morning, the 6th of June, the Composite Regiment recrossed the River Bresle and took up defensive positions to check the German advance, paying particular attention to the left flank along the coast. "B" Squadron was to block the road Eu—Beauchamp, "A" Squadron to move towards St. Quentin via Yzencremer in support of the 8th Argylls. This battalion, commanded by Lieutenant-Colonel Hamish Grant, an old friend of the Regiment, was having a very unpleasant time, being heavily shelled and mortared, and its forward companies were cut off by the Germans. "A" Squadron tried to help by taking on some machine guns which were causing them a lot of casualties.

Meanwhile, at 9.15 a.m. Regimental Headquarters, a mile away at Woincourt, were having an encounter with the enemy. Major Macdonell, Second-in-Command, seeing the head and face of a German popping out of the ground periodically about three hundred yards from Regimental Headquarters, suggested an investigation. Lieutenant-Colonel Peto agreed and led the reconnaissance accompanied by Major Macdonell's tank and two scout cars (Lieutenants Wright and Kingscote). They opened fire on twelve slit trenches full of enemy infantry. After ten minutes the Germans crawled out and surrendered. The "bag" was one officer and forty-three other ranks. We had found it impossible to depress the guns on our tanks sufficiently to bear, and Lieutenant-Colonel Peto, firing from his turret with his pistol, was badly wounded in the right hand. He carried on until the Germans surrendered, and was then evacuated, Major Macdonell assuming command.

Lieutenant-Colonel Peto's departure was a great loss to the Regiment. He had been a splendid commanding officer; he was a very sound and practical soldier and expected and achieved a very high standard of efficiency. He was always calm and, having a keen sense of humour, saw the funny side of the most depressing situation. He had a great insight into human nature, and radiated confidence. Only six officers and men in the Regiment had seen action in the previous war, and he was an ideal commander of a body of men who had never before been in battle.

From the 13th General Hospital at Rouen on the 8th of June he sent a despatch to Brigadier R. L. McCreery, describing the action of the Composite Regiment during the 5th and 6th of June.

It is a strange coincidence that when Lieutenant-Colonel Peto was wounded and lying out in No Man's Land in March, 1918, he was rescued by a corporal of the Queen's Bays: in this action twenty-two years later he was in a Queen's Bays tank driven by a sergeant of the Queen's Bays.

The Germans had by now crossed the river at Pont-et-Marais and Eu. The Composite Regiment was ordered to recross the Bresle to assist the 154th Brigade to hold the bridgehead at Beauchamp, as this brigade needed a tank squadron to call on if necessary. At 10.30 a.m. on the 6th, therefore, "A" Squadron reluctantly withdrew its support from the hard-pressed Argylls, with whom by this time it had established most friendly relations.

There was some dive-bombing that night. There were no casualties, but it was a spectacular attack and the Composite Regiment withdrew into harbour with difficulty. Haute Forêt d'Eu was full of artillery and transport of the 51st Division. "C" Squadron brought in a French naval officer badly burned after his ammunition column had been blown up, who showed great fortitude in bearing his wounds. Besides Lieutenant-Colonel Peto wounded, there were two others that day—Sergeant Edwards and Lance-Corporal Ashfield.

No orders came to the forest the next morning. The Composite Regiment had a long lie-in and a wash and brush-up. The transport withdrew to St. Leger and German reconnaissance planes flew overhead. At midday Colonel Broomhall and Major Vere-Laurie arrived with information and orders. A German advance down the coast from Le Tréport to Eu was threatened. Both places were only lightly held by the 51st Division and the bridges were not completely destroyed. The Composite Regiment must move immediately therefore to Criel and block any movement down the coast. "A" Squadron was sent to take position astride the threatened road. By 2 o'clock on the 7th the move was completed. As the Regiment moved into the woods at St. Martin-le-Gaillard a Messerschmitt was shot down by two Spitfires. The message of congratulation from one pilot to the other was picked up by one of our wireless sets.

In the middle of a bathe in the River Eu, while most of us were stripped, Major Vere-Laurie arrived with fresh orders. Any feelings that the situation on the 51st Divisional front had seemed a bit better that morning were dispelled by

Colonel J. R. MACDONELL, D.S.O.

the news that the Germans had broken through the French lines near Amiens and that German armoured columns had reached the area Poix—Grand Villiers —Formerie and were moving fast south-westwards towards Rouen. The Composite Regiment was ordered to send out patrols and itself to move to Fresnoy ready to protect the right flank of the 51st Division. Accompanied by French liaison agents and consisting of three scout cars each, two patrols went out: one in the area Cuverville—Grandcourt—Foucaiment—St. Leger—Aumale, and the other in the area Cuverville—Fresnoy—Smermesnil—Vatierville— Auvillier. By 6 o'clock that evening their reports began to come in, confirming the news of a break-through at Amiens. It took two hours to relay these reports by W/T because traffic on the group to which the Composite Regiment was netted was very heavy.

There was great congestion on the roads round Fresnoy as the Composite Regiment went into harbour that night in some woods south-west of Bailly. Some troops got lost and came in very late. "B" Echelon arrived and refilled the Regiment. They had been bombed, "A" Squadron ammunition lorry receiving a direct hit which had killed Trooper Duxbury. Taken prisoner that day were Sergeants Teate and L. C. Brain and Lance-Corporal Lewthwaite.

At 5 a.m. on the 8th Brigadier Morgan and Colonel Broomhall arrived with urgent orders. General Evans was at that moment receiving a message, which had taken over four hours to get through to him, from Headquarters, 51st Division, telling him that the Composite Regiment and the Support Group were reverting to his command. He sent a wireless message to Colonel Broomhall, who was with General Fortune, ordering the Composite Regiment to move to the road junction at Point 170 near Vieux Manoir to assist the 3rd Armoured Brigade, and the Support Group to extend the front from the left of the 3rd Armoured Brigade about Serqueux to Neufchatel. Colonel Broomhall, however, had discussed the German break-through with Brigadier Morgan in conference at Headquarters, 51st Division, and had already received General Fortune's permission for the move of the Composite Regiment and the Support Group. It was a lucky coincidence, for it was not until much later that Major Vere-Laurie, bearing General Evans's message, caught up with Colonel Broomhall. Thus ended the Regiment's brief period of service with the ill-fated 51st Division.

Colonel Broomhall's orders were quickly put into effect. The Composite Regiment set off to rejoin the 1st Armoured Division in the area Forêt de Lyons. The line Fleury—Forges—Neufchatel—Dieppe was being occupied by all available troops and the bridges would be blown as soon as ready. It was very necessary, therefore, to get west of that line as soon as possible. The route of the Regiment was by St. Aubin—St. Saens—Buchy to Les Hogues in the Forêt de Lyons. As we drove along we overtook two French cavalry regiments on the march—the same 11th Cuirassiers whom we had previously met at St. Leger-aux-Bois, and the 4th Hussars. It was interesting to see the difference between

D

them: the Cuirassiers were mostly large, heavy men on large, heavy horses, while the Hussars were small men on small, active horses.

At 11 a.m., as we were passing through Buchy, we were overtaken by Colonel Broomhall with further orders telling us to occupy a position in the area of Point 170 west of Buchy, and to stop the German tanks on the line of the railway Pierreval—Estouteville—Critôt. The column was being continually bombed and machine-gunned from the air, and there was much wireless interference. Thus, these orders did not reach "A" and "B" Squadrons until 12.30 p.m., when they arrived at the original destination at Les Hogues. There was therefore some delay, since all tanks were by now short of petrol and a halt had to be made to fill up from a dump which was fortunately found near by.

At 4 p.m. the Regiment was roughly disposed along the line of the main road passing north and south through Point 170, with "C" Squadron on the right and "A" on the left. The story of the next few hours is best told by describing the activities of 3rd Troop, "C" Squadron, commanded by Second-Lieutenant D. E. C. Steel:

"The troop, now reduced by breakdowns to S.S.M. Blandford in a light tank and the troop leader in a cruiser with a 2-pounder gun, was ordered to hold the line of a railway where it cut the Aumale—Rouen road about one mile northeast of Point 170. Up to a hundred enemy tanks had been reported near Aumale *en route* for Rouen.

"Forced to deploy off the road by a large bomb crater just short of the level crossing, the troop took up a position astride the road with the light tank on the left covering the crossing and the cruiser on the right looking across the railway along the road for about a mile to a point where it disappeared into a wood.

"It was a grilling hot afternoon; three hours elapsed during which time two trains and a stream of refugees, mostly in cars, passed by and enemy aircraft buzzed overhead. Then, just after Major Prior-Palmer, the squadron leader, had been up to detail night positions, a burst of machine-gun fire sounded ahead. The squadron leader was seen travelling at speed along the road on his motor-cycle and at the same moment three French artillery lorries came racing past. A few seconds later a man on a white horse galloped out of the wood in the distance, as though the devil was after him, followed closely by the cause of all the excitement.

"Three 'snarlers' crept out of the wood moving along the road towards the level crossing in line ahead. ('Snarlers' was the name given by Major Prior-Palmer to the German heavy tanks in France at that time.) Through field-glasses they appeared as large as the Matilda II, but flatter on top, and they had a red, oblong mark painted on the roof of the turret. Could this really be the enemy at last?

"The cruiser opened fire at the leading tank with the range at 1,200 yards. At the first shot all three tanks came to a standstill on the road. The second shot must have struck the leading tank, for it appeared to topple over into a ditch with a telegraph pole on top of it and never appeared again. The second tank was then engaged while still stationary on the road, with the third behind it, but two more tanks had now come out of the wood and were moving across the open country towards a wood on the right. Fire was already being directed on the cruiser, but so far the shots were falling short.

"The fifth round from the cruiser caused a sudden flash on the side of the second tank and black smoke began to rise from it. The cruiser now found that it was the centre of too much attention and so withdrew by stages across very exposed ground, firing as it went.

"There was no sign of S.S.M. Blandford on the left, but it turned out that early on in the action he had been engaged by fire from infantry who had somehow infiltrated, and soon after he had been fired on by a 'snarler' from the orchard near the level crossing which had forced him back to join 'A' Squadron.

"The cruiser was now busy engaging three enemy tanks which were all stationary in the open and firing—but without much effect. Suddenly, when in full view, the cruiser leapt in the air and stopped dead in its tracks. The crew thought its end had come. Trooper Chaplin (Queen's Bays, attached) was concussed and no longer able to drive. The gunner, Trooper Dyer, was slightly hurt and bruised. The loader-operator, Lance-Corporal Kirk, was unhurt, but the wireless had gone dead, the aerial having been shot away. All orders had now to be shouted by word of mouth. Trooper Dyer, by no means a small man, was somehow pushed into the driver's seat; the engine was started and the tank crawled over the ridge. There Trooper Chaplin received probably the shortest instruction on record for loading the 2-pounder gun, and he loaded it for the first time in his life!

"The cruiser then moved up to the nearest ridge to have a further shoot, but owing to accurate return fire it had to keep on the move. Across the railway smoke was still rising from the second tank, and this was a satisfactory sight. Two enemy tanks which were manœuvring on the right flank were engaged and the crew claimed a hit on one of them as it went out of sight behind cover.

"The cruiser had been hit in one or two places and the tyre on the roller wheel had been shot away, so the troop leader now decided to break off. The tank eventually rejoined the rest of the squadron on the main Rouen road south of Point 170, where it had been waiting for some time. In fact, as the squadron leader had been out of wireless touch with the troop, he had sent two light tanks to try to bring the cruiser in, as orders to withdraw had been received.

"Thus, the one and only tank in the squadron with a gun worth firing was now in rather a sorry plight, but it carried on valiantly and brought its crew safely across the Seine that night just before the Pont de l'Arche was blown. Altogether it had fired forty-two rounds of 2-pounder and the only regret of the crew was that the other two cruisers of the troop had not been there to do the same."

* * * *

At 4.30 p.m. Brigadier Morgan had issued orders for withdrawal across the

Seine. The Composite Regiment was to pivot on the right flank and withdraw by Martainville—Ponte de l'Arche, and no rallying point was given. As the squadrons moved south, the German tanks attacked the position we had been holding so precariously. The left troop of "A" Squadron, which was at the junction of the railway and the main road, was out of wireless communication. Captain Scott in his tank went back to find it. By this time the German tanks had reached a strip two hundred yards east of the road up which he was travelling and they fired a lot of ammunition at his tank. However, their shots being at that time slow and poking, they were behind each time. They had improved considerably by the time we met them again in the Western Desert.

After a short halt at Martainville at 6 p.m. the Composite Regiment withdrew to Pont de l'Arche: movement was slow with columns of French troops crossing on the main road to Rouen. At Martainville Colonel Broomhall had asked Major Macdonell about the petrol situation. Learning that one tank had petrol for five miles only, he at once said he would go and find some. Unfortunately he drove straight into the arms of the enemy and was taken prisoner.

The bridge at Pont de l'Arche was being prepared for demolition under the control of French and British military police as the Composite Regiment began to cross at 7 p.m. to halt and rally in the forest north of Louviers. "C" Squadron was not yet in, so a guide was left for it. Major Macdonell's tank broke down in the square in Louviers, which was fortunate, as Brigadier McCreery came by in a utility car and was able to give him the position of Brigade Headquarters at St. Didier des Bois. Captain Scott brought in "A" Squadron's lost troop, and "C" Squadron harboured by itself and rejoined the next day. Casualties that day were Lieutenant S. Wright, missing and prisoner of war, and Lance-Corporal Wessel, wounded.

By the morning of the 9th of June the last troops of the 1st Armoured Division had been driven back across the Seine. The 51st Division was penned north of the river with the sea as its only line of retreat. We imagined that a great defensive battle would be fought south of the river, which formed a great natural tank obstacle, but we did not realize that our Division, always without guns, infantry or engineers, had been reduced to a handful of tanks, all in need of repair; that there were no effective French troops with us, and no strategic reserves behind us. All that the future could hold was a long, harassed withdrawal southwards, culminating in evacuation. The military commanders were agreed as to the necessity for keeping as much as possible of British armoured strength concentrated for counter-attack; the two essentials were: first, to support the French with every tank that was fit to fight; second, to get every unfit tank away to the back area for repair as quickly as possible.

For the Composite Regiment the 9th of June was a day of rest. The local French commander made various demands that tanks should be used as mobile pillboxes for local defence, but Major Macdonell visited Brigade Headquarters and got permission to move to harbour at Surville. Surville was reached just before dark, the village was put into a state of defence and the men settled down for the night while the inhabitants of Louviers streamed away westward along the main road. On this day Trooper Hutchinson was killed and Corporal Wiggans was wounded.

Early on the 10th Brigadier McCreery arrived with orders. The Germans were across the Seine at St. Pierre du Vauvray and were preparing to cross in the area of Venables, while some British troops were holding positions facing their crossings and the 2nd Armoured Brigade (less the Composite Regiment) was organizing defences along the River Eure on a considerable frontage west of Louviers. The Composite Regiment was to advance at once to the area of Heudebouville. T.S.M. Pope's troop was sent to the 10th Hussars in Louviers to assist in patrolling the river line held by that regiment. This was the last troop left in "A" Squadron, two having been destroyed on the River Bresle and the third, which had become detached at Point 170, not having yet rejoined. Regimental Headquarters and "B" Squadron went to the River Eure and occupied their positions. "C" Squadron at Heudebouville reported that touch had been gained with the British troops there. The Germans had established a bridgehead at St. Pierre but were not advancing and the greatest pressure was coming from the direction of Venables. Major Macdonell, being uncertain of the position towards St. Pierre, began to move up to Heudebouville on the west side of the woods between it and Acquigny, but, after losing "A" Squadron Headquarters (two tracks off on a very steep bank), Regimental Headquarters spent two miserable hours trying to get out of the woods, which had a high boundary wall with no gates or gaps. They at last reached Ingremare and made contact with some French "Dragons Portés" who had been fighting a rearguard action since Sedan. They were only a quarter of their original strength and were about to continue their retreat, but, encouraged by the sight of English tanks manned by cavalry, they delayed their withdrawal by about an hour.

That afternoon German infantry began to filter through our widely spread posts and "C" Squadron had two brisk engagements. Towards evening wireless reception became very bad. "B" Squadron on the River Eure tried repeatedly to tell Regimental Headquarters that a bridge over that river was to be destroyed. The whole message except the name of the bridge was received, including the time—"2000 hours." At precisely this hour a loud explosion was heard and at the same time the voice on the wireless said: "It does not matter—it has gone up."

At 8.15 p.m. Brigadier McCreery arrived. On learning the situation, and in view of the approaching darkness and the certainty of being surrounded that night, he issued orders for withdrawal over the River Eure. This was carried out in a pea-soup fog which made progress back to harbour at Les Mesnil Jourdain very slow. The fog was due to a huge pall of smoke hanging over the burning oil stores of Rouen which a slight wind was dispersing.

At 11.59 p.m. on the 10th of June a wireless message from Brigade, ordering the immediate withdrawal of all tanks except "strong runners," brought to an end the life of the Composite Regiment. All except Regimental Headquarters, one troop of "C" Squadron and one troop of "B" Squadron left at first light on the 11th of June, and went back to the Le Mans area to refit.

The "Composite Party," under Major Macdonell, was ordered to Surville and took up positions astride the main Louviers—Neubourg road, their tanks camouflaged to represent apple trees and straw ricks. We spent the next few hours watching the endless stream of refugees and wondering at what range we would be able to distinguish Germans. By 8.30 p.m. that night the complete rear party (i.e., Composite Party, one squadron of the Bays and Brigade Headquarters) harboured at a château just south of Quatremare. "B" Echelon were having great difficulty in finding us and rations were getting scarce. For some time there had been constant artillery and machine-gun fire from the woods in the direction of Le Mesnil Jourdain, and, realizing how near we were to the firing line, Brigadier McCreery ordered evacuation of the château and a rendezvous at Crestot near the main Elbeuf—Neubourg road. At 8 a.m. on the 12th of June, therefore, the rear party withdrew to rejoin the remainder of the Brigade, now on its way to Le Mans. We passed the 52nd Division moving up towards the enemy and heard that the 1st Canadian Division was also on its way. We felt sorry for them—it was so nearly the end.

On the 13th of June the Regiment moved into two châteaux a few miles from Le Mans, and spent the next day on maintenance, repacking loads and generally recovering from the past busy weeks. Some people even found time to fish in the moat round the château, though without success. The 2nd Armoured Brigade had been formally relieved of its role, and the Composite Party had returned to their respective regiments. For the first time in France we had time to carry out detailed maintenance and, having been at instant readiness for weeks, we were now put at twenty-four hours' notice. Our first reinforcements joined us from the reinforcement camp at Le Mans, and a training programme was even discussed.

At 1 a.m. on the 15th of June the Brigade Major, Captain John Anderson, of the 5th Royal Inniskilling Dragoon Guards, arrived at Regimental Headquarters, his orders "Code word 'Blighty'." General Sir Alan Brooke, who was in command of all British troops still in France, knew that the Battle of France had reached its end and had decided on immediate evacuation. We did not need twenty-four hours' notice: lorries were loaded in double-quick time and the Regiment, less a tank party, marched off at 3.15 a.m., being carried on the "B" Echelon vehicles. At 5 a.m. the remaining tanks, under the command of "C" Squadron leader, moved down to the railway station at Le Nous, where they were loaded on a train of flat trucks destined for Cherbourg. The crews then piled into three-ton lorries and followed the main body to Brest. Nothing more was heard of the tanks or tank train, which fell into German hands.

A protective detachment of three scout cars under Second-Lieutenant Kingscote was sent to report for duty at G.H.Q., and for the next five days they averaged three hundred miles a day on reconnaissances. They embarked from St. Nazaire at 5.30 p.m. on the 17th of June and were under continual attack during the voyage. There were no ships' guns and Lieutenant Kingscote's men (Corporals Chadwick and Hewitt, Lance-Corporal Thomas and Troopers Billett, Parker, Blunt, Woods and Crutchley) did anti-aircraft duty night and day.

The Regiment made slow progress along the congested roads and at 5 p.m. reached a point fifteen miles from Brest. Here the Brigade Staff Captain, Captain Sir Douglas Scott, of the 3rd Hussars, directed us into a wooded area just north of Landerneau. At 10.30 p.m. we moved again into the town of Brest, leaving Lieutenant Greenwood with a party to bring in the transport. Embarkation was very slow in the darkness, as, loaded with personal equipment, arms and ammunition, we climbed in single file up the narrow plank into the *Lady of Man*. The ship was already full, and it was some time before we found a space to lie down on deck.

At first light on the 16th of June we could look around at our fellow-passengers. There were over two thousand of them, not more than half of whom had lifebelts. The Bays were there and the remainder consisted of small detachments of various units, such as R.A.S.C., R.A.O.C., Canadians, R.A.F., etc. The 9th Lancers and the Bays had some rations and, with these and the limited amount of food already on board, a breakfast of sorts was produced and the troops were fed one deck at a time.

It had been intended to sail that morning, but the Germans had mined the harbour entrance and it was 4.30 p.m. before the *Lady of Man* and her companions cast off and steamed slowly out to sea, passing the French minesweepers on their way home. The convoy was unescorted, and once out of harbour it was a case of each ship for herself.

At dawn on the 17th of June we steamed into Plymouth and dropped anchor. There was no one there to meet us at first, but later some ladies arrived and proceeded to prepare a canteen on the docks. The troops expressed approval in no uncertain manner. Orders to disembark resulted in an indescribable muddle; much equipment, including arms and ammunition, was left on board, an omission which was probably due to the fact that most of the troops were stragglers and not formed bodies. The 9th Lancers salvaged what they could and offered to clean up the ship, an offer which was not accepted, as she was under orders to put to sea again at once.

We sat on the docks all day waiting for a train, and the tea and refreshments served by the ladies' canteen were a boon to us all. Eventually at 8 p.m. a train arrived. We left at 9.45 and proceeded on our way to Warminster. All ranks were pleased and surprised to see cheering crowds lining the railway almost without a break as long as it was daylight. We felt like heroes until we remembered that we were part of a defeated army and that our allies in France had that day capitulated to the Germans.

"The experiences of the 1st Armoured Division in France—a formation wholly new to our Army until then—were unfortunate," wrote Major-General R. Evans, its commander. ". . . For five weeks they were continuously in operations which quite obviously offered no prospect of a major tactical success. Day after day they saw a stream of not only destitute refugees but also hale and hearty French soldiers in flight steadily pouring past them. They looked in vain for a sign of a real spirit of offence; for the most part all they saw were feeble attempts at resistance, the abandonment of even such a formidably natural defence as the River Seine; they knew the enemy to be vastly superior on the ground and in the air. In spite of these things, in spite of continuous marching, fighting and repairing vehicles, in spite of fatigue and sleeplessness, all ranks kept their spirit unbroken."

Thus ended the 9th Lancers' part in the Battle of France. It could scarcely have been a glorious one in the circumstances of that inglorious campaign, but this was not the fault of the troops. They displayed throughout the toughness and powers of endurance which have always been the characteristics of British soldiers provided that they have had sound training and are well led. The tragedy was that this magnificent material was so poorly equipped and so ill-supported.

It cannot be too strongly stressed that the 1st Armoured Division was not a division at all. Armoured troops cannot fight effectively by themselves. Artillery, infantry and engineers are a vital adjunct and the co-operation of all arms is essential for success in battle. That the 9th Lancers and their fellow-armoured regiments bore themselves so magnificently in the face of such handicaps against a greatly superior enemy is to their lasting credit.

A tribute to the Composite Regiment by Major-General H. R. Swinburn. C.B., O.B.E., G.S.O.1, 51st (Highland) Division, will be found at Appendix X.

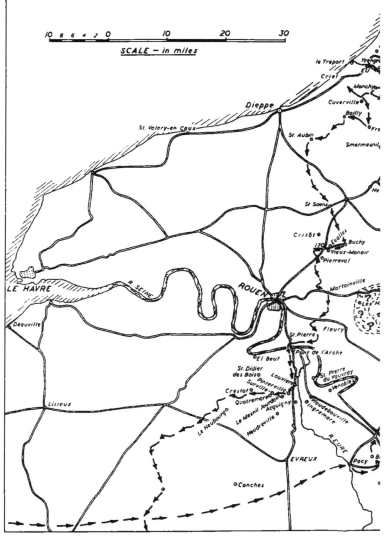

ROUEN—AMIENS AREA

← ROUTE OF 9TH LANCERS

SCALE – in miles

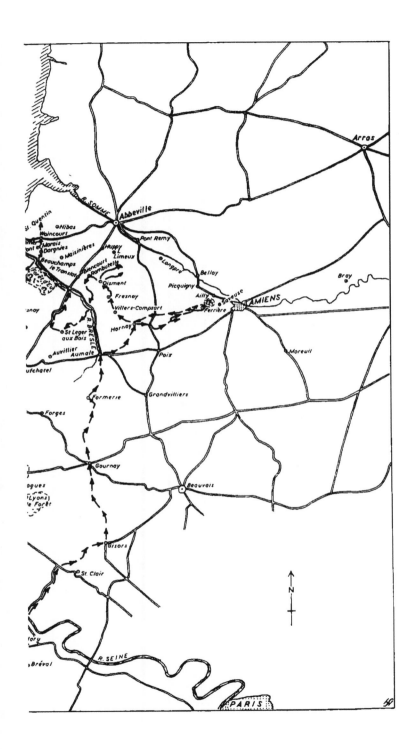

CHAPTER III

HAIL AND FAREWELL

AT first light on the 17th of June we found ourselves in a half-finished camp near Warminster on the Wiltshire Downs and we felt very vulnerable under our new white tents after the weeks of concealment in the woods of France. At roll call there were many absentees; two bus-loads had gone to the wrong camp in the dark, but turned up later in the morning. We set about checking up on the arms, ammunition and equipment, and found that we had brought with us rather more than our establishment of small arms: "A" Squadron, for instance, had thirty-six Bren guns instead of the five to which they were entitled; these were distributed so that each section was armed with a Bren as well as with rifles. A few lorries arrived a fortnight later and, on a dismounted basis, the Regiment was once more ready to fight.

On the 2nd of July Brigadier McCreery addressed all officers and non-commissioned officers of the Brigade on the international and strategic situation resulting from the fall of France, and the next day he held a conference of commanding officers to discuss the training and the immediate role of the Brigade.

In many ways the almost complete lack of equipment was a blessing, because we were able to concentrate on essential basic training and on the training of junior officers and non-commissioned officers. But in those strange days it was difficult to concentrate. In the space of one month we had been in action against a formidable enemy and had seen the collapse of a proud nation. We had sailed from France, one of the last units of a routed British force, and we were back at the beginning again. We had returned to an England which was not the England we had left. It was an England standing alone in the front line. Over our heads great battles were being fought which, though we did not realize it at the time, were delivering our country and making it possible for us to keep our next engagement with the Germans.

In September Major-General Willoughby Norrie succeeded Major-General Evans as Commander, 1st Armoured Division, and the 3rd Armoured Brigade was replaced by the 22nd (Yeomanry) Armoured Brigade.

On the 1st of October the *London Gazette* published the award of a Distinguished Service Order to Second-Lieutenant D. Steel, a Military Cross to Major Scott, and a Distinguished Conduct Medal to S.S.M. Blandford.

A week later the Division moved to the Bordon area and the 9th Lancers were billeted in Headley and Lindford. Here two changes took place: first, in

25

December, a new regiment was raised—the 24th Lancers—under the command of Major M. H. Aird. With him went Major Pettit, Captains Gilroy and Allhusen, Lieutenants Wills, Phillimore, Arbuthnot and Thwaites and sixty-nine other ranks. The other half was manned by the 17th/21st Lancers. The loss of so many officers, warrant officers and senior non-commissioned officers was a heavy drain on the Regiment, and it was fortunate that there were some experienced men to take their place. Secondly, an intake of eighty recruits from civil life came direct to the Regiment instead of going first to the Royal Armoured Corps Depot, but this draft contained some first-class men, many of whom were to do great service in the Middle East and Italy.

On New Year's Eve we read in the *London Gazette* that the following 9th Lancers had been mentioned in despatches for distinguished service in the field between March and June, 1940: Lieutenant-Colonel J. R. Macdonell, Major G. E. Prior-Palmer, Lieutenant S. Wright, Second-Lieutenant The Hon. Roger Mostyn, Sergeants G. R. Brain and P. Sandeman, Corporal W. Gorton, Lance-Corporal G. Mercer, and Troopers J. Snape and W. H. Watkins. In addition to these, the following officers serving elsewhere received mention: Brigadier C. W. Norman (who, in September, had been appointed Colonel of the Regiment in place of Brigadier-General Beale-Browne), and Majors L. W. Diggle, M.C., and J. F. Colvin, M.C.

On the 15th of February, 1941, the Prime Minister, Mr. Winston Churchill, accompanied by various notabilities, among whom were General de Gaulle (now the commander of all the Free French Forces) and General Sikorski (in command of the Polish forces), watched a demonstration of tanks advancing over open country. The Regiment took part with the 10th Hussars, the Queen's Bays and the 1st Battalion The Rifle Brigade. Two-pounder blank ammunition was used and the spectators said afterwards that the advancing tanks were an impressive sight. After the demonstration the tanks were formed up, the crews dismounted and lined the track, and the Prime Minister walked down the line, stopping to talk to officers and men here and there as he passed.

On the 1st of June the 1st Armoured Division had moved to the Marlborough Downs, and the Regiment went into camp at Tidworth Pennings. It was strange to settle down to life as a regiment after squadrons had been separated from each other in billets for so long.

On the 25th of July the Prime Minister talked to all officers of the 1st Armoured Division in the Garrison Theatre at Tidworth, and said he was sorry that once more their tanks had been taken away from them. (The 9th Lancers had had to hand over twelve Mark VI cruisers and these had been sent out East.) The tank strength of the Regiment at the end of July, therefore, was:

Cruisers:

Mark I C.S. (Close Support)	6
Mark IVA	3

Mark V	3
Mark VI	5
Lights:	
Mark VII	17
Mark VIB	11
	45

On the 30th of July Their Majesties The King and Queen paid a visit to the 1st Armoured Division and watched a demonstration. Whilst this visit was in progress the Regiment received orders to send two complete troops of light tanks, Mark VII, to form part of a composite squadron from Brigade. This composite squadron was commanded by Major "Margot" Asquith (Bays), with Captain Palmer (10th Hussars) as second-in-command, and Captain Pulteney and Lieutenants Carlisle and Astles, of the 9th Lancers, went with it. Part of it subsequently took part in the capture of Madagascar,* and then went to Burma. Captain Pulteney and Lieutenant Carlisle rejoined the Regiment at Tripoli in the summer of 1943.

The 1st Armoured Division now comprised the 2nd Armoured Brigade (Bays, 9th Lancers, 10th Hussars and 1st Battalion The Rifle Brigade, re-formed after its decimation at Calais), the 22nd Armoured Brigade and the Support Group (containing Royal Artillery, Royal Engineers, etc.). The 25-pounder regiment with whom we had most to do was the 11th Royal Horse Artillery (H.A.C.), which supported the 2nd Armoured Brigade right through until the end of the war. The confidence and feeling of comradeship which grew up between the Cavalry and the Horse Gunners were very great.

On the 5th of August we were told by the new Divisional Commander, Major-General H. Lumsden, that the 2nd Armoured Brigade would be following the 22nd Armoured Brigade abroad in six weeks' time. He did not say where we would be going, but the popular guess was Egypt. The general went on to say that as there were so few Mark VI cruisers we would be equipped with American M3's and, if we were lucky, one squadron of cruisers. The wind was taken out of our sails. Two days earlier we had received from the 4th County of London Yeomanry a collection of ancient Bren carriers and American M3 light tanks. We had thought they were due for the scrap-heap and had driven them back to the Pennings and parked them in the bushes. It was therefore with very mixed feelings that we backed them out again and began to undo the engine doors and dig into the thick layers of mineral jelly in which the guns were encased. Most troop leaders had at least one of the new Mark VI cruisers and had taken much pride in their low, clean lines, their powered traverse and their 340-h.p. Liberty engines. They had felt that at last they were going to fight in a tank which would do them justice and would enable them to meet the Germans on equal terms. However, it must be owned that we did the M3 (or "Honey" as it came to be

*See Appendix VIII.

known) a great injustice. It was old-fashioned and uncomfortable, the splutter-ings of its rotary engine filled the hearer with apprehension, but the little tank hardly ever broke down and later performed miracles of endurance. Its 37-mm. gun was no worse than the Crusader's 2-pounder, though, by German standards, both were inadequate.

On the 21st and 22nd of August the Regiment moved from Tidworth to a new standing camp at Ogbourne St. George. The Queen's Bays had been billeted in Marlborough town for some time—their tanks were parked all along the wide main street—while the 10th Hussars were in camp at Ogbourne. Our camp was barely finished, and there were heaps of mortar, tubs of whitewash and dumps of builders' materials lying all over the place. The new buildings leaked and there was an over-all air of bleak dreariness. However, there were concrete roads and tank standings and, after the constant drip of rain off the beeches in the Pennings and the candle-lit dampness of bell-tents, it was an improvement to have a roof over our heads and the benefits of electricity and hot showers.

The Brigade was to be fully mobilized by the 15th of September, 1941, approximately three weeks after moving to Ogbourne. Embarkation leave began on the 12th of August; on the 21st of August Divisional Headquarters closed down and the General Officer Commanding and his staff proceeded overseas.

The three weeks were filled with frantic efforts to get war stores, grab our own men who through sickness had been "Y" Listed, get inoculations, attend lec-tures and put the final touches to training. Fitters and crews worked like Trojans to discover the secrets of the Honeys. Signal exercises were held, small arms were zeroed and packed away, while issues of tropical kit matched withdrawals of thick clothing. Tanks and scout cars were sent away for modification, vast quantities of green and yellow paint went on to vast quantities of packing cases and baggage, partridges were shot in the nearby root fields, and a considerable quantity of rather dubious mushrooms were collected from the downs near Old Eagle.

On the 15th of August His Royal Highness The Duke of Gloucester visited the Regiment. He was due to arrive at 12 o'clock, but in fact the Royal party turned up at 11.45. Luckily "A," "B" and "C" Squadrons were already in position and H.Q. Squadron just marching on, so all was well, and the Adjutant, Captain Cecil Lomax, breathed again. After a quick inspection the Duke was invited to examine a Honey. He climbed in and drove himself round the field to the accompaniment of the ear-splitting bangs without which this tank cannot move.

Brigadier Norman arrived for luncheon, and with him Brigadier Joseph Kingstone, back from the Middle East on sick leave, and a strong contingent from the 53rd Training Regiment at Tidworth, among them Major Phipps-Hornby and Captain Pott. The Brigadier inspected the Regiment afterwards, and wished us all good-bye and good luck.

Preparations had by this time reached their peak. Between the 15th and 19th of September we handed in our weird collection of fighting vehicles and had left seven Crusaders and seventeen Honeys: the balance of twenty-eight would reach us at our destination. Of wheeled vehicles we had our full quota and on the whole they were in good shape, though all were deficient in tools. After tremendous efforts we eventually received two lorry-loads of kit and tools from Chilwell which had to be taken as unit baggage.

On the 19th of September the twenty-four tanks and nine Daimler scout cars left by rail for Birkenhead, and on the 22nd the three-tonners went to Hull, while the smaller vehicles went to Glasgow and Birkenhead. After the rush and commotion of the past few weeks a strange quiet stole over the camp. There remained only the medical inspection; this led to too many men being relegated to a lower medical category than the standard required for overseas service. A hasty visit to various training regiments produced sixty-four men, none of whom were even quarter-trained, such was the scarcity of equipment in the British Army at that time. However, it meant that the Regiment would sail at full strength.

On the 23rd of September a long and dirty train pulled out of Marlborough Station. In it was the advance party consisting of two officers from each squadron, the Ordnance Mechanical Engineer, Lieutenant "Jock" Henderson, and his Light Aid Detachment, ninety-two men and all the regimental baggage, with Captain Gardner, of "C" Squadron, in command. After an interminable journey this train ran down the centre of King George V Dock, Clydeside, and fetched up under the towering side of a liner, H.T. *Strathaird*, of 22,200 tons, once the pride of the P. & O. Steamship Company on the fast run to Bombay, now painted a sombre grey and refitted as a troopship. She lay there, making the quiet hissing noise peculiar to ships at rest, whilst throughout the day the freight wagons disgorged great quantities of baggage into the derrick nets and the darkness of her after-holds.

Although the Regiment was only a third of the complement, our advance party was first on the scene, and the best troop decks for the men and the best cabins for the officers and senior non-commissioned officers were successfully appropriated.

Meanwhile, at Ogbourne, final tidying-up was taking place, and, helped by a fleet of lorries from the 53rd Training Regiment, the Regiment entrained and arrived at Glasgow early the next day. The embarkation roll of officers was as follows: T./Lieutenant-Colonel J. R. Macdonell (Commanding Officer); T./Majors Sir P. Farquhar, Bart. (Second-in-Command), Hon. D. C. F. Erskine, K. J. Price and R. S. G. Perry; T./Captains C. C. Lomax (Adjutant), J. R. Greenwood, G. D. Meyrick, E. W. Hylton and R. O. G. Gardner; A./Captains M. S. Close and D. E. C. Steel, D.S.O.; Lieutenants D. A. St. G. Laurie, E. R. Donnley (Transport Officer), R. Merritt (Signal Officer), J. Marden, C. A. Steward (Intelligence Officer), W. T. Cadman, R. N. Kingscote, P. J. Oxley,

M.M., Hon. R. E. Lloyd-Mostyn, D. A. W. Allen and T. Montgomerie; Second-Lieutenants H. B. Hodson (Education Officer), W. G. Peek, H. J. V. Stevenson, D. C. Campbell, C. W. Heycock, I. H. Barber, C. G. A. Beer, B. P. G. Harris, J. W. Reid, A. J. Grant, R. P. Thomas, J. G. Wills, J. L. Walsh, R. C. Okell, T. Jenner-Fust, V. H. White, M. St. J. Wilmoth and J. H. Chadwick; and Captain W. V. Tully (Quartermaster). Attached: Lieutenant J. M. Dougan, R.A.M.C. (Regimental Medical Officer), and Second-Lieutenant G. S. Henderson, R.A.O.C. (Ordnance Mechanical Engineer Officer). It was a coincidence that exactly twenty years before, the 9th had sailed from Southampton for Egypt. The following who now embarked on the *Strathaird* were also present then: Lieutenant-Colonel J. R. Macdonell, Major The Hon. D. C. F. Erskine, Captains C. C. Lomax (Adjutant) and W. V. Tully (Quartermaster), Lieutenant P. J. Oxley, R.S.M. Blandford, T.Q.M.S. Sylvester, S.Q.M.S. Putman and Lance-Corporal Palser.

On board there was plenty of confusion as about 2,400 souls tried to settle themselves in, but by evening everyone had been given a cabin or a hammock on a troop deck and a good meal. We were tied up to the dock with all port-holes and doors closed at dusk, and the heat was overwhelming.

CHAPTER IV

THE CLYDE TO SUEZ

THERE is no greater distinction between the comfort of officers and senior non-commissioned officers and that of other ranks than in a troopship. H.T. *Strathaird* was no exception. The officers had small but clean and comfortable cabins, with running water and fans, and the company's stewards to look after them. They ate in an enormous dining-room, had the use of a small and stuffy smoking-room where Player's cigarettes cost one and sixpence for fifty and Gordon's gin twopence a glass, and for games and reading they had the boat deck.

The men were crowded in troop decks where the white walls and ceilings bristled with pipes and cables and the small port-holes frequently had to be shut to keep out the green seas. They slept in hammocks slung in rows from hooks in the ceiling, and they ate at long tables bolted down to the deck, taking it in turns to fetch the food in containers from the galleys. For exercise and fresh air they had the promenade deck, which was overcrowded, and the wells above the fore- and after-holds.

As each man accustomed himself to his surroundings, discomfort wore off and boredom took its place, and the innumerable fatigues, the washing up, the sweeping and the many guard duties became almost a blessing in disguise. Even so, many a grumbler looked back on that voyage with the nostalgia of remembering what it was like to sleep in peace.

Much to the relief of those on the starboard side who at last got some fresh air, on the afternoon of the 28th of September the ship was warped away from the docks. We drifted down the Clyde—past the yards where the skeletons of merchantmen under construction rose above the jumble of materials, past small towns bathed in the peace of a Sunday evening where all the people turned out to cheer the crowded decks—until, in the setting sun, we dropped anchor in the wide roads opposite Greenock and the ship swung slowly round into its place among a host of others whose grey shapes were just visible. A fresh breeze was blowing off the sea and the ship began to cool down.

The last mail went ashore the next day and the commodore of the convoy came aboard. The *Strathaird* was to be his flagship and, during the next two months a continuous procession of flag signals was going up the halyards, while Aldis lamps winked back from convoy and escort.

After lunch the anchor came up and we spent the afternoon moving in circles round the Firth—"swinging the compass" we were told. At nightfall our ship moved slowly out to the open sea, and a silence came over the crowded decks as the Scottish hills began to fade into the grey dusk. There were many for whom it was the last glimpse of their homeland—those many who now lie under the drifting sand of the Western Desert and beneath the olive trees of Tunisia and Italy.

Our first day at sea was occupied in boat drill and in watching the rest of the convoy. The *Strathaird*, being positioned third in the centre line of seven, was more or less the hub of this particular universe. On either side stretched long lines of merchant ships, ploughing through the green seas, and all round the outside steamed the escort. In all the convoy there were twenty-seven ships: Brigade Headquarters and the Bays were in the *Empire Pride*, and the 10th Hussars in the *City of Paris*. The escort consisted of the cruiser *Devonshire*, a light cruiser, an anti-aircraft ship, the *Argus*, and twelve destroyers. The destroyers kept disappearing into the troughs, while the steadier cruisers and, nearer in, the old *Argus* taking planes to Gibraltar, were pitching away at fantastic angles and appeared to be making very heavy weather indeed.

Our course seemed to be due west. It was changed continually and was in fact a series of zigzags, performed by the whole convoy in response to a signal from the *Strathaird*, repeated by each ship in acknowledgment. There were very few excitements, except for the brief appearance of a large enemy plane, which went back into the clouds on being fired at by a destroyer. Depth charges went off from time to time as escorts fancied there might be something about.

By the 5th of October it was becoming appreciably warmer and the sea was settling down. On the 9th battledress was discarded for drill and shirt-sleeves, and the swimming pool was filled. Permission for men to sleep out on deck at night brought instant relief to those on the overcrowded and unbearably hot troop decks.

Near the Cape Verde Islands the sea became flat and calm and oily-looking. The ship's officers suddenly became very active, and, by evening, a commotion was on. A pack of U-boats lay ahead guarding Freetown, so once more all ranks were ordered to sleep in their clothes (we had to do so on the first four nights of the voyage). We passed the boom without incident at 2 p.m. on the 14th of October, although we heard that the convoy ahead of us had been attacked and scattered, losing two or three ships.

We lay at Freetown until the 19th. No one was allowed ashore, and there was a daily issue of quinine. It was very hot and damp, but a relief to be free from the vibrations of the ship's engines.

Our main amusement was to throw pennies into the water and watch the native boys diving down after them. The practice of wrapping a half-penny in silver paper was much deplored by the natives, who seemed to have acquired a remarkable vocabulary of the simpler English adjectives. There was brisk trade between ship and shore—bananas and coconuts coming up in baskets which were pulled on board by means of a weighted rope. Payment went back in the basket at a rate of exchange of a shilling for twelve, plus "one for the King" thrown in. By the time we left, the market had deteriorated to sixteen for a shilling, because we demanded one for the King, one for the Queen, and one each for the Princesses.

When we left Freetown the escort had dwindled to the cruiser *Devonshire* and four corvettes. During the next few days there was much dashing about, dropping of depth charges and hoisting of black flags, but by the 23rd we were again permitted to leave off our life-jackets and relax. The north-east trade winds were blowing cool breezes which enormously improved sleeping conditions.

Of course, training was going on all the time—Morse learning, Bren-gun instruction, map reading, and, most important of all, lessons in the use of the sun compass for desert navigation, for by now there was no doubt that our destination was the Western Desert.

On the 24th of October the four corvettes turned round and sped back to take over the next convoy out of Freetown, leaving us the *Devonshire* as a guard against surface raiders.

On the 30th the convoy split into two, one half to go to Durban and the other —Brigade Headquarters, the Bays and 9th Lancers—to Capetown. The Commodore decided to push ahead and, after weeks of idling along at ten knots, the ship suddenly stepped up to sixteen or seventeen knots. A satisfactory bow wave appeared, the sea began to fizz and gurgle along the sides and the flying fish jumped more quickly out of the way. We drew ahead of the remainder and by nightfall they were mere smudges on the horizon.

During the next afternoon the great mass of Table Mountain gradually appeared through the mist on the skyline, and a stir of excitement swept through the ship. By 4 p.m. the town itself took shape—a clean town sprawling across the foot of the great mountain of which every detail stood out in the clear air. By 5.30 p.m. the ship had nosed its way round the mole and two tugs pushed her against the jetty. Once again the throb of the engines died away and peace reigned, as everyone crowded against the rails to examine this new world. Probably the thing which struck most of us was the incredible cleanliness of everything: even the docks made of brown stone were spotless, while on the quays were brand-new and shining American cars, newer than any we had seen for years in England. The South African girls, in their neat khaki-drill uniforms, looked wonderful to eyes accustomed to the stretching sea.

In the evening we were allowed ashore into a town brilliantly lit, a town which welcomed every single one of us with open arms. Never has such hospitality been shown before as that which greeted us in South Africa. It seemed that everyone who owned a car was there at the dock gates ready to take us into their homes, to show us the town and the surrounding countryside. The next three days were complete joy after so long at sea. After the Brigade, less the 10th Hussars, had marched through Capetown and the General Officer Commanding Capetown had taken the salute, we fell out, had a bath, and spent

E

the afternoon at the races. Our stay in that hospitable place was all too short, but many men left firm friends behind them and resolved to return to South Africa after the war.

Greatly refreshed, we prepared ourselves for more weeks of boredom and heat. The convoy formed up, and on the 4th of November we sailed up the east coast of Africa. On the 7th we heard that our ship was to call at Durban for mails, and hopes rose high, but when anchor was dropped in the outer harbour we were told that no one could go ashore. Many of our former convoy friends were there, and when we later compared notes with the 10th Hussars it appeared that much the same welcome had greeted them, and in fact to this day the question of who had the best time has never been settled.

Having picked up hundreds of mailbags the *Strathaird* bolted out and joined the other ships which were waiting for us with steam up. We could see coming up on the horizon the ships of our own half of the convoy from Capetown. As the sun set we all joined up and began the long journey up the coast. The battle cruiser *Repulse* was the sole escort.

The 9th Lancers and the Rifle Brigade held a sports meeting on the 12th of November, and on that same day Captain C. C. Lomax was promoted to major in command of H.Q. Squadron, Captain R. O. G. Gardner was appointed Adjutant, and Lieutenants D. A. St. G. Laurie and R. N. Kingscote promoted captains.

The next day the *Repulse* handed over to the *Revenge* and said good-bye, steaming up and down the lines of ships. As she passed, each ship's flag was dipped in salute to the White Ensign and those on board gave her three cheers. She left at once for Eastern waters, where she was so soon to be sunk.

On the 19th the Commodore learned that a Vichy submarine had escaped from Jibuti, so the tiresome business of zigzagging began all over again.

We arrived at Aden in the early morning of the 20th and tied up at the oiling wharf between the *Empire Pride* and the cruiser *Cornwall*. A more depressing spot than Aden would be hard to find—not one blade of green to be seen, just great slabs of deep-brown, sun-scorched rock over which countless buzzards wheeled interminably. The news that we had to remain there for a few days because Suez was too full to take our convoy was not very welcome.

Lieutenant-Colonel Tom Draffen, Queen's Bays, came aboard and brought the good news of the Eighth Army's offensive in Libya. The Bays' ship was leaving that afternoon, so our Second-in-Command, Major Sir Peter Farquhar, transferred himself and baggage to the *Empire Pride* with the good idea of going on ahead and making preparations for our landing. This almost resulted in his being thrown off by "O.C. Troops," an elderly officer lacking imagination, but it was still a good idea and his presence ahead of us was worth a great deal later.

On the 21st of November we left the oiling station and the harbour to anchor out in the bay. There was a strong ebb tide at the time and the ship bore down rapidly on a small sloop of the Royal Indian Navy, lying very spick and span, near to the boom entrance. The *Strathaird's* bows neatly removed two sets of davits, a length of railing and the gangway, and left the Indian crew in an advanced state of hysteria. Two officers of the 9th were severely censured by one of the passengers, a lieutenant commander of the Royal Naval Reserve, for seeing the humorous side of the incident.

There followed four days of inaction, during which we were able to see, and appreciate, the vast numbers of American freighters coming and going, all loaded to capacity with new equipment and aeroplanes. These were the first deliveries of the Tomahawks, which, although still no match for the Messerschmitts, were to play a great part in levelling up the unequal struggle in the air.

The ship weighed anchor early on the 25th and set out on the last leg of the voyage—three days through the Red Sea. On the way up we met the *Queen Mary* coming back from Suez behind a huge bow wave. At 11.15 a.m. on the 28th of November we passed the blackened superstructure of the s.s. *Georgic,* sunk a few months previously by bombs, and slid into Suez harbour, two months and three days after leaving the Clyde.

CHAPTER V

EGYPT

As the ship stopped, the Embarkation Staff Officer came on board and with him brought orders that the Colonel should go at once to General Headquarters, Cairo, taking with him his Quartermaster and Technical Adjutant. After a short conference the details of disembarkation were arranged. The 9th were to follow the Rifle Brigade, commencing at 12.30 p.m. In fact, it was 4.30 p.m. before the 1st Rifle Brigade got away, owing to the "go slow" methods of the natives manning the lighters. To those who were watching proceedings from the upper decks the activities of the lightermen were very amusing, but to those concerned with getting baggage ashore quickly they were maddening. The work was carried on with the maximum of noise and the minimum of effort—our first insight into the characteristics of the Arabs. Time meant nothing to them and they made it very obvious that it was not their war and they could see no reason for changing the habits of centuries by trying to do the job efficiently. The Arabs of this particular gang set to work with frenzied energy, however, when a sergeant of the Royal Engineers picked up a boat-hook and knocked the ringleader straight off the side of the lighter into the dirty water of the harbour.

Lieutenant Roger Mostyn was our baggage officer. His powers of self-expression, coupled with a nasty-looking leather cane, persuaded Abdul, Hassan and Company that at last they had met their match in the noble art of bawling-out, and they set to work with speed in an awed and admiring silence. The Regiment, less a rear party of nine men under Captain Robin Kingscote, crossed the brilliantly floodlit harbour and boarded a waiting train. Because the Western Desert Forces depended on this port as their only channel of supply, work went on night and day in Suez in spite of air raids.

The train, which was dirty and uncomfortable, crawled northwards through the cool night air and by daybreak was meandering along beside a deep canal through the Valley of the Nile, towards Benha. Those of us who had never been to Egypt before were astonished by the fertility of this rich land as field after field of sugar-cane, cotton, lucerne, potatoes, oranges and wheat, in every stage of growth from green shoots to golden stubble, moved before our eyes. Round the fields were long lines of date palms, and there were oxen, water buffalo and camels hauling water from the canals on to the fields as they revolved round big wooden wheels. In every field the "fellaheen" toiled before the heat of the midday sun grew too strong, while white egrets flew overhead or stood about with their long necks hunched into their shoulders. Along the banks of the many canals trotted tiny donkeys, each carrying a rider swathed in an enormous galabeih, and sitting well over the "back axle," with his leather slippers dangling off his big toes about two inches from the ground. All villages and most of the towns in Egypt are made of mud-brick, and look exactly as if they had suffered a heavy air raid the night before. For firewood the inhabitants burn a mixture of straw, mud and camel-dung which pervades the whole air of the Delta with a pungent smell, not unlike that of a blacksmith's forge when red-hot shoes are being burnt on.

The train drew into Alexandria at noon and then branched off up the desert line to Amiriya. Amiriya was the concentration area for all formations reaching the Western Desert and boasted no attractions whatsoever. The sand's crust had been broken by innumerable wheels and tracks, and whenever a wind blew there was an artificial sandstorm.

These sandstorms, or "khamseens," must be specially mentioned. They represented the peak of human discomfort in the desert and were the only freaks of Nature which made both sides "down tools" and suspend all battles until they passed. Previously limited to a few a year, they increased as the opposing armies grew in size and the areas fought over extended, until eventually in the dry season they came two or three times a month. A fierce wind blowing out of the ovens of the Sahara gave first warning of the miseries to come, and there would be a great airlessness in spite of the wind, which made tempers short. As the wind increased, so the sky grew darker, and then what looked like a black wall stretching up to the heavens came at terrifying speed from the south. This sign allowed some two or three minutes in which to take action. Then the storm hit, stinging sandblasts whipped the skin, and filled the eyes, nose and mouth with choking powder. Those who were frantically hammering in tent or "bivvy" pegs threw down their mallets and hid their faces in handkerchiefs or blankets, whilst in the open a complete silence reigned. The midday sun looked like an ice-blue moon, and such buildings or tents as there were looked like rooms opened after a century had passed. Uncovered food was ruined, and the oil on machinery and breech-blocks became green mud. Canvas was torn and loose papers whisked to far corners. In about half an hour it was all over and a great coolness followed as the storm moved away to the north. Faces began to appear, faces of millers, with red-rimmed eyes and clogged hair, as men crawled from beneath their cover to inspect the ruin of their homes.

Sometimes it rolled up to the coast and, meeting the cooler air above the Mediterranean, turned round and came back again, its energy spent but still spilling sand and bringing back the gloom of a thick snowstorm.

In the khamseen tanks passed within inches of enemy tanks, the crews having strange, fleeting glimpses of each other, and infantry found themselves within yards of enemy machine guns, neither being able to do anything. As a general rule, it was an unwritten law that both sides forgot their enmity in hatred of the common enemy, but as soon as the storm had passed the guns would bang out again.

One extraordinary part of a khamseen was that, as the millions of particles of sand hit metal surfaces, they charged tanks and lorries with electricity, and many a trooper touching his tank would get a shock. During the storm wireless sets crackled and reception was impossible, and, in order to earth static electricity, it was a standing order in the Middle East that petrol and ammunition lorries should drag a short length of chain from the towing bar.

The storms had only one advantage. They completely obliterated all signs of battle. The desert did its own housework and cleared the wreckage in a few hours. Tracks and skid-marks, empty ammunition cases, old tins, and all the soldier's sundry belongings were covered over, leaving only the blackened hulks of tanks, transport and aeroplanes above the sand's surface. A battlefield which, yesterday, was the scene of fierce fighting, today might well be a relic of a war long over. Even graves, dug hastily overnight, disappeared under the all-enveloping sand which obliterated for ever the resting places of countless soldiers.

*   *   *   *

Major Sir Peter Farquhar was waiting on the narrow platform of Amiriya station; so was a hot meal. While we were there a train from the desert pulled in, and on to the platform descended a crowd of wounded from the great Battle of Sidi Rezegh which had just started. They were unshaven, covered in dust and oil, in blood and bandages, and the sight of these men—and also a group of German Afrika Korps prisoners—brought home to us that the battle was now very near.

In a fleet of lorries we went to Perth Camp, Ikingi, which lay seven miles south-west from Amiriya. Here we found, thanks to the great efforts of the Second-in-Command and Major Peter Sykes, Queen's Bays, the tents pitched, cookhouses swept, and fires lit. We settled down in the first of our many camps.

THE WESTERN DESERT
SOLLUM—TOBRUK
AREA

SCALE in miles

20 10 0   20   40   60   80

LEGEND

Railways
Main Roads
Secondary Roads
Tracks
International Boundaries

N

Bomba
Timimi
Gazala
Tobruk
Bir Temrod
Acroma
Bir el Hamed
Gambut
Gabr el Abid
El Adem
Bardia
Knightsbridge
Sidi Rezegh
Trigh Capuzzo
Sollum
Halfaya Pass
Sidi Barrani
Maktila
Bir el Harmat
Trigh el Abd
Sidi Omar
Capuzzo
Bir Hacheim
Bir el Gubi
Tummar W.
Tummar E.
Bir Gibni
Nibeiwa
Bir Shefferzen
Sofafi
Bir Thalata
Maddalena
Jarabub
Siwa

CHAPTER VI

SITUATION IN LIBYA

A BRIEF summary here of the ebb and flow of the desert war will not be out of place.

In the autumn of 1940 the Italian army in Africa consisted of some two hundred and fifty thousand men, including a tank division (the Raggruppamento Maletti) and many hundreds of guns, commanded by General Graziani. They held a line based on the small seaport of Sidi Barrani and running through the forts of Maktila, Tummar East, Tummar West and Nibeiwa down to Sofafi in the desert near the Libyan border. Their chief port was Tripoli and their lines of communication ran along the coast road through the heavily garrisoned towns of Benghazi, Derna, Tobruk and Bardia. In the south they held a chain of outposts (Sofafi, Jarabub, Mekili and Kufra).

Opposing them were a bare one hundred thousand men, General Wavell's Western Desert Force. They made up a corps consisting of the 7th Armoured Division, the 4th Indian Division (which included several British regiments) and a division of New Zealanders, all under the command of Lieutenant-General R. N. O'Connor. Training in the Delta and in Palestine were two divisions of Australians and a number of Polish forces.

A small fleet under Admiral Sir Andrew Cunningham dominated the Mediterranean from June, 1940, to April, 1941. The Italian fleet was strong and well equipped, but in no other respect fitted to cope with the brilliant handling of the British fleet, which took risk upon risk and invariably won.

In the air the Italians enjoyed a numerical advantage of three to one, although British pilots had already set about proving that this was by no means to be the ratio of their opponents' successes. The Royal Air Force was equipped with Glosters, Wellingtons and Blenheims against the Italian Savoias, Macchis and Fiats.

General Graziani could wait until everything was ready. His camps and forts were being lavishly equipped and work was well in hand on the great new Via della Vittoria linking Sollum with Sidi Barrani. He overlooked the fact that he was sitting in the same wasteland that had once swallowed a Persian host; he forgot the old Arab proverb which says: "To the man who knows it the desert is a fortress; to him who does not it is a grave." Above all, he forgot the golden rule of always guarding your flanks against encircling attack.

It was inconceivable to the Italians that the British would attack. They represented a mere handful of the badly equipped troops of an already beaten nation;

it needed only a word for the rich Valley of the Nile to fall into the lap of Italy. Such was the situation given out daily on the Rome wireless.

When, therefore, on the 9th of December, 1940, this little army appeared as if by magic and sliced through the Italian outposts between Sofafi and Nibeiwa, the first essential of attack, surprise, was achieved. Nibeiwa fell, the Tummars fell, and then the British tanks were upon Sidi Barrani itself. With Sidi Barrani were captured General Gallina with his entire staff, an immense quantity of stores and guns of all kinds, and in quick succession fell Sollum, Halfaya Pass, Fort Capuzzo and Sidi Omar, all within a week of the beginning of the attack.

The Italian army rushed back into the perimeter of Bardia and slammed the door, but the Australians had them out by the 4th of January, 1941, capturing many thousands. By the 30th Tobruk and Derna had fallen, leaving no more fortified defences until Benghazi, which was to prove indefensible to both armies.

Whilst the main part of the army was pushing along through the green jebel country which stretches from Derna to Benghazi a small armoured force was being briefed at Mekili for a daring and ambitious march, the object of which was to cut off the retreat of the Italians along the coast road from Benghazi to Agedabia. Involving as it did a tremendous march of two hundred miles across unmapped desert, it was the throw of a gambler who feels that his luck is in. The force was divided into two: one half was to strike for Soluch, thirty-five miles south of Benghazi, the other for Beda Fomm, close to Soluch on the coast road. Speed was essential: yet speed could be had only at the cost of wrecked vehicles. Anything which broke down would have to be abandoned without hope of recovery, and there was no question of receiving any ammunition or supplies from the rear.

This famous march was completed in thirty hours and in the nick of time. Hardly had the two forces reached their objectives when a huge column came pouring down the coast road. Graziani and his eight senior generals were escaping with the remains of the Italian army (some twenty thousand men with one hundred and sixty tanks, upwards of three hundred guns and an immense amount of transport). Behind them came a great column of civilians leaving Benghazi with all the personal effects they could push or carry.

The British force gave immediate battle. Time and again the Italian attacks were broken up, until the British had little ammunition left, and after two days and one night of carnage the battle was over. Graziani's army was utterly smashed, Italy had lost an area the size of England and France, and Egypt and the Suez Canal were safe. Of the two hundred thousand men who had faced the Western Desert Force at Sidi Barrani half were either dead or captive. Nineteen generals were "in the bag."

The problem which then had to be decided was whether to go on to Tripoli or not. General Wavell's men were tired, their transport was worn out and their supply lines were stretched to the present limit. Tripoli was seven hundred miles away across the desert, but its capture would mean that the Axis could be prevented from landing in Africa.

Tied up with this was the problem of aiding Greece. Greece had been successfully holding the Italian attack, but now Germany was preparing to pull the chestnuts out of the fire for her disappointing partner. The War Cabinet in London decided that Greece must be sustained, and General Wavell's army was stripped of sixty thousand men, a great quantity of tanks, guns and technicians, and supplies of food and oil: all were shipped to Athens.

Meanwhile the Germans began to send the Afrika Korps to Tripoli. Composed of hand-picked troops, specially trained under artificial desert conditions, this force was equipped with the finest material Germany could produce. It consisted of the 15th and 21st Panzer Divisions and the 90th Light Infantry Division (a prototype of the divisions later to be called Panzer Grenadiers), and was commanded by General Erwin Rommel. To this force were added remnants of the Italian army, now reinforced, and the Luftwaffe in strength, based on airfields in Sicily and, later, Crete.

The first identification of Germans in Africa occurred one morning when a troop of British armoured cars, bowling down the road between Agheila and Tripoli, passed three strange cars coming from the other direction. "My God!" said the British commander. "Did you see who they were? Germans!"

General Wavell, with his Desert Army reduced to a skeleton, his attention seriously occupied with the disasters in Greece and Crete and the Nazi-backed Raschid Ali's threat in Persia, was in no position to withstand the punch which came from the wasteland beyond Agheila. In rapid succession Agheila and Agedabia fell. One part of Rommel's force made for Benghazi and the other shot across the desert south of the jebel and engaged the British at Mekili. Confusion reigned; Generals O'Connor and Neame, travelling along the Martuba bypass, were captured by a patrol of German motor-cyclists operating miles in advance of their main forces, and at Mekili General Gambier-Parry was taken and his small force routed.

The next possible stopping place for the British was Tobruk and here the scattered units assembled. The perimeter was manned and the back-to-the-wall siege began. Some of Rommel's forces sped on to the Sollum Escarpment, but here their impetus was lost, more through lack of supplies than because of anything the small British force could do. Rommel attacked Tobruk, but English and Australian troops fought back with success. At the end of a month the enemy's direct attacks ceased and siege warfare commenced: on the frontier both sides settled down to a further period of watching and waiting.

Rommel had recaptured most of the plums in Cyrenaica, but he had failed to do what General Wavell had done: destroy the opposing army. The retreat had cost us under three thousand men and a few vehicles.

At this period—the summer of 1941—General Wavell went to India and was succeeded by General Sir Claude Auchinleck. At sea Admiral Cunningham was

still in command and, against unremitting air attack, managed to supply Malta
and Tobruk and deal severely with Axis convoys going to and fro between Italy
and North Africa.

A steady stream of modern equipment, new commanders and reinforcements
came to Egypt. The long road from Cairo was jammed with vehicles moving up
to the front, while on unfinished landing grounds squadrons of new aeroplanes
continually touched down. General Wavell's Desert Force was changing to
become the Eighth Army.

During the lull Rommel was preparing to launch a knock-out blow at Tobruk,
while General Auchinleck was planning a great new offensive to regain Cyrenaica and sweep on to Tripoli. Both plans were due to mature in November, 1941.
The British got in first by a matter of days. On the 16th of November the dispositions were as follows : Tobruk was ringed by the Italian Pavia, Bologna, Trieste,
Trento and Brescia Divisions. The German 90th Light with some more Italians
held the frontier posts of Bardia, Sollum and Halfaya Pass. The 15th Panzer
Division, commanded by Major-General Neumann-Silkow, the 21st Panzer
Division, commanded by Major-General Ravenstein, and the Italian Ariete
Division formed the Axis armour in reserve. Thus Rommel had about one
hundred and twenty thousand men and four hundred tanks.

The British Army Commander, General Sir Alan Cunningham, had two corps
of some three divisions each disposed as follows : opposite Sollum and Sidi Omar
in the north were the Indians and New Zealanders with, in reserve, a South
African division. In the centre were three British armoured brigades, the 4th,
7th and the newly arrived 22nd. The south was held as far as Jarabub by another
South African division and more Indians. In Tobruk were twenty thousand
British and Polish troops with a hundred tanks. Altogether, he had about
one hundred thousand men and eight hundred tanks, the latter being largely
composed of Valentines, Matildas, Honeys and the new Crusaders.

The attack was launched on the 17th of November, 1941, and caught Rommel
on the wrong foot. He was about to make his "do or die" assault on Tobruk, but
suddenly found his desert overrun by fast-moving British columns. Calling off
his attack, Rommel concentrated his armour and waited to see what was happening. He found that the New Zealanders had rounded the German frontier
positions in the south and were now stretched with their supporting infantry in
a wide band all the way to Tobruk, while, simultaneously, the garrison of
Tobruk had sallied forth towards El Duda to meet the New Zealanders coming
along the coast.

In an attempt to surround the enemy the British armoured brigades were split
up. Rommel flung his weight against the 7th Armoured Brigade at Sidi Rezegh,
which became the decisive battleground. All day the 7th Armoured Brigade
withstood the onslaught; by the time the other two brigades had arrived to help,
it was down to a mere handful of men. That night the Axis put in a heavy attack
across the slopes of Sidi Rezegh and by the next day a state of utter chaos

reigned. A force of enemy tanks cut right through to the east, scattering head-quarters, shooting-up echelons, overrunning workshops and hospitals and sever-ing communications. They reached and passed the frontier wire again before they were stopped, and made contact with the force left on the Sollum Escarp-ment. This particular stage of the battle was thereafter known as the "November Handicap," involving as it did a stampede of echelons. Men were captured and recaptured several times in a day. XIII Corps Headquarters had to run for Tobruk and XXX Corps Headquarters was scattered and out of touch. Things looked very bad indeed, and the Army Commander was compelled to consider whether it might not be necessary to fall back into Egypt owing to the threat to the railhead and the risk of having his army cut off from its supplies.

General Auchinleck, however, refused to admit that Rommel's spectacular break-through had won the day. He realized that the enemy must have outrun his strength and he cast about for a method of offensive action which would take some of the pressure off his troops. He found it in the "Jock Column." Brigadier "Jock" Campbell had previously experimented with small columns, consisting perhaps of a troop of armoured cars, two or three troops of guns and some infantry in trucks. These were provisioned for a week or more and loosed into the desert to go behind the enemy, disrupt his supply lines, attack his soft vehicles, and generally cause as much damage and confusion as they could. Such columns were organized and quickly dispatched.

Meanwhile, the situation began to right itself. The enemy tank column had missed the railhead and our main dump, and had withdrawn. The Germans, who were surrounded at Sollum and Capuzzo, had tried unsuccessfully to break out. The New Zealanders were still defending the coastal ridge at Gambut, and Tobruk was held. The Eighth Army got its second wind and struck again. Once more Sidi Rezegh was the centre of the fighting, and, after one final desperate battle, the Axis force drew off under cover of darkness. In the desert the vanquished must always make a clean break and get back to the next line of defence as quickly as possible. In this event it was Gazala.

The Eighth Army withstood the onslaught by the skin of its teeth, and was nearly too tired to stand, but it staggered on after the retreating enemy, the garrison of Tobruk falling into place alongside the rest, and broke the Gazala Line.

Rommel cleared right out of Cyrenaica and went three hundred miles back behind the Agheila Line. Columns and the remaining tanks of the 22nd Armoured Brigade followed him up. There remained only the isolated garrisons of Halfaya and Capuzzo. Rommel had lost fifty thousand men and for the second time the Axis had been bolted out of the desert. The newspapers, which had daily been making synthetic victories, were at last able to give the British public some good news.

Such was the state of affairs when the 2nd Armoured Brigade arrived at Amiriya.

CHAPTER VII

APPROACH TO BATTLE

THE 9th Lancers spent the first two weeks of December at Ikingi, a few miles outside Alexandria. Parties of drivers were sent out daily to fetch the tanks, scout cars, water trucks and lorries needed by an armoured regiment. There came from Mena motor-cycles; from Tel-el-Kebir a fleet of yellow Canadian-made three-tonners and two Ford station wagons; from Hadra scout cars; from Dekheila more three-tonners, water trucks and office trucks. The big workshops at Wardian issued the tanks, which looked quite different from the ones we had brought from England, for they were sprayed with a peculiar shade of paint (interior decorators would call it "light stone") and their tracks were almost invisible beneath deep skirtings fitted to keep down the dust. Even the little Honeys looked better in their new paint, and modifications to their interiors made them seem almost modern. The technical store tent disappeared behind growing piles of sand channels, camouflage nets, picks and shovels, cases of sun compasses and tank binoculars, tarpaulins, jettison tanks and a host of suchlike.

All tanks fired-in their guns on the local range and commanders were instructed in the art of desert navigation. An officer of the 22nd Armoured Brigade spent a night with the Regiment and passed on all the advice he could about desert warfare. One of the first results of his advice was a succession of journeys to the local "officers' shop," where such commodities as desert boots, cord slacks and dozens of pairs of extra socks were purchased. The Eighth Army has often been accused of looking like nothing on earth and it probably did, but its manner of dressing (however unorthodox) at least spelled comfort under difficult conditions. It did not take the Regiment long to slip into the accepted rig.

On the 10th of December, 1941, an advance party, under Captain David Laurie and the Regimental Quartermaster-Sergeant, left for Mersa Matruh, and by that evening all tanks and vehicles were packed and loaded with petrol and ammunition. There was a terrible sandstorm and the orderly room typewriter, on which Trooper Spashett was trying to hammer out orders for the move, seized solid and had to be given a bath in petrol before it would function. Even then it was kept going only by blowing on to it with the air line of a cruiser tank backed up to the office doorway for the purpose.

Early on the 13th of December the move began. The wheeled vehicles, totalling one hundred and thirty, went by road to Matruh, refuelling at Daba, and the tanks were loaded on to war-flats at Amiriya. By 2 a.m. on the 15th the whole Regiment was concentrated in the desert two miles south of Matruh. Our

WESTERN DESERT, 1942

Approach to Battle

first night was spent in unparalleled discomfort owing to a torrential rainstorm which turned the surrounding plain into a lake. By dawn everyone was soaked to the skin and bitterly cold, but North Africa had a way of making up for its bad manners; by 8 a.m. the sun was shining in a clear, blue sky and all over the area steam arose from clothes and blankets as we cooked our first desert meal.

During the morning the whole brigade assembled at Bir Kanayis and brigaded "B" Echelon was formed and placed under the command of Major J. A. Cooke, 9th Lancers. The Divisional Commander's (General Lumsden) orders were that the Brigade was required as quickly as possible in Cyrenaica and there was to be no set period for adapting ourselves to the desert or for having special training in navigation: this must be done on the approach march.

Actually, the "intention" paragraph of the first operation order, which arrived from Brigade on the afternoon of the 18th, simply said: "1st Armoured Division will capture Benghazi." As this objective was at the moment seven hundred and fifty miles away, the Colonel and Adjutant, as they read the order, permitted themselves a slight smile of surprise.

We set out the next day (the 16th of December) on what seemed an all-time record approach march. A typical order for the day's march would be: "Forty-seven miles on two hundred and seventy-seven degrees, then forty miles on two hundred and ninety degrees," with almost no check bearings *en route* and positively no confirmation that you were where you thought you were at the end. It gave good practice in navigation, however, and squadrons took turns daily in leading.

We passed south of Thalata and reached the frontier wire at the Shefferzen Gap by midday on the 20th, where we were met by Lieutenant-General Willoughby Norrie, commanding XXX Corps, and where we drew rations and petrol before passing in single file through the gap and on to enemy territory.

So far the Honeys were going perfectly, but each day the route was strewn with broken-down cruisers all with the same fault: leaking water pumps. Squadron fitters and the Light Aid Detachment were permanently engaged in effecting repairs, catching us up each night, usually after dark. The serious part of such a defect was the scarcity of water. The whole desert was dotted with wells, dug hundreds of years ago by wandering tribes, but half of them were dry and where there was water it was usually so brackish that it was fit only for washing. The water-truck drivers very soon developed an uncanny ability to find the wells, and were adept at floating off into the blue, rejoining the moving regiment with the certain instinct of a professional homing pigeon. Perhaps we were especially fortunate in our drivers, but they never failed to provide the precious fluid and often drove their trucks twenty hours a day in order to satisfy the demands for radiators, washing and bigger and better mugs of the eternal "char" (tea).

There were to be times when water was more precious than petrol. Then we shaved in a mug of water, pouring it afterwards into the tank radiator, and the number of "brews" had drastically to be curtailed. The water trucks would slip quietly away and make a long pilgrimage to a far-away point which they remembered passing days before and at our next halting place back would come the drivers, grinning from ear to ear, with a hundred and thirty gallons of potential tea on board.

They shared the honours with the squadron fitters. "The black gang," as they were called, were the most independent of all. They could always be sure of being the last into leaguer at night and of having half a dozen repair jobs to do before they crawled into their blankets. They wrought miracles of repair and were never heard to grumble. All over the desert every night fitter sergeants turned up at squadron leaders' tanks, covered in oil from head to foot, and reported to a relieved officer: "All in now, sir." They lived permanently on tea. If all the mugs of tea consumed by fitters in North Africa were placed end to end they would encircle the globe. They seemed to run on tea as a car runs on petrol and if supplies of the life-giving leaf failed they became distraught and moody.

Their independent role gave them many opportunities for leaving the centre line and going to examine wrecks or abandoned vehicles. Spare parts and other valuables collected in this way gave the fitters a name for being light-fingered. But "all's fair . . ." and it was an unwritten law of the desert that an unguarded vehicle was an unwanted vehicle. Many a careless driver returned to find his machine deficient of a carburettor or coil. The fitters said that he was lucky to find anything left at all. Sometimes the regrettable happened and the vehicles themselves changed ownership without the formality of a voucher. As part of the equipment of a fitter's lorry included sets of regimental sign-plates and a tin or two of paint, the new acquisition was rapidly transformed. A certain well-known light infantry battalion lost a scout car one day under obscure circumstances. The company commander concerned met a 9th Lancer scout car shortly afterwards, stopped it and asked if it had seen the missing car near a certain well.

"Oh, no, sir! I've just come that way myself and there was no sign of it there."

In point of fact the inquirer was leaning on the missing car at the time.

The Germans left live mines and booby-traps on their abandoned tanks or vehicles, but our fitters developed the instincts of carrion crows; they took the meat and left the trap unsprung.

*   *   *   *

On the 22nd of December we were told that we were to remain for a week in the area of Bir Gibni. The shortage of petrol had become acute and, until Tobruk was functioning as a port once more, the supply side of the Eighth Army could not permit another armoured brigade to be sent forward. "G" were yelling for us to move on as quickly as possible, and "Q" were warning them that they could not supply us if we did.

This gave us time to repair our broken-down tanks and to enjoy a peaceful Christmas Day. Major Alex Barclay brought the Bays' band over and we had a good Christmas service. In the distance we could hear the guns firing at the garrison besieged on Halfaya Pass.

During this week great attention was paid to improving and perfecting leaguer drill. By the end of the period we had adopted a layout to which the 9th Lancers Group adhered until the end of the war. Briefly it was this. The three squadrons halted in double line ahead, one hundred and fifty yards apart and ten yards between tanks. "C" always took the right, "B" the left and "A" the centre. Regimental Headquarters, in single line, came in on the left of "A." "E" Battery had the big space between "A" and "C," "C" Company, 1st Rifle Brigade, the smaller space between Regimental Headquarters and "B." The Bofors (Light Anti-Aircraft) Troop and Anti-Tank Troop had a single column each on the left side of "E" Battery's piece. There were ten yards between vehicles and five yards between lines, so that the group in leaguer formed a tight rectangle in which all vehicles faced one way. The tanks on the flanks traversed their turrets outwards, except the end tank of each line, which turned its turret to the rear. The Rifle Brigade company established a listening post out in front and machine guns were mounted on fixed lines at each corner of the leaguer. Telephone lines were laid to each squadron, battery and company headquarters and the listening post, and all converged at the Colonel's cruiser.

When "B" Echelon came up the lorries carried out a "milk round" of the lines in the dark, handing out petrol, ammunition, food and water. They then formed up behind the leaguer and drove off to their own area, usually five to ten miles back.

It always worked perfectly and never once did we have to move because of enemy attack in darkness. The only disadvantage of this method of spending the night was that leaguer had to be broken before daylight to avoid presenting the enemy with a perfect target for shell fire.

The echelon was divided into two halves, an equal number of petrol and ammunition lorries in each. The forward half, "A" Echelon, was commanded by a subaltern from the Regiment and was directly under the Colonel's orders by wireless. This echelon supplied the fighting echelon with its requirements and replenished itself by going back to the "B" Echelon or straight to dumps. "B" Echelon consisted of the other half of the replenishment lorries and all the remainder, such as stores, office lorries, messes, signals and the Light Aid Detachment of the R.E.M.E. It was commanded by a major belonging to the Regiment, and was under Brigade command; the "B" echelons of all regiments within the Brigade were commanded by a field officer with a captain to help him. It replenished the "A" Echelon and itself from the R.A.S.C. or field dumps.

When a battle was imminent all vehicles which could be dispensed with for a week or so were detached and left out of the battle area under Brigade control. On these occasions there was a "B1" and "B2" Echelon.

On the 30th of December the Brigade moved on to Bir Harmat, a distance of sixty-seven miles. As we went the country began to get greener and the wadis were thick with grass and flowers, while here and there the Arabs had scratched up the soil and planted corn. The new green shoots were a welcome change from the endless miles of stony, dun-coloured desert.

We remained at Bir Harmat until the 4th, held up once more by lack of petrol. The bir itself was well constructed in stone, with a winch mounted on top for raising water, which, however, was unfit to use because a dead Italian soldier lay floating on the surface and had been there for some time.

The next three days were spent travelling. We used to go for two hours and then stop and cook breakfast. Rations were entirely "hard," consisting of bully beef and biscuit, and even these were scarce, but it was a healthy life and most of us felt very fit. Our route was uncharted and often lay among great crags and boulders. Halts were frequent while the experts checked our position. We finally reached Giof Ardun and went into open leaguer in the short camel grass, facing south-west. We were ten miles from Antelat to the west and sixty miles from Agedabia on the coast road. All tanks, except four on transporters, had completed the tremendous journey and were at last near the scene of action.

We were due to remain there until the 31st of January, 1942. Such was the shortage of petrol that even the practice of warming up tanks' engines at dawn had to be discontinued. On the 11th of January "E" Battery and "C" Company, 1st Rifle Brigade, reverted to the command of the Support Group and were soon moving on ahead to join the small army facing the enemy on the Agheila Line.

The weather was appalling, and day after day icy and torrential rain swept across from the Sahara in unbroken sheets. In the few fine periods we went afield and shot a few gazelle and sand-grouse and these, with some shaggy sheep purchased for silver from a wandering Arab family, were a welcome change from bully.

News from the front line was sparse. The coast and Agheila were held by the 201st Guards Brigade, while the left flank, down by the Wadi Faregh, was held by the combined Support Groups of the 1st and 7th Armoured Divisions. The only remaining armour was the 22nd Armoured Brigade with a strength of thirty tired tanks. The many gaps in between were covered by the armoured cars of the Royals and 12th Lancers. The Afrika Korps was being poked in the ribs in an effort to persuade it to continue its retreat towards Tripoli. If this happened the 1st Armoured Division was to carry on and take Tripoli.

On the 11th of January a battery of the 2nd South African Field Regiment and a battery of 2-pounder anti-tank guns of the Norfolk Yeomanry joined us, but the latter was withdrawn the same day. Brigade laid down a telephone line to each regiment which enabled the wireless set in the rear link tank to be switched off after seven hundred and forty-four hours of continuous running—no bad advertisement for the makers.

On the 22nd of January there came a sudden jolt. At ten minutes past four on a wet, cold morning the Brigade Intelligence Officer, Lieutenant Peter Laing,

9th Lancers, woke the Adjutant with a warning order to move ready for battle at first light and for the Colonel to be at Brigade at 7.15 a.m. Not really believing him, the Regiment packed up and cooked breakfast whilst waiting for the Colonel to return. The news as given to us was that a strong enemy raiding force had burst through the line and was making towards Antelat. In point of fact, the "defeated" enemy had received strong reinforcements of armour and men and had launched a massive attack, with one thrust up the coast road and another up the northern side of the Wadi Faregh. The Guards Brigade was too thin on the ground to hold Agedabia and had to fall back in the face of greatly superior enemy forces. The 22nd Armoured Brigade had been withdrawn two days previously to refit and the Support Groups were hopelessly bogged down in the soft sand of the Wadi Faregh. The latter learned of the enemy attack only because an officer tuned in his wireless to the B.B.C. early the next morning and heard from the lips of a dignified announcer in London that Agedabia had fallen and that they were already outflanked.

The chief reason for the complete surprise achieved by the enemy was that Antelat landing ground was flooded and consequently no air reconnaissance had been possible for three days.

However, the 2nd Armoured Brigade set off that morning under the impression that they were to round up and destroy an enemy column, composed mainly of Italians. After travelling only a mile we met a flock of armoured cars of the 12th Lancers coming at high speed from the opposite direction. We managed to stop one and learned that they were all that remained of the regiment and were going to Msus to refit. They warned us that they had had three cars captured intact and these might be used against us (in fact, they were).

The Brigade had crossed the deep valley at the Saunnu wind-pump at noon, when the order came to halt. After an hour course was changed to intercept a column of ten enemy tanks and two hundred vehicles reported as being north of Agedabia and moving towards Antelat. On the way the Regiment, which was leading, bumped into Divisional Headquarters retiring from the Wadi Faregh affair. We very nearly opened up on them, but recognition came just in time. Nothing happened during this day and the only sign of any hostility was a Stuka attack some distance away on the south flank. During the early hours of the next day the Bays were hurried off back to Saunnu to deal with an enemy column, presumably the one we were trying to head off, which had attacked the "B" Echelon during the night.

The rest of the Brigade moved at first light and began the move necessary to direct us on to Antelat. The 9th Lancers were advanced guard. At 10.40 a.m. "B" Squadron, in front, reported some transport at a great distance to its left front. At 11 a.m. its left troop reported four unidentified tanks about six miles away. By 11.15 a situation was developing. As the morning mist cleared reports came in fast and soon there was no doubt that we had bumped into the flank of a large enemy column moving from west to east. At first the great amount of

F

captured British transport within it confused us, and, even when known to be in enemy hands, we were disinclined to shell them, thinking that they would certainly contain prisoners.

Brigade's orders were to avoid becoming committed but to try to continue the move to the north. The Colonel ordered "B" Squadron to send a troop forward to have a closer look. Lieutenant John Marden's troop motored on over a slight ridge and ran slap into nine enemy anti-tank guns. One tank was hit at once and began to burn and Sergeant Dudeney was killed as he climbed out: his crew were saved by the gallantry of Sergeant Welham. The second tank seemed to put on speed and charge through the enemy gun line as if the driver had been killed. We never saw it again until a year later, when we were able for the first time to return to the scene and care for the unburied dead. Our guns went into action and the enemy sheered off and disappeared into the noonday haze.

Brigade now ordered the 10th Hussars to take the lead and resume the move up to Antelat, with the 9th Lancers as rear guard. The Second-in-Command went off in his tank to watch for the tail of the Brigade transport so that we would know when to move. By this time a veritable stream of traffic was passing behind us, including the whole of Divisional Headquarters and the echelons of the many columns which had been out in the south.

Whilst we waited "A" Squadron was watching a British armoured car creeping towards them in a suspicious manner. When it came within range they saw that it bore small black crosses; they shot it to bits and machine-gunned the very German crew which jumped out.

Eventually the mass of transport thinned out and it was reported to Brigade that the Colonel considered it no longer necessary to remain. At 2.30 p.m. the Regiment wheeled round and moved off with the intention of following the Brigade to Saunnu and Antelat. By this time the tanks were very short of petrol and "A" Echelon, being empty, was ordered to go north towards Msus and refill.

For miles there was not a soul in sight and the shadows were lengthening as we descended the steep side of the Saunnu Depression. A short halt was called to allow the guns to catch up and then the march was resumed across the flat bottom of the valley, with "C" Squadron in the lead.

As Regimental Headquarters began to move we suddenly saw on the escarpment ahead a black mass of vehicles. The sun was now very low in a wintry sky and for a few moments they were impossible to identify. However, we were not doubtful for long. The loud explosion of an air-burst overhead and a general crash as the whole enemy force opened up on the valley told us that we had arrived at the depression only a few minutes before the main German army. They had cut our direct course to rejoin the Brigade at Antelat.

The gunners immediately dropped their trails and went into action, unable to resist such a massed target. They did not acknowledge the Colonel's order that all squadrons should pack up and move on to the high ground ahead to the north-east.

The gravity of the position was apparent to all. Nearly every petrol gauge was showing "Empty" and between us and help was a force at least ten times as big as ours. After a running fight all three squadrons reached the northern escarpment and turned to face the enemy. "A" Squadron, which was the nearest, put down smoke and charged. Lieutenant Hugh Hodgson, the leading troop leader, ran his tank down a line of anti-tank guns, destroying several and killing their crews, but the last gun got his tank and killed him instantly. Captain John Greenwood's tank was seen to receive a direct hit which almost split it in two. This officer was later taken prisoner. Sergeant Loveless, of "C" Squadron, who had only just found the Regiment after collecting his tank from the workshop, announced to all and sundry over the wireless that he was "going in for a basinful" and joined the "A" Squadron charge. He and Trooper Lumley were both killed almost at once.

Meanwhile, behind us, twelve Mark IV's had come right down the escarpment and were making for the 25-pounders. These changed to open sights and fought back most gallantly. They were overrun and lost the guns, together with many of the crews, but before being put out of action they accounted for several of the Mark IV's.

Tanks had now begun to run out of petrol and the situation was saved only by darkness. Firing died away and by towing almost a quarter of the remainder of our tanks we managed to move about two miles and form a small leaguer.

It now proved impossible to communicate with Brigade—or anyone else, for that matter. The Adjutant and Sergeant Peterson tried for two hours with speech and Morse, but each time a German set jammed the transmission. Luckily, however, although we did not know it at the time, Brigade managed to receive the map reference of where we thought we were.

A council was held to decide the best course to adopt and it was resolved that the tanks of four of the most battered Honeys should be drained and the petrol given to the remaining tanks, allowing them a minimum of five miles' range. If no help was forthcoming by 2 a.m. we were to destroy the four tanks and hope to reach friends with the remainder. It was the only possible thing we could do.

In the quiet night we could hear the Germans in their leaguer filling up petrol tanks and shouting and singing. By 2 a.m. there was no sign of an echelon and still no communication with Brigade, so, unwillingly, the Colonel ordered the destruction of the four tanks.

Before this was completed a rumble was heard from the direction of Saunnu. It seemed to us that the enemy had decided on a night attack; we grabbed tommy-guns and pistols and swung our turrets round to face the rear.

The noise came nearer and nearer and the dim outline of the leading vehicle appeared. It was a truck and sitting beside the driver was Lieutenant John Reid, the "A" Echelon commander. Major Lomax and Captain Steel followed with "A" Echelon lorries and some of the "B" Echelon. We almost wept on their necks. Petrol! Hundreds of gallons of petrol and even some mail. Once more the echelon had not failed us.

After leaving the Regiment that afternoon "A" Echelon had motored north until they found an R.A.S.C. petrol convoy on the Msus—Agedabia track. They filled up and drove towards Agedabia looking for Brigade Headquarters. Just before dark they came across Major Lomax with some of the "B" Echelon lorries and Captain Steel, who was trying to get back to the Regiment after being detached. The combined party, together with the rest of the Brigade Echelon, reached Brigade Headquarters farther down the track at about 10 p.m., where they were given an approximate map reference of the Regiment's supposed position. Since the enemy were on the direct line between Brigade Headquarters and the Regiment it was decided to go back five miles up the track in a north-easterly direction and then to branch off on a compass bearing (approximately south-east) which after some ten miles should bring the convoy to the Regiment's position. There was a moon and a slight haze. In the stillness the convoy (which included the 10th Hussars' Echelon, who had decided to come too because the 10th were reported to be south-east of the 9th) seemed to make such a noise as must arouse the suspicions of the German outposts. After eleven miles there was still no sign of any tank leaguer when Captain Steel spotted some tracks of tanks which had obviously been travelling in a northerly direction, so it was decided to follow them up. John Reid went ahead of the rest of the convoy and after a short while a welcome challenge was heard: "Who goes there?" It was a 9th Lancer leaguer outpost. The echelon had arrived and their welcome was warm.

The "B" Echelon had had a narrow escape from being put in the bag the previous night. In his account of the incident Major Lomax said:

"The whole Brigade Echelon were halted in and around the Saunnu Valley in the afternoon of the 22nd, south of the Wind Pump, waiting for news from Brigade Headquarters. As dusk fell the regimental echelons close leaguered with the 9th on the east of the valley and Brigade Headquarters transport on the west. Tony Cooke, commander of the brigaded 'B' Echelon, took the precaution of collecting a few petrol and ammunition lorries from each regimental echelon to keep close to his own transport in case news came through during the night as to the respective regimental positions.

"During the afternoon and early evening a number of vehicles had been coming down the valley from the north, the drivers saying that an enemy column was round at the back of us shooting-up all and sundry. This made us slightly anxious, as we had no protecting troops or any weapons except the rifles and revolvers of the drivers, plus a few Brens, and we realized that the loss of the echelons would mean the immobilization of the tanks. Later that night I went across the valley in my car to find out if Major Cooke had any news. While I was there we heard gun fire from behind us near the Wind Pump. Tracer shells could be seen and we wondered if this was the enemy column we had heard about and if it was coming our way. I got into the car and drove back across the valley to rejoin my echelon, but there was no trace of it. Obviously, and very wisely as it turned out, George Meyrick, whom I had left in charge, had moved out of the valley. It was hopeless to try to find them in the dark, so I returned to the Brigade Headquarters transport.

"After a time we could hear the rumble of a column coming down the valley from the north. It was still dark and there was a ground mist, so we hoped that we would escape detection, and so it proved. We heard the enemy column pass close by and could distinguish the voices of the men above the noise of their vehicles. Just after this an excited non-commissioned officer arrived from the rear of our column to say that some Italians had run into the back of us and had been taken prisoner. Tony and I went to investigate and found two field guns with their crews and a truck with two officers. The whole party seemed to be little perturbed by their capture, but as they spoke no English and as we could not understand Italian we did not get much information from them.

"When dawn broke, Tony moved his echelon on to the high ground to the west of the valley, where he also collected the Bays' and 10th Hussars' echelons, and I went off to find George. I was about to cross the valley when I noticed some enemy armoured cars driving down it. After they had gone we went over to where the Regiment's Echelon had been and near by found a 9th Lancer truck stuck in some soft sand in a wadi, but on the flat plateau to the east of the valley there was nothing to be seen. We drove five miles due east and then five miles due north, but there was no trace of the echelon. There was nothing for it but to return to the rest of the Brigade transport. When we got down into the valley again there seemed to be a lot of vehicles about and I suddenly realized that they were all Italian or German. Luckily the mass of Brigade transport which I had left on the far side of the valley could not be seen from the valley itself.

"I suggested to Corporal Egmore, my driver, that we should try to capture an enemy lorry and that he should get in and drive it while I drove our car. He was all for this, so we drove alongside the nearest lorry and yanked the driver, who was an Italian, out of the cab and bundled him into the back of my car, where he and my servant, Trooper Mustoe, sat eyeing each other on the back seat like a couple of dowagers who had not been introduced. Poor Mustoe was later to die of his injuries when we drove on to a mine. Meanwhile, Corporal Egmore could not get the lorry to start and as by now there were a few bullets whistling about, I told him to get back into the car and drive as fast as he could to the shelter of the wadis on the western side of the valley. We were not molested and shortly afterwards rejoined the rest of the Brigade transport, handed over our prisoner and had some breakfast. Later in the morning Tony Cooke moved the whole Brigade Echelon back to our old position some miles north of Saunnu where we had been before the battle started.

"By that afternoon we were in touch again with Brigade Headquarters and met John Reid with his refilled 'A' Echelon just as we were forming up to go to Brigade Headquarters. The 'B' Echelon lorries I had with me, plus the 'A' Echelon, were sufficient to give the tanks all the petrol and ammunition they could want. How we eventually found the Regiment that night has already been told.

"The rest of the 'B' Echelon, under Captain Meyrick, turned up the next day."

Every tank was filled and, as dawn was not an hour away, we formed up in double line ahead with the transport in between and jogged off to more healthy parts.

Looking back afterwards on that night it seemed like a bad dream, but at the time our situation was very serious. Had the enemy not decided at the crucial moment to switch the main attack back on to the coast road, there would have been very little chance of our getting away and this part of the History would never have been written. To the mistake of committing to battle a brigade which had just completed a thousand miles without overhaul and was desperately short of petrol must be added the decision to split it up to fight three separate battles. This lesson was to take a great deal of learning and it was years before it became fully appreciated that in the desert the armoured brigade was the fighting unit and not the armoured regiment.

The next morning the Regiment was put under the command of Brigadier Valentin, 1st Support Group, and moved back again to the north side of the Saunnu Valley. The remainder of that day and all the next were spent in observation. Scattered parties and small columns kept coming in all the time and, apart from the inevitable Stukas, the enemy appeared to be taking a breather.

On the morning of the 26th of January orders came to us to revert to the command of the 2nd Armoured Brigade and join it at Msus. No sooner had this been completed when the enemy launched another attack. Luckily we had just refuelled from "A" Echelon, for the whole party suddenly came under heavy shell fire on a completely open piece of desert. The Division was ordered to get to Cherruba as quickly as possible. We were given a push in the form of a sudden salvo of shells from a semi-circle of Mark IV tanks which set on fire two petrol lorries.

It now became a case of "Home, James, and don't spare the horses." The Regiment was put in the lead, followed by Brigade Headquarters, with the remains of the Bays and the 10th Hussars in the rear. Good speed was made for three miles, after which the column turned north for Cherruba. As we turned a shell missed the armoured command vehicle by a few feet and embedded itself in the final-drive gearing of Lieutenant Percy Oxley's tank, much to the surprise of that individual, whose ruddy countenance deepened by several shades as he climbed out and inspected the wreck of his beloved tank. This reduced our strength to twenty tanks, ten cruisers and ten Honeys.

The remainder of the day and half the night were spent in fast travelling. By 2 a.m. what was left of the Brigade had reached Cherruba, where it refuelled. The long journey, henceforth to be known as the "Msus Stakes," had been completed with the loss of only one more tank. Sergeant Dickins, of "C" Squadron, whose tank was not in good running order, was left to guard "A" Echelon. It was very bad luck that just as a troop of Mark IV's started attacking the echelon his tank finally broke down and he was last seen engaging the enemy with his Besa. This unequal contest could have only one ending and Sergeant Dickins and his crew found themselves in captivity.

The 27th of January dawned fine and warm and ominously quiet. It was intended to hold the Cherruba Basin as long as possible with the 4th Indian Division on the right, the Polish Brigade on the left, and the 2nd Armoured Brigade, with the 201st Guards Brigade, in the centre.

The Brigade by now consisted of a Composite Regiment only, under the 9th Lancers. "A" Squadron was dismounted and sent away and was replaced by a composite squadron of Queen's Bays and 10th Hussars.

We sat and watched all day. Small columns of our own side kept coming in over the flat plains to the south. As the sun neared the horizon a stir went round the whole garrison of the Golden Valley. Away out on the plain a monster had appeared and was slowly making its way towards Cherruba. It was something the like of which had never been seen before—about forty feet long, black and immensely high. We racked our brains for details of any recent secret equipment, but could recall nothing resembling this juggernaut. On it came, occasionally disappearing from view as it crossed a wadi, until an armoured car got near enough to see that it was nothing more terrible than Lieutenant Roger Mostyn's cruiser towing Brigadier Valentin's armoured command vehicle. The circumstances surrounding the birth of this strange combination are best told in the words of the officer concerned:

"On the 22nd of January I was awakened by the Squadron Sergeant-Major and told that the squadron was to be ready by eight o'clock that morning. As it was already past six I replied that I could not do this, owing to the fact that on my own tank the fitters had only just finished putting in a new swash pump and consequently all the interior arrangements were out of the tank; also my Corporal's tank had the bearing supporting its offside final drive out and had the off-side track and sprocket off.

"I got the work under way. By nine o'clock my own tank was ready and rejoined the squadron while the fitters, under Corporal James, were still working on my Troop Corporal's tank. I was informed that some transporters were arriving and would bring on my Corporal's tank and another. By two o'clock in the afternoon the fitters had completed their work and both had been loaded on to transporters. So I set off with my column of two transporters, both with tanks on them, the fitters' lorry towing the office truck and a fitter riding a motor-cycle.

"The motor-cycle had to be abandoned after two miles; its front spring was broken and the crank-case kept hitting the ground. Next, the transporter I was riding on had a puncture. However, after an hour and a half we arrived at Saunnu, where I found in a valley the largest conglomeration of vehicles I have ever seen. Eventually I found the Brigade 'B' Echelon and made contact with Majors Cooke and Lomax. Major Cooke could give me no information beyond saying: 'The fog of war has descended,' and Major Lomax ordered me to join the 9th Lancers' 'B' Echelon, and to go up to the Regiment that night with the petrol lorries. At sunset I was about to join these petrol lorries when a major in the transporter company ordered me to close leaguer with the rest of the transporter company, as it was not safe to travel at night on these transporters. I therefore joined the transporter company close leaguer.

"At seven o'clock that evening the Germans started shelling the Valley of Saunnu from close range and the transporter company commander decided to move eastward out of the shelling area. Therefore, the transporter company moved, flat out, with no attempt at any formation. The going was bad and my tank got shifted six inches on the transporter over one bad bump. After this I dismounted the tank in the dark and eventually came up with the company, who had stopped for the rest of the night about twelve miles north-east of Saunnu. After a lot of talk and orders we eventually went to sleep.

"Reveille on the morning of the 23rd of January was at 5.30 and all vehicles were started up ready to move at a moment's notice. Half an hour before dawn, at about 6.15, a column of transport drove up from the direction of Saunnu and halted abreast of the transporter company and about three hundred yards away. After a quarter of an hour this column suddenly opened fire and much confusion prevailed. Some transporters drove off at high speed; some were deserted with their engines still running, and their crews either ran off into the desert or jumped on a passing lorry. In this manner the corporal's tank of 3rd Troop, which was still on its transporter, was lost. My own tank at first would not start up, but by dint of 'ki-gassing' eventually it did.

"We then advanced slowly and I had the guns swung round towards the enemy. However, we were unable to shoot owing to the number of transporters and lorries between us and the enemy. The enemy's fire, though fierce, was inaccurate and I saw no vehicle hit.

"I followed on behind the transporter company, intending to act as a rear guard in case of pursuit. However, this did not materialize, and after going five miles north-east I ran into the 9th Lancers' 'B' Echelon under Captain Meyrick. He also had a lot of oddments with him, such as gunners and R.A.S.C. lorries. I therefore joined forces with Captain Meyrick, who said he was pleased to see me. We motored for about fifty miles and close-leaguered for the night four miles south of Msus on the Msus—Saunnu track.

"On the morning of the 24th of January we moved on down the track and after about fourteen miles found the Brigade 'B' Echelon, and I made contact on the wireless with the squadron. The squadron leader expressed delight on hearing from me and gave me directions as to how to rejoin the squadron. This I eventually did, having as guide Second-Lieutenant Reid.

"After I had rejoined the squadron they moved on and thereupon my tank broke down again with the same trouble. The fitters, under Sergeant Maloney, managed to obtain the necessary spares from an abandoned tank and by nightfall had half finished the job, when they had to leave me to rejoin the squadron. I spent the night alone.

"On the morning of the 25th Sergeant Maloney came back to me to finish the job. I was ordered to rejoin the squadron as soon as possible and was told that they were moving east. Whilst Sergeant Maloney was working I could see German columns to the west and south-west, and even south of me, only about three miles away at one point. Eventually the job was finished and we moved off east. However, I could find no signs of the Brigade or the Regiment and I caught up with the Support Group under Brigadier Valentin, who gave me directions to the east. I went east and suddenly heard on the wireless the squadron leader ordering the squadron to slow down to twenty-five! After that I was out of touch with the squadron on the wireless.

"I then saw, through my glasses, about a mile distant, a tank which I thought was a Honey, and as it was to the east of me possibly that it belonged to the 9th Lancers. I drove to within seven hundred yards of it and looked again, to discover that it was a German Mark III. Some shooting then ensued, both tanks being very inaccurate with their fire—the German one so much so that it was almost hitting Sergeant Maloney and his fitters' lorry behind me. Then the German turned north and made off, and I refrained from following from fear of getting lost and running into a large force of Germans, and therefore being at a numerical disadvantage with only one tank and one lorry.

"I found the Support Group again, and Brigadier Valentin ordered me to be his advanced guard, as we were cut off by the Germans. He further ordered me not to fight if the enemy was encountered, but to patrol around them and pretend I was not just one tank but a whole squadron. We then pushed on as far as the big salt marsh south of Msus, where we halted and brewed up. After dark Brigadier Valentin held a conference and said that, as we were cut off by the enemy, we were going to try to get through by a forced night march. He was going to travel in three columns, himself leading the centre column in the armoured command vehicle, and I was to follow directly behind him. Our objective was Cherruba.

"At 9.30 that night we started. We could see all round us the flares from the German leaguers and once we could see a column of their transport moving across our path. However, by 3.30 on the morning of the 26th we had pushed through the German leaguers without incident, except for my tank running into a truck in the dark. We then halted for two hours' sleep. At a quarter to six on the 26th we moved on and just after daylight we hit the Mechili—Cherruba track, about ten miles from Cherruba. Here the armoured command vehicle ran out of oil and I was ordered to tow it. This I did and eventually we arrived in the Cherruba Valley, where I regained wireless touch with the squadron.

"I stayed with the armoured command vehicle all day, as we had no fuel oil. I sent Sergeant Maloney back to the squadron with two Honeys that he had salvaged soon after I had started towing operations. By night time the armoured command vehicle was running again, and I rejoined the squadron the following morning on the 27th of January."

All morning on the 29th of January reports came in which indicated the enemy's intention to push across the desert on the old Msus—Bir Tengeder route. At midday an order was received: "Prepare to advance," and the force formed up down the Golden Valley in the order Guards Brigade, Divisional Headquarters, 2nd Armoured Brigade. Leaving the Support Group to hold the approaches to our mountain fastness, we set forth.

After covering about twenty miles the Guards bumped into some enemy, including a few tanks, and had a fight. Nothing came of this by dark and the entire army was preparing to leaguer when the order came to return to Cherruba. So, like the noble Duke of York, we marched back to the Golden Valley in the moonlight and snatched the remaining hours of sleep lying beside our vehicles.

Even this little jaunt had taxed severely the remaining strength of some of our tanks and we spent the next morning sweeping up the bits. At 3 p.m. the order came for the Brigade to withdraw to a position south-east of Mechili, so we packed up hurriedly and moved off down the dusty east-bound track.

We spent two days at Der Grima, where we were joined by the remainder of the Regimental Group, "E" Battery and "C" Company, 1st Rifle Brigade, both rather battered but only too glad to be back again in their proper place. There were no signs of the enemy and everyone managed to catch up with some much-needed sleep.

The Regiment's first battle in Africa had turned out badly, yet every man had acquitted himself well. We emerged from Saunnu and Msus and Cherruba with a feeling of frustration and bewilderment and a wish to be allowed to meet the enemy again soon on proper terms.

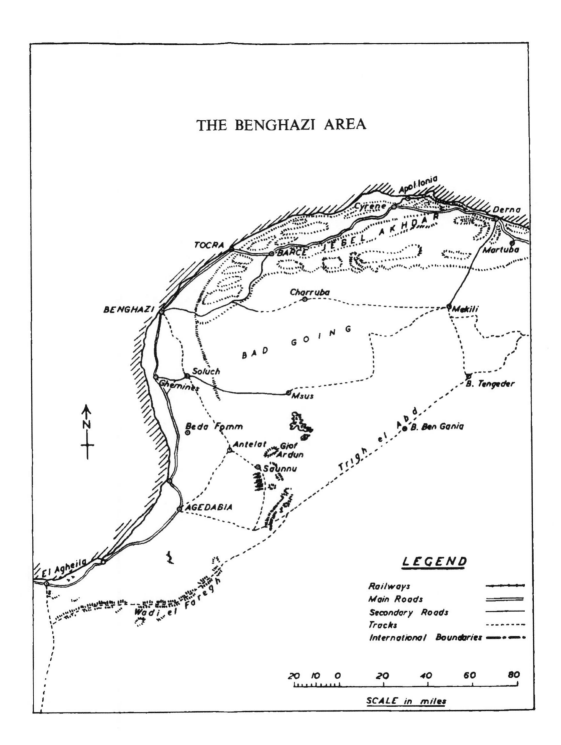

THE BENGHAZI AREA

Apollonia

Cyrene

Derna

TOCRA

BARCE   JEBEL   AKHDAR

Martuba

BENGHAZI

Charruba

Mekili

BAD   GOING

Soluch

Ghemines

Msus

B. Tengeder

N

Beda Fomm

Antelat

Giof Ardun

Trigh el Abd

B. Ben Gania

Saunnu

AGEDABIA

El Agheila

Wadi el Faregh

LEGEND

Railways	
Main Roads	
Secondary Roads	
Tracks	
International Boundaries	

20   10   0   20   40   60   80

SCALE in miles

CHAPTER VIII

THE GAZALA LINE

GENERAL ROMMEL seemed to be taking little interest in the open desert and it was to be presumed that his armour was in no better condition than ours. Provided that we kept abeam of the force delaying his advance in the north, thus securing it against encircling attack, there was little else we could do. The armoured-car patrols out in front had only the gazelle and desert fox for company.

On the 2nd of February, 1942, the order came to fall back once more. All movement had to be confined to the night hours because enemy air reconnaissance was very much on the alert, and at dusk the squadrons formed up in single file nose to tail awaiting the order to move. It was icy cold on those night marches, but the dust hung closer to the ground and the strain of driving was thereby eased. We moved off under a brilliant desert moon down the centuries-old camel track, the Trigh Enver Bei. In the past the Bedouin caravans had used it to make their annual journey from Agedabia and Msus to Egypt, trading in camels, wool and corn in exchange for sugar, tea and cloth. It was a queer business. Hour upon hour with never a sign of human life, only the interminable desert of silvery sand, dotted with the black shadows of camel scrub and boulders, stretching for hundreds of miles in every direction.

Dawn on the 3rd found the Regiment at Gabri el Abid, spread out and facing westward. That night the march was continued to Sighfet el Sidia, south of Acroma. During that day we could hear the dull rumble of explosions far away to the north. Warning came over the rear link that the Germans were using captured British cars and trucks to do reconnaissances.

At dusk a small column of trucks and three-tonners came into the leaguer from the east, and to our great joy it turned out to be Major K. J. Price and sixteen complete crews of "A" Squadron. Although the march was due to continue as soon as it was properly dark, a rapid change-over took place and we said good-bye to Major George Streeter and his Bays' squadron, who left at once to rejoin their regiment. The 9th were once more a regiment, forty-seven tanks strong, all of great mileage and in desperate need of repair. We were still served by a Bays' echelon.

That night we moved again, down the Trigh, and halted after fourteen miles. Although we did not know it at the time, we had reached the Gazala Line, to be held in comparative peace from then until the end of May. The line was based on the rocky and impassable heights at Ain el Gazala, and ran due south into the Libyan Desert to Bir Hacheim, an area of ground just a little less flat than

59

its surroundings. In the centre it was sown with mines and guarded by strong-points behind which the bulk of the armour could manœuvre. As a line it was weak and too much reliance was placed on artificial obstacles, but it was the only one possible between Agheila and the frontier. To keep Tobruk it was necessary to hold it.

On the 5th of February Major Cecil Lomax rejoined with our own echelon, and R.Q.M.S. Putnam doled out some much-needed kit. Our boots in particular had become very dilapidated.

In the afternoon we moved again, three miles east, to allow the 201st Guards Brigade to move in and occupy our present position. Whilst this was going on three Dorniers came over and had a good look round. They returned early the next morning and bombed the "B" Echelon area.

When the Colonel was satisfied that no more immediate moves were likely, the order went round to dig in. One of the few advantages of being in the desert was the ease with which holes of almost any dimension could be dug. During the next weeks all soft vehicles began to sink below ground: in many cases it was possible to get engines and wheels well in, a precaution which proved later to be a sound one when the area became the happy hunting ground of machine-gunning fighters.

The orderly-room staff constructed with loving care a deep, circular pit in which they mounted their private .300 Browning. They had to put up with a considerable amount of advice on the subject of the pen being mightier than the sword, but they persisted, and on any fine evening when the drone of distant motors indicated a visitation they could be seen leaping off the tailboard of their lorry into the pit. No aircraft was considered too high to engage and by the end of the month their heap of empty cartridges reached monumental height. As a punishment for firing one evening at our own tactical reconnaissance aircraft, they had to be suspended for three days, and it can truly be said that for that period the light went out of their lives.

Everyone was encouraged to fire at hostile aircraft, more as a means of keeping up morale than in the serious hope of doing much damage. Undoubtedly the hail of tracer which greeted the enemy aircraft (and, regrettably, sometimes our own) was a source of comfort and amusement. The pilot of a Hurricane who was incorrectly identified by the whole Division reported two hundred and seventeen hits on his machine. In point of fact, the danger from the enemy planes was negligible in comparison with that from neighbours whose enthusi-asm ran away with their ideas on safety angles. There came a time when no one was allowed to fire until a Bofors gun opened up, but then it happened just the same.

On the 8th of February the new Corps Commander, Lieutenant-General W. M. E. Gott, visited the Regiment. He told us that a new establishment for an armoured brigade was to be tried out. The 2nd Armoured Brigade was to consist of two armoured regiments, the Queen's Bays and the 9th Lancers, twenty-four 25-pounders, sixteen anti-tank guns, and the 1st Battalion The Rifle Brigade. At a time when the 25-pounder was the mainstay of the Army it was an attempt to overcome the inequality of tank armament by increasing the gun power within the brigades.

A few changes took place within the Regiment. Lieutenant V. H. White, of "C" Squadron, relieved Lieutenant Percy Oxley on Regimental Headquarters, the latter still suffering from the direct hit on his tank during "the Stakes." Captain George Meyrick became second-in-command of "B" Squadron, Captain E. W. Hylton being detached to the Polish Brigade, and Lieutenant Charles Heycock took over the duties of Navigation Officer from Lieutenant T. Montgomerie, who rejoined the Black Watch.

On the 9th General Lumsden, fully recovered from a mine accident, resumed command of the Division and General Messervy left. The composition of the 1st Armoured Division at this period was as follows:

2nd Armoured Brigade
The Royals (armoured car regiment).
The Bays and 9th Lancers (armoured regiments).
11th (H.A.C.) Royal Horse Artillery (twenty-four 25-pounders).
A battery of anti-tank guns (sixteen guns).
1st Battalion The Rifle Brigade.
A detachment of Royal Engineers.
A troop of light anti-aircraft guns (Bofors).

201st Guards Brigade (Motorized Infantry)
3rd Battalion Coldstream Guards.
1st Battalion Scots Guards.
9th Battalion The Rifle Brigade.
2nd Royal Horse Artillery.
51st Field Regiment, Royal Artillery.
A battery of light anti-aircraft guns (Bofors).

By now it seemed certain that we were in for one of the many quiet periods during which both sides prepared themselves for future battles. The enemy held an outpost line running from Tmimi, on the Bay of Bomba, through Mekili to Bir Tengeder, with patrols operating to the south. There was thus a No Man's Land of about forty miles opposite our position. In this vast area the armoured cars played "Tom Tiddler" to their hearts' content with the German six-wheelers. For us it was a period of rest, training and refitting, although we were always at about an hour's notice. Enemy aircraft, operating in pairs, were active and on most days there was a wild scamper for guns and slit trenches.

One evening the Ordnance Mechanical Engineer, Lieutenant "Jock" Henderson, was returning to leaguer up the Trigh el Abd in his 15-cwt. truck when two Messerschmitt 109's descended on him from the sun. He and Private Patterson took refuge underneath whilst the machine guns ripped into the engine. There was some very hard swearing that evening.

The Regimental Group practised forming up in every possible direction and very soon became very handy. A Brigade exercise took place on the 14th of February, a dull, cloudy day. The Bays were leading and the 9th were rear guard. All was going well when we passed Bir Harmat, heading south, but suddenly the sky was full of aircraft as a force of thirty Macchis and Messerschmitts burst out of the low clouds. They pounced on our "A" Echelon, which was just behind the tanks, and in seconds one "C" Squadron petrol lorry was blazing and another smashed to bits, until the scene was blotted out in thick waves of black smoke. Everyone was firing back as hard as they could and a great cheer went up as a Macchi spun blazing into the sand. This was credited to Corporal Ritchie's Bren, which had already spent seven magazines.

By this time we had halted and the next moment the attackers turned for home. By one chance in a million a British fighter patrol happened to pass and saw what was going on. They turned. Each pilot picked his target and dived. We were too excited to put our heads under cover as the hail of bullets whistled down and we had a perfect view of the most complete victory to date. The enemy tried to run for home, but the Tomahawks had full belts and all the advantages. Two more Macchis thumped into the ground and blew up. The chase was on, and of the twenty-eight attacking enemy planes twenty-two were shot down. The most serious damage on our side was to one of our two precious Scammell recovery lorries, which had thirty-six bullets in the engine. No one had been scratched.

The exercise was concluded and on return to leaguer it appeared that a situation was developing. The armoured cars reported fifty to sixty enemy tanks twenty miles away moving east. By evening they were halted sixteen miles away, the wireless net was opened and the Regiment stood-to at dawn. For three or four days everyone remained at instant notice, but the affair fizzled out.

By the 16th of February all enemy columns were stationary. The Royal Air Force had by this time flown a number of sorties against them and groups of the new Boston medium bombers were passing over several times daily. Derna and Martuba aerodromes were water-logged and the enemy was consequently unable to protect his ground forces from this sudden onslaught from the air. On the 19th air reconnaissance reported no enemy nearer than Mekili.

The remainder of the month passed without incident, except for continual strafing attacks from the air. The rainstorms began to give way to finer weather and the first signs of spring appeared. We had not expected to see flowers in those barren wastes and their arrival came as a welcome surprise. Their life was brief, but they possessed an intensity of beauty which was enhanced by the bleakness of their surroundings. Mostly of miniature variety, the forerunners of the cultured garden plants, there were scarlet pimpernels and little blue angel's tears, while in the rocky wadis bloomed miniature saffron snapdragons and gold or amber rock roses. In the valleys there were great clusters of purple mallow and in the most unexpected places we found the tall, white lily-of-the-field. Perhaps they did not stand comparison with the flowers we saw later in Tunisia, but they had a rare beauty which filled many of us with a great longing for home.

On the last day of the month we received an unexpected visitor—Mrs. Clare Booth, of the American Press. It was strange to set eyes on a woman again, particularly such a fair one. In the absence of the Colonel, the Adjutant had to answer some very-much-to-the-point questions, not the least awkward being: "How do you account for the recent defeat of three famous cavalry regiments?" The only possible answer was to ask Mrs. Booth to step outside and examine first an American Honey and then a German Mark III which we had found and towed into leaguer. She took a ride in the Honey, looked at the Mark III, and said: "Yes—I see."

The Second-in-Command of the 10th Hussars, Major J. Archer-Shee, came to see us on the 4th of March and told us that we were to be relieved by them on the 7th so that we could go back to the "wire" to take over new tanks.

During the interval a penetration test was carried out against the German Mark III. The 2-pounder on the Crusader and the 37-mm. on the Honey did not make more than a shallow impression on the front plate at four hundred yards. Even at one hundred yards they failed to penetrate the lower plate, but did so on the upper one. These results were depressing, and the Brigadier was invited to come and have a look.

On the 6th of March the 10th Hussars arrived from Capuzzo. As each squadron was relieved it moved across the Trigh el Abd to a new leaguer north of the Bays. Here the best fifteen cruisers were handed over to the Bays, together with six good Honeys, three scout cars and the Signal Section. Fifteen old crocks were taken over from the Bays for driving back to Capuzzo.

It was understood that whilst waiting for new tanks the Regiment was to find a clean rest area on the sea east of Tobruk. So we moved off in the afternoon and leaguered for the night on the escarpment four miles west of El Adem. The Colonel, who had been to Division, joined us with the news that we were still "operational" (no wireless, forty-two very old crocks and a few guns). Major Price and Captain Meyrick had been left behind with the Bays and 10th Hussars respectively in case we had to move back again in a hurry into the front line. Hoping very much that our services would not be required, we moved off the next day and pitched camp one mile north of the Tobruk—Gambut road two miles from the sea. The Second-in-Command had found a sheltered wadi covered in wild flowers and we looked forward to a good rest and unlimited bathing.

The next morning, when the camp was nicely arranged and a great deal of laundry was spread out to dry, Major Sir Peter Farquhar arrived from Brigade with orders to move back immediately to the Sidi Rezegh area. In high dudgeon the Regiment packed up, took one last look at the sea, and by sundown was again leaguered two miles south-west of the little white mosque round which so much desperate fighting had taken place the previous autumn. The area was covered with wreckage: graves and explosives littered the ground; piles of unfired and rusting shells lay among the scrub; lines of derelict tanks, burnt to cinders inside, stood out on the skyline; every yard of the desert was covered with expended bullets, splinters of shells or unexploded grenades. It was a cheerful place in which to put a regiment supposed to be resting and recuperating.

There was a tragedy on the first evening when Major Lomax, who had the echelon leaguered in the low ground, came up to look at the new area. On the way back his car hit a teller mine which was buried on the edge of the track, and blew up. Corporal Egmore, the driver, had both ear-drums burst, and Trooper Mustoe (Major Lomax's servant) was so seriously hurt that he died the next day. Major Lomax escaped with a few skin wounds, but his precious staff car was completely written off. Poor Mustoe was the first victim in the Regiment of what must be regarded as one of the rottenest devices of war—the mine laid indiscriminately by a soldier who does not even have the satisfaction of seeing the result of his handiwork.

The Adjutant went off immediately to Brigade, now forty-three miles away, to ask permission to move to a less unhealthy place. Brigadier Briggs promised to see the Divisional Commander and telephone the result. Permission came shortly afterwards and leaguer was moved about two miles due south on to a cleaner piece of desert.

The Regiment remained at Sidi Rezegh until early April. During this time "A" and "C" Squadrons went back to Capuzzo and exchanged the old tanks for new. By the time this was finished the tank position was as follows:

"A" Squadron: sixteen Crusaders.
"B" Squadron: twenty-three Honeys and two old cruisers.
"C" Squadron: three new Crusaders, eight Honeys and one old cruiser.
Regimental Headquarters was mounted in two new Crusaders and two new Honeys.

Rumour had it that a new American medium tank had arrived and that shortly we would receive enough to equip a squadron. This was excellent news. It must be remembered that at this time we were hopelessly behind the Germans in armour, fire power and reliability. The "splendid new 2-pounder tank gun" was a miserable little thing; its shell simply bounced off the standard Mark III, and the German panzer crews treated it with contempt. They measured their armour in inches whilst ours was reckoned in millimetres, and the high-velocity 50-mm. German gun cut easily through Crusader and Honey alike. They could sit down comfortably at fifteen hundred yards and with their magnificent telescopic sights pick off British tanks at leisure, whereas our orders were, of necessity, not to open up at anything greater than six hundred yards. To be able to do this there was much concentration on training in the use of smoke. In theory one squadron blinded the enemy by a curtain of 3-inch smoke whilst the remaining two squadrons closed the range as quickly as possible and, pushing their noses through the screen, did what damage they could. Sometimes it worked out as intended, "A" Squadron being particularly brilliant at these tactics, but usually the attackers found themselves silhouetted against the white phosphorus and suffered many casualties.

In those days any mention of "enemy tanks approaching" filled us with dismay, not because normal courage was lacking but because if we could not stop them no one could. The worst bogey of all was the 88-mm. anti-tank gun, converted originally from the "flak" gun common throughout the Wehrmacht. This was arriving in the desert in increasing numbers and was rapidly becoming a nightmare to all tank crews. Its range was colossal and, by virtue of an elaborate and extremely powerful telescope, it seldom missed its target. It fired a 23-pound armour-piercing shell or a 20-pound high-explosive with air-burst or instantaneous fuses. In the sights were coloured lenses which enabled the gunlayer to see through the mirage or the glare of the midday sun. On a still day nearby tank commanders would see a furrow in the sand streaking towards one of their neighbours. This was made by the shell speeding a few feet above the ground. A miss would hit the ground and then go shuddering and skipping away down the desert, still able to kill or maim anything or anyone who lay in its path. A direct hit felt as though a gigantic sledge-hammer had hit the tank. The shell made a neat, round hole about four inches in diameter, and then filled the turret with red-hot chunks of flying metal. Such a hit usually meant death, or at least loss of limbs, to two or three members of the crew. Often the shell passed through the fighting compartment into the engine and there set the petrol tanks on fire. Many men died trying to extricate helpless comrades from blazing wrecks. Right up to the end of the war the 88-mm. remained our most bitter enemy and was quite the most successful weapon the enemy possessed.

At the end of February Lieutenant John Marden and two "B" Squadron non-commissioned officers, Sergeant Hillary and Corporal Simpson, were sent back to Abbassia schools to learn the gunnery details of the new tank, the Grant. On the same day Lance-Corporal O'Connor, of "A" Squadron, stepped on a mine and was instantly killed. He was buried at Sidi Rezegh cemetery. That afternoon Lance-Corporal Randall, a tank driver on Regimental Headquarters, stubbed his toe on a 20-mm. shell. The shell exploded and Randall was removed to hospital suffering from leg injuries. It was here that someone found a German Mark III in good order lying out in the desert to the south. For several days it was driven about the leaguer before being removed by Division. Eventually it found its way back to England, where it was seen some two years later by 9th Lancers officers on a tactical course at Oxford. Indeed, Major K. J. Price was once invited to recount the circumstances under which it was collected.

By the 4th of April all new tanks were camouflaged and fitted with "sun-shields." These were monstrous cages of tubing covered with hessian which from above made a tank resemble a large lorry. They were fixed on in two halves, and, in theory, could instantly be jettisoned by the commander pulling a slip

G

cord above his head, but in practice they fell off regularly and remained immovable when required to come off.

On the 5th of April news came through that the Medical Officer, Captain John Dugan, had been awarded a Military Cross for gallant rescue work of wounded men in the Saunnu battle, and Sergeant Welham a Military Medal for his great courage in saving the lives of Sergeant Dudeney's crew. These were our first awards in the desert.

"A" and "B" Squadrons and Regimental Headquarters loaded on to transporters during the morning of the 5th and moved up to a cross-tracks called "Knightsbridge." Here they off-loaded and drove the remaining six miles to a position one mile south of the 10th, near Bir Aslagh. "A" and "B" Echelons followed, and "C" Squadron remained at Sidi Rezegh until the 8th in order to shoot-in their new guns.

We arrived to find ourselves at instant notice. Strong enemy columns were out in front, twenty miles away, and shelling our patrols. The 50th Division had a column in contact and the Royals and 12th Lancers had a screen in observation. The Colonel ordered a troop out to watch the south, and heavy gun fire could be heard to the west, but by evening things quietened down.

The next morning brought news that several enemy columns were cruising about in front of us, all of them containing strong tank guards and the general trend seemed to be southwards. "Welcol," a "Jock" column, reported that they were withdrawing under considerable pressure on to the centre of the main line and until sundown their gun fire could clearly be heard. The temperature that day rose to 105 degrees. It looked as if things were working up to a major encounter. Heavy enemy bombing and strafing on the southern end of the line indicated a turning movement that side, and the arrival of "C" Squadron after lunch on the 8th made everyone feel happier. The Regiment was rested, equipped with new tanks and ready for anything.

On the 9th "Welcol" had two minor engagements and the South African Division, holding the high ground at the extreme north, took one hundred and sixty-eight Italian prisoners. "B" Squadron went out on the 10th and joined "Welcol," and tension remained until the 16th, when "B" Squadron returned to the Regiment having had some very useful experience.

On the 17th the Brigade was relieved by the 1st Army Tank Brigade and moved off to an area south of Bir Gubi, taking two days and an exercise on the way. From here "B" Squadron began to collect its new Grant tanks, and by the end of the month had seven and quickly learned the maintenance details of the engines and guns. The Grants looked a bit tall and clumsy after the cruisers, but their 75-mm. gun appeared to be a real weapon at last. The unceasing work that this squadron put in during the next few weeks was to pay handsome dividends in a very short time.

April blew itself out in the worst "khamseen" we had yet experienced. It raged for three days, leaving everyone limp and dirty.

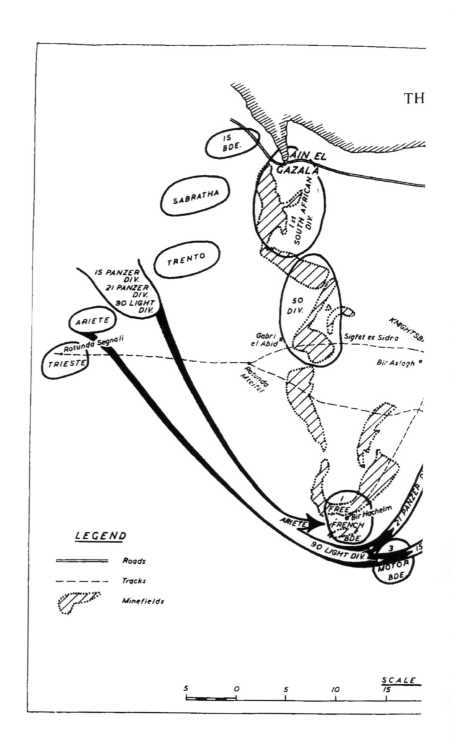

TH

15
BDE.

AIN EL
GAZALA

1st SOUTH AFRICAN DIV.

SABRATHA

TRENTO

15 PANZER DIV.
21 PANZER DIV.
90 LIGHT DIV.

50 DIV.

KNIGHTSB.

ARIETE

Gabr i
el Abid

Sigfet es Sidra

Rotunda Segnali

Bir Aslagh

TRIESTE

Rotunda
Mteifel

1 FREE FRENCH BDE.
Bir Hacheim

ARIETE

27 PANZER

90 LIGHT DIV.

3 15
MOTOR BDE.

Roads

Tracks

Minefields

SCALE

5   0   5   10   15

THE BATTLE OF KNIGHTSBRIDGE—
E OPPOSING FORCES AND ENEMY PLAN

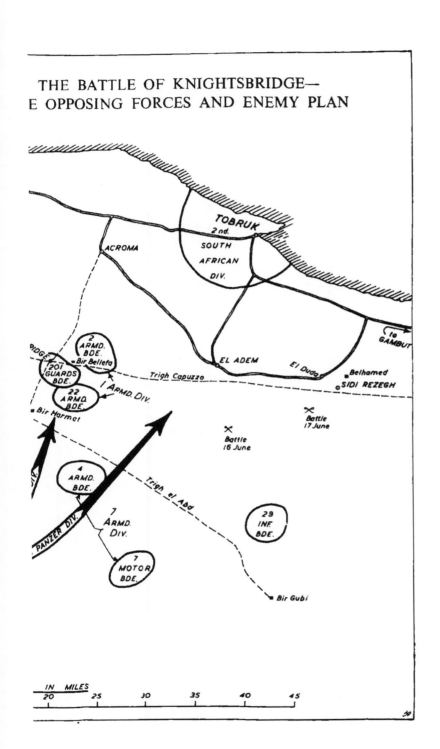

CHAPTER IX

KNIGHTSBRIDGE

THE heavy sandstorms continued during the first weeks of May, 1941, and on two occasions the regimental office tent became airborne. Each time this happened it took an hour to recover all papers.

Early in the month two distinguished visitors came to see us. On the 2nd His Royal Highness The Duke of Gloucester inspected the Regiment before lunching with the 10th, his own regiment, and on the 7th His Majesty King George of the Hellenes came to see us fire the 75-mm. guns. By this time "B" Squadron had mastered the technique and their shooting was good. They exchanged ideas regularly with the Queen's Bays and the 22nd Armoured Brigade.

There was a general feeling of restlessness in the air. Rommel's reconnaissance in force during the previous month could have had but one object: to test our defences and discover our dispositions. There were indications that both the 15th and 21st Panzer Divisions had concentrated in the area of Rotunda Segnali, so it was no surprise when, on the 12th of May, orders were received to re-form regimental groups and move up first to El Gubi and then to a battle position south of El Adem. The 12th Lancers were placed under the command of the 22nd Armoured Brigade and the Royals under the 2nd Armoured Brigade.

The move to El Gubi took the form of an exercise. On arrival there "B" Squadron received more Grants, making their strength up to twelve, and the echelons and all load tables had to be reorganized to carry the larger ammunition and more petrol.

By now the Regiment was mounted as follows: "A" and "C" Squadrons and Regimental Headquarters were in Crusaders; and "B" Squadron had twelve Grants, with a Crusader and two Honeys on squadron headquarters. A thirteenth Grant arrived on the 22nd, bringing the Regiment up to strength.

From the 22nd of May onwards an attack seemed imminent. We stood-to at 5 a.m. each day, practised forming up in almost every direction and received many long and complicated operation instructions designed to cover every contingency. At this time the officers and warrant officers of the Regiment were:

Regimental Headquarters
   Lieutenant-Colonel J. R. Macdonell.
   Major Sir Peter Farquhar, Bart.
   Captain R. O. G. Gardner (Adjutant).
   Captain E. R. Donnley (Technical Adjutant).

Lieutenant R. Merritt (Signals Officer).
Second-Lieutenant C. W. Heycock (Intelligence and Navigating Officer).
R.S.M. A. Blandford.

"A" Squadron
Major K. J. Price.
Captain M. S. Close.
Lieutenant W. T. Cadman.
Lieutenant W. G. Peek.
Lieutenant A. J. Grant.
S.S.M. B. Coleman.

"B" Squadron
Major R. S. G. Perry.
Captain G. Meyrick.
Captain D. A. St. G. Laurie.
Lieutenant J. Marden.
Lieutenant The Hon. R. E. Lloyd-Mostyn.
Lieutenant R. C. Okell.
Lieutenant R. P. Thomas.
S.S.M. H. Huxford.

"C" Squadron
Captain D. E. C. Steel, D.S.O.
Captain R. N. Kingscote.
Lieutenant D. A. W. Allen.
Lieutenant V. H. White.
Lieutenant T. J. Jenner-Fust.
Lieutenant J. Wills.
S.S.M. T. C. Hardwidge.

H.Q. Squadron
Major C. C. Lomax.
Captain (Quartermaster) W. V. Tully.
Lieutenant J. W. Reid.
Lieutenant M. St. J. Wilmoth.
R.Q.M.S. W. Putnam.
T.Q.M.S. A. Sylvester.
S.S.M. L. Dale.

Major D. C. F. Erskine left us on the 20th of May and went to Australia as an instructor to the Australian armoured troops.

On the 24th of May the Brigade moved again to a new battle position. That day everyone seemed to be doing the same thing—the whole desert was filled with moving columns and there were many stops to avoid bumping and boring. The Regiment eventually reached a very "second-hand" bit of ground on the edge of the escarpment north-east of the Knightsbridge cross-tracks.

On arrival, six Crusaders, including the Colonel's, were found to have leaking water pumps, a disaster of no small magnitude. The alternative to sending them into the workshops for about ten days was to mend them within the Regiment, and, as Captain Donnley could produce the necessary packing, work was ordered to commence at first light. By working in relays, regimental fitters got all tanks back on the road again in the nick of time. Four transporters stood by during this time in case of need.

The 25th of May brought news of general pressure all along the line. The 50th Division was under heavy shell fire all day and as soon as night fell great air activity began. Twin-engined German bombers roared round the sky singly, bombing and machine-gunning everything they could see in the moonlight, and El Adem and Tobruk aerodromes were heavily attacked. One Heinkel dropped a stick of bombs across "A" Squadron without damage, and passed so low over the guard that they shot at it with their revolvers. The rear gunner retaliated with a burst from his twin guns and the guard hastily flattened out.

All night long the thud of bombs and the crackle of machine guns filled the air. Some of us stood in the cold air watching the terrific barrage of Tobruk. Bofors shells sailed lazily upwards in groups of five, like red balls which disappeared as the tracer burnt out, and ended in a little white twinkle as the shell burst. Up above were the bursts of the heavier anti-aircraft shells and, even at that distance, the roar of the barrage could be heard. Stand-to was ordered for 5.30 a.m. and everyone went to sleep wondering what the morrow would bring.

The 27th of May dawned calm and clear. We had just finished a peaceful breakfast when the Brigade Major, Major John Scott, M.C., 9th Lancers, rang up and put us at instant readiness. The Colonel left at once for Brigade, which lay only half a mile away, and within ten minutes he came on the air to order the Adjutant to take his tank over to him and bring the Navigating Officer.

In a quarter of an hour they were back and the Colonel told the squadron leaders the news—which was sufficiently startling. Rommel, by a forced march in the darkness, had rounded the southern end of the Gazala Line. Leaving the Italians to invest the Free French Brigade at Bir Hacheim, he had hurried all his armour, with its supporting artillery and infantry, northwards *inside* the British defensive minefields. The 22nd Armoured Brigade was already in action near Bir Harmat with about seventy-five German tanks, and, worst of all, the 4th Armoured Brigade, of the 7th Armoured Division, had been caught napping and had been overrun.

Packing up was completed in record time and muzzle covers were removed as the Brigade formed up three miles to the south-west, facing south, with the Bays leading, 10th Hussars right and 9th Lancers left. Sunshields were discarded and all preparations made for immediate action.

The Brigade moved slowly southwards and then wheeled west. Soon afterwards the Bays reported that they were in action against an enemy column moving fast across their front and northwards. The Brigadier ordered the 9th to move across and fill in the gap between the 2nd Armoured Brigade and the 22nd Armoured Brigade, which, by this time, had disengaged and turned south. Visibility was extremely bad because of the heat and dust and, as always in the desert, it was extremely difficult to tell friend from foe.

The moment we had taken up position on the right of the Brigade a liaison officer from the 3rd County of London Yeomanry arrived at the Colonel's tank and told him that his regiment intended attacking the mass of vehicles in front of them and would be grateful for any help we could give them. Brigade gave us permission, so the Grants of "B" Squadron were moved up into line with the 22nd Armoured Brigade and "E" Battery put their trails on the ground behind. "A" and "C" Squadrons moved up on to the flanks and "B" Squadron and the 25-pounders started shelling. Fires and tall columns of black smoke soon showed that both were shelling to good effect. Then the Colonel ordered the cruiser squadrons to attack. At this moment Major Perry was severely wounded in the head by a shell splinter and, as Captain Meyrick was still away on a course, command of "B" Squadron fell to Captain David Laurie.

As was afterwards discovered, our opponents were the 90th Light Division, who had been moving north when both brigades hit them in the flank. The enemy had rapidly thrown out a screen of anti-tank guns, but this was being destroyed by the combined shelling of the Grants and artillery. Both cruiser squadrons shot through the smoke laid by "B" Squadron, and, carrying the fight on to the enemy's doorstep, completely overran his position. They did terrible execution, first as they passed over the remaining gun crews, and then as they got amongst the lorried infantry behind. Tank commanders were dropping grenades right and left and using their pistols and tommy-guns at point-blank range.

By this time the enemy had had enough and the remainder pulled away over the skyline. The two squadrons came back through the smoke and wreckage and re-formed. Sergeant Welham had been killed, several crews were unaccounted for, and four tanks were missing. On the credit side a number of anti-tank guns had been knocked out, including four 88-mms. and over a hundred prisoners taken. The desert was a mass of flaming trucks and lorries and a great number of Germans had been killed; many prisoners came in at the double pursued by very angry Indian soldiers waving large knives. The Indians, who had been captured the evening before and were in the enemy lorries when the attack began, had been given no water since capture and we handed them our water-bottles when they came up. Like the good soldiers they were, they refused to do more than moisten their lips, although we assured them that we had plenty.

It was interesting to read later an extract from the diary of an officer of the 15th Panzer Division, Captain Hubner:

"*27th May, 1942.*—Arrived two kilometres north of Bir Hacheim. First contact with enemy 0730 hours in form of second HQ Sect. coming under artillery fire with the result that many panicked and a number of supply columns fled.

When moving north in wedge formation an English Tank attack took place in the afternoon whereby No. 2 Battalion, 155th Lorried Infantry Regiment, was practically wiped out. Later we received heavy artillery fire. Our men slowly began to regain their composure but not so others, who fled senselessly from the direction of march.

"If we had not got excellent leadership and a first rate corps of officers, things would look black indeed."

Dusk was falling. The enemy guns were blown up by the Royal Engineers and Sergeant O'Connor towed back two of the "A" Squadron cruisers which had been hit. After a short conference at the Bays' headquarters we "brewed-up" and then, turning north, moved about a mile, and leaguered for the night with our head on the Trigh Capuzzo. The night was quiet and gradually the fires from burning vehicles died down. Although no enemy tanks had been encountered, "round one" had gone in our favour.

At dawn on the 28th of May leaguer was broken forward and protected by watchers of the Carrier Platoon of "C" Company, 1st Rifle Brigade, under Lieutenant Mark Culme-Seymour, we cooked breakfast. As a plate of two very nice-looking sausages was being handed up to the Colonel he was sent for by the Brigadier. A force of seventy-five enemy tanks was approaching Acroma, whilst another, presumably Marcks Column (a German column of all arms briefed to reach the Halfaya Pass), had reached Sidi Rezegh, where it was creating havoc among the supply echelons. The only other news was that the 7th Armoured Divisional Headquarters had been overrun and General Messervy and most of his staff were prisoners.

The Brigadier ordered the Regiment back up the escarpment to join the other two regiments. He said he expected to have to give orders for us to do one of three things: to attack the Acroma force, to attack with the 10th Hussars an enemy concentration building up in the south, or to continue the attack westwards. The Colonel ordered "A" Squadron to push a patrol out to watch the south and this was joined by Lieutenant Culme-Seymour's carriers. They had no sooner got out when the troop leader, Lieutenant Tim Cadman, reported three suspicious-looking vehicles approaching him from the south and fired on them when they were in range. Two of them, German armoured cars, wheeled about and fled, but the third kept confidently on. As it was a staff car and nicely covered by the tanks it was allowed to come right up. It halted and disgorged Padre Mawson, of the Bays, blissfully unconscious of either the dangerous company he had been keeping or how nearly he had been shot by us.

During this time "A" Squadron of the Royals kept reporting much enemy movement from the left flank and the 10th were moved out in that direction. They began shelling gun tractors which were trying to tow guns out into position and then attacked with their Grant squadrons but suffered rather heavily.

At this moment the Stukas appeared: they did little damage, but for the next four days we were constantly attacked. Twelve of them, looking like great black vultures, peeled off one by one and screamed down in their almost vertical dive and the yellow bombs could be seen leaving their racks as they pulled out before climbing back into the safety of the sky. After two or three visits, soft-vehicle drivers needed no encouragement to dig slit trenches; they did this automatically at every halt, with the result that casualties were remarkably light.

The Brigadier's third alternative materialized at 3 p.m. on the 28th of May. The 9th Lancers were ordered to lead the attack westwards and after about three miles bumped an enemy column moving across the front from south to north, protected on the flank by Mark III tanks. Hot fire was quickly exchanged and "E" Battery dropped its trails and began ranging. "B" Squadron found that enemy infantry had dug in in front as well, and after having disposed of the Mark III's it began to shell them out and to move slowly forward against a hail of armour-piercing shot from anti-tank guns.

The Royals now reported a second enemy column moving west to our south. The 10th Hussars moved up and engaged, but their "A" Squadron was wiped out in this encounter, being caught in the fire of a concentration of 88-mm. guns. It turned out later that this column was Rommel's tactical headquarters, which was always extremely well guarded.

"B" Squadron was now in control of its own immediate situation and the Brigade moved on again across the Harmat—Hacheim track, where it was held up by another line of guns. As the light was failing we called it a day and drew off and formed close leaguer facing west with our right flank resting on the Knightsbridge Box held by the Guards Brigade.

It was a moonlight night and the Germans were leaguered within gunshot to the west. The Second-in-Command, feeling in need of exercise, walked out across the desert and listened to them shouting and clattering their petrol tins. The Guards were fired on during the night, and their machine guns could be seen blazing away in retaliation westwards. In spite of this and several bombing attacks, most people were too tired not to enjoy six hours' sleep.

When Major Lomax brought the echelon into leaguer in the early part of the night he told a story of such excellence that it spread round the desert like wildfire, eventually appearing weeks later in the London *Times*.

At dusk he had set out with his party of laden three-tonners to find the Regiment, then known to be lying to the south and in advance of the Guards Brigade box at Knightsbridge. Shortly after starting he ditched his car, which was fully equipped with a binnacle compass and all other aids to navigation, in a slit trench and had to transfer into a 15-cwt. truck, which he steered with the aid of a prismatic compass and the stars, and eventually found the Regiment.

On the return journey, just before dawn, followed by long lines of now-empty lorries, he lost direction and veered too far to the north. Suddenly, ahead of him, by the light of an almost hidden moon, he saw one of those low trip-wires which denote the boundary of a minefield. Some way off two shadowy figures were standing. He shouted to them and found that they were two Guardsmen sentries

WESTERN DESERT, 1942

Driver's view through a Grant tank

German Mark III burning

WESTERN DESERT, 1942

Crusaders at speed

Captured 88-mm. gun

and asked if this was the Knightsbridge Box. On being told that it was, Major Lomax said: "How very fortunate! Another few yards and we would all have been in the minefield." "On the contrary, sir," said one of the Guardsmen, "another few yards and you will be out of it."

The angel who guards the welfare of echelons must have been well up on his job that night and the entire echelon drove unscathed in single file in each other's wheel tracks out of the minefield.

There is another tale which, although it did not concern Major Lomax, will bear repeating. The colonel of an armoured regiment near by was also waiting for his echelon and was trying without success to direct the commander over the wireless. His efforts were interrupted by a salvo of enemy shells which sailed overhead and burst a mile or so behind, resulting in the orange glow of a burning vehicle.

"Now, then," said the colonel, resuming his efforts. "Where are you in relation to that bright light?"

To which, after a pause, a miserable voice replied: "I *am* that bright light."

The 29th of May began at 5.30 a.m. and will not be forgotten by anyone who took part in what was probably the stiffest day's fighting of all. The guns were deployed where they leaguered and the Brigade began shaking out to face westwards. Hardly had this been done when a positive rain of shells came down on the 11th H.A.C., and our Medical Officer was soon busy patching up the wounded gunners.

The three regiments were laid out in a triangle, with the guns in the centre and the northern apex resting on the Knightsbridge Box, itself under continuous shelling and assault.

All day long the German panzers attacked, first from one direction, then from another. The fighting was confused and incessant. As each regiment became hard pressed the others moved squadrons across to its help. The Grants were shooting magnificently and time after time brought the squat, black Mark III's and IV's to a standstill. Accustomed to the 2-pounder, the Germans were slow to realize that a new gun was hitting them very hard indeed.

The most critical period of the day came when the 10th Hussars, who had lost almost all their Grants the day before, came over the air with an urgent call for help. They were being pushed in on top of their battery and the situation was serious. Colonel Macdonell ordered "A" and "C" Squadrons to attack under a smoke screen laid by "B." Both squadrons formed up, charged the encircling enemy most gallantly and restored the situation, but at a cost. Lieutenant Tom Jenner-Fust was killed and his entire troop knocked out. Lieutenant John Marden, whose Grant had begun to burn at the canvas dust shield round the big gun, was killed as he climbed out to extinguish it with a Pyrene. "A" Squadron came back with five tanks and "C" with six. "B" Squadron Grants remained intact, but were running desperately short of ammunition. "A" Echelon was dispersed behind the gun line, each driver and his mate lying in slit trenches within yards of their three tons of high explosive—theirs a task which no one envied and which received all too little recognition.

Two lorries were driven up to the Grants and the ammunition racks were replenished under cover of a smoke screen, but the Germans must have seen, for they at once opened up with heavy machine guns. Lieutenant Charles Heycock, who was helping to pass in the rounds, was hit in the stomach and died shortly afterwards. He had been a brilliant navigator and on many occasions his calculations had been proved right when everyone else's were wrong. His death was a very bad blow and left a gap in the Regiment which was very hard to fill.

As dusk fell things began to quieten down. For an hour we watched and waited and during this time one of our precious Grants suddenly burst into flames for no apparent reason and became a total loss, though, fortunately, the crew escaped. On the skyline to the west an enemy force opened up on our guns, which replied promptly, while to the north a huge column of enemy vehicles could be seen moving slowly in a cloud of dust towards the setting sun.

The Regimental Group leaguered in battle order. The two troops of "E" Battery remained unlimbered about a quarter of a mile apart, with "B" Squadron in line between. What remained of "A" and "C" lined out behind "B." "A" Echelon moved in and replenished, and at 11 p.m. "B" Echelon, intact, came rolling up through the darkness. Five minutes later an enemy lorry drove straight up to us. It contained an Italian medical officer and his staff of nine, rather off their course. They were quietly told to dismount and transfer to "B" Echelon lorries. Our own Medical Officer inspected the medical equipment with glistening eyes.

The results of the day's fighting were hard to assess. "A" and "C" Squadrons had lost three officers and eleven men and were reduced to pitifully small strength. "B" was our mainstay and had lost only one tank. Every day the shooting of this squadron was becoming more accurate, their fighting more deadly. Thirteen enemy tanks were knocked out for certain, and there was no doubt that the day's bag was considerably more.

It had been a day when it seemed time and time again as if the weight of the enemy's armour must overwhelm us, yet each time their impetus broke at the critical point. There were moments when the gunners of "E" Battery had to ignore the orders coming in from the observation posts and lower their pieces ready to shoot it out with the German tanks should we fail to stop them. All day those gun detachments had been under constant shell fire, quietly and efficiently loading, laying and firing their 25-pounders as if they were at practice camp at Larkhill. From that day the Regiment took "E" Battery, 11th H.A.C., to its bosom, and there began a partnership which was to continue in mutual trust and affection right up to the "Cease Fire" on the Venetian plains.

Before dawn on the 30th of May the Regiment moved out on to the ridge east of Bir Aslagh, facing north-west and on the right of the Bays. The enemy seemed to have cleared right out of the neighbourhood, leaving twenty of their burnt-out tanks behind as witness of the previous day's struggle, but on the skyline some three miles away we could see a line of enemy tanks, evenly spaced thirty yards apart and looking like grouse butts on a distant moor. We counted thirty-five. The Brigadier went forward to have a closer look and then decided that the 9th Lancers should attack, the Queen's Bays remaining in reserve. At this point the Bays had sixteen tanks left, only five of which were Grants, whilst the 10th Hussars were reduced to one Grant and two cruisers.

Whilst the Colonel was arranging a quick fire-plan with our battery commander, Major Roger Croxton, General Lumsden arrived and gave us a broad outline of the situation. Rommel had not succeeded in his plan for blitz warfare and had been compelled to fall back through the gaps in our minefields. The Royal Air Force had been doing great execution among his supply columns and some of his units had been overheard calling for petrol. He had formed a defensive ring of tanks and anti-tank guns round what became known as "The Cauldron" and was extricating his battered forces under cover of this ring. It was these tanks and guns that we were to attack.

The general wished us good luck and we started off up the slope, "B" Squadron leading, with "C" left and "A" right. The only other vehicle which accompanied the attack was the "White" scout car belonging to Major Scott, the Brigade Major. He could not resist joining in and, although the large map-board which he was waving about must have made him even more conspicuous than usual, he came through unscathed.

As the leading tanks topped the crest they were met by the murderous fire of anti-tank and field guns, but "B" Squadron kept on until it was within effective range and then settled down to steady shooting. Its guns made repeated hits on the enemy tanks, but not one went on fire. After carefully watching individual tanks we came to the conclusion that many of them were derelicts towed into the "shop window" to swell the ranks, but behind them were many 88-mm. guns and these were taking heavy toll of the cruisers. One by one the 75-mm. guns of the Grants were hit and put out of action. "B" Squadron was also running out of ammunition. The Colonel therefore ordered the close-support cruisers to put down smoke, under which the Regiment disengaged and returned to the start point below the ridge. We had made no apparent impression and had obviously taken on far more than was suspected of being there.

"A" Squadron came out with only two tanks, both useless; "B" had eleven Grants; and "C" Squadron was reduced to four cruisers and had suffered one casualty, Lieutenant David Allen, wounded.

It was proved later that the position we had attacked was held by thirty-six tanks and ninety guns, so there was good reason why the Regiment had been unable to make more impression, but this was not known at the time and we were ordered to attack again.

For this we were given "A" Squadron of the 3rd County of London Yeomanry and a composite squadron from the remainder of the 22nd Armoured Brigade. The Commander, Royal Artillery, arrived to organize a 25-pounder smoke screen and barrage, and altogether the 9th Lancers had sixty guns in their support that evening—probably a record.

Our immediate front was the key to the whole battle. If only the crust could be broken and Rommel pushed back through the minefields, the holes could be plugged and the British line restored.

General Lumsden returned. He said to the Colonel: "Well done, Ronald; just once more and we've got them"—a remark which did a great deal to raise our spirits. Shells were falling close by, and his presence with us was an example of his usual method of commanding a division—from the front end.

By 3 p.m. the guns had completed registration. The smoke was timed for 3.20 and our attack for 3.30. Through an unfortunate misunderstanding the guns began to fire ten minutes too soon, and by the time the tanks reached the ridge the air was as clear as a bell and there was no more smoke shell available.

The same thing happened as before: if anything, the enemy's fire was more deadly. The Colonel's cruiser was soon hit and his wireless set went silent. Sergeant Peterson was frantically changing fuses when Major Sir Peter Farquhar, realizing what had happened, brought his cruiser alongside and he and the Colonel changed mounts.

This second attack was no more successful than the first, and on learning that a counter-attack was coming in on our right flank the Brigadier recalled the Regiment. We reversed out of direct gunshot and held a watching brief on the crest.

The Stukas, which had been much in evidence all day, unloaded stick after stick of bombs on our positions and during the day Trooper Elbourne was killed and his store lorry, full of valuable tank spares, was destroyed. S.S.M. Paddy Byrne was also killed and Captain Pat Kelly, 9th Lancers, A.D.C. to General Lumsden, was fatally wounded. Their final attack destroyed a gun tractor belonging to "E" Battery, our medical stores three-tonner and the Medical Officer's own truck. Captain Dugan, M.C., who with his usual courage had been wherever he was most needed, was seriously wounded. As there were many other casualties we had to ask the Bays' medical officer to look after them.

The area of the desert on which we had been fighting for the past three days was by this time an incredible sight. Every yard of it was criss-crossed with tracks and pockmarked with shell-holes, while everywhere lay piles of empty cases. Slit trenches and gun pits had been dug all over the place and round the circumference lay the wreckage of our own and enemy tanks, burnt-out armoured cars and the skeletons of lorries and trucks. Every puff of wind raised a white, powdery dust.

There had been no time for shaving or proper washing, and everyone was tired out through lack of sleep and nervous strain. We looked like a lot of ragged tramps, with sweat-stained shirts and bloodshot eyes.

That evening leaguer was formed in the same way as on the night before. No sooner had we got in than two small high-explosive shells landed slap in the middle of Regimental Headquarters, without damage, but the knowledge that we were under observation and within range of German tanks was disquieting. "A" Echelon was sent out of leaguer again, out of harm's way. For an hour enemy bombers roared round the sky bombing wherever they saw the fires of burning wrecks, and we could see their red-hot exhausts as they passed over.

Crews manned their tanks all night. We knew that the enemy were barely a mile away and were determined not to be surprised.

At about 2 a.m. on the 31st of May a rumble was heard in the east and, some eight hundred yards away, the dim outline of a big column could be seen. The Adjutant walked out across the desert and identified it as British. Subsequently we learnt that it was a Guards column from the "box," but it was too far away and moving too fast to contact, and as it swung north from the enemy in front it came under heavy fire.

At dawn the Brigadier found us and told the Colonel that the time had come to form the inevitable Composite Regiment. We had not got much to subscribe to it: "A" Squadron had no tanks at all, only six of the Grants could still fire, and there were four almost useless cruisers in "C" Squadron. Two troops of Grants (Lieutenants Roger Mostyn and Roger Okell) were sent to join the Bays, and the remainder of the Regiment made its way to "B" Echelon, six miles in the rear.

Those four days' fighting had been fierce and hard, but the Brigade had kept together, each regiment had helped its neighbours, and we had reason to believe that the loss of life and machines, heavy as it was, had at least given others sufficient time to prepare for further plans.

The 9th emerged from Knightsbridge desperately tired but battle-hardened and confident. "B" Squadron, in its battered old Grants, had destroyed nearly forty panzers and under the cool leadership of David Laurie, then only twenty-three years old, had begun to establish a great reputation for itself and the Regiment, proving that British tanks, meeting the Afrika Korps on level terms, could more than hold their own.

The following illustrates the complexity of desert fighting, and is the story of Sergeant Hunt, of "A" Squadron, who was, for a short period, a prisoner in enemy hands a mile behind the battle line:

"During the Knightsbridge battle my tank developed engine trouble and we had to pull out. A recovery Scammell was called for, the cruiser put on tow and off we went to workshops, past the airfield at El Adem and the cross-tracks, where we were waved on by a military policeman. A few hundred yards farther on we passed a truck on the side of which was painted the black German cross. Having withdrawn some distance from the battle we could hardly be blamed for believing this to be a recaptured vehicle. We were wrong, as we soon found to our cost. Within half a mile of the military policeman at the cross-roads we suddenly halted. At the time I was down in the turret and thought little of the halt. However, on putting my head out to see why we had stopped, I received the shock of my life: the Scammell driver and the sergeant were standing with their hands in the air covered by two Jerries with machine guns. Two more were standing by another truck similarly armed.

"Before I could traverse my turret there was a shout from behind and there was a fifth Jerry, standing on the back of the cruiser pointing a machine gun into the turret.

"We'd had it! The situation struck me as being so ridiculous that I could not help laughing—coming out of battle and being taken prisoner with a military policeman on point duty half a mile away. The Germans covering us also saw the funny point and began to laugh too.

"We dismounted, were disarmed and then driven off to where the German column was parked. There were quite a hundred vehicles of ours parked around, and even more of our own men under guard. These seemed quite disgusted with us and failed to see the humour of the situation as we saw it.

"At midday a Spitfire flew over low, waggling its wing-tips, and was promptly shot down by a 20-mm. gun mounted on a truck. At 3 p.m. a battery of 25-pounders opened up on us and quickly found the range, but in three hours' heavy shelling they only hit a captured quad and damaged a German truck, nor were there many casualties among the men.

"The column spread out and moved around and the majority of our fellows moved with them out of the shelling. A few of us decided to risk our own shells and hung on in the hope that we would not be missed when the Germans moved away. At six o'clock Grants opened up with 75's and machine guns from the rear, and I began to wish then we had moved. The Grants were firing at anything that moved, and at that range could not distinguish one uniform from another. Four 50-mm. anti-tank guns had set themselves against the 25-pounders and were now being fired on from front and rear, but they did not move until the German column was safely over the ridge to the south, just as it got dark.

"At about nine o'clock we managed to creep away towards the Grants and found they were units of the 7th Armoured Division. Later we returned to our cruiser and the next day continued the interrupted task of getting it mended."

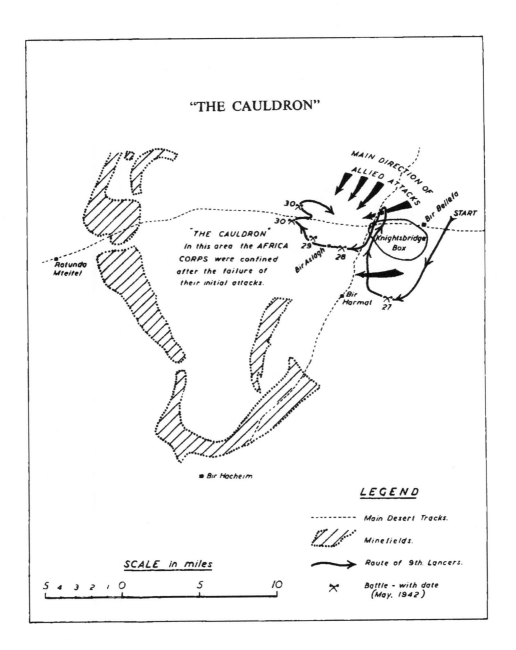

"THE CAULDRON"

"THE CAULDRON"
In this area the AFRICA CORPS were confined after the failure of their initial attacks.

MAIN DIRECTION OF ALLIED ATTACKS

Bir Bellefa
START

Knightsbridge Box

Bir Aslagh

Bir Harmat

Rotunda Mteitel

Bir Hacheim

LEGEND

- - - - - Main Desert Tracks.

//// Minefields.

→ Route of 9th. Lancers.

✕ Battle - with date (May, 1942)

SCALE in miles

5 4 3 2 1 0   5   10

Facing Page 78

CHAPTER X

RETREAT TO ALAMEIN

THROUGH the first days of June we remained in the "B" Echelon area at Bir Bellefa. They were uneasy days and we were wondering how the battle was going, and how the two troops of "B" Squadron were getting on.

Two nights' good sleep and a change of clothing restored us to normal. Efforts were made to account for all the wounded and missing and the total cost since the 27th of May was found to be three officers and fifteen other ranks killed, two officers and thirty-four other ranks wounded, some of whom were believed to be dead, and four men missing. Of the forty-seven tanks which set off for battle on the first morning, twelve had been burned out, two were missing and eighteen had been evacuated as beyond local repair.

Visits were paid to "E" Battery, still fighting with the Queen's Bays, and on one of these it was learnt that Major Croxton had been wounded, happily not seriously.

All three brigades, 2nd, 4th and 22nd, were down to a composite regiment each and the newly arrived 1st Armoured Brigade had been split up to reinforce all three. The 2nd Armoured Brigade was fighting in the area of Maabus el Rigel.

On the 8th of June "A" Squadron took over thirteen new cruisers from the Tank Delivery Squadron and set about making them ready for battle. Whether these were for us or whether they were to be handed over to another brigade we did not know. In fact, sitting back where we were, we did not know very much and we could only sift the many rumours which kept coming in, trying to believe the best of them and hoping that the worst were not true. The most cheering was the one which recounted the story of a U-boat, containing German officers for the administration of the port, surfacing in Tobruk harbour and being sunk by gun fire.

During the afternoon orders came for the 9th and 10th to move back to Bardia. We said good-bye to Major Price and his squadron and moved off on to the tarmac coast road, spending the night at Menastir. Early the next morning Colonels Macdonell and Harvey went ahead to ask the commander of the area for a good place to camp. He seemed anxious to use both regiments in a scheme for the defence of Bardia and required a good deal of persuasion before consenting to give us an area on the sea east of the pass. Both commanding officers had difficulty in keeping a straight face as they argued that without tanks they were of no great value to anyone: out of the window of the hut they could see their regiments already rolling down the Sollum Pass.

By midday we were leaguered among the white foot-hills by the sea, seven miles east of Sollum. To be able to look over the Mediterranean on one side and at the steep, brown mountains on the other was a welcome change from the endless flatness of the desert. To a man the Regiment tore off shirts and shorts and plunged into the sea.

The place was almost too good to be true, and we remarked that we would not be allowed to remain there long. The vehicles were spread out on the land-ward slope of a low ridge running parallel to the beach which towards the sea was of pure white sand in contrast to the amazing blue of the Mediterranean beyond. First the sea was light blue, then it turned quickly into a dark, kingfisher blue and merged into the crystal-clear sky. Two landing craft were out at sea, moving steadily towards Tobruk.

Here we stayed for four days, revelling in complete peace and idleness. "A" Squadron returned on the 11th, having handed over its tanks to the 22nd Armoured Brigade. During this time Captain M. S. Close had been blown up on a mine and had suffered serious leg injuries which kept him out for the remainder of the war. On the 12th of June Major J. H. Scott, M.C., relinquished his appointment of Brigade Major and returned to the Regiment to take over command of "C" Squadron.

It was on this day that we heard the news that Knightsbridge was lost and realized that the campaign was taking a serious turn. The deadlock in the Cauldron had ended and the enemy was coming on again with renewed energy. Tank strengths on both sides were down to a quarter of the original, but the Germans had enough left to force a decision. Everyone realized with a sudden chill that once again the pendulum must swing back. The 88-mm. gun and the superiority of the German tank had won the day and it remained only for the Eighth Army to cut its losses and fall back again.

On the night of the 13th/14th of June orders came for the 9th Lancers to take over the last reserve tanks from the Tank Delivery Regiment at Capuzzo. As these were only sufficient for two squadrons, "C" Squadron remained behind to make its own way back towards the Delta.

A dust-storm raged all day on the 14th. On the dreary spaces which sur-rounded the remains of Fort Capuzzo the tanks were taken over. Of all places in the desert this was the most depressing. Fought over time and time again, smelling of death and desolation, it was littered with wreckage, broken rifles, tumble-down barbed wire, isolated graves, and abandoned field guns. As each tank was taken over the crew set about putting it in fighting trim. Guns had to be stripped, cleaned and tested, the power traverse checked, ammunition stowed and all engine adjustments carried out, while lockers were filled with tinned food and bedding was strapped on. Sergeant Squires and his helpers moved from tank to tank screwing on "86 Rhino" plates and painting yellow squadron signs on the turrets. The Signals staff tuned and checked wireless sets and the Light Aid Detachment and the fitters lent a hand wherever wanted.

By dusk we had Regimental Headquarters mounted in three Honeys, "A" Squadron in sixteen cruisers and "B" Squadron, made up to strength with two troops from the 10th, under Second-Lieutenants Loney and Heathcote, in twelve Grants and three cruisers. At 7 p.m. "White" and "Diamond T" transporters arrived to load up and by 8 p.m. we set off to join the 7th Armoured Division.

All day on the 15th we travelled. The transporters gave their usual trouble and eventually the Grants had to be dismounted and driven. By evening the flash and rumble of guns were getting nearer and by dark we were once more in the front row. No one knew exactly what was happening and there were several columns out in front.

On the 16th "A" Squadron, on the left, rang up to say that there were some suspicious-looking vehicles in front and could these be attacked? The Colonel gave permission and the remainder of the Regiment then witnessed as nice a bit of tank handling as ever was seen.

Twelve graceful, putty-coloured cruisers were standing in a semi-circle, their guns pointing inquiringly towards the west where a column of dust rose on the still air. Behind them stood in line the two close-support tanks of squadron headquarters. Suddenly all four fired, their guns elevated high and the shells making an arc of smoke trail in the sky, and there was a puff of blue smoke behind each tank as their engines were started. The 3-inch guns were firing smoke as hard as they could be loaded and after the fourth salvo the front line began to move, slowly at first, until, gathering speed, each tank was soon throwing up a plume of sand. The squadron disappeared in a cloud of dust. The watchers saw no more, but from the bank of dust could be heard the slam of tank guns and the rapid hammer of Besas. For ten minutes the curtain remained drawn and then "A" Squadron came slowly back through the clearing smoke.

The Colonel's cruiser nosed its way over to them and stopped as each tank swung around to face west again.

Out in front a cruiser crackled and burned, surrounded by a semi-circle of debris, a wrecked truck and a few anti-tank guns with broken wheels. Four guns had been destroyed and thirty of the enemy killed. Another fifteen of the Panzer Grenadiers from the 90th Light Division sat in a German lorry behind Major Price's tank looking pale and shaken. "A" Squadron had lost Trooper Stringer, killed, Trooper Pash had been wounded, and one cruiser was lost and two others slightly damaged. For this bold and brilliant example of "private war" Major Price afterwards received a Military Cross.

On that same day Egg Column, a "Jock" column, reported the loss of an observation post, which had been stalked and captured, and asked for a guard for its successor. Lieutenant Bill Peek took his troop out and within an hour, when the enemy tried the same trick, he reported the capture of two troop carriers and a further twenty prisoners.

The day wore on to evening. The 4th Armoured Brigade were in action

H

against strong forces and asked for help. We had no idea where it was and, by the time it had sent us its position in a code we could translate, the enemy had retired and all was well. "B" Echelon found us and we leaguered alone.

On the 17th of June the Regiment found the 4th Armoured Brigade and became attached. The general situation became more clear. There had been a last-minute decision to hold Tobruk again and the attention of the German armour must be engaged while the last convoy of supplies was rushed into the perimeter. We were given the job of helping to hold the ridge south of the long Sidi Rezegh feature. Here there were sixteen anti-tank guns well sited and a battery of 25-pounders on either flank. The Brigadier in command of the 4th Armoured Brigade asked us to "keep a fatherly eye on the guns" and said that he considered that the position was quite secure.

The Colonel deployed "B" Squadron in a line on the top of the ridge. "A" was positioned on the right flank, and a half-dozen cruisers under Major G. Willis, 3rd County of London Yeomanry, which turned up during the morning, took the left.

In these positions we sat for over two hours watching the Bostons drop bombs on something making dust to our left front, and the two 25-pounder batteries intermittently shelling the El Duda and Belhamed crest lines. S.S.M. Huxford went out from "B" Squadron in a scout car and erected cairns at the key ranges.

At 3 p.m. the Brigadier came up and told the Colonel to attack a concentration of German tanks west of Sidi Rezegh aerodrome. This seemed rather a strange order, but there was nothing for it but to obey, and the Colonel was just beginning to give his orders to squadron leaders when the Germans attacked us.

S.S.M. Huxford came steaming in from out in front and behind him all along the skyline appeared a mass of Mark III's and IV's coming fast down the slope and across the dip facing us. We counted forty-five. According to the Brigadier's view, this was exactly what it was hoped would happen. The concealed anti-tank guns and the 25-pounders would be able to have the shoot of their lives. The black German tanks were coming on fast. "B" Squadron were holding their fire until they reached killing range, but we could not understand why the field guns were not shelling them. The next thing we saw was the anti-tank battery limbering up and disappearing over the horizon: then we looked round and saw the two 25-pounder batteries doing the same. All this was happening without a word from Brigade. We seemed to have been left holding the fort.

"B" Squadron opened up with their 75's. The range had shortened to one thousand five hundred yards and the first two shots set tanks afire while others stopped and began shooting back. Within a minute both sides had settled down to a terrific slogging match. The air was filled with flying metal and cordite fumes, and soon six or seven German tanks were blazing and two of the Grants were hit and ceased firing, whilst a third went up in a great explosion. Twice the enemy faltered and broke and twice they were pressed on from behind. The Adjutant asked Brigade for orders and whether we were fighting this battle alone, but got no coherent reply. The Colonel then spoke and suggested that a squadron of a tank regiment which we knew to be on our left might move up alongside and help. Surprisingly, an answer came this time to the effect that "they considered that they were very well placed where they were." After that we knew we had to fight it out by ourselves.

A dozen or so German tanks had by now worked their way round our right flank and were beginning to take toll of "A" Squadron, whose 2-pounders were trying hopelessly to stop them. In front the range had closed to seven hundred yards, and the Grants were outnumbered by three or four to one. One by one their guns stopped firing as they were hit or the gunners killed. Lieutenant Thomas had his 75-mm. and his machine gun shot away, but remained in position and fired a tommy-gun at the heads of German commanders and baled-out crews.

The Colonel realized that in a very few minutes the whole Regiment would be wiped out. We had no orders and not a soul was to be seen in the whole wide desert behind us.

The problem was a hard one. All our tanks were firing at a semi-circle of Germans who were gradually closing in on "B" Squadron, and the sun was, as usual, in our eyes: to turn round and retire would mean disaster. The 75-mm. on the Grant is mounted in the hull and once you turn the tank you also turn the gun. He therefore ordered the whole Regiment to begin reversing slowly and for all guns to prepare to load smoke. After reversing for a mile he ordered "Fire smoke and turn round quickly." This was done successfully, and as soon as everyone was facing east we put on speed. The enemy came through our smoke and for fifteen minutes there was a running fight. By now some 88's had been hauled into place on the ridge and were adding their blows to the hail of fire. One of their shells penetrated the turret of Sergeant Jackson's Grant, killing him and Lance-Corporal Hodgson, while another hit Lieutenant Tim Cadman's cruiser and killed him instantly. "A" Squadron would never again seem quite the same without him. Lieutenant Heathcote's operator reported that his commander was dying in the turret.

Gradually we began to outdistance our pursuers and the enemy tanks stopped firing. German artillery had taken over and their shells dropped on us for about two miles until it became too dark to see.

Then Brigade came on the air and told us to continue for another twenty miles to a point just west of the Shefferzen Gap in the frontier wire. Forming double line ahead, the remnants of the Regiment moved on for five miles, towing two cruisers which had been hit in the engines. Petrol was getting very short, but we were faintly in touch with "A" Echelon, which, at the commencement of the affair, had been told to "float."

After five miles we stopped and told "A" Echelon to watch for a tracer signal. To our great relief it was only about a mile away and soon joined up. We took the dead off their tanks and buried them in the desert. In the quiet moonlight night the officers collected round the Colonel's tank to discuss the day. There was not much to say. The Regiment had been prepared to stand and fight to the bitter end, but we had been left, with no orders and no help, to take the full force of the attack and we felt bitter over our losses. For the first time we really appreciated the advantages of being in our own brigade where help was given and taken automatically, and one's own gunners were as much a part of the Regiment as a fourth squadron.

The following, written by Corporal Brooks, concerns the fortunes in the battle of one of "B" Squadron's Grants:

"The squadron leader gave us the order to hold our fire until we could see the 'whites of their eyes.' By this time the three groups of enemy tanks had converged and formed one. When they were about twelve hundred yards away we received the order to fire. Our squadron strength stood at nine Grants and two Crusaders—not a very imposing figure to face the opposition.

"Every gun in the squadron was firing as fast as it could be loaded, each and every shot registering a target, either tank or telegraph pole! Things were rather warm in my tank, which was being hit repeatedly. Lance-Corporal Wilson, who was doing 75-mm. loader, was greatly surprised when the gun recoiled without being fired, due to a hit on the gun barrel.

"I could see the trails of dust left by fast-moving 88-mm. projectiles, and I kept moving the tank around to keep out of the way of these very unpleasant things. This carried on for about half an hour. Inside the tank it was an inferno, with heat, sweat, swearing, fumes and dust all combining to make things very unpleasant. By this time the 37-mm. gun had run out of ammunition, having accounted for one certain and two probable enemy tanks. We had only four rounds of high-explosives and no armour-piercing for the 75-mm. and things began to look a little grim, as there was no hope of obtaining any more.

"I was keeping a sharp look-out to my front and acting as observer for our 75-mm. gunner, Lance-Corporal Groves. I looked to my left and right, but could see nothing at all of the rest of the squadron, but was not worried, as I thought they would be slightly echeloned to my left and right rear.

"Suddenly we received a heavy hit low down on the front of the tank, and when I went to move I found it was impossible. I realized that the shot had penetrated the differential casing and smashed one of the half-shafts. I reported this to Sergeant Jackson, and at the same time could hear the squadron leader giving the order to withdraw. I had not finished reporting the damage to Sergeant Jackson when two deafening explosions came from the turret, and a second later the order to bale out. The wireless operator, Trooper Jackson, was unhurt, though badly shaken, but both Sergeant Jackson and the 37-mm. gunner, Lance-Corporal Hodgson, were killed outright, both 88-mm. shells having entered the turret. Inside the tank it was pitch black, with pieces of metal flying everywhere, and we quickly did the only thing possible to do—baled out and got behind the tank.

"We had a very big shock when we reached the back of the tank. We found that the rest of the squadron were about four hundred yards to our rear, and in our position it looked about four miles. We could still hear plenty of armour-piercing hitting the front of the tank, and machine-gun bullets were flying around and under it; and the four of us took as best cover as possible behind the two tracks, which seemed nothing at all to us.

"We certainly could not stop in that position and none of us wished to be taken prisoners, so we decided to make a dash for it. We ran from the shelter of the tank separately and began our nerve-racking return to the squadron. We could never have attempted this had it not been for the squadron leader, who laid smoke to cover us, and laid it absolutely perfectly and undoubtedly saved our lives. It was certainly a terrifying dash—running for about a hundred yards with streams of bullets pinging round, and then dropping flat on our stomachs for a short rest, then up again and on.

"S.S.M. Huxford came forward in a scout car and picked us up, and it was not until then that we discovered that Lance-Corporal Wilson had been hit in the foot. How he made that four hundred yards he does not know himself. The Squadron Sergeant-Major took us back about half a mile, where we transferred to the doctor's scout car, which took Wilson to the ambulance, and the other three of us to the echelon.

"It was not very pleasant in the echelon, as they were directly behind the tanks, and spent armour-piercing was bouncing around the lorries in a most alarming way.

"The squadron eventually returned with six Grants and the two Crusaders left, and every gun was out of action as the result of the furious hammering the tanks had taken. However, as usual, 'B' had given more than they got, and accounted for fifteen German tanks."

After a few hours of troubled sleep, the Regiment moved off again before dawn on the 18th, and by 7.30 a.m. came upon a mass of transport which turned out to be the 4th Armoured Brigade. Here we were ordered to make up one cruiser squadron and hand over the few Grants still battleworthy.

"A" Squadron was equipped to the best of our ability, for it was still necessary to keep in battle order in case of further pursuit. As it happened, the German armour had gone back to commence the assault on Tobruk and there was no sign of them that day. Tobruk fell within two days to a massed onslaught of tanks and dive-bombers, and with it were captured twenty-three thousand British and Dominion troops and a great quantity of stores. This event probably shocked the British people as much as any other in the whole war.

Only one Grant out of nine could be passed as fit for battle, and the remainder were handed over to workshops to be transported back to Egypt. The rest of the Regiment, by now very small indeed, then left in the "B" Echelon vehicles for Sofafi by way of the Shefferzen Gap and Conference Cairn, with much misgiving about leaving "A" Squadron behind.

The Second-in-Command and the Adjutant went on ahead to try to locate the remainder of the 1st Armoured Division, and on reaching Mesheifa found them on the coast road west of Sidi Barrani.

Course was changed the next morning and we headed north-east. Passing through Bir Thalata and Ember, we reached Sidi Barrani at midday. We were told that the Division was regrouping at Bir Kanayis, south of Mersa Matruh, so we drew more maps from the depot, filled up with petrol and leaguered for the night south of the road, some twenty miles east of Sidi Barrani.

The next day, the 20th, we moved off again. After going a few miles we saw a familiar sign on the left of the road, the number "71" and a white rhinoceros, and sure enough there was our own Brigade Headquarters leaguered in the low ground by the sea. Thankfully we pulled in and joined it, finding "C" Squadron there too. Our first inquiry was for the two troops of "B" Squadron which had been left with the Bays. Although they had had some very fierce fighting their casualties had not been too heavy and the Bays could not say enough for the way they had fought. Trooper McGinty had been killed, and Trooper Perry wounded. Lieutenant Roger Okell had been seriously wounded and this most gallant officer died later in Palestine as the result of his wounds. He had been badly hit in the thigh and rescued from his burning Grant by his crew. Owing to the heavy shelling all had to lie low, and before they could be rescued the remaining tanks were ordered to retire before a group of German tanks. Lieutenant Roger Mostyn and Sergeant Edwards then raced forward in their tanks, and under covering fire from the latter Lieutenant Mostyn dismounted and managed to get Lieutenant Roger Okell on to the back of his tank and away. This courageous rescue was not recognized in any way.

The news was not good. The Axis army had reached Capuzzo, where "E" Battery and "C" Company, 1st Rifle Brigade, were helping to fight a rear-guard action. These troops had now been fighting incessantly for twenty-five days.

General McCreery visited the Brigade on the 21st and told us that we were to go back to the Delta to refit. The next morning we joined in the endless stream of traffic moving back—all the bits and pieces that make up an army, hospitals, workshops, bulldozers, Air Force ground crews, transporters and road construction companies, jammed nose to tail all the way from Sidi Barrani to Alexandria. Any German aircraft would have had a field day, but none came, for they were changing their airfields and the R.A.F., operating first from one landing ground and then from another, was keeping constant watch over the defeated army.

We reached Amiriya on the afternoon of the 24th of June, and pulled into Sidney Camp, a rather depressed lot of individuals. It was not possible just then to imagine what was going to stop the Axis from reaching Alexandria.

In the evening we received a warning to move the next day to Sidi Bishr, just east of Alexandria. Before breakfast on the 25th that order was cancelled and all hopes of a peaceful refit were abandoned. By 11 a.m. we were on the road again, toiling back to the desert against a stream of east-bound traffic and heading for Fuka, a hundred miles away.

Here, we were told, were enough tanks to re-equip the Regiment less one squadron, but on arrival in the evening we managed to scrape together only seven very old cruisers and four scout cars. The Queen's Bays, however, had been given a squadron of Grants and two of Honeys, so our few cruisers, under Captains Meyrick and Laing, were attached to them and the whole party moved off at about midnight. Enemy tanks were reported as being at Charing Cross, so the Bays were warned to be prepared to fight their way up to join the 22nd Armoured Brigade.

By this time the Regiment was in a fairly parlous state. We had no idea what was happening to "A" Squadron and neither "B" nor "C" was capable of finding enough crews to man a full complement of tanks, had they been offered any. The only reinforcements we had been sent so far was a lorry-load of 11th Hussars' and Royals' men, all armoured-car specialists. We regarded this as a joke in poor taste on the part of Base, and sent these men off to find their own regiments, as both the 11th and the Royals would have had the kindness to do for our men similarly placed.

After a night of bombing we packed up again and set off down the coast road, strangely empty of traffic. As we moved off, the last train came down the single desert line, a tremendous affair of some three hundred trucks hauled by three engines and pushed by two. In the rosy dawn the last squadron of fighters took off from Fuka aerodrome and wheeled eastwards. By midday enemy tanks had cut the main road where we had spent the night of the 26th/27th of June.

Feeling like a lost tribe of Israel, we camped that night on the staging ground at Imayid, thirty miles from Alexandria, still wondering who was going to stop the rot, and hoping hard that "A" Squadron was all right. On the 30th of June we got a few tanks, six Grants for "B" Squadron and nine cruisers. "C" Squadron left in wheeled vehicles for Khatatba, and we were given "C" Squadron, 4th Hussars, under Major T. I. Taylor, to make up to two squadrons. A composite echelon was formed and, much to everyone's relief, the Medical Officer of the 4th Hussars took over the medical arrangements of the Regiment; it was a great comfort to feel that there was a capable doctor with the tanks of Regimental Headquarters. Horrible things can happen in tanks, and many lives were saved by having a doctor on the spot. We were always lucky in our doctors: all three received Military Crosses, and never hesitated to dive into the thick of the fighting when a call for help came.

On the 1st of July we moved across to the Tank Delivery Regiment at Ikingi and took over all the available tanks remaining in Egypt at that time. The Army Commander had issued the order "Send up your best team—suggest 9th Lancers," a message of which the Regiment had every right to be proud.

With twelve Grants and four Crusaders, "B" Squadron was ready first and moved up alone to join Brigadier Carr and the 22nd Armoured Brigade. By the

2nd, "C" Squadron, 4th Hussars, had eight General Lees and four Grants, and a composite squadron of "A" and "C" crews had eight rather old cruisers. These were commanded by Captain George Meyrick. We moved off through Burg el Arab, and spent the night by Hammam station.

Our orders were to report to the 22nd Armoured Brigade as soon as possible. Early on the 3rd of July we moved up, and on reaching Rear Divisional Head-quarters the Colonel went in to ask for twenty-four hours in which to test guns, adjust sights and telescopes and carry out the hundred-and-one other things necessary to a new tank. The answer was startling: "Get down that ridge as fast as you can—there's an enemy tank attack coming in and there's very little to stop it."

The Colonel hopped back into his tank and we hurried on down the ridge— the now-famous Ruweisat Ridge—passing Main Division, then Brigade, through the gun lines and then into a curtain of shell fire with which the enemy saw fit to greet our arrival. Here we joined "B" Squadron, which had already had trouble with its cruisers. Captain Laurie, with his tank, was towing Captain Laing's, which in turn was towing S.S.M. Huxford in a scout car. Captain Laurie's explanation of this rather odd spectacle was: "Well, I do like having my headquarters where I know what they are doing."

There was no sign of enemy tanks, so "B" Squadron was deployed across the hog's-back of the ridge, with the 4th Hussars' squadron in reserve. They were new to tank fighting and the Colonel was anxious to give them time to watch and shake down. In the hour's lull there was time to look round.

Though we did not fully realize it at the time, this was the centre of the Alamein Line. To the north stretched a sand-sea for nearly eight miles, ending on the low escarpment over which ran the one and only coast road. The north end was held by the Australians and South Africans. To the south the ground fell away to the lip of the Qattara Depression, an impassable obstacle even to tanks. In the centre was the Ruweisat Ridge, running for ten miles east and west. Our enemies held the far end.

As we waited, evening drew on and from out of the west came a familiar sound —the drone of a squadron of dive-bombers. Everyone who was outside his tank climbed briskly in, and then watched whilst nine Stukas began circling overhead. Then we saw, high up in the sky and heading for home, a patrol of Hurricanes. Would they see the Stukas? No; they kept steadily on. Then, as the first black vulture came diving down, the leader of the Hurricanes spotted them. The whole patrol seemed to fall out of the sky and in a few seconds they were tearing into the bombers. Eight of them crashed in flames in as many seconds and the ninth was trying to get away at a hundred feet with two Hurricanes on its tail. Every-one stood up and cheered themselves hoarse.

No sooner had the excitement died down than "B" Squadron rear link, Captain Peter Laing, reported a strong force of enemy tanks coming along the south side of the ridge. "B" moved up a bit and then began shooting. In the dusk the red tracer behind the armour-piercing shells sailed down on the enemy tanks and soon they began to burn. "One—two—three—there's five—no, six! —no, eight on fire!" an excited voice came on the air. They tried to dodge the fire, but within ten minutes twelve tanks were blazing. That stopped them and for a few moments they tried to shoot it out with "B" before turning tail. "B" Squadron's shooting that evening was superb. Later on a message came from General Ritchie: "Well done, the Ninth!"

Shortly after this we received the bad news that Major Sir Peter Farquhar had been badly wounded. He had gone back to the Tank Delivery Regiment to bring on a few more tanks, and was returning in his Fordson car when two Ju.88's, diving out of the sun, riddled it with bullets. Trooper Kelly had also been seriously wounded and died shortly afterwards. We could ill afford such a loss.

This attack proved to be the last real attempt of the Afrika Korps to break through to Alexandria until the next big offensive in August.

The thirty enemy tanks which were routed that evening represented all that Rommel could muster, yet they would have been enough to break through the fragile line which was just beginning to take shape. By the grace of God the remaining British armour, represented by a mixture of Queen's Bays, 4th and 10th Hussars and 9th Lancers, under the command of Lieutenant-Colonel J. R. Macdonell, was in exactly the right place and took such toll that the enemy was afterwards unable to mount more than local attacks until the Eighth Army was again organized.

The British public knew nothing of events that evening except perhaps an announcement of "another armoured clash." How much had depended on "B" Squadron's gunners that night was known to only a few, but some weeks later General McCreery said, in his quiet way, to the Colonel: "You know, Ronald, you saved Egypt that evening." And we like to think that it was true.

*　　*　　*　　*

The Regiment leaguered for the night of the 3rd/4th July in the soft sand on the north side of the ridge with a small force of six Honeys under the command of Captain Lord Knebworth, Queen's Bays, and six 6-pounder portees. Because of the depth of the sand no wheeled vehicle was able to come anywhere near us, so no replenishment was possible. One of the portees had received a direct hit during the evening's shelling and a neighbouring medical officer had to perform an amputation under a tank sheet with the aid of torches, an operation which was entirely successful.

The echelon was having tremendous difficulties in maintaining the Regiment; the impossible surface of the ground and constant attention from dive-bombers made it extremely hard. Sergeant Philpott tells of one incident:

"As dawn broke on the morning of the 4th of July I reported to my echelon commander, Major Lomax. On receiving my orders I began the sorting and loading of the petrol, ammunition, water and ration lorries which later I would have to take up in column to the tanks which were holding the line on Ruweisat Ridge. At 2 p.m. the Brigade column was ready lined up in staggered formation and at a quarter-past we moved off.

"The nature of the ground over which we were travelling slowed up progress considerably, as we had to force our way through dunes and drifts of deep sand. In those days we had no four-wheeled drive vehicles, and were continually having to tow the lorries out of the soft sand. The cursing and screaming of engines straining in low gear were beginning to have their effects when, from the direction of the setting sun, came the drone of planes.

"They were soon recognized as Stukas, but fortunately, or so we thought, they passed over us at a height of about two thousand feet. We were soon disillusioned, however, as they turned, spiralled into formation, and began their well-known and terrifying dive. The sight and sound of dive-bombers coming straight at one are not quickly forgotten, and the first yellow bombs had hardly left their racks when arms of every description opened up at the planes.

"My own particular vehicles caught the full force of the attack and, in less time than I care to think of, lorries were blazing and exploding from direct hits. During the attack a squadron of the famous Boston taxi service, returning from a raid, noticed our plight and dispatched its escort to our aid. In the fierce battle which followed, eight of the Stukas were shot down and the remaining one chased and brought down before it could reach its own lines.

"Meanwhile, the main column of supply lorries had moved on, and I began the thankless but necessary task of checking up. Of the ten vehicles which set out, I had only four left. Four drivers were dead and three seriously wounded.

"By this time it was practically dark and I set off with the remaining lorries to find the squadron, which, by the sound of the gun fire, was still fighting."

The enemy, who seemed tired and jittery, spent the entire night firing Spandaus in our direction, but did not succeed in robbing anyone of a night's sleep.

At dawn on the 4th the squadrons moved back on to the ridge. Quite soon two Italian M13 tanks came creeping along the crest towards "B" Squadron. These tanks were inferior even to our own cruisers, and, in soldier's language, were regarded as "a piece of cake." Interest, therefore, rose sharply as they meandered on towards Lieutenant Mostyn's troop on top of the crest. Not troubling to use his big 75-mm. gun, he picked both off in two quick shots with his 37-mm. mounted in the turret, setting them on fire. Such of the crews as baled out were knocked over before they had gone five yards by the concentrated machine guns of the rest of the troop.

Another incident indicating that the enemy was losing his grip occurred about an hour later. A yellow Mark III came forward, all alone, along the northern slope of the ridge towards a serried line of 4th Hussar General Lee tanks. As it was well in range and not a shot yet fired, the Colonel spoke to the 4th Hussars and inquired what they intended doing about it.

The 4th, being unused to desert warfare, replied that they thought it was a Grant. "Grant be damned! It's a Mark III and it wants shooting," said the Colonel.

After a second's delay practically all twelve Lees fired at once. The turret of the Mark III sailed into the air and two men jumped out and began to run for shelter. There was a ripple of Brownings and both of them collapsed.

In the middle of the morning we were relieved by a small force of the 4th County of London Yeomanry under Major Harry Scott (Royals), so that the tanks could go back to the echelon and replenish. The 4th Hussars' squadron, which had not expended much, was left under the command of the relieving force.

No sooner had we reached "A" Echelon and were just beginning to fill up when an urgent order came to return at once, as another attack was coming in. Down the ridge again we went, being thoroughly shelled on the way. There appeared to be nothing afoot, so we remained behind the 4th County of London Yeomanry squadron. At 4 p.m. enemy infantry began to attack. The six Bays' Honeys moved up to deal with them and then charged. In the heat of the moment they went too far and ran into anti-tank guns. Two tanks were lost and Major Lord Knebworth's cruiser was hit. As he walked back he was shot through the heart by a sniper. One of his remaining Honeys brought him back and we buried him on Ruweisat Ridge. The day, which had begun in a spirit of light-heartedness, now took an ugly turn. Sudden death is always a shock, but in his case it seemed more tragic than usual. Fifteen minutes before he had been leaning against the Colonel's tank full of life and laughter: now he lay in a hastily dug grave on a ridge whose name a week before few knew.

We now noticed that the 4th Hussars' squadron, which had also moved along the ridge, was in difficulties. Not being at this time under our command, we had no means of knowing what was happening, but soon a 6-pounder portee drew up alongside the Colonel's tank with Major Taylor lying on it, his leg terribly smashed. He was conscious and cheerful, but very soon afterwards he, too, died. Immediately on top of this second tragedy a third occurred. A General Lee came slowly back up the ridge with Major Taylor's second-in-command, Captain Eric Jones, lying dead on the back. Apparently there had been trouble with the wireless; both officers had climbed out of their tanks to pass and receive orders and one 88-mm. shell had struck them down.

So ended the 4th—a very sad day—and we leaguered on the ridge with Major Mark Kerr's company of the Rifle Brigade for protection. That evening a message arrived from General Auchinleck congratulating the Regiment on holding the line on the 3rd of July.

That day had really marked the end of the danger period. The enemy forces, having failed, but only just, to bounce the Eighth Army out of its final stop line, after their tremendous advance had now perforce to wait for reinforcements and supplies. If we were utterly exhausted so were they, and already there were signs that, although on their side they had success and bright hopes, their morale had sunk lower by far than ours.

Those days were probably the finest in all the history of the great Eighth Army. For weeks it had retreated, fighting by day and travelling by night, after one of the most vicious pitched battles in history. There was little equipment left and on reaching the completely unprepared Alamein Line the survivors had had to turn and stand and fight while defences were dug, minefields laid and newly landed reinforcements brought in. They fought with the courage of desperation, beating off attack after attack and falling asleep over their weapons in between. In the terrible thirst and glare of the desert summer they had endured, giving no ground. The Afrika Korps had expended itself as a wave breaking upon solid rock.

In Alexandria the sound of gun fire had caused some panic and passport offices were besieged while pro-Axis sympathizers prepared to welcome the conquerors. They had reckoned, however, without that singular British characteristic, of which our enemies always complain, that we never know when we are beaten.

The line held and from then onwards the fortunes of war began to change.

CHAPTER XI

RUWEISAT RIDGE

THE next period in the history of the Regiment was the most exhausting of the whole war. From the 5th until the 25th of July it remained on Ruweisat Ridge and spent twenty days so packed with incident that their events would fill a book.

Because of the shortness of the night we were in battle positions from 4.30 a.m. until it was dark enough to leaguer, which was usually at about 8.30 p.m., and by the time refuelling was finished it was 10.30 p.m. At the most we could expect five and a half hours' sleep, bombers permitting. By 9 a.m. the sun was already unpleasantly hot and shone down mercilessly from a cloudless sky until 6 p.m. Between 11 a.m. and 3 p.m. the mirage took charge and fighting was usually confined to the period before or after it. We all suffered from desert sores, our lips were parched and split, and our eyes so tired that we often saw things which were not there. To add to the misery, the flies buzzed round us all day. Dysentery was rife, but it was a greater menace to the enemy than to us because the Italians' ideas of sanitation were crude and their German allies suffered accordingly. Out in front, in No-Man's-Land, lay the unburied dead of both sides and as the weeks wore on the area became most unpleasant.

During this time our reserves of energy and mental stability were drained to the dregs. The man in the tank suffered most. He had to sit inside a furnace for fifteen hours a day, without proper meals or sufficient water, and had to watch the haze like a lynx and never relax his guard against sudden death. In leaguer, in the blessed cool of the night, he had first to maintain his tank, to fill it, to load it and to change the batteries of his wireless set before he could roll up in his blankets.

It was not surprising that some of the strongest nerves cracked under the strain and men whose courage had never been in question temporarily broke down and they lost their nerve. The only good part of this bad month was the increased comradeship among all the small units on the ridge. Friendships were forged which existed throughout the campaigns that followed and beyond. That between the 9th Lancers and the Royal Horse Artillery—2nd, 4th and our own 11th—grew strong. Through the long, fiery days we never had to ask for fire from their guns, for it came automatically and the observation posts shared in the hardships of the leading squadrons.

The daily log, written up each evening in the Colonel's tank, gives a fair summary of events up to our relief by the Queen's Bays on the 25th of July:

"*July 5th.*—Heavy mist; therefore we managed breakfast. Nothing much

93

happened all morning except that, being the leading troops on the ridge, we were thoroughly shelled from time to time. . . . Major K. J. Price has been wounded on column work. 'Bostons,' as usual, were very busy over the enemy MET (transport) to the north west. Smoke-screens and movement behind them at 1700 hours made us a little suspicious, but some of the enemy transport only moved off north west. Brigadier Carr, commanding 22nd Armoured Brigade, came up shortly afterwards in his tank. In response to the Colonel's request for a short maintenance and rest period for 'B' Squadron, whose 'Grants' were in a very debilitated state, he made arrangements for a new 'Crusader' Squadron of the Royal Gloucester Hussars, under Major Sam Lloyd (known as 'SAM' Squadron), to come up at last light so that 'B' Squadron could go out of the line. The 4H squadron moved up to hold the front, and 'B' Squadron retired to 'A' Echelon. It was an uneventful day, only remarkable for the amount of shelling which took place around 'B' Squadron and RHQ.

"Owing to soft sand in the vicinity of the tanks, topping-up was a most difficult operation.

" 'B' Squadron, on the way back in the dark, ran into a new minefield and damaged two 'Grants,' which Sergeant Maloney repaired.

"*July 6th.*—Opened leaguer at 0500 hours with 4H 'Lee' Squadron holding the ridge and astride the track; RHQ and Captain Meyrick's force of 4 'Cruisers' in the same places; and 'SAM' Crusader Squadron in reserve.

"The customary morning shelling by 155-mm. guns passed uneventfully, and the remainder of the morning was entirely peaceful. At noon 'A' Squadron's four 'Cruisers' moved further on down the valley to see what was going on, and were shot up by 50-mm. guns, Lieut. Harris's tank having its near-side front bogie shot clean away. It got back all right and no casualties were sustained.

"It was probably the hottest day of the year, and the usual visitors kept coming to see us. . . . 'B' Squadron, with 8 fit Grants and two new 'Crusaders,' rejoined us in the evening; and a large leaguer of 'B' Squadron, 9 L, 'C' Squadron, 4 H, one squadron Gloucester Hussars, Captain Meyrick's four 'Cruisers,' eight 6-pdrs and a number of Rifle Brigade trucks, was formed in the same place on the ridge.

"*July 7th.*—The 4th Hussars' 'Grant' Squadron left at first light. 'B' Squadron moved along the ridge and took up the usual 'stone-walling' position. . . .

"It was a very dull day indeed; apart from the usual 'hate' shelling on us in the morning, nothing happened at all. Our own batteries kept up a constant fire, and the 'Bostons' and 'Kittyhawks' were busy all day—on one occasion setting on fire two German ammunition lorries, which went up very satisfactorily. In the evening Major Hugh Meldrum, 1 RB, arrived with six more 6-pdr Anti-tank guns. The plan is for 6-pdrs and minefields to hold the North ridge, thus releasing 9 L for mobile reserve. This plan was put into effect during the night 7/8 July, only 'B' Squadron remaining until first light to see the guns well dug in. The remainder of the regiment: i.e. RHQ, Captain G. D. Meyrick's three tanks, and the Gloucester Hussars' 'Cruiser' Squadron, moved back at dusk to the area of the Brigade Headquarters.

"*July 8th.*—'B' Squadron came back to RHQ at 0700 hours. They sent away two very sick 'Grants' and took over three of the 4th Hussars' 'Lees' instead. At midday we moved up on to the Southern ridge, relieving a squadron of 'Valentines' with the three 'A' Squadron 'Cruisers' and the RGH's thirteen 'Cruisers.' 'B' Squadron 'Grants' remained in reserve behind RHQ. The ridge was shelled a little in the afternoon. Tac/R reports 47 tanks and 1,000 MET, moving South East, some 12 miles away in four different parties. Soon after we had taken up position on the South ridge, it was heavily shelled by 105-mm. guns—ineffectively, but unpleasantly all the same. . . .

"*July 9th.*—Opened out into the same positions. At 1200 hours the Commanding Officer went to see Brigadier Fisher concerning a small plan to deal with some enemy infantry and guns on the two ridges. Whilst there, 'SAM' reported thirteen Mark III and IV coming over the ridge in his front. 'B' Squadron was warned off, and we moved up nearer to 'SAM's' Headquarters. Twenty-two enemy tanks were then reported by 'L' Battery, 2 RHA, to the North of the other thirteen. Brigadier Fisher came up to 9 L HQ in his charger, and, as things seemed quiet, we ate a delayed lunch. Reports finally boiled down to 22 enemy tanks due West, and no more. . . . General Lumsden came to see us at 1830 hours.

"*July 10th.*—About four 25-pdr. batteries opened up in our immediate area at 0330 hours and fired salvo after salvo for an hour and a half, thus considerably shortening our night's sleep. However, it's all in a good cause. 'SAM' Squadron and 'A' Squadron's five 'Cruisers' took up their overnight positions and reported Barrel Ridge clear of the enemy: consequently they were pushed on a further 1,000 yards to deny observation to the enemy. The R.E. had laid more mines during the night, and unfortunately failed to complete erecting the trip-wire. This resulted in two 'Jeep' cars belonging to the Rifle Brigade being blown up. Lieut. Robin Fellowes lost one leg, and Captain Noel Kelly was injured. Captain Vere Nicholls, our M.O., was on the scene within ten minutes and performed an amputation under accurate shell-fire from enemy 105s.

"General Lumsden arrived at 1130 hours. His appreciation was that the enemy were preparing a tank assault on the New Zealand Brigade to our south— at the same time holding a considerable reserve opposite our centre. Should this occur, the 6th RTR, under Lieut.-Colonel Mitford, would go and assist N.Z. Brigade; 9 L would take their place, coming under command of 2nd Armoured Brigade once more; whilst 9 L sector would be taken over by the Scots Greys, who had just arrived today with two 'Grant' and one 'Stuart' squadrons.

"Early today the 1st S.A. Division put in an attack on the north and over-ran the Bersagleari, capturing 600 prisoners and the Commander. Stukas attacked the El Alamein position at 1100 hours. The 1st and 2nd RHA continued shelling hard practically all day. At 1215 hours 'SAM' Squadron shot up a German

Mk II at extreme range. The crew of three, of the 15th Panzer Division, were taken and the tank towed in. As Division had just said they wanted identifications most urgently (the 15th Panzers having been indiscreet on the air) this was most satisfactory. The tank was towed to Division by a 'Cruiser.'

"The Colonel and three officers of the Royal Scots Greys came, and were shown over the ground and positions. Desultory shelling by both sides during a very dull afternoon. Information points to all Rommel's tanks which are being repaired in workshops coming up either on tracks or transporters to a position in the south—on the northern edge of the Qattara depression. Reports in the evening stated that the South Africans had destroyed 18 enemy tanks and taken 150 prisoners (including 20 Italian Officers and 20 transport).

"*July 11th.*—On moving out to the same positions at 5 a.m. 'Stuart' troops of the Scots Greys were attached to 'A' and 'SAM' Squadrons; and a 'Grant' troop to 'B' Squadron; with the idea of first giving them some idea of the form, and, secondly, letting them get accustomed to the positions. By 0545 hours a battle began on our left front between 2nd Armoured Brigade and 13 enemy Mk IIIs supported by 88-mm. guns. By 0730 hours a lull had occurred, and news was not available. Later it was reported that an 8-wheeled armoured car and some transport had been destroyed. At 0950 hours Brigadier Fisher ordered the Regiment to side-step to the left to cover a gap caused by the southward and westward movement of 2nd Armoured Brigade. The Scots Greys were to take over our line of observation.

"The Regiment was in position east of Pt 71 by 1200 hours, with 'B' Squadron on the ridge in observation and 'SAM' Squadron in reserve to the left rear. 2nd Armoured Brigade could be seen advancing along the plain to the south, with New Zealand Infantry walking in lines with them. Four officers from the 8th Armoured Division arrived to see the country. There was heavy shelling towards evening. Four Junkers 88 bombed the area without damage, and one Messerschmitt was shot down, the pilot baling out and being taken prisoner. (He was a most offensive man. Whilst waiting at RHQ for an escort he was asked, quite civilly, what the Germans really thought of their Italian allies. He put on his best Nazi sneer and replied, 'We think the same of the Italians as the Russians think of you.' He was advised not to rely too far on the protection of the Geneva Convention and mend his manners. At that time this answer was a bit too near the bone to be amusing!)

"We were to move in support of the Essex Regiment on an attack at dawn, but this was postponed, the South Africans having been made to withdraw the previous afternoon. . . .

"*July 12th.*—The Regiment moved out at 0445 hours to the Barrel with the object of supporting the Essex Regiment in a general attack. However, on reaching the start line, no Essex Regiment was seen, and the attack was off owing to affairs in the north not having gone too well. Consequently we sat all day under a boiling sun with the 'Grants' on Barrel Ridge, 'SAM' Squadron in reserve on the right. 'C' Squadron The Scots Greys under command of Major The Lord Roborough on the right, and Captain Meyrick's six 'Crusaders' out to the left front in observation. Nothing occurred all day, except shelling on both sides. . . .

'The Regiment leaguered back to the same area at dusk. An extremely dull day. Three officers, recently arrived from England, were posted to the Regiment: 2/Lieutenants Bentley and Marsh and Lieut. Wyndham.

"*July 13th.*—Same procedure at 0500 hours, except that a dense mist came down and all squadrons had to wait until it cleared before finally moving on to their correct positions. There we sat until noon, when the Brigadier came and ordered us to revert to command of 2nd Armoured Brigade, who were understood to be moving up from the south to the north of the North ridge to meet a threat which appeared to be developing. 'C' Squadron, The Scots Greys, took over 'B' Squadron's position and remained under command of 22nd Armoured Brigade.

"We returned to our old position, north of the North ridge, opposite a gap in the minefield recently laid, and made contact with 'A' Column, a strong Guards Column. Here we sat whilst the sun set. . . .

"*July 14th.*—During the early part of the night we could hear a tremendous artillery bombardment to the north, in the direction of the El Alamein Box. This turned out to be the repulsing of a German tank and infantry attack on the South African Division, apparently with success.

"At first light leaguer was broken, and the same position occupied. It was a quiet morning, except for a long and inconclusive 'dog-fight' over our heads. At 1200 hours Captain Trevor Moorhouse, 10 H, arrived from 2nd Armoured Brigade with details of two alternative plans for a sortie by the Brigade which included an advance by 9 L to join up with the Brigade. At about the same time familiar sounds came over the air, heralding the approach of the refitted 'A' Squadron under command of Captain R. N. Kingscote.

"By 1445 hours the above squadron came in alongside 'B' Squadron and was amalgamated with Captain Meyrick's six 'Cruisers.' Whilst the reorganization was going on, and Regimental Headquarters was just about to enjoy some tea, several 75-mm. A.P. shells came whistling over and rolled to a standstill quite near the three tanks. Much hurrying about of carriers and vehicles on the ridge, and one vehicle on fire, confirmed our suspicions of an enemy tank attack. However, we then received orders to move south over the ridge and join up with 2nd Armoured Brigade, then composed of 3/5 R. Tanks and 6 R. Tanks: so the Regiment rejoined its own Brigade again, and received orders for a general advance on the next day. News came through that the C.O. had been awarded the D.S.O., to the great delight and satisfaction of the whole Regiment. (As it turned out, this was to become a Bar to a D.S.O. awarded long after his sad death for conspicuous gallantry in France, 1940. . . .)

"*July 15th.*—Our role is to support and protect the advance of the New

I

Zealand Brigade in a N.W. direction. We set off, with 'E' Battery, 1st RHA, in support, at 0700 hours. At 1000 hours we bumped an enemy strong point, mined and wired in. The 'Grants' did a little shelling, and the O.P. from 'E' Battery got the 25-pdrs on to the enemy infantry, who were well dug in. From time to time small white flags were shown—but we knew this turn, and continued shelling. . . . From now on the visibility deteriorated rapidly, and the heat became extremely trying. With a little more fire from the 'Grants' and 'E' Battery, all the enemy infantry on the ridge began to run across towards our tanks until a considerable number were massed for removal. 3/5 R. Tanks reported that they had taken 600—700 prisoners on their sector. The 'Grants' now moved up to a hull-down position on the ridge, where they could see twelve anti-tank guns. Even the crews of these began to show signs of nervousness, and, in order to assist them to make up their minds, a further sprinkling of shells was put down. . . . It was reported that Pt 64 had been taken—the New Zealanders' first objective. The Regiment turned and advanced slowly north at 1500 hours over the ridge, across a flat valley and on to the next ridge. Approximately twelve enemy tanks were forced back, one being destroyed. There were a number of enemy anti-tank guns also; and these accounted for one of 'E' Battery's Honey O.Ps. and one of 'C' Squadron's 'Cruisers' (the crew of the latter, except for the driver, being wounded). By 1845 hours the position was one of stalemate, but the 3/5 and 6 R. Tanks came up one on either side of us. In the dusk enemy tanks came up on our front, and a shelling match started.

" 'C' Squadron lost two 'Cruisers' disabled; 'A' Squadron had a track blown off. In exchange, 'B' Squadron destroyed one Mk III. The shelling round Regimental HQ was extremely hot and accurate, and frequent dives into the tanks were necessary. This went on until dark, the general tempo being raised by the addition of heavy machine-gun fire and night bombing. We leaguered back over the second ridge with the Battery and a Company of the KRRC.

"*July 16th.*—Shelling began early, at 0430 hours, but not on our leaguer; and we pushed out N.W. to the same ridge again. Shelling continued all around the tanks most of the morning. At 0540 hours the enemy began a tank attack on our position, which was beaten off—'B' Squadron destroying seven enemy tanks by 1000 hours, without loss to themselves in tanks or men. The 3/5 Tanks on our right also beat off a tank and infantry attack—reporting a 'bag' of five tanks. Until 1945 hours the day was uneventful: the enemy seemed to be performing some odd evolutions, and it was thought that he was disposing himself for an evening attack on the North ridge. At the above time a tank and artillery fight began, and went on until it was too dark to see. Result: another seven enemy tanks destroyed—our losses NIL.

"A message was received stating that Sergeant Edwards of 'B' Squadron and Corporal Thomas of HQ Squadron had both been awarded the Military Medal.

"*July 17th.*—We moved out at dawn on to the same ridge. No attack was made by the enemy during the day, and we only did minor shoots on some eight tanks in the valley, who returned our fire. Shelling by both sides all day. Some anti-tank guns were brought up during the mirage period, and these made us rather uncomfortable in the evening. There was no change in the general position. . . .

"*July 18th.*—Since the New Zealand Brigade had been ordered to take over our ridge overnight we merely moved out into open formation—and for once had sausages instead of A.P. shot for breakfast.

"The morning was spent in maintenance and cleaning up. . . . At 1400 hours the Brigade Commander held a conference. The Brigade would support an attack by 5th Indian Brigade on the North ridge, commencing at 1730 hours. Our role would be to counter attack any counter-attack by tanks. Barrages and concentrations were to be put down by the combined artillery of the N.Z. Division, the Australian Division and 1st Armoured Division.

" 'A' Squadron and RHQ moved up to the ridge, leaving the 'Grants' and 'SAM' Squadron behind. The barrage commenced, and the attack went in, but the chance of consolidation appeared to be lost by the tank regiment on the right failing to move sufficiently far up the valley. In the middle of these operations the Corps Commander, the Divisional Commander and the Brigade Commander came up by the C.O.'s tank and stood on the Brigadier's charger looking at the battlefield. A sudden concentrated Stuka attack very nearly had the most disastrous results. The C.O. and Adjutant just managed to get to ground in their tank in time, one bomb bursting a few yards away. However, when the smoke cleared we were horrified to see everyone around the Charger lying on the ground. The Colonel, after one glance at the mass of bodies on the ground, turned to the Adjutant and said 'Guy, I think I'm a Corps Commander!'

"If the pilot of that particular Stuka had only known, his bag included the Corps Commander, General 'Strafer' Gott, the Divisional Commander, General Lumsden, and the Brigade Commander, Brigadier Briggs. All three were wounded, happily not seriously. But the Corps Commander's A.D.C. died later and Sergeant-Major Gibbons, who was in a Scout Car behind RHQ, received a fatal head-wound. Major John Scott was wounded in two places and had to be taken away to hospital. Both the Generals' cars were 'written off.' What a disaster!

"The attack was successful, and it was not necessary for us to move or intervene—so, at dusk, we retired to our usual leaguer area for a peaceful, if short, night.

"*July 19th.*—In view of the fact that the New Zealanders had by this time put a holding force of machine-guns and 6-pounders on the ridge, only RHQ and 'A' Squadron went up at dawn. During the morning a tragedy occurred: Lieut. B. P. G. Harris moved forward to have a closer look into the depression where enemy tanks and guns were known to be; he went too far. Having seen some New Zealand carriers and men walking about on the slope without being fired on, he pushed on 400 yards west and his tank was hit three times by a

50 mm. gun dug in on the next ridge. Lieut. Harris, Lance Corporal Elder (driver) and Trooper Tyson (operator) were killed. The gunner (Trooper Reynolds) managed to get out with multiple cuts and burns, and was able to get back under cover of smoke from Captain Meyrick's close support tank. The 'Cruiser' went on fire, and the three dead could not be recovered. This, coupled with the news that the Orderly Room Sergeant-Major had died, made it an extremely sad day. Sergeant-Major Gibbons was a man of many qualities, who had an intense pride in the Regiment, and his death is a very great blow. To counter the bad, the arrival of Major Gerald Grosvenor, 9th Lancers, Brigade Major of 22nd Armoured Brigade, to take over Second-in-Command of the Regiment, was as good a piece of news as we had had for a very long time.

"*July 20th.*—The day was spent in open leaguer, one and a half miles behind the ridge, ready to move if required. . . . Lieut.-Colonel Roscoe Harvey, D.S.O., came up to command the Brigade while the Brigadier went back to rest and recover from his wound. Brigadier Gatehouse took over command of 1st Armoured Division whilst Major-General H. Lumsden, D.S.O., M.C., also rested. . . .

"Captain P. M. Laing had an extraordinary and nearly fatal accident in the afternoon: a pick head, which was being used to hold down a rope by his tank, was jerked up by the wind as he was resting in the shade. It struck him in the throat, cutting an artery and making a large gash. As it was, he lost a great deal of blood; but when evacuated to the New Zealand A.D.S. he was doing well. Lieut. Grant was transferred temporarily from 'A' Squadron to act as rear link. Of the 41 officers who came to Egypt with the Regiment, 17 only are left— although five are expected back when they have recovered from their wounds. . . .

"*July 21st.*—'A' Squadron took over the line of the ridge at dawn, and all was peaceful except for the usual shelling. Three of 'B' Squadron's nine 'Grants,' which were so debilitated that they were unable to do more than 5 m.p.h., were removed on transporters; and 'B' Squadron took over two of the Bays' tanks, giving them a total of eight and the Bays ten. Powerful reinforcement arrived at noon in the shape of Captain D. E. C. Steel, D.S.O., Lieuts. Allen and Thomas and Signal Sergeant Peterson (the last three now recovered from wounds or sickness). The acting Brigade Commander, Brigadier John Curry, arrived and discussed plans for a general attack to-morrow. The 5th Indian Brigade were to complete the capture of Ruweisat Ridge, whilst the newly-arrived 23rd Brigade of the 8th Armoured Division were to attack along the valley on the south. The New Zealand Brigade were to advance on their south flank whilst the 7th Motor Brigade were directed on the frontier. The role of 2nd Armoured Brigade was to exploit success, and march northwest on Daba. The 23rd Brigade had 150 'Valentines' and a Support Group.

"The Gloucester Hussars Squadron were to hand over their eight 'Crusaders' to 'A' Squadron and were to rejoin their Regiment; their place being taken by a

'Crusader' squadron of the Queen's Bays under command of Major James Dance. This would give 9 L a total of 18 'Grants' and 41 'Crusaders.'

"By dusk the required spare crews were up, and the eight 'Crusaders' of the Gloucester Hussars were taken over in the dark. The Bays' 'Cruiser' squadron was understood to be behind schedule, and did not arrive in time. Major Lloyd and his squadron of Gloucester Hussars went off in 'B' vehicles and we were extremely sorry to see them go. The Regiment had done its best to make them feel at home and could not have wished for stauncher support than that which they gave in return. We hoped that if ever the time came again for 'composite regiments' we might be fortunate enough to have the Tetbury squadron sent to us.

"From 2030 hours a tremendous bombardment started and only died away two hours after, the horizon to our N.E., East and S.E. being one continuous glow from gun-flashes. The R.A.F. did their full share, and sorties of 'Havoc' bombers added to the discomfort of the enemy. The attack on Pt 64 commenced at 2030 hours; and the objective was in our hands by dawn.

"*July 22nd.*—Two troops of 'A' Squadron, on patrol on the ridge, reported that eight enemy tanks were coming up out of the El Mreir depression: so 'B' Squadron got mounted and moved up behind them. RHQ followed, and the C.O. talked to Brigadier Gatehouse. The Navigating Officer went off to contact the New Zealand Brigade. Here he was told that one of their Battalions was out to the west, and that between them were some German tanks. So we turned slightly west and went to see what we could do. However, an enemy minefield prevented any further forward movement.

"For the remainder of the morning we remained in position, with a great number of shells falling around us—and one Stuka attack. At 1330 hours a detachment of Sappers arrived and commenced to clear a lane twenty yards wide through the mines. They were in full view of the enemy who allowed them to do their job in peace. At 1600 hours the Regiment received orders to advance through this gap and clear the enemy from the depression on the north side. The enemy was obviously clearly aware of this intention. It was learnt later than an Italian signal, reporting the clearing of the gap, was intercepted by Division. The project was difficult in fair light, but with the sun setting low and shining straight in our faces, it was a very forlorn hope. However, orders were given out, and exactly at 1700 hours we moved up to the gap—'B' Squadron leading; second, Bays; RHQ; then 'A' Squadron 'Cruisers.' As soon as the leading troop of 'B' Squadron got into the lane, very heavy and accurate fire from 105 mm. field guns came down, one tank receiving two direct hits almost instantaneously and exploding. 'B' Squadron were then under very heavy fire from anti-tank guns, including 88-mm., on both flanks; nine enemy tanks to the front and eight to the right; whilst the whole Regiment was receiving liberal attention from a 105 mm. battery. Owing to the fact that the squadron had to go through the lane in single file, all the enemy's fire was concentrated on each tank as it came forward; and the remainder were powerless to help. In this way 'B' Squadron lost two more 'Grants,' which burst into flames. Lieut. R. E. Lloyd-Mostyn lost his tank. He and his crew got away as it exploded but all were badly burnt. Trooper Roberts was killed. Lieut. Ralph Thomas, having to leave his blazing tank under shell-fire, jumped into a slit trench occupied, as he thought, by three others. To his request 'Hey, shove up a bit,' he got no answer and then he found his company consisted of three dead Italians.

"The C.O. then ordered 'B' Squadron to push on in spite of the intense fire, so that a bridgehead could be established and the Bays' Squadron sent through to their aid. This was done, but took time and resulted in congestion. About this time, Captain Robin Kingscote was killed by a shell—a sad and serious loss to the Regiment—which added to the gloom of an already desperate venture.

"It was now apparent that we were not able to get forward, and that every minute was costing a tank; Brigade, therefore, ordered us back. This was achieved with considerable success, in spite of the fact that every 'Grant' had to reverse through the lane, which was blocked by two burning tanks. Our gratitude is due to 'E' Battery, 11 RHA, who quickly and accurately laid a smoke screen to cover the above operations. . . . This operation cost us five 'Grants' destroyed and seven so badly damaged as to be useless. In addition, three 'Crusaders' were hit and had to be evacuated. . . .

"The following account of the experiences of an individual tank in this action was written by Sergeant Collier of 'B' Squadron :

" 'To-day we again took up our usual position facing the enemy across what has been aptly named Death Valley. It seems we are destined to spend yet another day watching the enemy and perhaps adding a few more to the great number of burnt-out vehicles and tanks already lying out in front.

" 'However, soon after midday our fortunes took a turn. The first information of this was the cry "All tank commanders to the squadron leader." Something must be on. We gathered around in the usual group and Major Laurie detailed very plainly the task we had been set to accomplish. A narrow lane was to be cleared through the minefield on our left front and it was intended that "B" Squadron should pass through first, head due west, then, changing direction make for Daba. We felt relieved to be really on the move at last although, having watched the sappers clear the lane in broad daylight without interference from the enemy, we were rather apprehensive as to the reception he had in store for us.

" 'Already I had seen and reported the enemy positioning one gun but had seen no further movement. At approximately four o'clock orders were received to advance, 1st troop leading in single file followed by 4th, 2nd, Squadron HQ and 3rd. 1st Troop were ordered to fan out to the right after passing through, 4th Troop to carry straight on and 2nd Troop to fan out to the left, thus forming a half-circle in front of the minefield gap.

" 'All three troops reached their respective positions without incident. The Squadron Leader then gave orders for us to push on to make room for the people behind us. I was on the right of 2nd Troop Leader, Lieut. Mostyn, and Corporal Dickens was on his left. As soon as we moved forward the fun commenced. A.P. came at us from all directions. My immediate concern was an anti-tank gun firing from the right rear, but after a few rounds we disposed of this menace. Then, hearing a terrific explosion to my rear, I looked over my shoulder to see a 'Grant' disintegrating in the air. Soon after Sergeant Edwards came up on the air and told me my tank was on fire. After a quick look round I felt sure he was mistaken, but he repeated his warning and I climbed out of my turret to investigate. I found that the bedding on the back was on fire. This little episode cost the crew several blankets, and two gallons of precious water!

" 'The enemy fire to our front now became very intense and I spotted a small anti-tank gun some 800 yards to our front and an 88-mm. at about 1500 yards. The latter "brewed" Lieut. Mostyn's tank after four shots, killing the 37-mm. gunner and seriously wounding the remainder of the crew. I put my 37-mm. gun on to the small gun, at the same time engaging the 88 with H.E. from my 75-mm. Having got a good bracket I gave further corrections and the order to fire. The tank lurched in the normal manner and I waited patiently for the shell to burst. Seeing nothing, I repeated my order to Trooper Stevens below and received the astonishing reply: "I can't—I can't." The lurch of the tank had not been caused by the 75-mm. firing but by a direct hit on the gun barrel from the 88.

" 'Trooper Stevens then illustrated his inability to fire by tossing both travers-ing and elevating wheels into the turret! I then gave orders to the turret gunner to engage the 88, but again bad luck came our way. After a couple of rounds it jammed. The only remaining means of bringing fire to bear on the 88 was the machine gun and this we did with great gusto, until all our ammunition was expended. With all guns out of action we were now nothing more than a sitting target, but at this moment we received orders to withdraw. A smoke screen was put down but we had great difficulty in reversing back through the lane as it was partly blocked by a burning "Grant" and one of our tracks had been hit and damaged. This was however achieved by the great skill of my driver.

" 'This was not the end of our troubles for, on reaching our own side of the minefield, a wave of thirty-five Stukas came over and dropped their load. This fell perilously close but did us no further damage.'

"During the morning the acting Divisional Commander, Brigadier Gatehouse, was hit by a shell splinter, and followed his predecessor into hospital. We heard that the 23rd Brigade had lost seventy 'Valentines' on the minefield on their centre-line, no gap having been made for them the previous night.

"*July 23rd.*—What remained of 'B' Squadron handed over their two service-able 'Grants' to the Bays Squadron, and the officers (two) and men went back to 'B' Echelon. Two patrols of 'A' Squadron and the Bays 'Grant' Squadron went out on to the ridge, the latter unfortunately putting two tanks on the minefield in the half-light. It is apparent that the length of time which the Regiment has now been in the desert (seven months), combined with the constant battles and lack of sleep, is having its effect; most of us are at the extreme limit and it is getting hard even to think clearly. Yesterday, three men—all normal, stout-hearted men—went temporarily out of their minds and others were showing the same signs of mental and physical strain. The 'Crusader' squadron of the Bays, under Major Dance, arrived at 1600 hours. The Regiment then moved two and a half miles east to a Brigade concentration area, in readiness for a night march over the North ridge. A dawn attack, in conjunction with the 9th Australian Division, was proposed and later cancelled.

"*July 24th.*—A quiet day—being in Divisional reserve and out of range except for the largest enemy guns. Everyone managed to get some extra sleep during the day. In the evening, Colonel Tom Draffen, D.S.O., and the Adjutant of the Bays arrived with the welcome news that they were taking over command next day. As the Composite Regiment now consisted of two Bays' Squadrons and one 9th Lancers Squadron, this seemed reasonable. . . .

"*July 25th.*—At 0800 hours the take-over began, and at 1100 hours RHQ personnel left for 'A' Echelon, where all unwanted vehicles were picked up; thence to 'B' Echelon for a meal. We are leaving complete 'A' and 'B' Echelons for the Bays until their own can be sent up. Unfortunately the Composite 'A'/'C' Squadron cannot yet be relieved—but it is being left in good hands. . . ."

A tribute to the Regiment's part in this battle by Brigadier R. Briggs will be found at Appendix X.

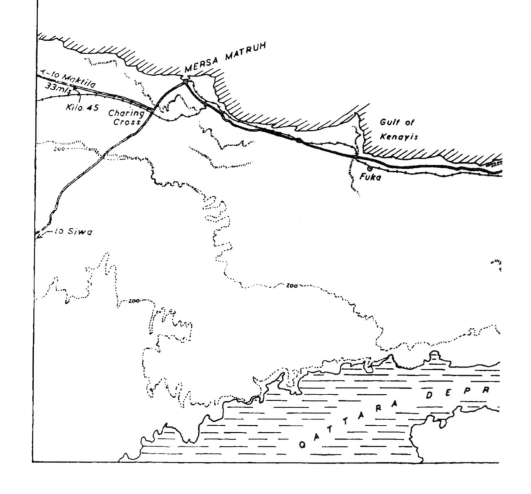

SCALE in miles

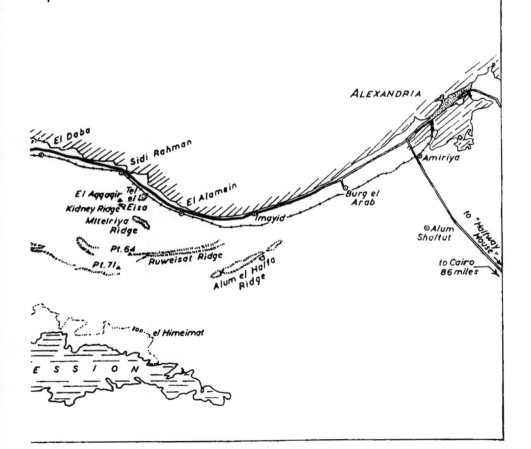

RN DESERT
MATRUH AREA

LEGEND
Railways
Main routes

N

ALEXANDRIA

El Daba

Sidi Rahman

El Alamein

Amiriya

Burg el
Arab

El Aqqaqir   Tel
             el
Kidney Ridge Eisa

El Alamein

Imayid

Alum
Shaltut

Miteiriya
Ridge

to "Halfway
House"

Pt. 64

Ruweisat Ridge

Pt. 71

Alum el Halfa
Ridge

to Cairo
86 miles

el Himeimat

E S S I O N

CHAPTER XII

REFITTING AT KHATATBA

WITH the exception of those who had to continue the weary struggle with the Composite Regiment on Ruweisat Ridge, the rest of the Brigade was from the 1st of August to enjoy two and a half months of peace in the desert between Alexandria and Cairo, a period in which the Regiment was reorganized, re-equipped and retrained for the tremendous battle which lay ahead. It was hard work, but at the end of the day it was possible to throw a suitcase into the back of a truck and slip away to bathe and dine in Cairo.

During this time the Eighth Army underwent a great change. In the melting-pot of desert warfare the finest metals were coming to the top which, tested and retested in the furnace of Libya, needed only a touch to be shaped into the finest steel that the Empire has ever produced.

Mr. Winston Churchill flew out to Egypt at the beginning of the month, bringing with him Mr. Averill Harriman, the American Lend-Lease administrator, General Sir Alan Brooke, the Chief of the Imperial General Staff, and many of his senior advisers. The admirals, the generals and the air marshals of the Middle East were gathered together and the course of the next phase of the war was decided upon.

General Sir Harold Alexander succeeded General Auchinleck, and Lieutenant-General Sir Bernard Montgomery took over command of the Eighth Army, other generals being replaced and reshuffled. If it was new blood we needed, here it was. New formations and reinforcements were arriving in a continual stream: the derricks at Suez and Alexandria were swinging ashore quantities of new and better equipment—Sherman tanks, 6-pounder anti-tank guns and the first of the Spitfires, as well as thousands upon thousands of new vehicles. Slowly the pendulum began to rise for the last time, ready for the great blow which was to sweep the Axis out of Africa once and for all.

As we moved down from the desert at the end of July we knew only that we were to have a short rest before going back again: we did not know of the great battle to come.

The first few days of August were spent on the edge of Lake Maryut, a pink lake which lies a few miles south of Alexandria, and on the 4th we moved to Khatatba and encamped on the open desert for two days whilst a new standing camp was made ready. The first officer reinforcements—Lieutenants H. O. D. Thwaites and G. G. A. Gregson—joined the Regiment.

On the 7th we moved into the camp which was to be our home for many

105

weeks—a camp of wooden cookhouses, standing on quite the barest piece of desert we had ever seen. The monotony of the scenery was broken only by Mr. Shafto's jerry-built cinemas, but by walking a short way to the east one could look down upon the rich green fields of the lower reaches of the Nile Valley. By evening everyone felt that they had reached a place that they could call home, and tents and marquees sprang up like mushrooms. R.S.M. Hardwidge got busy with a fatigue party and, mindful of Mooltan Barracks, surrounded every tent of importance with neat lines of whitewashed boulders, and the regimental lance, burnished by Lance-Corporal Phillips until it twinkled, was placed in its customary position outside the orderly room. As we fell asleep that night the silence seemed uncanny—the guns were beyond our hearing for the first time in nine months.

As the composite squadron was still away reorganization was difficult. One hundred and thirty-seven other ranks arrived the next day and were allocated to squadrons, but we soon discovered that very few of them were trained men and regimental classes in every trade had to be organized.

Command of "C" Squadron was given to Captain G. D. Meyrick, and Captain David Laurie retained command of "B" Squadron, being shortly promoted to major and receiving the Military Cross for the magnificent handling of his squadron in the recent battles. Major Price returned from hospital and resumed command of "A" Squadron. Major Perry came back. He was soon to become Second-in-Command in place of Major Sir Peter Farquhar, who, after a brief period as Officer Commanding H.Q. Squadron, 8th Armoured Division, was given command of the 3rd Hussars. When he left, the 9th lost an officer who had always given far more than his share and who in battle and out of it had never spared himself. The two D.S.Os. which he earned whilst commanding the 3rd Hussars are included in the list contained in this History because we regard him as a 9th Lancer and take as much pride in those awards as do the 3rd Hussars.

On the 20th of August General Lumsden, our Divisional Commander, was promoted to command X Corps, and the Brigadier, Raymond Briggs, assumed command of the Division. In turn his place was taken by Brigadier Fisher, whose first order was for the formation and preparation of a composite regiment to stand by, because General Headquarters expected an attack to coincide with the next full moon on the 25th of August. At first this consisted of twelve Grants manned by 9th Lancers and a small cruiser squadron manned by Queen's Bays and 10th Hussars, and was designed to act as longstop in the event of an enemy break-through. Full moons were not popular, because they normally meant an attack from one side or the other. Later on General Montgomery broke the time-honoured custom and attacked at the Wadi Akarit on a pitch-black night, but this was considered by his opponents to be an unpardonable thing to do, especially as he achieved a remarkable success.

By this time training was progressing and all young officers as they arrived were given a few days in which to shake down and were then sent up to the composite squadron to be entered to shell fire. The health of the officers and men of this squadron was causing concern, however, as they had reached a stage of utter exhaustion, were covered with desert sores, and the months of going without fresh meat, bread or vegetables were exacting their price.

"C" Squadron was overjoyed to learn that it was to become the second heavy squadron and set about learning the new tank with the greatest energy. Major Meyrick's previous experience in "B" Squadron and his aptitude for anything to do with figures and gunnery soon brought "C" Squadron's gunnery up to a very high standard, as day after day they practised in the gravel pit behind the tank park.

On the 27th of August all leave was cancelled, and on the 29th the Striking Force, as it was now known, did a practice turn-out. By this time it had had added to it a composite squadron of Valentines from the 1st Army Tank Brigade and a reconnaissance troop of scout cars under the command of Lieutenant Grant Singer, 10th Hussars. A second practice to polish up the forming-up drill took place on the 31st, but as the first squadron was leaving the lines the Brigadier rang up to say that the Germans had attacked during the night and we must all be prepared to move out in battle order at instant notice. "B" Echelon was ordered to load up operationally and remain in camp until further orders. The force moved westwards for some thirty miles, halting near Halfway House, a roadhouse on the main road between Cairo and Alexandria, whence it could either protect Rear Air Headquarters or move as required to intercept enemy raiding columns. We sat there for a week, in direct touch with the Eighth Army Headquarters by wireless.

Rommel's attack was contained and repulsed and the Striking Force was not called upon.

As the tension died down we found time to indulge in a little snipe shooting in the marshes of the Wadi Natrun, but there was little else to do through the long, hot days except to write letters, read or try to reduce the millions of flies which lived with us. The Doctor invented a fly trap which most people regarded as a double-edged weapon. He put a saucer containing a solution of arsenic and sugar in the middle of the table in the mess tent and then sat by the hour hoping for results. Some of the flies did behave a little oddly after refreshing themselves with the mixture before tottering off to recover, probably in the cookhouse, but he had eventually to admit that the old-fashioned swat gave a better performance.

On the 6th of September the composite squadron returned from Ruweisat Ridge, having taken a leading part in the defeat of the Afrika Korps' attack, and all members were immediately sent off to Cairo for some much-overdue and well-deserved leave. It was on this day that we heard that the Colonel had been promoted and posted as Second-in-Command of the 23rd Armoured Brigade. Although we knew he would have to leave us one day, the announcement came as a shock, for he had served with the Regiment for twenty-four years and it can truly be said that each man in the 9th felt on that day that he personally was losing not only a great Colonel but a kind friend. It was he who had commanded us during the dark days and his calm, clear voice had always been there, reassuring and helpful, never asking for a useless sacrifice to be made. He later became Second-in-Command of the 2nd Armoured Brigade and was still able to watch over the fortunes of his beloved Regiment until the sad day, almost at the end of the war, when a chance shell hit his tank at San Savino and killed him instantly.

He was succeeded by Lieutenant-Colonel G. H. Grosvenor, who had come out to the Middle East as Adjutant to the Nottinghamshire Yeomanry in the 1st Cavalry Division, and we were delighted to receive him as our Colonel.

At 9 a.m. on the 7th of September we were told that we could return to Khatatba. The next day the new Sherman tanks began to arrive and the remainder of the month was spent in learning their secrets. They were a great advance on the Grants and, powered by two immense General Motors Diesel engines, they were faster and much easier to maintain. Their greatest blessing was their slowness to catch fire when hit. The Grants had been driven by radial aero engines running on high-octane aviation spirit and they went up in flames in seconds, usually exploding as well. In the Shermans the 75-mm. gun was mounted in the turret instead of in the hull, which meant being able literally to get hull-down behind the slopes in the desert, exposing only a foot or so of turret against the skyline. The telescopes were better and the gun longer and more accurate. We were to have two squadrons each of sixteen Shermans and we began to look forward for the first time to meeting the enemy and his Mark IV's.

Until the middle of October the Brigade carried out intensive training by day and by night—all exercises having but one object, the crossing of minefields—until it gradually dawned upon us that we were practising a set-piece, because in every case the layout of the minefields was identical.

It was whilst returning from one of these night exercises that we were asked to pose for some Army photographers and unknowingly produced many of the "battle" scenes which afterwards appeared in the film *Desert Victory*. Had we known this at the time we would have removed muzzle covers for the scenes to be entitled "Massed tanks sweep into action"!

The Colonel of the Regiment, Major-General C. W. Norman, C.B.E., came to see us the next day. Not having seen him since Ogbourne St. George, we had a great deal to tell him and he must have noticed many changes within the Regiment.

On the 6th of October the Brigade moved out of Khatatba camp on to the desert and returned to hard living. Exercises continued, the Regimental Group was re-formed, our old allies "E" Battery of the 11th (H.A.C.) Royal Horse Artillery returned to us, but in place of the Rifle Brigade we now had "B" Company of the Yorkshire Dragoons, recently converted from horsed cavalry to motorized infantry and under the command of Major Edward St. John.

[Photo: P. A. Harding

Lieut.-Colonel G. H. GROSVENOR, D.S.O.

Training at Khatatba

The weather had begun to cool off and the first of the winter storms arrived. There was a familiar feeling of suspense in the air. For weeks we had watched mile upon mile of new equipment rolling northwards and had seen one of the new infantry divisions, the 51st (Highland), carrying out battle practice in the area. Something was undoubtedly going to happen and this time we felt ready for it.

On the 20th of October a sudden order arrived to move. As dusk fell, all the tanks were loaded on new "Diamond T" transporters and the whole Brigade rumbled off up the main road. As each tank left its parking place a swarm of workmen rushed out and erected an extraordinary-looking object made of hessian and timber which, we were assured, from the air looked exactly like a tank. The same thing was done when the wheeled vehicles left.

We spent the night at Alam Shaltut in a new "training area." Our orders were to remain quiet and still all day and the next evening we moved on to an area south of Hammam station. Here the entire area for the Brigade had been covered for weeks by a mass of canvas dummies representing large lorries and big enough to cover a tank, and as each tank arrived it was driven straight under its own cover. This was the biggest deception yet carried out. A whole armoured division was moved from its training area in the Delta to a point very near the enemy's front line. As far as the daily German reconnaissance aircraft were concerned the armoured division at Khatatba was still there and the mass of general transport vehicles at Hammam was still a mass of general transport.

Early the next day we received our orders. The attack, which was timed for 10.30 p.m. that night, would be preceded by a real old-fashioned barrage. The infantry would go in, followed by the Royal Engineers, who would clear lanes through the three known enemy minefields, and the armour would then pass through to "seek and destroy" the enemy armour.

The day was spent quietly under our "sun-bonnets" checking wireless nets, issuing code-signs and maps, cleaning already spotless guns and priming grenades. The old hollow sensation in the pit of the stomach began to make itself felt. After lunch the Brigadier addressed all ranks; the theme of his talk was "Revenge": revenge for past defeats, revenge for having been made to endure so much in the desert, revenge for our dead. We promised him to take it to the full.

CHAPTER XIII

THE BATTLE OF ALAMEIN

AT sunset on the 23rd of October, 1942, we warmed up engines. The squadrons pulled out of their concealment into single file and at 7.30 p.m. the whole Regimental Group began to move off on to the track leading to the start point. There was a brilliant moon and the route was clearly marked by hurricane lamps set inside petrol tins, the tins being perforated in various patterns; our route was "Moon." If people in England found hurricane lamps hard to obtain that winter the reason was not hard to find: they were all at Alamein. We jogged on steadily, passing lines of men waiting by the side of the track, then through the gun lines, heavies, mediums and field. Beside each gun, deep in its sandy pit with its snout pointing westwards, lay stacks of shells and boxes of charges, and the gunners rested on the ground alongside.

As we reached the start point the barrage began. As if fired by a single hand, eight hundred guns roared out, tearing the sky into crimson shreds. Guns bounced in their pits and before they had come to rest a new shell was slammed home into the breech. The entire front, from the Qattara Depression to the sea, was a solid mass of flickering lights and the ground shook with endless concussions, whilst the air overhead was filled with a gentle sighing as the shells sped towards the enemy. The noise was terrific at our end and we wondered happily what it must be like at the receiving end.

At the start point we halted and topped up our fuel tanks with the two spare cans of Diesel carried by each tank. Gun covers were removed and machine guns loaded. In the distance on either side we could see the dim outlines of the tanks of the Bays and 10th Hussars all waiting the word "Go." By this time the initial fury of the barrage had subsided. The guns had lifted the range and were now dealing systematically with the enemy batteries, which had been carefully plotted and recorded during the past few weeks. So far not a single shell had arrived from across the way.

It was 2 a.m. and bitterly cold. Most of us were frozen to the marrow and not feeling particularly brave. The first flush of excitement had given place to the knowledge that in a very few hours we would once more be at grips with the enemy armour and that the slaughter would begin all over again. Napoleon once said: "I have very rarely met with the two-o'clock-in-the-morning courage," and certainly only the most bloodthirsty among us derived any satisfaction from that slow, cold approach to battle.

We reached and passed our own minefields without incident, the big tanks

110

WESTERN DESERT, 1942

Two Shermans of "C" Squadron

Regiment loading on to transporters near Halfway House on the Cairo—Alexandria Road

C.O. holding a conference near Halfway House

L. to R.: Major D. A. St. G. Laurie, M.C., Capt. J. W. Reid, Major K. J. Price, M.C., Capt. E. R. Donnley, Capt. P. Thompson-Glover, Capt. T. Butler-Slaney, Major R. Croxton. (C.O.'s head can be seen in centre foreground).

lumbering through the narrow, white-taped lanes whose entrances had been marked by red and green shaded lights. There followed a long journey through neutral ground and the entrances to the first enemy minefield, where we were told that the second enemy belt was not yet clear owing to the attacking infantry having passed over some strong-points which were mortaring and machine-gunning the sappers of the Minefield Task Force. The troop of "A" Squadron cruisers under Lieutenant Newman which we had lent to the Task Force was busy clearing up the enemy until they were silenced. After an hour this minefield was cleared and we passed through, but at the third the enemy was putting up a stubborn fight and our company of the Yorkshire Dragoons was ordered up to the front of the column to help.

By this time it was nearly dawn and it was unpleasant to realize that the Regimental Group was still in column nose to tail and hemmed in by minefields, with no means of deploying to avoid the shells and bombs which would surely come with the daylight. Neither the Bays nor the 10th were any farther on than we were.

At 6.45 a.m. the first shells came over and vehicles were soon burning. "B" Squadron, Yorkshire Dragoons, suffered casualties, and called for medical aid. With daylight we could see where we were. Ahead the ground rose gently for some three thousand yards to the skyline, behind which the enemy guns lay. So far there was no sign of enemy armour, but the shelling was increasing each minute. No Stukas appeared, thanks to the Royal Air Force, who had raided on a large scale all forward landing grounds. By midday the last of the minefields was clear and the Germans who had been making a nuisance of themselves had been killed.

The Colonel ordered "C" Squadron, in the lead, to push on up to the crest and "B" Squadron to follow closely. To our right we could see the Bays just beginning to emerge from their minefield gap, and to the south another armoured brigade was climbing out on to the Mitiriya Ridge.

"C" Squadron had advanced a few hundred yards when another minefield was reported in front of them, round which a way could not be found. The Brigadier ordered us to drive straight through whatever the casualties, so, after a quick check back to make certain that he really meant it, "C" drove into the mines. On the skyline could now be seen the grey shapes of approaching German tanks, and a considerable amount of small-arms and anti-tank-gun fire began to come down, followed by the ugly sizzle of 88-mm. shells.

That we got through at all was due entirely to the gallant conduct of the two leading troops of "C" Squadron, Lieutenant Agate's on the left and Lieutenant Thwaites's on the right. Lieutenant Thwaites solved his problem by the simple but dangerous expedient of disembarking from his tank into a hail of flying metal and guiding his troop through on foot, occasionally trying to remove the mines himself. He continued to do this until ordered by Major Meyrick to stop. Lieutenant Agate was more fortunate: the sappers of the 1st Field Squadron, with detectors in one hand and rifles in the other, swept a path for him through the minefield. Both troops then crammed through and began to make for the high ground beyond. A moment later Lieutenant Agate's tank was hit by an enemy tank and set on fire. For some minutes under circumstances in which no one could have been blamed for getting as far away as possible from a tank liable to explode at any moment, he and his crew stayed calmly in their blazing turret and slogged away at the black shapes ahead. The part which this officer and his crew played in winning the immediate battle was exceptional. They baled out only on the direct orders of their squadron leader, by which time many of the German tanks were blazing away on the skyline.

Major Meyrick deployed his squadron on the crest, where he was shortly joined by "B" Squadron and Regimental Headquarters.

After further violent fighting the enemy decided that discretion was the better part of valour and disappeared into the haze of evening, leaving twelve of his tanks as proof of the excellent shooting of both squadrons.

Major Perry ordered up some lorries from "A" Echelon, as by this time ammunition racks were getting empty. As they entered the minefield defile a truck belonging to the Yorkshire Dragoons and loaded with 3-inch mortar ammunition blew up with a tremendous roar, temporarily blocking the lane, but the lorries got by and carried out their unenviable task of doing the "milk round" with both squadrons engaged in a particularly vicious battle and confined to an area of ground swept by shell fire. Before they had finished the fight ended and the air in front of the Regiment began to thicken as one German tank after another caught on fire.

Some of our own were burning, too. "C" Squadron had lost three tanks; Sergeants Worswick and Hole had been killed; and "B" Squadron had one tank on fire. The Regiment was by then firmly on the high ground and the Bays were alongside. When darkness came both regiments leaguered where they were. It was uncomfortable with bullets whistling through most of the night and the Royal Air Force dropping flares and bombs very near the safety limit. "C" Squadron had done magnificently and, thanks to them, we were through the great obstacle and could now set about the next part of our orders—"to seek and destroy the remainder of the enemy armour."

That night Major David Laurie, who had done the approach march in one of our two ambulances and had got into his tank only at the last minefield, was sent back with a severe attack of jaundice, his squadron being taken over by Captain Laing, his second-in-command.

At dawn on the 25th of October we shook out and began to probe forward. We and the Bays soon ran into trouble—an anti-tank-gun screen which seemed to include a large proportion of 88-mm. guns. The Bays lost six tanks in as many minutes and we lost one in "B" Squadron, Sergeant Raynor's. He was terribly wounded and, although the doctor risked his life to get him out of his tank and away, he died later in the casualty clearing station.

WESTERN DESERT, 1942

Corporal Dickinson is "brewed"

WESTERN DESERT, 1942

Refilling from "A" Echelon

Wreck of the Ariete Division

Both regiments realized the futility of going on until the 88's had been dealt with, but as they could not yet be spotted it was a difficult job. The mirage came on at noon and with it an increase in the shelling and the 88-mm. fire. We stood our ground and shelled back whenever a target presented itself, but the enemy armour did not put in much of an appearance that day except for one Mark IV, which was seen moving away on our right front. It was well out of accepted range, but someone in "C" Squadron had a go at it and the very first shot was a direct hit. It stopped dead and through our glasses we saw the crew bale out and run for dear life. The range was taken with a Barr & Stroud range-finder and found to be four thousand yards—over two miles. It may have been a fluke, but it was the best shot of the whole war and no one could have been more surprised than the four "Krauts" in the Mark IV.

As day advanced the light grew better and each squadron began to pick out targets. At least two 88's and several strong-points were destroyed. Captain John Reid, the Signals Officer, who manned the rear link to Brigade, had an unpleasant shock at about lunch time. He was in the tank decoding a message while the crew cooked a belated meal on the ground in the lee of the tank. A long-barrelled gun, of Russian origin and mounted on a tank chassis, crept up to the skyline and fired two shots at his cruiser in quick succession, scoring bullseyes which passed into the engine. The Signals Officer left the tank like greased lightning and landed beside his operator with a mug of tea in one hand and a bacon sandwich in the other. A second later "C" Squadron picked off the offending gun.

A plan was made for a limited attack by the 10th Hussars on our left, but before they could do this the enemy attacked the Bays and us. The Bays had only three Shermans left, but our combined fire accounted for eighteen enemy tanks—a "killing" which decided the enemy to call it a day and draw off. There followed a sharp shelling of the whole area by 105-mm. and 88-mm. guns. Sergeant Stocks, the Colonel's driver, who was stretching his legs behind his tank, ran to help an infantryman mortally wounded by a shell, but as he reached the dying man a second shell landed in exactly the same place and killed him instantly. For the rest of the day the Adjutant had to drive the tank. We missed Sergeant Stocks greatly. He came from Norfolk, had the reddest and most cheerful face you ever saw, and was a great companion. He had driven the Colonel's tank thousands of miles and was also "chef" of the tank, a job he enjoyed and performed admirably. He gave his life trying to save another and will not be forgotten.

In the late evening the 10th put in their attack. We knew what was going to happen to them and loaded smoke. They lost seven Shermans, but most of the crews got back under cover of our smoke.

In an effort to eliminate the 88's, which were holding up the armour, the Gordon Highlanders and Black Watch attacked the ridge that night. Lying

K

beside our tanks under the starry sky we slept oblivious of mortars. For a tired man the desert is a good resting place and the sand is soft and warm.

Enemy shell fire continued intensely on the 26th of October and the 24th Armoured Brigade moved up on to our left flank. Rommel seemed to be at a loss to know what best to do with his tanks. All day they could be seen moving backwards and forwards several miles away, but none appeared within range. The situation was becoming something of a deadlock. Our own tanks as they moved forward were immediately destroyed by the 88's, which no one could locate, while the infantry, whose losses were mounting seriously, seemed unable to get ahead. The only people making any progress were the bombers, who ran a sort of bomb-ferry service all day long.

The day ended with a night attack by the King's Royal Rifle Corps, again directed against the 88's, but in the darkness we saw some of their Bren carriers burning; at dawn the 88's were still there.

The next morning, the 27th of October, the Regiment side-stepped a little and managed to advance a few hundred yards. We found that the low ridge in front of us was strongly held by German infantry and decided to have a go at them. The Shermans did some accurate and concentrated shelling on their trenches which resulted in a party raising their hands and walking towards us. The Reconnaissance Troop fetched in about twenty-five rather sour-looking Panzer Grenadiers, none of whom seemed particularly enthusiastic about the war. Among them was an officer who had a map in his pocket showing the layout of his company and, with the aid of this, some more judicious shell fire was applied. After a pause a dirty white flag went up and a further thirty prisoners were taken.

At 3 p.m. fifty-six German tanks formed up opposite us and seemed to be about to attack. The "reception committee" stuffed the last of the bully-and-biscuit sandwiches into their mouths and cleared decks, but the tanks remained stationary until nightfall, which was a pity, as we had everything ready for a big "kill." A few did attack the 10th Hussars, but gave up after losing nine tanks. Stumps were drawn for the day as far as tanks were concerned.

Again that night our infantry—the 139th Lorried Infantry Brigade—attacked under a tremendous barrage. Enemy counter-battery and defensive fire was equally strong and a good number of shells fell into our leaguer as the Sussex walked through in extended order, their rifles at the high port. As an example of the weariness of battle, quite a number of us were unaware of the falling shells until the next morning, when we saw the dead lying in the leaguer.

By dawn on the 28th we had to be up with the infantry to prevent them being counter-attacked, but there was a very thick mist and none of the squadrons were able to find them. The Colonel decided to try himself, and, with the Adjutant, went poking forward in his tank. The Adjutant, mindful of his responsibility for the Colonel's safety (and possibly his own!), had just suggested that they had gone far enough when the tank shuddered all over from a direct hit.

Luckily it was still whole and they beat a hurried retreat. Investigation showed that a 50-mm. shell had hit the side, gone through a road wheel and finished up in the gearbox casing.

The infantry, when found, were nearer than we had thought and were faced by fifty or sixty enemy tanks beyond the ridge. We could not attack immediately because of a battery of 88's on our right flank, so "B" Squadron moved across to the left and forward, where they took up positions immediately behind the dug-in infantry. Sergeant Edwards's Sherman moved quietly ahead and surprised two M13's busily trying to get at the Scotsmen: two rounds from Corporal Nicholls's gun set them both on fire and the remainder of the enemy tanks disappeared.

On the right "A" Squadron was looking closely at the flat ground to the north-west and discovered that it was full of slit trenches and Germans. Major Price decided to attack. It was the usual "A" Squadron charge. After putting down a smoke screen to blank out the 88's the squadron wheeled round in a big circle, overran three 50-mm. anti-tank guns, two 81-mm. mortars and a good number of Germans and returned to the start point. Three tanks were lost, one hit in the tail as it came back and two which had run on surface mines and lost their tracks. Unfortunately Lieutenant Henry Wyndham had gone too far and did not return, and neither he nor his crew were seen for some time. Some days later his body was found in a fire-ravaged tank; the rest of his crew were prisoners. Under cover of a second smoke screen two cruisers had steel tow-ropes fixed to their rear shackles and, with a man lying on the engine covers, dashed up behind the casualties. The second shackle was bolted on and both machines tore back, pulling the two mined tanks behind them.

Sergeant Edwards and Corporal Nickolls were still having a game of their own with the enemy tanks. The former was lying in the open on the ridge with his tank below. As soon as the enemy tanks appeared Sergeant Edwards beckoned his tank up and it slowly rose up the slope until the periscope appeared. Then Corporal Nickolls would demonstrate the benefits of long experience in a good trade (his self-confessed occupation in civil life was poaching) by picking off one tank after another. Quite soon they had the whole skyline silhouetted with blazing tanks, and the Highlanders, standing up in their holes regardless of bullets, yelled their appreciation.

Sergeant Williamson, the wireless operator in Sergeant Edwards's tank, tells the story as follows:

"We advanced to within a few yards of the crest, taking great care not to raise tell-tale dust, and took up positions of observation without exposing our tanks more than necessary. Our task was made more difficult owing to a group of snipers who lay just beyond the top, machine-gunning our commanders every time they showed their heads above the turret. Our range of vision was good, the morning light had not yet given way to the customary midday haze, and we could see about four thousand yards to our front and rather more to our right.

"Scattered in the low valley below us we reported a mixed formation of German and Italian tanks numbering approximately thirty. There were also some anti-tank guns, which opened up spasmodically, but these we were unable to see. Sergeant Edwards spotted a couple of German Mark III's well within range, and we at once traversed on to the nearer of the two and engaged it. After four shots I saw several of the crew bale out and run to the neighbouring tank, but Corporal Nickolls had already swung his gun on to the second target, and their refuge was soon a mass of flames.

"Sergeant Edwards then observed three German tanks approaching us from our right flank, and we began ranging on these, supported by the other two tanks in the troop. There was a brilliant flash as Corporal Nickolls scored his third bullseye, and the enemy tank stopped dead, the crew baling out. The two remaining tanks meanwhile were being hotly engaged by the rest of the troop and both were destroyed after a sharp duel. The enemy snipers were particularly troublesome about this time and we had to withdraw a few yards before resuming our task.

"From time to time large formations of Bostons flew overhead and dropped their respects upon the enemy forward positions, and the consequent clouds of dust and smoke made observation pretty difficult for us. However, shortly afterwards we engaged another German tank at extreme range. He escaped and disappeared into the low ground and out of our line of vision. At this stage the squadron leader decided to recall us for replenishment of ammunition, and—equally important, we felt—a hasty brew.

"In the afternoon we again crept forward to our old beat and found that visibility had deteriorated considerably, but despite the mirage we could see that the enemy tanks were still more or less in their original positions. Sergeant Edwards selected an Italian M13 moving on our right flank and we had a few shots at him. The tank gave a sort of hiccoughing jerk and stopped, smoke belching from the turret. A few degrees left of this late member of the Axis we could see two more Italian tanks in a hull-down position, but owing to the formation of the ground we could not engage these without taking up a rather exposed position to our right. Ordering the rest of the troop to remain where they were, Sergeant Edwards moved cautiously on to this open ground and we hurriedly laid the gun on to the tanks.

"Corporal Nickolls scored a direct hit on one of them and chunks of metal went flying in all directions. Then, owing to the extremely unpleasant anti-tank fire which was coming at us, we withdrew for a time to a more sheltered position. Later we again eased forward and observed that the remaining Italian tank had been joined by others.

"Knowing the exact range, we quickly opened fire and registered direct hits on the nearest of them; the turret crew came tumbling out as flames appeared out of the turret. By this time an 88-mm. was ranging on us, but we got the next tank on fire before drawing back.

"Shortly afterwards we saw the turret of a German Mark IV to our left front, where visibility had been extremely poor. We decided to have a go at it and, although it proved to be a very tricky target, we eventually got him too, the tank bursting into flames.

"This was Corporal Nickolls's eighth scalp of the day, and brought his tally for the Middle East campaign to over the thirty mark. The other two tanks of the troop had accounted for a further three, and this proved to be our last engagement of the day. Taken all round it had been a very satisfactory day for 4th Troop, with the close-of-play score eleven for none."

It so happened that the Army Commander was listening on an intercept set to the conversation between Captain Reid and Major Fitzpatrick, the Brigade Major, and as each new victim was announced the excitement at Army Headquarters grew intense. At the end of the day a message came from General Montgomery that Corporal Nickolls was to be put in for an immediate Military Medal as an encouragement to all the other gunners in the Eighth Army. Certainly his shooting that day boded ill for the pheasants in Rutland whenever he got back to his normal occupation.

It was one of those days when the shelling was not bad enough to compel one to remain "indoors" all day, but sufficiently bad to make walking about from tank to tank a fairly exciting pastime. The 88's were firing those horrible things which hit the ground, bounced up into the air—and then exploded. One of these landed under the back of the Colonel's tank and a piece hit Lieutenant David Campbell, the Reconnaissance Troop Leader, in the leg as he was standing talking up to the Adjutant. Unluckily it severed a tendon and, apart from causing him great agony, put him out of the war for good. We thus lost one of our very best officers.

By evening we heard that we were to be relieved by the Sherwood Rangers and their squadron leaders came up to look over the ground. After dark we formed up in single file and went back, the Germans firing a few parting shots at our glowing exhausts as we went. Going back through the gun lines, we were just in time for the start of an enormous barrage and had to drive under the muzzles of the guns as they fired. It was a fitting finish to a very noisy four days.

It will be remembered that at this stage of the battle General Montgomery realized that his initial tactics were not going to win a victory. He had bitten an enormous hole in the enemy line, and at its strongest point, and by attacking in the north had compelled the enemy to concentrate his tactical reserve in that area. But the infantry were getting very tired, and could no longer afford the nightly casualties. They had fought all night and slept in their foxholes all day, but sleep in the middle of a tank battleground does not come easily.

General Montgomery decided to draw out some of his armour for refreshment and refit, and then push it right through as on the opening night. In other words, to back down the hill again and take another rush at it. The last three days of October were therefore spent refitting just out of shelling, but not Stuka, range.

We reshuffled crews and were made up to strength in tanks taken from another armoured brigade. Our casualties had been one officer killed and three wounded, three sergeants and seven men killed, and one sergeant and thirteen men wounded; all these had to be replaced.

On the 1st of November came the second phase of Alamein. It was carried out as far as we were concerned without a single written order. Briefly, the plan of attack was as follows: a barrage on a monumental scale was to precede an attack by the 151st and 152nd Infantry Brigades. In the dark before dawn the 9th Armoured Brigade, consisting of the 3rd Hussars and the Wiltshire and the Warwickshire Yeomanry, would go through the enemy anti-tank-gun screen, and then the 2nd Armoured Brigade would pass through on to the open ground beyond. By this means it was hoped to bring the 21st Panzer Division to battle on the morning of the 2nd of November.

The task of the 9th Armoured Brigade was not an enviable one, and it was expected that casualties would be heavy, but the Army Commander was prepared for one hundred per cent. casualties provided that the enemy's anti-tank screen was broken. The only hope was for the Brigade to get through before a glimmer of dawn appeared in the sky.

The 2nd Armoured Brigade set off at 1 a.m., with the 9th Lancers leading, and passed through the minefields without trouble. As we climbed the gentle slope on to the plateau of Aqqaqir, dawn was breaking. The enemy artillery was laying a curtain of fire on the crest and we had to pass through it before we could deploy. One large shell hit the O.P. tank of our battery commander, Major Croxton, which was directly behind Regimental Headquarters, and killed the driver, setting the tank on fire. Major Croxton was very badly wounded and had to leave us for good. He had gone through a great deal with the Regiment and his going was deeply regretted.

It soon became obvious that the 9th Armoured Brigade had had a disaster: tanks were burning all over the desert in front of us. As we afterwards learned, they had reached the enemy's anti-tank guns just as it grew light, the very thing which had been dreaded, and, silhouetted against the sky, the tanks were sitting targets for the enemy. Many individual battles had taken place at point-blank range and, though the tanks had taken a terrible hiding, the German guns had suffered severely and the officers and men who died that morning had not died in vain.

As we arrived we pushed on through the now pitifully small Wiltshire Yeomanry; what was left of them withdrew through us. To the right the Bays were taking over from the 3rd Hussars, commanded by Lieutenant-Colonel Sir Peter Farquhar. He had lost fourteen officers and about sixty men and his strength was reduced from fifty-two to four tanks.

From then on the day was about the worst we had ever had. The enemy line from Aqqaqir to Sidi el Rahman was held by a line of anti-tank guns with a strong backing of tanks, and all day we were fired at continually from three sides by 88's and 105's. For hours on end the whack of armour-piercing shot on armour plate was unceasing.

Then the enemy tank attacks started. Out of the haze in serried lines they came, the low, black tanks. "B" and "C" Squadrons repulsed no fewer than six determined attacks and the Regiment finished the day with a score of thirty-one, of which twenty-one were set on fire. In addition, five guns were knocked out by putting air-bursts just over their pits. Passing the gunpits later we saw whole crews lying dead across their guns.

Officer casualties started early. Major Meyrick was hit in the head and both Lieutenants Milne and Zissu received wounds from which they subsequently died.

The terrific cross-fire was taking its toll. Two of "C" Squadron's Shermans were burnt out, one cruiser destroyed and five other Shermans knocked out. Our own infantry, dug-in on the battlefield, suffered terribly, being killed by shells meant for us. In that torrent of shot and shell any man who moved was killed. We did what we could for them, but our attention was taken up in fighting for dear life.

Time and time again the tanks ran out of ammunition and as we could not afford to have one single tank out of the line the lorries had to rush forward to them across the shell-swept ground, taking what cover they could behind each tank. One tank at least was so placed that it did not get through as much ammunition as its fellows. In the words of Corporal Cook, M.M., of "C" Squadron:

"I had gone up to Sergeant Harris's tank to give him some ammunition and found that he did not require any. He was not in a very good firing position and, owing to the close proximity of the Bays, could not get into one. As I drove up to him he popped his head out of the turret, complete with stubby and furiously smoking pipe, and asked me if I had any good books for him to read."

Eventually the firing quietened down. We formed leaguer where we had fought and were machine-gunned throughout the night.

The next morning, the 3rd of November, before daybreak the Sherman squadrons moved out into line with the Bays and the 10th and the entire day was spent in shooting. The enemy tanks tried again, with no better results, and the 75's took great toll. The German infantry dug-in in front began to lose their nerve and ran from cover to cover all the time. They were shelled and machine-gunned whenever we could spare them attention.

That day was the crucial day. By evening reports began coming in that the Afrika Korps was streaming westwards and that the Royal Air Force was having the time of its life bombing and strafing the flying columns.

The great tank battle of Aqqaqir had proved the turning point in the desert, and indeed of the whole war. The enemy's armour was reduced to a handful and we were through his gun lines. Behind us fresh armoured brigades were waiting to pass through in pursuit.

On the 4th we crossed the Sidi Rahman track and passed through the results of our work. Dead men, abandoned tanks and guns lay all over the desert. A strong rearguard caused a good deal of trouble about a mile on. Sergeant Frost, of "A" Squadron, lost his cruiser, his gunner and driver being killed, but in return another eight tanks and half a dozen guns were destroyed. Prisoners began coming in in scores and it really did look as if the battle were nearly over.

The afternoon, which was spent in mopping up the remainder of the rearguard, was uneventful except for the capture by Lieutenant Grant Singer, of the 10th, of the commander of the Afrika Korps, General von Thoma, an event which after all does not happen every day. Lieutenant Singer was moving ahead in his scout car when he came upon a single tank. He was too near to it to turn and get away, so he decided to rush it. After firing one wild shot at him, the commander raised his hands and Lieutenant Singer bore off his rich prize.

As we leaguered that night it began to occur to us that the struggle was over. Not a shell or a bomb fell that night and the Germans were retreating across the desert as hard as they could go. Their allies, the Italians, abandoned in the south, were captured the next day in tens of thousands.

For the first time the British Broadcasting Corporation announced the happenings of recent days and gladdened the hearts of the British people. In a few days the church bells in England, silent for three and a half years, rang out the triumph of a great victory.

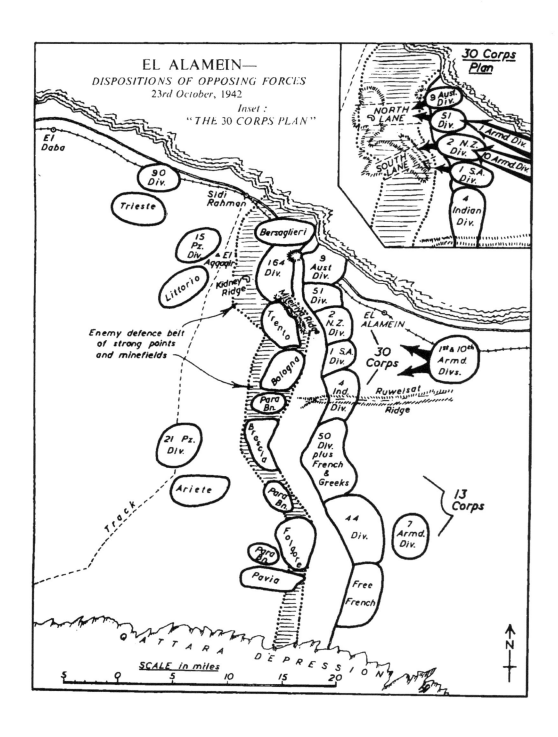

EL ALAMEIN—
DISPOSITIONS OF OPPOSING FORCES
23rd October, 1942

Inset :
"THE 30 CORPS PLAN"

30 Corps Plan

9 Aust. Div.
51 Div.
1 Armd. Div.
2 N.Z. Div.
10 Armd Div.
1 S.A. Div.
4 Indian Div.

NORTH LANE

SOUTH LANE

El Daba

90 Div.

Trieste

Sidi Rahman

Bersaglieri

15 Pz. Div.

El Aqqaqir

164 Div.

9 Aust Div.

Littorio

Kidney Ridge

51 Div.

Miteiriya Ridge

2 N.Z. Div.

Trento

EL ALAMEIN

Enemy defence belt of strong points and minefields

1 S.A. Div.

30 Corps

1st & 10th Armd. Divs.

Bologna

4 Ind. Div.

Ruweisat Ridge

Para Bn.

Brescia

21 Pz. Div.

50 Div. plus French & Greeks

Ariete

Para Bn.

13 Corps

Foligno

44 Div.

7 Armd. Div.

Para Bn.

Track

Pavia

Free French

QATTARA DEPRESSION

SCALE in miles

5   0   5   10   15   20

N

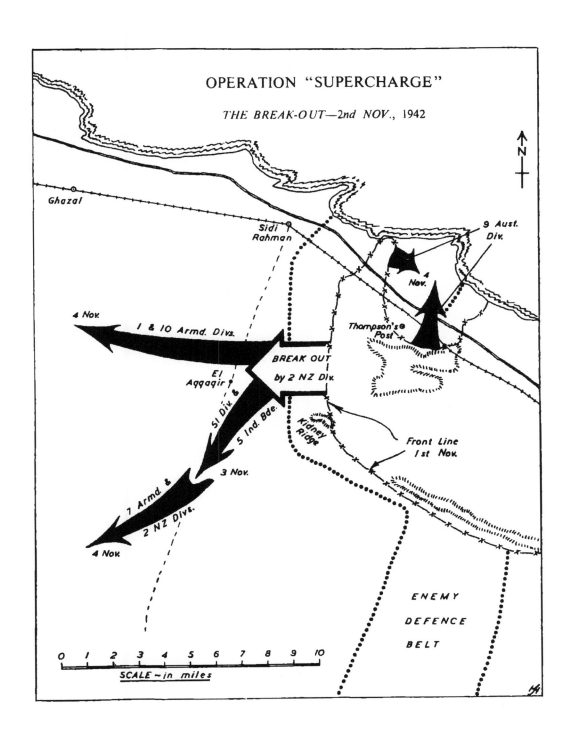

OPERATION "SUPERCHARGE"

THE BREAK-OUT—2nd NOV., 1942

N

Ghazal

Sidi
Rahman

9 Aust.
Div.

4
Nov.

4 Nov.

1 & 10 Armd. Divs.

Thompson's
Post

BREAK OUT
by 2 NZ Div.

El
Aqqaqir

51 Div. &

5 Ind. Bde.

Kidney
Ridge

Front Line
1st Nov.

3 Nov.

7 Armd. &

2 NZ Divs.

4 Nov.

ENEMY

DEFENCE

BELT

0 1 2 3 4 5 6 7 8 9 10

SCALE ~ in miles

CHAPTER XIV

PURSUIT

THAT night, the 4th/5th of November, we slept the sleep of the just. Men simply tumbled on to the ground and remained motionless until dawn.

The first thing we saw as we opened our eyes was a cold and untidy German private standing over the Colonel as he slept and saying, in a querulous voice and in English: "I've been trying to find someone to surrender to for three hours."

To which a sleepy voice replied: "Shut up and sit down."

We had a proper breakfast for once, and then, mounting our tanks, set out for the chase.

We reached Daba at noon and saw the airfield littered with dozens of wrecked Axis aircraft. Two 88's which had been left behind to delay us were silenced, but not before one had killed Lieutenant Grant Singer and another officer of the 10th Hussars by a direct hit on the scout car.

We turned due west and raced along the railway line to Fuka and Galil. The "A" Echelon came up at Galil and fuel tanks were replenished with the last of the petrol and oil. The pace was getting a bit hot for some of the older tanks, which began to fall out, giving the squadron fitters a golden opportunity to explore some of the many abandoned lorries and other equipment.

The intention was to go by way of Bir Khaldar and, by a forced march, to cut the coast road west of Matruh, so the march was continued through the night of the 5th/6th by the light of flares dropped by the Royal Air Force to the north. There were more breakdowns and these involved many change-overs and much renetting of wireless sets.

Farther back, in the Alamein area, it was raining hard, a torrential rain which robbed the Eighth Army of complete triumph. The ten-ton lorries of the Royal Army Service Corps petrol companies got bogged down and for twenty hours we got no more fuel to refill either the tanks or the echelons. Tanks were running dry when we reached the escarpment three miles south of the 45-kilometre stone west of Matruh. Below us, on the plain, there stretched many miles of German transport, guns and tanks, and what made it even more maddening was the fact that they were our old friends, the 90th Light Division. They, too, were out of petrol.

The Brigade sat and fumed, watching them until it became too dark to see. Petrol was promised by midnight, and so, hoping that ours would arrive before theirs, we got some sleep. At 9.30 p.m. on the 7th of November the lorries

121

arrived and tanks were filled, and the "A" Echelon took on the rest. An hour before dawn on the 8th we formed up in battle order and raced over the top and down the escarpment—but the birds had flown. Our disappointment was bitter and our anger was increased by a German 50-mm. gun firing at us as we neared the road. "B" Squadron vented its wrath on the crew, who should have known better anyway, and then we were across the tarmac road.

Here we halted and were joined by an armoured-car squadron of the 12th Lancers. The road was a shambles and a credit to the Royal Air Force. Burnt-out transport lay all along the ditches and a good number of their passengers lay dead. As we waited for further orders a single lorry came tearing down the road from the direction of Matruh. It passed through the squadron of the 12th which was on the road and careered off westwards. Captain Rex Hitchcock, who was inspecting an abandoned Italian office lorry in the hope of gain, suddenly realized as it passed him that it was driven by a German. He and Sergeant Charlton leapt into a jeep and gave chase. Slowly they began to gain on the bouncing lorry and Sergeant Charlton put in some bursts from his Bren gun at its rear tyres. After a while he hit both wheels and it slowed down and stopped. In the back of the lorry were two Germans, one dead and the other wounded, and a rich haul of canteen stores—Danish butter, chocolate, fruit juice and many other delicacies. A small offering was sent to the 12th with a note thanking them for leaving it for us!

Orders arrived telling us to stand fast, so we spent the remainder of the day on maintenance. A squadron of Spitfires came down to have a look at us during the morning and opened fire: the only casualty was Captain Peter Laing, who barked both shins while making a hasty entry into his turret.

The next day (the 9th) Captains Laing and Macpherson drove across the desert in a jeep to examine an almost new German Mark IV tank, but unfortunately there was a teller mine laid beside it which exploded, wounding Captain Laing so badly that he eventually lost both legs; Captain Macpherson escaped with minor cuts. Captain Laing had fought with the Regiment since France, 1940, and it was hard luck on him and the Regiment that this should happen just as the worst of the fighting seemed to have ended.

The Regiment now consisted of thirteen Shermans and seven cruisers, and to our great regret we were told that we were not to continue the chase. The supply situation was such that until Benghazi could be opened as a port, only one armoured brigade could be maintained forward of Tobruk, and, for the pursuit, a less battle-weary brigade was chosen. We had to be content with following its fortunes on the news. We remained at kilometre 45 for four days and then moved on by easy stages and on transporters to Tmimi, forty miles west of Tobruk, which became our home for three months.

We spent the three winter months November, December and January in comparative comfort. Although we had no tents, the resourceful British soldier soon produced "houses" of a sort, usually made of canvas and tied to the side of tank or lorry. These served fairly well to keep out the howling winter gales and rain. The carpenters found an abandoned repair shed on Martuba airfield and worked like blacks to construct a "village hall," complete with stage and dressing room. It was a properly equipped theatre, with footlights, spotlights, a curtain that really drew, and some very good scenery and wings. In fact, the only E.N.S.A. party which ventured so far into the desert were so delighted with it that they wanted to stay with us.

The 12th Lancers were leaguered only a mile away and we had some very good football matches with them, as well as with the Bays and the 10th Hussars. We organized a rifle meeting, a concert party and a dog show, and had some excellent duck shooting in the salt marshes of the Bay of Bomba (the bag for three months was fifty-six snipe and two hundred and fifty-four duck).

We trained, we had courses and lectures, and we sent leave parties back to the Delta. Our already dilapidated transport ferried tens of thousands of gallons of petrol from Tobruk harbour to Tripoli, journeys which made it more doubtful than ever whether it would survive until the end of the North African campaign.

We sent lorries back to Cairo to collect comforts and stores and had a splendid Christmas dinner. The cooks did marvels and every man had as much as he could eat and drink. Trooper Berryman, a teetotaller, claims to have put the whole of his squadron to bed with the assistance of a wheelbarrow, and then cooked their breakfast for them!

In January a completely new lot of tanks were received, only to be taken away again to reinforce the regiments beyond Tripoli. The Eighth Army had reached Ben Gardane, where opposition was stiffening, and the First Army was having some serious reverses in Tunisia. We were becoming bored with inactivity and it was a great relief when orders came to move forward again.

On the 20th of February, 1943, the tanks (new ones) were driven to the water-point at Tmimi and loaded up on transporters. The next day they left for Tripoli under Majors Laurie and Steel, the latter having been given command of "C" Squadron after Major Meyrick had had a serious accident in a jeep. Major Lomax had left to take up an appointment as Deputy Assistant Adjutant-General at General Headquarters, Cairo, and his place was taken by Captain Gardner, who, in turn, handed over his duties as Adjutant to Captain Rex Hitchcock.

The wheeled vehicles of the Regiment left Tmimi with the rest of the Brigade on the 1st of March. The longest journey we had ever had then began, the first night being spent at Martuba. For the next two days the road wound through the green and hilly country of the jebel, past the old Roman towns of Cyrene and Apollonia, and through Mussolini's great farm colony, now abandoned to the Arabs. We dropped down the Tocra Pass, its hillsides covered with the wrecks of Stuka dive-bombers from past fights, to Barce, and then, skirting Benghazi, joined the coast road running through Beda Fomm and Ghemines and round the Gulf of Sidra. We passed through Agedabia and Agheila, Nofilia and Sirte, to Buerat el Sun, where the route left the coast and cut across the Misurata headland, through Sedada and Beni Ulid and Tarhuna to Castel Benito, the big Italian airport south of Tripoli. Here among the white settlement farms built by Mussolini the wheeled party joined the tanks and we spent a day together under the tall eucalyptus trees. On the journey the Adjutant, Captain Hitchcock, went sick and his place was taken by Lieutenant Francis Pym, who, except for a short break, remained there until the end of the war.

By the evening of the 12th of March the Brigade was leaguered at Ben Gardane, and the next day's run to Medenine brought us once more within hearing of gun fire. We had six days to prepare for the next big battle.

Rommel had attacked the Eighth Army just before we arrived and had been "seen off" to no small tune, losing a large number of his tanks to the anti-tank guns of the Guards Brigade. This failure marked a further step in his decline and from then on the brilliant "Desert Fox" began to lose his reputation as a genius.

Although there was now small danger to the Eighth Army, which was by no means as yet up to its proper strength, General Montgomery was being pressed to take action in order to relieve the First Army, which was suffering serious reverses in the Fonduk and Kasserine sectors. He therefore planned an attack for the night of the 20th of March.

The Mareth Line was the toughest obstacle he had yet had to face. Constructed by the French to guard Tunisia against the Italians in Tripolitania, its left flank ran from the sea, down the almost impassable Wadi Zigzaou, to the village of Mareth. Its right flank lay in Toujane, high up on the northern scar of the Matmata Mountains. In the low ground it had triple anti-tank ditches, concrete gun emplacements and numerous minefields. It was, in fact, a miniature Maginot Line which the Germans had adapted to suit their own purposes. From the tops of the Matmata, looking down into the pretty white town of Medenine, the German gunners watched the hub of the British defence and responded immediately to every movement.

On the morning of the 20th the Army Commander addressed his commanding officers and issued one of his famous messages. It ran as follows:

"EIGHTH ARMY

"1. On 5th March Rommel addressed his troops in the mountains overlooking our positions and said that if they did not retake Medenine, and force the Eighth Army to withdraw, then the days of the Axis forces in North Africa were numbered.

"The next day, 6th of March, he attacked the Eighth Army. He should have known that the Eighth Army NEVER WITHDRAWS; therefore his attack could only end in failure—which it did.

"2. We will now show Rommel that he was right in the statement he made to his troops. The days of the Axis in North Africa are indeed numbered.

"The Eighth Army and the Western Desert Air Force, together constituting one fighting machine, are ready to advance. We all know what that means; and so does the enemy.

"3. In the battle that is now to start, the Eighth Army will:

    (a) Destroy the enemy now facing us in the Mareth position,

    (b) Burst through the Gabes gap,

    (c) Then drive northwards on SFAX, SOUSSE, and finally TUNIS.

"4. We will not stop, or let up, till Tunis has been captured and the enemy has either given up the struggle or been pushed into the sea.

"5. The operations now about to begin will mark the close of the campaign in North Africa. Once the battle starts the eyes of the whole world will be on the Eighth Army, and millions of people will listen to the wireless every day—hoping anxiously for good news. We must not let them be anxious. Let us see that they get good news, and plenty of it, every day.

"6. With faith in God, and in the justice of our cause, let us go forward to victory.

"FORWARD TO TUNIS! DRIVE THE ENEMY INTO THE SEA!"

His plan was to launch a frontal attack, with the usual violent barrage, and at the same time to send the New Zealand Corps round the southern flank aimed at Gabes. The armour was to be kept in one group and launched as soon as the break-in was made.

On the night of the 20th of March we watched the guns light up the sky and all the next day the bombers were going over on their errands of destruction.

Following the principle that "time spent on reconnaissance is seldom wasted," the day was spent in examining all possible routes and obstacles. During the afternoon a particularly intense discussion was abruptly terminated by a German shell which arrived out of the blue and landed near enough to bespatter the whole group. Thereafter a little more respect was shown for the German observation posts on the Matmata hills, and further discussions took place under cover.

On this occasion, however, reconnaissance was a waste of time. We never went near the ground we had so carefully studied, because the frontal attack on the Mareth Line was a failure. The 50th Division, attacking in the darkness across a deep wadi, got bogged down and failed to get its anti-tank guns across. When day came it was assaulted by the 15th Panzer Division.

The Army Commander, refusing to reinforce failure, made another of his courageous decisions. He ordered the 1st Armoured Division to steal away after the New Zealanders to the south, through Wilder's Gap and round the Matmata hills.

As darkness fell on the 23rd of March the Brigade moved down to the Medenine—Ben Gardane road and loaded up on transporters. At Foum Tatahouine the tanks dismounted and we began the most arduous march we had ever experienced. The country was wild beyond imagination and it seemed as though the New Zealanders had been the first living beings ever to pass through it. The surface was either ragged outcrop or deep, white sand, the latter being an alkaline powder which produced a raging thirst in us and completely clogged our eyes and nostrils. Water was at a premium and very soon we were all acutely uncomfortable. Engines became overheated and wheels spun and dug themselves deep. For the lorry drivers it was a case of dig, dig, dig, and time and time again they had to get out tow ropes to help each other along. The one gleam of comfort was that the enemy so far seemed unaware of what was going on. One single reconnaissance plane would have given the whole show away.

The story of the remainder of this astonishing march and the action which took place at the end of it is best told by Colonel Gerald Grosvenor:

"On the 24th of March we moved on for a further thirty-three miles over some of the grimmest desert country I have ever seen. The going was, for the most part, soft sand and the 'B' vehicles had a lot of difficulty, and did a lot of digging. We had orders to cross the Wadi el Aredj before we leaguered for the night. However, owing to the bad going, we were ten miles short of our destination when darkness fell. As the column was very strung out, and we had had a long march, I asked if we could stop where we were, and was told that I could. We duly pulled off the track and cooked a meal and had just formed close leaguer, preparatory to going to bed, when Lieutenant-Colonel Jackie Bowring, Second-in-Command of the Brigade, appeared out of the darkness on foot—his car having got stuck in the sand. He said that it was not the intention to stay where we were for the night, and that we were to cross the Wadi el Aredj. I protested that if the Brigade tried to cross in the dark a wadi which had only one crossing place and was covered by a French minefield it would take all night. Jackie passed on my protest, but to no avail, and we were told to move as soon as the moon came up at about 2200 hours.

"We duly moved off. The tanks gave no trouble, but getting the wheeled vehicles across was the very devil. We eventually made the ten miles and close leaguered at about midnight. Due to superhuman efforts on the part of the 'B1' Echelon commander, most of the replenishment vehicles arrived shortly after the Regiment and we were filled up with petrol right away. I subsequently heard that the people behind had even more difficulty in crossing the wadi than we had and never got their echelon at all that night, but I refrained from saying 'I told you so.'

"As we had no orders from Brigade since Jackie Bowring's unwelcome appearance during the night (strict wireless silence being enforced during the march), we opened out at first light on the 25th of March and had breakfast.

At 9 a.m. the Brigade Liaison Officer arrived with news of considerable loss of both formation and temper back down the track and orders for us to continue the march as soon as the 12th Lancers had passed through us.

"The march was continued under much the same conditions as on the previous day, except that it was rather more complicated owing to the inaccuracy of the map. By this time several of the more venerable of the tanks we had drawn at Tripoli were overheating badly and falling by the wayside. At about 1 p.m. we eventually reached our destination fifteen miles north-west of Bir Sultane. The country had remained exactly the same since leaving Wilder's Gap and there was not a vestige of civilization. On arrival we started doing all possible maintenance to the vehicles and I was sent for by the Brigadier for orders at 6 p.m. The situation on the New Zealand Corps front was as follows: the Germans were holding a position astride the El Hamma road, which ran through a valley six miles wide and eighteen miles south of El Hamma village. The flanks of their position rested on the high, rocky hills on each side of the road. They were strong in anti-tank guns and we had reason to believe that they were being reinforced by tanks and artillery. There was only one minefield, as far as was known, and that was astride the road and now behind the line of our own forward defensive localities.

"General Horrocks had arrived with the X Corps Headquarters, and the whole force (New Zealand Corps and the 1st Armoured Division) had been put under his command. The plan was to attack the German position as soon as possible before it could be reinforced, and the details were as follows:

"The attack was to be made at 4 p.m. the next day, the 26th of March. This hour was chosen with a view to surprise, as we had never attacked at this time before. The initial attack was to be made by the 8th Armoured Brigade with three regiments up, less their cruiser squadrons, which were to follow in support of the New Zealanders behind the rest of the Brigade.

"The attack was to be supported by all the Corps artillery and twenty-one squadrons of bombers (the heaviest air support yet given in any attack).

"The start line for the attack was the line of forward defensive localities just beyond the Roman wall, and the 8th Armoured Brigade and the New Zealanders were to penetrate to a depth of four thousand yards. The 1st Armoured Division, with the 2nd Armoured Brigade leading, was to follow up the attacking troops to their objective and to penetrate a further four thousand yards before dark. It was to halt astride the road until the moon rose, then continue its advance and capture El Hamma village. Brigaded 'B1' Echelons were to move with the Brigade, guarded by the tanks of the 10th Hussars, so that if the road was blocked behind us (as it subsequently was) the Brigade would be self-contained. Each tank was to carry five days' rations.

"The Brigade order of march was: 9th Lancers on the right with the road inclusive; Bays on the left; Brigade Headquarters on the centre line (the road), followed by 'B1' Echelon in five columns escorted by the 10th Hussars. The batteries and companies of the 11th H.A.C. and Yorkshire Dragoons were to move with their respective regiments.

"A very bold plan; and not one, I must admit, that I felt very confident about, as I remembered only too well the desert at Alamein littered with the burning tanks of the 9th Armoured Brigade. The other complication was that the whole Brigade Echelon (except for 'B1') was a long way behind, and each regiment had dropped a lot of stragglers.

"I gave out orders on the morning of the 26th of March and decided to move with two squadrons up—'C' on the right, 'B' on the left and in touch with the Bays.

"The Regiment moved out at 1.25 p.m. down the track to the deployment area north of Brigade Headquarters. A reconnaissance had been made of the route to the Roman wall that morning, but as time was short and the 'khamseen' still blowing strongly, no one was very confident of finding the way. The Bays, who were the directing regiment, said that they thought they knew, so I decided to stick to them like glue and hope for the best.

"Deploying in an area already covered with vehicles and with the visibility only about twenty yards was somewhat complicated and bad for the temper. The going was very rough and hilly and we had our whips out to keep up, as the Bays were mounted in Mark III Shermans throughout. We eventually fetched up much too far to our left, and the whole Brigade had to take ground to the right so as to reach the lanes through a New Zealand artillery regiment just as they were starting their barrage. However, they did not seem to mind, which was quite remarkable, considering that we must have given their position away, cut their telephone lines, and generally caused them a lot of inconvenience.

"As far as I can remember we had been allotted tracks 'A' to 'F' through the minefields. These were well marked to start with and as each squadron found them it turned left along its own track. For some reason the tracks disappeared before they reached the minefield! It was no place in which to dawdle about, as the first German shells were beginning to arrive in the area of the minefield, so I led on with Regimental Headquarters, found a lane and hurried through. On looking round I saw considerable congestion, as there appeared to be only three badly marked lanes to which the whole Regiment converged. Two tanks ran on to mines and had their tracks blown off. Mercifully the German shelling was very slight and soon stopped. I can only suppose that they were short of ammunition, as a whole armoured regimental group feeling its way through a minefield must have presented a wonderful target.

"I was very thankful to find the Roman wall and to see the New Zealand infantry disappearing in the dust about eight hundred yards away. We were a bit late, but so was everybody else, so all was well.

"We followed the New Zealanders for about three thousand yards. Visibility had improved during the approach march to the Roman wall, but now, with so many vehicles moving and so much shelling, we found ourselves in what closely resembled a London fog. Both armour-piercing and high-explosive shells seemed to be coming from every direction. The German gunners on the high ground on the flanks were obviously blinded, but were firing very fast and a variety of projectiles seemed to be coming from behind our right flank but too high to be doing much damage. Nothing could be seen of the 8th Armoured Brigade—but a lot of unescorted and badly shaken prisoners kept appearing in small parties.

"At one period there were no fewer than five tanks containing officers in red hats—namely, the Corps Commander (General Horrocks), the New Zealand Corps Commander (General Freyberg), the Divisional Commander (General Briggs), the Brigadier, Royal Artillery (Brigadier Fowler), and our own Brigadier (Brigadier Fisher)—between me and my leading squadron! However, as by this time we were passing through the Staffordshire Yeomanry—the centre regiment of the 8th Armoured Brigade—a few extra tanks on the ground did not add much to the general confusion.

"As we passed through the New Zealanders and the 8th Armoured Brigade, 'B' and 'C' Squadrons were being engaged by about five German tanks, but without effect. Two of these tanks were knocked out for certain, but it was impossible to say what happened to the remainder, as there were so many burning vehicles and so much shooting going on.

"By this time the break into the enemy positions had been accomplished and, apart from a few tanks and some very unwarlike German and Italian infantry hiding in the wadis, not much opposition was encountered during the next leg of the advance—i.e., the next four thousand yards to our forming-up position.

" 'C' Squadron encountered quite a large body of infantry in a wadi just short of our objective, who sniped at them in rather a half-hearted manner, so a ferreting party of Yorkshire Dragoons was sent off to deal with them. They returned shortly afterwards, grinning from ear to ear, with about seventy prisoners and a lot of assorted loot.

"It was now dark enough to form up in our night-march formation, and all firing had died away. I intended to move with 'B' Squadron leading, in line, 'C' Squadron echeloned on the right flank, followed by 'A' Squadron. Regimental Headquarters was to follow close behind 'B' Squadron, which in turn was to be followed by 'E' Battery, H.A.C., and 'B' Company, Yorkshire Dragoons. One scout-car patrol was to move along the road and keep in touch with the Bays on the left of the road.

"Up to this moment, and in fact until first light the following morning, the 9th Lancers Regimental Group did not suffer a single casualty.

"Just before we reached the forming-up position we met a large wadi—the first of a series which were to cause us a lot of trouble during the night. There seemed to be considerable congestion at the only crossing place on the right of the road, so I sent 'Stug' Perry to sort it out. It was by then quite dark, and

L

he found a Grant tank in the middle of the crossing place which he proceeded to address in no uncertain terms for five minutes before he found out that he was addressing the Corps Commander.

"Regimental Headquarters closed up on 'B' Squadron, but in the dark we drove through them and set off up the road to El Hamma towards the Germans. However, after about three hundred yards we decided that all was not well and returned very shamefaced and very nervous of being shot at by 'B' Squadron.

"After we had formed up there was nothing more to do but wait for the moon. It was a curious and not altogether pleasant sensation to be sitting in the middle of the German position with such a vast phalanx of vehicles. We could hear vehicles moving in the darkness and naturally could not tell whether they were friend or foe. One large gun kept firing spasmodically from the direction of Hamma village, but its shells were going well over our heads.

"At last the moon appeared, and the order to move was given at a quarter to midnight. We had discussed what action was to be taken if we met the 15th Panzer Division in close leaguer, but, as it could only result in a shooting match at under a hundred yards' range, there did not appear to be much that a colonel could do beyond keeping his head well inside his tank. Orders had been given that any tank that fell out was to be fought where it stood to the last round.

"Progress was very slow, and nothing very exciting happened to start with— except that the two leading scout cars motored into a wadi and went down about thirty feet. No serious damage to the crews resulted, but the scout cars are probably still there. This wadi, and several others like it, necessitated the whole Regiment and some of the Bays closing on to the road and fanning out again on the other side.

"We soon began to meet small parties of vehicles and guns, which were duly shot-up, and very soon the whole valley was brilliantly lit up by burning vehicles and exploding ammunition. German supply columns, ignorant of the fact that their entire front line had gone, were driving up the road towards us and being shot up in dozens. A number of Germans could be seen running about in the light of the burning wrecks, and the majority soon surrendered. The noise made by such a large number of tanks and the shooting must have been very alarming, and for the first nine miles of the advance there was no retaliation of any kind. In fact, it soon became a competition between the two leading regiments as to who could shoot up the most vehicles and there were complaints by both regiments of poaching on their side of the road. Occasionally an enemy vehicle would appear from behind us, trying to escape up the road. The results of this were most dangerous, as everyone fired inwards.

"We were, however, brought back to the sordid realities of war about five miles from El Hamma by an 88-mm. firing from our right front, and a tank of the Bays was hit. Michael Marsh, who was commanding one of the leading troops of 'B' Squadron, succeeded in getting to within a hundred yards of the gun and overran the enemy position. When dawn broke an 88-mm. and a 50-mm. gun were found abandoned. 'C' Squadron, in the meantime, had been sent up on to some very steep and rocky ground on the right. This feature was reported unoccupied by a patrol of the Yorkshire Dragoons and with great difficulty 'C' Squadron succeeded in establishing one troop on top.

"By this time it was about an hour before dawn and we received orders to halt and consolidate the ground that we held. I am sure that we could have got into El Hamma village that night, although we would undoubtedly have been heavily counter-attacked shortly afterwards. I can only assume that the order to halt was given because of the situation behind us. It was certainly very complicated. There were masses of Germans and Italians, and a certain number of tanks, wandering about between us and the Roman wall; our line of communication was cut for four days and the 8th Armoured Brigade and the New Zealanders had a stiff fight to get through to us. Quite a number of the surviving German tanks broke out to the north-east towards Gabes.

"The attack on El Hamma on the morning of the 27th of March failed. The enemy could be seen pouring into the village from the north, and we were very heavily shelled all day. The Regiment lost two tanks and suffered a number of casualties. El Hamma was eventually captured on the 29th. The value of the village was obvious and, had we been able to hold it in any strength, the Gabes Gap would have been partially closed and it is questionable whether many of the garrison of the Mareth Line would have been able to escape.

"So ended a brilliant operation which just failed to achieve its object. Its chief interest lies in the fact that it was the first time that we had achieved a successful break-through by armour in the dark. The possibilities of such an operation had been discussed even before the Battle of Alamein, and during the battle the 9th Armoured Brigade were given just such a task. They failed, with very high casualties, because they were not allowed enough time in the dark and, at first light, found themselves a few hundred yards in front of the enemy anti-tank guns instead of being well through them.

"In our case the break into the enemy position was achieved in daylight and the various factors contributing to the success of the operation were as follows:

"(1) There were no mines once we were through the minefield by the Roman wall.

"(2) There was just enough moonlight to march by.

"(3) Keeping direction was made very easy by having the road, with telegraph poles along its entire length, as a centre line.

"(4) It had never been done before and the Germans were taken completely by surprise.

"(5) Although I say it as shouldn't, the very high standard of training of the 2nd Armoured Brigade was undoubtedly the factor which contributed more than anything else to the success of the operation.

"I find that I have been referring to a 'successful operation' that failed in its object. I think it is fair to say that it was successful in that it swept away all German resistance south of Gabes and inflicted very heavy casualties on them. It failed, however, in cutting off the whole enemy force in the Mareth area."

WESTERN DESERT, 1943

9th Lancers' graveyard at Saunnu, dedicated whilst the Regiment was at Tmimi

H.Q. Squadron Cookhouse at Tmimi

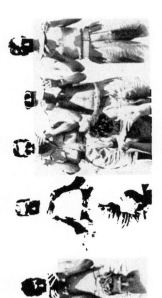

"C" Squadron upset on road to Medenine

Water melons

NORTH AFRICA, 1943

In the Kourmine area

L. to R.: Capt. R. P. Thomas, M.C., Lieut.-Colonel G. H. Grosvenor, D.S.O., Capt. R. K. B. Hitchcock, M.C., and Major J. H. M. D. Scott, M.C.

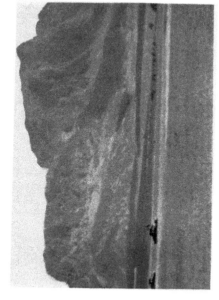

Creteville Pass, Tunisia

"Dead Horse Farm" and Jebel Kourmine

German Tiger at Kourmine

CHAPTER XV

WADI AKARIT

On the evening of the 28th of March the Brigade was warned to prepare for another night attack, commencing at 12.30 a.m. on the 29th. Our nocturnal excursions were controlled by the moon, which at that time did not rise until 2 a.m. During the night the plan was cancelled, rather to everyone's relief, and a second order came to be ready to advance at dawn. Before this was carried out news came from the forward patrols that the enemy were pulling out of El Hamma. The Mareth garrison had by this time got clear of Gabes and presumably Rommel had told his flankguard that their task was now completed.

At 8 a.m. the Regimental Group formed up and sailed through El Hamma, which then contained only a few dead Germans and a lot of wildly cheering inhabitants, and turned left-handed across a sort of desolate swamp. "B" Squadron soon made contact and began engaging guns and infantry, and for three hours we advanced slowly in the face of stiffening opposition until by midday we had to halt and admit that there was more to it than met the eye.

A flock of Stukas arrived shortly after noon and attacked "E" Battery, who suffered rather severe casualties, although the guns were not damaged. By evening our "bag" was one armoured car, eleven lorries and a few guns, and the day ended with the news that Gabes had fallen.

On the morning of the 30th a patrol of the Reconnaissance Troop went out and tried to make contact with the enemy, but two cars blew up on buried teller mines and Lance-Corporal Billett was killed. The next patrol could find no trace of the enemy, so the Regiment moved on again for about three and a half miles. This brought us under a range of sheer and jagged hills, rather like the back-cloth in a Gilbert and Sullivan play, with a marsh stretching away to the left. Nothing could be seen and the Colonel was just wondering what we were expected to do when heavy and accurate shelling began. We could not do anything about it, as the German guns were behind the mountain and no observation posts were visible. Unfortunately Major Laurie was wounded in the arm and had to be sent away. "B" Squadron was taken over by Major Gardner.

A night attack was made by the 7th Battalion The Rifle Brigade, under Colonel Douglas Darling, to capture the Haidoudi Pass on our left front, and the next morning, the 31st, the Regiment was ordered to move up in support. The pass had been reported captured and the Reconnaissance Troop went off to make contact, but it then became all too clear that the pass had not in fact been captured. In the dark one company had mistaken the objective and had sent up the success signal, with the result that the whole battalion dug-in in such a position that, when day came, it was overlooked and pinned down by the enemy. Colonel Darling asked for any assistance we could give him to get his men out, as they were being mortared and suffering terrible casualties. There was not a great deal we could do, especially as a great bog lay between us and them, and there were no visible Germans to fight. However, "B" Squadron dumped all their armour-piercing, loaded as much high-explosive as they could carry and moved off gingerly across the marsh left-handed. "E" Battery and "B" Squadron were to try to put down a curtain of shells along the top of the crags, under cover of which the Riflemen could escape from the hill.

"B" Squadron managed to get over the worst of the bog, more by good luck than anything else, and lined out about half a mile from the foothills. Here some 50-mm. anti-tank guns began firing at them, rather optimistically, as the shot was no more than denting the hulls, and a few return rounds stopped that. Then our gunner friends over the hills took a hand, but most of their shells failed to go off in the peaty soil: soon they, too, gave up, so "B" Squadron ranged each troop on its own sector of the crest line and waited in silence until 11 o'clock for the barrage. At the appointed time it crashed out. There was a ripple of shell-bursts all along the top and any Germans who were looking over the crest must have had a very uncomfortable time. Inside the tanks the cordite fumes thickened and stung the eyes, and towards the end it was necessary to start the engines to clear them away.

As the firing ceased the remains of the 7th Rifle Brigade were seen walking towards us across the marsh, leaving behind them in the hills many for whom help had come too late.

During the barrage two cars of the Reconnaissance Troop had become bogged down to the axles. Captain Reid went over to tow them out with his Crusader and himself got bogged. "B" Squadron sent a Diesel Sherman to tow him out and then that got stuck too, although it did succeed in freeing the Crusader. More tanks were sent to assist and more tanks got stuck. The Germans did not help in any way by sending shells over from time to time, one of which hit our Doctor, Captain Dison, in the foot and shattered his ankle. This was a severe blow to us all and no one much liked to think of future battles without his courageous presence wherever men lay wounded.

Eventually all the tanks or scout cars belonging to Regimental Headquarters were extricated and, in response to an earnest request from the Officer Commanding "B" Squadron not to do it again, the Colonel took his headquarters away on to ground more suitable for thirty-ton tanks.

By now some of "B" Squadron's Shermans were so deep in the mud that they looked like remaining there for ever, so the famous old Scammell was sent for. Its arrival was noisily greeted by the German gunners and the group of perspiring officers and men standing round the morass hastily took cover as it drove up. Owing to the noise of its venerable engine, Private Hickman, the driver, had remained ignorant of the fact that his beloved "wagon" had been the object of a dozen near-misses all along the marsh, and asked everyone blandly "where the fire was." The thirteenth near-miss answered his question.

With the Scammell's winch, anchored to two Shermans, the ditched tanks were soon recovered and "B" Squadron put away its brew-tins and made off on to firmer ground as fast as it could.

The next day, the 1st of April, was a holiday. At least there was no fighting and all crews got down to some much-needed maintenance. General Horrocks came to see us and said that XXX Corps would put in a major attack against the line ahead in a day or so. We remained where we were, being shelled occasionally, but otherwise enjoying the rest. Corporal Middleditch and his lorry came up and brought our store of tinned goods up to strength. The only excitement during the next few days was when "E" Battery suddenly decided to fire twelve rounds' gunfire—at what we were not sure. These so disturbed the peace of the parish that the Colonel sent across and told the gunners that if they were going to do that sort of thing they would have to go.

The big attack went in during the night of the 6th/7th of April. At 4.30 a.m. the barrage began and because it was late and a moonless night the Germans had all gone to bed. The Gurkhas had been sent up the main hill an hour before and they got among the enemy with their long knives. Those who climbed the hill the next day were appalled at the result of their handiwork. Our part in this operation was a minor one. We were required to move out to the left again and create a diversion. On the evening of the attack we went out to draw fire and, although we made as much dust as we could, the enemy appeared to be sulking in their tents. The next morning, however, the required fire was drawn and we spent a few unhappy hours sitting out a shower of shells of every calibre, with no visible enemy to shoot back at. We had no casualties to men or machines, though Major Gardner had a narrow escape when a shell splinter removed the field-glasses he was holding up to his eyes. When he mentioned the matter to the Commanding Officer the only comment he received was: "Well, there's nothing to see, anyway."

The rest of the day was spent awaiting the order to advance through the hills. In the evening we saw a very fine bit of shooting by a battery of Bofors guns which were guarding the road leading into the hills. Six Messerschmitt 210 fighters came flying up the road from behind at very low level, apparently having made a mistake in their map reading, and four were almost instantly shot down in flames. We discovered later that the battery commander was the Colonel's brother.

At 11.15 a.m. the next morning the entire Division moved off through the Zemlet el Beida Pass. Beyond the pass we fanned out and struck across country. The enemy was in full retreat and as we went the news came through that the 12th Lancers had made the long-awaited link-up with the Americans of the First Army.

CHAPTER XVI

WE JOIN THE FIRST ARMY

THE fox we had put up this time was a good one. He ran as straight as a die through the olive groves to Sfax and on to Sousse. Stopping there but an instant, he again headed north and finally went to ground in the formidable hills north of Enfidaville.

To our desert-weary eyes the country began to take on a different appearance and there was a distinct feeling of getting "nearer home." First we had to plough through miles and miles of dreary wasteland, with frequent bogs, but gradually the landscape changed. Near Sfax we came into the biggest olive-producing country in the world and saw acre on acre of the graceful, silvery trees, in geometrical rows, with the good red earth in between. There were great plains of standing corn, still green but affording all the cover we could want. The whole land smelt of olives, and fresh vegetables were there for the picking; how good they tasted after months of tinned food! In the valleys there were white farmsteads, with drives leading up to them lined with cactus and almond trees in full bloom. The Promised Land could not have looked sweeter to the Israelites than Tunisia looked to the dusty Eighth Army.

At first there was very little opposition, except from some rearguards who thought that they had better fire a few shots at us just for the look of the thing, and the odd broken-down tank or lorry struggling to get away. These were quickly dealt with and we picked up some very useful additions to our vehicles and, as the Germans seemed to be liberally supplied with food and equipment which they had captured from the Americans at Kasserine and Thala, we relieved them of these also.

Eventually we paused at a small farm which went by the name of "La Fauconnerie," and here were told that we were not to go any farther. In an orchard of old olive trees we rested for three days, catching up with some laundry and enjoying the calm of the country. On the first day a group of about thirty Italians came marching down the road, carrying a huge white flag and telling a pathetic story about having been trying to surrender for two days. Somebody told them not to bother us, but to keep on marching and perhaps someone would take them prisoner soon. In the evening, just as everyone was feeling really peaceful and enjoying the twilight, three Junkers 88 came tearing over and dropped their sticks of high-explosive in the next field.

On the 12th of April we were told that we would be at twenty-four hours' notice, so the "luxury" vehicles were sent up from "B" Echelon. Majors Price

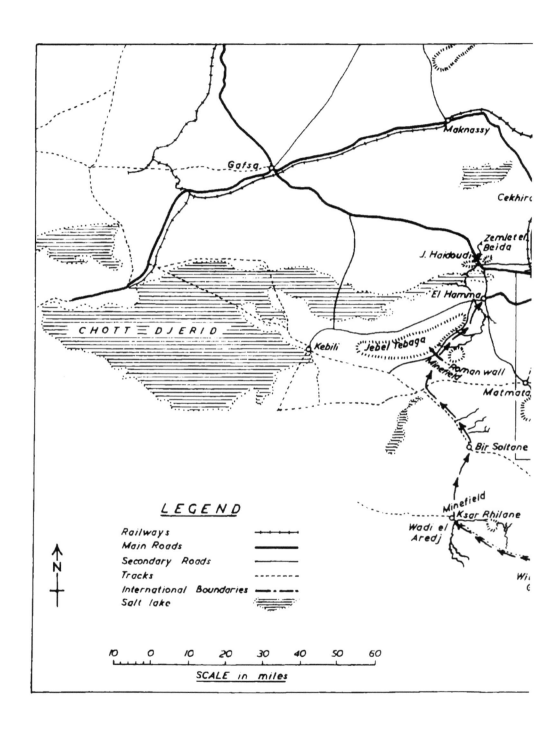

Maknassy

Gafsa

Cekhira

Zemleten
Beida

J. Haidoudi

El Hamma

CHOTT DJERID

Kebili

Jebel Tebaga

Roman wall

Minefield

Matmata

Bir Soltane

Minefield

Ksar Rhilane

Wadi el
Aredj

Wi...

LEGEND

Railways   +++++++
Main Roads
Secondary Roads
Tracks   -------
International Boundaries   —·—·—
Salt lake

↑
N
┼

10   0   10   20   30   40   50   60

SCALE in miles

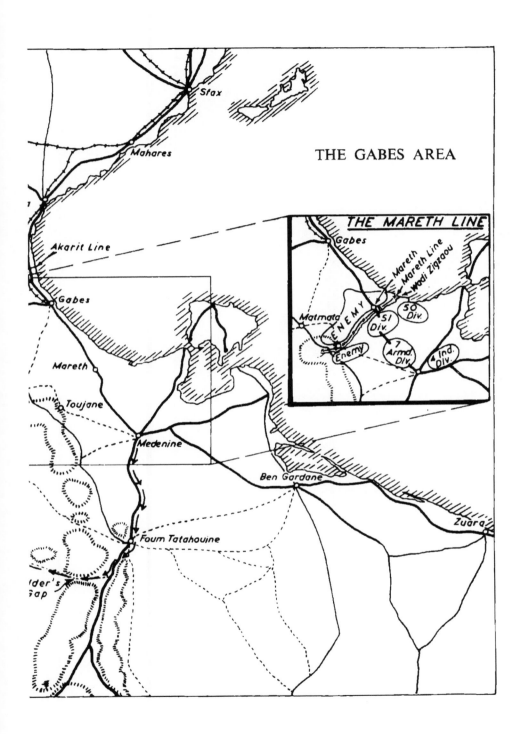

THE GABES AREA

THE MARETH LINE

and Gardner paid a visit to Sfax, which they found bombed inside out, and returned with some very nice willow-pattern crockery.

On the 13th of April the Brigade Commander came to lunch and told us the plans. The bulk of the Eighth Army was to be transferred on loan to the First Army, and the enemy at Enfidaville was to be contained by a skeleton Eighth Army. We were not likely to move for another two days. Actually it was not until the 16th of April that we loaded up on transporters at Telil and began the long march to the First Army. All tanks were supposed to be painted a dark green prior to the move, to deceive the enemy and to make them less conspicuous against the green foliage of Tunisia, but the paint never arrived, so we left looking just as sandy as we had ever been and as complete with our livestock, our goats, chickens and dogs.

We crossed the start point at 10.30 p.m. and covered the sixty-five miles to Sbeitla by 2 a.m. on the 17th. After that progress became increasingly slow. We passed through Sbiba, with its modern-looking shops—shops!—and modern-looking inhabitants, and here we met the first troops of the First Army. To those of us who had been away from England for so long it was a shock to realize exactly how far we had wandered from the accepted appearance of a British soldier. The First Army men were wearing neat battledress with blancoed gaiters, web equipment and steel helmets. They looked pale and cold and a little formal, and rode in dark-green lorries or trucks. Wherever they were halted they spread camouflage nets and it was a long time before we saw a brew-can. Our first impressions can best be summed up in the words of a member of the leading tank crew, who took one look and said:

"My God! *Soldiers!*"

On the other side there was equal amazement. If we thought they looked odd, what must they have thought of us? We had rolled into the town, a squadron of tanks which had once been painted a light yellow, and which were now blistered and had faded into a pale beige. All round the tanks hung bed-rolls and packs and water-cans, the sort of property contained on a tinker's cart, while, swinging at the back of each, rattled a couple of blackened tins used for cooking and washing. Slung round the turret of one tank were five tin hats, which had been there since the tank was last repainted. And behind came the fitters' lorry. To the men standing open-mouthed on the pavement this must have looked like a travelling circus. It boasted the same pale-amber shade as the tanks and had no windscreen. On its bonnet sat a large and phlegmatic black dog, and on the driving seat there was a black-and-white nanny-goat. As it passed by, a crate of chickens could be seen lashed to the tailboard.

The tank commanders wore shirts and moleskin slacks which had faded to a pale cream, while on their feet were old suede boots and round their necks some sort of silk handkerchief. The hats on their heads had holes in them and the peaks were badly frayed; their faces and throats were burned a deep copper.

When these extraordinary beings stopped, dismounted and proceeded to brew-up on the pavement, the eyes of the onlookers almost popped out of their heads. Then a Frenchman in the crowd tumbled to it and began shouting "La huitième Armée!"

After a quick breakfast the tanks drove on and by noon had reached the new concentration area by Le Krib. The journey was a most pleasant one, as there had been no fighting in the district and the Germans had not been in occupation. Our new leaguer area was in the fields surrounding a very attractive French farm which stood in a group of pine trees. The owners were most hospitable and were delighted to see us. We spent four days in this haven and occupied ourselves in painting the tanks and other vehicles to suit the darker landscape, though the paint when it arrived turned out to be black; however, we put it on in the hope that it would tone down a bit when it got dusty. It made the tanks look smaller but more formidable and it came off all over one's clothes.

On the 18th of April General Sir Harold Alexander paid us a visit and walked round the squadrons, and in the afternoon we had a pleasant surprise when Captain Hitchcock returned to resume his duties as Adjutant.

On the 21st of April, two days before the big attack was due to start, the Brigade moved out of the area and into a bowl in the hills north of El Aroussa, just behind the front line. We had begun to realize that there would have to be a slight change of tactics to suit the kind of country we were now in. Hitherto each squadron leader had been able to control his own squadron and had always had it under his nose. Now the troop leaders would have much more responsibility and would have to fight individual battles. Also we had yet to meet the new Tiger or Mark VI tanks, monsters which mounted an 88-mm. gun and were still spoken of in whispers.

The First Army attacked all along the line in the early morning of the 22nd, at first making considerable progress, but they found their impetus petering out against the desperate resistance of such crack German divisions as the Hermann Goering and 10th Panzers and some of the parachutists. On our front the 6th Armoured Division captured the high ground overlooking the salt lake at the foot of an immense peak called Jebel Kournine, but was unable to get any farther. The next morning we were ordered to move up on the left of the 6th over the Goubellat Plain.

Almost immediately we sustained the first two of many mine disasters. An "A" Squadron cruiser, pulling on to the side of the road to allow an ambulance to pass, went up in a cloud of black smoke, and Lieutenant Hainsworth, hitting another mine in his scout car, damaged his eardrums. The enemy had reduced the laying of mines to a fine art and could choose from a selection of different coloured teller mines to suit all kinds of soil: there were green for unripe corn and grass, yellow for ripe corn or sand, blue for water, and assorted browns for anywhere else. He had also developed a nasty habit of putting several mines on top of each other in a deep hole so that quite a few tanks could pass over them safely, but as soon as the weight of a few vehicles had sufficiently compressed the soil the mines went off and the resulting explosion had to be seen to be believed.

We now found ourselves on the edge of a vast plain, running east and west with a long hog's back bordering its southern edge. The tanks of the 17th/21st Lancers were just visible on its skyline. The plain was almost all deep green corn intersected with small but deep wadis, while scattered here and there were farm buildings, every one of them surrounded by buried mines, as we found to our cost.

We had not gone very far when "A" Squadron, in the lead, flushed some Germans in one of the farms. They had anti-tank guns with them, so the tin cruisers had to proceed warily. "E" Battery put down some very effective fire and the enemy decamped, leaving some dead behind. Motoring slowly on for another half-mile, "A" Squadron again bumped into dug-in infantry and more guns. Major Price accounted for one of the latter with his own gun, a 3-inch howitzer, and the leading troop got in among the infantry. They captured twenty-five, who turned out to be from the Hermann Goering Division, and the remainder bolted like rabbits through the long corn. It was our first sight of the men of this division and they were not very prepossessing. Chosen specially as fanatical Nazis, they were up to all sorts of dirty tricks and in captivity had that sullen, sneering look common to Nazi youth. One of their worst habits was to lie low until a tank came to within point-blank range, and then shoot the commander before standing up and raising their hands. After a few such incidents we gave them no mercy, and in the end they were the losers, but not before one of them had killed Sergeant Kretzer, M.M., of "A" Squadron, a very serious loss.

The Brigadier ordered us to move across on to the road to our left. On the way "A" Squadron found another strong-point and asked for a patrol of the Yorkshire Dragoons to help in digging them out. Major Price got another 50-mm. gun, while the patrol took four prisoners and killed nine for the loss of one man dead.

The German gunners had by this time switched most of their attention to our Brigade and, until dark, we had to put up with a great deal of heavy shelling.

Early the next day, the 24th, the advance was resumed. Very soon there was a long argument about the maps, the ones we were using being overprints of a French map and very inaccurate. We thought that we should be more to our right and the Bays and Brigade said we were all right where we were. At this moment Major Price's cruiser ran over a bunch of tellers hidden in the soil of a small track. The tank went up in a shattering explosion and burst into flames. To those of us who were watching it seemed impossible that anyone inside could be left alive in a tank which was practically split in two. To our great relief, Major Price and the entire crew were safe, though suffering from burns and shock. We lost Major Price for some considerable time and he eventually ended up as the only Englishman in an American hospital at Algiers.

Captain Grant took over command of the now-depleted squadron and then Brigade said that we were right about the map after all. We turned right and "A" Squadron hurried across our front in order to resume the lead.

No sooner had we straightened out again when a terrible thing happened. In front of "A" Squadron there was a rise and beyond that a deep wadi. The squadron topped the rise, had a good look in front and then began to cross the wadi. The leading tank, Lance-Sergeant Booth's, was just climbing out of the wadi when, from a cactus thicket only a few hundred yards to the left, four 88's opened fire. The thinly armoured cruisers had no chance and in a minute it was all over. "B" and "C" Squadrons fired all the smoke they could, but five tanks went up in flames. Captain Grant was killed instantly and his wireless went dead. Corporal Monks and Trooper Clarke were also killed, and six others were wounded. At first it looked as if the whole of the squadron had gone, but it was not quite as bad as that. The Bays, who were on our left, had also lost some tanks and the burning cruisers were not all ours. They rang up and told us that Captain Peek and Lieutenants Dudding, Kilgour and Marcks were safely into the wadi with the bulk of their crews. Sergeant Booth had managed to drop back into the wadi also and, although he could not get his tank out, it was all right.

The German guns had lain low until the tanks were almost on top of them and the result was inevitable. Both the Bays' battery and ours had at least a troop ready to fire and within a few minutes the cactus grove was being pounded from end to end. On the right flank "B" Squadron saw something suspicious in the corner of another patch of cactus and fired at it. The second round blew away the cactus and disclosed another 88 which had not yet been in action, and this was destroyed. "A" Squadron had four tanks left and these were withdrawn under Lieutenant Crampton, and attached as couriers to Regimental Headquarters. It was getting dark, so Brigade ordered us to spend the night where we were.

At first light on the 25th a change of orders came in. We were to move round again to the Kournine side of the hill to assist the 6th Armoured Division. Our side was taken over by anti-tank guns and we moved off round the long hill. The Regiment was put into reserve whilst the Bays and 10th moved up the hill and on to the left of the Lothians and Border Horse and the 16th/5th Lancers. "B" Squadron was ordered to line out in front of the Regiment as local protection and was heavily shelled on the way there. One shell scored a direct hit on Captain MacPherson's tank, buckling in the armour and killing the front gunner, Trooper Mirfin. The driver, Trooper Billington, was temporarily knocked out and until he recovered the tank ran round in circles, Captain MacPherson and the turret crew having to move with it trying to keep on the lee side away from the bursting shells. It was rare for a tank to be hit from such a distance by a field gun.

Late in the morning the 17th/21st Lancers put in an attack down the valley to the left of Kournine. We watched in amazement as they went by, sixty Shermans strong. They had no cruisers and one regiment seemed about as big as our whole brigade. They got right down the valley and fought against a number of German tanks under a hail of shells, the smoke of which completely hid them. They came slowly back and passed through us again, having suffered rather heavily.

In the afternoon there was great activity in the air as Messerschmitt fighters buzzed about trying to get at the guns, and our own Bostons passed over regularly on bombing expeditions. At one moment we could see five layers of aircraft; high up in the sky was a Spitfire patrol, below it a squadron of Stukas and its escort; lower down sixteen Mitchells went by on a bombing mission, and below these a single Focke-Wulf chased one of our own Taylorcraft observation aircraft round and round the peak of the Kournine. Apart from these two, none of the others seemed to be taking the slightest interest in each other. In leaguer that night German night bombers came over and dropped hundreds of small anti-personnel bombs which as they came down made a sharp crackling noise. Some fell in the leaguer and Trooper Quinn, of "A" Squadron, was wounded. One of "B" Squadron's Shermans caught fire inside the engine compartment as it was being filled up with Diesel oil, but prompt action by one of the crew, who luckily happened to be inside the turret and near the triggers of the built-in extinguishers, resulted in the blaze being put out before any damage was done. A burning tank in leaguer at night was a serious business, as it meant not only a probable shelling but a move by the whole Regimental Group.

On the 26th of April we took over from the Bays on the high ground on the left. "C" Squadron took the left and "B" Squadron took over from Major Crosby-Dawson's squadron at Dead Horse Farm. Both squadrons looked down a steep slope which ended in a shallow bowl, in the middle of which was a small salt lake. Beyond the lake the ground rose over a field covered with crimson poppies to a small ridge, and behind the ridge, not half a mile away, were the enemy. It was not a very nice place. As the name implies, the stables of the farm were full of dead livestock, which smelt horrible, and the clouds of flies were up to desert standard. The slightest movement by either squadron on top of the ridge brought immediate reaction from the enemy in the shape of 105-mm. shells fired from behind Kournine or 88-mm. shot from the German tanks behind the poppy field. We left the tanks behind the crest and took it in turns to watch from the cover of the farm buildings. It was rather a distressing job on account of the smell, and at times a little exciting, as the tanks fired a burst of solid shot every now and then through the corrugated-iron buildings.

In front of "C" Squadron, in the bowl, two companies of the Rifle Brigade were dug in. During the afternoon "C" Squadron pushed a troop of Shermans up to them with orders to try to get on a bit if it could. It seemed to be doing quite nicely, edging its way bit by bit, when two Mark IV's rose slowly over the skyline to the left and fired. Two Shermans went on fire at once and most of their crews were wounded. The troop leader, Lieutenant Hartley-Heyman, had his thigh shattered and could not be got out immediately. One of the 7th Rifle Brigade carriers pluckily ran up behind the tank and succeeded in getting him on to the back. The carrier turned and raced for shelter and at that moment a Tiger tank appeared and fired one shot at it. Although the carrier was moving fast and zigzagging like a snipe, the shot was a direct hit and killed Lieutenant Hartley-Heyman. "B" Squadron immediately engaged the Tiger before it disappeared again, and although it was hit twice no impression seemed to be made on it.

Another man, Trooper Dawson, was still lying wounded in his tank and when the firing had died down a smoke screen was put up to allow Sergeant Millington to go out and try to get him in. He managed to get there and give him some morphia, but failed to get him out of the turret because of the heavy machine-gun fire. Poor Dawson was dead the next time anyone could get to him.

After this Brigade was convinced that it would be a major operation to dislodge the enemy in front. They had mined themselves in and any attempt to get at them would only result in giving them an easy shoot. An infantry attack by night was the only way of doing it and there were too few.

So we remained behind our ridge. Our role was to contain the enemy armour and not to waste tanks and lives unnecessarily, because greater things were being planned for the future.

Brigadier Fisher was injured one morning when he asked Major Perry to take him to the top of the cornfield to see the ground ahead. The enemy chose that moment to "stonk" the crest and the Brigadier broke a collar-bone while trying to get out of the way.

We all became very familiar with that particular piece of country. Each tank moved out every morning to its appointed place and any deviation invariably brought some sort of retaliation. We lost Sergeant Maloney, "B" Squadron's Mechanist Sergeant, one morning. He was leaning against his squadron leader's tank after breakfast when the Tiger fired two rounds of high-explosive over the crest. The first fell within a few feet of the small group by the Sherman and a piece of jagged metal nearly severed Sergeant Maloney's wrist. He was an Irishman and it proved impossible to get him under with morphine, so it was not until the Doctor arrived with a syringeful that he was put out of pain. He returned to the Regiment, after spending a period as instructor at Sandhurst, and became Sergeant-Major of "A" Squadron.

During these days important things were happening farther back. The Eighth Army had sent both the 7th Armoured and 4th Indian Divisions to join the First Army. The 6th Armoured Division had been withdrawn and was refitting farther north. The 11th H.A.C. was taken away from us and lent to the 6th Armoured Division, a move of which we did not approve at all.

Major Perry was sent to command the Lothians, whose Colonel had been wounded, and his place as Second-in-Command was taken by Major Scott, who had been commanding "C" Squadron.

Apart from the Free French, who by a limited attack had improved their position in the Pont du Fahs sector, the last few days of April passed in comparative peace for the two hundred thousand Germans holding the Axis perimeter. They must have felt that something was brewing up for them, however, for their reconnaissance planes came over more and more frequently.

The stage was being prepared for the final act in North Africa. The enemy had no alternative: he must either fight it out or take to the sea, and either event looked like being well worth watching.

On the 6th of May it began.

CHAPTER XVII

THE END IN AFRICA

By 4 a.m. on the morning of the 6th of May the front was in an uproar. The guns, spaced one to every five yards of the narrow front, had been firing as hard as they could go since midnight and in the distance bursting shells were making a colossal tattoo. The Germans, cowering in their dug-outs, were blasted by the explosions, while those directly in the path of the main assault never knew what had struck them. By daylight a great swathe had been cut right through their positions.

The main attack was made by the newly formed X Corps under General Horrocks in the Medjez el Bab sector. X Corps consisted of the 4th Indian and 4th British Divisions, and the 6th and 7th Armoured Divisions, half from the First Army and half from the Eighth Army—a happy choice which allowed each army to share in the final honour of entering Tunis. The infantry and the sappers swept forward, their onslaught carrying them right through the outpost line and deep into the main defences, at that point some two miles thick.

Behind the infantry the two armoured divisions were waiting. At midday General Horrocks gave them the word to go and a mass of tanks with their attendant artillery and supply columns swept through the gap. By evening they were well on their way up the road to Tunis.

The success of these operations had an immediate effect on our front. The bulk of the German armour had been facing us, but when both "B" and "C" Squadrons moved out to their accustomed positions at dawn there was no trace of the enemy. Like Arabs the enemy had folded their tents and stolen away in the face of the threat from their right flank. Brigade ordered us to move on the centre line Ain-el-Asker—Cheylus—Creteville—Grombalia.

All day we kept on, meeting only an occasional enemy rearguard, and by evening halted some ten miles from Creteville at the southern end of the Cap Bon peninsula. Here we heard that Tunis had been captured by patrols of the 11th Hussars and the Derbyshire Yeomanry, who had entered in the late afternoon, to the consternation of Germans who were still strutting about in the town.

· The many prisoners we took that day seemed bewildered, as well they might be, for coherent orders from their high command had ceased. R.A.F. pilots were returning to their base with the astonishing news that they could find nothing to bomb or fight. The dislocation of the German army and the Luftwaffe was complete and absolute. There remained only one thing for them to do—to withdraw into the peninsula and stave off the advancing army while making arrangements to evacuate by sea and by air.

The next morning (the 7th) the Bays, who were leading, came up to the southern entrance of the Creteville Pass, a narrow and precipitous defile running north through the centre of the mountain range which stretched from Hammam Lif, outside Tunis, to Hammammet on the east coast. On the left front was a tall mountain, again called Jebel Kournine, and to the right towered the rocky mass of Jebel Rassas. They were brought up on their hocks by 88-mm. guns at the entrance to the pass, and once more the dirty-grey smoke of enemy shells was seen wherever a tank showed itself in the open.

On our left the 6th Armoured Division had reached Hammam Lif. Here the enemy had a perfect defensive line. The town lay on the edge of the Bay of Tunis and behind it the ground rose steeply to the crags of the mountain range. It took General Keightley only thirty-six hours to force a way through, however. He sent the Welsh Guards to attack the high ground on the right and put the Lothians along the level ground towards the town. After a tremendous battle, during which one squadron of the Lothians forced its way by the edge of the sea and the breakwaters, most of the German guns were knocked out and the enemy withdrew. For this action Lieutenant-Colonel Perry, then commanding the Lothians, was awarded a D.S.O. and, although we were missing them badly, "E" Battery did such a piece of work in giving close support to the attack that we were glad they were there.

The 7th Motor Brigade prepared to attack the hills guarding the pass, so for the rest of the day we remained where we were, trying to locate some of the 88's. In the morning of the 8th we were ordered to take over from the Bays, and "B" Squadron moved up towards their right flank. To do this it had to pass under the heights of Jebel Rassas, on the top of which were several enemy observation posts, which meant some hard and uncomfortably accurate shelling. At 10.30 a.m. the squadron engaged five German tanks on the lower slopes of the hill and forced them to withdraw.

When "B" Squadron had linked up with the Bays, two German officers came down off the hill and up to the Bays' leading tank. They were from the Hermann Goering Division and said that as they were out of ammunition they would like to surrender. The Colonel of the Bays said he would give them one hour in which to return to their battalion and bring it in. So off they went to collect their men.

The Colonel then ordered "C" Squadron to pass through "B" and enter the pass. As "C" Squadron began to climb the pass road the Hermann Goering men came marching down it in threes and headed by their officers. They were singing and looked as "pleased as Punch." As we passed the many 88's sited to fire down the road we noticed quite a lot of ammunition standing ready by the guns!

M

"C" Squadron topped the pass and began to descend the other side. As it reached the first cornfield more 88's opened fire. The road was blocked by felled trees and the squadron deployed on to the rise to the right of the road, where it found some infantry of the Italian Superga Division and sent two hundred of them back to Regimental Headquarters.

"B" Squadron was ordered to pass through "C" once more and resume the advance if possible. Ahead lay a long valley with steep hills on either side and the road running down the middle. To the right, just beyond "C" Squadron, another valley ran away to the east. About a mile down the main valley lay a small village with a big, white factory in the centre. It was from this village that the 88's were firing. "B" Squadron moved on down the left-hand side of the valley, but found that owing to the steepness of the sides it was not possible to bypass the 88's, which were now dividing their attention between the two squadrons. "B" Squadron Headquarters were passing through a belt of trees when a horde of Italian soldiers rose up out of the ground and clustered round them. At the same time someone began firing air-bursts into the tops of the trees and the Italians had to go to ground again. This sort of jack-in-the-box procedure went on for some time until the Squadron Leader got tired of it and reached for his tommy-gun. With it he managed to persuade the Italians to begin walking back towards Regimental Headquarters and the German guns shelled them thoroughly the whole way. Regimental Headquarters had by this time followed "B" Squadron and moved into the yard of a small farm behind it. The farmer came out and presented the Colonel with a large bunch of roses and carnations and the whole family showed signs of wanting to embrace him. He was saved by the arrival of "B" Squadron's Italians and their attendant shells, which impressed the French people with the fact that the war was still not yet over.

The 88's had been located and were being picked off one by one, when another complication arose. Down the valley to the east came a number of enemy tanks, which deployed and began firing at us, and, although the range was long, their shells were bouncing off the Shermans in such a way that they could not be ignored. The day ended with an inconclusive tank duel and a great deal of shelling from a battery of 105's sited at the end of the valley. We leaguered in the standing corn below Regimental Headquarters' farm and were told that the 6th Armoured Division had taken Hammam Lif and were streaming along the road towards Hammammet.

Before dawn on the 9th we moved out and down the road. "B" Squadron, in the lead, reported that the same enemy tanks were just moving out into position again, but got past before they fired any shots. Brigade was sceptical about this, but was soon persuaded otherwise when it had to pass the entrance of the valley. We entered and passed the village without a sign of the enemy, and a little farther on a large group of Germans were waiting by the roadside to give themselves up. Among them was a splendid figure dressed in white duck and gold lace, who turned out to be a German admiral; he was quite unable to account for being so far off his beat.

The valley became a defile and all the tanks had to converge on to the road. Passing a battery of abandoned 88's, we speeded up and after a mile or so turned the last corner before the small town of Grombalia, where the leading tank found itself looking down the barrel of a British 17-pounder and we were surrounded by a company of Grenadier Guards, all wanting to know what had happened. We were not quite sure ourselves. The 6th Armoured Division had swept down the road through Grombalia the night before and had by that time reached Hammammet, thus completely cutting off the Cap Bon peninsula. Behind us in the hills the 10th Hussars were having quite a brisk battle with the tanks we had passed in the early morning, and farther back still Divisional Headquarters were being shelled. Towards Enfidaville two British forces were converging on the 90th Light Division, which was, as usual, putting up a great fight. When eventually contact was made with General von Sponeck, the divisional commander, he said that he was ready to surrender but only to the Eighth Army. Somewhat nettled, and rightly so, General Keightley gave him the option of surrendering to the 6th Armoured Division or being blown to kingdom come: von Sponeck chose the former.

In Grombalia we decided that the war really was over and, dismounting, had a really magnificent breakfast. We found a bakery with a batch of bread just baked and had hot rolls for breakfast. The reception we had from the local French people was positively embarrassing. Tanks were garlanded with flowers and anyone getting out of his tank was immediately embraced by young and old alike. We finished our breakfast and had a wash and shave before pushing on over the road and up into the peninsula. "C" Squadron was ordered to go on to Beni Khalled and "B" Squadron to Menzel Bou Zelfa to take over from the 4th Infantry Division, which was going on to round up prisoners. Groups of prisoners stood about all over the place and every wood was full of abandoned enemy transport. It was not, however, until the late afternoon, when both squadrons were sitting astride their respective roads, that we fully appreciated the situation.

Down the road leading from the north came the enemy army. Mounted in its own transport, hour after hour the enemy rolled by as though coming away from some gigantic race meeting. Panzer grenadiers, parachutists, artillerymen, Luftwaffe ground staff and men from all the supply and base formations rode by in ten-ton lorries, staff cars and small four-seater Volkswagens. In an orderly manner they passed us on their way to the huge cages which were being hurriedly erected on either side of the Tunis road. We sat by the roadside with our mouths open and watched them go.

The end had come so suddenly that no attempt at evacuation by sea had been possible. The Royal Navy was waiting to pounce on any ships which attempted to get away, but, apart from the odd fishing boat, none tried. Even the German

Commander-in-Chief, von Arnim, with all the rest of the German High Command, was now a prisoner.

By night the stream of traffic had not ceased. As it grew dark the defeated enemy stopped by the roadside and went to sleep, continuing their self-controlled march into captivity as soon as it was light. In the twilight we fished out our remaining bottles of whisky, kept for such an occasion, and, tired though we were, sat up into the small hours discussing the incredible thing that had happened. There was not a sound; not a gun fired and not a plane was heard. After so long a period of bitter and remorseless fighting our brains were incapable of digesting the fact that the entire German and Italian armies had laid down their arms and were filling our barbed-wire cages.

Eight minutes to eight o'clock on the 12th of May is the official time given for the end of the war in Tunisia. At that time General Alexander sent the Prime Minister a message:

> "SIR,—It is my duty to report that the Tunisian campaign is over. All enemy resistance has ceased. We are masters of the North African shore."

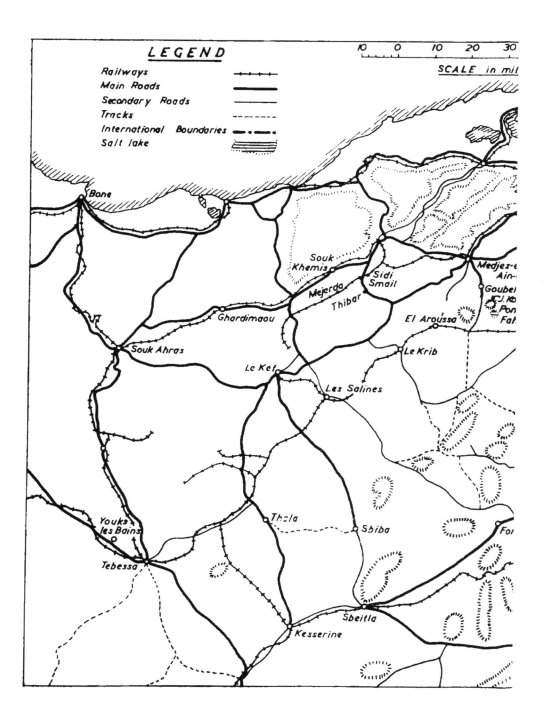

Bone

Souk
Khemis

Sidi
Smail

Medjez-e
Ain-

Mejerda

Thibar

Goubel
J. Ko
Pon
Fal

Ghardimaou

El Aroussa

Souk Ahras

Le Krib

Le Kef

Les Salines

Youks
les Bains

Thala

Sbiba

Fo

Tebessa

Sbeitla

Kesserine

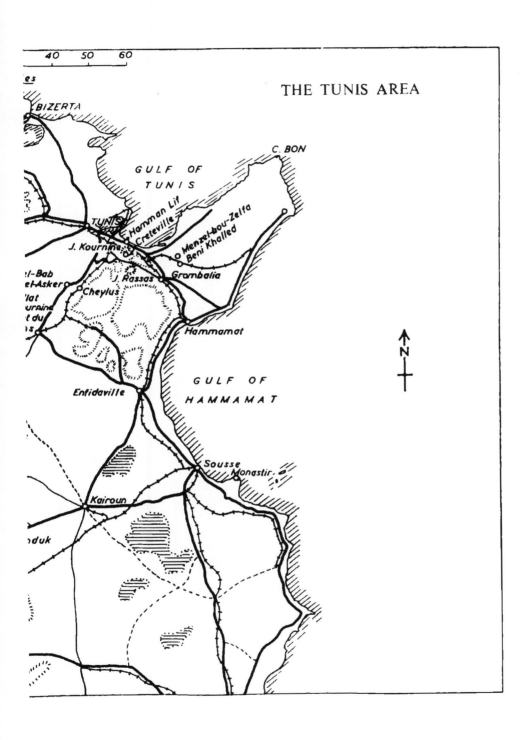

THE TUNIS AREA

CHAPTER XVIII

BACK TO THE DESERT

IT took a little time to become accustomed to it all. It was queer to lie in our blankets until well after sun-up and to consider gravely when and where we would have the next meal. Throughout the Regiment wireless sets were switched off and each tank was given a good spring-clean. Then we all had a bath and put on clean clothes before exchanging a round of visits with friends in other squadrons.

Every private soldier seemed to have acquired a motor-car and large supplies of cigars, and the roads round Grombalia were soon buzzing with traffic. The skies were blue, the sun was hot and there was no more fear of sudden death. The soldier suddenly realized that, for the first time in years, the whole width of the Mediterranean lay between him and the enemy and that panzer grenadiers and parachutists had become something to be seen in cages. The ordinary British soldier had made this thing happen—he was a millionaire for a day.

By tea time on the 13th of May half the Regiment was in Tunis and the other half was lazily enjoying this pleasant existence. But we had forgotten that, although the Afrika Korps was in the "cooler," our staff officers remained at large and they now ordered a move of six miles by 5 p.m. to Soliman. The old cry "Pack up!" from squadron sergeant-majors brought us back to earth. Somehow the move was carried out. Tanks were driven that evening by men who had never before risen higher than a three-tonner, and one troop leader who had been over-generous with his leave passes was seen driving his own Sherman. At Soliman peace reigned for a few happy days. The tanks were parked in the olives and forgotten, and every afternoon the greater part of the Regiment went off to bathe from the lovely beaches of Hammammet or St. Germain, or to see the sights of Tunis or Carthage.

The great Victory Parade took place in Tunis on the 20th. As usual, the only people who did not enjoy it were those taking part. It was a sweltering day and the parade carried them over five miles of red-hot tarmac to reach the saluting base. General Eisenhower and General Giraud took the salute on a platform at the end of the wide, palm-lined Corso, on both sides of which were long lines of tanks and guards of honour. The column was led by a regiment of Spahis, quite magnificent with their long, red cloaks and white horses. The band of the Guards Brigade and the pipes of the 51st (Highland) Division played the parade past and all the while squadrons of fighters and medium bombers flew overhead. The Regiment was represented by Captain Rex Hitchcock, M.C.,

149

R.S.M. T. Hardwidge, and thirty-three other ranks, under the command of Major Gardner.

The 60th Rifles were at this time guarding the cages containing our old foes the 90th Light Division, and on one afternoon they challenged them to a game of football. The Germans won and when subsequently the 60th were hauled over the coals for playing and being defeated into the bargain they replied that, as we had beaten the Germans so soundly at their national game, it was possible not to mind them beating us at ours.

Great was the grief the next day when an edict came round that all the recently acquired cars and lorries were to be handed in to a Brigade dump on the main road to Tunis, and by evening an extraordinary collection was assembled, ranging from forty-two-seater buses and generals' caravans to Volkswagens and tracked motor-cycles.

A few changes took place within the Regiment at this time. Captain Hitch-cock assumed command of "A" Squadron and Captain Francis Pym became Adjutant once more. Major Perry returned from commanding the Lothians and Border Horse, so Major Scott, M.C., relinquished the post of Second-in-Command and took over "A" Squadron again. Captain W. V. Tully, the Quartermaster, was posted to command the 152nd Transit Camp, Abbassia, and to the great regret of everyone left for Cairo, in company with T.Q.M.S. Sylvester. Their combined service with the 9th totalled fifty-five years. Captain Donnley became Quartermaster and Lieutenant Brutton took over his duties as Technical Adjutant.

Our "fifth squadron," of great renown, "E" Battery of the 11th H.A.C., left the Division to train for combined operations and we did not see them again until almost a year later in Italy. They fought through the Sicilian campaign, adding lustre to their name, and were back in their accustomed place just behind Regimental Headquarters when the Regiment fired their first shot in the Battle of the Pisa—Rimini Line. A farewell dinner attended by the Battery Commander, Major David Morris, and three of his officers marked their departure.

The 23rd of May brought two pieces of news. The first was that Major Perry had been awarded a D.S.O. for his brilliant handling of the Lothians in the attack on Hammam Lif. The second, not so good, was that the 1st and 7th Armoured Divisions were to return to Tripoli. The first reaction was one of disappointment. There seemed to be an attitude of "we've-finished-with-you-now-you-can-go-back-to-your-old-desert," but, on second thoughts, it was realized that Tripoli was as good a port as any from which to sail for Italy— or home.

On the 26th, in a high wind, we struck camp and in the small hours of the 27th a ghost column crept out of the olive grove and headed east. It consisted of a number of German touring cars which had unaccountably been overlooked when the others were handed in.

Early the next day the Brigade set forth, most of the tanks being left behind because they were too old to take back to Tripoli. By evening we were leaguered on a rolling plain outside Kairouan, where the grass was dangerously dry and the Queen's Bays soon had a good blaze, followed by the 10th Hussars with an even better one. The Regimental Sergeant-Major stood with the Adjutant watching the efforts of both to gain control with a "look at the poor fools" expression on their faces, when a huge tongue of flame shot up in the middle of our leaguer. We saw Mr. Hardwidge about two hours later: his face was too black for us to read his thoughts, but he was offering large sums of money for either the culprit's name or a pint of beer.

By the next night we were across the Wadi Akarit after passing our old leaguer of La Fauconnerie. The almond blossom had withered and the crisp greenness of the orchards had given way to the dry, brown coat of an African summer.

At midday on the 29th the column had passed through Medenine, crossed the frontier at Ben Gardane and was in Tripolitania once more. On a day of blistering heat we were back to the old dust and bumps, the diversions and the minefields, the lonely graves and the fire-blackened, derelict tanks.

At noon on the 30th of May the Regimental column pulled into a forbidding-looking area twenty miles due south of Tripoli and five miles north of Azizia. If you take the trouble to look up such places you will find that Azizia is listed as the hottest place on the North African coast and no one in the 2nd Armoured Brigade will contradict that statement. The area had been "colonized" by that great optimist Benito Mussolini. The waste of deep and powdery sand was divided off into squares by long lines of gum trees which provided shade only in the early morning or late evening. In the centre of our portion lay a small farmhouse of white plaster, the only building in sight, which was taken over by Regimental Headquarters.

Into this impossible place went the tanks and wheeled vehicles, half of them being pushed or towed through the soft, pink sand. Here at least was one leaguer which would not be left in a hurry. The Regiment remained there for three weeks—twenty-one days of complete misery. From 10 o'clock in the morning until tea time the strength of the sun was such that only essential movement was possible, and during these hours training ceased, everyone retiring to whatever shade he was able to find. Frequently the thermometer rose to one hundred and twenty degreees in the shade.

All forms of training were a burden at Azizia, but in any case the Regiment had only a few tanks, so after a few lectures and discussions as many men as possible were sent off to the sea to bathe.

On one such evening, when the sea was full of Queen's Bays, 9th Lancers and 10th Hussars, a British destroyer came into the bay and dropped anchor. The first picket boat to come ashore contained a most unusual-looking individual, half soldier and half sailor. This eventually resolved itself into Major

Price, who had escaped from his Algerian hospital by jumping on board just as the ship was sailing, and was now on his way to the Delta to recuperate. It was good to see him again, looking surprisingly well considering the frightful explosion in which he had disappeared.

There were two important events during our stay in this unhealthy place. On the 15th of June General Montgomery visited the Regiment and spoke to the senior officers. Each in turn expressed his feelings about Azizia and said how much better it would be if we were somewhere where we could either train or rest in comfort, sentiments with which the Army Commander agreed. He said that as the Eighth Army had conquered eighteen hundred miles of coastline he could see no reason why there was not enough for everyone, and ordered the Divisional Commander to find a more suitable area on the sea.

The second event was the visit of "General Lyon," His Majesty The King. Great preparations and scrubbings had taken place and it was a very tidy Regiment that lined a section of the Azizia—Tripoli road at Suani Ben Adem on the roasting-hot morning of the 21st of June. Much water had flowed since he last inspected the Regiment in England, and everyone deeply appreciated his coming to that outlandish place to do so again.

On the 22nd a large party of two hundred and forty-eight men from the Division left Tripoli by sea for the Delta to fetch up by road new vehicles for the Corps. The party was commanded by Major Gardner, and as Division had allotted him no senior non-commissioned officer he asked and was granted permission to take Sergeant Salt, of "C" Squadron, as Temporary Sergeant-Major. The party returned on the 18th of July with one hundred and forty jeeps, thirty staff cars, thirty Humber armoured cars, three ten-tonners and sundry trucks. They were rather angry at having had only three days in the Delta and then having to drive the fourteen hundred miles which they knew so well at a running-in speed of ninety miles a day. In addition they had had to transport the entire staff of the newly formed base at Tripoli.

On the 23rd, with the utmost relief, the Regiment moved to a leaguer a few miles west of Oliveti and right on the edge of the sea. Tents were pitched on the low cliffs, from which one could jump straight into the water. It was ten times cooler and life became tolerable once more.

"A" Squadron heard with satisfaction that it was at last to be relieved of its cruisers and equipped with Shermans. It had fought for too long in the temperamental and undergunned cruisers and the prospect of thicker armour and a proper gun gave the necessary incentive to begin intensive training. The other squadrons concentrated on teaching every man to swim, though the sea at this point was not ideal for the purpose. There were no shallows and a strong swell, so that the unfortunate learners had to be thrown in and a strong swimmer detailed to rescue them if they became water-logged. This had the effect of teaching them in a remarkably short time to remain on the surface. Under the Brigade Commander's guidance, loading tables and tactical plans for an assault landing on European soil were worked out. Tripoli yielded light recreation, where the Divisional concert party and the newly arrived Leslie Henson show were playing to packed houses. Mr. Henson brought his cast out to lunch in the Regimental Headquarters mess on the 6th of July, which included Beatrice Lillie, Vivien Leigh, Dorothy Dickson, May Craven and Kay Young, all of whom temporarily greatly improved the appearance of the tattered old mess tent. Corporal Rescaniere produced a most excellent meal, and after an entertaining luncheon they returned to Tripoli in time to give the afternoon performance.

July wore on. The few almost derelict tanks the Regiment possessed were handed in and the Colonel went off to Egypt in command of a thousand men from the Division to bring up new vehicles of every description. This party did considerably better than the previous one in the matter of leave, and did not return until the 10th of September.

On the 15th of July word came that the Division was to move again about the end of the month. As was to be expected and because we were hoping to move east, we were to move west and back into Tunisia. Moreover, we were destined apparently for the inglorious task of guarding prisoners, docks and dumps. To the oldest and most senior armoured division this was indeed bitter medicine.

Accordingly camp was struck on the 1st of August and the long drive westwards began. At lunch time on the 4th the Regiment turned into the olive groves near Enfidaville, the one-time gun lines of the Eighth Army's artillery during the final attack on Tunis. Here we were met by Major Perry, who had gone on ahead and who gave us the distressing information that our destination was not Tunis but a remote and wild place called Ghardimaou on the Algerian— Tunisian frontier, half-way between Souk Ahras and Souk Khemis, and that our chief occupation was to be the guarding of ten thousand prisoners of war.

The Regiment, then only two hundred and forty-two strong, arrived at Ghardimaou on the 6th. "C" Squadron went separately to Thibar. As a place Ghardimaou was hardly better than Azizia and the cage stood in a bowl of burnt-up grass surrounded by hills of the same quality. We took over from the 6th Battalion The Gordon Highlanders, who confessed that the place had nearly driven them crazy.

Needless to say, there were no prisoners in the cage, so Major Perry, in command, wisely decided that as the sole asset of the place was the view, camp should be pitched as high up the hillside as the road would allow, even if it meant ferrying guards to and fro. The only signs of human life for miles around were a few small and dirty Arab tents from which the inhabitants crept every night to pilfer what they could from the Regiment. So expert were they that several soldiers had their blankets stolen from them as they slept. The Regimental Sergeant-Major lived in a state of constant rage and eventually put an end to these thievings by the simple but effective method of taking a punitive expedition to the nearest village whenever a theft occurred. Here he would explain to the headman in his best Arabic what had occurred, draw his forefinger across his throat several times, and then impound the best looking of the community's pigs. The pig was returned only when both the stolen goods and the culprit had been handed over. The system appeared to be one which the locals easily understood, and before very long they conceived a profound respect for R.S.M. Hardwidge's legislative powers and the stealing soon ceased.

On the first day of our stay at Ghardimaou the one and only prisoner arrived. He was an Italian who had fallen out of a train and hurt his arm. He undertook to behave and was given a job in the cookhouse.

One night a Wellington bomber ran out of petrol and crashed in the hills above the camp. It had been on a nuisance raid over the Straits of Messina and made a bad mistake in its return navigation to Kairouan. The crew had mistaken the light of a heath fire for a flarepath and had to jump. Pilot Officer Strong and Sergeant Pollard walked into our leaguer both suffering from minor injuries and were later joined by the remaining three of the crew, all unhurt. They remained with the Regiment some ten days before the Royal Air Force sent a truck to collect them. By this time we had got to know them well and when they left they took with them a Regimental cipher which was destined for the fuselage of their new aircraft.

On the 12th of August a signal arrived from Mejerda Area inquiring whether we had any bakers among our prisoners. This gave us the impression that they were not reading the return which the Adjutant diligently sent in every day. However, we asked the prisoner if he was a baker and he said "No." This incident drew the attention of the authorities to the fact that one armoured regiment was engaged in guarding one Italian, who had no desire to escape, anyway, and our camp was "closed." On the 17th we moved to join "C" Squadron.

Thibar was a great improvement. The grapes were ripe, there were quail and French partridges in the maize and scrub, there were the buildings of an old lead mine to live in. Immediately we arrived Brigade started a series of tactical exercises without troops which began after lunch on about three days a week. Because of the great heat it is doubtful if much was achieved, and the health of the only two field officers available for such training, Majors Scott and Gardner, went into a rapid decline.

The only outstanding event which occurred at Thibar was the celebration of Mons Day. It began with the sending of a cable to Major-General Norman and the Old Comrades informing them that the Regiment was proposing to celebrate the day as suitably as possible in the circumstances. In the afternoon all the local Arabs were persuaded to bring their ponies, mules and donkeys to a big, flat field in the valley below the monastery and there we held a race meeting. The tote realized £9 15s., which was forwarded to Mrs. Macdonell for the 9th Lancers Prisoner of War Fund. In the evening there were special dinners. A prize bullock had been purchased from the monastery home farm which cut up very well indeed. Every man had a bottle of beer (almost unheard of in those days), supplemented by the good wine of Thibar. Entertainment was provided by two Austrian prisoners from the German hospital we were guarding, who played accordions as only their countrymen can. They brought the house down at the conclusion by playing "Hanging out the washing on the Siegfried Line," a possibility which at that time still seemed fairly remote.

On the 10th of September Lieutenant-Colonel Grosvenor and his staff, Captain R. P. Thomas, M.C., the Quartermaster, Captain Donnley, and the Adjutant, Captain Pym, arrived back from the Delta, having delivered their vehicles. It took the Colonel a considerable time to wade through and assimilate the mountains of correspondence which had come in during his absence.

It gradually became clear that the Brigade would not go to battle in the immediate future. We were offered courses in Egypt and some in England and no attempt was made to bring our transport or equipment up to standard. We were soon destined to leave Tunisia and move farther west. The end of the Thibar leaguer marked the end of a distinct phase in the history of the Regiment. Desert warfare, into which we had been so hurriedly pitched, faded into the past and, as in all experiences, perhaps we were inclined to remember only the good things and forget the bad. Desert days will always be remembered as the best days, and every man in the 9th, including those attached from the Royal Corps of Signals and Royal Electrical and Mechanical Engineers, will ever look back with pride on the part which the Regiment played in the sands of Egypt, Libya and Tripolitania.

CHAPTER XIX

ALGIERS

THERE had been talk for some days of a move westward, so when the telephone rang on the 24th of September and Major Sloan of the 2nd Armoured Brigade staff told us that we were moving from Thibar to Algiers early in October we were not surprised.

The move began on the 4th of October. Most of the Regiment travelled by a train which was due to leave Sidi Smail station at 2.33 a.m. on the 5th, actually left seven and a half hours later, and then developed engine trouble twenty miles away. There was a four-hour halt at Ghardimaou while another engine was produced. At Souk Ahras engines were changed again, this time from steam to electricity, and the next day there was a third engine change. Lieutenant John Goldsmid, a keen admirer of the Great Western Railway, mounted the footplate and, though the driver was unenthusiastic, his presence led to a miraculous increase in speed and the engine never broke down again. By now fifteen hours late, we eventually reached Bou Farik at 9 o'clock on the morning of the 8th.

Meanwhile the Regimental Transport formed itself into an unorthodox convoy, most of the lorries being captured ones and very unreliable, and set off at 6 a.m. on the 5th, with the technical staff, Captains "Jock" Henderson and Tony Brutton, under no illusions as to what was likely to occur. It was not long before their fears were realized: Captain Brutton's technical stores lorry collapsed at Souk Ahras, followed shortly afterwards by the medical inspection lorry. The rest reached Guelma at 5.30 p.m. and leaguered there for the night. The rain came down and it was very wet. Early the next day the Padre, Captain Davison, got bogged and the lorry that came to his rescue did the same. The column continued in leaps and bounds to Setif, eventually reaching its destination after lunch on the 8th. Many stragglers dribbled in for days afterwards.

We spent the next seven months at Bou Farik. Regimental Headquarters was seventeen miles south of Algiers near the village of Chebli in the middle of a small but fertile plain. This plain was some fifty miles wide and twenty miles deep and stretched from the sea to the range of mountains immediately behind "A" Squadron. The land was intensively cultivated with many vineyards and other crops growing between the rows of vines. A farm unit consisted of from four hundred acres upwards and had its own wine vats and large barns. These made admirable barrack rooms, though the sickly smell of fermenting wine was overwhelming at first. Regimental Headquarters was in Monsieur Martel's farmstead, the largest in the neighbourhood, and across the road Captain

156

Henderson and his Light Aid Detachment turned a barn into the service garage, with Sergeant Squires, the carpenter, next door. "B" Squadron was in another farm a mile away, and, having made friends with the owner and his family, gained a number of important concessions which resulted in each troop having one or two rooms to itself. Sergeant Hughes collected a huge pile of timber and built a magnificent Sergeants' Mess, which was decorated by Trooper Makin with a series of murals. "C" Squadron was the farthest off, just outside Rovigo, where the whole squadron lived in one huge barn, sleeping on top of the vats, and the officers occupied two rooms in a house across the road.

The first few days were spent in settling in and, despite all the drawbacks, the squadrons declared themselves happy. As the months slipped by many improvements were made—notably a stage on the top floor of H.Q. Squadron's big barn. There was floor space enough for about four hundred people and good use was made of this by visiting cinemas and variety shows, though in winter it was very cold and draughty. Trooper Gilpin painted the scenery and made an excellent stage curtain out of an old barrage balloon. A small vicarage was built for the Padre and he kept the Regimental library there, while Mr. Hardwidge built himself a small house. Football pitches were made and anything else that could relieve the monotony of life. Captain John Kemp, the Doctor, commonly called "Kempy," was busy advising on the more sordid details of our everyday life, as no accommodation stores were available. The annual inoculations were due and this kept him occupied for several days. The Colonel avoided this ordeal for some weeks, until "Kempy" marched into his office at 9.30 one morning.

Major Jack Price, having recovered from his wound, returned from Cairo with Captain Hitchcock and both rejoined "A" Squadron. A week after our arrival Major Derek Allhusen had returned to the Regiment from the 24th Lancers and taken over command of "B" Squadron. Lieutenant John Foy, who came with him, also went to "B" Squadron.

With squadrons thus disposed, preparations were made for training. This promised to be more interesting than it had been, as there was more equipment. We had had no tanks since leaving Tripoli in the summer and we had no roadworthy lorries. A new war establishment had authorized an increase in men of three officers and one hundred and twenty other ranks, all of whom would have to be trained, so, to begin with, individual training continued, with emphasis on gunnery, wireless and map reading, and after Christmas a class was run for young officers. As the equipment began to arrive, however, our main effort was directed towards troop training. For this we were allowed to run each tank up to two hundred miles and in addition we had six training tanks on which no restrictions were imposed. This gave us good scope for the job. Each squadron was given a training area and each produced its own programme.

The new tanks were Sherman Mark V's, the same as the others except for their Chrysler engines. All three squadrons were being equipped with them, and "A" Squadron no longer suffered from the thin armour of Crusaders. The Reconnaissance Troop got Honeys, which were a tremendous improvement on the Daimler scout car and with their turrets removed they could hardly be bettered.

Apart from training, November was devoted to the study of indirect fire. This had been tried in an amateurish way as early as Alamein and after the fall of Tunis some experiments had been carried out. Every squadron had its own ideas on the subject, so the Brigadier gave us one month in which to argue and test our various theories, at the end of which he said he would hold an inter-regimental trial. We made no marked progress until the 9th of November, when Major David Morris, commanding "E" Battery, 11th H.A.C., gave a lecture to squadron gunnery officers. At the end of his lecture Lieutenant Ivor Fitzpatrick (an officer who had just joined the Regiment from the 6th South African Armoured Division) produced a new theory which won support from all sides, and the Colonel ordered experiments to begin at once. It proved to be the right answer and was in fact the genesis of the present-day system, though it took several months, numerous modifications and a few inventions to perfect. On that day we went to work under Major David Steel, who in a week had had several tanks suitably modified, and held the first test. It was obvious that we were working on the right lines and the Colonel was pleased with our progress.

The Brigadier's trial was fixed for the 29th of November at the 10th Hussars Regimental Headquarters. The methods employed by each regiment at the gun position and observation post were studied and several targets were engaged by each, not so much for the sake of competition as to give everyone an idea of how each separate method worked. At the observation post everyone worked on the same general lines, though the detail varied widely—particularly in wireless procedure—but at the gun position the 9th Lancers' ideas were regarded as a kind of secret weapon. It so often happens that things go wrong on these occasions, but all was well that day and some time was spent in explaining our system. At 6 o'clock we all went home. For the next four days the Brigadier, wishing to achieve a uniform drill within the Brigade, studied the ideas which had been produced. He then called a conference and announced his decision, which, in the main, followed our technique. A week later there was a high-level discussion on the matter at Royal Armoured Corps schools where training in indirect fire had already begun.

To have reached agreement on drill was an advance, but now we had to train every crew to know it so well that there was no fear of a mistake. The results obtained later in Italy from this training were invaluable, for there were several occasions when indirect fire was the only way by which success could be achieved. During our last practice in Africa "C" Squadron lost a tank in crossing the river, which was abnormally full. It developed a hard list to starboard and the crew were rescued with difficulty and largely because Lieutenant

Pat Buchan was a very strong swimmer. Sergeant Smith, the tank commander, was for ever afterwards known as "The Admiral."

Once a fortnight there was a demonstration in the Division, usually by one battalion with one squadron under command, to practise the co-operation of infantry and tanks in close country and get ideas from the commanding officers and squadron leaders who were watching. Sometimes new weapons and equipment were tried out, and there were penetration trials of anti-tank guns. On one occasion it took a self-propelled artillery weapon, the M10, eighteen shots to hit the target against four shots by Corporal Nickolls.

The two most interesting days were those devoted to tank-driving trials. The 48th Royal Tank Regiment sent four Churchills over and these, with three of our Shermans and two Honeys, were to be driven across country, not as a demonstration or competition but as a practical means of comparing the performance of the three different kinds. Captain John Reid was "clerk of the course," and had laid out flags in point-to-point style. The spectators' stand was on top of a ridge and there were "race cards." The first pair, Churchill and Sherman, broke tracks within a quarter of a mile; the second pair were more successful and completed the difficult course in five minutes under the hour, though neither achieved the steepest obstacle which was a 50-degree gradient twelve yards long. Another Churchill and Sherman and two Honeys then started. Captain Geoffrey Gregson overturned his Honey and Trooper Probert bogged his Sherman, but when the Churchill had towed him out he gave a truly magnificent demonstration of driving for the rest of the course.

When the first two tanks had broken their tracks simultaneously the respective fitters' trucks dashed up to attend. The Churchill's fitters produced a pile of tools and set feverishly to work. Our fitters produced a dirty old tin, petrol and water and, under the shocked noses of the high-ranking spectators, proceeded to make and consume three large mugs of tea. When the ritual was over they put more water on to boil and set to work. The Sherman left five minutes before the Churchill; and then they had another cup of tea.

Five days later the trial was continued in wet conditions and soon all tanks were hopelessly bogged. Major Frank Barrett, the Brigade Mechanical Engineer, said that only a D8 tractor could extricate the tanks and he believed there was only one in North Africa. The next day Colonel Macdonell brought over an American officer who commanded a Grant recovery vehicle. This American, who was one of General Eisenhower's personal bodyguard, made an attempt but failed to move any of them. It was not until eight days later that they were recovered.

For most of us training stopped at lunch time and the rest of the day was spent in recreation, which took every conceivable form and often continued well into the night. There was football nearly every day and the Regimental team was better than it had been for many years, partly on account of Trooper Baylis's professional qualifications. "B" Squadron did well in winning the

Brigade Inter-Squadron and Company Competition, its team being led by Sergeant Helps and supported by the deafening roar of Captain Roger Mostyn's voice on the touchline. The hockey team never really got going, probably because our late Doctor, Captain Dison, was not with us. There were some entries for the Divisional Boxing Competition and Captain Michael Marsh, A.D.C. to the G.O.C., got into the finals, which were held at the 1st King's Royal Rifle Corps' billets on the 9th of December. Mr. Anthony Eden and the American Ambassador to Britain, Mr. Winant, who were on their way back from the "Big Three" Conference at Teheran, were among the spectators. Both made speeches afterwards and found it difficult to answer the shouts of "When are we going home?"

Some officers went shooting and the "bag" sometimes amounted to two or three snipe and five or six duck. Lieutenant Thwaites arranged a boar shoot once with the Mayor of Rovigo and set out at 5 a.m. one morning accompanied by Major Pulteney and Captains Bruce Carlisle and Gregson. But they did not reckon to be out for thirty-six hours and walking for thirty-two miles. Twenty Algerians and a pack of hounds went too, and the food and kit were carried on mules.

On the 7th of January "B" Squadron gave a dance which coincided with a visit from Leslie Henson, Hermione Baddeley and their concert party, and a week before Christmas "C" Squadron had an all ranks' dance in the Bosphor in Algiers. Other squadrons followed suit and "B" Squadron gave a dance almost every week in a hall in Cheragas.

The little village of Chrea, three thousand feet up behind Blida, was a popular resort for Sunday lunch. When the snow fell, there was a nursery slope there where a few people tried to ski. There were no long runs, but then there were very few experts.

There was close liaison with the Royal Navy during our stay. The officers of H.M.S. *Ronaldshay* more or less lived with "C" Squadron. H.M.S. *Dido* was also most hospitable, and several parties visited her. On the 20th of December Major Perry, the Second-in-Command, took five officers on board when she was "on the ranges" just outside the harbour.

Bandmaster Allen arrived shortly before Christmas with the 9th Lancers Band disguised as the 53rd (R.A.C.) Training Regiment Band. The festivities began on Christmas Eve and continued for three days and nights. "A" Squadron had an excellent "smoker" and the performance of Captain Bill Peek, who sang Irish ballads, and Trooper Lythe, who was just himself, made it an evening to be remembered; there were the usual rounds of carol singing and visits to the Sergeants' Messes. The service on Christmas morning was held in H.Q. Squadron's theatre and then the squadrons had their Christmas dinners and, according to custom, the officers and sergeants waited on the other ranks. The Colonel, Second-in-Command, Adjutant and Regimental Sergeant-Major visited each squadron in turn and the Colonel wished everyone a merry Christmas.

On Boxing Day the annual football match between officers and sergeants was played to the accompaniment of the Band, which in the evening gave a concert in the theatre.

Then training began again. The object of the Brigade training plan was to provide three fully trained regimental groups. Long before Christmas each regiment had told the Brigadier when its troop training would be completed— in our case, the 16th of January. As the Brigade area was suitable only for troop training, another was found at Bouira, some seventy-five miles to the south. We were ready first, so we were told on the 28th of December that we had to move during the second week in January. A standing camp had to be erected, which the Queen's Bays and 10th Hussars would use after us, exercises had to be worked out and written, all the tanks had to be modified, and the guns had to be calibrated. The move took place between the 11th and the 14th of January.

The camp measured three hundred yards by one hundred and fifteen yards, and into this crowded the 9th Lancers Regimental Group, four batteries of artillery, a troop of Royal Engineers, part of Brigade Headquarters Squadron, a platoon of the Royal Army Service Corps, sections of the Royal Electrical and Mechanical Engineers, Military Police, Field Security, light field ambulance, hygiene and mobile baths, and later the 14th Foresters. Our position stood in the middle of an undulating plain some two thousand five hundred feet above sea-level and fairly intensively cultivated. The weather was much colder than down at Chebli and there was a frost every night.

At 9.15 on the first morning the Brigadier addressed all ranks—about one hundred officers and fifteen hundred men—and then the fortnight's training began in earnest. For the first half we followed the Colonel's programme; for the second half we were in the hands of Brigade. For the first two days each squadron set off in a prearranged direction to practise its own drills and manœuvres while the Colonel, the Second-in-Command and the Chief Umpire, Major George Rich, M.C., Queen's Bays, worked out two regimental exercises. These were successfully completed and were followed by exercises set by the Brigade. We felt that our mettle was being tested and were determined to succeed.

The first day under Brigade orders was devoted to a field firing exercise which went well, though it upset the neighbouring farmers. That evening we got possession of a "secret weapon"—an air observation post. Major Perry had met "the type" in the mobile bath at Bouira, and asked him if he would like to lend the 9th a hand for a few days. The O.P. was delighted at the prospect, and brought his flying jeep to the field behind Regimental Headquarters. He at once became our guest and informer. Brigade Headquarters heard rumours of our visitor and dispatched Lieutenant Mike Bird to ask us all about him.

N

Bird arrived in the middle of dinner and sat down two places away from the pilot. He stated his business and we denied all knowledge. The pilot was wearing his pilot's wings at the time, but Corporal Stevens, the mess corporal, rose to the occasion admirably by bringing his overcoat and saying: "I think you're feeling a little cold, sir!" A puzzled Lieutenant Bird left to make his report.

At 9.30 the next morning the Colonel received orders to capture a nearby village and after twenty-four hours of vigorous manœuvre this was successfully accomplished. The O.P. was of the greatest help and gave information which led to the destruction of five "enemy" self-propelled guns.

The end of the exercise on the 29th of January was the end of our collective training. We had learnt a great deal and got our eye in once more. The weather had been kind to us—bright sunshine and a clear sky every day.

"A" Squadron ran two gymkhanas in April and the 10th Hussars had a race meeting early in May. Polo started; mules were used instead of ponies and there was an inter-regimental tournament which the Queen's Bays won. The 9th encountered the 42nd Light Anti-Aircraft Regiment in the first round, and only just managed to defeat them! We lost to the Queen's Bays in the semi-final.

During all these months preparations for the invasion of North-West Europe were proceeding in England, and General Montgomery, now commanding 21st Army Group, was collecting together a number of battle-experienced commanders from the Mediterranean theatre. Under this scheme Lieutenant-Colonel G. H. Grosvenor was recalled in the middle of March, 1944. He was on a course in Italy at the time, but returned at once to collect his belongings and say good-bye. We gave a tremendous party for him on the 17th, and all his officers, as well as some of the Brigade staff, crowded into the Regimental Headquarters mess. The Colonel left the next morning. Since September, 1942, he had commanded the 9th Lancers, who now lined the drive and cheered him farewell. When he was seriously wounded in Normandy three months later the entire Regiment was anxious for good news of him.

Lieutenant-Colonel R. S. G. Perry, D.S.O., then assumed command of the Regiment.

[*Photo: Janet Jevens, W.1*

Lieut.-Colonel R. S. G. PERRY, D.S.O.

CHAPTER XX

AND SO TO ITALY

THE reason for keeping the 1st Armoured Division in Algeria for so long remained a well-guarded secret. Up to the end of the summer of 1943 we had been kept well informed about the reasons for our moves, so when explanations were no longer forthcoming troops became a little perplexed. Then, on the 8th of April, 1944, the Colonel was called to Brigade Headquarters. On his return he summoned his squadron leaders and we learned that we were going to Italy.

We had become so well dug in at Chebli that to move was a complicated process. Staff conferences were frequent, clerks put in hours of overtime, and movement instructions came in by the quire, more tanks were issued and we began to approach our war establishment. Twenty of the tanks had to go to Italy ahead of us, however, and be handed over to the Canadians. Captain Reid and Lieutenant Lacy-Thompson took them and were a great help to our advanced party.

On the 1st of May the bulk of the Regiment went to the Divisional rest camp at Surcouf, a very nice spot by the sea ten miles east of Algiers. No one had had any leave for months, primarily because there was no suitable place to which to send them during the winter, so the main body returned in a week, and the rear party, some fifty strong, took four days off. The officers did not go to Surcouf, but toured North Africa, going as far afield as Fez, Marrakesh and Rabat. The Quartermaster and the Acting Adjutant did not get much of a holiday—but, then, they never do.

At 9 o'clock on the 14th of May the first tank left the Chebli leaguer and by midday the last lorry was clear. The first stage of our journey was short, only fifteen miles to Blida. It was an upheaval for such a short distance, but it had obvious advantages in that we were on a mobile—as opposed to a static—basis, and the whole Brigade was collected together in one transit camp which made communications and the issue of orders easier. The camp was better than most, with tents carefully laid out and adequate cookhouses; it was clean and dry, two conditions seldom found in transit camps, and only fifteen minutes' walk from Blida. We had no indication of how long our stay would be, so daily leave facilities were given as usual.

Blida boasted some enterprising black-market restaurants, a couple of cinemas, and some savage Arabs. These gentlemen inflicted serious knife injuries on several soldiers, including Trooper Tomlinson, of "A" Squadron, who had to have eighteen stitches put round his scalp.

163

Meanwhile Captain Bill Peek and a few men were handing back our billets. There was a matter of £100 damage at one farm, but Captain Peek, supported by an old German motor-bike he no longer required, was able to drive a bargain which satisfied everyone. The owner of "B" Squadron's farm presented Major Derek Allhusen with five thousand francs (about £25) for their Benevolent Fund.

It was at Blida that Major Price returned from England, where he had been on a course since February. He went straight off to Italy in a destroyer to get things ready for us over there.

The Divisional Commander visited the Regiment. He arrived at an opportune moment, when crews were manning their tanks and practising regimental wireless nets.

After breakfast on the 21st of May Brigade Headquarters announced that our vehicles would be loaded the next day or the day after that. If it was the next day, they said, we should be told by 4 p.m. At 4.30 nothing had come through, so the daily exodus to Algiers began. Half an hour later orders came to load the next day. One hundred and six trucks and lorries were involved and fifty-six tanks. Captain Foy, the Technical Officer, had worked out the loading tables beforehand, though we did not know how many different ships there would be or how many vehicles of each type would be loaded on to each until the final orders came. As ill-luck would have it, that officer had gone to Algiers for the evening. For the Adjutant it was a very hectic night. He did his best to match the vehicles shown on the loading tables with those actually in the camp, but this was difficult because allowances had been made for certain unspecified lorries for which no place on board could now be found. The one hundred and sixty-two vehicles had to be divided into eight convoys travelling by various routes and at different times to the docks, each under the command of an officer, and on arrival they had to be loaded into four ships in varying proportions. The 10th Hussars had reported that guards would have to be detailed because equipment was being stolen on the quayside during loading operations. As the first convoy would leave at 6 a.m., everyone had to have his orders that night. The issue of seven days' rations to all ranks going to the docks was not made easier by the absence of the Quartermaster in Algiers!

From 11.30 p.m. onwards officers and men began to return from their sorties, each quite naturally wanting to be informed of the situation. It was a relief to see the Regiment sorting itself out at dawn the next morning and starting as arranged for the docks. The total number of men involved was two hundred and ten, of whom about one hundred and fifty were to guard the docks. There were several sheds on the quays and permission was obtained for us to use these for accommodation. There was no difficulty over personal baggage, as this was stored in lorries.

Loading began soon after midday, but when the dockers knocked off for

ITALY—
GENERAL

lunch, went to sleep for the afternoon and refused to work in the dark, it was clear that the Algerian Arabs were no different from their brothers in Egypt.

On the 23rd the remaining lorries went down to the quay to be loaded on to the *Samoa* and *Samwash,* and "B" Squadron's nineteen Shermans went on to the *Fort Marin.* The staff work had been well done and there was room for everything. Captain Dison appeared on the docks that morning. He had been our Doctor from Knightsbridge to El Hamma and was now Medical Officer on H.T. *Winchester Castle.* This had not been converted like the other troop-ships and so was very comfortable. A request to send us in her was politely refused, but Captain Dison gave some of us an excellent lunch on board.

The next day "Reveille" was at 5 a.m. In the pouring rain the Regiment entrained at Blida station and reached Algiers central station at 10 o'clock. Everyone from the train and the dock guards formed up beside our ship in alphabetical order by squadrons, irrespective of rank, while the Queen's Bays went on board, and when our turn came we embarked in under an hour, which was regarded as a record by the embarkation staff. The Colonel's car and the motor-bicycles were also loaded on to our ship. These proved invaluable on arrival, because all other vehicles were going in a different convoy, by a different route, to a different destination.

H.T. *Durban Castle* was much more comfortable than the *Strathaird* and all ranks were accommodated above the water-line. We left Algiers at 5 a.m. on the 25th of May, and hugged the coast towards Bizerta all day. The voyage lasted for only two days, so there was no training except for fifteen minutes' P.T. on the first morning, which was done in relays on account of the limited deck space.

At 7.15 a.m. on the 27th the convoy passed in line ahead through the straits between the Isle of Capri and Sorrento and entered the Bay of Naples. Many travellers regard this view as one of the loveliest in the Mediterranean, and we were not disappointed. The multi-coloured landscape from the Isle of Ischia and Posilipo on the north round to Vesuvius on the south, with the vivid blue sea in the foreground, made a perfect picture. It had a special significance for us, because this was one step nearer home, an overriding consideration in every move we made. "See Naples and die" is a statement we endorsed at once. Out in the bay it was plain what the author meant. Equally plain was the alternative meaning of this phrase when we entered the town itself. No one had ever seen a more squalid or filthy place. It was not the bombing or shelling that accounted for it, but the unhygienic way of Neapolitan life, which had to be seen to be believed.

The convoy was originally meant to take us to Taranto, but during the voyage this plan had been changed. Consequently no proper arrangements had been made for our reception. Luckily, Major Bill Manger, Queen's Bays, was in Naples and he gave us great assistance. Disembarking after the 10th Hussars at 11 o'clock, we marched to the transit camp at Afragola, some nine miles inland. It was an unpleasant way to spend such a hot afternoon, but no one fell out—perhaps because Captain Carlisle was bringing up the rear with his immense crook. All the baggage had to be landed by lighter on another quay, and in order to ensure that it all arrived that evening Captain Peek remained behind with Mr. Hardwidge.

If Naples was bad, Afragola was worse. Our transit camp was sited in a vineyard just outside the town. The meals were badly cooked and inadequate, the wash-houses were dirty and there was no lighting. The officers' mess was equally poor and complaints produced no improvement. The Colonel saw the Commandant and offered to take the place over while we were staying there, but the suggestion was turned down.

The Regiment went for a route march every morning, and after lunch about three hundred men went out on pass. They hitch-hiked everywhere, since the only Regimental transport available was the Colonel's car and a few motor-bikes. Many took the opportunity of visiting Pompeii and seeing the damage caused by the recent eruption of Mount Vesuvius. The Opera House in Naples gave at least one show a day, and this was always well attended. Lieutenant Thwaites was delighted to occupy Mussolini's chair in the royal box one night.

We waited in the transit camp for eight days, during which time advance parties from each squadron went off to our ultimate destination, Matera. Because of the discomfort the Colonel went to see if we could all move there at once, but this was not possible, as all the vehicles in the Division were still afloat and it would have been impossible to maintain us. At last, at 7.45 a.m. on the 4th of June, the Regiment marched to Casoria station and boarded their allotted cattle trucks. Punctually at 10 o'clock, with a jerk the train moved off. We lunched at Benevento, whence an electric engine gave us a smoother run over the Apennine Mountains. At dusk we stopped at a wayside station near Foggia, and the R.T.O. there promised to arrange a "brew" for us farther on at Barletta, but when we arrived at 9.15 p.m. there was no sign of it. Major Pulteney, who was commanding the train (he always seemed to get saddled with that job), sent for the R.T.O., but he loftily said that our train could not stop there and hold up the trucks of ammunition required at the front. Major Pulteney won, however, and put an armed guard on the footplate to ensure that the train did not move. There were eight soyer stoves available and a team of three on each competed for the quickest "brew." Fifty-two minutes later we continued our journey. Early the next morning we reached Altamura and dismounted. While we ate breakfast the engine got up steam and gave the Regiment shaving water. Major Price and Captain Tubbs arrived and an hour later twenty 10th Hussar lorries came to transport us to Matera.

Matera is about fifty miles inland from the port of Bari on the Adriatic; it is in a monotonous and torrid neighbourhood, but the town itself was above average in cleanliness. Each squadron was billeted in a block of flats and had plenty of room: "B," "C" and H.Q. Squadrons were within fifty yards of each other next to the station, and "A" Squadron was about half a mile away. This compactness helped administration, but the tanks when they came had to be in the Brigade park two miles away. There was an excellent "gelati" (ice-cream) shop next to the orderly room and this did a roaring trade until put out of bounds by the police.

There were two pests which never ceased to be a source of aggravation and a danger to health—mosquitoes and flies. In 1943 the Army learnt its lesson about malaria, and after that every kind of device was invented and measures taken to ensure that the devices were used properly. It was mainly a question of taking mepacrine tablets every day, sleeping under a net, rolling down sleeves at sunset, and so on. Of necessity there were constant and tedious inspections, but as a result the Regiment suffered only two or three casualties. By erecting muslin and netting over windows and doors, spraying gallons of "Flit" everywhere and conducting an enthusiastic swatting campaign, the flies were partially conquered, but out on the street they were thick everywhere, and floors and walls seemed to move with them.

Meanwhile, Captains Allen and Foy were supervising the unloading at Taranto docks, and on the 11th of June the last vehicle drove into Matera. Captain Henderson took his L.A.D. down to the park and began modification of the tanks.

CHAPTER XXI

HARD WORK AND A HOLIDAY

ON the 7th of June Brigadier Goodbody, the Brigade Commander, returned. He had taken over command of the Brigade from Brigadier Peake in Algiers, but he had been sent straight away to do a special job in the Anzio beach-head and had thus lost several valuable months in directing our training. He had commanded the 11th H.A.C. and was very well known to the troops now under him.

The next day he began a programme of intensive training devoted to the study of co-operation in the attack between tanks and infantry. He had been at the front for over two months, and had seen how the 25th Army Tank Brigade and the 1st U.S. Armoured Division met the peculiar conditions of fighting in Italy. He had seen various techniques employed against the determined methods of our ingenious and unorthodox enemy, and consequently he was able to teach his Brigade the systems of attack which he knew would be successful. It was this training which led us from victory to victory in the later stages of the campaign, although much took place before we got a chance to try it out.

This idea of mutual co-operation was nothing new. It had started in the First World War and had been taught during the intervening peace. In Africa and Italy in this war it was practised again, but never seemed to run smoothly. The problem of reliable communications was always acute, and misunderstandings sometimes resulted in high casualties to both arms. Clearly this was an unsatisfactory state of affairs, particularly when the nature of Italian terrain convinced the whole army that, except in the mountains, mutual co-operation was the only answer. Both infantry and armour, therefore, set about perfecting the technique.

As this is a story and not a training memorandum the precise details are of only academic interest, but put in the most general terms this is what happened.

The infantry were the senior partners. They first decided how a position should be attacked, and were then given an appropriate number of tanks to support them. The rest of the tanks were responsible for helping and supporting the leading tanks from behind. The infantry scoured all bushes, hedges and ditches to clear out any bazookamen or snipers who might be in a position to pick off tanks or their commanders at ranges of a hundred yards and less. The bazooka was a highly effective anti-tank weapon used by infantry. It consisted of a long tube out of which was fired a hollow-charge projectile that was capable of penetrating the armour of any British or American tank. One man could carry it and it was effective up to ranges of seventy-five yards. The Germans were very artful in its use and the bazookamen and snipers sometimes held their fire until the leading troops were a mile or more beyond them. To overcome this it was necessary for the attacking troops to advance in great depth, so that when the leading infantry reached the objective their rear had only recently crossed the start line. In this way the infantry and the tanks were well spread out over the ground just won and in a position to help each other to deal with the snipers. All-round observation in each tank as well as each troop was vital, because the enemy were just as likely to fire from either flank, or from behind, as they were from in front.

There was no hard-and-fast rule as to who should lead. It might change as much as three or four times in a mile, depended on the terrain and on whether opposition was more likely to be anti-tank or anti-infantry. In this way the best tank tactics possible in the circumstances were superimposed, as it were, on the infantry tactics. Each partner was aware of the difficulties and limitations of the other. If in the event tanks suffered heavy casualties, they saved the lives of many infantrymen and their sacrifice was worth while. All this sounds easy, as generalizations usually do. It was the mass of small details that had to be solved correctly which made the complications.

In the second week of June, therefore, while the crews were getting their tanks ready, the Brigadier talked to all officers in the Opera House in Matera and explained the subject lucidly and convincingly. He then ran a series of sand-table discussions and organized demonstrations by the 1st King's Royal Rifle Corps so that each officer could see for himself what was required. Thus instructed, but not practised, we moved out from Matera to the Brigade training area on the 15th of June. We arranged six regimental exercises: each squadron would do two exercises in their tanks and four exercises as infantry. Apart from the fact that no proper infantry were available to take part in our schemes, it was our first duty to understand the main problems of an infantryman's job; and what better way was there of doing this than acting as infantry ourselves?

The first three days were spent in doing three preliminary tasks: first, a day's ordinary troop training to refresh everyone's memory; second, teaching all tank commanders what the Brigadier had just taught the officers about co-operation; and, third, teaching all the soldiers elementary platoon battle drill, for which "C" Company, 1st King's Royal Rifle Corps, kindly provided instructors. H.Q. Squadron were included in this infantry training, for they were to act as enemy. After this we were ready to begin.

Our training area was ideal in every way. The undulating country was covered in scrub and young self-seeded trees, and lent itself to the enemy tactics already described. It was varied enough to necessitate changes of lead between infantry and tanks and to show many of the different ways in which tanks could best give support. The whole area was only just big enough for the Brigade, and in order to introduce maximum variety of ground the Brigade

Major rang up about every third day and said "General Post," upon which we all moved round one.

The Colonel and Second-in-Command prepared the exercises, which all took the same form: moving to the forming-up place, "marrying-up" with the infantry (a convenient expression which we soon redesignated "wedding"), crossing the start line; then the attack itself, consolidation, and sometimes exploitation. Sometimes we formed up by day, sometimes by night. On two occasions minefields were included. Some attacks were in one phase at dawn, others in two phases by day. H.Q. Squadron made realistic enemies and fired Very lights, thunder-flashes and smoke bombs from 2-inch mortars. These caused two fires, but the Regimental Sergeant-Major and his fire-fighting squad were always close at hand, though once all the "infantry" had to help too. The Reconnaissance Troop staged a sharp counter-attack in their Honeys, for this was an invariable practice with the Germans. In these ways interest was always maintained. The 1st King's Royal Rifle Corps lent an officer to command our infantry for each scheme so that we should work on the right lines. By the end of the month we felt a sense of achievement. We had started almost from scratch, for our training with the 1st Buffs in Algiers had been rather superficial. We now felt that we knew the secrets of this difficult form of warfare and that we had added another and far stronger string to our well-tried bow.

Besides the co-operation training we practised indirect fire on a regimental level and called it Exercise "Minden." In spite of some opposition the Colonel was determined to order "one round regimental gunfire." This made an impressive noise for the guns were equal in number to two field regiments of artillery. A linear target was engaged and an area target, and then Lieutenant-General Allfrey (G.O.C. V Corps), who was watching, ordered the Regiment to switch quickly to another target. The Colonel pointed to Captain Reid, who acted with speed and fair judgment. We did "Minden" twice, as it was a good way of practising and the observation post was ideal. Under the shade of trees, on the edge of a sheer drop, the observing officers had a panoramic view as far as the eye could see. The tanks had to motor less than a hundred yards to their gun positions and this saved track mileage. Someone hit a tree immediately ahead one morning, but otherwise they shot well.

Each troop practised direct and indirect fire on the artillery ranges. There was also a Browning field-firing exercise for each squadron, which included individual targets as well as area shoots. A Browning was a type of machine gun fitted in Sherman tanks. Another exercise demonstrated how to knock a house down. The only available building was a kind of shepherd's bungalow made out of sandstone. Different types of shells were fired at different points on the house, which rapidly disintegrated; then a high-explosive shell, set on delay, penetrated the wall, exploded inside and removed the roof; this was a tip to remember.

Lieutenant-Colonel Kidd, 4th Hussars, gave us a lecture on the Armoured

Reconnaissance Regiment one day. His regiment had just joined the Division in this new capacity. Another day Major Price and Captain Peek took part in a Divisional artillery exercise. It ended unhappily, since the last shot landed among the crowd of spectators, which included the G.O.C., Major-General Galloway, and two brigadiers. Brigadier Goodbody was among the casualties, but luckily he was in hospital for only a few weeks.

It was the current policy to regard tanks as expendable "tin cans," and it must have been this which set the Colonel wondering about the possibilities of a robot, crewless, remote-controlled tank. The L.A.D. fixed one up for him by attaching a cable to the ignition and starter motor at one end and to a switch on the ground at the other. A hundred yards of cable was wound round a drum which stood on the ground by the switch. Colonel Macdonell (the Brigade Second-in-Command) and the Brigade staff came to see it one day. First the ignition switch was put on from a point twenty yards behind the tank, then the starter-motor switch, and, sure enough, the tank moved forward about six inches under the power of the starter. Then the engine started (for the tank had been left in gear) and away it went to the limit of the cable, when the switches were turned off and the robot halted. Mechanically it worked, but it was a great strain on the starter-motor to move thirty tons with a gear reduction of about fifty to one. The guns were fired electrically, so it was possible to attach another cable to them. The sort of situation the Colonel had in mind was one such as faced the Regiment at Kournine in April, 1943, when the enemy would disclose his positions only if tanks motored down the forward slopes.

Though our training was varied, our pleasures were monotonous. The one unfailing attraction was ice-cream. The nearest village, Gravina, was about two miles away and there the Italian reputation of being good "ice-cream merchants" was maintained at the highest level. It was only a small place, but it had two establishments, one in a side-street which made ice-creams with a chocolate or coffee flavour, the other in the square. Some days later a letter arrived from the Base Censor saying that he had noticed that the troops had written home about their ice-cream sessions and that it was against orders to eat such food. He quoted three extracts as evidence. Quite by accident the letters were burnt and three exceptionally graphic descriptions of the art of eating ice-cream were lost to posterity. These shops also sold an astonishing drink called "dragon's blood." No one knew what were its ingredients, but those with a small capacity for ice-cream gained certain relief by washing it down with this drink.

Soon after we began training near Gravina Major Steel returned from England, where he had been on a course, bringing Major David Laurie with him. The latter assumed command of H.Q. Squadron in place of Captain Mostyn. It was good to see Major Laurie back with all his paraphernalia. No one in the Eighth Army could have had so complete a kit. He had battledresses lined in three different thicknesses; high sheepskin boots; specially made black boots which fastened with two straps and buckles; a weatherproof tank suit;

hats, scarves, waistcoats, and trousers of divers natures; an Orilux lamp with a special strap; tables, chairs, a library of books, and anything else likely to alleviate the realities of campaigning in the hottest or the coldest weather. He wasted no time in organizing dinner parties in the "Bedford Drivers' Club" ("B" Echelon officers' mess), with a well-balanced menu of good, plain food. The club staff consisted of Troopers Mallard, "Herman" Fink (Captain Henderson's servant) and Lee, the cook. It would have been hard to find such a consistently high standard of messing in the whole Army.

At Gravina we were told that after Rome had fallen the Army was being regrouped and that the 1st Armoured Division was now in V Corps with the 1st Infantry Division and the 4th Indian Division. This Corps was originally going to assemble in the Foggia neighbourhood, but owing to the good progress of the campaign, assembly was now to take place at Rome. The 1st Infantry Division was already there and the 10th Hussars moved up at the end of June to join them and help in their training. At first we feared that the Division might be split up, but happily this did not happen. The G.O.C. talked to all officers and tank commanders in the Regiment. He wisely avoided making any promises, but it seemed that we must go on waiting and spend at least three more weeks at Gravina. This was depressing news. After such an excellent month's training morale was high. One sensed the feeling of "Oh, well, we've got to fight soon, so let's get on with it."

At this time the Division were given some ferry duties. Fifty lorries and trucks were ordered to stand by at three hours' notice for four days to transport petrol from Bari to the front, but the move was cancelled. We lent a hundred drivers to take vehicles from the docks to various ordnance parks; we lent eighteen lorries to move a Polish hospital; we lent one and a half sections of jeeps for essential operational work and sent men to build transit camps. The men on loan quite enjoyed themselves because it made a change, but their absence interfered with training and we seemed to be farther away than ever from the battle front. It was terribly hot and as it was obviously no use being idle in that climate Major Price arranged a rest camp on the sea-shore near Bari. H.Q. Squadron provided the small staff required and all squadrons sent their men there for short periods in relays.

At the end of the second week, when the weather showed no sign of improving and our numbers were further reduced by odd jobs, serious training was abandoned and the Regiment moved *en masse* to Bari. The tanks could not be moved, nor could Brigade Headquarters, so there were some problems in administration and communication. The best solution was to line up all tanks in column of squadrons and leave one man behind with each. The Light Aid Detachment, Signal Troop and carpenters stayed to continue modifications and other jobs, as well as a few cooks, a water-truck driver, and so on. Officers took it in turns to command this force. Towards the end of the month Brigade Headquarters moved too, and then things became easier.

At Bari the sea breeze was refreshing and the bathing excellent. While in the camp we lived in our bathing pants and daily became a deeper colour—white at first, then pink, then brown and then, in the case of Sergeant Hughes and several others, almost black. The sun was very hot and the hazy outline of Bari docks shimmered in the distance. "Kempy" modified his gas-mask in a curious fashion, so that he could swim with his head under water while breathing through the tube. We had been there a week when the Brigadier declared a ten-day holiday. This amounted to "official sanction" for what we were already doing and we enjoyed it all the more.

Many officers lived in the Grande Albergo Imperiale. This was really the Officers' Club and no one was allowed to stay for more than five days. By adopting a new alias every fifth day, however, it was possible to get round the rule and Majors Price and Laurie held the record with twenty-seven consecutive days.

Meanwhile, officers in twos and threes were visiting fighting armoured regiments in order to keep up to date and gain as much knowledge as possible of the enemy's methods and the nature of the country. On the 31st of July ten officers from each regiment in the Brigade listened to a short talk by Major-General Galloway, who was unluckily forced to leave the Division on account of ill-health. That afternoon Major Guy Gardner rejoined the Regiment from Headquarters, 6th Armoured Division, and everyone was pleased to see him back again.

It was as well that we made the most of this ideal existence at Bari.

CHAPTER XXII

CONCENTRATION

THE way we moved around Italy during the month of August would have been incomprehensible to an outside observer. Indeed there were times when we ourselves did not understand what we were doing.

It all began on the 2nd of August and sounded very simple. The tanks were to move from Gravina to Bari, whence they would go by train to Alife, forty miles north of Naples. The rest of the Regiment was to move to the vicinity of Mondragone on the west coast and return to Alife when the tanks arrived. We were then to train with the two new infantry brigades in the Division, the 43rd Gurkha Brigade and the 66th British Infantry Brigade. When this was finished, or even before, the Division would move into battle. We were told, furthermore, that eighteen new tanks would meet us there, two fitted with 105-mm. guns for each squadron, and one fitted with a 76-mm. gun for each of our twelve troop leaders.

During the next three days orders were issued. Captain Gregson went off with the advance party; two report centres consisting of one officer and seven men each went to help Divisional Headquarters control the move; the tanks were placed under Major Gardner's command and reorganized with minimum crews plus the necessary administrative staff. All our detachments out on odd jobs rejoined, and "Doncol," consisting of a few Regimental Headquarters vehicles under the Quartermaster's command, motored on ahead to save time on arrival. While the Regiment was engaged in these preliminaries the Bishop of Lichfield visited us and talked to a group of sun-bathing soldiers for a few minutes about England and some of the difficulties of running a home there, now and after the war, all of it welcome information.

The echelon—that is, all the wheeled part of the Regiment—left at 5 a.m. on the 6th of August. They were due to cross the start point at 10.40 a.m., but the circuitous route to get there was seventy miles long. They passed through Barletta and Foggia and leaguered for the night at Giardinetto, near Bovino.

After breakfast the Colonel and Adjutant drove straight through to Mondragone. Arriving at the junction of Routes 6 and 7, thirty miles north of Naples, they were met by Captain Gregson, who said that the proposed area was an American training ground and not available. Moreover, he had condemned the site near Alife, but had found a suitable spot in between, and Regimental Headquarters (the Colonel, Adjutant, Captain Gregson and "Doncol") arrived there at 6 p.m. The 10th Hussars were across the road, having just returned from Rome. Captain Donnley's quick ears had learned that all plans had been changed. Major Price, who had been staying with the 10th Hussars, came over in the evening and confirmed this, but was unable to say what the new plan was, except that it might involve a move to Ortona on the other side of Italy.

The next day an early visit to Division yielded the information that the Brigade Staff Captain had motored to the echelon at Giardinetto during the night with orders to direct them to Ortona. The Brigadier, who was acting Divisional Commander, had flown to Allied Armies, Italy, Headquarters that morning to find out exactly what the Division was supposed to do. While drinking a mug of tea, the Colonel saw an aeroplane fly overhead and guessed that it was the Brigadier's. He motored to Division again with the Adjutant and found the Brigadier with orders for the Division. There then began a series of conferences.

We were going into battle soon and we were to concentrate secretly in the Ancona area. This concentration would not be easy, because at that moment each regiment was divided into several parts across an area of two hundred miles long, each part being out of touch with the other. The Brigadier decided that in spite of the extra distance involved the Brigade must reassemble as far as possible in one place. For numerous reasons Alife was the best place, and signals had been sent accordingly to the echelon. The plan for the move of the tanks was not altered: they would go by train from Bari direct to Ortona and then continue on their tracks in short stages by night.

These orders simplified the move considerably, but there were still some complications. The long drive was likely to wear out bogey wheels and tracks and there might not be enough time to change them; Ortona was over a hundred miles distant from Alife and the tank crews had to be transported there; for security reasons only two or three lorries could be sent forward from Ortona with each convoy of tanks.

All went well until Lieutenant Newman arrived at Regimental Headquarters at ten o'clock the next morning with news that the echelon had advanced to Termoli the day before. This was almost diametrically the opposite direction from Regimental Headquarters and it took four hours to contact the Brigade Major, Major Gordon Fox, and tell him. He said that the echelon orders were changed three times in one morning, without the second and third orders catching up with the first in time to stop the move. Furthermore, communications were not easy between the various parts of the scattered Divisional Headquarters. When Majors Steel and Laurie arrived at Regimental Headquarters at 4 p.m. the next day it was a relief to hear that the echelon was on its way. Being on the echelon was like being a tennis ball: whichever way you were sent someone always appeared and sent you back again.

After this confusing start, things sorted themselves out. There was delay in ascertaining the time at which our tanks were expected to arrive at Ortona, but the balance of the crews left Alife at 7 a.m. on the 14th of July under the command of Major Price. We were to get our 76-mm. tanks at Ortona and he would supervise their calibration and firing practice. As might have been expected, the trains became more and more delayed and finally nothing arrived at all until the 17th. The crews waited patiently and bathed all day, for the sun was very penetrating.

After two changes in orders, that part of the Division still in the Alife area advanced on the 15th of July. The route lay across the Apennine Range to Vasto and was winding and dusty. Contrary to expectations, the scenery was dull. Hour after hour the convoy climbed upwards, entering the village inevitably perched on the summit and surrounded by terraced vineyards, and then descending the far side and over the river to the next hill. We went into leaguer at 6.30 p.m. and at once went to the beach to bathe.

At 11 o'clock the next day the convoy continued without a halt to Francavilla, passing the tank crews in their leaguer at Ortona. We were glad to know that the whole Regiment was at least on the same side of Italy. At 5 p.m. on the 17th of July the convoy arrived at Porto Civitanova and was guided to its appropriate place by Captain Gregson, who was our representative on Colonel Macdonell's brigade advance party.

Major Gardner occasionally sent us a message about the situation at what he called "the blunt end." He had had his full share of counter-orders, but in the end had loaded our tanks on to three different trains. To cover the last ninety miles from Ortona in secrecy each train-load was sent off at 5 a.m. on the morning after it arrived, and allowed to go on for four hours only. They took three days to do the journey, stopping at Rosetto and Pedaso for the two intermediate periods of twenty hours; consequently the first tanks arrived at Porto Civitanova on the 20th of August, and the last lot, the 76-mm.'s, on the 23rd. The firing practice for those at Ortona was cancelled and rearranged to take place on the sea-shore at Porto Civitanova.

It would be difficult to invent a more complicated way of getting a regiment from A to B. But the circumstances had been unavoidable and it was a merciful relief to have everyone collected together again.

The fact that we had to regard ourselves as being "in a forward area" meant that we had to observe precautions like camouflage and black-out. This left no choice of leaguers, though we were fairly lucky compared with the Queen's Bays and 10th Hussars. The shape of our leaguer was that of a lollipop. A straight drive under an avenue of pines represented the stick of the lollipop and housed the entire echelon in line ahead, except for the Quartermaster, Light Aid Detachment and Signals, who claimed their independence whenever possible. Then round the oval part of the sweet, so to speak, the tanks were packed one behind the other. This track was narrow, but provided excellent concealment. Apart from the first few tanks at either end of the column, any movement was quite impossible without extensive shunting. In the middle there was a country house, tennis court and small wood covering half an acre where the officers' lines were located and most of the crews slept. It was a curious arrangement, but worked well. Traffic control was a little difficult, especially when some of the tracks on the tanks had to be changed.

The 76-mm. tank was an impressive weapon with its gun protruding several feet in front of the hull. The engine was almost identical with other Sherman tanks, and the turret was larger and incorporated all-round-vision slits in the commander's cupola. The guns were targeted on the 25th of July. Tests showed that the recoil action damaged the end of the deflector guard and might even break the wireless set, but the guard was strengthened and the trouble stopped. There was much talk of collecting 105-mm. tanks and, although we were prepared to have them at short notice, they did not in the end arrive for several weeks.

The new Divisional Commander, Major-General Hull, visited the Regiment on the 18th of July. He walked round with the Colonel and at tea produced some interesting facts about the invasion of France, all now well known. The 43rd Gurkha Brigade had arrived with the Division, but the 18th Lorried Infantry Brigade was joining us again in place of the 66th Brigade originally suggested. A number of liaison visits were paid to both these, particularly the 2nd/8th Gurkha Rifles, to whom we were affiliated. The 1st King's Royal Rifle Corps also came back to the 2nd Armoured Brigade after a short period with the 9th Armoured Brigade, and gave a party to mark the occasion. This meant that "C" Company, with which we had trained so often, would be part of our Regimental Group. "E" Battery, 11th H.A.C., was leaguered half a mile to our north, while near by lay the 1st Field Squadron, Royal Engineers. Once more the Regimental Group was a physical reality and not a series of wooden tokens on a sand table.

At 10.30 a.m. on the 20th of August ninety men and all officers from each regiment in the Brigade assembled for an address by the Army Commander, Lieutenant-General Sir Oliver Leese. He spoke for forty-five minutes about the war in general, the history of the Division, some tactical lessons peculiar to this campaign, and something of the future battle. It was a good talk and we were conscious now of our imminent employment and the importance of success.

Three days later the Colonel was away all day attending a conference. It was obvious that all officers of his rank were being briefed for battle in true Eighth Army style. The next day the squadron leaders and the Adjutant went to the Bays' regimental headquarters to meet the V Corps Commander, Lieutenant-General Keightley. He had a word with everyone, and afterwards drove off with a flourish, saying: "Meet you on the Po." So that was it—the Po!

Back in Regimental Headquarters the Colonel explained the Army plan to squadron leaders and the Adjutant. Their lips were sealed until the Brigadier addressed the entire Regiment at 11.30 on the 27th. His brilliant oration lasted exactly an hour, and never once did he lose the keen attention of his audience.

o

He began at the top and concisely reviewed the war in general, explaining the three attacks on Germany, from France, Italy and Russia, which were designed to meet somewhere in Germany in the not-too-distant future. Coming down to our particular front, he described the situation in Italy and the nature of the Gothic Line. At that moment the Eighth Army was some fifteen miles away from it and during the previous night a big attack had been launched. The intention was to go on attacking hard right up to the line; immediately it was reached an attempt would be made to "bounce it." V Corps was the exploitation force and would be led by the 1st Armoured Division.

When the Gothic Line was penetrated and the leading troops were almost on Route 9, the Rimini—Bologna road, we should have to fight our way out of the last part of the gap and then pursue in the proper role of an armoured division. The first day would be the worst, the break-out into the Po Valley, but we had to get there, at great cost if need be. Starting from the moment we arrived "we will go on and on and on, day and night, until we are too exhausted to see the target." Those were the Brigadier's exact words and the light of battle was in his eye. It was a grand opportunity and we were certainly going to take it. But there was an obstacle, a danger greater than the enemy himself for all his Tigers—the country. It would be close, overgrown with vines and full of wire, and, worse still, there were many irrigation canals with their steep flood-banks. Getting over it would demand the most ingenious initiative. The Brigadier did not tell us our objectives or even our route, but if all went very well maybe we should reach the Brenner Pass and even Germany. The great secret of success in this kind of operation was teamwork, and there was no brigade so well able to work as a team as this one.

It was a rousing speech, lucidly argued and simply put. It caused every man to set about his job with redoubled energy. Tactical conferences were going on all day and every day; the sand table was gazed upon for hours at a time to achieve the right application, in this particular case, of the principles we had thought about for months. Traffic control over such big distances had to be worked out. We were told to be ruthless with the refugees who would assuredly throng the roads. The centre line must be marked. And what was the best organization for the echelons in these circumstances? With so many water courses to cross and never a hill to be seen, could we fix on any special drills for capturing bridges? What was the best way for a troop to advance down an autobahn? Ideas were legion and under skilful direction well harnessed.

Foot-square baulks of timber the length of a railway sleeper arrived by the ton, and four were tied on to most tanks for casting off into deep ditches. Steel frames called cribs, measuring six feet by two by two, also came for the same purpose and one was tied on the back of each tank. Charges of ammonal were packed in to knock down obstacles. Steel tracks were changed for rubber, because we preferred that type. Lieutenant Donat, R.E., instructed troop leaders in the methods of assessing bridge classifications. Major Morris re-

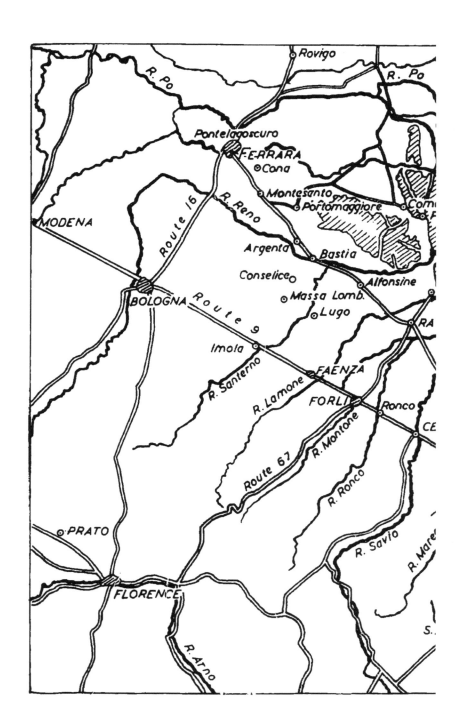

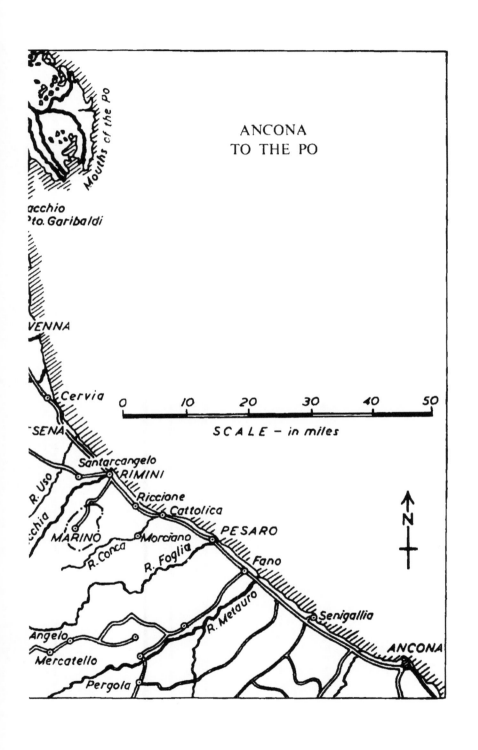

ANCONA
TO THE PO

Mouths of the Po

acchio
Pto. Garibaldi

VENNA

Cervia

SENA

0   10   20   30   40   50

SCALE – in miles

Santarcangelo
RIMINI
Riccione
Cattolica
PESARO
MARINO   Morciano
R. Conca   Fano
R. Foglia
R. Uso
chia

N

R. Metauro
Senigallia
Angelo
ANCONA
Mercatello
Pergola

minded them of the cardinal point method of correcting artillery fire, in case no forward observation officer were available. The Brigadier had ordered an hour's walk for everybody every morning before breakfast as an aid to fitness, and map reading and the use of ground were taught *en route*. There was a wireless exercise to refresh our memories and to practise the new codes. An Italian liaison officer called Raimondo arrived to interpret the language, help with the refugees and buy food for the mess.

The administrative staff was no less busy. The orderly room poured out *pro formæ*, aides-memoire, instructions, codes and orders. They set up an all-time record one afternoon by putting four thousand sheets of foolscap through the Roneo duplicator and completely emptying Lance-Corporal Philip's oil-can. The Adjutant worked into the small hours of the morning, the Quartermaster issued emergency rations, the Technical Officer tried to quench Brigade's insatiable thirst for returns, Major Gardner worked out the composition of our echelons, and Lieutenant Hainsworth, the Intelligence Officer, was practically invisible amid bales of maps and a bucket of gum.

Owing to the compact nature of our leaguer it could genuinely be described as a hive of industry. This description well fits the diversion inadvertently created on the 24th. After dinner a fire was seen in the vicinity of the Light Aid Detachment, fifty yards from the tanks. A haystack was alight. "A" Squadron crews were nearest the fire and leapt for extinguishers, which they squirted furiously. On account of the dryness of the stack and the rapidity with which the fire caught hold, their efforts failed to have any visible result. Water-carts soon arrived and began pumping water on the surrounding grass and adjacent rick. After an hour or so, while the heat increased, the 10th Hussars rang up to say that all the farmers for miles around thought they were being bombed and had evacuated their houses. Colonel Macdonell rang up to know what steps we were taking to prevent the fire spreading. He did not sound altogether convinced that the biggest "brew" in the 9th Lancers' experience had only by some remarkable chance coincided with Mons Night.

And then at last we were ready. Reports came in showing steady progress up at the front. Surely we would be moving soon? All preparations had been made with the greatest care; our equipment was in working order down to the last nut and bolt; every man had been briefed in detail so that he knew just how much was expected of him; the Regimental Group was at maximum efficiency. We knew that any time now would see the culmination of our year's training. We went down to the beach for a swim and then sat in deck-chairs and waited.

CHAPTER XXIII

THE SAN SAVINO—CORIANO RIDGE

At 2 a.m. on the 31st of August a message arrived warning all tanks to be ready to move that evening. It was learnt at a Brigade conference at breakfast time that the Gothic Line had been "bounced" and the advance was progressing with encouraging speed. Consequently, the exploitation force, which was rather far behind, had to move up to a concentration area in the Gothic Line as quickly as possible.

For the sake of speed and mechanical economy it was decided to send the tanks of each regiment in three separate convoys, of which two would go on their tracks and one on transporters. They would assemble at a staging area five miles north of Senigallia and after a twelve-hour halt continue complete to the concentration area near the River Foglia. "B" Echelon was to move after the tanks by a different route, and, with an intermediate halt of four hours only, it was timed to arrive at the River Foglia at the same moment as the tanks. The Regiment was therefore due to be assembled by the morning of the 3rd of September, when battle formations would be adopted.

The story of this move explains in part the fiasco which followed. The fact that we were so far behind was itself unfortunate, and had it been possible to motor straight up the road all might still have been well. As it was, the circumstances could not have been worse.

At 10 p.m. thirteen tanks under Captain Carlisle set out. They crossed the start point at Porto Recanati at midnight and reached the staging area five hours later. Soon after midday on the 1st of September thirty tanks under Major Allhusen pulled out and, loaded on to transporters, reached the staging area in the middle of the night. At 9 p.m. the last of the tanks, including the Reconnaissance Troop, left the leaguer under Major Pulteney's command. Crossing the same start point at 10 p.m., they reached Ancona in safety and turned sharp left up the tank track. This was exceedingly dusty and, as ill-luck would have it, the last tank of Brigade Headquarters just in front, got lost in a cloud of sand and ditched itself in a position so awkward that it could be moved only by a tow from in front. It was impossible for anyone to get by and a bad night followed for Major Pulteney. After two hours he succeeded in contacting a tank ahead which returned to open the road. As a result of this his convoy did not come in until dawn on the 2nd of September.

The echelon left Porto Civitanova at 2 a.m. on the 2nd of September and had a gruelling drive to their staging area near Castelleone, fifteen miles west of the tanks. As it drove in at 10.30 a.m. the personnel and vehicles were covered in Italian dust.

Colonel Macdonell, commanding the Brigade tracks, announced that there would be no move before nightfall. After a short sleep Captain Gregson, accompanied by Major Price, walked over to Eighth Army Headquarters, which was sited in a field across the road. He wanted to visit his brother, Major Charles Gregson, M.C., 12th Lancers, who was then G.S.O.2 (Liaison). Arriving at the armoured command vehicle, he learned that an order had been issued that the march should have been continued and that the Group should by then have been forty miles farther on. It was obvious that all was not well. Presumably we were required to start exploiting very soon and we were not there.

The crews were ready when the order to advance was sent round in the late afternoon, but the echelon, moving under a different command, was taken by surprise. At 3.50 p.m. it was ordered to continue in fifteen minutes; hastily packing up, it managed to do so. In order of march, it was behind the Queen's Bays, but the staff tables for road convoys had been so completely thrown out of gear by now that there were many other road users besides. Mile after mile of lorries nose to tail ground sluggishly on, winding up and down the third-class ravines on third-class roads. Two of the older vehicles boiled, but otherwise there were no breakdowns. As the echelon approached its leaguer at St. Ippolito the dust-cloud became so thick that visibility was reduced to five yards. Eventually it halted on the Metauro river bed and everyone rushed into the deep stream at the side. Some were still there at 10.15 p.m. revelling in its refreshing coolness.

It was some thirty-eight hours since anyone had been to bed, so the echelon thankfully lay down to sleep, but not for long, for at ten minutes after midnight Lieutenant Hainsworth returned from Brigade to say that the march must continue in twenty minutes. The order was slightly altered: the 1st King's Royal Rifle Corps led, followed by all the "A" Echelons, and then all the "B" Echelons. The destination was given as Montecchio and the route "One Bar."

Never before and never since has the echelon undertaken such a perilous and unattractive journey. The hills became steeper, the road narrower, the corners sharper, the dust thicker, and the drivers more weary. As they gained height the hot wind increased to a gale which was almost alarming on the knife-edge mountain ridges along which "One Bar" had been engineered. The heavy armoured command vehicles in front of the column had to reverse to get round corners, which reduced speed to an irksome series of fits and starts. One ammunition lorry overturned and the battery-charging lorry caught on fire. We were indeed fortunate not to lose more. In their fiftieth hour of exertion the last drivers halted by the River Foglia.

The tanks had been even less fortunate. When a soldier is told that his regiment is going to motor up a tank track he knows that the drive will take far longer than it should and that he will get tired and covered in dust. As the miles crawled by it was clear that "Boat Track" was no exception. The worst road is selected for the movement of tanks and "Boat Track" had much more unattractive characteristics than "One Bar." At the time that the echelon was bathing at St. Ippolito the tanks arrived at a point eight miles up-stream, the drivers tired and dusty. Within two hours they, too, were commanded to continue.

To the amateur it sounds easy to say: "Oh, yes, the tanks can motor on." But they have their limitations. They did not only motor that night, they mountaineered as well. The earth, churned into powder, rose in thick, choking clouds hundreds of feet high and hung as an impenetrable fog. Each tank followed the one in front by sound and not by sight. It was not surprising that some got ditched and fell over cliffs, though luckily none of ours. The path was constantly blocked and Captain Gregson in the lead took diversions, some on the spur of the moment, which provided driving problems difficult even by day, but they had to get there. Blindly they rumbled on, straining every nerve to keep on the narrow path. One hundred and fifty tanks in mass create an ear-splitting noise which makes all thought, except about the job in hand, impossible. Tanks burnt four or five gallons of petrol to the mile and consequently a dozen of the oldest ran out of fuel, while others suffered from mechanical failure.

When dawn came it seemed as though some dark age had passed. The tanks began arriving in leaguer, a mile from "B" Echelon, at 8 a.m. The drivers and commanders were in an advanced stage of exhaustion. There was no question of doing any maintenance; they were asleep before they lay down. Fifteen tanks were still out, mostly for lack of petrol, and Captain Mostyn started back to fetch them with petrol loaded on a White half-track. (A White half-track was an American semi-armoured vehicle which carried tracks in place of back wheels, thus giving it a superior cross-country performance to that of an ordinary wheeled vehicle.) Meanwhile, fitters worked without rest on those that needed repair.

Few men can have had so human an insight into the everyday life of a regiment under battle conditions as the Brigadier. We knew that he knew the effects of the past fifty hours. He told us in training that in his experience one of the really vital needs of a regiment was the certain knowledge of how long it would be in one particular spot. Because so often in the past valuable hours had been wasted when this question was left unanswered, he told us to be ready to move tactically grouped at 6.30 in the evening. Although many people had more than enough to do, this at least gave the vast majority of crews a few hours' sleep. In times of unusual strain it is wonderful how a few hours of rest can bring back a high degree of vitality. In the middle of the afternoon everyone was up and in good fettle. We could hear the guns and things did not seem so bad.

At 6.30 p.m. on the fifth anniversary of Great Britain's declaration of war on Germany the 9th Lancers, after over a year's interval, were formed up for battle and ready. At 7.15 we crossed the River Foglia and an hour and a half later went into leaguer five miles to the north-west.

In the course of this move an irate officer of another formation stopped Lance-Corporal Philson, who was quietly doing his job as despatch rider on the echelon, and slanged him without taking breath for ten minutes. His anger seemed to be based on the assumption that the echelon was using the centre line without permission. This was, in fact, an entirely false accusation. Lance-Corporal Philson sat quietly and when he could get a word in replied innocently: "Beg pardon, sir, but in spite of the fact that I am a lance-corporal I was not consulted before the Brigade was sent up this route." No man could have been rebuked more tactfully.

As soon as we arrived in leaguer the Colonel was called to Brigade to receive orders. He issued his own at 11 p.m. The Gothic Line had been broken. The plan was for the Division, led by the 2nd Armoured Brigade, to cross the River Conca that night and reconcentrate in the neighbourhood of San Savino village at dawn, in readiness to pass through the 46th Infantry Division by the River Marano and exploit to the valley beyond. A series of objectives was given, but these were likely to be altered in the light of the situation the next day. The 1st King's Royal Rifle Corps, supported by the 10th Hussars, were to lead this advance and the 9th were at the rear of the Brigade.

The advance began at 1.30 a.m. For us "Reveille" was at 2.30. The traffic was thick in front and the centre line itself on a narrow lane, so progress was slow. We waited patiently with the wireless perpetually screeching in our ear-phones and did not move until 5.45. A convenient thirty-minute traffic block enabled us to eat a welcome breakfast and then we crossed the River Conca. Listening on the Brigade link it was plain that the leading troops were involved in an unexpected delay. The 1st King's Royal Rifle Corps and 10th Hussars were being fairly heavily shelled two miles north of the river and two miles short of San Savino. A change of plan was announced, and the Colonel went to Brigade for new orders at 12.15.

Battle was imminent, and we "brewed up" for lunch. Squadron leaders collected at the Colonel's tank while he explained the forthcoming attack. The enemy had been hit hard; they were tired, depleted, and "on the run." The Brigade was therefore going to attack the San Savino—Coriano Ridge, which was still in enemy hands, with two regiments up, the Bays and 10th Hussars, supported by four field regiments of artillery, 11th H.A.C., and four medium batteries, and then seize crossings over the River Marano. The 1st King's Royal Rifle Corps and "B" Squadron, 9th Lancers, were to exploit success, and the rest of the Regiment was in reserve. At 2.20 p.m. Major Allhusen took his squadron off to join the 1st King's Royal Rifle Corps and the rest of the Brigade began forming up. The attack was due to begin at 3.45 p.m.

It was then that we got into difficulties. One of the reasons for a start line is to allow a force to give itself the best possible send-off. After several changes the start line for this attack ran from a point one mile east of Coriano south-west to San Savino. While approaching this line the 10th Hussars were subjected to accurate shell fire from the ridge in front, and the Bays were engaged from Monte Colombo and Montescudo to their left rear. The latter was of only nuisance value, but as events to our front were disconcerting the attack was postponed until 4.50 p.m. At that hour the barrage came down and the attack began. As the Regiment reached the San Clemente—Cevolabbate Ridge we were surprised to see so many tanks of the leading regiments still there, but the truth was that the start line itself was in enemy hands.

At Cevolabbate there was a superb view of the country ahead, which was composed of a series of ridges and deep valleys. The slopes were steep, in some places sheer, and gashed with impassable gullies. From the Adriatic on the east the ridges became higher and higher, culminating in San Marino on our left. The land was tilled with average intensity, chiefly with vines and maize. The San Savino—Coriano Ridge in front was sharply outlined against the setting sun and the spire of the church on top stood defiantly opposite us. Down in the valley the 10th Hussars were struggling to reach the start line, as were the Bays, only they were hidden by a shoulder of hill.

As events were developing so unexpectedly the Brigadier ordered the 9th to come up in between the two leading regiments and try to capture San Savino. This was going to be a little tricky with only two squadrons and the Reconnaissance Troop under our command, but the lie of the land was ideal for the straightforward tactics of fire and movement. The Colonel ordered "C" Squadron to move on the left and "A" Squadron on the right and support each other forward. Alas, they did not get far. We were of the opinion then—and still are —that we could have succeeded if the crews had been fresh. But after four days and three nights of almost continuous effort gone were their confidence, their high spirits and some of their skill. They had indeed gone "on and on and on, day and night, until they were too exhausted to see the target," not in pursuit of the enemy, however, but in an endeavour to gain victory over time and distance.

Major Pulteney's tank and one other overturned in a gully, and others became hopelessly ditched on the hillsides. We advanced half a mile, but dusk was falling and the day would soon be over. The Colonel was ordered to a conference at Brigade Headquarters. The map reference given was over a mile beyond Coriano, still in enemy hands. It took two hours of hard work by Captain Allen on the rear link to obtain a corrected reference, by which time we were on our way back to Cevolabbate to leaguer. There was only one thing the Regiment needed, and that was a long, sound sleep. It had been a black day. In a matter of minutes the situation had changed from thrilling prospect to disillusionment. There was no disguising the fact that the operation had failed.

At the conference that evening it was decided that the complete Regimental Group should set out to capture the southern end of the San Savino Ridge.

In addition, the Regiment would be supported by the 1st King's Royal Rifle Corps.

On the morning of the 5th of September San Savino looked like a quiet village. The odd shell was bursting here and there, but there was no other movement. At 7 a.m. Captain Gregson and Corporal C. Smith patrolled to the village in their Honeys to ascertain the whereabouts of the enemy. By skilful manœuvring they reached the objective unobserved and surprised a platoon of Germans. They killed a number of these before being subjected to intense mortar fire. Corporal Smith's Honey was "brewed up," but Captain Gregson rescued the crew before coming home, and killed some more Germans on the way. His information was invaluable.

By 8 o'clock the Regiment was formed up. "A" and "C" Squadrons were in position five hundred yards in front of Cevolabbate cross-roads, well placed to give direct fire support to "B" Squadron, which was to make the assault. Major Morris had arrived at Regimental Headquarters and was ready to help with artillery, but there was no sign of any infantry. After an hour's wait the Colonel decided to begin without them.

1st, 3rd and 4th Troops, "B" Squadron, started into the valley in line abreast at ten minutes past nine, supported by 2nd Troop and Squadron Headquarters. Picking its way down the steep slopes, the squadron reached the treacherous wadi at the bottom. Two tanks of Lieutenant Birch-Reynardson's 4th Troop lost tracks, but the remainder got through and at once encountered bazooka-men hiding in vines and haystacks. This clearly indicated the need for infantry, so a halt was made. One platoon of "C" Company, led by Lieutenant David House, arrived and performed yeoman service for the rest of the day, ably directed by Major James Cunningham from Regimental Headquarters. Meanwhile, a new artillery fire plan was worked out for "B" Squadron's uphill assault. The Colonel ordered the attack to continue at 11 o'clock, and the Brigadier came to watch it from our command tank, "Scylla."

And then a tragedy happened. Colonel J. R. Macdonell, D.S.O. and Bar, was killed. Shelling had been intermittent all the morning and it was sometimes necessary to duck into the turret. One shell in "A" Echelon had already killed Corporal Cowie, Lance-Corporal Hayden and Trooper Pimm. At 11.10 the Germans fired the shot which to the 9th Lancers was the most evil shot of the war. By chance it struck the front of the Brigade command tank and blasted the wooden dummy gun back into the turret, where Colonel Macdonell was working. It was a terrible blow to the 9th, and the whole Brigade lost a very great friend. He had had the opportunity to return to England, but preferred to stay and fight beside his Regiment and his friends. His place could never be filled. The Colonel considered that this news would be so great a shock to the 9th Lancers that he did not send it over the wireless during the attack. When they heard, the heart went out of their day.

The second phase of our attack went in at 11 o'clock as planned. Bazookamen and snipers were much in evidence and progress was slow. Some of those who were not killed gave themselves up and were a great embarrassment on account of the inadequate infantry. 3rd Troop, under Lieutenant John Joicey, was held up by bazookas in front of a vineyard below the church. 1st Troop worked up the Agello—San Savino road on the left. Sergeant Thomas's tank was hit by a bazooka which seriously wounded Lance-Corporal Rooney, and Sergeant Thomas himself later lost an eye as a result of it. However, Lieutenant Peter Caro and Sergeant Parfitt continued. A Mark IV, as it transpired later, knocked out the troop leader's tank and all his crew were reported missing. Later it was found that they were prisoners, except Trooper Powell, who succeeded in regaining our lines the same day. Sergeant Parfitt quickly reversed and dealt with numerous Germans as he extricated himself from the village. 2nd Troop, commanded by Lieutenant John Goldsmid, moved up into 1st Troop's place, thirty yards from the cemetery on the extreme left of the village and near the end of the ridge. Whenever they advanced farther they were greeted by a hail of armour-piercing shells. There were Germans hiding in the sunken road between the church and cemetery, and Corporal Moffat got his Honey in a position to fire down the road at them. After a few minutes his tank was hit and set on fire and the crew were killed.

The situation then settled down. Shelling was light and a counter-attack was expected any minute. Two patrols of the Reconnaissance Troop went up to watch the flanks; "A" Squadron advanced on to "B" Squadron's right; a section of Lieutenant House's platoon tried to clear the church, but was forced to withdraw, as it was weak in numbers. The persistent enemy began to infiltrate back down hedgerows and vines, and this demanded intense vigilance. Speed was vital; the members of "B" Squadron either saw the bazookaman or sniper within three seconds of his taking aim and shot him within the next two, or they were shot themselves. Lieutenant Newman careered about in his Honey inflicting many casualties and seemed to be thoroughly enjoying himself.

We had asked for infantry from the moment "B" Squadron was approaching the ridge, and even before. Certainly the Colonel had been led to expect them the night before, and during the day he repeatedly described the situation and the nature of the country, appealing in the strongest terms for at least one battalion. This demand was passed on by Brigade, but no one appeared. The 1st Buffs were promised us, but they were still miles behind. They were urgently needed to prevent the enemy from stalking "B" Squadron's tanks and to defend the ridge against counter-attack. Until they should come, our position remained in grave danger. The crews had never had to be so alert before, and Major Morris gave his battery no rest. With his "ack" Bombardier Bennett he worked behind "Scylla" all day in a jeep which afforded no security whatever from the crumps and bangs. Major Morris put down defensive fire all the afternoon, and in the evening had fifty guns firing for us in addition to his own battery. To land shells just over the ridge was difficult and sometimes they landed only sixty yards in front of "B" Squadron, but in the absence of infantry there was no alternative.

As darkness fell the 1st Buffs arrived and were guided forward from San Clemente by the Reconnaissance Troop. As they were getting into position our own shells caused them a number of casualties. "A" Squadron then relieved "B," who retired in line ahead, negotiating the ditch successfully in spite of the darkness, the rough going, the shelling and enemy patrols, and joined the Regimental leaguer just behind San Clemente.

"C" Squadron on the left of Regimental Headquarters had had some good shooting. Captain Carlisle and his gunner, Corporal Allen, between them destroyed two German tanks. After that most of Captain Carlisle's fire orders began: "Reference my last 'brew' but one." The squadron also knocked down the church tower, which was thought to harbour a German observation post, and shot-up all the places likely to endanger "B" Squadron's advance.

It had been a great day for "B" Squadron. They had captured sixty prisoners, killed thirty Germans, including six bazookamen on the point of taking aim, and above all captured the southern end of the San Savino Ridge. What is more, they had done it with a mere handful of infantry, whose leader was later awarded the Military Cross for his gallantry. The cost to us was one Sherman and two Honeys destroyed, and five Shermans ditched (later recovered). Lieutenant Caro was missing and Second-Lieutenant The Viscount Stuart was seriously wounded in the head. He died in hospital and the Regiment lost one of its most lively and cheerful troop leaders. In addition, the casualties among other ranks were: Troopers Baylis and Webster killed, Corporal C. Smith and Trooper Wilson wounded, and Corporal Williams, Lance-Corporals Cliff and Morris missing, later reported prisoners.

Just before dawn on the 6th the 18th Infantry Brigade, supported by the 10th Hussars and "A" Squadron, made an unsuccessful attack on San Savino village, and then dug in on the reverse slopes. Owing to the noise and dust created by tanks on the move, the infantry would not permit "A" Squadron to leave the forward area until 7.15 p.m.

On the 7th of September the Brigadier visited all squadrons and congratulated them on their performance. He explained the attack by the 43rd Gurkha Brigade which was going to take place that night, and described the help needed from us. "C" Squadron was given the task of indirect firing. Having found a suitable gun position, Lieutenant Thwaites drove his tank out and tested for crest clearance. His first shot hit a house on the skyline and three Germans emerged to surrender. This incident gave us the probable explanation of the continual and accurate shelling in our leaguer which had seriously wounded Lance-Corporal Geary and several others that morning.

The attack by the Gurkhas was postponed for a week to conform to a V Corps plan. While this was being prepared there were several warnings of counterattacks. The worst threat necessitated "C" Squadron motoring forward to fire positions, and Lieutenant Newman, acting as liaison officer with the 7th Armoured Brigade on our left, was "brewed up" in his Honey for the third time in four days, but escaped without a scratch.

After a night under a rain of spent anti-aircraft shrapnel the Regiment relieved the 10th Hussars on San Savino Ridge on the 10th of September, under command of the 18th Infantry Brigade. "C" Squadron was forward under command of the 1st Buffs, and got into position by 5.50 a.m. "B" Squadron remained on the Cevolabbate Ridge, ready to come up and fire if trouble began. Regimental Headquarters was split for the first time into Tactical and Main. Tactical consisted of the Colonel, Adjutant, Intelligence Officer, two tanks, the command White car, two scout cars and a jeep. It was in fact the minimum headquarters from which the Colonel could command the Regiment. The rest of the Regimental Headquarters was left at Main, often under the Second-in-Command. This sub-division was convenient and easy to manage.

Major Price and Captain Donnley used to visit Tactical Regimental Headquarters and procure their dinner on the way. They were adept at catching young cockerels to supplement their rations, which were never quite adequate under battle conditions when the minimum working day was about seventeen hours. In fact, whenever the Second-in-Command went "swanning" in his jeep he was certain to return with something worth eating.

Sergeant Maloney returned from the Royal Military College, where he had been since recovering from his wounds received at Kournine, and was appointed Sergeant-Major of "A" Squadron.

An analysis of casualties shows that the number incurred by unexpected "stonks" was disproportionately high compared with those resulting from direct anti-tank-gun fire. When a tank is in position hour after hour, just observing, interest wanes. It is sometimes an irresistible temptation to get out and visit next-door tanks, sometimes a necessity. That day two unfortunate "stonks" cost "C" Squadron nine casualties. All of them were dismounted for one reason or another. While mending a track Captain Carlisle, Lieutenant Thwaites and Troopers Brown and Legg were all wounded, also Lance-Corporal Pritchard when he was in the Main Regimental Headquarters leaguer. Just before 9.30 p.m. another shell killed Lieutenant Buchan and Corporal Moore and wounded Troopers Butler and Storr, the latter dying later. Captain Tubbs was standing five yards away, but was not touched.

The next day, the 11th of September, the 7th Armoured Brigade took over the commitments of "C" Squadron, which returned with Tactical Regimental Headquarters to the main leaguer. This was not as comfortable as it might have been because the Brigade area was bombarded with shells, but fortunately eighty per cent. were duds.

At 6 p.m. on the 11th "A" Squadron, after extensive reconnaissances and a patrol by Lieutenant Moule, moved to the 18th Infantry Brigade assembly area behind San Clemente. At 7.40 "B" Squadron took part in the cover plan and motored about on the top of Cevolabbate Ridge to attract the enemy's attention. At 7.50 Regimental Headquarters moved through dense traffic to the spot it had vacated twenty-four hours earlier. At 11 p.m., after four twenty-minute artillery concentrations from four hundred and sixty guns, the attack began. The Canadians captured Coriano; the Gurkhas, supported by the Bays, captured Passano in the centre of the ridge; and the 18th Infantry Brigade, supported by "A" Squadron, at last secured San Savino itself. At dawn fighting was confused, but by 4 o'clock the ridge was entirely in our hands and one thousand prisoners as well. "A" Squadron had greatly assisted in clearing San Savino village, demolishing houses and firing much ammunition. The Regiment then moved up one; "B" Squadron to the bottom of San Savino Ridge and "C" Squadron to Cevolabbate.

At 4.10 p.m. on the 12th the 9th Lancers, with the full Regimental Group and followed by the 1st King's Royal Rifle Corps, were ordered to seize Ripa Bianca Ridge overlooking the River Marano. While Regimental Headquarters and "C" Squadron were advancing to San Savino the command tank "Scylla" seized up and the command crew had to change on to the Second-in-Command's tank. The Regiment was ready by 5 p.m. and under considerable artillery and mortar fire. There was no sign of the infantry, so we were told to go cautiously forward.

"B" Squadron and one section of the Reconnaissance Troop led. While navigating the dangerous forward slopes they ran into a minefield and at the same time came under a heavy artillery concentration. Three tanks received direct hits and six were knocked out in about ten minutes. Visibility was reduced to nil on account of the dust and smoke. By some miracle no one was hurt, but progress was impossible on account of the mines. Then a message came over the air from Main Brigade that the attack was postponed. "B" Squadron took up the best positions possible and waited for the infantry. As the moon got up at about 10.30 p.m. it slowly made its way back to leaguer, bringing its dehorsed crews and arriving about half an hour after midnight. The Germans shelled the forward slopes all night.

After Regimental Headquarters had sorted out its vehicles and "B" Squadron its crews, we slept until 6 a.m. on the 13th, when a message arrived that the 18th Infantry Brigade, with the 9th Lancers and 1st King's Royal Rifle Corps under command, were to achieve the task we had embarked on alone the night before. The Colonel got his orders from Brigadier Erskine. Only one squadron was required to support the 1st Buffs, so Major Steel took his. He lost two tanks early on owing to bad going, and a third to a mine. Progress was slow, though the troops on our right and left were making good headway.

Tactical Regimental Headquarters, consisting of the command White scout car, the Intelligence Officer's scout car and Major Morris's tank, established themselves at 18th Brigade Headquarters. This was shelled with consistent accuracy, probably because heavy wireless traffic was being transmitted. At five minutes to one o'clock an 88-mm. landed on the command car's bonnet. The Colonel was crouching just outside and was unfortunately wounded in the hand. The Adjutant and Sergeant Jenner were hurled to the floor amidst broken glass and choking smoke. After a five-second black-out Sergeant Jenner came up on the air with characteristic imperturbability:

"Roger 7, take over, please—over." (Roger 7 was the Second-in-Command.)
"Roger 7. O.K.—out," came the answer.

Thus relieved of responsibility of command, we surveyed the damage. There was a casualty clearing station in the farmhouse, so the Colonel got speedy attention among other and more serious victims, but he was told that he would have to be evacuated. The command car was in fragments, the second one in ten days. Major Price was sent for, and in twenty minutes he arrived in his tank, to assume temporary command of the Regiment. Tactical Regimental Head-quarters then decided to move.

"A" and "B" Squadrons, which had not moved far from night leaguer, also suffered through enemy shelling. Lieutenant Moule, Sergeants Dickinson and Dow and Lance-Corporals Flinn and Jones were wounded. Sergeant Dickinson died later—a great loss to his many friends.

The tactical situation was that the 1st King's Royal Rifle Corps and the 1st Buffs were almost on their objectives, but about ten Panthers and self-propelled guns were pin-pointed in among them and these the artillery could not engage because the infantry were too close. "C" Squadron did all that was possible to help the infantry forward. After it had tried three different ways, losing a tank each time, Brigadier Erskine realized that it could do no more. The squadron had a very unpleasant day and Sergeant Winch, Corporal Pickles and Lance-Corporals Swan, Allen and Pulman were killed. Major Steel was himself "brewed up," again without injury, but three of the above casualties were in his crew.

During the night of the 13th the infantry consolidated the objectives, though they failed to destroy the Panthers. "C" Squadron had the task of advancing at dawn to give anti-tank protection to the infantry. A hazardous wadi barred the path over which the sappers prepared a crossing. Four tanks got over, but the two H.A.C. observation-post tanks got bogged. An attempt to overturn them failed. It was essential to clear them, as many other vehicles had to pass that way, and after two hours' delay a bulldozer arrived to make a new crossing. Intermittent shelling went on all night. The Commanding Officer visited "C" Squadron after breakfast and, on relief by "A" Squadron, "C" was back by 2 p.m.

The Brigade Major visited the Regiment and spoke of the attack by the 43rd Gurkha Brigade and the 10th Hussars across the River Marano which was due to go in at 7.30 p.m. that night (the 14th). They expected to get to Mulaz-zano Hill without difficulty and then the Division was to have a few days' rest and refit until another break-through was almost complete, when we would

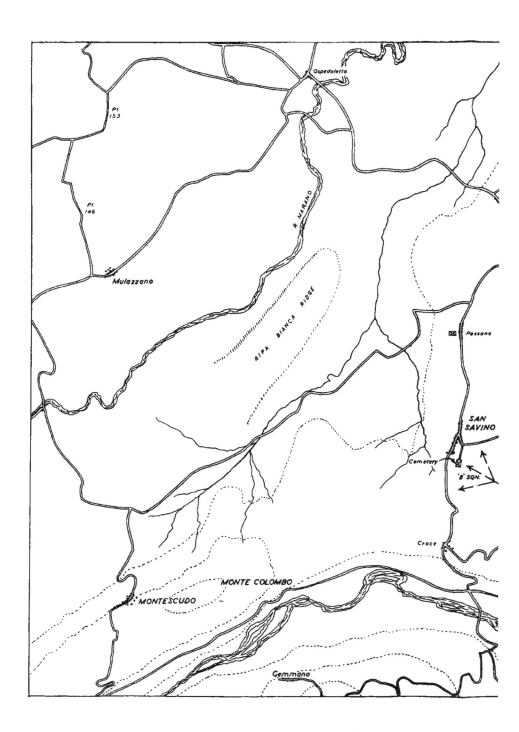

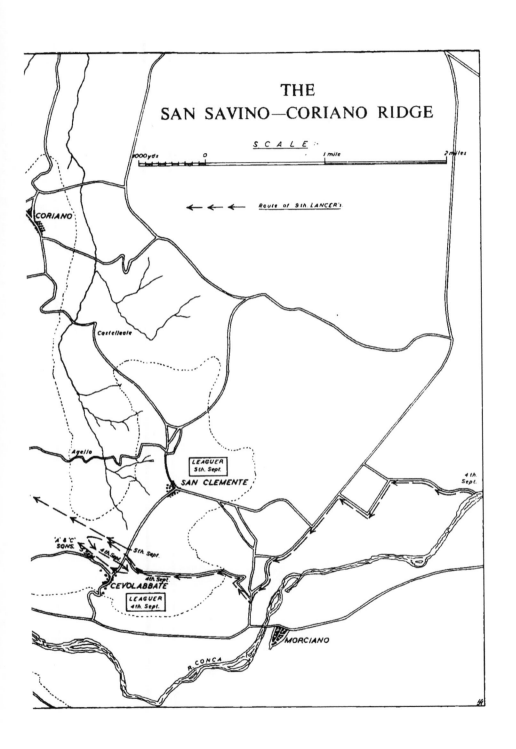

THE
SAN SAVINO—CORIANO RIDGE

S C A L E

1000 yds   O   1 mile   2 miles

← ← ←   Route of 9th LANCER's

CORIANO

Castelleale

Agello

LEAGUER
5th. Sept.

SAN CLEMENTE

4th.
Sept.

'A' & 'C'
SQNS.

4th. Sept.   5th. Sept.

4th. Sept.

CEVOLABBATE

LEAGUER
4th. Sept.

MORCIANO

R. CONCA

again attempt exploitation. We were still eager and determined, but any mention of the Po fell on rather sceptical ears.

Captain Foy worked hard all day recovering the ditched tanks on Cevolabbate Ridge. They had nearly all been looted, but we got back the most essential kit. The supply of tanks was excellent, better than we had ever known it before. The only trouble was the dirty condition in which they arrived, but "B" Echelon lent a hand to the crews in cleaning them.

The attack was successful and on the 16th of September "A" Squadron came back to the rest of the Regiment, which was now completely disengaged. Our leaguer was just below San Savino and Brigadier Goodbody ordered us to spend two days resting and preparing for further battle. Fifteen new tanks arrived, including six 105-mm.'s, also ten reinforcements. "A" Echelon came and leaguered with the tanks. The orderly room came up and paper work was brought up to date.

The last seventeen days had gone quickly: the frightful drive, the fatigue and disappointment, the hard fight and the watching; and now the capture of the ridge and valley beyond.

The famous Gothic Line had been breached on the Eighth Army front and a break-through achieved, but a number of natural obstacles still lay in our path before we could hope to reach the Po Valley proper. On the opposite coast the Fifth Army had progressed slowly through Lucca and were in contact with the Gothic Line. The Germans, however, were putting up a stiff resistance and made a strenuous effort to plug the hole that had been drilled by the Eighth Army. The weather, which had been perfect, was expected to break any day. That would be a grave disadvantage to us. Could we dislodge the enemy from their next position, not only before they were ready for us but before the rain? It was decided that there was a reasonable chance. If luck was on our side we still might achieve a break-through; if luck was against us no harm could be done.

CHAPTER XXIV

POINT 153

Meanwhile a further effort to reach the Po Valley was being planned and during most of the 18th the Commanding Officer was at Divisional Headquarters gaining information and receiving orders.

The Brigade was ordered to capture Point 153, some six miles south-west of Rimini, as a prelude to the plan of pursuit. The Canadians were to capture the conical hill of Fortunato on our right, and the 7th Armoured Brigade was in support of an infantry attack on our immediate left. The 1st King's Royal Rifle Corps and the Bays, supported, of course, by the 11th H.A.C., were to carry out the assault, followed by the 9th Lancers, whose exact employment would depend upon events.

The forming-up place for the attack was ten miles away and the following is an extract from the War Diary of that day: "The difficulty is for everyone to get where they ought to be by dawn, for there is no moon; the roads are inches deep in dust; bridges are blown and diversions frequent; and every formation seems to be using the same road. The events planned to take place from to-morrow morning onwards are based on the movements that are to be carried out in the next ten hours under conditions so unfavourable that the outcome cannot be foreseen with any degree of certainty."

The expected delays occurred, but at 5 a.m. on the 19th of September we were put at one hour's notice to move.

During the morning the attack was further postponed, but when it was learnt that the dominating Fortunato feature on our right and Point 146 on our left had been partly taken, the Bays Group was ordered to attack at 2 p.m. Owing to the exceptionally difficult going, they were unable to get far before nightfall, so they prepared for an assault at first light.

Meanwhile, the 9th Lancers began their approach march at 4.15 p.m. on the 19th. In San Savino itself there was a traffic block and, as we continued, the various bits of the Regimental Group tagged on behind the column. At 8.5 p.m. we were in position on the north side of the River Marano at Ospedaletto. Fifteen minutes later we were ordered to continue to our forming-up place behind the Bays in readiness for the "first-light" attack. We were under heavy artillery fire all the way, particularly at the crossing over the River Ausa. An "A" Squadron tank caused a blockage there, but a bulldozer quickly reopened the route. Several houses and haystacks were on fire around us, which was indicative of stalwart resistance. For the first time in Italy artificial moonlight was used to help our move. We went into leaguer at 1 a.m. on the 20th of September and filled up with petrol.

During the night patrols of the 1st King's Royal Rifle Corps had determined that Point 153 was strongly held, so the Bays advanced cautiously. Before light, on their way to the start line, they had lost several Honeys to armour-piercing fire, and as dawn broke they were heavily engaged from high ground on their left rear which had been reported as clear. They met strong opposition as they tried to get on to the ridge from which they were to launch their attack. As on the 4th of September, the Brigade plan was based on inaccurate information. Now that the facts were known, the plan was readjusted and the Bays were ordered to capture the ridge which was to have been their start line. Against resolute opposition from every type of gun they succeeded in winning the reverse slopes at the expense of considerable casualties. It then seemed pretty clear that the tanks could not capture Point 153 that day. However, in order to conform to the V Corps plan, in which speed was of vital importance, the Bays were ordered to attack again within fifteen minutes. The 9th Lancers, who had been supporting the Bays with "A" Squadron from a ridge behind, were ordered to send one squadron forward under command of the Bays to help them. "B" Squadron, after sniping a German tank from the ridge in front of Regimental Headquarters, was selected for this, while the rest of the Regiment was to be prepared to follow up and pass through the Bays. This delayed the start until 10.50 a.m.

To those who were watching, the result was a foregone conclusion. The Bays gallantly drove over the top of the hill and were met by devastating fire. The forward slope was bare, affording no protection whatsoever, while the supporting tanks on the ridge were equally exposed. The Bays were reduced to eighteen tanks in a matter of minutes, and suffered heavy casualties in crews, who were machine-gunned and sniped as they jumped from their burning vehicles. Major Allhusen then issued his orders over the air for "B" Squadron to follow suit—an advance which seemed to have no future.

Such was the situation when the 9th Lancers were ordered to pass through. To make matters worse, the command tank shed a track, so another hasty change was made, this time under heavy artillery fire. The command crew was installed in four minutes, during which time the Commanding Officer discussed the situation with Lieutenant-Colonel Asquith, Queen's Bays. He then spoke on the air to the Brigadier and suggested that, whereas he could repeat the performance of the Bays with similar consequences, it was obviously desirable to begin from another point. He waited anxiously for the answer while he pored over the map, amid explosions whose suffocating fumes pervaded the turret. It came: "Hold on to the ground already won."

"B" Squadron now reverted to the Regiment's command and took up a position just below the ridges. Then came Regimental Headquarters and behind them "C" Squadron, while "A" Squadron remained in support.

P

From the moment we came up behind the Bays enemy shelling was intense, but it caused us only two losses: Major Pulteney, commanding "A" Squadron at the rear, was one; an 88-mm. landed in front of his tank, shattering his binoculars and earphones, but luckily only one bit of shrapnel hit his face. Major James Cunningham, commanding "C" Company, 1st King's Royal Rifle Corps, was also wounded; he was a great loss to us.

The country was ideal for concealed Spandaus and snipers, who quickly engaged any tank commander who put his head out too far. The going was more perilous than ever; the slopes and the ditches were steeper, though the ridges themselves were lower; in our area there were many places where a tank could not go at all. Enemy infantry and tanks were infiltrating up the forward slopes and sniping at us from the top. Captain Kemp motored forward on to the ridge in his scout car and tended the wounded crews of the Bays. In one house which he entered he was attacked by a German sniper. For his courage that day he was later awarded the Military Cross.

Eventually the 14th Foresters came up to take over from the 1st King's Royal Rifle Corps. By 4 o'clock the shelling was very much lighter, a thick concentration arriving only about every ten or fifteen minutes. The necessary reconnaissances were made in safety, and three troops of "B" Squadron remained forward for the night of the 20th in support of the infantry.

When it was getting dark and all seemed settled we were ready to go into leaguer, so the Commanding Officer ordered "A" Squadron and the Reconnaissance Troop to leaguer in the place they had occupied the night before. Soon after 9 p.m. Regimental Headquarters, with "C" Squadron, began moving there too, leaving "B" Squadron to help the infantry.

Scarcely had we gone a mile and a half when the rain came down, the rain which was destined to impede our every move during the next six months. It was abnormal rain. Within ten minutes the countryside was transformed into a quagmire and not a tank in the Regiment could move. All crews closed down their wireless sets and endeavoured to spend as dry a night as they could where they were.

The bleak, wet morning of the 21st found us somewhat dejected, but there was an element of humour about it as well. The crews dismounted under an overcast sky to take stock of the situation. The first thing to do was to eat breakfast; the second to see if we could extricate ourselves. Both were achieved, the latter thanks to the skill of Sergeant Rule, the Fitter Sergeant of "C" Squadron, but it was a long process. The tanks were in line ahead on a steady slope facing uphill. Starting from the rear, each reversed or skidded down on to the road at the bottom. We continued up the road for a mile, and eventually reached our leaguer. Captain Mostyn had succeeded in getting petrol, ammunition, water and food to the leaguer, and every tank filled up as it turned off the road. Tarpaulins were rigged up as tents, ditches were dug to prevent water running into the blankets, and clothes were changed as far as possible. Practically the whole Division was immobile except on the roads, and later in the day even they became impassable to some vehicles.

Meanwhile, "B" Squadron had spent a quiet night, though the 14th Foresters did not arrive complete until 3 a.m. During the 21st this battalion advanced unmolested to the objective. A Polish deserter surrendered to them and said that the Germans had withdrawn over the River Marechia. If it could be called a joke, the laugh was on us, for we were no longer physically able to pursue. "B" Squadron withdrew to a farmhouse which they described as "untouched by the war" and dried themselves out.

Regimental Headquarters was next to a battered farmhouse. The infantry occupied the farm buildings, for they did not have so much as a tarpaulin for protection. Though the houses were full of insects and rats, these were better companions than rain. We called this leaguer "Muddy Field," not because it was worse than any other but because it was the scene of our initiation into the refinements of Italian wet weather.

From a conference at Brigade the Commanding Officer brought unexpected news: Brigadier Goodbody was leaving the Brigade, a matter of great regret to the whole Regiment, and the 1st Armoured Division was to be broken up. Naturally this was a shock. It was the original armoured division in the British Army, had been in existence for over seven years, and possessed unique traditions which all ranks had given much to win.

Thus the White Rhino was handed down to the 2nd Independent Armoured Brigade, to whom it had originally belonged.

CHAPTER XXV

FIUMICINO

ON the 26th of September the new Brigade Commander, Brigadier J. F. B. Combe, D.S.O., accompanied by his Second-in-Command, Colonel Peter Payne-Gallwey, D.S.O., visited the Regiment. The Brigadier addressed all officers and tank commanders on the Regimental Headquarters melon bed, which happened to be the driest spot in Muddy Field. He told us that the 2nd Armoured Brigade was now under command of the 46th Division, that the 9th Lancers would be under command of the 128th Infantry Brigade, and that we would probably begin fighting again in a few days' time.

Once again we prepared. The tanks were cleaned and mended. Reinforcements arrived and were divided between squadrons and the Reconnaissance Troop. The Medical Officer's "troop," in contrast to the amenities at his disposal in the desert, now consisted of two armoured half-tracked cars fitted with stretchers, one jeep with two stretchers, one 15-cwt. truck, one three-ton medical store lorry, and for himself an armoured scout car fitted with a wireless. "B" Squadron rejoined, new tanks arrived, and each squadron got two 105-mm. tanks, while 17-pounder tanks were promised to us shortly.

Several expeditions were made to the independent State of San Marino, which was surrounded by police endeavouring with partial success to prevent British troops violating neutral territory.

One morning a liaison officer arrived from the 128th Infantry Brigade. For close co-operation in battle the essential condition is that everyone should know everyone else, not merely by name and by sight but as a person. Often this is difficult, and obviously depends upon the time available. Whenever there was time our officers got to know their opposite numbers in the infantry. The 128th (Hampshire) Infantry Brigade consisted of the 2nd, 1st/4th and 5th Battalions of the Hampshire Regiment. It was commanded by Brigadier Kendrew, who in earlier years played rugger for England. On the 27th of September two officers from each battalion visited the Regiment. Numerous tactical problems were discussed on a squadron level and detailed methods of communication and target indication were worked out.

It would be true to say that the infantry regarded tanks with some suspicion, as they had not always been well served by them. From the outset, therefore, and in spite of our inexperience, we were determined to support them in every way possible.

The axis of advance of the 46th Division was in a north-westerly direction along the foothills of the Apennine Mountains on the edge of the Po Valley. The original plan was for the Hampshires, with the 9th Lancers under command, to take over a sector of the line just west of the River Uso from the 139th Brigade (also in the 46th Division) on the 28th of September. This was slightly amended on that date and at first the 5th Hampshires advanced alone to help the 139th Brigade against further counter-attacks, two respectable ones having been launched the night before. The 128th Brigade also moved their headquarters forward and Tactical Regimental Headquarters conformed, leaving Major Allhusen in command of the tanks with brief instructions for their future moves. A wireless link with them was maintained. Major Steel and Captain Peek, commanding "C" and "A" Squadrons respectively, followed Tactical Regimental Headquarters so that they could receive orders and make preparations while their squadrons were on the move the next day.

It rained hard on the 29th. Lorries without chains were unable to move uphill, traffic became blocked and interference obstructed wireless traffic at even normal range. The command and rear-link tanks made remarkable progress along the tank track, arriving before dark. The River Marecchia was rising rapidly and some vehicles were unable to cross. However, by 9.15 a.m. all Tactical Regimental Headquarters had reached a brick factory, half a mile from the 128th Brigade Headquarters.

Captain Mostyn arrived at breakfast time on the 30th of September with the news that the River Marecchia was a torrent five feet deep and all crossing places were impassable. There were only two bridges, one at Timini and one four miles up-stream on the 4th Indian Division front. The tank track was quite impassable, so the Regiment did not expect to move, as the existing roads were too valuable to cut up. At 11 a.m. the Commanding Officer learnt that the proposed attack on Montalbano was postponed for one night, but that the Hampshire Brigade had begun taking over a sector of the line. Before the wireless had become unserviceable a message was got through to the tanks ordering them to be ready at 6 a.m. the next day.

At 10 p.m. the Adjutant was summoned to the telephone. The enemy was reported to be withdrawing from Montalbano Hill immediately in front of the 128th Brigade. Was it possible, inquired Major Brian Harris, the Brigade Major, for one squadron to motor up that night in readiness to support the 5th Hampshires, who as a result of this information were going to advance on to Montalbano at dawn? Very reluctantly the Adjutant explained that under the existing conditions of ground and weather such an operation was unlikely to succeed, although we were prepared to try it. It was unfortunate to have to shy at the first request made upon us, but under such unfavourable conditions night moves always end in tears. Major Harris discussed the question with Brigadier Kendrew, and then asked us to send off one squadron at 5 a.m. This was agreed at once and Lieutenant Hainsworth drove back to the tanks with detailed orders.

By 5.30 a.m. on the 1st of October "A" Squadron was well on its way, and at 7 a.m. "B" and "C" Squadrons left Muddy Field and reached the brickworks in two hours.

The 5th Hampshires had started their advance at dawn, but found elements of the enemy still on Montalbano Hill. "A" Squadron sent one troop to their assistance. One tank was blown up on the way, in spite of the fact that the road had been swept for mines and the two leading tanks had driven over the same spot. However, in spite of this tank being ditched, the troops were reinforced successfully. The 5th Hampshires did not use the troop at first and secured Montalbano Hill by lunch time. A second troop was then ordered up the road, which ran over half a mile south of our axis. This had not been mine-swept, so 2nd Troop, 1st Field Squadron, R.E., in support of the 9th Lancers, began work. They reckoned to take two hours, but the local inhabitants turned up trumps by announcing that they had put a bamboo stake over each mine after the enemy laid them, for the benefit of their own farm carts, and this considerably accelerated the work.

Appreciating that the enemy had withdrawn over the River Fiumicino, the 128th Brigade made quick plans that afternoon for the 2nd Hampshires to cross that river and capture the next objective, Montilgallo, supported from first light onwards by "A" Squadron. The 2nd Hampshires reached the river without incident, but it was plain that Montilgallo Hill, half a mile beyond, was strongly held. The forward troops of "A" Squadron could not help much, as the exact positions of the leading infantry were not known, visibility was bad and movement was slow because of scattered mines. However, it was only a matter of time before these difficulties were overcome, and the infantry were delighted to see the tanks in position, though they gave them no specific task to fulfil. "A" and "C" Squadrons resorted to indirect fire, with Lieutenant Whately and Captain Reid acting as observers. A battery of nebelwerfers was engaged and one was claimed as knocked out. All houses unfavourably regarded by the infantry were destroyed, and a camouflaged gun, observed by the colonel of the 2nd Hampshires, was hit. Numerous other targets, infantry and self-propelled guns, were engaged. At first the infantry were a bit sceptical about our ability as gunners, but by midday they were indicating more targets than we could cope with.

It had by then become clear that an attack on a larger scale was necessary, so it was decided to await the V Corps attack on the next night, the 2nd of October. Meanwhile, in order to try to ascertain the enemy defensive fire plan, concentrations of artillery were fired which produced retaliation but no damage. Crossings over the river were also reconnoitred during the night. 128th Brigade Headquarters moved up under the lee of Montalbano Hill and Tactical Regimental Headquarters went too, setting up shop across the road in a field. "B" and "C" Squadrons crossed the River Uso and leaguered on the first lateral road, as movement across country was impossible. The infantry temporarily dispensed with "A" Squadron's services and they also withdrew to the Uso lateral.

The next day, the 2nd of October, the attack was put off until the 7th, but the Commanding Officer attended many conferences and produced many suggestions as to how the 9th Lancers might help. Air photographs were invaluable, the usual practice being to have the map on one side of a board and the corresponding photographs on the other. The route of each tank was then marked in and the commanders concerned actually had their route pointed out to them on the ground from the observation post in Montalbano. It should here be explained that such minute detail had not usually been possible or even necessary before. But now the number of routes passable to tanks was so very small that we could tell the infantry exactly what we could do.

The problem of crossing the river was the primary concern of our tanks, and an "Ark" was asked for. An Ark is a turretless Churchill tank with long ramps on each end. It is driven into a river and the ramps are then let down on either bank. Its efficiency depends on the height of the banks above the river bed, forty feet being a fair span. On this occasion no Ark was available, so we collected more sleepers and tied them on the tanks to drop into the river bed. All landmarks were given code names to facilitate control. As the days went by and the plot developed, everyone's map became almost invisible under a maze of chinagraph marking that looked like some exotic doodle.

As soon as the postponement was announced, Tactical Regimental Headquarters moved back to the main tank leaguer. As usual, the White car was bogged and while being towed out a "stonk" arrived and wounded Corporal Norris, the driver.

That night most of the Regiment gathered in "C" Squadron's tiny house. We had to sleep under cover to keep dry and were packed close, but nobody minded. Two days later our neighbours, the 46th Reconnaissance Regiment, moved out of their billets and the Regiment was able to expand. "B" Squadron had been living in Camerano Church for several days and the local Father was relieved to see them move into more secular surroundings.

While waiting to attack, indirect fire was carried on each day. Whatever effect this may have had on the battle, it was at least good practice. Houses on Montalbano Hill were admirable observation posts and genuine targets were legion. The gun position on the Uso lateral road was ideal because no tank had to move from its position in leaguer. All houses in the path of battle were destroyed, and any movement seen was instantly engaged. Remote-control mechanisms for the wireless led out from three or more scout cars to a house actually on the hill-top. We had many visitors and every room facing west and north on both floors was crammed with officers craning their necks to get the best view. One morning a certain officer (of "B" Squadron, they say) caused alarm and despondency among his brother "observation posts" by putting down on to them five accurate rounds of gunfire from eight 75-mm.'s. All the assurances of Captain Laurie failed to persuade them that his squadron was innocent. One day we emptied the ammunition point of 105-mm. and the R.A.S.C. thought we were involved in a terrific battle. But it was excellent practice and a good occupation for all.

Major Gardner made frequent visits from "B" Echelon, bringing with him clothes, groceries and almost anything anybody asked for. His task was thankless. In that rain the echelon was bogged anywhere except on roads. V Corps laid down devious traffic circuits and, although "B" Echelon was only three miles away by the shortest route, it took two hours to reach the tanks. He was constantly asked to send up this man's socks and that man's shirts, and to see to piles of laundry. In addition, he had to produce gallons of petrol and tons of ammunition, and deal with the piles of paper the Adjutant had no time to tackle. The commander of "B" Echelon was a versatile man.

The day before the battle Lieutenant-Colonel Perry returned from hospital. He did not take command of the Regiment at once, since Major Price had been responsible for all the preparations.

On the afternoon of the 7th of October "A" and "C" Squadrons moved to their forming-up places. They did not use the tank track for fear of bogging and fortunately no one complained about their using the road. Only these two squadrons were to be employed in direct support of the infantry. "B" Squadron was to fire indirect. Tactical Regimental Headquarters now returned to 128th Brigade Headquarters. The weather had been fair for four days, and if it continued there was every chance of our movement becoming less restricted. Zero hour was 7.15 p.m.

"B" Squadron opened fire at 7.10 p.m. and in thirty minutes dispatched two thousand rounds. Their target was the eastern end of Montilgallo Hill and they effectually silenced the opposition in that area. By 9 p.m. the 2nd Hampshires on the right and the 5th Hampshires on the left had each got one company across the River Fiumicino. Soon afterwards, Montilgallo itself was captured, but a few strong-points containing machine guns caused trouble. "B" Squadron was ready to repeat its concentrations, but the infantry were too close to the targets for safe engagement. One officer from "A" Squadron and one from "C" Squadron were with the 2nd and 5th Hampshires respectively, reporting their progress and ready to reconnoitre crossings.

At 1 a.m. on the 8th of October the rain came down again. The sappers were at first unable to begin work on the crossings because their Sherman dozers could not negotiate the mud without the help of a bulldozer, and the bulldozer could not operate since it had no protection against the severe fire along the line of the river. They made a start at 2 a.m. and had completed a crossing fit for wheels in three hours. The infantry battalion commanders were anxious for the tanks to come up to them at once, but Brigadier Kendrew quite rightly refused to allow tanks on the wheeled crossing because they would ruin it for everyone else. Captain Reid and a sapper made a close search up and down our stretch of water, but could find no suitable alternative crossing place.

Just before first light on the 8th things were a little critical for the infantry, who were still without anti-tank protection, but at dawn a few jeep-towed anti-tank guns got over and helped to relieve the situation. Meanwhile, as arranged, the 1st/4th Hampshires passed through the 2nd Hampshires and continued the advance five hundred yards. They were held up there and later withstood a counter-attack.

For us the situation was depressing. We knew the Hampshires quite well by now and were determined to help them, but there was nothing we could do. We could not cross the river; we could not deploy off the road; we could not even see to fire on account of the fog which hung on until 10 a.m. and was followed by pouring rain. We manned fifty-two Sherman tanks, which were useless because they could not even cross a ploughed field. Our patience was severely tried.

At 2 p.m., however, information was received that a strong counter-attack was due to be launched from the north against Montilgallo at 4 o'clock. "A" Squadron sent one troop to the north end of Montalbano Hill, where it destroyed five houses beyond the river. Lieutenant Donat, R.E., went in a scout car to reconnoitre possible routes for tanks on the far side of the river in case it was decided to send tanks over the wheeled crossing. His report was not encouraging. A plan was made for "C" Squadron to drive a long way round to the left and come to the aid of the 5th Hampshires via the 10th Indian Divisional area, but this had to be abandoned, as the enemy shelling of the unfinished Bailey bridge in that area was so heavy that the R.E. could not get on with it.

However, "B" Squadron was warned to get ready to fire on the supposed enemy concentration area. At 4 p.m. they opened fire and shelling on both sides was intense. The counter-attack was partially successful, as one corner of Montilgallo was lost, though the actual houses involved had been flattened by "C" Squadron's 105-mm.'s. "B" Squadron fired off its entire complement of ammunition, plus a further two hundred rounds per gun which had been dumped the night before.

All night the Regiment remained in readiness to repeat this performance, but was never actually asked to do so. The night was appalling, with drenching rain, and the roads became so dangerous under inches of mud that a dumping programme of a hundred rounds per gun for "B" Squadron could not take place. The river rose to a depth of five feet and the infantry had to be supplied by mules. Two companies of the 2nd Hampshires were reduced to forty men, but in spite of this they recaptured the corner of Montilgallo which they had lost the previous evening. The 5th Hampshires on the left established themselves on Point 205, having bypassed Lorenzo. A German prisoner captured the next morning, the 9th of October, revealed that their counter-attack force had been reduced from two hundred to some forty-six men before they even began. He stated, furthermore, that they knew that tanks were firing at them, because they recognized the high velocity of the shells, and the house in which he had been was hit ten times.

The Colonel came up to Tactical Regimental Headquarters on the 9th and resumed command of the Regiment. The 5th Hampshires cleared Lorenzo of the enemy, so the 128th Brigade had achieved its objective. It was relieved in the evening by the 139th Brigade. The 9th Lancers continued firing all day, both direct and indirect. Every house that was known or suspected to contain enemy was flattened, so that by evening scarcely a building was standing. "A" Squadron sent two troops to the north end of Montalbano Hill, which brought down heavy "stonking." Unluckily Captain Paul Glenny-Smith's tank (the forward observation officer attached to "A" Squadron from "E" Battery) was hit. "C" Squadron observed numerous gun flashes which, though accurately located, were difficult to deal with because observation of fire in the Po Valley was often misleading.

Shortly before midnight the 139th Brigade had taken over and the 9th Lancers passed under its command. The 10th Hussars had been assigned to this brigade, but it was impracticable to change over the two regiments in the existing circumstances. A probable enemy withdrawal during the night covered largely by bazookamen and mines was reported. It would be difficult to follow up, but there were several possible methods.

Before first light on the 10th the 16th Durham Light Infantry had advanced half a mile to the north and the 2nd/5th Leicesters had captured Point 147 to the west on the way to Longiano. Meanwhile, a crossing place for us was reconnoitred on the extreme right flank and declared suitable with half an hour's "dozing." On the far side of the river, however, the patrol found the enemy in fair strength, so it was decided to improve the crossing made on the original 2nd Hampshires' front. Work began at once, though shelling was increasing. Lieutenant Newman was slightly wounded in the face.

By 11 a.m. the crossing was complete. "A" Squadron sent one troop forward at first to see how it fared, since the going beyond the river, even on the tracks, was doubtful. This troop was supported by two troops still on Montalbano Hill. "B" Squadron was ready to bring fire down on the exposed right flank at short notice, though the 56th Division was now making good headway. Four hundred yards beyond the river the second tank collapsed a culvert and, in the absence of a tractor, there was a long delay. Eventually the troop got through, followed by two more tanks of another troop, and these five took up fire positions on the extremity of Montilgallo Hill, about a thousand yards behind the 16th Durham Light Infantry, who had just captured the village of La Crocetta.

"C" Squadron had a boring day, but claimed that it had seen a German on Gambettola tower five miles away. On engagement, ten direct hits were scored with a 105-mm. which blew the roof off. "B" Squadron had one unfortunate casualty. Sergeant Simpson was hit by a spent .303 bullet fired behind us from the other side of the River Uso.

In the small hours of the 11th of October the 16th Durham Light Infantry took Balignano, the 2nd/5th Leicesters advanced a few hundred yards westward, and the 138th Brigade, supported by the Bays, captured Longiano. At first light Sergeant Gates, the Reconnaissance Troop Sergeant, advanced towards La Crocetta in his Honey to find a route by which "A" Squadron could join the infantry. Some three hundred yards from the village he met with an impassable bomb crater. On taking a closer look he blew up on a mine which shattered the auxiliary charging engine and seriously wounded him in the leg. The mine had been driven over once already but had not exploded. "A" Squadron could not get farther than this crater and did not fire all day.

Major-General Hawkesworth, G.O.C. 46th Division, visited the 139th Brigade soon after dawn on the 11th and later ordered the Regiment to revert to the 2nd Armoured Brigade's command. Tactical Regimental Headquarters returned to Main; "B" Squadron stood down but did not have to move, for it had fired from positions next to Main Regimental Headquarters; "C" Squadron occupied half a dozen houses one mile south of Montalbano; and "A" Squadron remained in the area of the crossing, but it was three days before permission was obtained for its five tanks in front to return. This left the Regiment too dispersed for convenience, but as competition for housing was keen it was wise to keep what one had.

For the first four days we did not know how much respite we should get and there was plenty to do, especially in the way of gun cleaning and general maintenance. There were a number of conferences at which tactical and domestic matters were discussed. We borrowed a mobile bath, which functioned on the banks of the Uso and accomplished a highly necessary improvement in our condition. We held a church parade on Sunday, the 15th of October, and the next day the 46th Divisional concert party gave us an excellent show. Captain Kemp left for England, having completed four years' overseas service. We missed him badly, but he had earned a rest. Major Price had to leave us to recover from jaundice.

It was then announced that we were likely to have a week more out of the line. This suited us well, because the Colonel had decided to change the entire Regiment to 76-mm. tanks. He had been offered the choice of our remaining as we were or changing to 76-mm.'s complete, apart from the admirable 105-mm. close-support tanks, and he had chosen the latter. On the 16th and 17th of October the new tanks were drawn, but they all had to be modified. One week would just give us time for this, and to fire in the new guns. Thus we were able at last to dispose of the old 75-mm. tanks; the merits of the 76-mm. have already been described.

There were several conferences on indirect fire. Our training in Algiers had stood us in good stead, but now the procedure could be slightly altered in the light of experience. Twenty half-trained wireless operators were sent back to "B" Echelon for further instruction. This arrangement was made by Brigade, since we were told that we were unlikely to get any more fully trained operators. The Brigadier invented two new bridging tanks. One was a Sherman Ark, which worked on identical lines to the Churchill Ark, and the other was a fascine carrier. A fascine consisted of a large bundle of faggots perched on the top of a turretless Sherman with a mechanism to release it into a ditch. We regarded these two inventions as a menace, but on one occasion, yet to be related, a fascine did come into its own.

On the 18th of October "A" Squadron began to move back to Ciola, a small village between Regimental Headquarters and "C" Squadron. The Brigade had been allotted definite areas for billets so that we now had more room in the neighbourhood of Regimental Headquarters. Part of "B" Echelon also came up and occupied a nearby house, and this saved many hours of travelling time every day. However long the journey might be, the prospect of lunch in the Bedford Drivers' Club was worth the effort. Here visitors from the tanks felt transported into another world as Major Gardner, immaculately dressed and armed with a long crook, conducted them round his demesne. He showed them "Squiresville," where the carpenters and Trooper Gilpin, the painter, produced regimental signs by the dozen; the "Quartermaster-General's Branch," where Captain Donnley toiled with abrupt efficiency; Sergeant Joe Middleditch, centre of 9th Lancers' "big business," the "universal provider" and "Regimental banker"; Captain Henderson and his Light Aid Detachment; Lance-Corporal Parker, the saddler, sitting cross-legged sewing. Then on past the cookhouse, the office, the despatch riders and fitters, to the centre of the community, the canteen, which sold every manner of produce and was a social centre. They were a happy and essentially individualistic crowd in the echelon. To anyone but the Commander and Sergeant-Major Dale, their composition was a labyrinth of specialists, each section of which tried to encase itself behind a wall of "private rights." This bid for democracy caused considerable amusement to all ranks and demanded a nimble brain from those in authority.

On the 30th of October Major Gardner left us to become an instructor at the Haifa Staff College. We hated to see him go as much as he wanted to stay. Captain Laurie was promoted to the rank of major again and assumed command of H.Q. Squadron, commonly called "The Wing." Major Pulteney, recovered from his wounds, returned to lead "A" Squadron, and Captain Hitchcock was transferred from "A" to "B" Squadron.

During our week's interlude there was one alarm. The hill outside Cesena, called Madonna Del Monte, was captured and a bridge over the River Savio was observed intact. We were told to be prepared to exploit over this bridge, though we had not yet finished modifying our new tanks. However, five hours later the plan was abandoned and we continued working.

It was an opportunity to examine objectively our first innings with the Hamp-

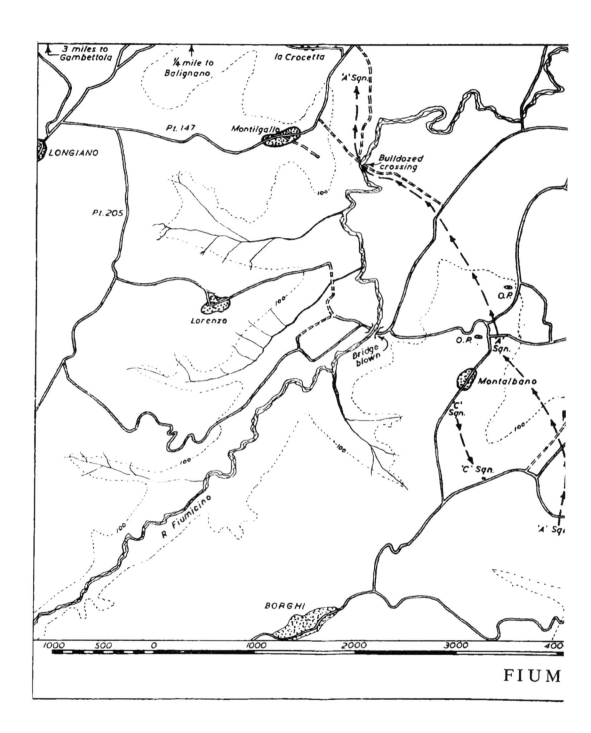

3 miles to
Gambettola

¼ mile to
Balignano

la Crocetta

'A' Sqn.

Pt. 147   Montilgallo

LONGIANO

Bulldozed
crossing

100

Pt. 205

O.P.

Lorenzo   100

O.P.   'A'
Sqn.

Bridge
blown   Montalbano

'C'
Sqn.   100

'C' Sqn.

100   'A' Sqn.

100

R Fiumicino

100

BORGHI

1000   500   0   1000   2000   3000   400

FIUM

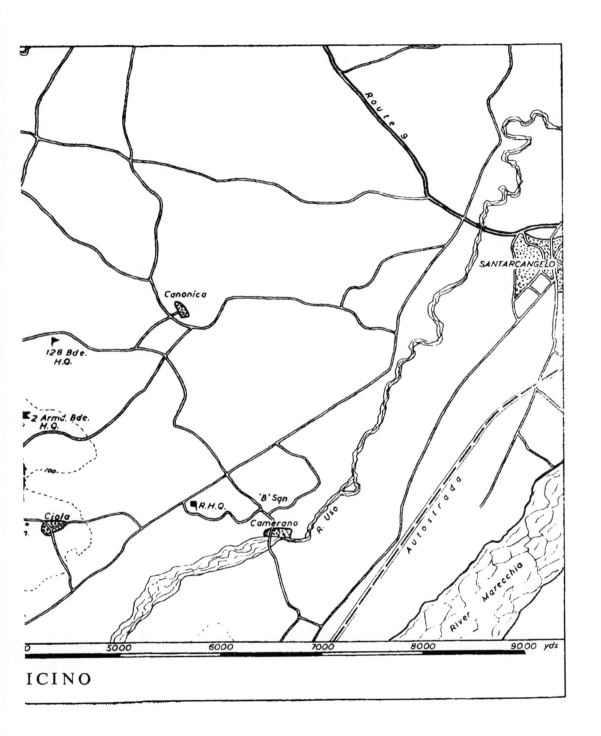

Route 9

SANTARCANGELO

Canonica

▶ 128 Bde.
H.Q.

◀ 2 Armd. Bde.
H.Q.

100.

Ciola

■ R.H.Q.

'B' Sqn.

Camerano

R. Uso

Autostrada

River Marecchia

| 0 | 5000 | 6000 | 7000 | 8000 | 9000 yds |

ICINO

shire Brigade. From the beginning they impressed us. Brigadier Kendrew was a man of powerful physique, of an unbounded energy and enthusiasm which electrified the troops under his command. His profound knowledge of warfare was unquestionable and he inspired confidence. His staff were the essence of efficiency and teamwork, and Tactical Regimental Headquarters considered themselves exceedingly lucky to work with such steady and delightful soldiers. There was never any fuss, indecision or even ambiguity. They were hospitable, helpful and polite. We were no judges of the three battalions, but they reflected the characteristics of the Brigadier and his headquarters, and we were earnestly resolved to do everything possible to keep with them in future.

From a tactical point of view the rain had dictated our every move and restricted our methods. We had been unable to put into practice the principles we learnt at Gravina in June, but we had taken one important step forward: we had had a little practical experience of working with infantry. It demanded quite different technique from anything we had known before. Indeed, it demanded a different attitude of mind. Armour is taught to go into battle at a few minutes' notice and to act with speed, applying certain basic principles to suit the nature of the terrain and the opposition encountered. But there is nothing impromptu about mutual co-operation, when emphasis must always be placed on detailed preparations. We saw that we should have to plan for a week before capturing two square miles of Italy, instead of receiving half an hour's notice to pursue without limit. The tempo would be reduced to its slowest. This necessitated two alterations in wireless methods. First, we had to scrap the idea that the speed of advance allowed for less secrecy on the air. If we gave our position away the consequent shelling could do us no harm, but to the infantry it was fatal. No word could be said of their location, casualties or (most important of all) future intentions. Conversation veiled in jargon was too unreliable. Therefore a new Regimental code was invented, and served us well for the rest of the war.

Secondly, the days of retiring into leaguer every night were over. We should be expected to be on the alert for an indefinite number of days and nights. Accordingly, Regimental Headquarters and squadron headquarters had to carry a higher proportion of wireless operators. This was easier said than done, and on nights when little was likely to happen full use had to be made of soldiers with hardly any wireless training.

"Ah," said someone, "here comes Corporal Heather, just back from Brigade with a sack of mail"—and our thoughts were far from soldiering.

CHAPTER XXVI

THE RONCO, RABBI AND MONTONE RIVERS

WE were soon brought back to battle consciousness, for we received three days' notice of our next engagement, which was timed to begin beyond the River Ronco on the 2nd of November, 1944. To save the tanks and the crews this move was to be made in three stages, with a probable pause of two or more days at the end of the second stage, near Bertinoro, after which we should cross the River Ronco and assemble in the village of Magliano.

At 11.30 a.m. on the 1st of November the tracked vehicles left under Major Allhusen and after a difficult drive arrived in leaguer before dark. Tactical Regimental Headquarters and "A" and "B1" Echelons motored up Route 9, leap-frogging the tanks to the second staging area near Bertinoro. We were again under the 128th Brigade's command and were to cross the River Ronco that day by a ford two miles south of Route 9. Speed was essential because of threatened rain. 25th Army Tank Brigade Headquarters gave details of the crossing and Lieutenant Hainsworth, the Intelligence Officer, was sent to reconnoitre the ford and select a leaguer on the far side. The Colonel and the Adjutant then visited 4th Infantry Division Headquarters, in whose area lay the crossing. The General said that in no circumstances would the 9th Lancers be allowed across; the approaches were nearly ruined already, and he was not going to permit any more of his own tanks to go near it, let alone ours. The Colonel explained the situation to Brigadier Kendrew, and the Engineers undertook to begin work on a Class 40 Bailey bridge.

At dusk there were two short, sharp storms and later came the heaviest downpour of the winter. In the morning we were told that the River Ronco had risen fifteen feet. Four officers in a jeep set off for Magliano. They found one bridge, an aqueduct: all the others had been swept away. They crossed this by driving beside the parapet, but the roads on the far side were too deep in mud even for the jeep. Magliano was inaccessible, so they had to wait. The R.E. needed four days to build the bridge and had not been able to begin. The only alternative was to reconnoitre the tank track from Cesena onwards. This was done by Captain Gregson, while "B" Echelon with a section of 925 Company, R.A.S.C., advanced through Cesena and leaguered on the west bank of the River Savio, which flows through that town.

On the 3rd of November squadrons carried out elementary engineer training in blowing up banks with explosive and collected baulks of timber to tie on to the tanks to help in crossing ditches. The River Ronco subsided almost as quickly as it had risen, and on the 4th of November "B" Squadron was ordered to cross by the ford on the 4th Infantry Division front. It left Cesena at 3 p.m. and, as darkness was falling, successfully navigated the river. This was quite a remarkable feat because the approaches were hazardous and, once in the water, it meant driving two hundred yards down-stream on a ridge of the river bed to reach the point of egress. By 7.30 p.m. the squadron was installed in some farmhouses two miles north of Magliano.

The next morning "B" Squadron passed under command of the 5th Hampshires, who were the right-hand leading battalion of the 128th Brigade. They were up to the River Rabbi as far north as Grisignano, where the line turned east for two and a half miles and then north again. The River Rabbi runs roughly north and south through the town of Forli, which lies four miles to the north of Grisignano. At first "B" Squadron was to have gone forward to the river to destroy houses and towers, but Brigadier Kendrew decided that it was best to conceal the tanks, so Major Allhusen and his tank commanders reconnoitred on foot all day. In the evening, however, 4th Troop advanced to the village of Grisignano—three hundred yards from the river—to be ready to support the 5th Hampshires if necessary. To cover the noise of its movement "E" Battery—back with the Regiment again—fired concentrations on the far side of the river, an operation which resulted in the troop being shelled all night. Lieutenant Birch-Reynardson, the troop leader, visiting the infantry commander, was almost shot on his way back because the Armoured Corps type of steel helmet was almost identical with the normal German type. This point had not occurred to us before, and we hastily warned the infantry to look out for us. As he was about to get into his tank a very heavy "stonk" arrived and wounded him in the fingers, which was bad luck.

Meanwhile, Tactical Regimental Headquarters crossed the River Ronco by the now established Bailey bridge—Class 12, not Class 40—and occupied a house a quarter of a mile away from 128th Brigade Headquarters.

Lieutenant Lacey-Thompson brought "A" Echelon across in two parts, because of the limited number of vehicles allowed to travel in one convoy, and arrangements were made to get the rest of the Regiment over later. This movement was not so straightforward as it sounds. Permission to move at all was not easily obtained, and only a few tanks were allowed to move at a time and then on a tight time-table. All traffic was one-way because the lanes were so narrow, and the circuits were sometimes changed at short notice. The R.E. and the police were apt to despair as they saw tanks ruining their roads and they could hardly be blamed.

A day later, on the 5th, the Reconnaissance Troop left Cesena at 1.30 p.m., followed by "C" and "A" Squadrons. The Honeys arrived in two hours and settled down in a white house opposite Regimental Headquarters. The Shermans were much slower in the clinging mud, but just completed the journey in daylight. "C" Squadron leaguered near the village of Maratello, which was a good gun position for indirect fire as far north as Forli, and close to the head-quarters of the 1st/4th Hampshires. There was a better house farther forward, but it often came under mortar fire and there were liable to be unnecessary casualties. "A" Squadron leaguered immediately north of "B" Squadron.

It was the most perfect autumn day with a light blue, cloudless sky and brilliant sunshine. It was what we had imagined Italy ought to be from pre-war posters and advertisements. We now knew better—and the winter had hardly begun.

Under the warm sun we made our preparations to continue the advance. The ground was drying fast and if movement off the road was possible we might be able to reach the next river, the River Montone, in a day. Captain Gregson and Sergeants Riley and Ralph reconnoitred the River Rabbi, a mile south-west of Grisignano, in search of possible crossings, but there were none. There were several conferences during the day and the squadron leaders received orders from their respective battalion commanders. The three squadrons checked with the infantry their complex wireless communications, and worked hard to make their co-operation fool-proof.

The object of the battle was the capture of Forli aerodrome by the 4th Infantry Division on our right, while the 46th Division, employing the 128th Brigade only, was to secure the left flank of the 4th Division; to do this it would attack northwards towards Forli up the east bank of the River Rabbi.

Down went the barrage at 10.50 p.m. on the 7th of November, and the infantry moved forward at 11 p.m. There was nothing we could do to help them in the darkness, but since we had remained inactive and immobile until then, in order to conceal our presence from the enemy, we spent the night motoring into position. "B" Squadron, with the farthest to go, started at 11 p.m., reaching its assembly area in Grisignano by a round-about route at 1 a.m. the next morning. At 2.30 a.m. "C" Squadron advanced to the hill behind Collina village, whence it could support "B" Squadron and the infantry by direct fire. "A" Squadron moved one mile west, up to the 2nd Hampshires, in two halves, one at 3 a.m. and one at 5.30 a.m.

The infantry made little progress during the night—house-to-house fighting is a slow business—but as the sun rose the Regiment came into its own and tackled the village of San Martino-in-Strada. "B" Squadron, under command of the 5th Hampshires, approached from the south; "A" Squadron, under command of the 1st/4th Hampshires, approached from the east, encountering many ditches and having to use its "scissors" bridge. Progress was slow, and the squadron had to halt on the outskirts of the village while the 5th Hampshires and "B" Squadron did the actual clearing. This was executed perfectly and "B" Squadron's performance was a constant delight to the 5th Hampshires as they watched its accurate and intelligent shooting of each house in the street. The 5th Hampshires then rushed in, going from room to room and killing or bolting any Germans who were still alive. If they bolted, "B" Squadron swung

S.S.M. H. Huxford, M.B.E., D.C.M.

Sergt. Simpson and crew

Lieut. D. Wentworth-Stanley,
February, 1944

A "B" Squadron tank knocked out at
San Savino

ITALY, 1944-1945

"B" Squadron firing indirect
(S.S.M. Huxford, Lieut. Birch-Reynardson, Sergt. Parfitt)

Corporal R. Irvine, M.M., and crew at San Savino

Lieut. C. Parnell and 4th Troop, "B" Squadron, 86th
Regiment of Foot

"Oxhill" after destruction

its turrets with agility and let no one get away. One gunner accidentally fired the 76-mm. gun instead of the machine gun and scored a direct hit on a German. Shouts of applause went up from the infantry who saw it.

They were through San Martino-in-Strada by midday without a single casualty, and encountered an enemy tank half a mile beyond. Ditches prevented tanks leaving the road, so Sergeant Blunt carefully edged forward and finally brewed it up. A few minutes later he examined it—and found that it was a Tiger. The squadron also killed a number of Germans and took fifteen prisoners.

"B" Squadron and the 5th Hampshires then reorganized for an assault on the bridge a mile to their north and a mile south of Forli. An hour before dark they were ready. In spite of numerous mines they succeeded in capturing the crossroads two hundred yards short of the bridge. There they consolidated, and sent strong patrols on towards the bridge itself, but it was heard to crash into the mud below. It was a sad end to their otherwise splendid day. At first the 5th Hampshires wanted to keep two troops forward in an anti-tank-gun role, but Brigadier Kendrew overruled this, and the squadron came back to San Martino-in-Strada to replenish and rest.

The left flank of the 4th Division had been secured and some of our efforts could now be turned in other directions. As soon as the 5th Hampshires and "B" Squadron had cleaned up San Martino-in-Strada the 1st/4th Hampshires and "A" Squadron moved in. A shell unfortunately landed among the fitters, wounding Corporal Griffiths, Lance-Corporal Wilson and Troopers Dunn and Roberts. The plan was for the Battalion Group to attack over the River Rabbi that night and then fight to the River Montone. This was made possible because the 138th Brigade was coming up on the left of the Hampshires. It seemed that the best hope of a crossing for us was in the vicinity of that village, and Captain Gregson organized a search during the afternoon. One man in the Reconnaissance Troop swam the river, but declared the water five feet deep. This was not encouraging, but it was difficult to have a thorough look because the enemy was still on the far side. A further search would have to be made that night.

128th Brigade Headquarters with Tactical Regimental Headquarters had moved to the extremity of Grisignano and a conference was held there at 5 p.m., when Brigadier Kendrew gave out his orders. At 9 p.m. the 1st/4th Hampshires crossed the river in silence and without artillery support, since opposition was weak and likely to be unprepared. They circled round a loop in the River Rabbi and formed a bridgehead. "A" Squadron then went down to the river in strength and on foot and proceeded to paddle up and down. These efforts were duly rewarded and a ford found, but the crossing did not begin until just before first light.

From 7.30 p.m. on the 8th "A" Echelon began to bring up its supplies. Replenishment was complicated, as every squadron had different requirements and was leaguered several miles apart. No difficulties were too great for "A" Echelon, however, and throughout the winter it continued to perform wonders.

Q

By 7.15 a.m. on the 9th "A" Squadron was over the River Rabbi. The 1st/4th Hampshires, who had made no contact with the enemy, captured the village of Vechiazzano and patrolled to the bridge in front of the 5th Hampshires. The two battalions met there and found only the centre span blown. The 1st/4th Hampshires also reached the River Montone at the ford opposite San Varano. "A" Squadron had difficulty in reaching the infantry on the bank because of the many craters in the road, but it got there in the end.

The air observation posts did splendid work. They were mounted in "Taylor-craft," which are small, frail planes carrying only one man and a wireless set, and capable of landing in a five-acre field in almost any weather. They flew at low speeds close to the ground, spotting all movements of the enemy and directing artillery fire on to them. They were unarmoured, unarmed, relying for their protection on their unique manœuvrability and on the fact that they could bring a rain of shells down on any German who disclosed his position.

The fact that the inhabitants of San Varano were hanging out their washing was considered evidence that there were no Germans. A plan was made to cross the River Montone that night, but luckily it never materialized because it began pouring with rain again after dark, and the move would have left us stranded on the far side. As it was, one platoon of the 138th Brigade on our left was sent over and had the ill-luck to be captured.

The next morning when the ford was examined it was found to be passable in spite of the rain, though it was mined on either side. Civilians reported a German withdrawal, but we knew that this was incorrect, because we could see the enemy ourselves.

Meanwhile, "C" Squadron vacated its fire position behind Collina and went into leaguer behind "B" Squadron. On the 11th of November "A" Squadron, after destroying a 75-mm. anti-tank gun, was relieved by "C" Squadron and returned to the Magliano area.

That same week the first three 17-pounders arrived. Here at last was a real gun. The ammunition was so large that the crew had to be reduced to four men. The barrel was very long, and, when out of action, travelled clamped down to the engine cover, beyond which it still protruded several feet. Though it had its limitations and was designed for anti-tank work only, Lance-Corporal Stevenson, a "B" Squadron fitter, spoke for everyone when he described the 76-mm. as a fountain-pen in comparison.

At 2 a.m. on the 13th of November the 1st/4th Hampshires crossed the River Montone. They were two hundred yards outside San Varano at dawn and had cleared it by 7.30. "C" Squadron, assisted by the infantry's pioneer platoon, cleared the mines on either side of the ford, and the squadron passed over. Having taken up preliminary positions to protect the 1st/4th Hampshires, it was ordered to get ready to support the 2nd Hampshires, who were going to exploit north-west towards Villagrappa. This was done with speed, and "C"

Squadron was straining at the leash for half an hour before the infantry commander finally lifted up his voice and said: "Come along, chaps."

The country was enclosed and difficult to cross, and the roads were frequently cratered, but the co-operation was confident and flawless. The platoon commanders asked for fire to be put down in certain places, and this was done instantly. All houses and hedgerows received appropriate treatment: a number of prisoners came in, and, though self-propelled guns gave trouble, the line gradually advanced. Lieutenant Thwaites was "pinned" by one self-propelled gun and an accurate shot from another struck Sergeant Crayton's tank, wounding him and Trooper Williams and killing Lance-Corporal Clark and Trooper Stott.

The Reconnaissance Troop crossed the ford behind "C" Squadron and then deployed and sent back extensive and useful information about the enemy positions. They found numerous craters and mines on all roads, but, working their way round with the confident rapidity of a highly trained team, they surprised many Germans and inflicted considerable losses upon them.

In a fluid battle, when the infantry are divorced from their telephone and have to rely on their wireless, the armour's communications can be of great assistance. The early information which we were able to transmit about the exact positions of the stiffening opposition enabled the Brigadier to decide the night's positions quite early. Two troops of "C" Squadron remained with the 2nd Hampshires all night, and the remainder, with the Reconnaissance Troop, withdrew into leaguer in San Varano. Owing to the ever-present risk of rain "A" Echelon sent two ammunition and two petrol lorries over the ford and some supplies were ferried forward to the leading troops in two Honeys.

At first light on the 14th of November the Reconnaissance Troop and the disengaged part of "C" Squadron deployed. Brigadier Kendrew decided to move the 1st/4th Hampshires up on the left of the 2nd Hampshires, and two troops of "C" Squadron under Captain Reid's command formed up to support them. Up to Villagrappa their advance was delayed more by craters than by Germans, and Captain Gregson contacted the Bays in the village. Several craters on the east of the village brought the Shermans to a standstill, and as they were covered by machine-gun fire the tank crews were unable to get out to remove the mines. This state of affairs continued all day, the 2nd Hampshires making little progress, but Lieutenant Thwaites's troop systematically destroyed houses and Spandau posts. One self-propelled gun was encountered, but the thick country prevented direct observation.

That night the 139th Brigade relieved the 128th Brigade. The 10th Hussars were to relieve us, but at first they only succeeded in taking over our commitments on the right. It rained hard during the night, and consequently the road to Villagrappa was unnavigable until 11 a.m., when the complete change-over was effected.

Two days earlier the Regiment—less "C" Squadron and the Reconnaissance Troop—had concentrated in Forli. Tactical and Main Regimental Headquarters amalgamated and occupied a suburban villa next door to 128th Brigade Headquarters. It was a typical Italian building, made of reinforced concrete, and was ideal for Regimental Headquarters. The squadrons and echelon occupied similar houses within a radius of half a mile.

Because of the rain it took "C" Squadron and the Reconnaissance Troop a long time to return. The first two troops to be relieved got back early in the morning on the 15th, but with only one inch clearance under their maximum fording depth. When the rest of "C" Squadron was ready to cross, the river had risen a further twelve inches, and as the only bridges available on either side were no stronger than Class 12, Captains Tubbs and Foy took over supplies of food and rum, and returned with three men from each crew, leaving the minimum of two on each tank. By breakfast time on the 16th of November the river was down and the stragglers got back in safety.

The cycle of our winter's adventures had thus been repeated twice. Every few miles we ran against a river line defended by the enemy, and on each occasion we followed the same principles, the same procedure, varying only in the particular. We wondered how many more times this cycle would be repeated. Yet compared to our efforts in September there was a large and heartening improvement at little cost. Though teeming rain hindered us at every turn, gradually we were conquering Italy. The Regiment had made a host of new friends. We had given the Hampshires every ounce of support that circumstances allowed. That was far below our potential, but they understood. Some of our ideas and methods caused them amusement. About three times a week a cartoon used to appear in the *Eighth Army News* depicting some of the idiosyncrasies of the Eighth Army as it was in the desert. The characters featured were called the "Two Types." They were pictured as two bewildered and rather irresponsible captains, hopelessly in the dark about what was happening all around them. They motored about Italy in a battle-scarred jeep, unable to resign themselves to the realities of fighting outside the desert. They made fatuous but apt remarks to each other in the jargon language of the Desert Army, and constantly bemoaned the fact that they had ever crossed the Mediterranean Sea. The 9th Lancers did not reflect all these characteristics except in their dress and their kit, both of which were astonishing. Major Price was rightly regarded as the first "Type" in the Regiment, and there was considerable speculation in 128th Brigade Headquarters as to what he would wear next. Perhaps his best effort was a bright-coloured silk scarf—chiefly scarlet—a white waistcoat, a Jaeger battledress coat made in Cairo, cream corduroy trousers, and a bowler hat! But that was unconventional even for the Eighth Army. Scarves and corduroy trousers were the rule rather than the exception, while pullovers worn outside trousers were a universal habit. Troops who joined the Eighth Army after desert days never learned to appreciate its eccentricities; these eccentricities had grown up

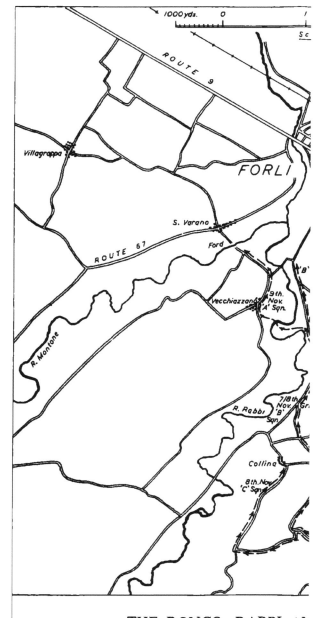

THE RONCO, RABBI AN

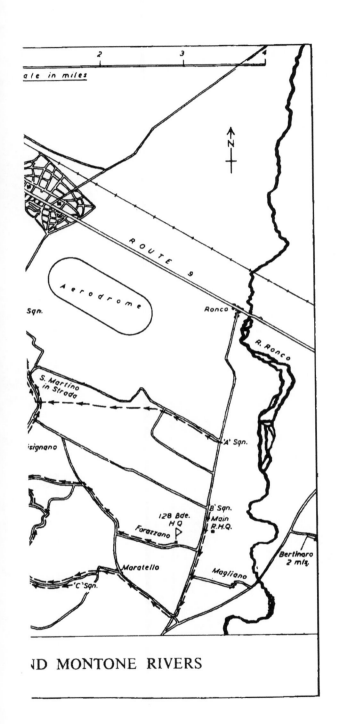

ND MONTONE RIVERS

in the sand hundreds of miles from civilization and had made the Eighth Army the most high-spirited and unique force in the world.

On the evening of the 14th of November a despatch rider from Brigade Headquarters came at speed into Forli and pulled up at Regimental Headquarters with a screech of brakes. Out of his inside pocket he produced a "Top Secret" document entitled "L.I.A.P." That piece of paper inaugurated the first leave to England—Leave In Addition to "Python" ("Python" was the scheme whereby troops with five years' continuous service overseas automatically returned to England for six weeks' leave, after which they went to Germany). It was a great moment. Only eight men could go this time and they had to be chosen for long and meritorious service in the face of the enemy. The whole Regiment qualified on this basis, so it was hard to be fair in selection, but more would follow soon and it gave everyone something to look forward to. In the end the leave quota settled down to four or five men every three weeks, and we numbered six hundred! Four days after the first "Liap" contingent left Forli local leave began. This was worked on a roster so that each man got four days in Florence or Rome, which gave him some relaxation from the rigours of winter campaigning.

Northern Italy is a country of climatic extremes and the winters are hard for campaigning. Progress became inevitably slow. In addition, our forces were soon to be appreciably diminished by the removal of three divisions to Greece and the withdrawal of the Canadian Corps to the Western Front, balanced by a loss of only two German divisions. Luckily our air superiority was unchallenged.

A period of local engagements ensued with a view to improving our tactical situation in readiness for the final blow when spring should come.

CHAPTER XXVII

THE COSINA CANAL AND THE MARENZO AND LAMONE RIVERS

AT 9 p.m. on the 19th of November Brigadier Combe came in and told us that we were to become gunners and by indirect fire to put down concentrations which would thicken up the artillery programme in the next attack.

We had to be in position and ready to fire by dusk the next day, the 20th of November. Lieutenant Hainsworth collected the particulars of the targets that we had to engage, and Major Price took two jeep-loads of officers to reconnoitre the gun position, which they selected near the hamlet of Ciola, three miles south-west of San Varano. At 11 a.m. the tanks of the Regiment left Forli, crossed back over the River Montone by the same ford at San Varano, and drove into their appointed positions.

There were twenty targets in all, eight of which were being engaged by two squadrons of the Bays. That left twelve targets for the 9th Lancers, and these were subdivided among squadrons, whose observation posts visited Point 212 —the obvious viewpoint in the neighbourhood. From there visibility was bad and even artillery officers were unable to observe the fall of 25-pounder shells among the monotonous rows of vines growing on cushion-like mud which threw up no dust. We had no choice, therefore, but to fire a predicted shoot, making the necessary calculations down to the smallest detail off the map. Major Morris came and helped us and surveyed our gun position. The squadrons registered in turn throughout the afternoon, and as the results could not be observed we could only hope for the best.

At 2 p.m. the Colonel visited 128th Brigade Headquarters and was told that the attack had been postponed for twenty-four hours.

At 4.45 a.m. on the 21st of November we opened fire and continued without further orders at the rate of one round gunfire every two minutes. We expected to be told to double the rate at 6 a.m., when the battle would reach a more critical stage, but, as Brigadier Kendrew had appreciated, the timings forecast by the leading troops were optimistic. The 139th Brigade, for instance, for whose benefit we were firing, made little progress that morning and did not even reach the Cosina Canal, let alone establish a bridgehead. The 4th Division on the right got one company over, but we heard that it was forced to retire with a bloody nose. The Polish forces on the left advanced about a hundred yards.

Consequently at 8 a.m. we were ordered to reduce our rate of fire to one-quarter, and later in the day we stopped altogether. Tank guns are not designed to fire artillery programmes and if fired too often they lose some of their high velocity, so vital in their normal role, especially against enemy tanks.

The terrain permitted only one tactical solution, which was for the 4th and 46th Divisions to await the further advance of the Poles, who were tackling the dominating high ground. For us this meant a few days' delay, though we fired occasionally to enable the 139th Brigade to clear the ground up to the canal itself. This they accomplished successfully.

On the afternoon of the 22nd of November, while fresh plans were being made, the Regiment relaxed. There was a slight variation this time in that the 139th Brigade was to make the bridgehead through which the 128th Brigade and the 9th Lancers would pass. As the Poles had entered Oriola and were about to capture Monte Ricci we expected to begin advancing the next morning. Squadron leaders attended their battalion commanders' order groups, and Tactical Regimental Headquarters joined 128th Brigade Headquarters.

During periods of waiting throughout that winter we got much enjoyment from watching the "Hurribombers" dive down to drop their bombs on enemy tanks and strong-points. The rocket-firing Spitfires were specially thrilling to watch. They used to circle overhead until they had located their target, swoop down in a shallow dive, fly horizontally for the last two hundred yards, and then fire their rockets, which trailed red spurts of flame behind them. Above these flew the medium bombers, in compact formation, to release their load some two miles behind the line. No anti-aircraft shells or bullets could change them from their course until they had dropped their bombs. We owed a lot to the Desert Air Force for keeping us free from hostile air activity.

At 5 a.m. on the 23rd, when the Regiment was packing up the tanks with bed rolls and brew cans, all movement was suddenly cancelled. The 139th Brigade had not made its bridgehead. The 5th Foresters had got two companies across and that was all. The 16th Durham Light Infantry had put one company over, but this was forced to withdraw. The 2nd/5th Leicesters had captured a bridge intact on the left, but it was inadequate for the 46th Division's needs and the sappers had been unable to start bridge building. That night, however, the 139th Brigade enlarged its bridgehead and an Ark was put into the canal. Our plan remained unchanged.

At 5 a.m. on the 24th of November the Reconnaissance Troop crossed the Ark without difficulty. One section was sent to watch the exposed right flank and another to maintain contact with the 1st King's Royal Rifle Corps supported by the Bays, who together had relieved the 2nd/5th Leicesters on the left. "B" Squadron crossed ahead of schedule and began forming up with the 5th Hampshires. The new Sherman bridging equipment went next, but broke down on top of the Ark. It was towed off, but the Engineers had to put in half an hour's work before "C" Squadron could go over and form up with the 2nd Hampshires on the right. The 1st/4th Hampshires and "A" Squadron did not cross but remained in reserve.

At 8 o'clock the advance began. The 139th Brigade was passed within a few minutes and the two battalion groups continued side by side all the morning. "B" and "C" Squadrons used all available roads and tracks, so deployment was at its maximum. Mines caused delay, but the crews and the infantry picked them up fast. As each farm was passed the inhabitants said the Germans had left only five or ten minutes before, so it was a race to catch them up. The Reconnaissance Troop got as far north as Route 9, and protected our exposed right flank. A few prisoners walked in and our spirits were high, which is natural when the enemy is withdrawing. "B" Squadron was nearly involved in an unfortunate accident: the Bays reported a self-propelled gun to their north, which they engaged. It proved to be Sergeant Edmunds's tank and firing was stopped only just in time. At 1 o'clock the River Marenzo was reached, making the advance one of three miles that morning.

This river cut our line of advance obliquely, with the result that the 5th Hampshires and "B" Squadron met it first. At the south-east corner of Faenza it joined the River Lamone, flowing north-east round the eastern edge of that town, while on the near bank stood the village of Borgo-Durbecco, which contained the main Route 9 bridge. This bridge was found to be utterly destroyed and the enemy installed in strength in Faenza on the far side. A German motor-cycle was seen going over the next bridge a mile to the south. Five minutes later a loud explosion blew it. On moving closer to investigate, "B" Squadron found the surrounding vines hewn down to give good fields of fire to anti-tank guns. Further reconnaissance therefore had to be done on foot. From a study of the map and air photographs there appeared to be two possible crossing places. The 1st King's Royal Rifle Corps were using the most southerly one and this in the end proved to be the only possible one.

It was the right moment for 128th Brigade Headquarters to move. Tactical and Main Regimental Headquarters joined up and quartered in a farmhouse which was soon to be christened "Stonk Hall." During the move the Colonel met Brigadier Kendrew in "Auld Reekie," the "A" Squadron scout car he had been lent, and received an optimistic account of the battle. Because there were no enemy on the River Marenzo and they were probably withdrawing over the River Lamone, he was anxious to reach that river as soon as possible. Majors Allhusen and Steel were out on their feet conferring with the infantry and neither squadron was under the command of Regimental Headquarters. In the afternoon the 139th Brigade arrived and took responsibility for the Hampshires' right flank. This released the 5th and 2nd Hampshires, who crossed the River Marenzo in that order. "B" and "C" Squadrons were preparing to follow them and the Reconnaissance Troop returned to Regimental Headquarters. At that moment Colonel Payne-Gallwey arrived and gave a very different picture of the 1st King's Royal Rifle Corps bridgehead. It was not a walk-over nor were the enemy withdrawing; the bridgehead was tight and it was not certain that it could be held.

The two infantry battalions got over. Half of "B" Squadron were already across and had become involved in a chaotic block of men and vehicles with tanks and lorries stuck fast. Such was the situation at last light and the over-crowding in the bridgehead defied any plan other than a rearrangement of the troops already there. Brigadier Kendrew did this himself by crossing the river and issuing his orders on the spot. The Germans began firing energetically and A.P. came whistling over "B" and "C" Squadrons from the north-west. "Stonk Hall" was "baptized," so to speak, with shells and "moaning Minnies," which continued all night, while Spandaus rattled continually. Sergeant Rule and Corporal Tyler were killed by a direct hit on a shelter in which they were seeking cover. They were the two senior fitters in "C" Squadron, among the most skilled men in their trade. Both had done their same jobs since before the Regiment left England and had won admiration and respect by their unfailing efforts and cheerfulness. In Regimental Headquarters Trooper Moat, the "B" Squadron scout-car driver, was killed, and Captain Tubbs and Troopers Carey, Fairs and Woodcock were wounded.

At dawn on the 25th the bridgehead was expanded in three stages. The 5th Hampshires and "B" Squadron started advancing north-west, which enabled "C" Squadron to cross the river, enter the salient and form up with the 2nd Hampshires, who then set off westwards. And then the 1st King's Royal Rifle Corps, supported by a squadron of Bays, attacked Belvedere to the south-west. The day's fighting resulted in the bridgehead being extended by three-quarters of a mile. "B" Squadron met a number of tanks and self-propelled guns and was exceedingly lucky to escape without casualties: two of its tanks were hit by armour-piercing shot, one of which bounced off and the other half-penetrated the gun mantlet but did no damage. Two German tanks were "brewed-up" in front, but the squadron was moving against the grain of the country and was therefore slower. "C" Squadron was very unlucky in losing Lieutenant Paddy Holt, killed by a shell which chanced to explode on a tree when his tank was passing underneath. He had been with the Regiment since Algiers. It did not encounter any enemy tanks. Walking over that ground after the battle it was interesting to note the exact courses taken by the German tanks. The track marks conclusively proved that their cross-country performance was far superior to that of a Sherman in spite of their greater weight.

As no anti-tank guns could reach the leading infantry, our tanks remained in position all night, during which no incident of note occurred. The 1st/4th Hampshires relieved the 1st King's Royal Rifle Corps, so that at dawn on the 26th of November the 128th Brigade had three battalions up. While the 5th Hampshires and "B" Squadron remained where they were, the 2nd and 1st/4th Hampshires, each supported by half of "C" Squadron, advanced two miles due west almost to the river. The Brigade then side-stepped to the left, as the 139th Brigade had crossed the River Marenzo and come up on its right.

By midday the Hampshires were within striking distance of the River Lamone without having gained contact with the enemy. The Brigade front was therefore divided into three roughly equal parts, and each battalion with its respective tanks made a quick plan to patrol to the river, reconnoitre crossings and find out the strength of the enemy beyond. This was carried out during the afternoon, when it was established that the enemy was in strength on the far bank. A full-scale attack in the usual style would have to be prepared. Later in the afternoon the rain came down in earnest and it became clear that the cycle must be repeated once more. At least it was consoling to know that in three days we had advanced five and a half miles as the crow flies and had taken one river in our stride.

Tactical Regimental Headquarters left Stonk Hall at 3 p.m. and took four hours to travel six miles. The cause of the slow progress was the teeming rain, which transformed the approaches to the River Marenzo into a marsh. After every twelfth vehicle the Engineers had to bulldoze away the soft mud from the surface and the Pioneers had to tip some twenty tons of rubble on top. Traffic was in single file for two miles and a change-over from up traffic to down meant the loss of an hour. It got dark soon after 5 o'clock and a strict black-out was essential.

During the last week in November the rain, though not the heaviest we had known, was so persistent that the River Marenzo became a rushing torrent and swept all before it, including the Ark. Cut off from behind, it was plainly impracticable to cross the next river. It was hard enough to supply us as we stood. An overhead ropeway did splendid service until the weight of Captain Clavil Mansel, of "E" Battery, strained it unduly. A bridge fit for jeeps was eventually opened, but neither Regimental Headquarters nor "C" Squadron could be reached by day, as they were in full view of the enemy.

The Colonel wanted to bring "A" Squadron forward, but it would have been fatal to the roads, so permission was not granted. The crews left a guard on their tanks and returned to their billets in Forli. Main Regimental Headquarters wisely evacuated Stonk Hall at the same time and returned to their villa in Forli. This move was hastened by the continual bombardment, and on several occasions the Second-in-Command had to give the order to bale out of the mess on the top storey. Numerous shells landed in the yard and a hit on the house seemed certain. The odds were shortened as each "stonk" arrived.

The plan to cross the River Lamone, as far as it affected the 128th Brigade, was altered four times. It formed part of the Allied strategic plan, in which the Eighth and Fifth Armies had to contain the twenty-seven German divisions in Italy and prevent them from reinforcing on the River Rhine. The details were fixed finally on the 1st of December, and primarily involved "C" Squadron.

"B" Squadron, which was still supporting the 5th Hampshires in their holding positions, was given a separate task. It had been unlucky in suffering four casualties from one shell: Trooper Hunt was killed, and Lance-Corporal Wigglesworth and Troopers Poulton and Woodward wounded.

Briefly, the 128th Brigade plan was this: the 2nd Hampshires, on the right, and the 1st/4th Hampshires, on the left, were to cross the River Lamone together and establish a bridgehead some three thousand yards wide and twelve hundred yards deep, as far as Olmatello. The 1st/4th Hampshires were then to continue and capture Point 261 and the hamlet of Pideura, while the 5th Hampshires were to pass through the 2nd Hampshires and capture the high ground between Olmatello and Pideura. Securing those two places and the surrounding high ground was the key to the whole operation. Two troops of "C" Squadron were to support the 1st/4th Hampshires and the other two, initially the 2nd Hampshires and later the 5th Hampshires. Should it prove necessary the 1st King's Royal Rifle Corps would be introduced to guard the left flank.

The cover plan was twofold. First, artillery silence was to be observed and no targets, however tempting, were to be engaged before the battle began. Secondly, firing and general noise were to be created by the 2nd/7th Queen's, supported by one troop of "B" Squadron, half an hour after the attack began. It had been normal to fire a feint shoot before the genuine one, and by reversing this procedure the enemy might be foxed. The remainder of the two squadrons during the first night were to engage definitely located enemy strong-points by direct fire on fixed lines. "C" Squadron would have to support all three battalions instead of one, thus introducing new problems of control and of "weddings" with the infantry on the far side. Major Steel vigorously laid his plans, the merits of which he himself had to "sell" to the three infantry colonels. They, in their turn, were co-operative and understanding.

Major Steel, without whom the Regiment had never once gone into action throughout the war, cast his experienced eye over the map and the ground. He walked many miles so that he personally knew the lie of the land on his side of the river. From the hill behind his farmhouse he scanned the heights of Olmatello through powerful glasses. However, the map in no way adequately indicated the immense difficulties of the terrain and in particular failed to show the razor-backed approach to Pideura from Point 261 with a drop of five hundred feet on either side. Furthermore, from careful study through binoculars, the general opinion was that no tank could climb up the track from the River Lamone to the ridge leading to Point 261. In addition, a steep ravine which divided Olmatello from Point 261 was not revealed until it was actually reached and this prevented the 1st/4th and 2nd Hampshires from mutually supporting each other. The difficulties of the "going" in general were not underestimated, however. The selection of fire positions for our first night task was simple. "A" Echelon came and dumped one hundred rounds per gun, so that when it was time to advance no tank would be without its full complement.

Owing to the state of the river and the difficulties of patrolling, the attack was postponed each day for a week. This was a great strain, especially on "C" Squadron, sitting there in full view of the enemy. No movement was safe by day and no engines could be started. Each day the squadron was keyed up for the battle and each night it stood down.

CHAPTER XXVIII

PIDEURA AND OLMATELLO

AT 7 p.m. on the 3rd of December the Hampshires crossed over the river to the thunderous accompaniment of the artillery barrage. "B" and "C" Squadrons added their guns to the noise, concentrating chiefly on Olmatello and Castel Raniero—two small groups of houses on the first ridge. Until 11 p.m. one troop of "B" Squadron joined the 2nd/7th Queen's on the right and made a loud noise by firing freely into the area a mile to the north of the Hampshires' bridgehead. This diversion was successful, because heavy German defensive fire was soon heard from that stretch of the river. For the rest of the night both squadrons remained in readiness to fire again, but they were not asked to do so. Soon after midnight the 2nd Hampshires reached the foot of Olmatello hill and encountered stiff resistance. For hours they held on until, at 4 a.m. the next morning, they stormed up the hill and won their objective. When Brigadier Kendrew visited the position later in the day he declared that the 2nd Hampshires' success was one of the finest achievements of infantry fighting he had ever seen.

With first light there was a faint outline through the morning mist of ruined towers and houses. "C" Squadron could not cross the river because of mines; the bulldozer had been blown up; and the infantry reported two huge craters in the lateral road beyond, each of which would require a Bailey bridge. No advance was possible for the moment.

All day the Desert Air Force was overhead, their fighter-bombers in greater strength than we had ever seen them.

The 5th Hampshires passed through the 2nd Hampshires and were then held up by fierce opposition while the 1st/4th Hampshires made slight advances on the left. Both battalions, struggling through the night with small results, reported that the presence of "C" Squadron was vital for their further progress.

"C" Squadron had been at thirty minutes' notice since 7 p.m. on the 4th, but it was not until 5.15 a.m. on the next day that the Adjutant was able to order them over. During that night the Sappers, temporarily abandoning their original bridge site, had put a double Ark in the river five hundred yards to the north. The 138th Brigade had crossed the river and come up on the right of the Hampshires, while the 2nd/4th King's Own Yorkshire Light Infantry had relieved the 2nd Hampshires, who were holding the right flank between the river and Olmatello.

221

By 7 a.m. Captain Reid had crossed the Ark with two troops in an attempt to get at least one troop beyond Olmatello to the support of the 5th Hampshires. The only route for tanks lay along a track as far as Castel Raniero, where it turned left and ran back to Olmatello, finally taking a sharp turn to the right. Castel Raniero was still in enemy hands, so it obviously had to be captured. The 2nd/4th King's Own Yorkshire Light Infantry had tried once, but thick fog had confused the position and they were now re-forming for a second attempt.

The Queen's Bays were officially in support of the 138th Brigade, but, as they had not yet crossed the river, the Colonel ordered the leading troop of "C" Squadron to support the 2nd/4th King's Own Yorkshire Light Infantry. A troop of the Bays arrived, however, and took on the job. By 2 a.m. Major Steel and the rest of his squadron had negotiated the Ark and were established in a house on the main lateral road.

Three hundred yards short of Castel Raniero the leading tank of the Bays' troop was blown up by a mine and the King's Own Yorkshire Light Infantry came to a standstill until darkness fell. All that afternoon and evening "C" Squadron worked at full pressure, keeping in touch with the Hampshires and King's Own Yorkshire Light Infantry and at the same time, with the help of the Pioneers, they made good the craters in the hope that one troop could reach the Hampshires the next morning.

It was a dull, grey dawn on the 6th of December. By 8 a.m. Castel Raniero was captured and the disabled tank was extricated three hours later. At 11.15 a.m Lieutenant Fitzpatrick's troop, in company with a platoon of infantry lent by Lieutenant-Colonel Rotherham, set off to clear the houses on the route. Lieutenant Fitzpatrick's tank blew up on another deeply buried mine, fifty yards in front of the one that had given the Bays so much trouble. There were no Engineers at hand, so Lieutenant Fitzpatrick prodded the road with his own crew and continued, himself in the leading tank, until he reported at 1 o'clock to Lieutenant-Colonel Robinson, commanding the 5th Hampshires. The crews of the other two tanks did their best under heavy fire to remove the damaged tank, but without success; in the end, Sergeant Simpson found a way round and, by very skilful driving, arrived with the 5th Hampshires beyond Olmatello at 2 p.m. This diversion was so cut up by the movement of his tank that no more vehicles could pass that way.

Lieutenant Fitzpatrick and Sergeant Simpson took up fire positions in the forward infantry localities about four hundred yards apart.

This brave endeavour was well matched by events at Pideura. The 1st/4th Hampshires were being counter-attacked off Point 261 and as soon as it was light Lieutenant Hannen was ordered to try to reach them. Two of his tanks got bogged while trying to get round the two great craters. By 11 o'clock a Bailey bridge was in position over the worse of the two craters, and Lieutenant Thwaites's troop passed over and turned up what looked like a narrow goat track. After climbing for a mile they met the infantry and Lieutenant Thwaites reported to the Colonel of the 1st/4th Hampshires.

A plan was then made for the recapture of Point 261 and exploitation to Pideura. The attack went in at 2 p.m. and within two hours Point 261 and Casa Nova, which was close by, were taken. A mist hanging low over the hills reduced visibility to fifty yards and made tank-infantry co-operation a difficult task.

A further plan for the capture of Pideura was made and Sergeant Corbett set off down the road to help the infantry into the hamlet, while the other two tanks gave supporting fire from near Point 261. Sergeant Corbett soon lost touch with the infantry, who disappeared into the mist to mop up, and for over an hour the three tanks were left marooned and unguarded while darkness fell. Their crews could hear Germans talking around them. The minutes dragged by and there was still no sign of their protecting infantry nor was there any reaction from them on the wireless. Then three green Very lights soared slowly up into the sky. This was the signal which announced the infantry's success. At that moment Sergeant Corbett saw a German bazookaman rise up out of a ditch and take aim, but as he traversed his turret rapidly on to him the German dropped his bazooka and gave himself up.

The success of the infantry made no difference to the dangerous position of the three tanks. Lieutenant Thwaites decided to consolidate on Point 261 and hope for the best. Then by a lucky chance he encountered one of the Hampshires and learned that the enemy had launched a counter-attack against Pideura and that the 1st/4th Hampshires had been driven out. One company was going to spend the night in Casa Nova, so Lieutenant Thwaites moved his troop into its protection. During the night "B" Company of the 1st King's Royal Rifle Corps relieved the forward company of the Hampshires, who were by now completely exhausted.

At 6.30 a.m. on the 7th of December "B" Company attacked Pideura, again supported by Lieutenant Thwaites's troop, with Corporal Jamieson's tank leading. They had advanced a quarter of a mile down the track when, within fifty yards of the hamlet, the infantry charged into the buildings and ditches. The leading tank, left by itself, received a direct hit which killed Trooper Curtiss and wounded Corporal Jamieson and Trooper Rust. Lance-Corporal Harris, the driver, was also hit, but in spite of his wounds he reversed the tank single-handed and went back along the muddy track. He was under anti-tank fire all the way, but he managed to reach Casa Nova, which was the only place where tanks could pass each other.

Contact was regained with "B" Company, who said that they held the church and had taken a dozen prisoners. Thirty Germans, however, were established inside the priest's house alongside the church and were counter-attacking, so the company commander asked for a tank to knock the house down. Sergeant Corbett's tank was by now the only one fit to do this. He had to run the gauntlet of murderous fire for six hundred yards, so, to help him, "E" Battery put down a smoke screen. He reached the hamlet in safety, expecting to be met by "B" Company, but there was no one except Germans in sight. He proceeded to fire about six shots into the priest's house while being engaged from all sides by Spandaus. Then his 76-mm. gun failed because a cartridge case became stuck in the breech, but without hesitation Sergeant Corbett charged straight through a wall of the house. Half the roof and a wardrobe fell on to his tank, damaging the gun beyond repair. As the tank was driven through the parlour door it was covered with falling plaster and drapery. In fifteen minutes Sergeant Corbett had used up all the machine-gun ammunition, but he backed his tank alongside the church door and fired his tommy-gun through it, killing three Germans, while his operator fired through the turret. It was not until all his ammunition, including grenades, had been exhausted that he withdrew to Casa Nova.

Within five minutes of his return "B" Company reported that they held Pideura and had taken another thirty prisoners. It was then realized that Sergeant Corbett had arrived in the hamlet at the same moment that a counter-attack had driven out our infantry and for his great work that day he was awarded the Distinguished Conduct Medal.

Meanwhile, Lieutenant Hannen's troop had climbed the goat track from the river with supplies of ammunition for the infantry and, though smoke was laid to cover them across the last half-mile, shells and mortars came down thick and fast. They reached Pideura in the middle of the afternoon and relieved Lieutenant Thwaites's troop, who returned to the valley.

That night the 25th Indian Infantry Brigade relieved the Hampshires, who withdrew for a long period of rest and refit. We were extremely sorry to see them go. They had earned our profound respect and we were very happy to be with them. In their turn they were profuse in their gratitude and sincere in their desire to be supported by us. The end of our partnership had been marked by an engagement in which "C" Squadron had played a distinguished part and the Hampshires were very appreciative.

The 1st King's Own took over at Pideura, and the 3rd/1st Punjabis took over at Olmatello. No advances were made on the 8th of December, but there was intense and accurate mortar fire on Pideura and Casa Nova. Both battalions were new to us, and "C" Squadron had to visit each of them to make itself familiar with their methods and to discuss details of co-operation. The fact that they were new to tanks added to the responsibilities of Major Steel and the squadron.

In other circumstances the question of wireless communications could have been pleasantly puzzling, but now "C" Squadron had to use its limited resources to keep six separate links in simultaneous action. Sergeant Dolezal had the six sets lined up in a row in squadron headquarters, and tied a label on to each head-set marked "The Squadron," "3/1 Punjabis," "RHQ," and so on. Most of the wireless sets were left on day and night, which meant that none of the operators got more than four hours' sleep, the batteries wore out very quickly, and, to add to the confusion when the 25th Indian Infantry Brigade took over, many of the operators at the other end only spoke Hindustani.

The V Corps had only one road for supplies which for eight miles from the River Marenzo to the River Lamone was single line only. In some places it was actually under water. Hundreds of tons of rubble were put down every day by the Pioneers and "up" and "down" traffic was allowed on the road only for a period of two hours each day. This meant that the average time required for one lorry from "A" Echelon to replenish the tanks and return was twelve hours. Captain Mostyn and Lieutenant Mike Bird took it in turns to do the job and the "A" Echelon drivers did exceedingly well, overturning only one lorry during the whole period. Tactical Regimental Headquarters then crossed the River Lamone and occupied a house next to the 25th Indian Infantry Brigade Head-quarters; later half of the "A" Echelon remained on that side so that lorries would have to do the journey only one way each day.

Even this did not solve the difficulties. As it was impossible for a lorry to get beyond the Lamone lateral road, the two forward troops had to be supplied on foot. On the night of the 8th of December Captain Reid went to supply the Olmatello troop, while Major Steel with a party of six went to Pideura. They trudged uphill for three miles through the pouring rain and reached Pideura without mishap. Having delivered their stores they left. As they neared Point 261 they came under heavy shell fire and Trooper Longmire was killed by a direct hit. At that moment a heavy counter-attack had been launched by the enemy and had taken the Pideura troop completely by surprise. The company com-mander and Lieutenant Hannen had run straight into two Germans, who demanded their surrender, but luckily an alert Bren gunner prevented this. Inside their tank Corporal Perry and his crew knew nothing until somebody knocked on the turret and shouted "Hande Hoch!" Their reply was to swing the turret quickly round and press every trigger. As the gunner, Trooper Lythe, quite rightly said: "It's the bangs that count." On this occasion, anyway, the enemy was prevented from gaining an initial advantage in his counter-attack.

At that moment, just as the officers in Tactical Regimental Headquarters were remarking how quiet it was, news of the counter-attack began to come over the wireless. Major Morris quickly realized that the only way by which correct defensive fire could be brought to bear was by use of the tank wireless links from Tactical to "C" Squadron Headquarters and thence by another set to 4th Troop. In this way he organized a superb rain of shells and forced the enemy to withdraw.

At 2.15 a.m. the next day (the 9th) a second attack came in, which was also beaten back by artillery fire. The bag for the two engagements was ten Germans captured and fifty killed. Both were a prelude to the great counter-attack which began at 7 a.m. on the 9th of December.

This attack was carried out by the 90th Panzer Grenadier Division and stretched a distance of four and a half miles from Pideura to the outskirts of

R

Faenza. Fierce fighting continued all day and Lieutenant Fitzpatrick's troop beyond Olmatello was heavily involved. Though the battle was fluid the line remained unaltered. Once more Major Morris by his fire plan along the ditch Rio Canona was largely responsible for breaking up the attack which developed in the "C" Squadron sector. On the left the 138th Brigade and the Bays, though heavily engaged, held firm. The enemy had suffered a crushing reverse and documents captured later revealed that they had intended to drive us back across the River Lamone.

Towards last light a German self-propelled gun in Pideura crept up and scored four hits on Sergeant Salt's tank. Sergeant Salt was wounded and the crew had to bale out, but not before they had damaged the self-propelled gun, which was later found abandoned. Soon after midnight, the 1st King's Own Yorkshire Light Infantry altered the position of their companies and, by a misfortune, when the new company was installed at Pideura, a hand grenade exploded in the crowded cellar of the priest's house, killing four men and wounding eleven others, including Lieutenant Hannen, Lance-Corporal Walker and Trooper Laundy.

Lieutenant Thwaites's troop was at the end of its tether, and because of casualties "C" Squadron could not send relief. Accordingly "A" Squadron sent up Lieutenant Michael de Burgh and his crews. They could not start until 3.30 a.m. on the 10th because a 17-pounder anti-tank gun was blocking the knife-edge ridge outside the hamlet; however, the relief was uneventful and, in addition, a third tank was able to motor up and replace that of Sergeant Salt.

Before dawn Lieutenant Thwaites and his troop were back at squadron headquarters, where they collapsed into sleep. Some of the crews had spent over sixty hours in their tanks and had been subjected to continuous mortaring and shelling. By this time Pideura lay in ruins and the only three complete rooms were occupied by seventy infantrymen; facilities for cooking were nil.

Meanwhile, on the right Captain Reid took Lieutenant Moon and two relief crews to Olmatello. Lieutenant Fitzpatrick's troop had been committed longer than Lieutenant Thwaites's troop and its members were almost asleep before they got back.

When the Colonel visited "C" Squadron that morning he realized that the men were dead beat. He accordingly sent for "A" Squadron Headquarters and six more crews. Captain Peek was commanding "A" Squadron, as Major Pulteney was in hospital with jaundice. At midday "C" Squadron got away in lorries to Forli, and Major Steel followed later after having taken Captain Peek to visit the three infantry commanding officers.

From then on the Pideura front was comparatively quiet, and, though spasmodic shelling continued, the enemy seemed to have abandoned all hope of capturing it.

CHAPTER XXIX

"HARRY"

DURING that first fortnight of December when "C" Squadron was engaged so closely at Pideura and Olmatello, "B" Squadron was also having an unpleasant time. It was called upon to send half a squadron in support of the 169th Brigade of the 56th Division on the 5th of December in an advance up the west bank of the River Lamone to capture Faenza.

At 8 a.m., therefore, twelve tanks under the command of Major Allhusen crossed the river, but the 2nd/7th Queen's, the leading infantry battalion, did not arrive until midnight that night, when detailed plans were finally made. The first objective was to be a large cross-roads, locally known as "Harry," one and a half miles south-west of Faenza.

At first light on the 7th of December they started off up the road, crossing the rear of the Hampshires and the 138th Brigade under ever-increasing shell fire. All went well until, two hundred yards short of "Harry," the leading tank blew up on a mine. It was, however, possible to pass, so the half-squadron continued in line ahead to the cross-roads, which was found to be cratered and mined.

Lieutenant Goldsmid, the leading troop leader, dismounted and found a way round. On regaining the road on the far side of "Harry," two alternative routes into Faenza presented themselves: the right-hand one was straight and without cover, so that as soon as the first tank advanced it was fired on with armour-piercing shot; the left-hand road was safe for two hundred yards, when, on turning the first corner, it also became dead straight for a mile. On reaching the bend Lieutenant Goldsmid found a minefield which was being covered by armour-piercing fire. As owing to heavy shelling most of the Engineers and Pioneers had become casualties on the way up to "Harry," they were not available to pick up the mines. Moreover, tanks could not deploy off the narrow road for at least five hundred yards and in line ahead would have presented the target of an anti-tank gunner's dreams.

At 4 p.m. a great increase in enemy shelling made it clear that the Germans proposed to stop any further advance. They had the advantage, as from the high buildings in Faenza they could see much of the battlefield, whereas "B" Squadron's observation was restricted on that flat, thickly covered and boggy plain.

So deadly was the shelling that four direct hits were registered on each tank which blew off every wireless aerial and shattered twelve periscope heads. To meet a German counter-attack which had its general axis southwards down the

227

railway line, one troop of "B" Squadron moved back half-way round the diversion on to the road running north-west from "Harry" to Celle. German infantry were infiltrating down the ditches and along the hedgerows and "B" Squadron's machine guns hardly ceased fire. Sergeant Help's tank blew up on a deeply buried mine which he had driven over already two or three times. Darkness was falling when another tremendous "stonk" enveloped the squadron in noise and smoke—a sure sign that the first counter-attack had been beaten.

All communications with the infantry had by now broken down, so Lieutenant Joicey was sent back to the 2nd/7th Queen's Headquarters to find out their news and act as a reliable wireless link to them. The battalion had suffered over a hundred casualties in this short and fierce engagement and were no longer in a position to protect the tanks during the night. Appreciating the extreme importance of the cross-roads, Major Allhusen decided to hold his ground alone. He organized his tanks and his crews for defence and prepared for a rough night. He sent back a report on the air to Regimental Headquarters, but the Adjutant and Sergeant Jenner could only just hear him because the enemy was stalking up so close that he dare not raise his voice.

Luckily the enemy made no determined attempt to retake "Harry" and at 4 a.m. on the 8th of December a new battalion, the 2nd/5th Queen's, arrived to take over. When it got light Second-Lieutenant Barton and 5th Troop remained in support of the infantry while the remainder of the squadron withdrew south of the cross-roads. The enemy continually infiltrated forward all day, but no ground was given. Heavy shelling was frequent. After four direct hits Lieutenant Patrick Dudding decided to close down the cupola lid in the turret roof and the next shell actually landed on it, causing him mild head wounds only. One bazooka patrol got very close to 5th Troop, but it was forestalled in time. The troop remained in position all night.

The next day enemy tanks were very active, and, though they were invisible to "B" Squadron, the air observation posts kept a close watch on them. Major Allhusen had a wireless set netted on to these Taylorcraft so that he could hear all the information about the Tigers. As soon as one had been definitely located a battery of medium or heavy guns immediately engaged it while the air observation post directed the shots. A direct hit was seldom scored, but a near-miss by a 7.2-inch shell was enough to cause damage or force the tank to move. This good work not only provided up-to-date news of the enemy's movements but saved "B" Squadron several tank casualties.

There was little that tanks could do now—apart from giving encouragement by their presence—but a plan was made for two to attempt to motor up each of the roads that led to the town. The mines having been lifted, this was achieved with the aid of twilight, smoke and heavy high-explosive concentrations. By 1 p.m. Lieutenant Goldsmid's was the only tank in position, so he was asked to support an infantry patrol as it investigated a house four hundred yards in front of him. They reached the objective and immediately heard small-arms fire. Both the opposing forces were in the house together, so there was little a tank could do. On withdrawing, the patrol had three men missing and reported fifteen Germans there. By 4.15 p.m. the other three tanks were in position just off the two roads.

As these tanks were likely to remain out there for an indefinite time a frequent relief of crews was necessary. Therefore the crews of the rear half-squadron came up from their house near "Journey's End," walking round by the 46th Division crossing, a distance of at least five miles, while their kit took a more direct route. Captain Hitchcock built an aerial ropeway over the River Lamone at its nearest point, and Heath Robinson would have been envious of this remarkable contrivance. It worked perfectly and all kit was ferried across in safety. Unfortunately, however, Sergeant Helps was badly wounded during a "stonk" which landed near the receiving end.

That night the tanks right forward were heavily camouflaged, though it was difficult to achieve surprise with the enemy so close. Second-Lieutenant Barton and crew relieved Lieutenant Goldsmid and Lieutenant Joicey relieved Corporal Irvine. This was a grim business because shelling was continually heavy and Spandaus firing on fixed lines only narrowly missed the two tanks.

The next morning, the 9th of December, while the great counter-attack was coming in on their left, Second-Lieutenant Barton saw what looked like a German tank move out from behind a farmhouse half a mile away. As he was about to engage it, his own tank was hit by a round of armour-piercing and "brewed up." Trooper Pattison was killed and Trooper Thomasson wounded. Major Allhusen had been at 169th Brigade Headquarters all the morning and now motored forward round "Harry" to take up a fire position near the bend in the left-hand road. Second-Lieutenant Barton then crawled forward with a No. 38 set in an endeavour to find the enemy tank and report its position to Major Allhusen. He never saw it, however, and it was not "brewed," though Major Allhusen and a troop of M10 anti-tank guns a thousand yards behind the squadron fired a number of rounds in its direction.

On the 11th of December the New Zealanders took over that sector of the line and the 2nd/5th Queen's were relieved by a Maori battalion. The next day they sent out a patrol of twelve to examine another house in "No Man's Land" and occupy it if it were vacant. There was a sharp engagement inside the house which resulted in four Maoris being wounded and all the Germans killed or wounded. A Tiger then appeared and plastered the house with armour-piercing and high-explosive shells under cover of which the enemy counter-attacked. Realizing the hopelessness of its position, the patrol gathered its wounded and withdrew. This operation made the enemy all the more sensitive to movement and noise in "B" Squadron's area.

This sensitiveness made more hazardous the change-over of crews. This had to be done every night now because the tense and close nature of the fighting demanded such alert vigilance that a crew could remain really efficient for only twenty-four hours. There was little respite from shells, mortars or machine guns and while walking out or back the intervals in the enemy's fire had to be judged. In this unhurried manner no casualties were suffered during reliefs.

Before dawn on the 13th of December one battalion of the New Zealand Armoured Brigade had crossed the River Lamone by a newly completed Bailey bridge. It did not relieve "B" Squadron that night, as originally intended, because it was relieving the Maori battalion and a fire plan was indispensable in safeguarding what amounted, in the circumstances, to a large-scale movement of tanks. Since V Corps was firing a barrage the following night it was decided to wait until then.

"B" Squadron's last day in this position saw heavier shelling than usual, including single-barrel rockets. After dark Lieutenant Charles Parnell and two drivers relieved their opposite numbers in the two right-hand tanks in readiness to withdraw. At 11 p.m. the New Zealand attack to the River Senio was heralded by a really impressive artillery barrage. "B" Squadron took its cue to retire, but because their batteries were by now very weak only one tank—the left-hand one—managed to start up and withdraw. The other two ran their Homelites to charge their batteries, but the Germans' defensive fire plan must have included concentrations on positions they knew we occupied, for these they saturated with shells. Both tanks were hit several times, their aerials were blown off twice and communication became impossible. When after more than two hours there was no sign of them, Major Allhusen dispatched Lance-Corporal Emerson of Sergeant Collier's crew to get in touch with Lieutenant Parnell. In spite of heavy fire, Lance-Corporal Emerson got through and reached them. Eventually both tanks got going and, running the gauntlet of armour-piercing fire from enemy tanks shooting straight down the road from Faenza, finally became disengaged at "Harry" at 3 a.m. on the 15th of December. For eight days this half-squadron had remained in the infantry outposts and had been largely responsible for holding the cross-roads on which the subsequent operations of the New Zealand Division were based.

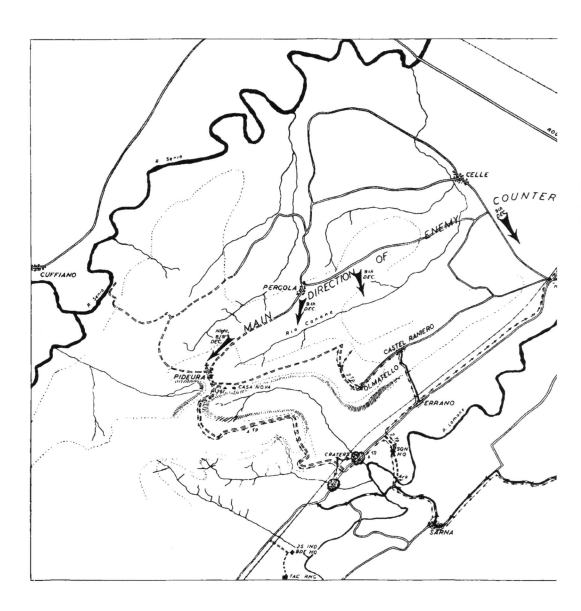

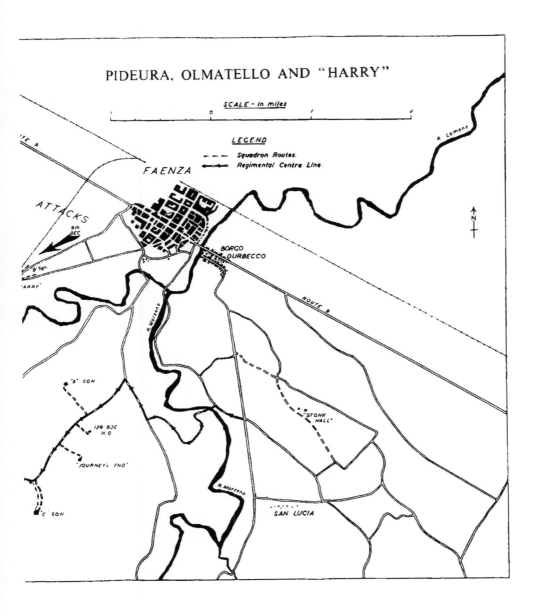

PIDEURA, OLMATELLO AND "HARRY"

CHAPTER XXX

PERGOLA AND PESARO

THE object of the next attack was to reach the River Senio, south of Route 9. The 10th Indian Division was the centre of the three divisions in V Corps and was going to employ two brigades up, the 10th and the 25th. Their first objective stretched from the village of Pergola on the right to Point 155, which was half a mile from the banks of the river. In order to support this attack by five battalions of infantry "A" Squadron was to employ three troops, one on each of the only possible lines of advance for tanks. One troop would advance from Olmatello to Pergola and the other two north-west and north-east respectively from Pideura.

Because of "C" Squadron's tank casualties it was necessary to bring forward three more. The nearest belonged to "B" Squadron, so Lieutenant John Berry and the remaining troop of "A" Squadron came forward to mount those tanks whose crews were taking their turn in the engagement at "Harry."

For some reason the Indians seemed to doubt our ability to destroy houses and were not even convinced when the 105-mm.'s shooting indirect hit a number of "by request" targets for them. They asked for some flame-throwing Crocodile tanks, as they foresaw that the enemy would blockade a number of these houses and be difficult to eject, and Crocodiles would be ideal for such a situation. After some delay two duly arrived on the morning of the 14th of December.

The barrage came down at 11 p.m. on the 14th and the battle began. The infantry made some progress at first, but then the counter-attacks came in and ground changed hands several times in various parts of the front. Lieutenant Berry and his troop slowly climbed the goat track to Pideura, followed by a Shermandozer and a Crocodile in case of need. This little convoy left the main lateral road at 3 a.m. on the 15th of December and within three-quarters of a mile of Pideura the road collapsed beneath the leading tank. The Shermandozer did its job, however, and all five tanks reached Pideura.

The 1st King's Own and the 4th Sikhs were having great difficulty in clearing the enemy out of a group of houses called Camillo, four hundred yards north of Pideura. They wanted help from the Crocodile, but Lieutenant Whately said he could deal with the situation alone. It was still night, so he fired several belts through his machine gun until he observed the bullets striking Camillo; then he pressed the 76-mm. trigger and that was the end of Camillo. The infantry were pleased with the display, but they did not get much farther before the sun

231

rose. At first light, under cover of a smoke screen, Lieutenant Whately's troop advanced. One tank got bogged *en route,* but the other two reached the leading platoons. No further progress was made here all day.

On the left the 3rd/18th Royal Garhwal Rifles successfully captured Casa Zula and Monte Corelli. At first light on the 15th 1st Troop advanced up the track west from Pideura with its 17-pounder tank in the lead, reaching Casa Zula, but were stopped by the soft mud. One tank got hopelessly bogged, so the troop took up the best possible fire positions and gave what help it could.

Lieutenant Crampton's troop was never called upon to advance from Olmatello. A Durham Light Infantry battalion and the 3rd/1st Punjabis had been driven back from the outskirts of Pergola and their position at dawn afforded no scope for tanks; in any case, the route was hazardous and it was doubtful whether the troop could have got there. Farther over on the right the New Zealanders captured the village of Celle after a tough fight and held on all day, though they were faced by about twenty Tigers and were being heavily shelled.

During the day the Crocodile at Pideura sprang a leak in its flame-fuel tank, so it was decided to send up another from the valley, but this one overshot the turning up the hill and became ditched while turning on the main road.

The enemy withdrew during the night and the infantry reached their objectives. At first light on the 16th Lieutenant Whately's troop started to advance to Pergola, but soon ran up against mines. To save time it started to lift them, but stopped when wooden Schu mines were discovered surrounding the anti-tank mines. Shermans could not go round the minefield across country, so the Crocodiles were tried, since their cross-country performance was superior. But they also failed and Engineers had to be sent for, who lifted mines all the morning until the road was clear. Lieutenant Whately's troop continued through Pergola and went to the support of the 10th Indian Brigade from Point 132 beyond. This left the 25th Brigade with no tank support other than Lieutenant Berry's bogged troop. The 3rd/18th Royal Garhwal Rifles did well on the left, capturing the hill feature overlooking the River Senio, while the Baluchis captured the end of the Pergola Ridge and the road which extended to the north-east to the New Zealanders' boundary.

That night the infantry patrolled to the banks of the River Senio and the New Zealanders found several possible crossings. All along the Lamone Valley yellow streaks flashed out from the guns as they harassed the enemy and there is no doubt that this last crossing over the River Lamone and the subsequent fierce fighting inflicted very heavy losses on three of the finest divisions in the German Army—the 90th Panzer Grenadiers and the 26th and 29th Panzer Divisions. By last light details of the take-over by the 20th Indian Infantry Brigade were completed and early the next morning, the 17th of December, a squadron of the 8th Royal Tanks relieved our "A" Squadron.

The Regiment assembled at Forli, where the billets, though they could not have been called civilized by any normal standard, seemed the acme of comfort.

Night had followed day eighty-eight times since that first stiff dash up the hill at Point 153. During that period we had advanced thirty miles as the crow flies and assisted in forcing crossings over five major rivers. To the listening-in and reading public our achievements were described as "patrol activity" and only those who were there could understand our happiness at being out of the line and our feelings of pride at the success which had attended our efforts.

"I have admired the determination of all ranks to surmount the great natural difficulties of the terrain," wrote the Army Commander to the 2nd Armoured Brigade, "and your fighting spirit, enterprise and endurance have led to great achievements. On many occasions your support of the infantry with tanks has turned the scale, and you have developed the closest co-operation with the other arms, which is the key to success."

Christmas was barely a week ahead when Brigade ordered us to move back out of the Corps area. Pesaro was our destination, a town on the Adriatic coast eighteen miles south of Rimini, where it had originally been intended that Field-Marshal Alexander's Allied Armies Headquarters in Italy would be situated. The place was never used and there was plenty of comfortable accommodation.

The tanks came back down Route 9 from the Lamone lateral the night after we were relieved. Faenza itself was not yet clear of the enemy, but the bridge constructed there by the New Zealanders was open and, after twenty-four hours in Forli, they were loaded on to transporters for the trip to Pesaro.

Packing up the echelon was not easy, chiefly because of the furniture problem. Pesaro had none and even though we looked like a travelling circus our baggage did not include any armchairs or good tables. We made good this shortcoming from Forli to the distress of the various owners, who did not expect to see any of it back and were very pleased when we returned it all a few months later.

The Regiment was assembled in Pesaro by lunch time on the 20th of December. We were in the residential quarter of the town, along the sea front. Each squadron occupied six or more villas and our whole area did not measure more than two hundred by one hundred yards. The echelon was decentralized to squadrons which parked their lorries and tanks on one side of their streets.

At 10.30 a.m. on Christmas morning there was a Brigade church parade in the Garrison Theatre, after which the Brigade marched past, Brigadier Combe taking the salute. Then the Colonel, the Second-in-Command, the Adjutant and the Regimental Sergeant-Major made their usual tour of the squadrons.

For the next ten days after Christmas we worked hard. Twenty-six reinforcements joined the Regiment; there were the usual reports of Germans making sea landings along the coast and we had to keep a force permanently on the alert in case they tried Pesaro; the Regimental Band, under Mr. Allen, spent six days with us, and on New Year's Eve played at the Regimental church parade, while every night its dance section entertained in the Sergeants' Mess. The Colonel succeeded in borrowing four horses from the Remount Depot. Lieutenant Pat Stevens, a half-trained vet., was in charge of them, assisted by Troopers Whittal and Thursfield as grooms. The stables were refitted by Sergeant Squires and in spite of many more battles before the end of the war the number of horses began increasing from that day.

Major John Scott returned to the Regiment, but within a few days he got jaundice. There was a great deal of sickness among the officers at this period; half a dozen went down with influenza and an equal number with jaundice. There were generous grants of leave: contingents of four or five had left for England every month, and Rome and Florence were as popular as ever. We knew little about the future. The 10th Hussars were in the line supporting the 56th Division just beyond Faenza, and though we knew we were going to relieve them shortly nothing seemed definite.

CHAPTER XXXI

THE 86TH REGIMENT OF FOOT

THE snowstorm on New Year's Day, 1945, was an all-too-accurate sample of the weather we were to enjoy for the next two or three months. On the evening of the 9th of January the Colonel returned from leave in Rome and all was calm and quiet, but then the telephone in the passage rang and we received orders to take over as infantry a mile of the winter line in forty-eight hours' time and come under the command of the 9th Armoured Brigade.

The next morning saw a transformation. Soldiers rushed round counting up rifles, Bren guns and ammunition while the Colonel and squadron leaders hastened from one conference to another. How many tanks could we take? What should we do with the rest? How should we be armed? There were many problems to be solved and time was very short.

The first and main decision was our organization. The Regiment was divided into six main parts: three infantry squadrons, each of one tank troop and three infantry troops; H.Q. Squadron for administrative purposes as usual; the Reconnaissance Troop in their Honeys as a mobile reserve; and the 105-mm. tanks centralized as one battery for the Regiment's own use. We promptly christened ourselves "The 86th Regiment of Foot"—eighty-six having been our divisional serial number since 1941.

Up until then the Allied armies in Italy had continued their offensive action in spite of the draining away of their forces to other theatres. For some months past the two sides had been equal in numbers, yet the Allies kept pushing ahead. At the turn of the year, however, it was obvious that no further progress could be made until the spring. The infantry divisions were under strength and tired, so it was essential for many of them to be withdrawn into reserve to retrain and reorganize for the future offensive. It was to fill the gap thus created that the 9th Lancers and other armoured regiments found themselves on their feet.

The forty-eight hours' dead line was increased to sixty hours, and later to five days. Even so there was not time for any infantry training. We armed ourselves to the teeth with our numerous automatic weapons and took in addition one machine gun from each tank we left behind. These tanks were left closely parked along the streets under Captain Henderson's command and a small rear party from each squadron also remained behind. Pesaro looked utterly deserted as, on the 12th of January, in a blinding blizzard the Regiment turned north up the main road.

Our intermediate destination was Cervia, a small Adriatic resort more bleak than Pesaro. The billets consisted of a luxury hotel, completely stripped of furniture and fittings, and several small seaside bungalows. All the water pipes were frozen and the drains were out of order, so life was truly miserable. The Colonel, the squadron leaders and most of the officers went forward to make many reconnaissances of our sector and peer grimly into our future trenches, now water-logged because the snow had turned temporarily to rain. No one was sorry to leave Cervia on the 15th of January.

That evening "A" and "B" Squadrons relieved "D" Company, 1st King's Royal Rifle Corps, and found themselves holding a one-thousand-five-hundred-yard sector of the front. The 1st King's Royal Rifle Corps were on their right and the 7th Hussars on their left, with the 1st Welch on the left of the 7th Hussars. The rest of the 9th Armoured Brigade was on the right of the 1st King's Royal Rifle Corps and consisted of the 27th Lancers, 1st Buffs, Royal Devonshire Yeomanry (Field Artillery), two anti-tank batteries, and one field company of the Royal Canadian Engineers. The 10th Hussars joined the Brigade later. Major Johnson commanded a battery of the Royal Devonshire Yeomanry and came to stay in Regimental Headquarters as our affiliated artillery commander.

The squadrons were much relieved to find a farmhouse situated in each of their troop localities and, as the weather was still bitterly cold with snow falling, there seemed no alternative but to base our defence on these houses after the manner of our more professionally qualified predecessors. Later this proved to be to our cost. Fortunately it took our immediate opponents, the 16th S.S. Reichsfuhrer Division, some time to realize that they were not being opposed by crack infantry troops; at the time of our arrival they were too much preoccupied in harassing the unfortunate Italian Cremona Division on our right. This allowed the squadrons time to prepare their forward positions unmolested.

The width of "No Man's Land" varied from thirty to one thousand yards and we amateurs were given sectors at the widest points. In front of us ran three small canals and beyond these lay the town of Alfonsine, the local German forward headquarters. Our forward posts lay on the edge of the nearest canal, except for our most southerly one, which was on the second; the enemy manned strong-points in between the canals by night. They were all marked on our large-scale maps—Bosco Bruciato, La Giorgetta, and so on, all of which became household names within a few hours. We gave names to our own positions—Oxhill, Mallory, Shaw, Oaks and Gorse.

The Po Plain is an area of nearly ten thousand square miles, triangular in shape with its apex near the French frontier. It is entirely agricultural and with its rich soil has immense productivity. It is divided up geometrically into hundreds of rectangular "fields" measuring about a hundred and fifty by thirty yards. This symmetry is broken only by roads or water-courses. The "fields" are divided by vines which vary from four feet to twelve feet in height and are supported either by stakes or by wires stretched between mulberry trees specially grown for the purpose. The view from the air seemed to be of an endless chessboard of elongated squares with a white house at almost every corner. From the ground the field of view was limited.

In these surroundings, enlivened by shell fire, "A" and "B" Squadrons spent busy days sandbagging, wiring and mine-laying. Regimental Headquarters and "C" Squadron were less than a mile behind in the village of Villanova, eight miles west-north-west of Byzantine Ravenna, while the echelon was four miles south of Ravenna.

Four days after we arrived "C" Squadron relieved "A" and thereafter reliefs were carried out every six days so that each squadron had three days out and six in, alternating between the right- and left-hand positions. Propaganda leaflets had already been showered on us and the Reconnaissance Troop had shot down a Stuka. On the 21st of January we had our first brush with the enemy. The following is a graphic description of the incident by Lieutenant Berry:

"I don't think it was a surprise to any of us in the troop when we were attacked by a small raiding party of the enemy on the third night of our first spell of duty at 'Oxhill.' The house was generally accepted to be the first likely point of attack in our area, so our preparations were complete.

"The great uncertainty which played on everyone's nerves was how an attack would come, and whether we should be able to see and get due warning. Numerous stories were current about what was supposed to have happened to other people who had been attacked. And so it was with a certain tension that the troop would shut up the house each evening at 5 o'clock to await what darkness would bring.

"In the event of an attack our dispositions inside the house mainly centred round various loopholes on the top floor. There were only a few men at the doors and other vantage points downstairs. We numbered twenty-two, including myself and two sergeants. We also provided a patrol of two men each hour who would go out to the flood bank one hundred yards to our front and act as a listening point for about twenty minutes.

"The attack was one to inspire confidence in such 'green' defenders as ourselves, for it came from the most easily observed quarter. I had just let out our patrol—Corporal Clark and Trooper Duxbury—from the back door and had returned to the main night post when Trooper Ling, the sentry, reported two men approaching from the open ground. I told him not to fire, as I thought it was one of our patrols going out. I observed carefully and saw that they were in truth *approaching*. They appeared to be carrying some large white objects, to which Trooper Ling drew my attention as being map boards. As the two men continued to come on and were about to shelter behind some haystacks, I ordered Trooper Ling to fire. The moon permitted us to see them clearly at the range of one hundred yards, and it was obvious that they were enemy.

"Besides killing the first two, the staccato chatter of Trooper Ling's Bren gun sent the remainder of the troop, who were having their evening brew, to action stations in double-quick time.

"Soon there was lively fire from all sides of the house. Sergeant Corbett was looking after the No. 38 set, which became our only means of communication while the battle was on owing to bad positioning of the telephone. He also went round the posts to ensure that all the men had enough ammunition, and were in good heart.

"It was about five minutes after the alarm that two explosions were heard. These turned out to be bazookas, but the men who had shot them had been so unnerved by our withering fire that their aim was considerably put off and the projectiles burst harmlessly, only causing Troopers Greenfield and Smith to be blinded for a few moments by the blast. Both remained at their posts and carried on firing.

"Meanwhile, Private Raine, our rather deaf cook, caused amusement among us by wandering round the upstairs rooms bumping into various people on his way and immediately saying in a very audible whisper, 'Blanco'—the password I had given everyone for use in the event of the enemy breaking into the house. He was very useful, however, in passing the ammunition, and later in providing us with an impromptu and 'off the ration' meal in the early hours, after the battle was over.

"After about half an hour the firing died down and a hushed silence descended on the whole place. It became apparent that the enemy had withdrawn, but we did not think he would be content to leave us the victors of the encounter, so we anticipated a renewed and surprise assault in the early hours. All remained at their posts until after 2 o'clock in the morning, only a few chaps being relieved at a time for a smoke and a rest. Morale was high, though we all got rather fed up with two moaning Teds (our term for Germans, being an abbreviation of the Italian name 'Tedeschi'). One was quite near and merely groaned. He was found dead in the morning. The other let out piercing yells from away out in the open ground, anything up to half a mile from the house. Both Sergeants Corbett and Aris were keen to take a patrol and get these men in, but I refused to allow this, as I did not want to lose any of our small number to an enemy ambush party which might well have been laid for that very purpose."

The next morning seven abandoned weapons as well as the two dead men were revealed. The same night Lieutenant Tony Moon's troop in the next position captured a rather uninterested Bavarian, who apologized for getting lost. All this gave us confidence and encouragement, though the activity in Regimental Headquarters was too much for the Second-in-Command's dog, "Forli," who was sick all over the Intelligence Officer's maps.

Our night patrolling was on a very limited scale. The ground was covered with snow and the sight of five or six surly troopers dressed up in white smocks and cap-comforters was uncouth in the extreme and caused much amusement. There is no doubt that our lack of experience in patrolling eventually gave the initiative to the Germans, although it was not for lack of trying on our part. The Germans had an unpleasant habit of taking on patrol "panzerfausts" (tank-destroying weapons which fire hollow-charge projectiles) and several of our houses were holed in this way, luckily with few casualties. This difficulty was largely overcome by putting up Somerfelt tracking (a kind of heavy wire netting) which caused the missiles to explode before they struck the wall.

Life in the winter line was more unpleasant than anything we had experienced before. Indeed we might have died from exposure but for the crates of comforts which arrived from our relatives in England. Mrs. Erskine organized extensive knitting, and every man had something woollen to wear in addition to his ordinary clothes. We were profoundly grateful for this as we cowered in our foxholes. Later, when the thaw set in, we still needed them, for the penetrating damp was as cold as ice and snow.

The horses gave great pleasure, and on a quiet afternoon it was possible to ride up to "No Man's Land" and look across to the German positions. We often wondered if the German intelligence summaries ever reported cavalry on the Villanova sector.

Racing started at Cesena and drew a peace-time crowd, though only a few 9th Lancers could go.

At night the Germans sometimes stopped firing at us and played dance music instead. Once they had the audacity to broadcast to "C" Squadron. Needless to say, this was rapidly dealt with by the Regimental Battery of 105-mm. tanks. "Bullock-head" (our term for the unloading point of German bullock-carts) was a popular target for us too, because the enemy used to replenish his forward positions with ox-drawn carts and we discovered that most of the unloading was done at that point. The Reconnaissance Troop, not to be outdone, assisted in this by dismounting their five Browning machine guns and rearranging them for indirect fire. This generally caused more alarm among our own troops than the enemy. In fact, the dismounted regiments often accused each other of faulty aiming. The three Partisans were another menace. They were given to us to assist in controlling the civilians, but Mr. Hardwidge decided to teach them to fire a rifle. The usual result was that the "observation posts" in the front line had to climb down from their trees.

After a month the Regiment had settled into its new role and the conversation revolved round the subject of leave to England. Captain Reid and six men were dispatched on the next boat-load. Major George Meyrick returned and took over command of "A" Squadron after an absence of two years as a result of his jeep accident in Cyrenaica.

With the improvement in the weather we began to think about the future. The first indication came on 18th February, when Lieutenant Joicey and Sergeant Simpson, of "B" Squadron, were sent back to Bertinoro to train with the 78th Infantry Division. The following week Brigadier Musson, commanding the 36th Infantry Brigade in that division, and one of his commanding officers were entertained by the Colonel and squadron leaders, and it appeared that we were going to be affiliated to that brigade. Throughout our term as infantry we kept up with the latest armoured developments and we tried some experiments with "platybus grousers." These were steel plates fitted as an extension to tank tracks so that the weight of the tank was distributed over a much greater surface and did not sink down in the mud so easily.

All this time the six-day reliefs were continued and the forward positions were improved and strengthened. The roads were getting into a lamentable state and working parties, assisted by twenty-two sturdy Basutos, maintained them daily. So far we had had very few casualties, and those were through shelling and mortaring at night. Apart from Lieutenant Ribton Crampton, who unhappily had walked on one of our own mines and been injured, no officers had yet been evacuated. It was known that the 42nd Jäger Division was now opposing us, but at first its behaviour towards us was unprovocative.

At 7.15 a.m. on the 25th of February the enemy suddenly began shelling "Oxhill" very heavily with a self-propelled gun. This gun dashed from one direct fire position to the next on the far canal bank and, after firing some eighty shots over a period of an hour and a half, only the bottom half of "Oxhill's" four walls stood—and this after a month of strengthening. Everything possible was done to pin-point this gun, but without success, since it was so nimble in changing positions. Unfortunately 4th Troop, "C" Squadron, under Lieutenant Hannen, was having breakfast inside the house at the time and consequently was caught before it could get out and man its slit trenches. This incident cost the troop twenty-five casualties out of a strength of twenty-eight, and eighteen had to be evacuated, including Lieutenant Hannen and Sergeant Hardwick, who later lost one of his legs. Otherwise the casualties were not serious, being caused mainly by falling rubble.

The Colonel was enraged at the enemy's behaviour and that evening the 105-mm. battery drove forward to direct fire positions between "Oxhill" and "Oaks" with orders to flatten at least four selected enemy houses. Within half an hour these orders had been carried out. We hoped the enemy would realize that we had now embarked on a "four houses for one" policy. Early the next morning a further "bait" was fired called "Stug's Benefit" and encompassed most of the area opposite us, but the self-propelled gun was never pinned down; perhaps it had withdrawn already. The remains of "Oxhill" were pieced together with the help of the Engineers, but the occupying troops were forced to live in trenches, as the house was now only a pile of rubble.

The next day there was a tragic and fatal accident. Sergeant Simpson, an old and trusted Troop Sergeant of "B" Squadron, was accidentally killed by a tommy-gun bullet.

From then on "Oxhill" was shelled and mortared continually. On the 1st of March, under cover of this fire, the Germans sent out a very skilful patrol. Its exact movements were only found out the next day. What actually happened was that the patrol entered "B" Squadron's area from the lines of the 1st Welch, who had relieved the 1st King's Royal Rifle Corps on the right, and then lay up in the ditch beside the track connecting "B" Squadron Headquarters with "Oxhill," determined to get a prisoner. The patrol had realized that the firing on "Oxhill" would produce reinforcements or casualties or both and that this was the obvious track for us to use. They must have seen our one casualty, Trooper Jordon, being evacuated—for by now the shelling had ceased—and must also have seen Major Derek Allhusen go up to "Oxhill" and back, but he was protected by an escort. The man they finally seized was Trooper Jennings, who was returning unescorted with the empty stretcher.

The patrol plus prisoner then moved off westwards and crossed the first canal not far from "Oaks." On its way it chanced to stumble across two men, Lance-Corporal Waddell and Trooper Brown, who had both been killed by mortar bombs while repairing the telephone line. The Germans stripped these two of their boots, equipment and identifications, and returned to their own lines. As far as "B" Squadron was concerned, the two linesmen were missing for several hours before eventually being discovered long after the patrol had passed by.

That was the last patrol we saw, though self-propelled guns continued to batter at the ruins of "Oxhill." We were only too thankful to give someone else a turn when the 2nd Palestine Regiment relieved us on the 4th of March. The usual reconnaissance and advanced parties had arrived beforehand, so the change-over was extremely smooth. It was the first time that the Jewish Brigade had been into action, so they were even "greener" than we had been. They were amazed at the number and nature of automatic weapons we possessed and did not easily fall into the swing of things, but they were most co-operative and soon gave a splendid account of themselves. Any Germans they took prisoners were made to feel thoroughly uncomfortable.

The 9th Lancers were happy to wave good-bye to Villanova. We had held nearly a mile of the winter line for eight weeks in cruel weather at a cost of two officer and thirty-six other-rank casualties. Spring was coming, the sun was beginning to shine, and the ground was drying up. Let us get back to our tanks. Give us some infantry. It's time the war was won!

The following is a list of our casualties while operating as infantry:

KILLED

Sergeant G. Simpson.	Trooper N. R. Brown.
Lance-Corporal J. W. Waddell.	

DIED OF WOUNDS

Trooper A. E. Lowry.

WOUNDED

Lieutenant G. P. C. R. Crampton, M.C.	Trooper I. J. Clift.
Lieutenant L. G. M. Hannen, M.C.	Trooper H. W. Cross.
Sergeant S. V. Hardwick.	Trooper A. C. W. Fisher.

s

Corporal E. Pritchard.
Lance-Corporal T. C. Yeaman.
Lance-Corporal J. T. Edington.
Lance-Corporal C. J. Radley.
Lance-Corporal J. A. Simmons.
Trooper Livesey.
Trooper A. J. Payne.
Trooper J. E. Finnis.
Trooper H. H. Williams.
Trooper E. S. Brooks.
Trooper C. R. Clement.

Trooper M. Gregory.
Trooper G. Livingstone.
Trooper C. L. McCann.
Trooper N. Nuttall.
Trooper W. J. Pledge.
Trooper R. C. Saunders.
Trooper S. Simms.
Trooper D. A. Jones.
Trooper G. E. Jordan.
Trooper W. Duxbury.

SLIGHTLY WOUNDED BUT REMAINED IN ACTION

Trooper J. C. Black.
Trooper J. E. L. Butler.
Trooper J. Gabbey.

Trooper G. S. Hawkins.
Trooper W. S. Reid.
Trooper W. H. Yates.

PRISONER

Trooper P. Jennings.

CHAPTER XXXII

THE SENIO FLOODBANKS AND A NEW TOY

As there is little to choose between one bit of the Po Plain and the next we had no false hopes about our new leaguer at Carpinello, three miles north-east of Forli. Regimental Headquarters picked Villa Monti, the only reasonable house, and the remainder of the Regiment was dispersed over an area of two and a half square miles. The absence of operational responsibility temporarily made up for the shortcomings of our leaguer, and, though there was an exceptionally heavy month ahead of us, the trials of winter were over and we felt we had been given a new lease of life.

We had less than a week to prepare for a return to the line, this time in our tanks and with two squadrons only. As had been expected, our new colleagues were the 36th Infantry Brigade and no time was lost in getting to know each other. Being out of the line gave us an excellent start and, furthermore, each had had experience in "mutual co-operation" fighting. First we had to get our tanks up from Pesaro and they came on transporters in small batches. On the 10th of March "A" and "B" Squadrons motored forward to a staging area near the River Montone, and the next day "A" Squadron moved into positions supporting the 36th Brigade while "B" Squadron remained in 78th Division reserve. Tactical Regimental Headquarters, under the command of Lieutenant Hainsworth, now the Signals Officer, also advanced to the Divisional area in case "B" Squadron was called into action.

Two troops of "A" Squadron were in support of the 6th Royal West Kent Regiment and one troop in support of the 5th Buffs. Their tanks were in position several hundred yards behind the infantry outposts in the floodbanks of the River Senio close to Bagnacavallo, and their commanders spent most of the day conferring with the infantry officers. In the evening the squadron announced its presence by firing a hundred rounds of 105-mm. shells at five selected targets.

"No Man's Land" here was very different from Villanova, as the Germans were determined to hold the west floodbank, and to do this they had to hold their own side of the east floodbank. Therefore it was common for our own infantry to be tunnelling away quite happily to improve their positions and meet Germans also tunnelling in the same bank. Sometimes the infantry observed German digging parties on the far bank, and as it was unwise to put heads up they used periscopes. Through these they could see the blades of the shovels flinging away excavated earth. As they could not take any action themselves, a

243

76-mm. tank was driven forward to a suitable position. Direct fire was impossible, but the lay of the gun was calculated from the map and a shot fired. Through the most devious channels of communication the men on the spot reported it ten yards left. The necessary adjustment was made and the second shot found its mark. Fifteen more rounds were fired in rapid succession and the Germans were seen running for cover. Then a stretcher party appeared, proving that at least one man had been hit. This target was named "The Buttress" and received rough treatment during the following three weeks. Otherwise nothing exciting or unusual happened.

"B" Squadron was never called upon to fight while in reserve. It began training with the third battalion in the 36th Brigade, the 8th Argyll and Sutherland Highlanders. A nearby squadron of air observation posts became its friend and took several members of the squadron up to look at the German positions. In the circumstances this was not as dangerous as might be supposed, because the enemy seldom fired for fear of disclosing their position. The American Congresswoman Mrs. Clare Luce Booth visited the squadron one day—a great social event. She had visited the Regiment before, at Knightsbridge in 1942, and remembered the squadron and Major Laurie too. She inspected a few tanks, accepted some light refreshment and departed with a promise to come back one day.

On the 21st of March "B" Squadron relieved "A," coming under the command of the 36th Brigade, and the tedious vigil continued. It was difficult to do any positive damage, though four Germans were killed on its second day. Tactical Regimental Headquarters returned to Carpinello, since there were now no squadrons forward under our command. Lieutenant Hainsworth had spent ten days learning Italian and was now a competent interpreter. Finally, on the 28th of March "B" Squadron was relieved by the 4th Hussars and returned to join the rest of the Regiment outside Forli. It had been a boring interlude, but we now knew and liked the 36th Brigade and this was an important achievement.

Soon after we arrived at Carpinello Lieutenant-Colonel Perry was taken ill. Medical tests revealed that he had a kind of diphtheria and he had to go to hospital. It was a long time before he was fit again, so he was not able to return to the Regiment. He had commanded the 9th Lancers for exactly a year, through perhaps the most difficult period in our war history, and it was unlucky that he missed the thrilling finale which lay in store for us in April. He was succeeded by Lieutenant-Colonel K. J. Price, M.C., and Major Allhusen became Second-in-Command.

There were some radical changes. Major Laurie returned to command "B" Squadron; Captain Carlisle took "The Wing," with Captain Allen in charge of "A" Echelon. Captain Mostyn moved to "A" Squadron, Captain Gregson to "C," while Lieutenants Newman and Parnell were given the Reconnaissance Troop.

Lieut.-Colonel K. J. PRICE, D.S.O., M.C.

While "A" and "B" Squadrons were up at the front, big schemes were developing at the rear. A programme of work was produced so that squadrons could see how they stood, and as no one knew how long we had, the Colonel selected the 9th of April as his dead line. This gave the Regiment an interlude of twenty-five days and in that period each squadron was to do ten days in the line and five days on our ranges at Cervia. The Brigadier was anxious for us to carry out tank-infantry co-operation training, but the Colonel wanted to postpone this complicated work until the end. So we started on our programme without delay. It had to be altered eventually because we went to battle earlier than expected.

The real cause of the change, however, was the sudden appearance of the word "Kangaroo." This was the official code-word for an armoured infantry carrier, a new weapon which no one had ever heard of before. It consisted of a turretless Sherman tank or a gunless Priest self-propelled gun, inside which the infantry were carried. Each Sherman type Kangaroo carried one section, whereas the Priest type carried two. Each had a wireless set and of course an equal cross-country performance to that of a tank. The idea was that the infantry should travel in these vehicles close to the tanks, thereby keeping themselves well forward, immune from small-arms fire, and fresh. In future operations we were likely to fight with these and we therefore had to carry out three exercises with them—on each occasion a different battalion of the 36th Brigade being mounted inside.

Each regiment was to do the same three exercises, the 10th Hussars beginning first. The Colonel and Major Steel watched their first attempt and at the end there was a long and complex discussion on the way in which the Kangaroo had been handled. The Colonel was opposed to the tactics he had seen which featured centralized Kangaroos behind Regimental Headquarters. His own theory was that they should be subdivided and mixed with the troops of tanks. This led to a great controversy, but the Colonel eventually convinced his own officers that he was right.

There was no doubt that the Kangaroo was an excellent innovation. The country was unsuitable for an advance by tanks alone and in the past there had been endless delays in dismounting the infantry behind, moving them forward and explaining what was required before anything had happened at all. But now they would be in a position to see and hear all that the tanks themselves saw and heard and the rate of progress would be vastly improved. The only problem was their tactical handling.

Up until then all our attacks in Italy had been limited by distance. Now we should be called upon to go as far as we could. For this our technique needed much improvement, so when "C" Squadron set off to the Cervia ranges it carried out a scheme of its own on the way. It was very simple to fix an advance across country with a river crossing at the end, but after a few moments it was clear that moving across the grain of the vineyards was unexpectedly difficult and the actual speed was one mile an hour, which is slower than infantry pace. The lack of practice at this kind of movement had to be taken into account, but even so the troop leaders at first found difficulty in manœuvring their tanks. "C" Squadron also experimented with launching a borrowed Sherman bridge into a canal. It would have been a quick operation had not the crew stopped on the brink to remove all their kit, rations and brew cans. Altogether it was an instructive day and showed us that armoured infantry carriers were not the only problem to be mastered.

"A quiet night at the front: Kangaroos at the back," says the War Diary one morning. Both were full-time jobs. The Colonel ran sand-table discussions for all tank commanders while the Adjutant prepared for three exercises. Some officers were sent off to gain contact with the Desert Air Force who were going to make the exercise still more professional by practising their system of close-support bombing. Others visited the 4th Hussars who crewed the Kangaroos. Meanwhile, the infantry were briefed and consulted about all our ideas.

Possibly because of the imminence of Easter, the name chosen for the exercise was "Hosannah." The Brigadier planned it and the sequence of events was tactically straightforward. The Colonel had decided to collect the party together in a six-acre field so that everyone would be close at hand for order groups and any preliminary conferences. The field had only two entrances and the force arrived from different directions. It was a heterogeneous collection that converged on Carpinello on the morning of the 26th of March and came under the command of the 9th Lancers:

> 8th Argyll and Sutherland Highlanders.
> "A" and "B" Squadrons, 4th Hussars (the former of Kangaroos and the latter of tanks).
> "E" Battery, 11th (H.A.C.) R.H.A. (self-propelled 25-pounders).
> 138th Field Regiment, R.A. (towed 25-pounders).
> Two troops, "C" Squadron, 51st Royal Tanks (Crocodiles). (Crocodiles were flame-throwing Churchill tanks. Apart from the fuel trailer there was no significant difference between a Crocodile and an ordinary tank.)
> One detachment, Armoured Regiment, R.E.
> One section, 3rd Troop, 3rd Field Squadron, R.E.
> One section, Light Field Ambulance.
> Three armoured bulldozers (called Shermandozers).
> One scissors bridge.
> Rover David (R.A.F. liaison, of which more later).

This force exceeded three thousand men and two hundred vehicles and, according to Major Meyrick, its equipment was worth over three million pounds. The assembly took place without a hitch, as each vehicle was carefully guided to its appropriate position and in the end the entire group was tactically formed up.

The battle formation is complicated to describe, but it is important, since the rest of this History depends on it.

Two squadron groups were leading, side by side, "A" on the right and "C" on the left. Each of these groups consisted of one 9th Lancers squadron with, under command, one company of infantry, one troop of Kangaroos (which lifted that company), one Shermandozer, one bridge and a section of Engineers, and, in support, one section of the Reconnaissance Troop and one forward observation officer from "E" Battery. In addition, each squadron had its own fascine carrier.

Each of these two squadron groups was disposed with two troops leading, one on each side of its squadron's axis of advance, and each troop had in support a platoon of infantry mounted in a section of two Priest Kangaroos. This was the fundamental principle of the Colonel's theory and, moreover, had been recommended and tried out by the 9th Lancers in the old Tidworth days before the war. With this lay-out the leading troops had their own infantry motoring along with them, ready to leap out and help at a second's notice. Behind these two troop groups came a third troop, actually on the axis of advance, followed by squadron headquarters, the reserve platoon of infantry, also in two Kangaroos, and finally the reserve troop of tanks. Thus every Kangaroo had a troop of tanks in front of it which it carefully followed. Furthermore, every vehicle in the squadron group was netted on the same frequency so that they worked as a united team.

Behind the leading squadron groups came Regimental Headquarters, an immense conglomeration of vehicles. There were battalion headquarters in Kangaroos, battery commanders, the officer in command of the Crocodiles, a spare bridge, Rover David (two tanks commanded by Desert Air Force officers), the Reconnaissance Troop reserve—and all these in addition to our own party. After Regimental Headquarters came the two reserve squadron groups side by side and finally the assorted "hangers-on" already described. These were placed under the command of one of the reserve squadron leaders for movement purposes only. The reason for this is obvious: the Colonel had quite enough to do taking tactical decisions and, by deputing the task of moving the "tail," he saved himself having to think about the important but comparatively insignificant task of "whipping-in."

There was a mass of people in that field, but it was orderly because every man had had explained to him the layout and the reasoning behind it. The Colonel arrived on the scene at 8 a.m. with the obvious intention of enjoying himself. His tank was flying a lance flag from the top of the aerial mast, and a number of red-hatted officers had already collected to bombard him with questions. For the tenth time at least he explained again what he planned and then gave out his orders to the commanders of every part of the group, who declared themselves entirely happy about what was going to happen.

"Well, Brigadier, I think we're ready."

"All right, Jack, send them off when you like."

And then the Colonel picked up the microphone and gave the order: "All stations Able—'Hosannah'!"

We were out of the starting gate at ten minutes past nine and advancing at the rate of about two miles an hour. The enemy was represented by other troops in the Brigade, so umpires were numerous. The day was a tremendous success. The problem of control had been mastered automatically by the nature of the formation and the neatness of the grouping. There was no muddle or difficulty. The Shermandozers filled in the dykes and enabled all vehicles to cross. The infantry in their Kangaroos faithfully followed our tanks and enjoyed every moment of it. Every few hundred yards they were called upon to motor up past the tanks they were following to destroy an enemy strong-point. Sometimes they had to carry out a company attack which took longer, but as they could listen and talk to each other on the wireless and could always see their objective, it was made much easier for them. At midday the opposition stiffened, so a regimental attack had to be made. The ground was suitable for a left-hook movement and at the conclusion of this the exercise ended.

The next day there was a conference on "Hosannah" in Forli. All officers forgathered there for a harangue by four brigadiers followed by the G.O.C. 78th Division. Many theories were methodically analysed, but there was no doubt about it, the day belonged to Lieutenant-Colonel Price. It was a triumph for him, and the whole Regiment was delighted with its toy and the way in which it was being worked. Enthusiasm was sincere and we prayed to be given Kangaroos in the next battle.

Twice more we played "Hosannah," each time with increased confidence and pleasure. The infantry were changed and on the third occasion we used a different area of ground, but otherwise the exercise remained the same. The Desert Air Force support worked well. Whenever the Colonel or a squadron leader wanted some bombs, the two Air Force officers constituting Rover David were given the map reference over the air. Then, by a complicated process, they described the target and its exact whereabouts to the aeroplanes which flew overhead in readiness. There were six of these flying one behind the other, known collectively as a "cab rank" because they flew round in a queue awaiting their turn. Once the leader had spotted the target as a result of Rover David's indications, it took only about a minute before the "cab rank" had unloaded its bombs. Naturally, no bombs were released on exercise, but we tested their accuracy by asking them to "bomb" the command tank, which they did with consistent accuracy.

Meanwhile, much spadework was going on in the background. The usual classes were run for operators, gunners and drivers. Sixteen reinforcements arrived, and "A" and "B" Squadrons spent three or four full days on the Cervia ranges, now that "C" had returned. Tanks were cleaned and oiled; fitters adjusted the engines; the ammunition loading on echelons was recalculated; emergency rations were changed; summer clothing was drawn.

Easter Day was on the 1st of April and a more heavenly day could not be imagined. It was not a holiday, but somehow it felt like a Sunday. In battle one loses all sense of day and date, for each is just like the last, and the future is so uncertain that definite plans can only be made a few hours ahead. Even out of the line there is little difference unless it is for a long period of rest such as we had in Algiers. Apart from an occasional day off and the break at Christmas, the Regiment had been working seven days a week for eight months. Now our house was almost in order, the sky was bright blue and the buds were bursting into flower. One could not help pausing for a moment's contemplation.

It was not a day of rest, however. The guns kept on firing up the ranges. We still had one more "Hosannah" to do on the following Tuesday, and all the time speculation was growing as to the nature of the spring offensive. The Germans had had plenty of time to prepare: the rivers and canals would be expensive to cross, while the precipitous hills on the left were equally hazardous.

The Colonel was briefed by the Army Commander in the usual way and two days later the Brigadier disclosed the outline plan to our senior officers. The 15th Army Group intended to destroy the enemy south of the Po. The Eighth Army was to attack first, followed by the Fifth Army four days to a week later. The opening move had already been made by the capture of the spit of land on the extreme east of the line up to Porto Garibaldi. From here the 56th Division, with the 10th Hussars under command, had embarked on an amphibious operation across Lake Comacchio round the right of the German positions. This had not yet developed into a major operation but was proceeding satisfactorily. A cover plan was taking place simultaneously on the extreme west of the line, where the 88th U.S. Division attacked. The X and XIII Corps were in the centre, holding the line with a minimum of troops and at the same time doing everything in their power to make the Germans believe that we were going to attack straight up Route 9.

These were the preliminaries. The main Eighth Army assault was to be made by V Corps in the Bagnacavallo—Cotignola area, the very place where we had so recently been supporting the 36th Brigade. This attack was to go in at first light after an all-day fire plan of unique weight culminating in two minutes' intensive flaming by Crocodiles and Wasps. Once across the Senio the infantry were to capture Lugo and reach the River Santerno as soon as possible. When they had crossed this second river the 78th Division, with the 2nd Armoured Brigade (less the 10th Hussars) under command, were to advance due north alongside it. The 9th Lancers were probably going to work with the 38th Irish Brigade and not the 36th Brigade after all.

Such was the gist of the plan. It was ambitious, because to destroy the enemy south of the Po would mean that prodigious advances would have to be made by both armies.

On the 7th of April training finished and orders were issued for the move to our concentration area near Godo station. We said good-bye to the 36th Brigade, whom we were very sorry to leave, squadrons packed up and loaded their tanks and lorries, and the echelons were re-formed.

The next day the six 105-mm. tanks under Captain Peek advanced to their gun positions, whence they took part in the artillery programme by firing one thousand five hundred rounds. On the 9th April the Regiment left Carpinello at 6 a.m. and had an uninterrupted journey by devious side-roads to Godo, which lay six miles east of the River Senio at Cotignola.

CHAPTER XXXIII

"HOSANNAH" TO THE RIVER RENO

D Day for this particular battle coincided with our arrival at Godo on the 9th of April. Nothing happened all the morning, but just after lunch there was a distant drone and eight hundred Flying Fortresses, thousands of feet up in the sky, flew over, their silver paint glinting in the sun, for now it was no longer necessary to camouflage our aircraft. They dropped several hundred thousand fragmentation bombs between the Rivers Senio and Santerno over a period of ninety minutes.

At 3.20 p.m. a vigorous artillery barrage opened up. After each thirty minutes the gunners paused for ten minutes and the dive-bombers pounded away. Two hours later it was H Hour and a herd of Crocodiles and Wasps drove up to the banks of the river to belch flame on to the farther bank. Finally, after two minutes of this, the New Zealand and 8th Indian Divisions went over the top. From where we watched, six miles back, the rumble of guns and swelling clouds of thick, black smoke were most impressive.

The Brigadier looked in and informed us of further plans. If the enemy strongly opposed our advance up the Santerno the Bays would support two battalions of the 38th Irish Brigade in a deliberate advance. If opposition was light the 9th Lancers Group would be launched as for Exercise "Hosannah," with the 2nd London Irish Rifles—also of the 38th Brigade—as our infantry. This was excellent news, as it promised us Kangaroos and in any case no plan for exploitation could be more definite at that stage.

At 5.30 p.m. on the 9th, in two jeeps and a cloud of dust, twelve officers of the London Irish arrived at Regimental Headquarters. The Commanding Officer of the 2nd London Irish Rifles was Lieutenant-Colonel Bredin, D.S.O., M.C., and from the first moment our two regiments became firm friends. In three-quarters of an hour the operation, should it materialize, had been arranged, and after that it was just a question of chatting until dinner time. "Let us hope," says the War Diary, "that we do work with the London Irish and not change again."

The next morning it was learnt that the assaulting divisions had gained all objectives, taking six hundred prisoners. During the morning they sat along the line of the Canale di Lugo, half-way between the two rivers. Back came the Flying Fortresses, down went their bombs, again the artillery fired, and when this was over the attack continued to the Santerno. Everything was going according to plan.

251

At 9 p.m. on the 10th the Colonel issued orders for the move to Lugo the next day. The timing and route were changed during the night, but Major Allhusen and the reconnaissance party set off at 5 a.m. as originally arranged. The Regiment itself started at 8 a.m. on the 11th in the order: "C" Squadron, Regimental Headquarters, Reconnaissance Troop, "A" Squadron and "B" Squadron. Once on the tank track the move went smoothly. It was unusual to move up in daylight and, though the dust was beyond description, no time was wasted. We crossed the Senio over the New Zealand bridge three miles south of Cotignola, and from there the reconnaissance party guided us to leaguer just north of Lugo. "A" Echelon, under Captain Allen, also had a clear run, and we had all assembled by 12.30 p.m. The London Irish were there waiting for us, so we amalgamated into our various groups without delay: "A" Squadron with "G" Company, "B" Squadron with "E" Company, "C" Squadron with "H" Company, and "B" Squadron, 4th Hussars, with "F" Company. The Engineers had arrived and also three Shermandozers and an extra bridge. The party was taking shape.

The tactical situation was good, though progress up in front was slower than expected. We were at three hours' notice to move from 3 p.m. on the 11th, but actually we were stationary for forty-two hours. No bridgehead was made over the Santerno until the night of the 11th, and the first formation to go in and expand it was the 36th Brigade, which fought in the direction of Conselice and made steady progress. Then two battalions of the 38th Irish Brigade and the Bays began attacking due north. In effect, this amounted to a combination of the two alternative plans explained by the Brigadier at Godo. When this expanding process had loosened the opposition we should be launched to pass through.

During the waiting there were the usual conferences and changes of plan, and on the 12th all sorts of people arrived at Regimental Headquarters, saying: "I've been told to report to you." "A" Squadron, 4th Hussars, arrived with the Kangaroos and the London Irish got mounted. More doctors, ambulances and gunners joined us, and one squadron of Flails from the 51st Royal Tanks. (A Flail tank is designed for clearing mines. Across the front of the tank is attached a cylinder which can be made to revolve by the tank engine. Chains are fastened to the cylinder so that when the cylinder rotates the chains beat the ground and explode the mines.) We began to feel like a private army. "The more the merrier," said the Colonel.

In the evening we formed up to move so that if we were called forward in the night there would be no confusion. We could never afford to let our two hundred and ten vehicles get into a tangle. At 7 p.m. there was a final "O" Group (a conference specially convened for the issue of orders) at the Colonel's tank.

The Regimental column set off at 6 a.m. on the 13th of April and made a slow and uneventful journey into the Santerno bridgehead. The two battalions of the 38th Brigade and the Bays were making some progress against minor opposition, and the whole Regiment knew that the moment had come. There was no sign that we would be launched at once, however, and as the minutes became hours and there were still no orders, there began to be a feeling of tension and impatience. Then, at midday, the Colonel arrived back from visiting the 38th Brigade Headquarters.

"Come on," he said, "we're off!"

"A" Squadron Group was in the lead, followed by "C" Squadron Group, which had orders to come up on "A's" right as soon as the lie of the water-courses permitted. Then came Regimental Headquarters, "B" Squadron Group, "B" Squadron, 4th Hussars, Group and finally the Flails.

It took an hour to pass the 38th Brigade. There was much speculation as to the exact positions of their forward troops, which was unavoidable but meant that "A" Squadron had to go cautiously until the first German was seen or killed. However, they did not have long to wait. Spandaus and bazookas were scattered all over the place, and soon "G" Company had to put in a respectable attack against an enemy strong-point near the floodbank of the Santerno. While supporting this, Corporal Chapman's tank was struck on the gun mantlet by a bazooka which luckily did not penetrate, although the blast and bits of flying metal wounded Corporal Chapman and Troopers Williams and Atkinson in the face. The bazookaman was dealt with and Corporal Chapman remained in action for a further half-hour until ordered back by his squadron leader, as he was now nearly blind.

At about the same time, a sniper took a shot at Major Meyrick's head from fifty yards' range but luckily erred in his aim and the bullet ricocheted off the turret. This German was also killed.

A further strong-point was encountered at La Giovecca, where the Santerno turns sharp east. "A" Squadron could not bypass it because an impassable ditch lay ahead, so "G" Company, under the staunch leadership of Major Ted Griffiths, put in a rapid attack which destroyed the enemy and enabled the Shermandozers to get into action. Once across this obstacle the water-courses diverged and "A" Squadron struck north-east while "C" Squadron continued due north.

The country was very thick, for the foliage was well advanced, so progress was difficult for "A" Squadron working across the grain. At once Germans were met in increasing numbers, though some gave themselves up quite willingly when they saw our little "army." No sooner had the two leading troops of "A" Squadron crossed the main road just outside La Giovecca than Lieutenant Whately spotted a long-barrelled 75-mm. anti-tank gun. It was only three hundred yards away on the left flank and rapidly traversing on to them. Engaging it with his machine gun, Lieutenant Whately warned 2nd Troop on his left. Corporal Cumbers spotted it, fired two rounds of armour-piercing at the gun and knocked the barrel right off with the second one—a very good shot. During training we had instituted a rule of avoiding roads because the enemy usually expected us to use them. Naturally our speed was reduced, but this incident was the first justification for our rule, for the anti-tank gun was sited to shoot down the road and was spotted only because the movement of its traverse gave way its position.

"A" Squadron's objective was the railway bridge over the canal called Scolo di Conselice a mile away. As expected, the wires along which the vines were growing proved a formidable obstacle, especially for Kangaroos, and the smooth working of the group was impeded. In the end "G" Company dismounted completely and surrounded each tank troop as it slowly plunged onwards. Eventually they reached the Scolo to find the bridge blown and, as darkness was falling, they leaguered where they were.

Meanwhile, "C" Squadron Group was pushing northwards to its two more important bridges over the same Scolo at Cavamento. One of these carried the main road, the other a railway. 4th Troop, under Lieutenant Hannen, approached to within a hundred yards of the road bridge and found it intact. A quick plan was made in which one tank followed by one Kangaroo was to charge the bridge covered by the other tanks in the troop. Sergeant Salt set out and when he was only forty yards away from the bridge it went up in a cloud of dust. He continued right up to the canal bank and fired at the many Germans running about on the far side. The Kangaroo was right behind him and the two sections instantly dismounted, scrambled across the ruins of the bridge and shot-up the German demolition party who were just mounting their horse-drawn cart to make their getaway.

At the same time, Lieutenant Berry's troop had reached the railway bridge on the left and found it already partially demolished. The troop leader fired two rounds of 17-pounder armour-piercing at a movement on the far bank and a German officer with two Iron Crosses threw up his hands, waded the canal and surrendered.

A bridgehead was essential so that the Engineers could build a Bailey, and this was won by "H" Company. Later, "E" Company went to its assistance because all the houses on both sides of the river required clearing—a laborious business. However, the London Irish could not be left to hold the bridgehead alone despite its small radius of nearly a quarter of a mile. As luck would have it, part of an armoured assault regiment, R.E., had been added to our "tail" during the afternoon, and their commander now dispatched a Churchill Ark to span the canal. Once we feared it was going to lose its way, but eventually it turned up and was put in the canal between the two bridges. This enabled Lieutenant Mike Woodhead to get his troop safely across, much to the delight of "H" Company.

There was now no alternative but to call a halt for the night. Except for the two leading squadron groups, the Regiment leaguered by La Viovecca. The echelon came up the road and refilled us, taking back on the empty lorries the seventy-odd prisoners we had captured so far. More prisoners were coming in, and the recovery tanks under Captain Foy, the Technical Officer—commonly called the "Chinese Squadron"—excelled themselves by taking three more in the leaguer.

During the hours of darkness Lieutenant-Colonel Bredin assumed command of the group, since the infantry then became more important than the tanks. He held a conference at 11 p.m. which was attended by company commanders, squadron leaders and the Regimental Headquarters officers. He gave orders for certain patrols to go out and generally explained the defence for the night. Then Lieutenant-Colonel Price issued his orders for the continuation of the advance the next day. Finally, those who were not otherwise engaged slept, while the Engineers heroically hammered away at the Bailey to complete it by first light.

The next morning, the 14th of April, our objectives were the two bridges across the River Reno at Bastia, a furlong apart and one and a half miles north of our bridgehead. A double attack was planned, "C" Squadron Group, including "E" Company instead of "H," going due north through Lavezzola and "B" Squadron Group doing a right hook. Captured documents showed that the intermediate areas were full of minefields, so a troop of five Flail tanks was put under the command of "B" Squadron.

At 5.45 a.m. "C" Squadron set off towards Lavezzola, with 2nd Troop leading and the London Irish pioneers clearing the mines. The normal German rearguards and snipers were much in evidence and were ruthlessly dealt with. The road was mined the whole way and nearly every house contained booby-traps, so the advance demanded caution. By the luckiest chance Lieutenant Woodhead captured a party of Germans early in the proceedings and on being roughly handled they confessed that they were the very Germans who had laid the mines. This was too easy, and they were made to walk in front of the tanks and pick up the mines they had so carefully laid the night before. This considerably accelerated the advance, and by 9 a.m. "C" Squadron had reached the River Reno to find the main Route 16 bridge blown up as well as the railway bridge. The group took up a holding position on the bank awaiting further instructions. The civilians in Lavezzola were wild with excitement and lavish with "vino" and flowers. In a short time each tank looked more like a stall at a flower show than a tank.

"B" Squadron had a less easy passage. It reached Route 16 uneventfully, collecting a few prisoners on the way, but was then held up by a dyke and a minefield. The latter was cleared by the tank crews and the Shermandozer filled in the dyke, but it transpired that there was a solid minefield on either side of the road, so they had to proceed north-west up the road with the infantry prodding for mines just in front of them. Then suddenly they came under heavy fire and a huge crater prevented further progress that way. Major Laurie decided to reach the Reno floodbank five hundred yards to the north, and ordered the Flail troop to clear a path. The troop worked exceedingly well, making an admirable lane to the river and thence westwards along the floodbank. This enabled part of the squadron group to reach the river and later allowed the

Engineers to reconnoitre for a bridge site. More prisoners came in, making our total for the morning thirty-five.

The Reno was quite a large river, but the London Irish wasted no time in establishing a bridgehead over it so that we were ready for the Sappers to build another Bailey. However, none came. It transpired later that no one had expected us to reach the Reno so quickly, so no arrangements had been made.

Meanwhile, the London Irish bridgehead was counter-attacked and they were driven back at the cost of twenty-five men. Forty Germans had appeared and marched through the perimeter ostensibly to surrender, but had suddenly dis- persed and attacked the London Irish from behind. It was a lesson which no one forgot.

Ultimately it was decided not to erect a bridge until the 56th Division, approaching from the east along the far bank, had joined up with us. Accord- ingly all parts of the Regimental Group leaguered where they were, thoroughly displeased at the thought of unmolested Germans preparing for our return beyond the river.

That, however, was not our business. We had been ordered to reach the Reno and had succeeded in getting there. The cost to the enemy was one self-propelled gun overrun, one 75-mm. gun destroyed, and two officers and one hundred and five other ranks taken prisoner. We called this operation "Hosannah" because its form was almost exactly the same as our training exercises of that name and because it entirely vindicated the Colonel's ideas. It is true that the opposition had been only slight, but we had been by no means fully exerted or deployed.

Above all, we had cemented our friendship with the London Irish. The two commanding officers thought and acted as one man and each had confidence in the other. As with the commanders so with their regiments, and this spirit extended to the rest of the group. The Flails had made history because they were the first to go into action in Italy; the atmosphere of complete understanding and confidence was truly remarkable.

So we called ourselves "Price's Private Army," an appropriate name for the only force of its kind.

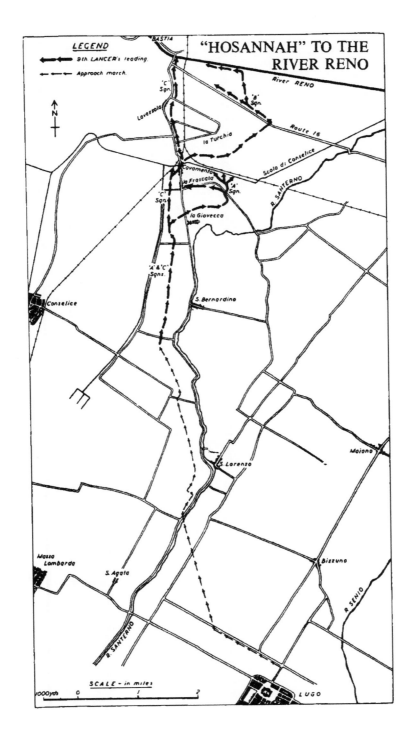

CHAPTER XXXIV

THE ARGENTA GAP

THE morning of the 16th of April found us still waiting. The Flails had gone, but the rest of the "private army" was under command of the 38th Irish Brigade. There was much uncertainty at this stage as to whether or not its life would be prolonged, and because of this one squadron was affiliated to each of the Irish battalions in case normal tank-infantry fighting was resumed. The 56th Division had just taken Bastia and the Bailey bridge on Route 16 was going up fast. As usual, plans were changed four or five times during the day, but the crews did their maintenance and cooking. At tea time there was every sign that we should be needed again and we were ordered to move to a concentration area north of the Reno. We were told to use the 56th Division bridge farther to the east because the approaches to the bridge in front of us were in danger of being spoiled by tanks. The London Irish were told to "stay put" for the night and rejoin us the next morning.

We started at 5.15 p.m. on the 16th in the order: Regimental Headquarters, Reconnaissance Troop, "B" Squadron, "A" and "B" Squadrons, 4th Hussars, and "A" and "C" Squadrons. All went well until the head of one column was just over the river. There we encountered the tail of a traffic block which stretched for miles. The 56th Division Police knew nothing of the arrival of a hundred tracked vehicles, so all their arrangements were upset. Though the journey was only seventeen miles, the last squadron did not arrive until after midnight. There were clouds of dust and the sky was black with mosquitoes, for we were on the edge of Lake Comacchio, now in flood. We leaguered in an orchard near Filo well clear of the road, and could see the guns of the 56th Division in action across the marsh. We watched them fire a new sort of shell consisting of three red flares on parachutes which acted as aiming marks for our bombers.

The operations which had been planned for the succeeding day or two followed the same general lines as those at the Santerno four days before. One battalion of the 11th Brigade (78th Division) was already in the attack by the time we were in leaguer, and at first light the 38th Irish Brigade, again with the Bays, was to pass through them and continue the good work. We were then to repeat "Hosannah," get the whips out and try to reach Ferrara.

The London Irish duly arrived in their lorries at 5.15 a.m. on the 17th and formed up by companies in the field adjoining our leaguer. The Kangaroos formed up on them and the infantry were mounted in half an hour. By 7 a.m.

T

they had joined their respective squadrons and the "private army" was re-formed and ready as ordered.

At 6.30 there was an "O" Group in Regimental Headquarters and the Colonel explained an unexpected delay. Two Arks in a ditch called Fosso Marina had capsized, so that a further crossing had to be made before the 38th Irish Brigade and the Bays could go forward. They were able to move at 10 a.m. and opposition was at once encountered, including Tiger tanks. No one was surprised at this, because the Argenta Gap was of great strategic significance. It is a narrow isthmus of land between Lake Comacchio and another more inland marsh, the town of Argenta being roughly in the centre of this gap. Obviously it was an ideal spot for defence because it was impossible to be outflanked unless boats were used. Furthermore, the Germans knew that if they could hold us here there was no immediate fear of the Eighth and Fifth Armies joining up. Therefore they put up the most stalwart resistance.

In the afternoon the leading troops had increasing difficulty in making any headway, and the Regiment's feeling of tense expectancy rapidly changed to one of anti-climax. We were not altogether surprised when the London Irish were warned to be prepared to fight on their feet in the normal infantry way, supported by one of our squadrons.

However, Lieutenant-Colonel Bredin had gone to a conference at V Corps Headquarters and there had heard what was going to happen that night. The plan amounted to a two-divisional advance up the gap, the 56th on the right and the 78th on the left. When the 78th Division had captured Argenta and was approaching Boccaleone, the "private army" was to be launched with the intention of seizing a crossing over the Fosso Benvignante and then exploiting northwards. As a result of this knowledge the Colonel was able to lay his plans and issue his orders at 7.30 p.m. The written orders arrived from Brigade Headquarters at midnight, but luckily there was no change.

These social "O" Groups were a speciality of the "private army" and much enjoyed by the many officers who came to them. They were held at the command tank, which was equipped with all manner of paraphernalia. Its crew consisted of the Colonel, the Adjutant, Sergeant Williamson, the Regimental Signal Sergeant (Sergeant Jenner being on leave in England), Sergeant Fox, the driver, and Trooper Kent. We carried no ammunition because there was not enough space. There were two wireless sets in the turret; a table, pigeon-holes and writing materials for the Adjutant; a cocktail cabinet on the turret floor; a reserve "cellar" under the turret; and an extensive supply of tins of fruit, lobster, tongue, biscuits, and every other sort of foodstuff that Sergeant Middleditch could obtain. In addition there were bales of maps, code boards and two thousand cigarettes, as well as all the essential tank kit, binoculars and clothes. On top of the engine were strapped two tarpaulins which made a spacious bivouac at night, a folding table, a bench, two deck-chairs, and two summer-house chairs, while on top of the turret there was a gigantic umbrella. This had been specially made in Bari and was about seven feet in diameter. Its stem fitted into a socket in the middle of the turret roof and protected the Colonel and his Adjutant from sun and rain. When motoring along we looked rather like two Indian maharajahs riding on an elephant.

As soon as we halted in leaguer up went the umbrella, the table and chairs. Every few minutes someone arrived with a problem to be solved or in search of news, and they greatly appreciated the little extra comfort and the small refreshment we were able to offer. Our tank was, in fact, the only one in the Regiment that could dispense with its ammunition and we made the most of the extra storage space for everyone's benefit. It will be understood from all this why our "O" Groups were called social. About twenty-four officers, and occasionally more, would forgather. When the party had arrived and was ready, the Colonel would give the latest information from the front and issue his orders. At the end, when everyone was absolutely clear as to what was required, they would stay and talk until they finally drifted back to their own squadrons or companies. It was a businesslike and disciplined procedure, yet informal, and all were thoroughly at ease.

After a peaceful night we were ready to move at 5.30 a.m. on the 18th of April. There was a short delay during which the previous night's orders were confirmed, and the column actually moved off at 6.45 a.m. We were in single file, closed up as tight as possible to reduce the length of the tail. Fighting still continued in Argenta itself and traffic blocks made progress difficult, but by making detours across country we wormed our way forward until we finally reached the 8th Argyll and Sutherland Highlanders, one of the leading battalions, on the line of the Scolo Cantonacci. "B" Squadron Group was leading, with "A" just behind, ready to go up on the right as soon as it could. We had the same difficulty as before in deciding when we had actually overtaken our own troops, and in this instance the information we had been given proved inaccurate. Within a very few minutes battle had been joined.

Boccaleone was supposed to be captured, but just as "B" Squadron was bypassing it on the east a tank started firing from the outskirts of the town. This Mark IV caused some delay, as we had to side-step to the right to avoid it. Like the self-propelled gun at Alfonsine, it was difficult to engage, as it kept darting in and out of the houses. It knocked out one Honey of the Reconnaissance Troop, luckily without casualties. Two Kangaroos were also pierced by armour-piercing shot going in at the front and out of the back; one 4th Hussar was killed, but the London Irish were extremely lucky to suffer only eight minor casualties. Inside a Kangaroo the infantry sit opposite each other in tube-train fashion, and these eight were wounded by bits of flying metal from the armour-piercing shot as it whistled between them. Shortly afterwards the Mark IV was knocked out by Lieutenant Birch-Reynardson and his gunner, Corporal Nickolls, who had been lying up in readiness for it to reappear.

"A" Squadron had now come up on "B's" right, and straightaway lost a tank

T1

to another Mark IV. Unhappily Corporal Marrows, Lance-Corporal Stackpool and Trooper Kinsman were killed. Within two minutes the Mark IV was hit by "B" Squadron and blown up by rocket-firing Spitfires. Soon afterwards, Sergeant Corney-Bond was also wounded. From then on we met very strong resistance and came under accurate shell fire. Both flanks were fully exposed and the whole column was harassed by machine guns and snipers from front to rear.

We had to fight every yard of the way. The country was difficult to cross owing to the innumerable ditches which had to be filled in with bulldozers, and the London Irish were constantly dismounting to destroy bazookamen and strongpoints. Going into action with lightning dash, they cleared up each pocket in a matter of minutes. By 1 o'clock "A" Squadron had reached the bridge over the Fosso Benvignante to find it blown and "B" Squadron was up to the impassable Scolo Cantonacci, having destroyed four vehicles *en route*.

Up to that moment eighty prisoners and one German ambulance had been taken. It is doubtful if we could have advanced so far without the wonderful support of the Desert Air Force. A "cab rank" was constantly overhead, bombing, machine-gunning and firing rockets only three hundred yards ahead of us. We actually saw them destroy two Mark IV's, two self-propelled guns and several half-tracked vehicles trying to escape northwards. We all agreed that their support saved us from losing at least six tanks.

After much bulldozing under heavy fire, "B" Squadron succeeded in negotiating the Scolo Cantonacci and from there swung left with the intention of seizing the two bridges over the Fosso Benvignante half a mile north of Consandolo, but almost immediately it was held up by another ditch running north and south. A fascine was put in and this combined with further bulldozing enabled it to proceed towards the bridges. Soon "B" Squadron reported that it could see the bridges two hundred yards away and both appeared to be still standing. Excitement was now intense, because if we could not cross the Fosso by one of these bridges we could not cross at all that day and our mission would have failed.

Without wasting a minute, Lieutenant Joicey's troop made a dash, and soon the news came through that it was safely across and that both bridges were intact. It was a thrilling moment.

Quickly "B" Squadron and "E" Company formed a bridgehead and collected many Germans who were completely taken by surprise. "A" Squadron and "G" Company, following close behind, slipped over the bridge and joined up on "B" Squadron's right. Both groups now advanced, with the London Irish dismounted, as the country was so dense, and after four hundred yards they halted to reorganize. The area was by now thick with crestfallen Germans: each squadron had already taken fifty prisoners, who were becoming an embarrassment to them, and reports of lorries, officers' messes and equipment indicated some very good loot.

Before allowing the advance to continue, the Colonel wisely decided to make

ITALY, 1944-1945

88-mm. gun overrun, 18th April, 1945

9th Lancer crew on captured German 155-mm. gun

Bailey Bridge over Po at Ferrara

Captain H. O. D. Thwaites, M.C., and crew

ITALY, 1944-1945

4th Hussar Kangaroos

Sergt. J. E. Edwards, M.M., "B" Squadron

Lieut. F. C. Hainsworth, Capt. P. J. Dudding, Major D. S. Allhusen, April, 1945

The C.O. and Adjutant (Lieut.-Colonel Price and Capt. Pym), May, 1945

certain that the bridges were not tampered with. Being in the heart of enemy territory, we should be completely cut off if the bridges were blown behind us. He ordered "B" Squadron, 4th Hussars, with "F" Company to overtake Regimental Headquarters and sit tight round the crossings. Just as Major John Oger, the 4th Hussar squadron leader, was walking over to get exact orders from the Colonel, a shell landed almost on top of him, seriously wounding him in the leg. This caused delay, but the squadron second-in-command eventually got his group into position round the bridges.

All this had taken some time and there was now only one hour's daylight left. So without more ado and in spite of their encumbrances, "A" and "B" Squadron groups continued the advance towards the Fosso Sabbiosola. Within five minutes both squadrons were engaged by 88-mm. and larger calibre guns shooting over open sights and scores of 20-mm. anti-aircraft guns, some with quadruple barrels. Both squadrons replied with all guns, and the whole area was plastered with high-explosive shells and machine-gun bullets. Immediately afterwards the leading troops of tanks and the London Irish on their feet charged straight into the German gun lines, whose crews were still manning them.

In an area of about half a square mile they "brewed-up" two more Mark IV's, overran a battery of four 88-mm.'s and a battery of four 150-mm. field guns, as well as twelve 20-mm.'s. The German gunners put up a very brave performance, for they all went on firing at point-blank range up to the end. Luckily the 88's had been sited for anti-aircraft fire and were taken by surprise. Nevertheless, they managed to load with armour-piercing and fire a considerable number of rounds at our tanks, but they were so cluttered up with camouflage and branches of trees and so overwhelmed with our fire that their aim was erratic. They hit Lieutenant Michael de Burgh's tank, but, though its suspension was holed, he was able to continue. Lieutenant Whately's tank was also hit by a 150-mm. shell, but he, too, continued despite two broken ear-drums.

Meanwhile, "C" Squadron and H.Q. Company had gone over the crossing and were being similarly entertained on the right, for the three squadrons were advancing in line. They encountered a battery of four 105-mm. field guns and a battery of three 88's, both of which they captured intact. They suffered only one casualty—Trooper Brown, who was wounded. The London Irish coped with the more tenacious strong-points and all the time prisoners came streaming in. They had never before had their gun lines entered and did not know what they should do. Many enemy vehicles and fortified houses were burning, set alight by the tracer from the tanks.

As it grew dark all squadron groups reported that they had gained their objectives on the Fosso Sabbiosola and were busy mopping up and consolidating. The Colonel would have liked to go on, but the squadrons were too cluttered up with prisoners and guns, and in any case the ground we had already taken was far from being clear of the enemy.

Regimental Headquarters advanced to a farm called La Fossa in the centre of the four squadron groups, and the Colonel has since written this account of his reactions at that moment:

"When I stepped out of my tank the countryside was an incredible sight. It was quite dark and we were completely surrounded by a ring of fire. There were twenty-one houses burning, with flames roaring through the roofs, innumerable German vehicles burning, and two ammunition dumps exploding and sending every sort of firework into the air. The whole countryside was alight for about two thousand yards in every direction.

"It was a very big thrill indeed to sit in the middle of this ring of fire and to realize the extent of the destruction wrought by the 9th Lancers Group and to know that we had burst the Argenta Gap wide open."

Throughout the day Lieutenant-Colonel Bredin had been an example of tranquillity. Since his battalion was under 9th Lancers' command he was relieved of his usual responsibilities. On arrival at La Fossa, however, he sprang into action. He gave out his orders and made a personal inspection of the company positions to co-ordinate the defence for the night. It was not easy, because Germans were around us and in amongst us, but in less than an hour he confirmed that the situation was under control.

Lieutenant Dudding, the Intelligence Officer, armed himself with a stout stick and herded prisoners into a barn—over two hundred of them, including six officers. They all said they never believed we could cross the Fosso Benvignante so soon and were therefore quite unprepared. They had had orders to withdraw that night, and were only waiting for a liaison officer to come out and give them final details. Such is the value of "bouncing" a bridge.

We had hardly got set for the night when "A" Echelon arrived. It had been following closely behind our tail all day quite unmoved by the strong-points we had failed to destroy, though unhappily Trooper English had been killed by a shell. We had left a number of "jagged edges" behind us and "A" Echelon had themselves captured thirty prisoners. Surely this is a record? The going had been tricky for lorries in spite of the fact that Lieutenant Dudding had made the Regimental Headquarters bulldozer prepare a suitable track for them. From Regimental Headquarters they went out to the squadrons and by midnight the "private army" was refilled with petrol, oil and ammunition. All prisoners were bundled aboard the empty lorries and we were thankful to see the last of them.

We spent the night amid crackling flames and palls of smoke, scouring the neighbourhood for Germans, and collected a further one hundred and twenty-five.

At 4 a.m. on the 19th of April two troops of tanks and two platoons of infantry advanced northwards to the double canal called Scolo Bolognese, where all bridges were found blown. It was then clear that we could not reach Ferrara that day even if we began attacking at once. Soon after first light, however, the G.O.C. 78th Division decided that the crossing operation should not begin before nightfall, and assigned the 11th Brigade for the task. In the meantime the London Irish were to reconnoitre as offensively as possible without incurring losses.

This meant a day off for most of the Regiment, and the Colonel sent Lieutenant Dudding to enumerate all the loot. The following is the total of the "bag" for the previous twenty-four hours:

Four Mark IV's ("brewed").
Two armoured cars ("brewed").
One self-propelled 88 ("brewed").
Two batteries each of three 150-mm. field guns overrun.
One battery of four 88-mm. guns overrun.
One battery of three 88-mm. guns overrun.
Four 88-mm. anti-tank guns ("brewed").
Two 149-mm. field guns overrun.
Twelve 20-mm. guns "brewed" and overrun.
One quadruple 20-mm. anti-aircraft gun.
Two 105-mm. anti-tank guns.
Three half-tracks.
Twenty-nine assorted lorries.
One ambulance.
Four hundred and fifty-five prisoners.
Twelve horses.
Two Alsatian dogs.
One pony and trap.

At least as far as enemy equipment was concerned this was our most successful day in the Second World War. The inventory speaks for itself. The "B" Squadron officers, under instruction from our friends of "E" Battery, amused themselves by firing one of the 150-mm. batteries against the Germans. They wanted to shoot across the River Po, but the range was too great. They fired a number of rounds, but soon had to stop when one failed to go off. It was heard sizzling in the breech and caused a hurried departure from the gun.

In the execution of their orders the London Irish carried out a brilliant operation in the afternoon and established a bridgehead over the Scolo Bolognese, encompassing both blown bridges, without the loss of a single man. This assault was preceded by flame-throwing from their Wasps and was supported by a troop from both "A" and "C" Squadrons. They were entirely successful and the way was now clear for the Engineers to build bridges. Seventeen prisoners were taken, including three sergeant-majors who were commanding the remnants of three companies. They stated that their soldiers were thoroughly demoralized and only with the greatest difficulty could they be kept in the line.

While this was happening Lieutenant Whately was winkling out Germans dug in on the far bank. The enemy had extensive tunnels there and all along various weapons could be seen protruding through the grass. Lieutenant

Whately got his tank on to the near bank and began firing armour-piercing into these slits at twenty yards' range. Soon a very "bomb-happy" and dejected "Ted" (our name for a German) emerged from the bank and surrendered. When he had finished firing at all visible positions, Lieutenant Whately got the "Ted" up on to his tank and made him shout across the canal to his friends to the effect that if they did not surrender immediately they would be blown to bits. This had the desired effect and several more men waded the canal with their hands stretched high. Altogether it was a profitable afternoon.

Thus ended our second innings. The "private army" began to feel more secure now. There seemed to be less danger of being split. The Colonel was now the recognized authority on Kangaroos and the Regiment's prestige stood very high.

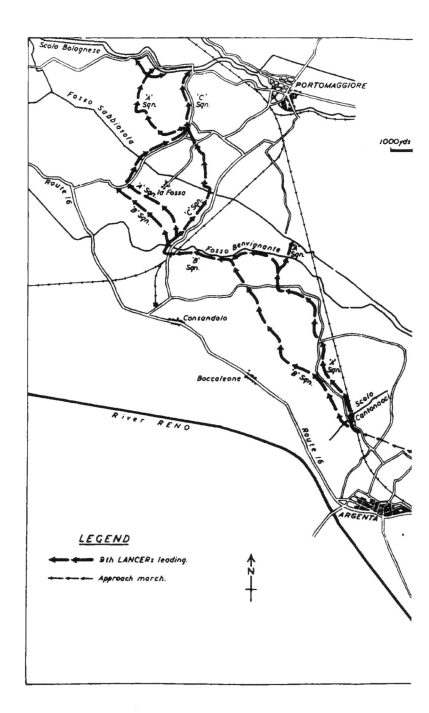

THE ARGENTA GAP

SCALE – in miles.

0   1   2   3   4

Route 16

BASTIA

FILO

CHAPTER XXXV

THE "PRIVATE ARMY" FIGHTS BY NIGHT

THE night after we got through the Argenta Gap the London Irish enlarged their bridgehead over the Scolo Bolognese at a cost of only seven wounded, including Trooper Wilkinson, of "A" Squadron, who was hit by a shell. By 1 a.m. on the 20th of April the Sappers had completed their bridges, so the 11th Brigade, supported by the Bays, crossed over. They advanced north-west, but were only a mile and a quarter farther on by the end of the day and had not reached the large diagonal canal beyond which they were to establish a bridge-head.

Once the 11th Brigade had passed through, the London Irish became a right-flank guard and throughout the day were subjected to considerable small-arms fire from the east. This came from an enemy stronghold near the town of Porto Maggiore and "B" Squadron, 4th Hussars, left our command to put in an attack from the right in the hope of destroying it, while the Desert Air Force dive-bombed the position. Sixty prisoners were taken, but there was no sign of the opposition weakening, and it was estimated that a further one hundred and fifty Germans remained. One troop of "C" Squadron therefore crossed the Scolo Bolognese and remained in support of the London Irish all day. This troop killed or wounded a number of Germans and was able to help protect the infantry.

Lieutenant-Colonel Bredin now had to decide what to do. He wanted to keep his battalion within the "private army," but his men had been in action for sixty hours on end and needed rest. If he could secure one night's sleep for them he would be able to bring them with us. So everything possible was done to get them relieved, and, luckily for the 9th Lancers, this was achieved soon after dark. Their night's sleep was not as long as they would have liked but sufficient to warrant their continued employment.

That night the 38th Irish Brigade, supported by the 10th Hussars, who had just rejoined the 2nd Armoured Brigade from the 56th Division, passed through the 11th Brigade and made a bridgehead over the diagonal canal in the vicinity of Montesanto. The "private army" was put on one hour's notice to move from 8 a.m. on the 21st so that we should be ready to exploit from this bridgehead when it had been adequately expanded. At 9 a.m. we re-formed by the Scolo Bolognese, because we had become somewhat dispersed during the preceding two days. We set about this at a leisurely pace, for there was no immediate sign of a move. At 11 o'clock we were ready, and time dragged by for two hours before we were ordered forward. The task we were given was to proceed north

265

from Montesanto and if possible to seize the bridge over the River Po di Volano at Cona, a distance of five miles. However, it was not expected that we should get as far as this.

We set off in single file in the order: "C" Squadron—"F" Company Group, "B" Squadron—"E" Company Group, Reconnaissance Troop, Regimental Headquarters, "A" Squadron—"E" Company Group, and "B" Squadron, 4th Hussars—"H" Company Group. The approach march was uneventful. We moved at full speed and our serpentine column, two hundred vehicles strong, made a tremendous noise. The troops we passed on the road were filled with amazement and Major Morris, now Second-in-Command of the 11th H.A.C., said we were a most impressive sight and sounded like a race at Brooklands. By 2.45 p.m. we were concentrating just over the canal and being subjected to very heavy shelling which seriously wounded the London Irish Medical Officer.

The tactical situation at that moment was far from inviting. Our right flank was going to be particularly dangerous because the two large villages of Voghiera and Voghenza were likely harbouring places for self-propelled guns and tanks. Major Steel was in the lead and gained all the information he could from the foremost 10th Hussar squadron leader, who gave him a very gloomy picture, saying that his squadron had just lost several tanks to self-propelled guns, and that a number of his tank commanders had been killed or wounded by snipers and heavy shell fire. He warned Major Steel to be exceedingly careful as to how he advanced.

The country in front was open with no cover for at least two thousand yards and beyond that it became very thick again. The usual impassable canals intersected it, but in this instance made a more complicated pattern which impeded the lateral deployment of the "army." After studying the map the Colonel decided that it was possible to advance only on a one-squadron frontage as far as the Canale Montiese. After this it looked as if it might be possible to get "B" Squadron Group forward on the right of "C." The Brigadier had been most anxious to advance on a broader front, but the lie of the land made this impossible.

The Divisional artillery was most efficient. It prepared a fire plan to lay smoke along our right flank, though as it turned out this was not needed. It had registered nearly every farmhouse in our line of advance as a Divisional target and whenever we wanted any one of these engaged we had only to give its code number over the air and down came the shells.

At 3 p.m. on the 21st, with some trepidation owing to the unfavourable reports, "C" Squadron Group passed through the forward troops. Simultaneously the fighter-bombers knocked out a Mark IV and a self-propelled gun four hundred yards ahead of them. Undoubtedly these would have caused our leading troop at least two tank casualties had they not been faithfully dealt with by the "cab rank." "C" Squadron had to advance in very extended order owing to the open country, and the supporting troops had to be anything up to one thousand yards behind. This fact meant that the rear half of the "army" was waiting outside Montesanto for over an hour, which made Brigade Headquarters unjustly conclude that no progress was being made. Lieutenant Hainsworth on the rear link, occasionally assisted by the Colonel himself, was _ pains to explain that the leading troops were advancing and meeting considerable opposition three thousand yards ahead.

"C" Squadron plodded on, constantly having to close in to single file to get over the canals at a bridge or bulldozed crossing. Strong-points and bazooka parties were ensconced in the most unexpected places and this necessitated small contingents of the London Irish having to dismount and attack. After an extensive and hazardous reconnaissance, "C" Squadron discovered a crossing over the Canale Montiese west of Voghenza, and all were across by 5.15 p.m. The Reconnaissance Troop was of invaluable assistance here, and one of its sections had the disappointment of seeing a bridge over the canal demolished when it was only fifty yards from it.

Across the canal "C" Squadron Group circled left-handed to avoid some difficult country and "B" Squadron Group was then able to go up on the right and strike for the village of Gualdo. At that point both squadrons would have to converge in order to pass through a four-hundred-yard gap between two deep ditches. Then "C" Squadron was to strike north-west to Cona and "B" Squadron north to the three bridges over a tributary stream at Quartesana. "A" Squadron was then to overtake Regimental Headquarters and capture the centre bridge between these two villages.

"C" Squadron was going strong when it suddenly ran into two fossas, both of which required the services of a fascine or bulldozer, and encountered determined enemy rearguards, including a self-propelled gun and snipers up trees. Consequently "B" Squadron reached Gualdo first, skirting it on the east. The Colonel ordered it to divide here, with half going to "C" Squadron's objective. At that moment opposition slackened so that "C" Squadron was able to catch up, and the original plan was resumed. The light was fading and both objectives were still one and a half miles away. The Colonel decided to push on as fast as possible and continue the advance in the dark, an operation rarely undertaken by armour. The moon was poor and our task proved to be exacting.

Almost immediately "B" Squadron was engaged by a self-propelled gun from its right. This caused delay until a dismounted patrol from "E" Company skilfully stalked and destroyed it. 5th Troop in the lead, under Lieutenant David Wentworth-Stanley, was then fired on by an 88-mm. anti-tank gun which scored a direct hit on Sergeant Parfitt's tank, putting both guns out of action. Corporal Irvine, however, by a dexterous manœuvre and one straight shot, quickly disposed of it. Five minutes later the same troop knocked out a 75-mm. anti-tank gun in the same way. As it was now dark Sergeant Parfitt, the leading tank commander, was a little worried because his guns were broken.

"Five Able. I have no guns. What am I to do?" he asked.

"You've still got your tommy-gun," replied Major Laurie, "so continue to the objective as ordered."

"Five Able," replied Sergeant Parfitt, "your orders are clear, and you'll be glad to know that I've got my Very-light pistol as well."

On arrival at Quartesana Sergeant Parfitt saw a German ammunition lorry coming down the road. He fired at it with the tommy-gun, killing the driver and "brewing" the lorry. At this critical moment the commander of the fascine carrier tank reported on foot to his squadron leader that his tank had been bazooka-ed and his driver, Trooper Gill, wounded in the neck. Later it transpired that an enemy sniper had climbed on to the vehicle and taken up a fire position right on top of the fascine itself, a situation for which no one had bargained.

To control the squadron group was impossible and the fighting became confused. Bazookamen were everywhere and armour-piercing fire came whistling down from the north. "E" Company were dismounted round the tanks because there was no other way of giving mutual protection. Just as Corporal Irvine's tank was escorting the infantry to the right-hand bridge it was knocked out by a Mark IV Special firing from an orchard fifty yards away. Unhappily Trooper Lloyd was seriously wounded and died soon afterwards. A platoon of the London Irish was cleaning up this orchard at the time and seeing four tanks in the dark assumed that they were ours. It was not until one tank fired that they realized their mistake, but before they had time to act the four Mark IV's beat a hasty retreat northwards. This platoon actually picked up some of the crews of these tanks who were resting in a farmhouse. On being questioned they said that they had no idea that we were right on them and that their tanks were being manned by the driver and gunner only while the rest of the crews relaxed. They must have been very heavy sleepers.

This vague but heated skirmishing continued until midnight, when the opposition had been quelled and all was quiet. The three bridges had been captured intact and positions were selected to defend them. "E" Company could put only one platoon across the river. This was really inadequate, but the company could not be reinforced because the bridge at Cona was the most important one. Enemy infantry continued to infiltrate during the night, but "B" Squadron was not giving an inch. So much for the right sector.

The rest of the "private army" struck for Cona. There was half an hour's pause at Gualdo to get ready. The London Irish dismounted from their Kangaroos and we quickly decided that they must surround each tank while stationary and ride on its back when moving. In this way we hoped to counter the bazookas. Then we all formed up facing the objective, including "A" Echelon. An advance by night demands the highest standard of battle drill and driving, so it was important to get straight before we began. A few houses were burning all round, but even so it was only just possible to distinguish the next tank as a black shadow. "We're starting now," said "C" Squadron over the air.

Slowly they surged forward, careful to avoid getting bogged in the ditches, for even now we still persisted in avoiding the roads. Guns were fired indiscriminately and bullets ricocheted up into the night. Gradually the number of fires increased until it seemed that the whole countryside was in flames. Every haystack, house and barn was set alight by our tracer bullets, with the result that the Germans had to evacuate their positions before they could open fire. It was a thrilling exploit, eerie and confused, but we could not hurry it and somehow we kept in formation. There was no question of clearing the enemy up as we went; it was a case of barging to Cona in a mass.

When within a thousand yards of its objective "C" Squadron came under intense armour-piercing fire from the north. This came from a battery of 88's firing straight down the road which we had taken such care to avoid. The projectiles were landing all down the side of the column and close to "A" Echelon. It reminded us of the old days in the desert to see the unmistakable tracer of an 88 coming towards us through the night and to have "A" Echelon under armour-piercing fire once more.

Rumbling steadily forward, "C" Squadron crossed the railway and entered the village of Cona. It had been fairly straightforward so far, but now it became pandemonium. The Germans were in all the houses, hedgerows and "fossas" firing for all they were worth. Bazookas shot this way and that, exploding against houses and trees like fireworks. One tank was hit, luckily not fatally, though one Irishman was killed and several others wounded. The noise was terrific with the fire from our tanks and the merciless spray from German machine guns. Tracer bullets of every description and colour streaked across the sky and overhead was the hum of a hundred engines. Suddenly there was a devastating explosion.

"There goes the bridge," said Regimental Headquarters unanimously. But they were wrong. Sergeant Smith, the leading tank commander, had had an unpleasant evening. He had had great difficulty in finding his way, and it was essential to avoid sudden jolts in case the infantry on the back were knocked off. Frequently he had caught glimpses of small parties of Germans running this way or that, and had had to give fire orders to his gunner, who could not possibly see the target. Just before entering the village he had put down the infantry and began setting the houses on fire. The road in the village ran across our front and was raised on an embankment. The only means of access was along a ramplike track up which Sergeant Smith had advanced, followed by other tanks in the squadron. Once on top they had been greeted with a medley of missiles which Sergeant Smith compared favourably with Blackpool illuminations. Slowly he had edged his way forward and as he turned the corner that led to the bridge he was greeted with a 150-mm. shell fired from seventy yards' range. That was the explanation of the bang. But the shell missed the tank and struck the house behind, so the crew were unhurt, though certainly not unmoved. Sergeant Smith rapidly reversed, almost slipping over the embankment, but found himself still engaged by the 150-mm. gun from in front as well as by two bazookas from the flank, one of which knocked out his guns. Sergeant Crayton's tank immediately came up beside him and 4th Troop took up a position on the left. Corporal Perry spotted the 150-mm. gun-flash fifty yards beyond the bridge and plastered it with armour-piercing and high-explosive. This covering fire enabled Sergeant Crayton to advance up to the bridge and support the infantry across. Sergeant Crayton himself then crossed and rejoined the infantry. Together they captured the 150-mm. with its crew of six, and in addition two other 150-mm. guns in the same farmyard. Having achieved this, they continued up the road and captured another 88-mm. with its crew, without doubt one of the guns that had been firing at us all the evening.

The bridge was now ours; that was the important thing. It had been prepared for demolition, but our timely arrival in the dark had preserved it. Meanwhile, the rest of Cona was in turmoil and "C" Squadron pressed for more infantry to help. Its old partners, "H" Company, under Major John Lofting, arrived from behind in their Kangaroos. Though tired after the fighting at Scolo Bolognese they quickly got organized. In a surprisingly short time the London Irish had subdued the Germans in the village and the fighting died down abruptly at 3 a.m. At that moment a large German lorry drove gaily down the street and Lieutenant Hannen shot the driver at the wheel. This lorry was carrying a load of 210-mm. rocket ammunition, which luckily failed to explode. Had it done so we should have suffered many casualties.

As it was so late it was decided to leave the centre bridge which "A" Squadron was originally going to capture, and consolidate where we were. So off went Lieutenant-Colonel Bredin to arrange for our defence during the remaining three hours of darkness.

As dawn broke on the 22nd we heard that the 11th and 36th Brigades were going to pursue north and west respectively with the Bays and 48th Royal Tanks under command. However, nothing happened and we began to wonder why we had spent so much energy on capturing bridges intact if no one proposed to use them. The Colonel did not hesitate to offer the "private army" to carry on with the good work, but was told that he must stay where he was until reinforcements arrived. In the end it was twelve hours before anyone continued the advance. But they had not gone far before they met another impassable "fossa."

We adjusted our leaguer, cleaned ourselves up and sorted out the hoard of heterogeneous kit and equipment that had somehow fallen into our hands.

Once again we had achieved our object. In addition to the weapons already mentioned, we had destroyed a further two self-propelled guns and captured forty-five prisoners. Our success had caused considerable surprise and for a short period we had been beyond the range of our artillery. It was our first night operation since El Hamma in March, 1943, only more intricate and adventurous than that had been. The operation was contrary to accepted tactics, but it had been made possible by a high standard of training and perfect understanding between all ranks in the group.

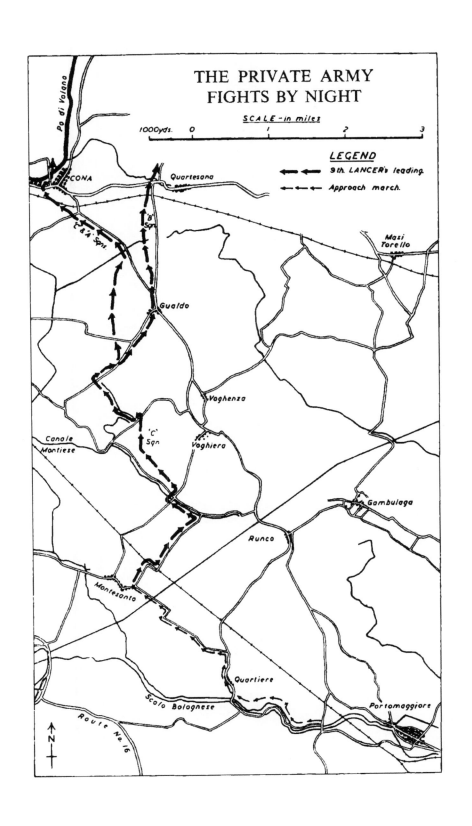

THE PRIVATE ARMY
FIGHTS BY NIGHT

SCALE – in miles

1000 yds.   0   1   2   3

LEGEND

⟵⟵ 9th LANCERS leading.
⟵-⟵- Approach march.

Po di Volano

CONA

Quartesana

'B' Sqn

'C & A' Sqns

Mazi Torello

Gualdo

Voghenza

Canale Montiese

'C' Sqn

Voghiera

Gambulaga

Runco

Montesanto

Quartiere

Scolo Bolognese

Portomaggiore

Route No. 16

N

CHAPTER XXXVI

THE RIVER PO AT LAST

THE 15th Army Group plan was developing favourably. The American Fifth Army had attacked on the west and were now pursuing northwards rapidly. Lieutenant Dudding could not possibly keep his maps up to date, but he frequently visited the squadrons to explain the latest available news to the crews. The 11th Brigade had succeeded in forcing a crossing over the Po di Volano to our north-east and this enabled a bridge to be built near Fossalta on the 23rd of April. The 78th Division had abandoned any idea of using our bridge at Cona because three miles beyond it there was a *cul-de-sac* where an irrigation canal called Diversivo del Volano flowed into the main Volano River, so the plan was to begin the next advance from Fossalta and thus avoid the main natural obstacles. Opposition was already stiff and it was expected to increase because the Germans were compelled to stand and fight now in order to complete the withdrawal of their troops and equipment over the River Po. The 8th Indian Division had actually reached it west of Ferrara, and most of the enemy lay to the east of that town in front of us.

While we awaited final orders we rested and "coffee-housed" with the London Irish. A stray shell landed in the middle of "C" Squadron leaguer, killing Trooper Fairs and wounding Sergeants Smith and Griffiths and Signalman Stewart. Lieutenant Hannen and Corporal Pickering were also wounded but did not have to be evacuated. "C" Squadron always seemed to be unlucky with "stonks," and this was a great blow after a successful night attack with few casualties.

At 2 a.m. on the 24th of April the London Irish left Cona in their Kangaroos to rejoin the 38th Irish Brigade. The circumstances were not considered suitable for launching the "private army," and at 5.30 a.m. "A" Squadron motored forward into the Fossalta bridgehead in readiness to support the London Irish with the usual "mutual co-operation" technique. The rest of the Regiment was put at two hours' notice to move, with the idea of exploiting north-east later with some other battalion if events permitted it. The Colonel visited "A" Squadron after breakfast and found that there was no indication of an impending move. He went on to see Brigadier Scott, commanding the Irish Brigade, to find out the form and arrange for the rest of the Regiment to advance across the river. At that moment the Regiment was ordered to Fossalta and the Colonel was called to meet Brigadier Combe.

The plan had changed. Instead of striking north-west we were now to re-form the "private army" and advance almost due west to seize the line of Route 16

271

running north from Ferrara to the Po at Pontelagoscuro, a distance of seven miles in front of the leading troops.

The enemy were not yielding a yard of ground unless engaged and defeated, and the 11th and 38th Brigades were experiencing considerable strain in advancing even with the normal tank-infantry technique. Therefore the employment of the "private army" was in the nature of a speculation. However, the Colonel hastily dispelled any doubts about the successful outcome of the venture, though he agreed that it was unlikely that we should reach Pontelagoscuro before dark. No one knew what we might meet on the way, but we were in the frame of mind in which nothing would surprise us.

This sudden switch from north to west caused chaos in our map arrangements and everyone hastily searched for the right sheets and reset them. All the report lines had turned into centre lines, so the Colonel had to issue his new orders from scratch. Having scrutinized the map, he decided to advance with two squadron groups leading and later on, when the ditches allowed, to send a third squadron group forward. "A" Squadron—"G" Company Group was already at Fossalta, so it was given its orders at once and then moved north to the farthest centre line. It formed up behind the East Surreys, then fighting in the village of Corlo.

As it moved out, the rest of the "private army" crossed the Po di Volano and reshuffled itself. This might have been a muddle, but constant practice had enabled everyone to take up his correct position without any shouting or bother. There was some delay before "C" Squadron arrived, as a military policeman had put the road out of bounds at the critical moment and diverted the squadron across country, where it had had great difficulty in negotiating the "fossas" and had to use its fascine and bulldozer. Nevertheless, it was possible for us to change plans, change direction, change maps, reissue orders, and still move in fifteen minutes—as opposed to the minimum official time of an hour—and when we were ready we started up the road in single file. "B" Squadron—"E" Company Group led and branched off the main road near Tamara, wending its way through a maze of ditches to Corregio, where the Northants were in action supported by the Bays. At five minutes past three, when "B" Squadron was level with "A," the Colonel gave the order to "Hosannah" and we were off. Once again we did not begin until a late hour, which was a great pity.

Passing through our leading troops proved particularly difficult on this occasion and almost immediately both the leading squadron groups reported being engaged by the enemy and troubled by sniper and Spandau fire. The country was exceedingly difficult with wide ditches involving heavy work for the bull-dozers. Many diversions had to be made, which kept the squadrons two thousand yards apart and out of range for mutual support. From the very outset the London Irish had to dismount constantly to winkle the enemy out. Cascinetto was strongly held and the bazookamen had to be cleared up before the advance could continue. Several were shot or run over and twenty prisoners were taken.

German 75-mm. S.P.

Senior Officers, 9th Lancers, with two captured Mark IV tanks
Major Allhusen, Major Meyrick, Colonel Price, Major Cooke, Major Laurie, Major Steel.

Tac R.H.Q., 9th Lancers, Francolino, May, 1945

9th Lancer Officers, 6th May, 1945

So for the first three hours progress had been slow, about one thousand yards an hour. Both squadrons pushed on as fast as they could, continually picking up prisoners, who again became a source of embarrassment. "G" Company had to leave one rifleman to guard more than fifty Germans, including three officers, until some carriers from "S" Company were sent to collect them. At 6 p.m. "B" Squadron reached the hamlet of Boara and at once the battle livened up with armour-piercing shot which suddenly began to land in our midst. "B" Squadron knocked out one Mark IV and one self-propelled gun and still kept on advancing. The Reconnaissance Troop reported that the bridges over the three canals between the two leading squadron groups were still intact, though under heavy shell fire. On this information the Colonel sent "B" Squadron, 4th Hussars—"F" Company Group forward over these canals so that the "private army" then had three squadron groups up. Regimental Headquarters followed "B" Squadron, 9th Lancers, on the left, and "C" Squadron Group brought up the rear, followed by "A" Echelon. There was now only one hour of daylight left and the entire "army" reported being engaged by armour-piercing fire from all round, including the rear.

"B" Squadron's leading troops reached Malborghetto and reported three Mark IV's driving rapidly down the road half a mile away. Within two minutes Sergeant Edmunds had "brewed" a couple of these with a right and left; the third got away to the north, but with smoke pouring out of its tail as a result of Corporal Nickolls's unerring aim—three magnificent shots, which proved that the high-class shooting performance at El Alamein had been no fluke. This third tank was later found abandoned by the roadside with two of the crew dead. Sergeant Riley in his Honey had a grand time with his machine gun, killing the crews as they baled out. Meanwhile, Lieutenant Moule's troop in "A" Squadron reported two further Mark IV's "brewed up" and that his squadron was encountering many more. 88-mm. anti-tank guns began to appear, and while the Colonel was discussing the situation with Major Laurie the latter reported a further two Mark IV's on fire and one 88-mm. destroyed. Enemy tanks were going down like ninepins and the figures on the Colonel's scoreboard mounted rapidly.

Once more the Regiment was engaged in a major tank versus tank battle, and on the wireless it sounded like a flashback to the days of Knightsbridge and El Alamein. We had no difficulty in remembering the tricks of the trade and our shooting was as straight as ever. The London Irish found themselves in the front row of the stalls and were greatly intrigued by the proceedings. They did their best to keep their conspicuous Kangaroos out of the way and sat back while our tanks plugged away.

The guns got hot as empty shell-cases were flung out of the turret port-holes. Thousands of bullets ripped through the sky. First one troop edged forward, then another. In a second, another Mark IV was a flaming wreck. Then we came upon an expanse of open ground with 88's firing from the far side. There was room for one tank behind a signal box. Other tanks had to jockey up and down firing one or two shots each time they stopped. Like the desert, there was no cover, so the tanks kept moving, then firing, and all the time the sun was setting straight in our eyes, just like old times, so that it was difficult for us to see the Germans and easy for the Germans to see us. Now only half the sun was visible and the bushes threw out long, narrow shadows which grew imperceptibly until suddenly the whole earth was dark yet pierced with glowing tracer.

By last light we were still a mile and a half from our objective, having lost one tank only to a self-propelled gun, which unhappily killed Lance-Corporal Coombes, of "A" Squadron, our last fatal casualty of the war, and slightly wounded Lieutenant de Burgh. The battle was still raging, houses and haystacks were in flames, and armour-piercing shot was everywhere. Again the Colonel had decided to fight on through the night, but suddenly the plans were changed. The Brigadier proposed two or three quite different tasks for us, but it was some hours before one of them was finally selected. In the meantime, the "army" began to concentrate at various convenient points and get organized for a night advance in any direction, so that we should be ready when a definite decision was made.

Disengagement proved a most difficult operation because the Regiment was pinned. Even though it was now night there was a moon and the countryside was lit up by burning farmsteads and Mark IV's. Whenever a tank moved it was silhouetted against the flames and attracted a hail of armour-piercing shot. However, by moving slowly, one tank at a time, all squadrons were disengaged and concentrated by midnight. "B" Squadron withdrew along the railway embankment to join Regimental Headquarters and "C" Squadron in a field west of Malborghetto. "A" Squadron had to mop up the greatest number of Germans, taking a hundred and thirty-one prisoners. It had also captured a Mark IV intact which it had found in a farm. The engine was still warm and obviously it was one of the tanks that had been firing all the afternoon. There was no apparent explanation as to why it had been abandoned by its crew.

The task we were finally given was to proceed north-east to Francolino and Borgo on the banks of the Po to capture the pontoon bridges which were suspected to be in use there. It was a tall order at so late an hour, as the Regiment had already advanced six miles and this entailed a further three. Furthermore, our axis of advance was switched by over ninety degrees, but we accomplished this turn with little difficulty in spite of the proximity of the enemy. The two commanding officers decided on a plan, and an "O" Group was summoned. There was no information about the enemy except what we knew ourselves, and this simply amounted to the fact that there were a number of tanks and guns to the north and that opposition might be heavy. Therefore it was decided to move to the two objectives with a platoon of infantry leading in each case, supported by a troop of tanks protected by another platoon of infantry, while the rest of the squadron groups backed them up from five hundred yards behind. A careful fire plan was laid on with the Divisional artillery, including medium guns, covering the whole length of both routes. This could be called on when required.

At 1.30 a.m. on the 25th of April "B" Squadron—4th Hussars Group set off for Borgo in this manner, and fifteen minutes later "A" Squadron Group started towards Francolino. The advance went smoothly but slowly, with the infantry walking all the way, and by first light both groups were established on their objectives, having met only mild resistance which was easily dealt with. There was no sign of any pontoons or even remains of them, so we were ordered to hold on to the ground won until relieved by the 56th Reconnaissance Regiment. At 9 a.m. "C" Squadron was attacked by the Lancashire Fusiliers and the Bays, who had not been informed of our activities during the preceding eighteen hours. Luckily no harm was done.

Regimental Headquarters moved to La Pavonara and the "tail" closed up. The whole area from the outskirts of Ferrara to Borgo was littered with German tanks, self-propelled guns and equipment of all sorts. The sudden arrival of the 9th Lancers had taken the 26th Panzer Division completely by surprise. They had begun to withdraw and then decided to stand and fight, but after losing ten tanks in a few minutes the remaining crews became so demoralized that they deserted their tanks and guns and destroyed them during the night. This was confirmed by the civilians on the spot. Never before had the Regiment so utterly defeated a German panzer regiment in so short a time. It is true that they had no Tigers and that their numbers were less than ours, but we did succeed in destroying practically everything they had. During the day and night we had advanced eight and a half miles into hostile territory, taking the following toll of the enemy:

Ten Mark IV tanks "brewed up."

Two Mark IV tanks captured in running order.

Eleven Mark IV tanks and one self-propelled gun found abandoned and destroyed at Francolino.

Two self-propelled guns destroyed.

Two large mortars destroyed.

One 20-mm. gun overrun.

Three officers and two hundred and twenty-seven other ranks taken prisoner.

It was another victory.

As a topographical feature the Po was disappointing. All the talk about "fighting to the Po" had automatically led one to the unreasonable conclusion that it was something out of the ordinary—almost one of the wonders of the world. But instead we found the same sort of floodbanks and muddy water that we had met so often—only, of course, on a bigger scale. On the other hand, militarily speaking, it was of the utmost importance. No one believed that we could "bounce" a bridge over it, and German propaganda had made the most of this by dropping leaflets depicting the dreadful consequences of an assault crossing. However, it was well known that the Po had not got an elaborate system of defences and that there were no fresh troops to hold it. What actually happened was that the spring offensive had progressed so fast that the enemy was pushed into the river with his few remaining troops. The situation bore a remarkable resemblance to Dunkirk, and the Po turned out to be the Germans' downfall, not ours.

With this consoling thought we set about the loot and proceeded to scour the neighbourhood: there were hundreds of horses which were quickly examined, the pick being brought back to leaguer. All the time, more Germans came on, asking to be taken prisoner.

The inhabitants of Francolino went mad with delight. "A" Squadron was fêted up and down the street, and the houses were covered with messages of welcome written in large letters with orange paint:

"Viva Tenente Crampton! Viva Caporale Cumbers!"

Thus ended the fourth and longest attack made by "Price's Private Army," and indeed our last battle in the Second World War. It had been a heaven-sent climax and crowned our Regimental pride with glory. The Irishmen felt just the same way, and Brigadier Scott wrote this letter to the Colonel:

"Although the 'Kangaroo Army' was only under my command on the first occasion, I feel I must record my tremendous appreciation of the way your Regiment fought with the 2nd London Irish. The degree of confidence your soldiers inspired in them was quite outstanding."

Above all, it was a triumph for the Colonel. He had overcome every obstacle to retain his group intact, and had carried his "army" along with him. He was subsequently awarded the D.S.O. for these actions—a fitting tribute to his work. He wrote a message to the "private army," at the end of which he said:

"I feel that the 9th Lancers have probably fired their last shot in Europe, and what a last shot it was!

"Tanks: 12 'brewed,' 1 captured intact, 11 'self-brewed.'

"Armoured cars: 2 destroyed.

"Self-propelled: 1 overrun, 6 destroyed, 1 self-destroyed.

"Guns: 150-mm., 4 overrun, 1 destroyed; 105-mm., 2 overrun, 4 destroyed; 149-mm. howitzer, 2 overrun; 88-mm. 4 overrun, 7 destroyed; 75-mm. anti-tank, 1 destroyed; 20-mm., 2 overrun, 12 destroyed.

"Mortars: 2 (large) destroyed.

"Miscellaneous: half-tracks, 1 overrun, 2 destroyed; transport (various), 29 destroyed and overrun; horses, 8 captured; Alsatians, 2 captured; ponies and traps, 2 captured.

"In addition, 7 officers, 2 medical officers and 870 other ranks were taken prisoner.

"Above is a list of enemy equipment destroyed by the 9th Lancer Group between 13th and 25th April during the advance from the River Santerno to the River Po."

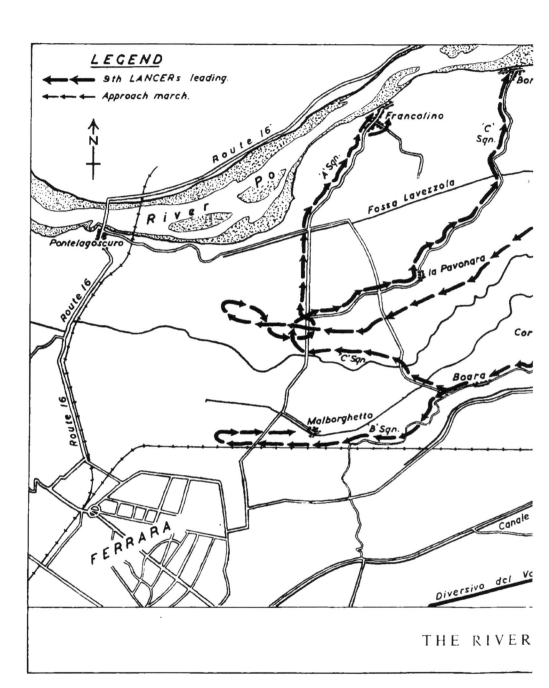

THE RIVER

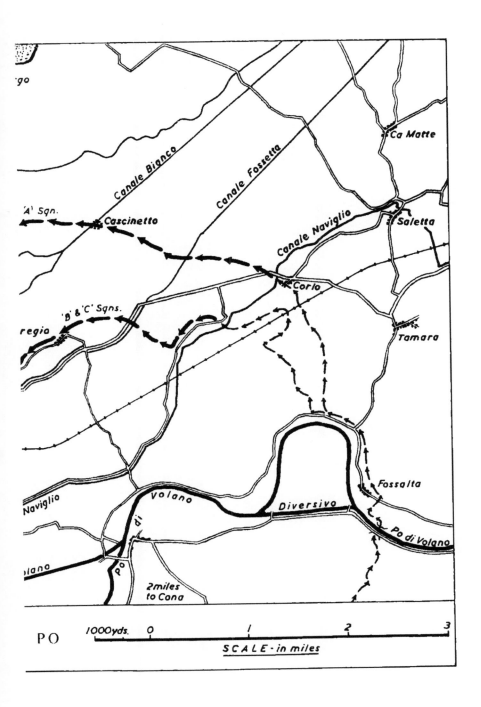

'A' Sgn.

Canale Bianco

Canale Fossetta

Ca Matte

Cascinetto

Canale Naviglio

Saletta

Corlo

'B' & 'C' Sgns.

regia

Tamara

Volano

Diversivo

Naviglio

Fossalta

Po di Volano

Po di

2 miles
to Cona

PO

1000 yds.   0   1   2   3

SCALE · in miles

CHAPTER XXXVII

THE END OF THE WAR

THE New Zealanders were across the Po, Berlin was surrounded, the Fifth Army had swept through Verona; it would be only a matter of hours before the Adige Line, the last defensive line in Italy, was reached.

The London Irish and 4th Hussars and the rest of the "private army" left us. We settled down in Francolino and Borgo. Expeditions were made to inspect the bridge being built over the Po, a pontoon Bailey. Orders were issued for our advance to continue northwards, but then it was postponed indefinitely. Trooper Hill, of "C" Squadron, took it into his head to swim the Po and be the first of the 9th Lancers across. Luckily someone tied a rope round him before he began because the strong currents forced him down-stream and he had to be pulled in when he was scarcely half-way across. Everyone paid a visit to Ferrara to satisfy their curiosity, for its name had loomed large on the map during the past eight months, but, apart from the ancient castle which had been used as a Fascist headquarters, it was a dull place. The Regiment sent three horses to the 78th Division Gymkhana in Copparo, and Major Tony Cooke, who had just rejoined us from G.H.Q., Middle East, won the hurdle race on "Rhumba." In other events the Regiment was competing closely with the Bays.

On the evening of the 1st of May General Mark Clark, commanding the Allied Troops in Italy, announced over the radio that all organized resistance in Italy had ended. We had succeeded in our task and had destroyed the enemy south of the Po. There were no Germans left to man the Adige Line and their remnants were scattering in chaos as the New Zealanders swept on through Padua and Venice to Trieste. Only Austria remained. There had been much talk of the "German Redoubt" in the Alps. Would they hold on to it? If so, how long could they last?

The Colonel went off to visit Venice for a night while others went to Bologna and farther afield. More horses were collected until the stables in the echelon were full. The asparagus was ripe and on sale by the stone, strawberries appeared at every meal, the blossom was flowering and the fields were green.

On the 2nd of May the great news came. Field-Marshal Alexander announced the unconditional surrender of General von Vietinghoff and the German South-West Army Group, which numbered a million men.

The firing had ceased and peace had come. It was all over. It takes time to absorb such news. The object of our military existence had gone and there was none to put in its place. For six years the 9th Lancers had done nothing but study the best methods of killing Germans. Now there was no one left for us to kill. We had thought quite casually about the post-war era of freedom, but those had been intangible thoughts compared with the solid aim of defeating the enemy. One could throw one's hat in the air and shout, but somehow that was inadequate. In a matter of minutes life had changed and it was difficult to adapt oneself to the fact that the past six years were finished. This does not mean that we regarded the news as anything but wholly good, for we had everything to be thankful for, but it was beyond our immediate grasp to recognize it for what it was.

The bells of Francolino Church were ringing and their echoing chimes heralded peace throughout the parish. All the bells in Italy followed suit until the whole country joined to rejoice in musical discord but spiritual harmony. The local fathers ordered thanksgiving services and the Italians came flocking to church for miles around.

As the day progressed we became gradually more conscious that the war was over, so that by dusk we were ready to give vent to our feelings.

Our celebrations finished soon after midnight and in the stillness that followed there was time for reflection. Not all the 9th Lancers were there to see the end: many who had died so that others might live now rested in the sands of Africa or in the fields of Europe. They had given their lives to reach this very day and were not here. Those far-off days in the desert, driving backwards and forwards in the dust and the heat, seemed as unreal as a dream. It had been a long, hard road along which we had travelled and at times it had seemed as though the journey would never end.

A few days later we joined in the special Eighth Army service of thanksgiving. It took place in the theatre of Ferrara, which was bedecked with flowers and greenery. The service sheets bore the signs of all the divisions that had fought in the Eighth Army. It was a short service and deeply moving, for we had come not to ask but to thank the Lord for answering our prayer:

> "Defend us Thy humble servants in all assaults of our enemies
> that we, surely trusting in Thy defence, may not fear the power of
> any adversaries."

On VE Night we listened to His Majesty The King and then gave ourselves over to enjoyment, but we all felt that our really great celebration had taken place when our own campaign had ended.

Under peace-time conditions our leaguer was unsatisfactory, so steps were taken to find a comfortable spot where the soldiers could have a good holiday. Captain David Allen achieved this for us and reserved a dozen or more villas in the village of Spinea near Venice. Thirty-five soldiers went at first and this figure was increased later to well over a hundred. Sergeant Deacon, two cooks and the "Bedford Drivers' Club" formed the basic staff, augmented by a similar contingent from each squadron. Spinea was a residential area and each villa had a garden behind and every convenience inside. The soldiers spent most of their time in Venice, but were free to do exactly what they chose. During all our peregrinations that summer we held on to Spinea and it was an excellent base for any expedition and always able to produce a meal for anyone passing through.

The horses, about ten, came up from the echelon and were stabled near Regimental Headquarters. It was almost too hot to ride in the day time and few people possessed boots or breeches, but what did that matter? On the whole our life was idle and very pleasant.

We moved at the end of the second week in May. The original destination was Treviso, near Venice, so the Regiment was given permission to occupy its holiday resort at Spinea. This was very satisfactory and all arrangements were made, but at the last moment the orders were changed and the Brigade had to go into the foothills behind Monselice. "C" and H.Q. Squadrons were in the village of Galzignano and shared a large seminary which housed both comfortably. Regimental Headquarters took a villa just outside, perched on top of a conical hill with gardens, vines and fruit trees growing round the slopes. "A" Squadron went into a manor, almost a castle, called Lispida, close to a hot spring, while "B" Squadron went to Valsanzibio and marched straight into a lovely house with an extensive garden.

Our life was by no means all holiday, however. No indication of future Army policy had been given, but it was obvious that the demobilization scheme would soon begin to operate. The Colonel began to organize training on the basis that within a short time all ranks up to Group 27 would have departed. Furthermore, the "Python" period was likely to be reduced to four years and this would involve nearly half the Regiment going home. Classes were begun for the remaining nucleus upon which the future 9th Lancers would be built. This was no easy task, as promotion had been rapid during the war, and we could not hope to find a new collection of fifty sergeants from our own resources. However, it was essential to begin training the younger men as soon as possible.

So we settled down to a quiet, unhurried, peace-time routine. We used to think how pleasant it was that the days of sudden moves were over and that there were no more frightful night marches, no more "brewing up," no more "O" Groups. But we deceived ourselves, all of us except perhaps the Colonel. On the 18th of May we were amazed and even stunned to hear that there was fighting in Yugoslavia and that we must move east immediately.

Having just reconciled ourselves to the advent of peace, this sudden reversion demanded further readjustment. The facts of the controversy were that the Yugoslav Partisan leader, Tito, was occupying that part of Italy known as Venezia Giulia which includes Trieste, and the country as far west as the Isonzo River. Several months before, Field-Marshal Alexander had concluded a treaty with Tito providing that the Allies should have the use of the port of Trieste in order that the troops in Austria could be supplied. Tito now refused to stand by this treaty and wished to keep Trieste under his own administration. Reports indicated that he had sixty thousand troops in the area equipped with Russian and German weapons, and it was apparent that if he persisted in his claim the Eighth Army might have to deal with him. Naturally negotiations continued, but if these failed we could not sit and watch him violate the avowed war aim of our own country. The San Francisco Conference was in session at this moment and Tito presumably realized that time was against him, and this aggravated the situation.

The 2nd Armoured Brigade passed under the command of XIII Corps and moved to the extreme north of the Adriatic Sea between the coast and Udine. The journey had all the signs of a rushed march and the tanks had to motor along the usual kind of meandering track coated in dust. One hundred and ten miles had been covered on the first day, the longest drive in one day for several years. Our tanks had seen long service now, and the oldest of them took some time to arrive, but none of them gave up completely. Parts of the echelon had now ceased being on a fully mobile footing. The horses alone required three lorries and another two for the fodder we had in store for them.

Orders were issued as soon as we arrived. Two corps were to advance across the Isonzo in an infiltrating movement limited to ten miles. The Bays and 10th Hussars were each to support one infantry division in this operation, while the 9th and 12th Lancers protected the base dumps and stores against pilfering. If circumstances warranted it the two corps would continue their advance later, but whatever happened our own job was clear-cut. The first task was to find the dumps and then guard them. This presented no difficulty and there turned out to be about five. The guards consisted of one non-commissioned officer and six or more men, who had orders to shoot anyone who began plundering.

We organized three flying columns, one from each squadron, consisting of three tanks, two Honeys, one scout car and two lorries, each carrying two sections of infantry and a wireless set. Two days after we arrived we were given nine armoured cars which were substituted for the tanks. One of these columns had to be at half an hour's notice, so the squadrons took it in turns.

Militarily speaking, our commitments were not arduous and involved only permanent vigilance. However, it was not really a military but a political problem, and as everyone knows proved one of the main difficulties of the peace.

Gradually the tension calmed down and it became clear that a decision must be given on an international level. Subversive activity and political demonstrations were renewed from time to time, but there seemed to be no prospect of any major clash.

All this time the Regiment was living in Palmanova Barracks. The town itself was octagonal in shape and encompassed by medieval fortifications and a

ITALY, 1944-1945

R.S.M. T. C. Hardwidge and "Lancer," with Tpr. R. Gilmour

4th Troop, "B" Squadron, "Python" Party, August, 1945

R.H.Q. Football Team (Sergt. Johnny Carey seated second from left)

H.Q. Squadron Sergeants' "Python" Party, August, 1945

moat of the same geometrical form. There were only three entrances into it, where the old drawbridges used to lie. It was of considerable historical interest, having withstood several sieges, the last one by Napoleon. Field-Marshal Alexander, keenly interested in the development of warfare through the ages, came to inspect the defences one day.

The barracks themselves lay two hundred yards to the east of the town and were in a most filthy condition because four thousand Chetniks (Yugoslav Royalist Partisans under Mihailovich) had occupied the place before us. The squalor in which they had lived was amazing. There were no hygienic arrangements, each room was thick with dirt, and the roofs leaked. Naturally we were disappointed, as we expected peace to bring us a modicum of comfort, but there was no chance of moving into billets elsewhere, so all who were not engaged in the political fracas became housemaids, decorators and plumbers, hosing out all the rooms and persuading the drains to function. The bulldozers came over from Brigade and filled in the slit trenches and potholes. It was some days before we made any impression on the place, but eventually we got it clean. Even then it was an unpopular leaguer, though it had several obvious advantages, and Mr. Hardwidge took a good view of having everyone under his eye. Apart from numerous out-buildings, there were four single-storeyed blocks and one squadron occupied each of these.

Across the road was the Campo Sportivo, where cricket and football began at once. Local leave was granted generously. Parties of two or three soldiers hitch-hiked all over Europe, from Amiens to Brindisi and from the Riviera to Vienna. Nobody minded where they went or how they got there as long as they returned on time, which they always did. Stresa, Lake Garda, Milan and the Italian resorts enjoyed a temporary boom. Austria was specially popular. Squadrons took over a schloss each and these were perhaps the best places for a quiet week-end. The London Irish on Ossiacher See near Villach were most hospitable and invited every troop in the Regiment to stay with them. Since leaving us they had had an exciting time sorting out several thousand assorted Balkan forces in the Austrian Alps.

The fishing was excellent either in the Isonzo itself or up in Austria. Captain Reid made serviceable rods from wireless aerials and the Colonel frequently visited the river. Once he and three officers went up to Turacher See and caught seventy trout in one afternoon. The mountaineers got busy with ropes and Major Meyrick and Captain Reid began climbing the Italian Alpine peaks in a methodical way. Then, of course, there was every kind of bathing, rocks to the south-east and sandy beaches to the south-west.

Recreation centred mainly round the horses. Riding school began soon after we arrived and some twenty officers turned out at 7 o'clock each morning under the instruction of the Colonel and Mr. Hardwidge. We were lucky in having No. 1 Veterinary and Remount Collecting Station established in the town. Lieutenant Carter, of the Royal Army Veterinary Corps, kindly gave a series of lectures and demonstrations on horsemanship and the care and management of horses. His invaluable knowledge and teaching were much appreciated by everyone. The first mounted competition in the Brigade was the Handy Hunter Trials organized by the 9th Lancers and held just outside the fortifications. There were fifty-eight entries in the open competition, which was won by Lieutenant Crampton, a fine achievement, as he had never ridden before he came to Palmanova. In the regimental pairs event Brigade Headquarters won and the 9th Lancers came second. It was an excellent day and was followed by many others like it.

At gymkhanas the Colonel was consistently successful in bending races, mounted on "Basuto." At the end of July, after weeks of hard work by a South African heavy engineering company, the first Aiello race meeting was held. Second-Lieutenant McInnes-Skinner, a newly joined officer, won the Brigade steeplechase on "Lydia." Major Meyrick, riding "Collaborator," and Lieutenant Birch-Reynardson, on "Quicksilver," took third and fourth places in the Ioannis Maiden Stakes. Captain Reid took a heavy fall riding "Mistake" in the open steeplechase. The meeting was a great success, although the heat was appalling on the unshaded grandstand, but a day at the races is always enjoyed and troops came from all over North Italy and Austria. Other meetings followed in August.

Meanwhile, training still continued with those in Group 27 and over, for the day was fast approaching when a new 9th Lancers must be made. There was a powerful education drive at this stage. Lieutenant Whately was put in charge of it, assisted by Lance-Corporal Brodie. The arrangements for teaching academic subjects were magnificent and the number of forms that had to be filled in about each man would have been the envy of the Civil Service. But the utilitarian aspect was rather overlooked, primarily because of the shortage of instructors. Any amount of school teachers were available for history, languages, mathematics, classics and so on, but hardly anyone was qualified to teach bricklaying, gardening, plumbing and all the other practical trades.

"Liap," "Python," "Lilop"—these were the key words. Since the end of hostilities the "Liap" rate had increased to one per day and more. This had been made possible by the opening of the overland route and later the rail route. By road, leave parties assembled in Villach and set off from there in a convoy of lorries. The first day led them behind the Dolomites and over the Brenner Pass to Innsbruck, and for five days they continued through Garmisch, Augsburg, Ulm, Mannheim, Mainz, Luxembourg and Sedan to Calais. Each night the convoy stopped in a staging camp staffed and managed by a different division in the Eighth Army. It was a thoroughly well-organized undertaking, and, although the seats became exceedingly hard, the staging camps and inward excitement were ample recompense.

The rail route opened in August. The reason for the delay here was partly demolitions and partly the vexed question of Swiss neutrality. It was a thirty-six-hour journey from Milan via the Simplon Tunnel, Montreux and Basle. There were no restaurant cars, but the trains used to stop at prearranged sidings for every meal. The food was cooked by a permanent staff and the troops detrained to consume it. The journey was more comfortable by rail, of course, and the high spirits of the soldiers led them to cheer out of the windows practically the whole way across Europe.

Early on in the war the qualifying period for "Python" had been over five years, but gradually it had decreased. All those who came out with the Regiment were therefore due for "Python" in September, 1945, and these amounted to about two hundred and sixty. In the meantime, no one with over three and a half years' service was allowed to go home on "Liap." This local rule was obviously fair.

"Lilop" stood for "Leave in lieu of Python," and if a man elected to take advantage of this he went home for sixty-one days' leave and then returned to the Regiment for a period not exceeding two years. It was a generous offer to those in a high release group, but few men accepted it, to the detriment of the Regiment and to the later regrets of many. However, it was entirely voluntary. All these exotic names and abbreviations led to the local invention of "Lolli-pop," which stood for "Lots of local leave in place of Python"!

Another alternative was to defer "Python" for six months. The main advantages here were twofold: first, you got back to England on "Liap" before you would have done on "Python"; secondly, you came back to the Regiment for the remaining five months of your deferment. This was an excellent offer for anyone in Groups 21 to 26 who did not want to stay in the Army. For those with over three years' service it was a generous offer and the remainder naturally had to await their turn on "Liap." For the benefit of the Regiment the Colonel took great pains to explain to everyone the advantages of taking "Lilop" or deferring "Python," but in the vast majority of cases the soldiers' minds were set on "Python" and there it was.

At the end of July we got orders to send our two hundred and fifty-eight men home on "Python" in September and a week later this date was advanced to August. A hundred reinforcements from the 12th and 48th Battalions of the Royal Tank Regiment arrived a few days before our "Python" party left. Dances, "smokers" and parties were organized and the pitch of the celebrations gradually mounted. Trucks drove miles to fetch enough "vino" and beer, all available dance bands were collected, decorations were put up and girls invited. Each squadron forgathered in turn, old faces and new, to take part in the rejoicings on so notable an occasion.

Finally the memorable day dawned—the 27th of August, 1945. A few had departed the day before and now the remaining one hundred and eighty-five men, under the command of Major David Steel, gathered up their belongings and their souvenirs to bid the 9th Lancers farewell. They were taken to Udine station, accompanied by all those who still remained. There, smiling broadly, they boarded the train, laden with kit and unable adequately to give expression to their feelings.

This was no ordinary parting: it was a profound wrench. These were the men who had carried on the 9th Lancers' traditions and now, with nothing more than a wave of the arm, they were handing them back. The occasion was both exultant and sorrowful, exultant because these above all men richly deserved their journey home, sorrowful because the 9th Lancers were saying good-bye to some of the finest of their kind.

The train steamed out at 11.30 a.m. under the scorching sun.

TYPES OF TANKS

USED BY THE REGIMENT

1939—1945

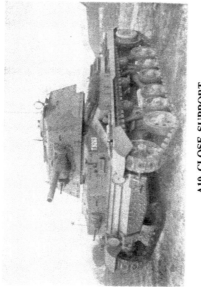

A10 CLOSE SUPPORT

GENERAL STUART I

A10

CRUSADER I

LIGHT Mk. VI B

LIGHT Mk. VI C

CRUISER Mk. IV A13

A 9

GENERAL GRANT

SHERMAN 76-mm.

APPENDICES

APPENDICES

APPENDIX I

ROLL OF HONOUR

ABBREVIATIONS

Accidentally killed	A.K.
Died of illness	Died
Died of wounds	D.O.W.
Killed in action	K.I.A.

OFFICERS

Rank and Name.	Casualty.	Theatre of War, or Country.	Date.
Arbuthnot, Major Sir R. D., Bt. ..	K.I.A.	N.W. Europe.	30/ 6/44
Buchan, Lieutenant P. H. W. W. ...	K.I.A.	Italy.	10/ 9/44
Cadman, Lieutenant W. T. ...	K.I.A.	Middle East.	17/ 6/42
Grant, Captain A. J.	K.I.A.	N. Africa.	24/ 4/43
Harris, Second-Lieutenant B. P. ..	K.I.A.	Middle East.	19/ 7/42
Hartley-Heyman, Lieutenant C. ..	K.I.A.	N. Africa.	26/ 4/43
Heycock, Second-Lieutenant C. W.	D.O.W.	Middle East.	30/ 5/42
Hodson, Lieutenant H. B.	K.I.A.	Middle East.	23/ 1/42
Holt, Lieutenant G. H. P.	K.I.A.	Italy.	25/11/44
Jenner-Fust, Second-Lieutenant T.	K.I.A.	Middle East.	30/ 5/42
Kelly, Lieutenant L. P. G.	K.I.A.	Middle East.	30/ 5/42
Kingscote, Captain R. N.	K.I.A.	Middle East.	22/ 7/42
Macdonell, Colonel J. R., D.S.O. ...	K.I.A.	Italy.	5/ 9/44
Marden, Lieutenant J.	K.I.A.	Middle East.	30/ 5/42
Milnes, Lieutenant J. T.	D.O.W.	Middle East.	4/11/42
Okell, Second-Lieutenant R. C. ..	D.O.W.	Middle East.	18/10/42
Pettit, Lieutenant-Colonel E. R., M.C.	K.I.A.	India.	4/ 8/44
Phillimore, Major The Hon. A. F.	K.I.A.	France.	23/ 5/40
Steel, Second-Lieutenant R. O. P. ...	K.I.A.	France.	24/ 5/40
Stuart, Lieutenant The Viscount ..	D.O.W.	Italy.	18/ 9/44
Tew, Lieutenant T. M. P. ..	A.K.	France.	23/ 5/40
Wyndham, Lieutenant H. S.	K.I.A.	Middle East.	28/10/42
Zissu, Lieutenant T. ..	K.I.A.	Middle East.	3/11/42

OTHER RANKS

		Casualty.	Theatre	Date.
Allan, Lance-Corporal T.	..	K.I.A.	Italy.	14/ 9/44
Ashworth, Lance-Corporal K. B. ...	..	K.I.A.	Middle East.	23/ 1/42
Bailiss, Trooper R. H.	..	K.I.A.	Middle East.	3/ 7/42
Baylis, Trooper C.	..	K.I.A.	Italy.	5/ 9/44
Bentley, Trooper K. C.	..	K.I.A.	Middle East.	30/ 3/43
Berryman, Corporal H. G. ...	..	K.I.A.	N. Africa.	30/ 4/43
Billett, Lance-Corporal E. W. J.	..	K.I.A.	Middle East.	30/ 3/43
Birks, Trooper N.	..	K.I.A.	Middle East.	30/ 3/43

Rank and Name.	Casualty.	Theatre of War, or Country.	Date.
Bond, Lance-Corporal W.	K.I.A.	Madagascar.	5/ 5/42
Bottomley, Trooper B.	K.I.A.	Middle East.	28/ 5/42
Bramhall, Trooper K.	K.I.A.	Middle East.	23/ 1/42
Brown, Trooper J. L.	K.I.A.	France.	26/ 5/40
Brown, Trooper N. R.	K.I.A.	Italy.	1/ 3/45
Bunting, Trooper H. B.	K.I.A.	Middle East.	30/ 5/42
Byrne, Squadron Sergeant-Major J.	D.O.W.	Middle East.	29/ 5/42
Carter, Sergeant E.	Died	United Kingdom.	17/ 6/42
Clarke, Lance-Corporal G. B.	K.I.A.	Italy.	13/11/44
Clarke, Trooper R. C.	K.I.A.	North Africa.	24/ 4/43
Coombes, Trooper C. K. L.	K.I.A.	Italy.	24/ 4/45
Cornwall, Sergeant F. J.	K.I.A.	N.W. Europe.	24/ 9/44
Cowie, Corporal L. J.	K.I.A.	Italy.	5/ 9/44
Curtis, Trooper W. H.	K.I.A.	Italy.	7/12/44
Dannatt, Corporal A. E.	K.I.A.	Middle East.	30/ 5/42
Darvell, Trooper E. T.	Died	United Kingdom.	29/ 9/39
Davidson, Lance-Corporal E.	A.K.	Middle East.	15/12/41
Dawson, Trooper D. T.	K.I.A.	N. Africa.	26/ 4/43
Dawson, Trooper G.	K.I.A.	Italy.	14/12/44
Dickinson, Sergeant M.	D.O.W.	Italy.	18/ 9/44
Donnelly, Trooper E.	K.I.A.	Middle East.	24/10/42
Dudeney, Sergeant E. L.	K.I.A.	Middle East.	23/ 1/42
Duxbury, Trooper F.	K.I.A.	France.	7/ 6/40
Eddison, Trooper J.	D.O.W.	Middle East.	3/ 7/42
Elbourne, Trooper V. J.	K.I.A.	Middle East.	30/ 5/42
Elder, Lance-Corporal W.	K.I.A.	Middle East.	19/ 7/42
English, Trooper A. C.	D.O.W.	Italy.	18/ 4/45
Fairs, Trooper S. J.	K.I.A.	Italy.	22/ 4/45
Gibbons, Orderly Room Sergeant-Major A. C.	D.O.W.	Middle East.	18/ 7/42
Gooding, Trooper R. H.	K.I.A.	N. Africa.	24/ 4/43
Gray, Lance-Corporal W. C.	K.I.A.	N. Africa.	26/ 4/43
Hamlett, Trooper G. P.	K.I.A.	Middle East.	4/11/42
Hayden, Lance-Corporal J. A.	K.I.A.	Italy.	5/ 9/44
Hayward, Lance-Sergeant E. J.	D.O.W.	Middle East.	25/ 1/42
Hetherington, Trooper H.	K.I.A.	Middle East.	27/ 5/42
Hodgson, Trooper J. D.	K.I.A.	Middle East.	17/ 6/42
Hole, Lance-Sergeant G. H.	D.O.W.	Middle East.	27/12/42
Horton, Trooper G. L.	K.I.A.	Middle East.	25/10/42
Hunt, Trooper R. G.	K.I.A.	Italy.	29/11/44
Hutchinson, Trooper B.	K.I.A.	France.	9/ 6/40
Izzard, Trooper W. C.	K.I.A.	Middle East.	3/ 7/42
Jackson, Lance-Sergeant N.	K.I.A.	Middle East.	17/ 6/42
Jagger, Trooper H. R.	K.I.A.	Middle East.	3/ 7/42
Jeans, Trooper C. F.	Died.	N. Africa.	26/10/43
Kelly, Trooper J.	K.I.A.	Middle East.	3/ 7/42
Kinsman, Trooper K. A.	K.I.A.	Italy.	18/ 4/45
Kretzer, Sergeant E., M.M.	K.I.A.	N. Africa.	23/ 4/43
Lloyd, Trooper T.	D.O.W.	Italy.	22/ 4/45
Longmire, Trooper W.	K.I.A.	Italy.	8/12/44
Loveless, Sergeant A. E.	K.I.A.	Middle East.	23/ 1/42
Lumley, Trooper E. R.	K.I.A.	Middle East.	23/ 1/42
Lowrie, Corporal J.	K.I.A.	N. Africa.	26/ 4/43
Lowry, Trooper A. E.	D.O.W.	Italy.	22/ 1/45
Marks, Trooper D. W. H.	K.I.A.	Middle East.	13/ 6/42
Marrows, Corporal J. W.	K.I.A.	Italy.	18/ 4/45
McGinty, Trooper P.	K.I.A.	Middle East.	13/ 6/42

Rank and Name.				Casualty.	Theatre of War, or Country.	Date.
Mifflin, Trooper L. T.			..	D.O.W.	Middle East.	25/10/42
Mirfin, Trooper S.			..	K.I.A.	N. Africa.	25/ 4/43
Mitchell, Trooper J. L.			..	K.I.A.	Middle East.	11/ 6/42
Moat, Trooper J.			..	K.I.A.	Italy.	25/11/44
Moffatt, Corporal D. M.			..	K.I.A.	Italy.	5/ 9/44
Monks, Corporal T.			..	K.I.A.	N. Africa.	24/ 4/43
Moore, Corporal J.			..	K.I.A.	Italy.	10/ 9/44
Moore, Lance-Corporal A. H.			..	Died.	United Kingdom.	11/ 9/39
Mustoe, Trooper E. C.			..	D.O.W.	Middle East.	9/ 3/42
Nelson, Trooper J. C.	..	..		K.I.A.	N. Africa.	26/ 4/43
Newell, Trooper E. J.	..	..	..	D.O.W.	Middle East.	30/ 5/42
O'Connor, Trooper R.	..	..	..	K.I.A.	Middle East.	29/ 3/42
Parker, Corporal G. A.	..	..	..	K.I.A.	France.	5/ 6/40
Pattison, Trooper R.	..	..	..	K.I.A.	Italy.	10/12/44
Pickles, Corporal G.	..	..	..	K.I.A.	Italy.	14/ 9/44
Pimm, Trooper D.	..	..	..	K.I.A.	Italy.	5/ 9/44
Pinkney, Trooper W. R.	..	..	..	K.I.A.	N. Africa.	25/ 4/43
Ponting, Trooper C. H.	..	..	..	K.I.A.	Middle East.	30/ 5/42
Pulman, Lance-Corporal C. J.	..	..	..	K.I.A.	Italy.	14/ 9/44
Quinn, Trooper M.	..	..	..	D.O.W.	N. Africa.	25/ 4/43
Ralph, Lance-Sergeant W. H.	..	..	..	Died.	Italy.	27/12/44
Raynor, Sergeant F. H.	..	..	..	D.O.W.	Middle East.	25/10/42
Rickerby, Lance-Corporal A.	..	..	..	D.O.W.	Madagascar.	12/ 5/42
Roberts, Trooper J.	..	..	..	K.I.A.	Middle East.	22/ 7/42
Rule, Sergeant A. L.	..	..	..	K.I.A.	Italy.	25/11/44
Salmon, Trooper A. W.	..	..	..	K.I.A.	Middle East.	30/ 5/42
Schofield, Lance-Sergeant C. R.	..	..	..	D.O.W.	Middle East.	27/ 3/43
Shelton, Trooper W.	..	..	..	K.I.A.	Middle East.	25/10/42
Sime, Lance-Sergeant H. R.	..	..	..	A.K.	United Kingdom.	11/11/39
Simpson, Sergeant G.	..	..	..	K.I.A.	Italy.	26/ 2/45
Sims, Trooper W.	..	..	..	D.O.W.	Middle East.	27/ 5/42
Smith, Trooper A.	..	..	..	K.I.A.	Middle East.	4/11/42
Smith, Sergeant J.	..	..	..	K.I.A.	N. Africa.	26/ 4/43
Smurthwaite, Trooper S.	..	..	..	K.I.A.	Middle East.	24/10/42
Stackpool, Lance-Corporal P.	..	..	..	D.O.W.	Italy.	18/ 4/45
Stocks, Sergeant F.	..	..	..	D.O.W.	Middle East.	25/10/42
Storr, Trooper H. S.	..	..	..	D.O.W.	Italy.	10/ 9/44
Stott, Trooper R. A.	..	..	..	K.I.A.	Italy.	13/11/44
Stringer, Trooper A. J.	..	..	..	K.I.A.	Middle East.	16/ 6/42
Swan, Lance-Corporal J. J.	..	..	..	K.I.A.	Italy.	14/ 9/44
Thomas, Trooper C.	..	..	..	Died.	United Kingdom.	26/ 7/42
Tipper, Trooper G.	..	..	..	K.I.A.	Middle East.	27/ 3/43
Tron, Trooper J. L.	..	..	..	K.I.A.	France.	2/ 6/40
Tyler, Corporal B.	..	..	..	K.I.A.	Italy.	25/11/44
Tyson, Trooper J.	..	..	..	K.I.A.	Middle East.	19/ 7/42
Waddell, Lance-Corporal J. W.	..	..	..	K.I.A.	Italy.	1/ 3/45
Watkins, Corporal W. H.	..	..	..	K.I.A.	Madagascar.	5/ 5/42
Webster, Trooper A. H.	..	..	..	K.I.A.	Italy.	5/ 9/44
Welham, Sergeant L. G., M.M.	..	..	..	K.I.A.	Middle East.	28/ 5/42
Williams, Trooper J.	..	..	..	D.O.W.	Middle East.	28/ 5/42
Winch, Lance-Sergeant E. J.	..	..	..	K.I.A.	Italy.	14/ 9/44
Wood, Trooper A. T.	..	..	..	K.I.A.	Middle East.	2/11/42
Woodcock, Corporal L.	..	..	..	A.K.	United Kingdom.	16/ 1/40
Worswick, Sergeant E.	..	..	..	K.I.A.	Middle East.	24/10/42

HONOURS AND AWARDS

OFFICERS

Rank and Name.	Campaign.	Gazetted.
C.B.		
Brigadier G. P. Hardy-Roberts, C.B.E.	N.W. Europe.	1945
C.B.E.		
Major-General C. W. Norman	Middle East.	1943
Brigadier G. P. Hardy-Roberts, O.B.E.	Italy.	1944
Brigadier J. J. Kingstone, D.S.O., M.C., A.D.C.	N.W. Europe.	1945
Colonel G. H. Phipps-Hornby	N.W. Europe.	1946
BAR TO D.S.O.		
Brigadier J. J. Kingstone, D.S.O., M.C.	Middle East.	1941
Lieutenant-Colonel Sir P. Farquhar, Bart., D.S.O.	Italy.	1944
Lieutenant-Colonel J. R. Macdonell, D.S.O. ..	France.	1940
D.S.O.		
Brigadier C. H. M. Peto	France.	1940
Brigadier G. E. Prior-Palmer	N.W. Europe.	1945
Brigadier O. L. Prior-Palmer	Italy.	1945
Lieutenant-Colonel Sir P. Farquhar, Bart.	Middle East.	1943
Lieutenant-Colonel G. H. Grosvenor ..	Middle East.	1943
Lieutenant-Colonel J. R. Macdonell ..	Middle East.	1942
Lieutenant-Colonel R. S. G. Perry	N. Africa.	1943
Lieutenant-Colonel K. J. Price, M.C.	Italy.	1945
Second-Lieutenant D. E. C. Steel	France.	1940
O.B.E.		
Colonel M. H. Aird	N.W. Europe.	1945
Lieutenant-Colonel J. R. Bowring	Middle East.	1941
Lieutenant-Colonel F. Flower	N.W. Europe.	1945
Lieutenant-Colonel G. P. Hardy-Roberts ..	Middle East.	1941
Major J. F. Colvin, M.C.	N.W. Europe.	1945
M.B.E.		
Captain E. R. Donnley		1946
BAR TO M.C.		
Captain H. O. D. Thwaites, M.C. ..	Italy.	1945
M.C.		
Major R. O. G. Gardner	Middle East.	1943
Major G. D. Meyrick	Middle East.	1943
Major E. R. Pettit	Burma.	1945
Major K. J. Price	Middle East.	1942
Major D. E. C. Steel, D.S.O.	Italy.	1945
Captain G. Dison, R.A.M.C. (attached 9th Lancers) ..	Middle East.	1943
Captain J. McD. Dougan, R.A.M.C. (attached 9th Lancers)	Middle East.	1942
Captain G. G. A. Gregson	Italy.	1945
Captain J. W. R. Kemp, R.A.M.C. (attached 9th Lancers)	Italy.	1945

Rank and Name.					Campaign.	Gazetted.
Captain D. A. St. G. Laurie	..		..	..	Middle East.	1942
Captain J. H. Montagu-Douglas-Scott		..	..	..	France.	1940
Captain F. L. Pym	..		..	..	Italy.	1945
Lieutenant B. S. Agate	..	..	..	..	Middle East.	1943
Lieutenant G. P. C. R. Crampton..		..	..	..	Italy.	1945
Lieutenant I. G. Fitzpatrick	..		..	..	Italy.	1945
Lieutenant L. G. M. Hannen	..	..	..	..	Italy.	1945
Lieutenant R. K. B. Hitchcock	..	..	..	..	Middle East.	1942
Lieutenant J. E. Joicey	..	..	..	..	Italy.	1945
Lieutenant The Hon. R. E. Lloyd-Mostyn		..	..		Middle East.	1943
Lieutenant M. J. W. Marsh	..	..	..	..	Middle East.	1943 '
Lieutenant J. P. Thomson-Glover, R.H.A. (attached 9th Lancers) ..	..	..	..	..	Middle East.	1942
Lieutenant H. O. D. Thwaites	..	..	..	..	Middle East.	1943
Lieutenant T. D. Whately..	..	..	..	..	Italy.	1945
Second-Lieutenant R. P. Thomas..	..	..	..	..	Middle East.	1942

MENTIONED IN DESPATCHES

					Campaign.	Gazetted.
Major-General C. W. Norman, C.B.E. ..		..	..	..	Middle East.	1940
					Middle East.	1943
Brigadier G. P. Hardy-Roberts, C.B., C.B.E. ..				..	Middle East.	1941
					Middle East.	1944
Brigadier C. H. M. Peto, D.S.O. ..					N.W. Europe.	1945
					N.W. Europe.	1945
					N.W. Europe.	1945
Brigadier J. J. Kingstone, D.S.O., M.C. ..					Middle East.	1941
					N.W. Europe.	1945
Colonel M. H. Aird, O.B.E.	..	..			N.W. Europe.	1946
Lieutenant-Colonel L. W. Diggle, M.C. ..					France.	1940
Major R. L. Benson, D.S.O., M.V.O., M.C.					France.	1940
Major J. F. Colvin, M.C. ..	..	..			France.	1940
					N.W. Europe.	1945
Major F. Flower ..					Middle East.	1941
					Middle East.	1943
					Middle East.	1944
Major R. O. G. Gardner, M.C. ..			..	..	Italy.	1945
Major C. Lomax ..	..	..	..	..	Middle East.	1943
Major J. R. Macdonell	..	..	..	..	France.	1940
Major R. S. G. Perry	..	..	..	..	Middle East.	1944
Major G. E. Prior-Palmer..	..		..	..	France.	1940
Major D. E. C. Steel, D.S.O., M.C.			..	..	France.	1940
					Italy.	1945
					Italy.	1945
Captain D. A. W. Allen	..	..	..	..	Italy.	1946
Captain E. R. Donnley	..	..	..	..	Italy.	1945
Captain P. G. Dudding	..	..	..	..	Italy.	1946
Captain G. G. A. Gregson, M.C. ..		..	..	..	Italy.	1945
Captain W. G. Peek	..	..	..	..	Italy.	1946
Captain F. L. Pym, M.C. ..		..	..	..	Italy.	1945
Lieutenant C. R. Lacy-Thompson		..	..	..	Italy.	1946
Lieutenant J. P. Thompson-Glover, M.C., R.H.A. (attached 9th Lancers) ..	..	..	..	..	Italy.	1946
Lieutenant T. D. Whately, M.C. ..		..	..	..	Italy.	1945
Lieutenant S. C. Wright ..	..	..	..	..	France.	1940
					N.W. Europe.	1946
Second-Lieutenant The Hon. R. E. Lloyd-Mostyn					France.	1940

FOREIGN DECORATIONS

FRANCE

Brigadier G. E. Prior-Palmer, D.S.O. . . . . . Legion of Honour, Chevalier avec Croix de Guerre.

Brigadier C. H. M. Peto, D.S.O. — Legion of Honour, Chevalier Croix de Guerre with palms.

BELGIUM

Brigadier C. H. M. Peto, D.S.O. . . Order of Leopold (Commander), Croix de Guerre with palms.

CZECHOSLOVAKIA

Brigadier C. H. M. Peto, D.S.O. . . Order of the White Lion (3rd Class) War Cross.

GREECE

Lieutenant-Colonel The Hon. D. C. F. Erskine — Commander, Order of the Phoenix.

HOLLAND

Brigadier J. J. Kingstone, C.B.E., D.S.O., M.C. — Order of Orange Nassau (Commander).
Lieutenant-Colonel F. Flower, O.B.E. . . Order of Orange Nassau (Officer).

LUXEMBOURG

Brigadier C. H. M. Peto, D.S.O. . . Order of Nassau (Commander), Croix de Guerre.

POLAND

Brigadier C. H. M. Peto, D.S.O. . . Polonia Restituta.

U.S.A.

Brigadier G. P. Hardy-Roberts, C.B., C.B.E. . . Legion of Merit (Officer).
Colonel M. H. Aird, O.B.E. . . . . . . Legion of Merit (Officer).
Major D. S. Allhusen . . . . Silver Star.

OTHER RANKS

Rank and Name.	Campaign.	Gazetted.
M.B.E.		
Squadron Sergeant-Major H. G. Huxford . .	Italy.	1945
D.C.M.		
Squadron Sergeant-Major A. Blandford . .	France.	1940
Squadron Sergeant-Major H. G. Huxford, M.B.E.	Italy.	1945
Sergeant V. F. Corbett	Italy.	1945
Sergeant W. Lloyd	Middle East.	1942
Lance-Sergeant D. Parfitt	Italy.	1945
BAR TO M.M.		
Squadron Sergeant-Major F. Edwards, M.M. . .	Middle East.	1943

M.M.

Rank and Name.	Campaign.	Gazetted.
Squadron Quartermaster-Sergeant A. G. Harriss	Middle East.	1943
Mechanist Sergeant A. J. Bennett..	Middle East.	1943
Sergeant A. J. Beswick	Italy.	1945
Sergeant G. P. K. Brennan	N.W. Europe.	1945
Sergeant J. A. Edmunds ..	N.W. Europe.	1945
Sergeant F. Edwards	Middle East.	1942
Sergeant F. Helps ..	Italy.	1945
Sergeant R. L. Hillary	Middle East.	1943
Sergeant E. Kretzer	Middle East.	1942
Mechanist Sergeant D. T. M. Maloney ..	Middle East.	1942
Lance-Sergeant E. G. Berryman ..	Italy.	1945
Lance-Sergeant A. W. Booth	Middle East.	1943
Lance-Sergeant F. Crayton	Italy.	1945
Lance-Sergeant R. J. M. Irvine	Italy.	1945
Lance-Sergeant S. J. Perry..	Italy.	1945
Lance-Sergeant I. C. Simpson	Italy.	1945
Lance-Sergeant L. G. Welham	Middle East.	1942
Corporal F. D. M. Chapman	Italy.	1945
Corporal R. S. Riches	Middle East.	1943
Corporal C. D. S. Smith ..	Italy.	1945
Corporal H. G. Thomas ..	Middle East.	1942
Lace-Corporal W. Charlesworth ..	Middle East.	1943
Lance-Corporal L. Cook ..	Middle East.	1943
Lance-Corporal R. Harris..	Italy.	1945
Lance-Corporal E. A. Instone	Middle East.	1943
Lance-Corporal A. Nickolls	Middle East.	1943
Trooper H. Ferner ..	Middle East.	1943
Trooper R. S. Jackson	Italy.	1945
Trooper J. Macfarlane	Middle East.	1943
Trooper C. L. Pine..	Middle East.	1942

MENTIONED IN DESPATCHES

	Campaign.	Gazetted.
Regimental Sergeant-Major W. H. Crook	Middle East.	1944
	Italy.	1944
Regimental Sergeant-Major T. Hardwidge	Middle East.	1944
Squadron Sergeant-Major H. G. Huxford	Middle East.	1944
Sergeant A. J. Beswick	Italy.	1945
Sergeant T. E. Blunt	Italy.	1946
Sergeant G. R. Brain	France.	1940
Sergeant T. Chambers	Italy.	1946
Sergeant K. H. Clews	Italy.	1945
Sergeant J. A. Edmunds	Italy.	1945
Sergeant E. Evans ..	Italy.	1945
Sergeant G. G. Gates	Middle East.	1944
Sergeant S. V. Hardwick ..	Italy.	1945
Sergeant W. A. Jenner	Middle East.	1943
Sergeant A. E. Loveless	Middle East.	1942
Sergeant W. Philpott	Italy.	1946
Sergeant C. H. Riley	Italy.	1945
Sergeant J. W. Salt ..	Italy.	1946
Sergeant P. Sandeman	France.	1940
Sergeant A. Wiggans	Middle East.	1943
Sergeant G. M. Williamson	Italy.	1946
Sergeant W. J. Wood	Italy.	1946

X

Rank and Name.	Campaign.	Gazetted.
Lance-Sergeant W. Frost	Middle East.	1944
Lance-Sergeant F. Grundy ..	Italy.	1946
Lance-Sergeant R. J. M. Irvine ..	Italy.	1945
Corporal A. Blackburn	Italy.	1945
Corporal J. S. Broomhall	Middle East.	1944
Corporal J. Burrows	Italy.	1945
Corporal W. Gorton	France.	1940
Corporal R. D. Loveday	Italy.	1946
Corporal F. C. Novels	Italy.	1946
Corporal G. Pickles	Middle East.	1944
Corporal T. A. Sleeman	Italy.	1946
Lance-Corporal R. Harris.. ..	Italy.	1945
Lance-Corporal G. Mercer ..	France.	1940
Lance-Corporal A. Nickolls, M.M.	Middle East.	1943
Trooper J. W. Andrews	Middle East.	1944
Trooper K. Shore	Italy.	1945
Trooper J. Snape	France.	1940
Trooper W. J. Thomas	Italy.	1946
Trooper W. H. Watkins	France.	1940

FOREIGN DECORATIONS

U.S.A.

Sergeant G. H. Dolezal ..	Bronze Star, 1947.

CITATIONS OF DECORATIONS AWARDED TO OTHER RANKS OF THE REGIMENT

As the exploits of most officers have been fully covered in the text, their citations for awards have been omitted. Because the same cannot be said for all other ranks, in their case the citations have been included in full.

OTHER RANKS

M.B.E.

Copy of citation dated 18th January, 1945

No. 310799 WARRANT OFFICER CLASS II HERBERT GEORGE HUXFORD, 9th Queen's Royal Lancers, Royal Armoured Corps.

During the period between March, 1941, and December, 1944, S.S.M. Huxford has been S.S.M. of "B" Squadron, 9th Lancers, where he has been continuously employed as chief gunnery instructor to the regiment. His squadron was the first to be equipped with heavy Grant tanks. He was largely responsible for the training of the gunners, and overcoming the very considerable fighting difficulties.

After only three weeks' training the squadron went into action at Knightsbridge; and, between 27th May and the end of July, 1942, his gunners knocked out and burned out no less than eighty-six German tanks. When the rest of the regiment was equipped with Shermans he went out and assisted each squadron in their training. Again, it was largely due to his efforts that the regiment claimed seventy-one burned-out enemy tanks during the Battle of El Alamein. Then again, when indirect fire had to be learnt, S.S.M. Huxford, by his skill and keenness, greatly helped the regiment to attain a very high standard, which has been found most valuable during the operations in Italy.

S.S.M. Huxford has not missed a single battle in which the regiment has taken part since the war started—always being in the thick of the fighting, helping with ammunition supply, directing fire or assisting to repair guns under fire. Without S.S.M. Huxford's untiring energy and keenness the standard of gunnery of the regiment would never have attained the high standard which has been such an outstanding feature in all the operations of the regiment.—*"London Gazette" dated 28th June, 1945.*

DISTINGUISHED CONDUCT MEDAL

No. 726541 WARRANT OFFICER CLASS II (S.S.M.) ARTHUR BLANDFORD, 9th Queen's Royal Lancers, Royal Armoured Corps.

On 5th June, 1940, S.S.M. Blandford was ordered to carry out a patrol at Toeufles, S.W. of Abbeville, to protect the right flank of the 153rd Infantry Brigade. At Toeufles he established contact with a patrol of the Black Watch, who reported the enemy in large numbers N.E. of the village. S.S.M. Blandford, with his patrol of two light tanks, immediately went towards the positions where these enemy were reported. He there surprised and engaged a large number of German infantry at close range. He inflicted heavy casualties on the enemy in position, and followed up those who ran away. While engaging these infantry an enemy anti-tank gun opened fire from a flank, hit one of his light tanks and set it on fire. S.S.M. Blandford was instrumental in having the fire put out, the tank driven out of action, and subsequently towed to safety.—*"London Gazette" dated 27th September, 1940.*

No. 310799 WARRANT OFFICER CLASS II (S.S.M.) HERBERT GEORGE HUXFORD, M.B.E., 9th Queen's Royal Lancers, Royal Armoured Corps.

W.O.II Huxford is S.S.M. of "B" Squadron, 9th Lancers, and by his initiative and enterprise has contributed greatly to the success of his squadron. He commands a 105-mm. tank and always supports one of the leading troops. In the advance north of Fosso Benvignante on 18th April the squadron was held up by two batteries of 88-mm. guns. S.S.M. Huxford was ordered to deal with the battery to the left front. By great speed and accuracy, under A.P. and H.E. fire shot over open sights at short range, he engaged each gun in turn, knocking out two. As a result of this, the tanks and infantry were able to advance to the objective. On the same day the squadron was held up by a fosso. This W.O. brought forward the fascine, and, under heavy H.E. and small-arms fire, supervised the crossing operation, which resulted in the capture of other bridges intact and the consequent havoc in the enemy gun lines. On 24th April, north of Ferrara, S.S.M. Huxford was supporting the leading troop which was held up by three Mk. IV's and an 88. The only cover available—the signal box—was occupied. So, regardless of great danger, he moved his tank up and down in the open under exceedingly accurate fire, and engaged the 88 from every angle, displaying the keenest determination and gallantry, which was an inspiration to the whole squadron. After an hour of such treatment the gun destroyed itself. This action greatly assisted the squadron in reaching their objective. His energy, cheerfulness and enthusiasm have been a magnificent example to his squadron.—*"London Gazette" dated 23rd August, 1945.*

No. 319399 SERGEANT VERDUN FRANK CORBETT, 9th Queen's Royal Lancers, Royal Armoured Corps.

On 7th December, 1944, Sergt. Corbett was commanding a tank in 3rd Troop, "C" Squadron, 9th Lancers, who were supporting a company of the 1st K.R.R.C. in the attack on the village of Pideura which was a key position and strongly held. Whilst the infantry were securing a foothold in the church the other two tanks of the troop were disabled by bazookas. Further tank support was urgently required by the infantry in the church in order to silence a German strong-point in the house next door. As no tank could cover him, Sergt. Corbett proceeded to advance the 400 yards into the village alone. The power traverse had been badly damaged by a bazooka the day before when infantry support during the advance had been impossible, so that he well knew that his tank was almost defenceless against any bazookamen. Furthermore, the whole 400 yards of the road was in full view of enemy S.P. guns shooting from the flank. In spite of this, he continued to advance and reached the village. On arrival at the church where it had been arranged that he should meet the infantry, he was surprised to find Germans taking up positions all over the village, and no sign of our own infantry, who, it afterwards transpired, had been driven out of it by a strong German counter-attack. Sergt. Corbett was able to kill one German as he ran to man his anti-tank gun and then to run over the gun. By now Spandau was being fired at him from all sides at ten yards' range, but undeterred he proceeded to engage the house which was the German strong-point with H.E. fire. He now saw that more Germans were entering the house, so decided that the only way to restore the situation was to charge his tank at them. This he did, causing the front wall and top floor to collapse on top of his tank. Reversing out, he found that both his 76-mm. gun and his two Brownings were jammed. He now proceeded to engage the enemy with his tommy-guns from an exposed position out of the top of the turret. His gunner-operator loaded one for him whilst he fired the other. He also engaged the enemy in the ditches with his hand grenades, and the rest of the crew used their revolvers out of the revolver ports. Sergt.

Corbett had by now killed and wounded many Germans and had got his tank alongside the church. Standing on the turret, he was able to look through the window and saw that the church was occupied by the Germans. He immediately fired his tommy-gun, killing several and clearing the church. Sergt. Corbett had now completely run out of ammunition, but at this critical moment the K.R.R.C. re-entered the village and were able to enter the church and house, consolidate the position and take several prisoners. There is no doubt that had it not been for Sergt. Corbett and the outstanding use of his tank the German counter-attack might have succeeded, and the key position of Pideura would have remained in German hands.

Sergt. Corbett, by the complete disregard for his personal safety, his exemplary offensive spirit and determination to fight his tank to the last round, was outstanding in the battle at Pideura.—*"London Gazette" dated 10th May, 1945.*

Copy of citation dated 10th August, 1942

No. 319036 Sergeant William Lloyd, 9th Queen's Royal Lancers, Royal Armoured Corps.

On 29th May, his troop leader having been killed in action, Sergt. Lloyd assumed command and, on many subsequent occasions, led his Grant tank troop with the greatest courage and determination. In particular, on 17th June at Sidi Rezegh, when the regiment was attacked by superior numbers of Pz.K.3 tanks, the determined resistance offered to the enemy by Sergt. Lloyd's troop was largely responsible for beating off the enemy attack. On 22nd July, south of El Ruweisat Ridge, Sergt. Lloyd again showed great courage and determination in leading his squadron, single file, through a gap in the enemy's minefield. From the moment Sergt. Lloyd reached the gap the squadron was subjected to the heaviest fire from tanks and anti-tank guns directed from both flanks as well as the front. Sergt. Lloyd continued through the gap, reporting locations of enemy tanks and guns. Subsequently, when it became necessary to withdraw the regiment through the minefield, Sergt. Lloyd covered the movement and was the last to come back. His determination, courage and complete disregard of personal safety have earned for him the admiration of all officers and other ranks of his squadron.—*"London Gazette" dated 15th October, 1942.*

Copy of citation dated 9th September, 1944

No. 320087 Lance-Sergeant Desmond Parfitt, 9th Queen's Royal Lancers, Royal Armoured Corps.

Sergt. Parfitt was commanding the third tank in 2nd Troop, "B" Squadron, 9th Lancers, during the attack by the regiment on the San Savino feature south of Coriano on 5th September, 1944. He led his troop under very heavy fire down into a very steep and rough wadi and up the other side into the enemy F.D.Ls., when he was fired on by a bazooka from a house. The bomb struck the back of the tank and blew off some bridging equipment. Sergt. Parfitt destroyed the house with H.E. His Troop Sergeant's tank was then knocked out by a bazooka from very close range. Sergt. Parfitt went on towards the objective. He had, in the meantime, got separated from his troop leader by a sunken road, and when he got up to his troop leader, some ten minutes later, he found his tank had been knocked out and was blazing. The same gun then opened up at him and just missed the turret. He reversed very quickly back, and, looking over his shoulder, he saw a bazookaman part the bushes behind and level his tube at the tank. He shouted "Traverse left," and his gunner traversed 180 degrees at full speed and blew the German to bits with an H.E. round. He then saw five men stalking him with what looked like sticky-bombs, and he shot all of them before they could attack. Shortly afterwards, as he was reversing, he saw a lot of Germans lying at the bottom of their slit-trenches. He shot one, and the rest came out with their hands up, laying two bazookas and their arms on the ground. He waved these back towards the squadron position. A face suddenly appeared at an upstairs window of one of the farms, and a moment later a grenade exploded on the top of the turret, smashing the periscope and temporarily blinding Sergt. Parfitt in one eye with dust and very small particles of metal. More Germans then appeared, running about, and, although he could not see properly, he told his gunner to traverse backwards and forwards as the tank drove out at full speed straight through a barn which was in the way, back to his squadron just behind.

Through this single-handed action Sergt. Parfitt showed the greatest gallantry against very great odds. On his return to the squadron his eye was bandaged and, although in great pain, he refused to be evacuated and came up into the line again when he was shortly dispatched with an infantry section to mop up some Germans in a vineyard. He remained in action until his squadron was withdrawn some time after dark, dealing with continuous sniper and bazooka attacks on the squadron. Sergt. Parfitt killed a great many Germans, and was responsible for accounting for four bazookamen. He very greatly assisted the squadron to hang on to this important feature and showed the very greatest courage, resource and devotion to duty throughout the whole action.—*"London Gazette"* *dated 8th February, 1945.*

BAR TO MILITARY MEDAL

Copy of citation dated 17th May, 1943

No. 317439 Squadron Sergeant-Major Fred Edwards, M.M., 9th Queen's Royal Lancers, Royal Armoured Corps.

On 24th April, 1943, Sergt.-Major Edwards was following his squadron in a scout car when they attacked a strongly held enemy position. As soon as the leading tanks crossed a wadi they came under heavy anti-tank fire at a range of only 300 yards and seven tanks were knocked out. In spite of very heavy fire, S.S.M. Edwards visited every tank that had been knocked out, in search of survivors, and succeeded in bringing three badly wounded men back to the wadi. The wadi was heavily mined and, by this time, it was under very heavy fire. In spite of this, S.S.M. Edwards evacuated all the seriously wounded on his scout car. In doing so, he made three journeys across a very exposed piece of ground. He then reported to Regimental H.Q. and gave a very clear account of the action and what he had seen of the enemy position.

During the whole action S.S.M. Edwards displayed the utmost courage, and by his coolness and devotion to duty undoubtedly saved the lives of several seriously wounded men.—*"London Gazette" dated 19th August, 1943.*

MILITARY MEDAL

Copy of citation dated 24th March, 1943

No. 317557 Sergeant (A./S.Q.M.S.) Arthur George Harriss, 9th Queen's Royal Lancers, Royal Armoured Corps.

This N.C.O.'s troop leader was killed at an early stage of the Battle of Alamein, and at a critical time Harriss took command of the troop and handled it thereafter with outstand-ing courage and ability.

On 24th October, 1942, Harriss was troop sergeant of the second troop to pass through the enemy minefield. His tank was brought to a standstill through the driver being hit. However, he calmly continued to fight his tank and use his field glasses under intense fire, destroying three enemy tanks and spotting two 88-mm. guns which the troop destroyed by shell fire. On this day this N.C.O. displayed outstanding courage and ability in a situation when much depended on the few tanks which had forced a bridgehead.

On 2nd November, 1942, his squadron was attacked by seventeen enemy tanks. Harriss had just lost his operator, but he continued to load his gun, use his wireless and at the same time command the troop. He fired eighty rounds in this action, scoring many hits on the enemy, who were eventually compelled to withdraw. His own tank was hit repeatedly.
—*"London Gazette" dated 14th October, 1943.*

Copy of citation dated 11th October, 1942

No. 318910 MECHANIST SERGEANT ALFRED JOHN BENNETT, 9th Queen's Royal Lancers, Royal Armoured Corps.

This N.C.O. is Mechanist Sergeant to his squadron and during the period 27th May to 6th September, 1942, he has been continually in the field. He has accompanied the tanks in an unarmoured vehicle during every action and, owing to his hard work by day and night and to his devotion to duty, the majority of tanks were kept running under what were frequently very difficult circumstances.

On several occasions, both at Knightsbridge and on the Ruweisat Ridge, he repaired tanks in the open, under heavy shell fire, without the slightest regard to his own safety.—*"London Gazette" dated 18th February, 1943.*

Copy of citation dated 19th June, 1945

No. 3529777 SERGEANT ALFRED JAMES BESWICK, 9th Queen's Royal Lancers, Royal Armoured Corps.

During the period 9th April to 2nd May, 1945, Sergt. Beswick was Troop Sergeant of an armoured squadron, R.E. Throughout that time he carried out his duties with the greatest zeal and courage, frequently under heavy enemy fire.

On five occasions he has commanded Arks when they have been placed in position under heavy fire, and in particular on 18th October, 1944, during the battle of the Gothic Line, near Cesena (map ref. M664032), he commanded an Ark which became ditched just in front of the obstacle in which it was to be placed. In spite of heavy mortar fire, Sergt. Beswick, with complete disregard for his own safety, got out of the Ark and by giving the driver visual signals enabled it to be moved sufficiently to allow another Ark to be brought up. This Ark he again directed by visual signals until it was in position, and Sergt. Beswick was satisfied that the crossing was suitable for tanks.

During the operations of the past two years Sergt. Beswick has shown outstanding courage and perseverance in the face of danger, and has set a fine example of devotion to duty to all his subordinates.—*"London Gazette" dated 13th December, 1945.*

Copy of citation dated 26th February, 1945

No. 319135 SERGEANT GABRIEL PATRICK JOSEPH BRENNAN, 9th Queen's Royal Lancers, Royal Armoured Corps.

This N.C.O., who is an expert in the mounting of air pick-up operations, was parachuted into the Vaucluse on 6th August, 1944.

The Dakota operation which he organized was of the greatest importance. On the night of 12th August, 1944, thirteen agents were landed in France, and twenty-one persons were safely evacuated, including agents whose information proved invaluable in the preparation and execution of immediate military operations and of subsequent work in the field. Sixteen members of the American Army Air Corps were amongst those who were evacuated.

It is significant that the organizer in the area considered this operation as the most successful which had taken place in his region.—*"London Gazette" dated 21st June, 1945.*

Copy of citation dated 1st May, 1945

No. 7901256 SERGEANT JACK ARTHUR EDMUNDS, 9th Queen's Royal Lancers, Royal Armoured Corps.

Sergt. Edmunds is Troop Sergeant, 4th Troop, "B" Squadron, 9th Lancers. On 18th April he commanded the point tank of the right leading troop in the advance up to and over the Fosso Benvignante. Passing through the F.D.Ls. S.E. of Boccaleone at 269630, the advance was stopped by an S.P. and Mark IV, which had already knocked out two tanks and two Kangaroos. So Sergt. Edmunds, under intense A.P. fire and harassed by snipers, moved his tank from one fire position to another until he had "brewed up" both. Had it not been for this N.C.O.'s gallant and skilful action the squadron could not have advanced without heavy losses. Again, on 24th April, N.W. of Malborghetto, 1487, the squadron met five Mark IV's, which were causing trouble to the infantry mopping up strong-points. Immediately, this N.C.O. drove his tank right forward, firing all his guns, being himself engaged by A.P. fire from all sides. This gallant dash forced the Mark IV's to withdraw, and amidst intense fire Sergt. Edmunds halted and knocked out three enemy tanks in six shots. By his disregard for danger, his courage and aggressiveness, Sergt. Edmunds was responsible for maintaining the speed of the advance, with the resultant destruction or capture of a very large number of enemy guns and tanks.—*"London Gazette" dated 23rd August, 1945.*

Copy of citation dated 21st June, 1942

No. 317439 SERGEANT FRED EDWARDS, 9th Queen's Royal Lancers, Royal Armoured Corps.

On 31st May the regiment [The Bays] was ordered to take over from the 9th Q.R. Lancers all battle-worthy tanks.

This N.C.O. joined my Grant tank squadron on this day. During the period 12th to 14th June Sergt. Edwards was continuously in the forefront of the battle, showing the greatest determination and skill in the handling of his tank. On 14th June this N.C.O.'s tank together with the Acting Squadron Leader were the only two Grant tanks left to fight.

They fought side by side continuously throughout the day, and by 2000 hrs., although surrounded by enemy tanks, had not given up a single yard of ground. It was at this juncture and only on my orders did Sergt. Edwards commence to slowly withdraw. In addition it was entirely due to this N.C.O.'s efforts that on the previous evening the crew from another burning Grant tank were rescued whilst under intensive fire. During the whole period that this N.C.O. has been under my command he has shown outstanding determination.—*"London Gazette" dated 13th August, 1942.*

Copy of citation dated 10th September, 1944

No. 7901379 SERGEANT FRANCIS HELPS, 9th Queen's Royal Lancers, Royal Armoured Corps.

Sergt. Helps was commanding the second tank in 2nd Troop, "B" Squadron, during the attack on the San Savino feature on 5th September, 1944. At the beginning of the attack Sergt. Helps was in reserve, but was soon sent to reinforce the left-hand troop as a result of the attacking force having lost four tanks. This involved Sergt. Helps leading his troop across the side of a hill under heavy artillery and anti-tank fire, to which he was extremely exposed above the turret, as he had to negotiate his tank in safety over the hazardous and hostile going and past a German minefield whose boundaries were unknown; and therefore had to be recced. on foot; and then on to the ridge into the enemy F.D.Ls. Here he killed pockets of infiltrating Germans without loss to himself. He was then ordered to work his way along the objective to the left. While doing this he came under further anti-tank-gun fire, obviously directed at himself. He immediately pulled down into dead ground and with a good eye for country worked his way still farther along the ridge. Constantly he was sniped and stalked from the ditches, bushes and tree-tops. These he destroyed, in addition to fifteen whom he observed crawling along a half-sunken road, including (as it turned out later) the company commander. As his tank came up on to the top again, an A.P. shot landed close to him, closely followed by two more. Sergt. Helps immediately jockeyed for position to engage this gun, which in the meantime destroyed the tank on Sergt. Helps's left. However, he could not find a suitable fire position at first, and knocked out two bazookamen rapidly approaching from his rear. Eventually he saw a good position forward, and, advancing at speed under a hail of every kind of fire, managed to reach it intact. He immediately put down fire in the gun area, but unluckily (though wisely) it had moved. Shortly after this he destroyed a bazookaman about to engage his troop leader's tank and, as a result, prisoners came in. Sergt. Helps stayed in this position for ten hours, completely surrounded by the enemy and in the gravest danger. In the evening he was withdrawn with the rest of the squadron, his tank and his crew unscathed.

His tireless energy, his determination and unspeakable bravery were the finest example to all who worked with him.—*"London Gazette" dated 8th February, 1945.*

Copy of citation dated 17th May, 1943

No. 317242 SERGEANT ROBERT LESLIE HILLARY, 9th Queen's Royal Lancers, Royal Armoured Corps.

On 10th May, 1943, Sergt. Hillary's troop was the leading troop when the regiment advanced through the pass west of Jebel Rassas. The advance was held up by four anti-tank guns covering a road block. Sergt. Hillary stalked and destroyed two of the guns and, by very well-directed small-arms fire at short range, forced the crews of the other two guns to abandon them. While this was going on he came under heavy enfilade fire from two more guns, and was unable to move his tank in daylight. As soon as it got dark Sergt. Hillary attacked the two remaining guns and silenced them before rejoining his squadron.

Throughout the action this N.C.O. showed great dash and determination to close with the enemy, and inflicted heavy casualties on them.—*"London Gazette" dated 19th August, 1943.*

Copy of citation dated 10th August, 1942

No. 317346 SERGEANT ERNEST KRETZER, 9th Queen's Royal Lancers, Royal Armoured Corps.

On 16th June, 1942, at Hagfet el Haiad (424392) Sergt. Kretzer's tank took part in a successful attack by a squadron of Crusader tanks on anti-tank guns which were guarding the flank of a large German column. Sergt. Kretzer's tank was hit and set on fire when close to the German anti-tank guns (50-mm.). He continued to close with the enemy until the flames made it impossible to remain in the fighting compartment. Sergt. Kretzer thereupon dismounted and with two hand grenades destroyed a German gun crew and wrecked the gun. He then returned to the tank, which was now a sheet of flame, and organized the rescue of the driver, who was trapped in his compartment and who was subsequently got out through the fighting compartment.

Sergt. Kretzer's resolute action and complete disregard of personal safety materially affected the success of the action.—*"London Gazette" dated 15th October, 1942.*

Copy of citation 26th June, 1942

No. 318917 SERGEANT DESMOND THOMAS MICHAEL MALONEY, 9th Queen's Royal Lancers, Royal Armoured Corps.

Throughout the period 27th to 31st May, when the regiment was hotly engaged throughout every day, in the Knightsbridge area, Mech./Sergt. Maloney was constantly up with the tanks of his squadron in a lorry carrying out repairs whilst the tanks were in action. His courage under fire, and his determination and skill were the means of keeping many tanks in action at a critical period of the operations.

This N.C.O.'s conduct was a great inspiration to all who saw it.—*"London Gazette" dated 24th September, 1942.*

Copy of citation dated 1st May, 1945

No. 7919191 LANCE-SERGEANT ERNEST GEORGE BERRYMAN, 9th Queen's Royal Lancers, Royal Armoured Corps.

Sergt. Berryman is Troop Sergeant, 3rd Troop, "B" Squadron, 9th Lancers. During this last battle he has shown great skill and courage. On 18th April, north of Argenta, when within 1,000 yards of the objective (229677), the squadron was held up on the left flank by a battery of 88-mm. guns covering a very open bit of ground. By swift and bold action Sergt. Berryman, regardless of intense A.P. and machine-gun fire, knocked out two and silenced the remainder. These guns would have caused great havoc to the squadron. Sergt. Berryman continued on to the objective as point tank, overrunning two 150-mm. guns complete, destroying much wheeled transport, and killing or capturing many Germans.

On the advance north of Ferrara on 24th April Sergt. Berryman was again the point tank of the leading troop. With unfaltering aim he shot up a Mark IV on the move at 900 yards. At last light, having moved down the railway about 500 yards in the open, suddenly two Mark IV's opened up at him on his right flank and a Mark IV and an 88-mm. S.P. on his left. Sergt. Berryman first took cover behind the signal box and then with great gallantry and coolness knocked out the two Mark IV's on the right and killed two members of the third Mark IV which caused the remainder of the crew to desert, leaving their tank intact. Sergt. Berryman was engaged by the 88-mm. for about an hour and he returned fire continuously, handling his tank with the greatest courage and determination. Finally the crew of the 88-mm. demolished their piece.

It was very largely due to this action that the squadron was able to reach its objective. This N.C.O., by his confidence and courage, has been responsible for the destruction of a large amount of enemy equipment.—*"London Gazette" dated 23rd August, 1945.*

Copy of citation dated 4th May, 1943

No. 5496801 LANCE-SERGEANT ARTHUR WILLIAM BOOTH, 9th Queen's Royal Lancers, Royal Armoured Corps.

This N.C.O., who has been in every action in which his squadron has taken part since their arrival in the Middle East and who has several times taken over command of his troop when his troop leader has been "knocked out," showed the greatest courage and determination during the fighting between Goubellat and Bou Arrada on 23rd and 24th April, 1943.

On 23rd April, 1943, L./Sergt. Booth's tank was blown up on a mine and left behind when his squadron advanced. Although unable to find any fitters, L./Sergt. Booth and his crew took some parts from another knocked-out tank and, by working through the night, managed to get their tank on the road by first light on the morning of 24th April. L./Sergt. Booth then started out, following the tracks of the regiment, and rejoined his squadron only a few minutes before they went in to attack a very strongly held position. L./Sergt. Booth's tank was the only one not destroyed by the enemy guns; he managed to get his tank into a concealed position only about 300 yards from the enemy; he then dismounted and went forward, under heavy machine-gun fire, in an endeavour to extricate Tpr. Pinkney, who was badly wounded, from a burning tank. He was successful and carried him back into a safe position and then to an ambulance. L./Sergt. Booth then returned to the burning tanks in search of survivors, and remained in observation of the enemy in that area. The information he collected greatly assisted the gunners, who were able to bring heavy and accurate fire to bear on the enemy positions. Later in the day, L./Sergt. Booth returned to his own tank and, despite enemy anti-tank fire, brought it safely back to the regiment.

This N.C.O. throughout the whole action showed a complete disregard for his own personal safety, and set a fine example to his squadron.—*"London Gazette" dated 22nd July, 1943.*

Copy of citation dated 1st May, 1945

No. 3598442 LANCE-SERGEANT FRANCIS CRAYTON, 9th Queen's Royal Lancers, Royal Armoured Corps.

This N.C.O. is troop corporal of 1st Troop, "C" Squadron, 9th Lancers. At 2300 hrs. on 21st April his troop had reached the road junction in the village of Cona, fifty yards short of its objective—the bridge over the Volano River at 188823—and was held up by bazooka and Spandau fire. It became clear that the bridge and canal banks were strongly held, for the leading tank—on turning the corner to support the infantry across the bridge —was bazooka'ed and engaged by a 150-mm. medium gun firing at 100 yards' range. This caused the infantry a number of casualties, and the tank was put out of action temporarily.

In order to get the infantry across it was essential to have a tank in direct support in the middle of the road ten yards from the bridge. Without hesitating, Sergt. Crayton drove his tank to this position and stayed there firing all his guns. The 150-mm. gun opened fire, but luckily missed, and the tank was spattered by machine-gun fire, but Sergt. Crayton shot two bazookamen, and by his gallantry enabled the infantry to cross. Then he crossed himself, captured the 150-mm. gun and crew intact, and engaged S.P. and more infantry. He killed the officer and about six other ranks, and fifteen prisoners gave themselves up to him, and the infantry were able to capture two more 150-mm. guns. By this courageous single-handed action Sergt. Crayton had dealt with an enemy rearguard of two officers and forty-five other ranks, with the result that the objective was seized and held.

Just before first light next morning Sergt. Crayton advanced with the infantry to expand the bridgehead, and captured an S.P. 75-mm. gun and crew intact.

Sergt. Crayton's complete disregard for great danger and his outstanding bravery were largely responsible for the seizing and holding intact of the bridge at Cona.—*"London Gazette" dated 23rd August, 1945*

Copy of citation dated 1st May, 1945

No. 7920353 LANCE-SERGEANT ROBERT JAMES MORGAN IRVINE, 9th Queen's Royal Lancers, Royal Armoured Corps.

Cpl. Irvine is Troop Corporal, 1st Troop, "B" Squadron, 9th Lancers. During the advance to Quatresana bridges on 21st April the squadron was being delayed by an S.P. 88-mm. gun. The light was failing and it was essential to knock it out to continue the advance in daylight. By quick, careful stalking, Cpl. Irvine withstood the enemy fire, and destroyed the S.P. After finding a fosso crossing under small-arms fire, he attempted to cross the embanked railway just short of the objective. There he was shot at by four bazookamen, all of whom he killed. With complete disregard for the enemy, he moved nearer the road where a strong-point was established, to see if he could cross there. The road was blown, but he succeeded in finding a way round in the dark, and by about 2200 hrs. reached the objective (with eight prisoners on his hands) and by his initiative enabled other tanks to follow him. There was only one platoon of infantry available to hold the bridges, so Cpl. Irvine crossed over himself to give support, when his tank was hit by A.P. fire at fifty yards' range from a Mark IV. He kept his tank in action and threw the enemy into such confusion that their tanks were forced to withdraw, as a result of which the infantry were able to consolidate the bridgehead, and the rest of the squadron could advance unmolested. Cpl. Irvine's driver had been badly wounded, so he pulled him out across the road, under very heavy Spandau and rifle fire, to administer first aid. Having done this, he noticed his knocked-out tank was alight. Quickly fetching an extinguisher from another tank, and with the risk of exploding ammunition, he tried to put it out.

The enterprise and gallantry of this N.C.O. was almost entirely responsible for the squadron's success that night.—*"London Gazette" dated 23rd August, 1945.*

Copy of citation dated 1st May, 1945

No. 7903134 CORPORAL SIDNEY JAMES PERRY, 9th Queen's Royal Lancers, Royal Armoured Corps.

This N.C.O. is troop corporal of 4th Troop, "C" Squadron, 9th Lancers. On three occasions during the last week's advance he has shown great initiative and dash. On 13th April he commanded the leading tank in the advance to capture the bridge at La Frascata. By moving at high speed under heavy fire he got within fifty yards of the bridge before it was partially blown. Without stopping he moved on to the canal bank and engaged the enemy on the far side—thus preventing any further demolition and enabling our infantry to cross and capture the enemy rearguard of forty men. On 18th April Cpl. Perry was first across a bridge just south of Ripapersico, though it was prepared for demolition, and immediately took thirty prisoners. As a result of this quick capture of the bridge 200 Germans were mopped up in that area during the next three hours.

Cpl. Perry was also in the lead when his troop was advancing after dark to capture the bridge over the Volano at Cona on 21st April. His tank was carrying infantry on the back, and he advanced 2,000 yards, avoiding three German tanks which were reported to be in the area and numerous bazookamen, and found his objective. On unloading his infantry he negotiated a 10-foot embankment to give supporting fire. In position he was attacked by bazookas and Spandaus, which he answered with both Brownings and tommy-guns, killing at least three Germans. Although engaged by a 150-mm. gun at point-blank range, Cpl. Perry kept his tank in action and so devastated the opposition with H.E. and M.G. fire that the infantry and one supporting tank were able to cross the bridge and secure the bridgehead. All this action took place in moonlight, and Cpl. Perry's presence of mind and cool gallantry under the most difficult and dangerous circumstances were largely responsible for the success of the operation.—*"London Gazette" dated 23rd August, 1945.*

Copy of citation dated 18th December, 1944

No. 7889188 LANCE-SERGEANT IAN CHRISTOPHER SIMPSON, 9th Queen's Royal Lancers, Royal Armoured Corps.

On the morning of 6th December, 1944, Sergt. Simpson was Troop Sergeant of the troop ordered to support the 5th Battalion The Hampshire Regiment in the area Duecento (254221). In order to get to the required position the troop had to use a road occupied by the enemy outside the infantry bridgehead over the River Lamone. Sergt. Simpson's Troop Leader's tank was blown up on a mine and completely blocked the track. As it was imperative for tanks to get up to the infantry, the Troop Leader left his own tank and continued in the leading tank, leaving Sergt. Simpson to get up to him as best he could. The mist now cleared, leaving the track and Sergt. Simpson's tank in full view of the enemy at very short range. Very heavy shelling and machine-gun fire were immediately directed on the tank. Using great initiative and determination, Sergt. Simpson succeeded after an hour's work in getting his tank past the obstruction. He organized both tank crews to dig, lay planks and cut down trees, and by this method he constructed a way round the blown-up tank. During all this time he was in full view and under very heavy fire. Sergt. Simpson was now able to proceed to join the infantry on the Duecento ridge and give them most valuable support, as a result of which they were enabled to hold the position.

This N.C.O. showed the most remarkable coolness under very heavy fire and his resourcefulness and determination to get his tank up to the hard-pressed infantry were an example to all.—*"London Gazette" dated 10th May, 1945.*

Copy of citation dated 6th February, 1942

No. 317405 LANCE-SERGEANT LEONARD GEORGE WELHAM, 9th Queen's Royal Lancers, Royal Armoured Corps.

On the morning of 23rd January, 1942, when his squadron was in action against German tanks and anti-tank guns west of Saunnu, L./Sergt. Welham was ordered to go in his tank to relieve a troop which had been in observation of the enemy and which had had two tanks of its three destroyed by enemy fire. On arrival he reported that he could see anti-tank guns in position at about four hundred yards from one of our tanks which was on fire. He also requested permission to go and pick up the crew of the burning tank whom he could see crawling away under fire. Permission was refused on account of the risk. Shortly afterwards, by changing his position, L./Sergt. Welham was able to fire on an anti-tank gun and an armoured car, silencing them both. He then advanced and picked up the three survivors of the crew of the burning tank and brought them to safety.

His courageous action and determination not to abandon his comrades undoubtedly saved them from capture, as the position had later to be abandoned.—*"London Gazette" dated 23rd April, 1942.*

Copy of citation dated 1st May, 1945

No. 7920337 CORPORAL FRANK DENNIS MEAD CHAPMAN, 9th Queen's Royal Lancers, Royal Armoured Corps.

During the advance north, out of the Santerno bridgehead, on 13th April, Cpl. Chapman was in command of the leading tank of the squadron. Soon after passing through our own F.D.Ls., along the line of the road running N.W. from S. Bernadino, 320495, a considerable number of enemy were encountered firing Spandaus at our infantry. Cpl. Chapman silenced and overran the enemy position at 317513, which was of two-company strength.

On continuing the advance the country became very enclosed and Cpl. Chapman's tank was hit by a bazooka which wounded him in the face and also wounded his gunner. Both Cpl. Chapman's eyes were affected, but he continued to fight and his tank killed a party of bazookamen in a house at 317521. His covering fire enabled our infantry to get forward and mop up four other houses which formed the enemy strong-point. At this moment another tank saw an anti-tank gun just north of the road at 320524, swinging round on to Cpl. Chapman's tank. On being warned, this N.C.O. immediately swung his turret, machine-gunned the gun crew, and directed his gunner with such coolness that the enemy anti-tank gun's barrel was blown off with the second shot from Cpl. Chapman's 76-mm. Only then, forty-five minutes after being wounded, did Cpl. Chapman withdraw and receive medical attention. His eyes by this time were so bad that he could hardly see and was evacuated immediately.

By his courage and devotion to duty Cpl. Chapman enabled the squadron to obtain its objective, and by his quick action averted almost certain casualties to other tanks.—*"London Gazette" dated 23rd August, 1945.*

Copy of citation dated 17th May, 1943

No. 7906967 CORPORAL RONALD STAMFORD RICHES, 9th Queen's Royal Lancers, Royal Armoured Corps.

This N.C.O. has been in command of his squadron's "B1" Echelon for the past twelve months.

On 23rd April, 1943, this N.C.O. brought some ammunition lorries up under heavy fire through a heavily mined area. Regardless of his personal safety, he led his echelon on foot through the mines and delivered the ammunition to the tanks whilst they were still in action. The same day he made a second journey through the same area, as guide to some recovery vehicles. Owing to his courage and determination, none of the vehicles under his command went on mines, and recovery and ammunition arrived when it was most needed.

By his complete disregard of his personal safety, and by his unfailing cheerfulness, he has set a very fine example to his drivers and he has always done his duty in a most exemplary manner.—*"London Gazette" dated 19th August, 1943.*

Copy of citation dated 9th September, 1944

No. 7920375 CORPORAL COLONEL DOUGLAS STEWART SMITH, 9th Queen's Royal Lancers, Royal Armoured Corps.

On 5th September, 1944, Cpl. Smith was commanding a Runney which was ordered to accompany his Troop Leader, Capt. G. G. A. Gregson, on a patrol to ascertain the whereabouts of the forward infantry and to find out whether the area of San Savino was held by the enemy or not. Cpl. Smith went off in the lead, covered by his Troop Leader, on the route ordered. They shortly came to a bridge which he discovered was mined; so Cpl. Smith, making a wide detour, found a way across and carried on. He pushed on here, at a fast pace and without hesitation, to a farm where he obtained information that the enemy were in the village. It was decided that this information must be confirmed, so, by skilful use of ground, he worked up with his Troop Leader towards the village. On reaching it, heavy and accurate mortar fire was directed on to the section and, at the same time, at least a platoon of German infantry was seen running in all directions. In no way perturbed, Cpl. Smith engaged the infantry very coolly and shot many of them. M.G. fire was then brought to bear on the patrol, so Cpl. Smith quickly put down smoke and withdrew. On the way out his Runney was hit on the back by a mortar bomb and it burst into flames. Quite regardless of danger to himself, he organized the removal of all M.Gs., hand grenades from the Runney and prepared to receive the oncoming Germans. There he waited until he was picked up by his Troop Leader.

The evening before, Cpl. Smith had done a ground reconnaissance in much the same area, and had brought back vital information which helped the operation of 5th September very greatly: and all this under continuous mortar and M.G. fire. Later in the day Cpl. Smith was wounded while assisting the crew of another Runney which had broken down.

Without the skill, courage and devotion to duty of Cpl. Smith vital information would not have been obtained and he set a fine example to his troop.—*"London Gazette" dated 8th February, 1945.*

Copy of citation dated 15th June, 1942

No. 7902457 CORPORAL HAROLD GLUYAS THOMAS, 9th Queen's Royal Lancers, Royal Armoured Corps.

During the period 27th to 31st May, 1942, this N.C.O. was employed as a despatch rider in a scout car. During this period he accompanied the tanks, and was almost continuously under shell fire and small-arms fire. Throughout these five days Cpl. Thomas showed great courage and devotion to duty. On 29th May one of our anti-tank guns received a direct hit, killing the entire crew with the exception of one man who was seen to be wounded. Cpl. Thomas drove the scout car forward to the anti-tank gun, under fire; dismounted; and, single-handed, picked up the wounded man, put him in his car, and carried him back to safety.

On 30th May, during an attack on an enemy position by our tanks, Cpl. Thomas, who was accompanying the tanks in a scout car, observed a tank crew getting out of their tank (which was on fire). He drove forward under heavy fire, picked up the crew and took them back to cover. The courage shown by this N.C.O. whilst under fire was a splendid example to all ranks with whom he came in contact.—*"London Gazette" dated 13th August, 1942.*

Copy of citation dated 11th October, 1942

No. 320824 LANCE-CORPORAL WILLIAM CHARLESWORTH, 9th Queen's Royal Lancers, Royal Armoured Corps.

This N.C.O. drove an ammunition lorry during the whole period that the regiment was in action.

On several occasions he brought ammunition up to the General Grant tanks while they were in action, and under heavy shell fire. By his courage and complete disregard for his own safety, and by his consistent hard work and cheerfulness under all conditions, he has set the highest possible example to all who have ever been in contact with him.—*"London Gazette" dated 18th February, 1943.*

Copy of citation dated 6th July, 1943

No. 317481 TROOPER (L./CPL.) LEONARD COOK, 9th Queen's Royal Lancers, Royal Armoured Corps.

L./Cpl. Cook has been driver and in charge of the squadron's "B1" ammunition lorry throughout the recent operations. At all times he has shown complete disregard for his own safety, and has set the highest example to all ranks in devotion to duty and concentration on his highly dangerous task.

At El Hamma village on 27th March, 1943, when the squadron was dangerously low in ammunition, L./Cpl. Cook drove his lorry up to within 100 yards of the battle line, where vehicles and tanks were blazing on all sides; and, while under heavy shell, mortar and M.G. fire, he refilled the whole squadron, which was completely out of ammunition by the time he arrived—thus enabling them to deal with the enemy's counter-attack with tanks.

Again, on 29th March, 1943, while under most heavy and accurate shell fire, miraculously escaping being hit, he continued to drive calmly round all the tanks of the squadron, replenishing them at a time of most urgent need, thereby enabling the squadron to continue the fight without having to break the line. Throughout the whole campaign L./Cpl. Cook has never hesitated to drive his lorry, knowing its dangerous cargo, wherever the tanks needed him. He always came to the tanks, instead of the tanks having to go back to him, thus saving valuable time.—*"London Gazette" dated 25th November, 1943.*

Copy of citation dated 7th April, 1945

No. 6981700 TROOPER (L./CPL.) RAYMOND HARRIS, 9th Queen's Royal Lancers, Royal Armoured Corps.

This N.C.O. is a tank driver in "C" Squadron, 9th Lancers. During the period from January to March, 1945, whilst the regiment were on their feet, he was a section commander. On 20th January one forward position ("Oxhill" 454448) was attacked by a strong fighting patrol. This N.C.O. took control of the defence on his side of the house. The battle lasted for two hours, during which time the room in which he was established was bazooka-ed twice. He was largely responsible for the defeat of this attack. On 24th February this same position was attacked by S.P. fire. The house was hit continuously, and the roof and ceiling collapsed on L./Cpl. Harris's troop. He organized the rescue of ten men who were trapped, courageously ignoring the continued S.P. and mortar fire. As a result of this hard work and fine example, the lives of his comrades were saved.

The record of this N.C.O. as a tank driver is remarkable. At Pideura in December, 1944, he was driving the leading tank in the initial assault on the hamlet. His tank was bazooka-ed, killing the co-driver and wounding all the remaining four. Although severely hit in the arm and face, and purely on his own initiative, he reversed the tank under heavy fire single-handed 400 yards along a mud track to safety. By his action the lives of his crew were saved and his tank preserved for further use.

This N.C.O.'s courage and cheerfulness over a long period have been a great example to his squadron.—*"London Gazette" dated 20th September, 1945.*

Copy of citation dated 3rd November, 1942

No. 5349069 LANCE-CORPORAL EDWIN ALFRED INSTONE, 9th Queen's Royal Lancers, Royal Armoured Corps.

ALAMEIN.—This N.C.O. was the driver of the second tank to pass through the enemy minefield on 24th October. His tank was hit ten times, the last shot killing the operator and seriously wounding his commander and the gunner. He was trapped in his seat, but pushed the spare driver out and sent him for help. He then got out from the same door and re-entered the tank by the turret. He gave morphia to the two wounded men, and then, single-handed and under heavy fire, got his commander (who had lost both legs) out of the tank. He broke the fall for his commander by letting himself fall under him from the top of the turret. He then got his gunner out, who was almost fainting. Having given his commander more attention, he led back his gunner, who was very weak, to the first aid post, where he got help for the commander. All this was done under heavy machine-gun and shell fire, and L./Cpl. Instone showed conspicuous gallantry in dealing single-handed with a most difficult situation.—*"London Gazette" dated 14th January, 1943.*

Copy of citation dated 22nd November, 1942

No. 550824 LANCE-CORPORAL ALFRED NICKOLLS, 9th Queen's Royal Lancers, Royal Armoured Corps.

ALAMEIN (24th to 28th October).—Throughout the recent fighting this N.C.O. was continually serving the gun in a Sherman tank.

Though frequently under heavy fire, he continued to sight and fire his gun with complete coolness and an utter disregard of events outside. By his determination to destroy, and his concentration on his task, he succeeded in immobilizing fourteen enemy tanks and one 88-mm. gun. On one single day of the battle he shot nine enemy tanks.

His marksmanship and concentration of effort have been an example to the regiment, and is already encouraging others to do likewise.—*"London Gazette" dated 14th January, 1943.*

Copy of citation dated 27th January, 1943

No. 792034 TROOPER HYMAN FERNER, 9th Queen's Royal Lancers, Royal Armoured Corps.

This man was driver of an ammunition lorry on "B1" Echelon during the battle of Alamein (23rd October, 1942). On the first evening of the battle the squadron went through a 20-yard gap in the minefield about one mile across, and deployed on the far side and was engaged in a battle with its back to the minefield. It soon began to run out of ammunition, and it was necessary to take the risk and send the ammunition lorries right up to the tanks. At the time, the gap in the minefield was under very heavy fire; both A.P. and H.E. were covering the entire gap. The first lorry to go was blown up in the gap. Trooper Ferner's lorry was fifty yards behind. When he realized there was just room for the lorry to go between the burning lorry and the mines he did not hesitate: he went straight on and took up a position about thirty yards behind the tanks, where they replenished. Trooper Ferner stood up on the lorry and passed the ammunition down—and by a miracle the lorry was not hit.

This man's disregard for his own safety and fine sense of devotion to duty made ammunition available for the tanks which was urgently needed.—*"London Gazette" dated 11th March, 1943.*

Copy of citation dated 2nd October, 1944

No. 7901373 TROOPER RICHARD SAMPSON JACKSON, 9th Queen's Royal Lancers, Royal Armoured Corps.

Trooper Jackson was the driver of Sergt. Parfitt's tank during the attack on the San Savino feature on 5th September, 1944. His magnificent exhibition of faultless driving over rough and treacherous going was largely instrumental in enabling Sergt. Parfitt to reach the objective to help his troop leader. His thorough understanding of the capabilities of his tank and quick eye for likely fire positions enhanced in full measure the security of his crew. On many occasions he indicated to the gunner targets of snipers and bazookamen whom he had seen approaching the tank. It was due to his speed with the gears that his tank commander was able to manœuvre out of sight of the anti-tank gun which had shot his Troop Leader's tank and missed his own with the first shot. He showed the greatest presence of mind and subtlety in driving out of action when completely surrounded by the enemy: he went at full speed straight at and through a farm building; then, while negotiating a very steep bank, one of his tracks came half off the sprocket. Without pausing for an instant, he leapt out of his hatch under exceedingly heavy mortar and machine-gun fire in order to examine the extent of the damage. After one quick glance, he returned to his seat and, by superb judgment, Trooper Jackson rode the track back on to the sprocket once more. Throughout this single-handed action Trooper Jackson showed the most magnificent courage and devotion to duty.—*"London Gazette" dated 8th February, 1945.*

Copy of citation dated 30th May, 1943

No. 3857764 TROOPER JOSEPH MACFARLANE, 9th Queen's Royal Lancers, Royal Armoured Corps.

During the action on 24th April, 1943, Tpr. Macfarlane was acting as gunner in the only tank that was not knocked out while attempting to cross a wadi. Tpr. Macfarlane's fire was so accurate that he temporarily silenced the enemy A./T. guns on the left flank, who were only 300 yards in front of him.

When his tank got back into the wadi Tpr. Macfarlane rendered the most valuable assistance to his tank commander, Sergt. Booth, in bringing in several badly wounded men. In spite of very heavy fire, they went up to the burning tanks and made a thorough search for survivors. Sergt. Booth and Tpr. Macfarlane then remained in observation, and passed back the most valuable information about the enemy dispositions.

Throughout the action he displayed great courage and complete disregard for his personal safety.—*"London Gazette" dated 19th August, 1943.*

Copy of citation dated 12th November, 1942

No. 61320 Trooper Cyril Leonard Pine, 9th Queen's Royal Lancers, Royal Armoured Corps.

In the action on the evening of 3rd/4th November Tpr. Pine was driver of a tank in the leading squadron. The tank was penetrated in the turret and both crew commander and gunner was seriously wounded. Tpr. Pine immediately baled out and under intense enemy machine-gun fire climbed on to the turret and managed to extract the gunner, whom he placed in comparative safety behind the tank. By this time the tank was on fire and by using all the available Pyrenes and all the fourteen gallons of water on board managed to extinguish the fire. He then tried to get the crew commander out, but he had been badly wounded and was now dead. Tpr. Pine had Tpr. Conley, the gunner, put on to another tank and evacuated safely. By his indomitable courage in the face of intense enemy machine-gun fire and individual sniping Tpr. Pine saved the life of one of the crew and also prevented the tank from being completely destroyed by fire, and is strongly recommended for an immediate award.—*"London Gazette" dated 31st December, 1942.*

COMMANDING OFFICERS, ADJUTANTS, QUARTERMASTERS, MECHANICAL ENGINEERS, REGIMENTAL SERGEANT-MAJORS, DOCTORS, AND CHAPLAINS OF THE REGIMENT

COMMANDING OFFICERS

Name.	Date.
Lieutenant-Colonel C. W. Norman, C.B.E. ..	March, 1936, to April, 1938.
Lieutenant-Colonel C. H. M. Peto, D.S.O. ..	April, 1938, to June, 1940.
Lieutenant-Colonel J. R. Macdonell, D.S.O.	June, 1940, to September, 1942.
Lieutenant-Colonel G. H. Grosvenor, D.S.O.	September, 1942, to April, 1944.
Lieutenant-Colonel R. S. G. Perry, D.S.O. ..	April, 1944, to February, 1945.
Lieutenant-Colonel K. J. Price, D.S.O., M.C.	February, 1945, to April, 1947.

ADJUTANTS

Captain K. J. Price	1937 to May, 1940; August, 1940, to January, 1941.
Captain R. H. S. Wynne ..	May to August, 1940.
Captain C. C. Lomax	January to November, 1941.
Captain R. O. G. Gardner, M.C.	November, 1941, to February, 1943.
Captain R. K. B. Hitchcock, M.C.	February to May, 1943.
Captain F. L. Pym, M.C. ..	May, 1943, to June, 1945.

QUARTERMASTERS

Major V. H. Tully	1935 to 1943.
Captain E. R. Donnley, M.B.E.	1943 to 1947.

O.M.E. AND E.M.E.

Major M. W. B. Phelps	1939 to 1941.
Captain G. S. Henderson	1941 to 1945.

REGIMENTAL SERGEANT-MAJORS

P. J. Oxley, M.M. ..	..	1939 to 1941.
A. E. Blandford, D.C.M.	..	1941 to 1942.
T. Hardwidge	..	1943 to 1947.

CHAPLAINS

Name.	*Date.*
The Reverend P. F. Kelsey	September, 1939, to May, 1940.
The Reverend C. T. R. C. Perowne	June, 1940, to August, 1941.
The Reverend J. L. Rowlands	March, 1942, to November, 1942.
The Reverend T. W. Baverstock	January, 1943, to August, 1943.
The Reverend R. G. Davidson	September, 1943, to August, 1944.
The Reverend W. C. Eggington	December, 1944, to May, 1945.

DOCTORS

Captain J. W. M. Owen	October, 1939, to January, 1941.
Captain J. Dougan, M.C.	January, 1941, to May, 1942.
Captain G. Dison, M.C	June, 1942, to April, 1943.
Captain J. W. R. Kemp, M.C.	May, 1943, to December, 1944.
Captain D. Moynagh, M.C.	December, 1944, to June, 1945.

RECORD OF SERVICE OF 9TH LANCER OFFICERS

NOTES

1. Rank is in all cases shown as the highest that it is known an officer reached during the war.

2. Symbols against an officer's name denote:
   * was serving as a Regular on 3rd September, 1939.
   † was a reservist on 3rd September, 1939.
   ‡ was serving with the Regiment on 6th May, 1945.
   § was serving as a Regular at the end of the war.

3. The abbreviation E.R.E. means extra-regimentally employed.

4. Extra-regimental employment is not shown in detail unless the officer concerned commanded a regiment or was employed in the rank of colonel or above.

5. The last employment shown was held until the end of the war.

Agate, Capt. B. S., M.C.‡ ..	From 4th/7th Dragoon Guards, August, 1942.
Aird, Colonel M. H., O.B.E.* ..	O.C. "A" Squadron to June, 1940; Second-in-Command June to December, 1940; C.O. 24th Lancers, December, 1940, to December, 1943; Second-in-Command, 27th Armoured Brigade, December, 1943, to August, 1944; Adjutant-General's Branch, H.Q., Second Army, September, 1944.
Alderton, Capt. A. C.*‡§	Commissioned October, 1942; E.R.E., August to October, 1944.
Allen, Capt. D. A. W.‡..	Joined February, 1940; Signals Officer, October, 1943, to March, 1945.
Allfrey, Capt. B. H.† ..	E.R.E. the whole war.
Allhusen, Major D. S.*‡§	E.R.E., February to April, 1940; with 24th Lancers, December, 1940, to October, 1943; O.C. "B" Squadron, October, 1943, to March, 1945; Second-in-Command, March, 1945.
Arbuthnot, Major Sir R. D., Bt.	Joined April, 1940; to 24th Lancers December, 1940; killed in action June, 1944.
Astles, Capt. W. R.	Joined August, 1940; E.R.E. from July, 1941.
Barber, Capt. I. H.	Joined July, 1941; E.R.E. from June, 1942.
Barton, Lieut. J. G.	Joined November, 1944; to hospital December, 1944; died August, 1945.
Batchelor-Taylor, Lieut. A.	Joined June, 1941; E.R.E. from August, 1941.
Beckett, Major Hon. C. J.*§	E.R.E. the whole war owing to ill-health.
Beer, Lieut. C. G. A.	Joined July, 1941; E.R.E. from August, 1942.
Benson, Colonel R. L., D.S.O., M.V.O., M.C.†	E.R.E. the whole war; Assistant Military Attaché, Washington, U.S.A., from 1941 to 1944.
Bentley, Capt. R. N. C. ..	From 4th/7th Dragoon Guards July, 1942; E.R.E. from June, 1943.
Berry, Lieut. V. F.‡	Joined January, 1944.
Birch-Reynardson, Lt. W. R.‡.. ..	Joined April, 1944.
Bird, Lieut. J. M. A.‡	Joined November, 1944.
Bishop, Major G. C.†	E.R.E. the whole war.
Bowring, Colonel J. R., O.B.E., M.C.*	E.R.E. the whole war; Second-in-Command, 2nd Armoured Brigade, December, 1943, to April, 1944.

Breitmeyer, Capt. G. W.†	E.R.E. the whole war.
Brutton, Capt. J. A. L. ..	Joined February, 1943; Technical Officer, May, 1943, to March, 1944; E.R.E. from March, 1944.
Bryant, Lieut.-Colonel A. D.† ..	E.R.E. the whole war.
Buchan, Lieut. P. H. W. W. ..	Joined July, 1943; killed in action September, 1944.
Burden, Lieut. R. A. M.†	E.R.E. February, 1940, to January, 1941; E.R.E. from September, 1941.
Burgh, Lieut. M. G. de‡ ..	Joined July, 1943.
Busk, Capt. W. R.†	E.R.E. the whole war.
Cadman, Lieut. W. T.†	Killed in action June, 1942.
Campbell, Major Hon. A. D., O.B.E., M.C.†	E.R.E. the whole war.
Campbell, Lieut. D. C.	Joined February, 1941; wounded October, 1942, and invalided out.
Carlisle, Major B. M. M.‡	Joined December, 1940; E.R.E. July, 1941, to June, 1943; O.C. H.Q. Squadron, March to April, 1945.
Caro, Lieut. P. A. ..	Joined November, 1943; prisoner of war September, 1944.
Chadwick, Lieut. J. H.	Joined August, 1941; E.R.E. from September, 1941.
Chisholm, Lieut.-Colonel C. J.† ..	E.R.E. the whole war.
Close, Capt. M. S.†	Wounded and E.R.E. from June, 1942.
Colvin, Lieut.-Colonel J. F., O.B.E., M.C.†	E.R.E. the whole war.
Cooke, Lieut.-Colonel J. A.††‡.. ..	E.R.E. January to December, 1940; O.C. H.Q. Squadron December, 1940, to September, 1941; E.R.E. September, 1941, to April, 1945; O.C. H.Q. Squadron April, 1945.
Cottee, Capt. S. J.*§	To 24th Lancers, December, 1940.
Crampton, Lieut. G. P. C. R., M.C.‡ ..	Joined November, 1942.
Crossley, Major J. F. F.†	E.R.E. the whole war.
Daly, Capt. J. H.†	E.R.E. the whole war.
Diggle, Lieut.-Colonel L. W., M.C.† ..	E.R.E. the whole war.
Donnley, Capt. E. R., M.B.E.*‡§ ..	Commissioned January, 1941; Technical Officer, January, 1941, to May, 1943; Quartermaster, May, 1943.
Dudding, Capt. P. J.‡ ..	Joined November, 1942; Intelligence Officer, March, 1945.
Eland, Lieut. C. A.	Joined June, 1941; E.R.E. from September, 1941.
Emsell, Major B. St. V.†	E.R.E. the whole war.
Erskine, Lieut.-Colonel Hon. D. C. F.†	O.C. "C" Squadron April, 1941, to April, 1942; E.R.E. from April, 1942.
Farquhar, Lieut.-Colonel Sir P., Bt., D.S.O.†	From 16th/5th Lancers as Second-in-Command, April, 1941; wounded July, 1942; C.O., 3rd Hussars, October, 1942.
Flower, Lieut.-Colonel F., O.B.E.† ..	E.R.E. the whole war.
Fitzpatrick, Lieut. I. G., M.C. ..	Seconded from South African Army November, 1943; reverted February, 1945.
Foy, Capt. J. K.‡	From 24th Lancers, October, 1943; Technical Officer, March, 1944.
Gardner, Major R. O. G., M.C.	Joined December, 1940; Adjutant, November, 1941, to February, 1943; O.C. H.Q. Squadron, February to March, 1943; O.C. "B" Squadron, March to August, 1943; E.R.E. August, 1943, to July, 1944; O.C. H.Q. Squadron, July to November, 1944; E.R.E. from November, 1944.
Gilroy, Major J.†	To 24th Lancers December, 1940.
Gisborne, Capt. W. G., M.C.†	E.R.E. the whole war.
Goldsmid, Lieut. J. M. F.‡ ..	Joined August, 1943.
Grant, Major A. E. G., M.C.† ..	E.R.E. the whole war.

Grant, Capt. A. J.	Joined February, 1941; killed in action April, 1943.
Gregson, Capt. G. G. A., M.C.‡	From 16th/5th Lancers August, 1942.
Greenwood, Capt. J. R.*§ ..	Technical Officer to January, 1941; prisoner of war January, 1942.
Grosvenor, Lieut.-Colonel G. H., D.S.O.*	E.R.E. to July, 1942; Second-in-Command, July to September, 1942; C.O., September, 1942, to March, 1944; C.O., 22nd Dragoons, March to July, 1944; wounded July, 1944, and invalided out.
Hainsworth, Capt. F. C.‡	Joined September, 1942; Intelligence Officer, December, 1942, to March, 1945; Signals Officer, March, 1945.
Halfknight, Major J. J.*	E.R.E. the whole war.
Hannen, Lieut. L. G. M., M.C.‡ ..	Joined June, 1944.
Hardy-Roberts, Brigadier G. P., C.B., C.B.E.†	E.R.E. from January, 1940; Deputy Adjutant and Quartermaster-General, XIII Corps, January, 1943, to April, 1944; Deputy Adjutant and Quartermaster-General, Second Army, April, 1944.
Hartley-Heyman, Lieut. C.	From 15th/19th Hussars February, 1943; killed in action April, 1943.
Harris, Lieut. B. P. G.	Joined March, 1941; killed in action July, 1942.
Harris, Lieut.-Colonel L. H. H.†	E.R.E. the whole war.
Heycock, 2/Lieut. C. W. ..	Joined February, 1941; Intelligence Officer, January to May, 1942; died of wounds May, 1942.
Hitchcock, Capt. R. K. B., M.C.‡§	From 5th Dragoon Guards September, 1942; Adjutant, February to May, 1943.
Hodson, Lieut. H. B. ..	Joined July, 1940; killed in action January, 1942.
Holt, Lieut. G. H. P. ..	Joined November, 1943; killed in action, November, 1944.
Hylton, Capt. E. W.	Joined November, 1940; E.R.E. from April, 1942.
Jenner-Fust, 2/Lieut. T. ..	Joined June, 1941; killed in action May, 1942.
Joicey, Capt. Hon. E. R., M.C.†	E.R.E. the whole war.
Joicey, Lieut. J. E., M.C.‡§ ..	Joined July, 1943.
Kelly, Lieut. L. P. G.†	Killed in action May, 1942, when E.R.E.
Kent, Lieut. R. P.	Joined November, 1942; E.R.E. from December, 1943.
Kilgour, Lieut. P. S.	Joined February, 1943; E.R.E. from January, 1944.
Kingscote, Capt. R. N.† ..	E.R.E. October, 1940, to February, 1941; killed in action July, 1942.
Lacey-Thompson, Capt. C. R.	Joined July, 1943; E.R.E. from November, 1944.
Laing, Capt. P. M.	Joined January, 1940; E.R.E. July, 1941, to June, 1942; wounded November, 1942, and never rejoined.
Laurie, Major D. A. St. G., M.C.†‡§ ..	O.C. "B" Squadron, May, 1942, to March, 1943; wounded and E.R.E. April, 1943, to April, 1944; O.C. H.Q. Squadron, June to July, 1944, and November, 1944, to February, 1945; O.C. "B" Squadron, February, 1945.
Laurie, Major G. H. F. P. V.* ..	O.C. "B" Squadron, June, 1940, to August, 1941; E.R.E. from August, 1941.
Lloyd-Mostyn, Major Hon. R. E., M.C.*§	Wounded and E.R.E. July, 1942, to November, 1943; O.C. H.Q. Squadron, December, 1943, to June, 1944.
Lomax, Major C. C.†	Adjutant, January to November, 1941; O.C. H.Q. Squadron, November, 1941, to February, 1943; E.R.E. from February, 1943.
Macdonell, Colonel J. R. M., D.S.O.*	O.C. "B" Squadron to May, 1940; Second-in-Command, May, 1940; C.O., June, 1940, to September, 1942; Second-in-Command, 23rd Armoured Brigade, September, 1942, to June, 1943; Second-in-Command, 2nd Armoured Brigade, June, 1943, to September, 1944; killed in action September, 1944.

Mackenzie, Lieut. I.†	E.R.E. from December, 1939.
Macpherson, Capt. E. F. D. ..	From North Somerset Yeomanry August, 1942; Intelligence Officer, August to December, 1942; O.C. H.Q. Squadron, October to December, 1943; E.R.E. from May, 1944.
Marden, Lieut. J.†	Killed in action May, 1942.
Marsh, Capt. M. J. W., M.C. ..	Joined July, 1942; E.R.E. September to December, 1943; E.R.E. from January, 1944.
Marx, Capt. F. R., M.C.	Joined March, 1943; E.R.E. from January, 1944.
Merritt, Capt. R.* ..	Commissioned January, 1941; Signals Officer January, 1941, to July, 1942; E.R.E. from July, 1942.
Meyrick, Major G. D., M.C.*‡§	O.C. "A" Squadron, July to August, 1942; O.C. "C" Squadron, August, 1942, to February, 1943; accidentally injured and E.R.E. February, 1943, to January, 1945; O.C. "A" Squadron, January, 1945.
Milnes, Lieut. J. T. ..	Joined June, 1942; died of wounds November, 1942.
Montgomerie, Lieut. T.	Joined September, 1941; E.R.E. from January, 1942.
Moon, Lieut. A J. R.‡§	Joined November, 1944.
Moule, Lieut. M. G.‡§	From 16th/5th Lancers August, 1942.
Newman, Capt. L. J.‡ ..	From 15th/19th Hussars September, 1942; wounded and E.R.E. October, 1942, to February, 1943; E.R.E. December, 1943, to April, 1944.
Norman, Major-General C. W., C.B.E.	Colonel of the Regiment from July, 1940; Inspector, Royal Armoured Corps, November, 1939, to March, 1940; Commander, 1st Armoured Reconnaissance Brigade, March to October, 1940; Commander, 27th Armoured Brigade, October, 1940, to October, 1941; G.O.C. 8th Armoured Division, October, 1941, to August, 1942; Major-General, Armoured Fighting Vehicles, G.H.Q., Middle East, August, 1942, to May, 1944; G.O.C. Aldershot District, September to November, 1944; G.O.C. East Anglian District, November, 1944, to February, 1945; G.O.C. East Central District, March, 1945.
O'Bryen, Lieut. C. J. R.*	Commissioned November, 1940; E.R.E. from March, 1941.
Okell, Lieut. R. C. ..	Joined August, 1941; died of wounds October, 1942.
Oxley, Lieut. P. J., M.M.*	Commissioned March, 1941; E.R.E. from May, 1942.
Parnell, Lieut. C. E.‡ ..	Joined November, 1944.
Peek, Capt. W. G.‡§ ..	Joined December, 1940; E.R.E. October to December, 1942.
Perry, Lieut.-Colonel R. S. G., D.S.O.*§	E.R.E. to August, 1941; O.C. "B" Squadron, August, 1941, to May, 1942; wounded and E.R.E. May, 1942, to April, 1943; Second-in-Command, April, 1943; C.O., Lothians and Border Horse, April to May, 1943; Second-in-Command, May, 1943, to March, 1944; C.O., March, 1944, to March, 1945; evacuated sick to United Kingdom March, 1945.
Peto, Brigadier C. H. M., D.S.O.*§ ..	C.O. to June, 1940; wounded; Second-in-Command, 23rd Armoured Brigade, December, 1940; Commander, 29th Armoured Brigade, January, 1941, to August, 1942; Commander, 137th Armoured Brigade, August, 1942, to October, 1943; Commander, No. 4 Liaison H.Q., October, 1943, to April, 1944; Chief Liaison Officer, 21st Army Group, April, 1944.
Pettit, Lieut.-Colonel E. R., M.C.*	To 24th Lancers December, 1940; killed in action, August, 1944.
Phillimore, Major Hon. A. F.*	Killed in action May, 1940, when E.R.E.

Phillimore, Major J. H. B.	Joined July, 1940; to 24th Lancers December, 1940.
Phipps-Hornby, Colonel G. H., C.B.E.†	E.R.E. the whole war.
Pilkington, Major R. W.*	O.C. H.Q. Squadron to January, 1940; E.R.E. from January, 1940.
Pott, Major W. T., M.C.†	E.R.E. from January, 1940.
Price, Lieut.-Colonel K. J., D.S.O., M.C.*‡§	Adjutant to May, 1940; Adjutant, August, 1940, to January, 1941; O.C. "A" Squadron, January, 1941, to July, 1942; wounded and E.R.E. July to August, 1942; O.C. "A" Squadron, August, 1942, to April 1943; wounded; O.C. "A" Squadron, November, 1943, to March, 1944; Second-in-Command, March, 1944, to March, 1945; C.O., March, 1945.
Prior-Palmer, Brigadier G. E., D.S.O.*§	O.C. "C" Squadron to April, 1941; C.O., 1st Derbyshire Yeomanry, April, 1941, to July, 1942; Commandant, Royal Armoured Corps Officer Cadet Training Unit, Sandhurst, July, 1942, to April, 1943; Commander, 27th Armoured Brigade, April, 1943, to July, 1944; Commander, 8th Armoured Brigade, July, 1944.
Prior-Palmer, Brigadier O. L., D.S.O.*§	Second-in-Command to May, 1940; C.O., 2nd Northants Yeomanry, May, 1940, to March, 1942; Commander, 30th Armoured Brigade, March to August, 1942; Commander, 29th Armoured Brigade, August, 1942, to October, 1943; Commander, 8th Armoured Brigade, October, 1943, to January, 1944; Commander, 7th Armoured Brigade, January, 1944, to March, 1945.
Pulteney, Major W. K. C.*§	E.R.E. July, 1941, to June, 1943; O.C. "A" Squadron, March, 1944, to February, 1945; E.R.E. from February, 1945.
Pym, Capt. F. L., M.C.‡	Joined September, 1942; Adjutant, May, 1943.
Radcliffe, Major E. C.†	O.C. H.Q. Squadron to September, 1940; E.R.E. from September, 1940.
Reid, Capt. J. W.‡§	From Royals March, 1941; Intelligence Officer, June to July, 1942; Signals Officer, July, 1942, to October, 1943.
Reynolds, Lieut.-Colonel G., M.C.†	E.R.E. the whole war.
Richardson, Major J. W.†	E.R.E. from August, 1940.
Scott, Lieut.-Colonel J. H. M. D., M.C.*§	O.C. "A" Squadron, June, 1940, to January, 1941; E.R.E. January, 1941, to June, 1942; Second-in-Command, July, 1942; wounded and E.R.E. July, 1942, to April, 1943; Second-in-Command, April to May, 1943; O.C. "A" Squadron, May to November, 1943; E.R.E. from November, 1943.
Seeley, Major V. B. J.	Joined November, 1939; E.R.E. from November, 1939.
Steel, Major D. E. C., D.S.O., M.C.‡	Joined January, 1940; O.C. "C" Squadron, February, 1943.
Steel, 2/Lieut. R. O. P.	Joined January, 1940; killed in action May, 1940.
Stephens, Capt. H. A. P.‡	From 24th Lancers August, 1942; E.R.E. November, 1943, to October, 1944; E.R.E. November, 1944, to March, 1945.
Stevenson, Major H. J. V.	Joined February, 1941; E.R.E. from April, 1942.
Steward, Major C. A.*§	Intelligence Officer to January, 1942; E.R.E. from August, 1942.
Stewart, Lieut. J.†	E.R.E. May to August, 1940; E.R.E. from September, 1941.
Stuart, 2/Lieut. Viscount	Joined June, 1944; died of wounds September, 1944.

Sykes, Major H. H. .. .. E.R.E. from April, 1940.

Taylor-Whitehead, Capt. H. R.*§ E.R.E. until April, 1940; E.R.E. from March, 1941.

Tew, Lieut. T. M. P.* .. .. Killed on active service May, 1940.

Thomas, Capt. R. P., M.C. Joined August, 1941; O.C. H.Q. Squadron, March to September, 1943; E.R.E. from September, 1943.

Thoms, Capt. P. W.* .. .. Commissioned to 24th Lancers April, 1941.

Thwaites, Capt. H. O. D., M.C.*‡§ With 24th Lancers December, 1940, to August, 1942.

Tubbs, Capt. V. H. From Gloucestershire Hussars March, 1943; wounded and E.R.E. from November, 1944.

Tully, Major W. V.*§ .. .. .. Quartermaster to May, 1943; E.R.E. from May, 1943.

Usher, Lieut.-Colonel Sir J., O.B.E.†.. E.R.E. the whole war.

Vesey, Lieut.-Colonel Hon. O. E.,
C.B.E.† .. .. E.R.E. the whole war.

Vint, Lieut. R. G. Joined February, 1943; E.R.E. from October, 1943.

Walsh, Major J. L. .. Joined September, 1941; E.R.E. from June, 1942.

Walwyn, Major F. T. T.† .. E.R.E. the whole war.

Wentworth-Stanley, Lieut. G. D.‡ Joined June, 1944.

Whately, Lieut. T. D., M.C.‡ .. Joined November, 1943.

White, Major V. H. Joined June, 1941; E.R.E. from November, 1942.

Wills, Capt. A. C. L. Joined July, 1940; to 24th Lancers December, 1940.

Wills, Lieut. J. G. Joined June, 1941; E.R.E. from June, 1942.

Wilmoth, Lieut. M. St. J. Joined September, 1941; E.R.E. from May, 1943.

Woodhead, Lieut. M. ff.‡§ Joined February, 1943; E.R.E. May, 1944, to February, 1945.

Wright, Capt. S. C.† .. Prisoner of war June, 1940.

Wright-Harvey, Lieut. A. D. .. From 24th Lancers August, 1942; wounded and E.R.E. from November, 1942.

Wyndham, Lieut. H. S. From Leicestershire Yeomanry August, 1941; injured and E.R.E. August, 1941, to July, 1942; killed in action October, 1942.

Wynne, Major R. H. S.† Adjutant, May to August, 1940; E.R.E. from September, 1940.

Zissu, Lieut. T. .. Joined September, 1942; died of wounds November, 1942.

OTHER RANKS WHO HAVE SERVED WITH THE 9TH LANCERS, INCLUDING THOSE WHO WERE KILLED IN ACTION OR DIED OF WOUNDS, AND INCLUDING THOSE WHO BECAME PRISONERS OF WAR OR WERE WOUNDED IN ACTION

Every effort has been made to get this appendix as accurate as possible, but no guarantee can be given that it is so. Any errors or omissions are very much regretted

317402 Abrahams, Lance-Corporal S.*
317287 Adams, Corporal L.
2183527 Adams, Trooper W.
7919657 Adams, Trooper P.
7903159 Addicott, Trooper J.
7920319 Addy, Trooper C.
7951740 Affleck, Trooper J.
14514339 Ainsworth, Trooper A.
7918666 Alaway, Trooper E.
7882979 Alderson, Lance-Corporal J.
553050 Alderton, Sergeant A. C.
6018961 Aldred, Trooper C.
7938364 Allan, Lance-Corporal T.
317220 Allen, W.O.II (S.S.M.) R.
317362 Allen, Corporal D.
537346 Allen, W.O.I (Bandmaster) A.
7918667 Allen, Trooper E.
316717 Allison, Trooper W.
7920320 Allison, Trooper P. V.
7926626 Almond, Sergeant G.
7899558 Amos, Trooper A.
4799173 Anderson, Trooper J.
7920321 Andrews, Corporal F. P.
7920322 Andrews, Trooper R. H.
7931073 Andrews, Trooper J. W.*
321723 Archer, Trooper R.
7882633 Aris, Lance-Sergeant C.
7937384 Arscott, Corporal R.
7917750 Arundel, Lance-Corporal W.
320196 Ashfield, Lance-Corporal R.*
7920323 Ashford, Trooper H.
7901715 Ashmore, Trooper J.
3528333 Ashworth, Lance-Corporal K. B.
317088 Aslett, Corporal A.
329626 Atkinson, Trooper T.*
771987 Atkinson, Corporal E.
7920324 Atkinson, Trooper C. W.
7941869 Audsley, Trooper J.
7920326 Aveyard, Trooper S.
7889357 Bacon, Trooper H.
321097 Bafico, Trooper W.
7942031 Bailiss, Trooper R. H.
7890107 Bain, Trooper W.

321076 Baker, Trooper A.
5724342 Baker, Trooper F.
558609 Baker, Trooper L.
5834027 Baker, Lance-Corporal F.
319698 Ballinger, Trooper C.
404889 Balsden, Trooper A.
731543 Banfield, Sergeant A.
3717773 Banks, Trooper R.
7918181 Banks, Trooper L.
317704 Barber, W.O.II (O.R.Q.M.S.) H.
317497 Barker, Sergeant B.
774621 Barker, Trooper F.
4041185 Barker, Trooper J.
7901287 Barnes, Trooper H.
7916837 Barnes, Lance-Corporal D.
7919699 Barnes, Trooper D.
316027 Barnham, Corporal G.
319525 Barrett, Trooper C.
319708 Barrett, Trooper D.
7920328 Barstow, Trooper E.
14375473 Bartlett, Lance-Corporal E.
7912779 Batley, Lance-Corporal N.
7952067 Bayes, Trooper C.
320750 Bayley, Trooper G.
3455039 Baylis, Trooper C.
319749 Bayliss, Lance-Corporal J.
310670 Beal, Corporal G.
7916089 Beare, Trooper R.
7914149 Beaumont, Trooper E.†
7920329 Beaumont, Trooper J. B.
7887731 Beddoe, Lance-Sergeant D.
14317794 Beerman, Trooper P.
7942692 Beeston, Trooper N.
6408834 Bell, Lance-Corporal V.
5492935 Bellenie, Lance-Sergeant C.
4124737 Bellis, Corporal W.
317270 Bendon, Trooper G.
14543420 Bendon, Trooper E.
310872 Bennett, Trooper G.
315987 Bennett, W.O.II (S.S.M.) H.
316693 Bennett, Trooper A.
320171 Bennett, Corporal G.
7902435 Bennett, Trooper J.

*Wounded.   †Prisoner of war.

318910 Bennett, W.O.II (Q.M.S./M.) A. J., M.M.
14539841 Bennett, Trooper E.
320511 Benson, Trooper J.
14382637 Benson, Trooper J.
317091 Bentley, Trooper W.
7920330 Bentley, Trooper H.†
7920331 Bentley, Trooper K.
314368 Berry, S.Q.M.S. A.
7899856 Berry, Trooper C.
319058 Berryman, Corporal H. G.
7919191 Berryman, Lance-Sergeant E., M.M.
3529777 Beswick, Sergeant A. J., M.M.
316400 Betts, Trooper W.
7903632 Betts, Trooper T.
7884403 Bevan, Lance-Corporal A.
7935402 Billen,Trooper F. J.*
317398 Billett, Lance-Corporal E. W. J.
7917753 Billings, Trooper R.
3604988 Billington, Trooper A.
6981221 Bird, Trooper W.†
14547296 Bird, Trooper E.
5888053 Birks, Trooper N.
317266 Bishop, Trooper J.
14504675 Bishop, Trooper V.
319709 Bisset, Lance-Corporal C.
7901293 Black, Trooper J. C.*
319107 Bladon, Corporal W.
3455767 Blakeley, Trooper C.†
726541 Blandford, W.O.I (R.S.M.) A., D.C.M.
316339 Bloxham, Trooper A.
317302 Bloxwich, Trooper R.
7901381 Blue, Trooper U.
7916839 Blundell, Trooper M.
4913944 Blunt, Sergeant T.
316336 Bodley, Trooper G.
317248 Bolton, Corporal A.
7883824 Bond, Lance-Corporal W.
320270 Bonsall, Trooper P.
5496801 Booth, Sergeant A., M.M.
14538690 Booth, Trooper F.
7920333 Bottomley, Trooper B.
7931078 Bourne, Lance-Corporal A.
407130 Bousfield, Trooper E.
7959323 Bowers, Trooper C.
7882318 Bowman, Lance-Sergeant J.
5330551 Boyce, Trooper N.
7920334 Boyes, Corporal C.
7902432 Boyle, Trooper H.
317189 Bradley, Trooper S.
319732 Bradley, Trooper E.
313370 Bradshaw, W.O.II (S.S.M.) G.
7960829 Bradshaw, Lance-Corporal F.
5569366 Brady, Trooper J.
14323703 Brady, Trooper T.

319126 Brain, Sergeant G. R.†
4464005 Bramhall, Trooper K.
318888 Branton, Trooper A.
319135 Brennan, Sergeant G., M.M.
3062962 Brewer, Trooper C.
7906341 Briggs, Trooper H.
7893702 Bright, Lance-Corporal T. H.*
7934080 Broadbent, Trooper A.
7920335 Brodie, Lance-Corporal H. H.
316764 Brooks, Trooper S.
2053066 Brooks, Trooper A.
7901822 Brooks, Corporal A.
7918674 Brooks, Trooper E. S.*
7933821 Brooks, Trooper F.
2040926 Broomhall, Lance-Sergeant J. S.*
315247 Brothers, S.Q.M.S. H.
316043 Brown, Trooper D.
320347 Brown, Trooper N.
322052 Brown, Trooper A. R.†
767398 Brown, Trooper J. L.
4389248 Brown, Trooper A.
7880514 Brown, Corporal J.
7901132 Brown, Trooper S.†
7901566 Brown, Trooper D.
7920336 Brown, Trooper E. D.
7947753 Brown, Trooper C.*
7949756 Brown, Lance-Corporal K.
14414385 Brown, Trooper N. R.
7882943 Browne, Trooper C. A.
7903155 Browning, Trooper L.
7914750 Buchanan, Trooper A.
7904730 Buckingham, Lance-Corporal J.
7901550 Buckley, W./Corporal S.
7902750 Buckley, Trooper A.
4124091 Bull, Lance-Corporal A.
6471701 Bull, Trooper H.
7901597 Bull, Trooper H.
7901597 Bull, Trooper A.
7947949 Bunn, Trooper P.
7917756 Bunting, Trooper H. B.
7882850 Burch, Trooper W.
5494226 Burgess, Trooper.
316998 Buriatte, Corporal H.
7902629 Burke, Lance-Corporal P.
318918 Burrell, Corporal S.
319407 Burrows, Corporal J.
5046513 Burrows, Trooper S.
6188181 Burrows, S.Q.M.S. L.
14382637 Burt, Trooper A.
7918184 Bush, Lance-Corporal S.
5124392 Bushell, Trooper J. G. M.*
7948535 Butler, Trooper J. E. L.*
14528694 Butt, Trooper.
405589 Byne, Trooper D.
7882362 Byrn, Lance-Corporal W.
312543 Byrne, W.O.I J.

*Wounded. †Prisoner of war.

7947448 Calder, Trooper R.
7945339 Caldwell, Trooper A. S.
14521820 Calloway, Trooper R.
14342560 Calvert, Trooper C.
830254 Cameron, Trooper J. M.*
7952547 Campbell, Trooper K.
551818 Cann, Trooper H.
7880238 Capper, Trooper E.
14548240 Cardew, Trooper V.
5735362 Careless, Trooper H.
317124 Carey, Trooper J. A.*
317120 Carnegie, Trooper A.
310752 Carpenter, Corporal A.
317290 Carroll, Trooper T.*
14415080 Carroll, Trooper V.
320790 Carter, Sergeant E.
558472 Carter, Trooper G.
5834567 Carter, Trooper R.
318974 Cartwright, Corporal R.
321531 Carver, Trooper E.
320733 Casey, Trooper F.
319718 Catchpole, Corporal F. A.*
553408 Catt, Trooper L.*
317552 Chadwick, Sergeant F.
7902560 Chadwick, Trooper H.
7920404 Chadwick, Corporal H.
7893325 Challacombe, Trooper F.
7896262 Chamberlain, Trooper D.
320679 Chambers, Sergeant T.
558623 Champ, Lance-Corporal N.
5889611 Champion, Lance-Corporal G.
7920243 Channon, Trooper R. A.*
7882875 Chant, Trooper D.
7913933 Chapman, Trooper A.
7920337 Chapman, Corporal F. D. M.,
M.M.*
14533759 Chapman, Trooper R.
7945641 Chard, Lance-Corporal R.
319729 Charlesworth, Lance-Corporal L.
320824 Charlesworth, Lance-Corporal W.,
M.M.
317333 Charlton, Sergeant F. J.*
7947927 Checkley, Trooper E.
7942589 Cheetham, Trooper M.
5053938 Chell, Corporal F.
320865 Clark, Trooper J.
7911215 Clarke, Trooper T.
7917760 Clark, Corporal W.
14533761 Clark, Trooper C.
317537 Clarke, Trooper R. C.
318890 Clarke, Trooper R.
321169 Clarke, Lance-Corporal G. B.
420143 Clarke, Lance-Corporal J.
7584025 Clarke, Lance-Corporal L.
7882686 Clarke, Trooper J.
7917760 Clarke, Trooper W.

7931158 Clarke, Trooper.
3455485 Clarkson, Trooper W. E.
317119 Clayton, W.O.II J.
322109 Clayton, Boy A.
3598442 Clayton, Corporal F.
5250832 Clayton, Trooper W.
7935409 Clayton, Trooper W.
7937787 Clayton, Lance-Corporal R.
7958666 Clement, Trooper C. R.*
7899561 Clews, Sergeant K. H.*
320763 Cliff, Lance-Corporal L.†
319381 Clift, Trooper I. J.*
7884198 Clifton, Trooper C.
316249 Clipston, Lance-Corporal H.
548034 Clutson, Sergeant A. C.
320111 Cockings, Trooper W.†
3711470 Cockram, Lance-Corporal F.
320485 Cody, Boy W.
7920338 Coldron, Trooper G. R.
550769 Coleman, W.O.II B.
317760 Collard, Sergeant B.
3596667 Collier, Lance-Sergeant F.
7902770 Collier, Sergeant R. J.*
7910095 Collins, Trooper D.
7945825 Collinson, Trooper H.
7918680 Comley, Trooper A.
7940796 Conlon, Corporal J.
7893624 Connor, Trooper F.
310728 Cook, Sergeant G.
316226 Cook, W.O.II C.
317481 Cook, Corporal L., M.M.
319728 Cook, Sergeant G.
328159 Cook, Lance-Sergeant.
403052 Cook, Trooper.
321312 Cookson, Lance-Corporal J.
7893807 Cookson, Trooper N.
7935883 Coombes, Trooper C. K. L.
317356 Cooper, Trooper T.*
7919701 Cooper, Trooper E.
7948445 Cooper, Trooper A.
7920619 Cope, Trooper L.
319399 Corbett, Sergeant V., D.C.M.
319752 Corbett, Lance-Corporal T.
7902415 Corney-Bond, Sergeant A. F.*
3448403 Corns, Trooper S.
319207 Cornwall, Sergeant F. J.
787898 Corrigan, Trooper F.
317116 Cossey, Lance-Corporal J. C.
320713 Costard, Trooper S.
310753 Cottee, W.O.II (R.Q.M.S.) S. J.
317566 Cowell, W./Sergeant H.
7944354 Cowell, Lance-Corporal J.
5890416 Cowie, Corporal L. J.
548807 Cox, Lance-Sergeant S.
5113862 Cox, Corporal L.
5882026 Cox, Trooper S.

*Wounded.   †Prisoner of war.

7947914 Cox, Trooper J.*
7954012 Cox, Trooper R.
14262246 Craddock, Trooper R.
7942483 Craft, Corporal D.
7920339 Craimer, Trooper S.
7920340 Cranmer, Lance-Corporal A.
319693 Craven, Trooper D.
3598442 Crayton, Lance-Sergeant F., M.M.*
7892606 Creech, Lance-Corporal A.
317159 Crew, Trooper J.
123298 Cridland, Lance-Corporal N.
7925430 Crombie, Trooper S.
317240 Crook, W.O.I (R.S.M.) W. H.
7893462 Crook, Trooper E. E.*
5575097 Crookes, Trooper R.
318986 Cross, Trooper W.
859873 Cross, Sergeant J.
7931083 Cross, Trooper H. W.*
319319 Crossey, Trooper C.
557545 Crossfield, Trooper R.
6142121 Croton, Trooper L. A.
317109 Crow, Trooper J.
14318814 Crowder, Trooper H.
316561 Crudgington, Corporal J.
7882125 Crutchley, Lance-Corporal D.
318911 Cubitt, Corporal F.
7945346 Cuddon, Sergeant G.
5381946 Cullen, Lance-Corporal P.
7942598 Cullen, Trooper S.*
7899552 Cumbers, Sergeant F.
319995 Cunningham, Trooper C.
4619400 Curtis, Trooper W. H.
742613 Dale, W.O.II (S.S.M.) L.
1442989 Dale, Trooper F.
316721 Damon, Trooper B. C.
820750 Dannatt, Corporal A. E.
318978 Darvell, Trooper E. T.
7917763 Davenport, Trooper A.
317768 Davidson, Lance-Corporal E.
316318 Davies, S.Q.M.S. A.
319696 Davies, Trooper E.
319738 Davies, Lance-Corporal W.
2565901 Davies, Trooper T.
3450430 Davies, Trooper G.
5733414 Davies, Trooper W. J.*
7916474 Davies, Corporal A.
7937322 Davies, Trooper R.
7943963 Davis, Trooper J.
14254176 Dawes, Corporal S.
14254176 Dawes, Trooper J.
312516 Dawkes, W.O.II (S.S.M.) S.
7914320 Dawson, Trooper D. T.
14433357 Dawson, Trooper G.
310014 Deacon, Sergeant J.
317106 Deakin, Corporal W.
319695 Dean, Trooper T. H.

7944339 Desney, Trooper H. J.
7920341 Deighton, Trooper C.
7916276 Dell, Trooper W.*
7914757 Dempster, Corporal R.
6470013 Denny, Trooper S.
7905050 Devey, Lance-Corporal A.
7887002 Dew, Sergeant J.*
7892581 Diamond, Trooper E.
317743 Dick, W.O.II (S.S.M.) J.*
320651 Dickins, Trooper D.
7011459 Dickins, Sergeant S. H.†
329309 Dickinson, Sergeant M.
320770 Dillaway, Sergeant R.
316712 Dinsdale, Trooper.
2316660 Dobson, Trooper F. J.
5829518 Dobson, Trooper P.
7680847 Dobson, Trooper G.
317329 Docherty, Sergeant D.
5835308 Doe, Lance-Corporal T.*
317487 Dolezal, Sergeant G., Bronze Star,
    U.S.A.
320057 Dolton, Trooper A.†
7045340 Donnelly, Trooper E.
315480 Donnley, W.O.II (T.S.M.) E.
3050571 Denoghue, Corporal J.
14507006 Doughty, Trooper R.
7940339 Douglas, Trooper J.
7940335 Douglas, Trooper J.
319703 Douthwaite, Trooper F.
7887002 Dow, Sergeant J.*
319151 Dowdeswell, Lance-Corporal G.
7934003 Downey, Trooper J.
317340 Downs, Sergeant S. G.*
804396 Doyle, Lance-Corporal G.
7915114 Dray, Trooper H.*
317697 Dudeney, Sergeant E. L.
6985271 Duke, Trooper T.
7881768 Dunbar, Trooper A.
864592 Duncan, Trooper J.
7911519 Dundas, Trooper C.
401333 Dunford, Trooper J.*
1940870 Dunn, Trooper C. M.*
321741 Duxbury, Trooper W.*
7879846 Duxbury, Trooper F.
310543 Dyer, Corporal W.
5614618 Dyer, Trooper E.
7918688 Eagling, Trooper L.
7915474 Eastwood, Trooper G. T.
7920394 Eddison, Trooper J.
320827 Edey, Trooper D.
7899904 Edington, Lance-Corporal J. T.*
7901256 Edmunds, Sergeant J., M.M.
316430 Edwards, Sergeant C.
316708 Edwards, Corporal G.
317439 Edwards, W.O.II (S.S.M.) F.. M.M.
    and Bar.*

*Wounded.   †Prisoner of war.

320486	Edwards, Trooper A.
319259	Edwards, Trooper C.
401743	Edwards, Trooper H.
7947342	Edwards, Trooper R.
317261	Egmore (aias Woods), Corporal H.*
14277248	Ekins, Trooper R.
317664	Elbourne, Trooper V. J.
404220	Elder, Lance-Corporal W.
555455	Ellery, Corporal.
7944496	Ellicott, Trooper T.
404227	Elliot, Trooper W.
319197	Ellis, Trooper E.
3766374	Ellis, Trooper W.
7914138	Ellis, Trooper G.
7943970	Ellis, Trooper J.
14387543	Ellis, Trooper G.
14679079	Ellis, Trooper E.
7944750	Elson, Trooper A.
7901628	Emerson, Lance-Corporal T.
6983014	England, Trooper F.
14293535	English, Trooper A. C.
319612	Enticknap, Trooper R.
550836	Evans, Trooper T.
883875	Evans, Trooper P.
7901267	Evans, Trooper W.
7938141	Evans, Trooper A.
6213255	Everest, Lance-Corporal R.
7920342	Ewan, Trooper A. W.
14546883	Fairs, Trooper S. J.
7903664	Faithfull, Trooper E.
7920343	Falkingham, Trooper E.
7884739	Farr, W.O.II (Q.M.S./M.) T.
406127	Fay, Trooper R.*
320108	Fearn, Corporal R.
320819	Feldwick, Trooper E.
7920344	Ferner, Trooper H., M.M.
5336984	Fielding, Trooper R.
319645	Fillis, Trooper G.
1063504	Fink, Trooper E. G.*
7920345	Finn, Trooper T.
7958274	Finney, Corporal T.
14216092	Finnis, Trooper J. E.*
7948371	Firmin, Trooper R.*
555101	Firth, Trooper R.
7915478	Firth, Trooper W.
7931171	Fishburn, Lance-Corporal W.*
7901481	Fisher, Trooper L.
7918194	Fisher, Trooper A. C. W.*
5772444	Flaxmer, Trooper P.
7937793	Fletcher, Trooper H.
5109706	Flinn, Lance-Corporal W. J.*
5829411	Flood, Trooper P.
317235	Flower, Lance-Sergeant L. R.*
3708673	Flyn, Trooper C.
5109706	Flynn, Lance-Corporal W.
7902362	Flynn, Trooper H.
319597	Ford, Trooper W.
310921	Fordham, Trooper J.
7945843	Foster, Trooper G. W.
7945801	Foster, Trooper J.
3781811	Foulkes, Trooper H.†
7935304	Fowler, Trooper A.
14290848	Fowler, Trooper E. G.*
317232	Fox, Sergeant J.
5569765	Fox, Lance-Sergeant D.
7920346	Fox, Trooper H.
7945002	Fox, Corporal.
7947162	Fowler, Trooper L. A.
321164	Francis, Trooper E.
317475	Francis, S.Q.M.S. W.
404286	Fraser, Trooper A.
320440	French, Trooper L.
7914322	French, Trooper E.
7945260	Frewer, Trooper W.
549072	Frost, Sergeant W.*
7947014	Furness, Lance-Corporal F.
7921042	Gabby, Trooper J.*
14681612	Gadsby, Trooper H.
7918692	Gaeschlin, Trooper L.
316631	Gallagher, Corporal J.
7956014	Gallagher, Trooper E.
316181	Galliers, Trooper J.
7901480	Gardener, Trooper G.
4468114	Gargett, Trooper J.*
319721	Garner, Lance-Sergeant D.
7938880	Garner, Trooper E.
2029474	Garside, Trooper W.
14379385	Garwood, Trooper F.
317462	Gates, Trooper A.
5497339	Gates, Sergeant G. G.*
7890110	Gatins, Trooper J.
7878001	Gatwood, Trooper S.
551609	Gayden, Corporal A.
7920251	Geard, Trooper J.†
317438	Geary, Lance-Corporal N. M.*
7901651	Gill, Trooper A.*
7942858	Geering, Lance-Corporal E.
6723115	Gerrlei, Corporal E.
7920347	Gibbins, Lance-Corporal J. R.
316705	Gibbons, Trooper R.
317681	Gibbons, W.O.II A. C.
7918525	Gibbons, Trooper J.
2572528	Gibbs, Trooper F.
7916852	Gibbs, Trooper W.
7901651	Gill, Trooper A.
2977636	Gilmour, Trooper R.
3460610	Gilpin, Trooper W.
549007	Gilpin, Corporal T.
7901919	Glover, Trooper H.
5182737	Goble, Corporal H.
7903132	Godkin, Trooper J.
7945031	Goff, Trooper P. H.

*Wounded.   †Prisoner of war.

1574536	Goode, Trooper.
7918307	Gooding, Trooper R. H.
556715	Goodman, Trooper A.
7920348	Goodman, Trooper L.
319602	Gordon, Lance-Corporal W.
7903154	Gordon, Trooper H.
4468104	Gorgan, Trooper A.
3714489	Gormley, Trooper A.
319125	Gorton, Corporal T.
7944983	Gosling, Lance-Corporal R.
317771	Gourley, Trooper S.
320924	Gowdy, Trooper W.
7877448	Graham, Trooper W.
3052349	Grahamslow, Lance-Corporal T.
3909711	Grans, Trooper F.
317432	Gray, Trooper H.
320504	Gray, Trooper H.†
320746	Gray, Lance-Corporal W. C.
7937795	Gray, Trooper E.*
14348162	Graydon, Trooper E.
320125	Green, Trooper R. H.*
122995	Greenfield, Trooper S. J.*
319415	Greenhough, Corporal J.*
7948633	Greenway, Lance-Corporal D.
7914369	Greenwood, Lance-Corporal D.
320660	Gregory, Trooper M.*
558728	Gregory, Lance-Corporal R.
1574106	Grey, Corporal S. F.*
7901635	Griffin, Trooper G.*
7879215	Griffiths, Sergeant T. E.*
14378043	Griffiths, Trooper E.
4468104	Grogan, Lance-Corporal J.
3706978	Groves, Lance-Corporal F. W.*
7908302	Groves, Lance-Corporal A.
2567452	Grundy, Lance-Sergeant F.
319276	Gullick, Lance-Corporal E.
6340416	Guymer, Trooper A.
7917770	Haggerty, Lance-Corporal J.
7915486	Haigh, Trooper C. N.
7194514	Hailwood, Trooper C.
548992	Halfnight, W.O.III (T.S.M.) J.
320036	Hall, Trooper M.*
4450258	Hall, Trooper J.
5722330	Hall, Trooper A.
7947930	Hall, Trooper D. W.
7906052	Hallam, Trooper G.
7938355	Hamblin, Trooper C.
7903158	Hamlett, Trooper G. P.
7917772	Hammersley, Trooper H.
7914326	Hammerton, Trooper J.
6012945	Hammond, Corporal E. W.*
1463702	Hammond, Corporal G.
7922668	Hannabess, Trooper E.
317224	Hancox, Trooper S.
7918200	Hankinson, Trooper N.
4922168	Harding, Lance-Corporal E. N.

317459	Hardwick, Sergeant S. V.*
7882386	Hardwick, Trooper.
310832	Hardwidge, W.O.I (R.S.M.) T. C.
7919710	Hardy, Trooper F. C.
319117	Harlow, Corporal J.
317557	Harris, S.Q.M.S. A., M.M.
4618939	Harris, Trooper J.
6981700	Harris, Lance-Corporal R., M.M.*
7920349	Harrison, Trooper T. H.*
14533784	Harrison, Trooper M.
319745	Hart, Trooper J.
7937576	Hatton, Trooper O.
7947235	Hatton, Corporal F.
317250	Hawkins, Trooper G.
317532	Hawkins, Trooper S.
321624	Hawkins, Trooper G. S.*
7920632	Hawkins, Lance-Corporal W.
407278	Hayden, Lance-Corporal J. A.
320172	Hayford, Trooper S.
317698	Haylett, Trooper H.
320768	Haynes, Trooper R.
7916855	Haynes, Trooper R. T.*
319322	Hayward, Lance-Sergeant E. J.
320668	Haywood, Trooper J.
7901251	Healey, Trooper T.
5123501	Hearn, Trooper A.
317436	Heathcote, Corporal C.
310661	Heather, Corporal W.
317138	Heaton, Trooper E.
7899398	Heaton, Trooper J.
7960013	Heggie, Trooper J.
7878348	Hehir, Trooper F.
7914005	Heighton, Trooper L.
7901379	Helps, Sergeant F., M.M.*
317515	Henderson, T.Q.M.S. J.
7938968	Henderson, Trooper D. B.
7904875	Herrington, Corporal G.
550700	Henstridge, Trooper H.
7935436	Herwood, Trooper G.
3460520	Hetherington, Trooper H.
317744	Hewitt, Sergeant R.
320697	Hewitt, Lance-Corporal C.*
321873	Hewitt, Lance-Corporal W. T.
5124405	Hiblen, Lance-Corporal T.
319970	Hill, Trooper A. W.
6203452	Hill, Trooper A.
6299822	Hill, Trooper D.
317242	Hillary, W.O.II (S.S.M.) R. L., M.M.*
549888	Hills, Sergeant B.
314664	Hilton, Trooper.
7918698	Hinckley, Lance-Corporal F.
6286421	Hipple, Lance-Corporal R.†
7893668	Hirschfield, Trooper A. W.*
4041086	Hobbs, Lance-Corporal J.
7919754	Hobley, Trooper A.

*Wounded.   †Prisoner of war.

7912796 Hobson, Trooper W.
317433 Hodgson, Trooper G.
7920350 Hodgson, Trooper J. D.
7915490 Hogarth, Trooper W.
549147 Hole, Lance-Sergeant G. H.
320767 Hollingsworth, Trooper W.
320439 Holloway, Boy H.
3393199 Holloway, Trooper S.
14728640 Holman, Trooper J.
320238 Holmes, Corporal F.
4040945 Homer, Trooper H.
7901249 Hooton, Trooper N.
2555336 Hopper, W.O.I (R.S.M.) R. G.
548655 Horton, Trooper A.
7920351 Horton, Trooper G. L.
7879769 House, Trooper L.
14320643 Howard, Trooper W.
4537404 Howarth, Sergeant F.
320646 Howe, Trooper P.
545273 Howes, Trooper J.
6096791 Hubbard, Trooper J.
4335261 Hudson, Lance-Corporal C.
6619774 Hudson, Trooper C.
7917776 Hudson, Lance-Corporal F.
317392 Hughes, Corporal F.*
317482 Hughes, Lance-Sergeant R.
320628 Hughes, Trooper C.
406142 Hughes, Sergeant S.
7893892 Hughes, Trooper J.
7896867 Hughes, Lance-Corporal V.
324416 Hull, Trooper J.
317359 Hunt, Lance-Sergeant J. W.*
4548298 Hunt, Trooper R. G.
317538 Hunt, Trooper G.
558717 Hunt, Sergeant R.
7899582 Hunt, Trooper A.
7920352 Hunt, Trooper F.
317289 Hutchinson, Trooper B.
321516 Hutchinson, Trooper D.*
310799 Huxford, W.O.II (S.S.M.) H.,
                    M.B.E., D.C.M.
321039 Humberstone, Lance-Corporal F.
7938613 Inns, Trooper H.
5349069 Instone, Lance-Corporal E., M.M.
317444 Irvine, Trooper I.
7920353 Irvine, Lance-Sergeant R., M.M.*
2047020 Ive, Lance-Sergeant.
5949066 Ives, Trooper M.
7876645 Izzard, Trooper W. C.
7904453 Jack, Trooper D. D.*
7901373 Jackson, Trooper R. S., M.M.*
7919222 Jackson, Trooper T.
7920354 Jackson, Trooper F. A.
7920355 Jackson, Lance-Sergeant N.
14392981 Jacobs, Trooper S.
7920356 Jagger, Trooper H. R.

317560 James, Trooper G.
7878139 James, Sergeant E.
7920357 James, Trooper A.
7939915 James, Trooper W.
7899924 Jamieson, Corporal J.*
7920357 Janes, Trooper A.
317264 Jarman, Corporal C.
7919427 Jeans, Trooper C.
1921474 Jeffrey, Corporal M.
7947915 Jeffrey, Trooper R. W.
5834384 Jelfs, Trooper L.
7914175 Jenkins, Trooper F. H.†
320118 Jenkinson, Lance-Corporal C.
318982 Jenner, Sergeant W. A.
4921835 Jennings, Lance-Corporal P.†
7899286 Jennings, Trooper B.
1525778 Jessop, Trooper C.
7947013 Johns, Trooper D.
317505 Johnson, Trooper.
548806 Johnson, Trooper J.
7920358 Johnson, Trooper J. W.
7920395 Johnson, Trooper C.
7941533 Johnson, Trooper R.
917966 Johnston, Trooper J.
7947510 Johnston, Lance-Corporal C. C.
320647 Jolly, Trooper A.
329272 Jones, Lance-Corporal D. A.*
398850 Jones, Trooper L.
1574174 Jones, Trooper H. L.
2566333 Jones, Trooper J.
5106955 Jones, Trooper M.
7878689 Jones, Lance-Corporal G.
7893806 Jones, Boy H.
7899984 Jones, Trooper H.
7901307 Jones, Trooper H.
7901397 Jones, Lance-Corporal A.*
7914627 Jones, Trooper D.
14382012 Jones, Trooper A.
7948345 Jordan, Trooper G. E.*
5053221 Judge, Trooper N.
3456319 Kay, Trooper T.
14521443 Kaye, Trooper H.
319021 Keeble, Trooper P.
769607 Kegg, Trooper J.
185620 Kelly, Trooper J.*
317638 Kelly, Corporal W.
7917778 Kelly, Trooper J.
7944725 Kemp, Trooper A. J.
7914631 Kempton, Trooper M.
7915707 Kendrick, Trooper E.
321690 Kennaugh, Trooper A.
5191322 Kent, Trooper A.
14624920 Kenway, Trooper B.
7945202 Kenyon, Trooper C. G.
317558 Kerler, Trooper L.
7944947 Kerry, Trooper T. C.

*Wounded. †Prisoner of war.

7901389 Kibler, Trooper A.
7947794 Kierlan, Trooper.
6847896 King, Trooper H.
7943927 King, Trooper H. H.
10511536 Kinsman, Trooper K. A.
7907510 Kirby, Trooper M.
317251 Kirk, Corporal C.
7893643 Kirwan, Trooper B.
7920396 Knew, Trooper F. E.
3060718 Knight, Trooper T.
4915029 Knight, Trooper W.
317346 Kretzer, Sergeant E., M.M.
7889988 Laing, Trooper F.
310859 Lake, Sergeant G.
3450234 Lamb, Trooper J.
7907423 Lamb, Lance-Corporal.
316532 Lambert, Lance-Corporal A.
4921796 Lambert, Trooper W. J.*
7937494 Lambert, Trooper G.
7942147 Lancashire, Trooper A.
6458711 Lane, Corporal H.
7893656 Lane, Trooper C.
7905201 Lane, Trooper G.
7945683 Langlands, Lance-Corporal D.
310588 Langridge, W.O.I (R.S.M.) H.
7937496 Large, Trooper S.*
810413 Latter, Trooper M.†
14258774 Laundy, Trooper P.*
869060 Lawrence, Trooper H.
7942230 Lawrence, Trooper D.
319758 Lawton, Lance-Corporal W.*
5620178 Leach, Trooper J.
7943984 Leach, Lance-Corporal H. C.
3596630 Leake, Trooper H.
329306 Leaver, Trooper E.
2047080 Lee, Corporal F.
3457150 Lee, Trooper G.
5833032 Lee, Trooper A.*
7920359 Lee, Trooper A.
2040925 Leese, Trooper F.
7920908 Legg, Trooper E. H.*
14352667 Leggett, Trooper A.
316703 Le Gresley, Trooper E.
7915140 Leighton, Trooper W.
7935445 Levick, Trooper G.
320381 Lewis, Trooper G.
320487 Lewis, Boy F.
7945295 Lewis, Lance-Corporal D. M.
7947729 Lewis, Lance-Corporal H. I.
14247743 Lewis, Trooper J.
861768 Lewthwaite, Lance-Corporal J.†
317221 Liddle, Lance-Sergeant G.*
4626697 Lindsay, Trooper R.
7932614 Ling, Trooper A.
7947326 Lintott, Trooper P. A.
3522406 Littleford, Lance-Corporal R.

320669 Livesey, Trooper E.*
7944094 Livesey, Trooper J. T.*
7899593 Livingstone, Trooper G.*
7893307 Llewellyn, Trooper J.
317758 Lloyd, Trooper W.
319036 Lloyd, W.O.II W., D.C.M.*
1574206 Lloyd, Lance-Corporal L.
7046686 Lloyd, Trooper T.
7899621 Lloyd, Trooper J.
421109 Lobb, Trooper C.
7951694 Lockitt, Trooper J.
7939217 Lockyer, Lance-Corporal A.
7947500 Longmire, Trooper W.
7923404 Loveday, Trooper R.
319400 Loveless, Sergeant A. E.
7958658 Loveless, Trooper K.
316221 Lovell, Trooper W.
317742 Lowrie, Corporal J.
14346578 Lowry, Trooper A. E.
316893 Lucas, Trooper E.
7893329 Lucas, Trooper R.
7583676 Luckham, Trooper A.
7914038 Lumley, Trooper E. R.
317145 Lupton, Trooper H.*
320866 Lyth, Trooper A.
7904511 Lyttleton, Trooper W. R.
319364 Macdiarmid, Sergeant G.
7893692 Macdonald, Trooper W.
7933211 MacFayden, Trooper D.
7947324 Macintosh, Lance-Corporal T.
7938200 Macken, Trooper J.
777005 Madden, Sergeant J.
7893050 Magee, Boy J.
3392563 Malaney, Trooper R. J.*
319473 Malcolm, W.O.II (S.S.M.) D.
7901262 Mallard, Trooper W.
7934343 Mallard, Corporal E. W.*
7893803 Mallette, Boy P.
318917 Maloney, W.O.II (S.S.M.) D. T. R.,
    M.M.*
317292 Malt, Sergeant J. H.
410827 Mann, Trooper H.
320899 Manuel, Lance-Corporal H.
406975 Mapplethorpe, Trooper F.
7920361 Margerison, Trooper A. L.
322307 Maris, Trooper E.
14346031 Markin, Trooper W.
7927015 Marks, Trooper D. W. H.
7893604 Marriott, Trooper A.
320593 Marrows, Corporal J. W.
7906653 Marsden, Trooper H.*
315457 Marshall, Sergeant I.
551076 Marshall, Sergeant G.
2653849 Marshall, Sergeant W.
317528 Marston, Trooper A.
310939 Martin, Trooper L.

*Wounded.   †Prisoner of war.

1578823	Martin, Trooper H. G.*
2752810	Martin, Trooper G.
7920362	Martin, Trooper J.
7939934	Martin, Lance-Corporal E.
7947672	Marvin, Trooper K.
319279	Maslin, Trooper G.
320723	Mason, Trooper B.
7958261	Massey, Trooper A.
14361363	Masterson, Lance-Corporal N.
317528	Marston, Trooper A.
317620	Mather, Lance-Corporal H.
1578635	Mather, Corporal J.
7920363	Matthews, Trooper R.
558615	Mayes, Lance-Corporal R.
7920397	McArthur, Trooper J.
7904410	McCabe, Trooper F.
7911431	McCann, Trooper C. L.*
3568501	McCormick, Trooper D.
14314696	McCormick, Trooper A.
14318760	McDonald, Trooper F.
7920360	McDowell, Trooper H. L.
7935835	McDowell, Lance-Corporal C. C.*
3857764	McFarlane, Trooper J., M.M.
7914782	McGinty, Trooper P.
319526	McGowan, Lance-Corporal W.
7901126	McGowan, Trooper E.
3599943	McGrady, Sergeant T.
7903136	McGrath, Trooper B.
3459367	McGumiskey, Trooper W.
6846828	McIver, Trooper E.
320888	McKrill, Trooper H.
317314	McLawlin, Trooper G.
2825030	McNeil, Trooper A.
5628628	McPherson, Trooper A.
3451349	Mellor, Trooper J.
7876446	Menzies, Lance-Sergeant W.*
320167	Mercer, Lance-Corporal G.
7919486	Meredith, Trooper J.
7945178	Merrian, Lance-Corporal A.
319274	Merriman, Sergeant E.
7954178	Merrion, Trooper A.
2317440	Merritt, Sergeant R.
313077	Middleditch, Sergeant J.
7917785	Middlemiss, Trooper J.*
3459880	Miffin, Trooper L. T.
317424	Millar, Trooper H.
4741024	Miller, Lance-Corporal G.
7917786	Miller, Trooper G.
7921394	Milligan, Trooper F.*
316695	Millington, Sergeant J. W.*
3714840	Mirfin, Trooper S.
7920364	Mitchell, Trooper J. L.
1872040	Mitchinson, Trooper F.
7918565	Mizon, Corporal.
7934142	Moat, Trooper J.
3064587	Moffat, Corporal D. M.

7901675	Monk, Trooper J.
317143	Monks, Corporal T.
2036221	Montgomery, Corporal A.
316842	Moon, S.Q.M.S. A.
7920365	Moon, Trooper F.
14363468	Moorcroft, Trooper C.
317452	Moore, Trooper S.
2570925	Moore, Lance-Corporal A.
3598081	Moore, Corporal J.
7932388	Moore, Trooper T.
316156	Morgan, W.O.II (R.Q.M.S.) S.
317178	Morgan, Trooper W.
7914336	Morgan, Lance-Corporal G. D.*
320239	Morley, Corporal J. W.*
4697822	Morley, Trooper R.
92288	Morris, Lance-Corporal G.†
316005	Morris, Trooper.
317301	Morris, Trooper S.
317339	Morris, Sergt. W.
548374	Morris, Trooper C.*
4537481	Morris, Trooper E.*
7918786	Morris, Trooper H.
7945178	Morrison, Trooper A.
317369	Morton, Sergeant F.
7938287	Moulds, Trooper G.
5834485	Mowatt, Corporal R.
7914337	Muldoon, Trooper W.
312521	Mullett, W.O.II (S.S.M.) G.
545291	Mullins, Trooper.
320189	Murphy, Trooper R.
2034394	Murphy, Trooper P.
3460094	Murphy, Trooper E. C.*
14249834	Murphy, Trooper D.
319316	Murray, Sergeant F.
319379	Murray, Corporal H.
7893603	Murray, Trooper D.
7920366	Musgrave, Trooper J. E.
14392175	Muskett, Trooper E.
7929040	Mustoe, Trooper E. C.
7946211	Mutch, Lance-Corporal W.
829982	Mutlow, Corporal R.
7920367	Naylor, Trooper H.
319608	Neill, Corporal A.
7901174	Nelson, Trooper J. C.
6024387	Nevills, Lance-Corporal.
7947188	Newbold, Lance-Sergeant G.
7932393	Newell, Trooper E. J.
320089	Newitt, Trooper O.
7938782	Newman, Trooper H.
14345566	Newman, Trooper E.
1397118	Nichol, Trooper K.
3064508	Nichol, Lance-Corporal J.
7916088	Nicholas, Trooper W.
14677453	Nicholson, Trooper D.
3064508	Nicol, Trooper J.
7890561	Nicolle, Lance-Corporal H.

*Wounded. †Prisoner of war.

550824	Nickolls, Corporal A., M.M.
319608	Niell, Lance-Sergeant A.
7901631	Noake, Trooper L.
7919726	Nock, Trooper R.
320716	Nolan, Trooper A.
319481	Norris, Corporal W. L.*
7920368	Northorp, Corporal T.
7912277	Northover, Trooper A.
7914181	Norwood, Lance-Corporal E.
6024387	Novels, Trooper F.
3710461	Nunnington, Corporal.
7903658	Nuttall, Trooper K. P.*
7920917	Nuttall, Trooper N.*
7917793	Nuttycombe, Trooper V.
317488	Nye, Trooper R.
318981	O'Connell, Sergeant P.
179221	O'Connor, Trooper R.
319621	O'Donnell, Trooper E.
7893272	O'Donovan, Trooper J.
7893273	O'Donovan, Trooper A.
14697356	O'Gara, Trooper J.
317354	Oglesby, W.O.III (T.S.M.) F.
5338280	Okell, Trooper R. C.
317434	Oldfield, Trooper.
320162	Oldham, Lance-Corporal B.
545273	Oldham, Trooper B.
7893670	O'Loughlin, Trooper N.*
837006	O'Neill, Trooper D.
1430352	Ongley, Corporal N.
5180815	Oppery, Trooper F.
320264	O'Reilly, Trooper R.
317608	Orwin, Sergeant J.
5378711	Ould, Trooper W.
7917794	Ovendon, Trooper P.
2079343	Owen, Corporal H.
5781678	Oxborough, Lance-Corporal R.
312899	Oxley, W.O.I (R.S.M.) P.
320855	Page, Trooper L. E.*
7932888	Page, Trooper R. E.*
410354	Paget, Lance-Corporal T.
7899432	Palmer, Trooper H.
7930566	Palmer, Lance-Corporal G.
825848	Parfit, Lance-Corporal C.
320087	Parfitt, Sergeant D., D.C.M.*
317389	Parish, Lance-Corporal H.
316688	Parker, Lance-Corporal T.
320035	Parker, Corporal G. A.
547040	Parker, Lance-Corporal W.
6292731	Parker, Lance-Corporal R.
7918299	Parker, Trooper K.
14557185	Parker, Trooper D.
4858667	Parkin, Trooper W.
7912322	Parrott, Trooper E.
320772	Parry, Trooper W.
14387318	Parry, Trooper O.
5508043	Parsons, Trooper G.
5570090	Parsons, Trooper E.
317623	Parton, Lance-Corporal F.
7879392	Partridge, Corporal R.
320648	Pash, Trooper S. C.*
4972873	Pashley, Trooper.
407872	Patterson, Trooper J.
321700	Pattison, Trooper R.
14386322	Payne, Trooper A. J.*
14279810	Peachey, Trooper A.
552410	Peake, Trooper G.
7920369	Pedley, Trooper H. O.
320153	Pegg, Lance-Corporal G.
317694	Penfold, Corporal A.
316228	Penny, Trooper A.
7903134	Perry, Lance-Sergeant S., M.M.
7903633	Perry, Trooper A. C.*
316473	Pert, Trooper T.
317300	Peters, Lance-Corporal F.
317619	Peters, Lance-Corporal S.†
317149	Peterson, Sergeant F.*
310853	Philips, Lance-Corporal H.
317085	Philson, Lance-Corporal A.
7880593	Philpott, Sergeant W.
314448	Phipps, Trooper F.
320170	Phoenix, Lance-Corporal P.
7914384	Pickard-Shackleton, Trooper.
317283	Pickering, Corporal W.*
5729586	Pickering, Trooper H.
7899606	Pickles, Corporal G.
7924871	Pike, Trooper F.
14399159	Pilbrow, Trooper J.
7945648	Pimm, Trooper D.
61320	Pine, Trooper C. L., M.M.
4386881	Pinkney, Trooper W.
7880351	Pirrie, Lance-Corporal G.
316459	Plant, Trooper R.*
320680	Plant, Lance-Corporal A.
7948498	Pledge, Trooper W. J.*
7901621	Plowman, Trooper A.
14330300	Pocock, Lance-Corporal W.
550182	Pollard, Trooper I.
319724	Ponting, Trooper C. H.
14339614	Poole, Trooper A.
7915056	Poole, Trooper G.
316130	Pope, W.O.III (T.S.M.) G.
410746	Pople, Trooper J.
317112	Popley, Sergeant R.
14370911	Potter, Trooper D.
7907119	Poulton, Trooper E.*
7882337	Povey, Trooper E.
329795	Powell, Trooper T. I. L.*
548929	Powell, Corporal A.
7920475	Power, Trooper H.
780742	Poyner, Corporal E.
316422	Precious, Trooper L.*
320775	Price, Corporal A.

*Wounded.   †Prisoner of war.

7932408	Price, Trooper H.
317387	Priest, Trooper A.
317523	Pritchard, Trooper W.
2004195	Pritchard, Trooper E.*
7901640	Pritchard, Corporal E.
7909121	Pritchard, Trooper A.
7916504	Probert, Lance-Corporal E.
7882075	Procter, Lance-Corporal J.
7881563	Prosser, Sergeant W.
321061	Pryce, Corporal E.
7925614	Pugh, Trooper E. M.*
7947653	Pullin, Trooper J.
7893701	Pulman, Lance-Corporal C. J.
751254	Purfield, Corporal W.
314726	Putnam, W.O.II (R.Q.M.S.) W.
320227	Putt, Trooper L.
1468939	Putt, Trooper A.
3451367	Quinn, Trooper G.
3599456	Quinn, Trooper M.
552453	Quinton, Trooper E.
7045131	Radley, Lance-Corporal C. J.*
7880376	Raine, Trooper H.
3445996	Ralph, Lance-Sergeant W. H.
7920371	Ramskir, Trooper G. N.
319688	Randall, Lance-Corporal S. T.*
14318839	Ratford, Trooper A. E.*
317626	Rawson, S.Q.M.S. F.
406127	Ray, Trooper R.
7899323	Ray, Lance-Corporal T. C.*
317662	Raymond, Trooper J.*
310896	Raynor, Sergeant F. H.
552360	Read, Trooper R.
314914	Ready, Lance-Corporal G.
7882250	Redshaw, Trooper J.
552360	Reed, Trooper R.
7935467	Reed, Corporal E.
317416	Reeves, Trooper J.*
317294	Reid, Trooper J.
7919159	Reid, Trooper W. S.*
317662	Remon, Trooper J. T.*
545207	Rennie, Corporal.
14378518	Rennie, Trooper W.
7931197	Rescanieres, Lance-Corporal R.
320764	Reynolds, Corporal E.*
321620	Reynolds, Trooper C.
552448	Reynolds, Trooper W.
7928069	Reynolds, Trooper W.
7951711	Reynolds, Trooper E.
1080599	Rhodes, Trooper G. E.*
320126	Richards, Trooper W.
402676	Richards, Trooper T.
14717007	Richards, Trooper J.
551449	Richardson, Lance-Corporal A.
7906967	Riches, Sergeant R. S., M.M.
3849778	Rickerby, W.O.II (S.S.M.) T.
7902718	Rickerby, Lance-Corporal A.

7928895	Riffkin, Trooper M.
317498	Rigby, Lance-Corporal G.
2047082	Riley, Sergeant C. H.
3652527	Riston, Trooper L.
319664	Robbie, Trooper G.
7931889	Robbins, Trooper F.
320289	Roberts, Trooper W.
320667	Roberts, Trooper L.
408211	Roberts, Trooper H.
409083	Roberts, Trooper G.
551840	Roberts, Trooper J.
3390362	Roberts, Trooper J.
7885934	Roberts, Trooper J. A.*
7893890	Roberts, Trooper V.
7932530	Roberts, Trooper H.
14362083	Roberts, Trooper E.
403723	Robertson, Trooper.
7931889	Robins, Trooper F.
317113	Robinson, Sergeant F.
317457	Robinson, S.Q.M.S. W.
320256	Robinson, Corporal J. R.*
552902	Robinson, Trooper T.
553048	Robinson, Lance-Sergeant H.
7343053	Robinson, Lance-Sergeant W.
552330	Rochelle, Trooper.
7920373	Roe, Trooper G.
315478	Roffery, Trooper S.
7899907	Rogers, Trooper V.
2574697	Rolands, Trooper J.
7920372	Rooley, Trooper A. G.
7894171	Rooney, Lance-Corporal E. J.*
7877199	Rose, Lance-Corporal F.
14505583	Rosewarne, Trooper A.
558524	Ross, Lance-Sergeant G. D.*
7936089	Ross, Trooper D.
916404	Routledge, Trooper H.
319716	Rowan, Corporal A.
3459600	Rowbotton, Trooper J.*
319002	Rowe, Trooper J.
320496	Rowe, Trooper D.
2574697	Rowland, Trooper J.
7015804	Rowland, Trooper C.
7929807	Rowland, Sergeant E.
5392956	Ruffles, Lance-Corporal R.
319109	Rufford, Corporal A.
317278	Rule, Sergeant A. L.
6023312	Rushbrook, Trooper G.
315787	Rushby, Lance-Corporal B.
315737	Rushley, Trooper B.
14532681	Rust, Trooper L. T.*
3653920	Ruston, Trooper R.
557247	Ryan, Corporal E.
3056035	Ryans, Corporal R.*
317206	Sadler, Trooper R.
5386392	Salmon, Trooper G.
7914719	Salmon, Trooper A. W.

*Wounded.　　†Prisoner of war.

Z

14508963 Salmon, Trooper F.	320182 Slack, Trooper J. H.
548548 Salt, Sergeant J. W.*	7931133 Slack, Trooper R.
7942870 Salter, Trooper F.	7913964 Sleeman, Corporal T. A.*
14326816 Samphire, Trooper H.	7041752 Smallbone, Trooper H.
7946874 Sams, Lance-Corporal G.	400635 Smallwood, Lance-Corporal J.
319361 Sandeman, Sergeant P.	403967 Smart, Trooper A.*
7946394 Sandham, Trooper R.	2811213 Smillie, Trooper F.
319420 Saunders, Lance-Corporal A.	310744 Smith, Corporal A.*
7941864 Saunders, Trooper T.	316235 Smith, Trooper W.
14324885 Saunders, Trooper R. C.*	317214 Smith, Lance-Corporal G.
3064722 Savage, Lance-Corporal G. L.*	319473 Smith, Sergeant D.†
4974928 Savage, Trooper J.	320180 Smith, Trooper C.†
7900068 Schofield, Trooper J.	320695 Smith, Trooper W.
7917803 Schofield, Lance-Sergeant C. R.	320698 Smith, Trooper A.
320734 Scott, Corporal W.	320720 Smith, Trooper H.
7937307 Scott, Corporal C.	403770 Smith, Lance-Sergeant W.
314525 Seager, Trooper W.	404138 Smith, Lance-Corporal R.
555226 Seaman, Trooper G.	406977 Smith, Sergeant T.
7946146 Secker, Trooper J.	532361 Smith, Lance-Corporal J.
316079 Sewell, Trooper V.	548292 Smith, Trooper F.
558611 Sewell, Trooper L.	551856 Smith, Trooper E.
317365 Seymour, Corporal W.†	552361 Smith, Trooper J.
4698408 Shakespeare, Trooper R.	814763 Smith, Lance-Corporal R. C. H.*
7892715 Sharp, Trooper J.	857371 Smith, Corporal J.
7928910 Sharp, Trooper T.	4124832 Smith, Trooper T.
849624 Sharpe, Trooper K.	4467410 Smith, Trooper R.
7917804 Sharpe, Trooper G.	5049473 Smith, Trooper L.
319235 Sharples, Trooper L.	5054167 Smith, Trooper L.
310969 Shaw, Trooper C.	5107448 Smith, Lance-Corporal S.
7915787 Sheard, Trooper T. C.*	5183389 Smith, Lance-Corporal A.
317243 Shelton, Trooper W.	5251252 Smith, Trooper C. A. W.*
4625885 Shepherd, Trooper J. P. L.*	5391336 Smith, Trooper A. G.*
5781114 Shepherd, Trooper W. J.	7893532 Smith, Lance-Corporal P.
7923080 Sheppard, Trooper L.	7897365 Smith, Trooper R.*
7938781 Shooter, Trooper E.	7899603 Smith, Sergeant L. G.*
317501 Shore, Lance-Corporal K.*	7902560 Smith, Lance-Corporal J.
551907 Shore, Lance-Corporal A.	7904594 Smith, Trooper G.
404341 Shortt, Trooper E.	7919742 Smith, Trooper S.
3451370 Shuttleworth, Trooper J.	7920375 Smith, Lance-Sergeant C. D. S., M.M.*
7894952 Sibley, Trooper E. G. R.*	
328805 Silver, Trooper H.	7923001 Smith, Sergeant J.
319298 Sime, Lance-Sergeant H. R.	7932534 Smith, Trooper R.
7916872 Simmond, Trooper R.	7936094 Smith, Trooper P.
7893978 Simmons, Sergeant W.	7943499 Smith, Trooper W.
14293229 Simmons, Lance-Corporal J. A.*	13021400 Smith, Lance-Corporal E.
7937057 Simms, Trooper S.	14254587 Smith, Trooper T.
4448818 Simpson, Corporal N.	14384535 Smith, Trooper N.
4448820 Simpson, Sergeant G.	7912769 Smurthwaite, Trooper S.
7889188 Simpson, Corporal I, M.M.	548375 Snape, Trooper J.
7886972 Simpson, Trooper M.	552882 Snook, Sergeant S.
317406 Sims, Trooper W.	558638 Sowerby, Lance-Corporal B.*
2022553 Sims, Lance-Corporal P.	7920376 Spashett, Corporal W. H.
5569789 Sims, Trooper A.	14368270 Speifal, Trooper M.
7937057 Simms, Trooper S.*	7926966 Spellman, Trooper G.
552411 Sitch, Corporal C.	317376 Spence, Corporal F.
317134 Skipper, Trooper K.	7903148 Spicer, Trooper G.

*Wounded.   †Prisoner of war.

320826	Spiers, Trooper N.
7934358	Spinney, Trooper J.
317114	Spratt, Trooper S.
7920377	Spurr, Trooper E.
320132	Squires, Lance-Sergeant L.
3974487	Stackpool, Lance-Corporal P.
7905135	Stafford, Trooper G.
7938708	Stafford, Trooper G.
7920378	Stainthorpe, Trooper J.
317530	Stanford, Lance-Corporal C.
317478	Staveley, Sergeant S. W.*
14380868	Staveley, Trooper R.
7920379	Stead, Trooper C.
14312212	Steel, Trooper J.
7903145	Steer, Trooper L.
310854	Stephenson, Trooper C.
329476	Stephenson, Trooper F.
551960	Stephenson, Corporal T.
3170844	Stephenson, Trooper A.
316100	Stevens, Lance-Corporal H.
317473	Stevens, Trooper J.
329848	Stevens, Corporal H.
7893617	Stevens, Trooper G.
7947770	Stevens, Trooper J.
7919168	Stevenson, Trooper W.
7916511	St. Ledger, Trooper B.
317441	Stocks, Sergeant F.
319124	Stokes, W.O.II (Q.M.S./T.) B. H.
6298741	Stokes, Trooper N.
6550123	Storr, Trooper H. S.
7909865	Storr, Trooper L.
14340156	Stott, Trooper R. A.
318836	Straker, Lance-Corporal L.
7916352	Stratton, Lance-Corporal W.
320717	Street, Lance-Corporal J.
14520641	Streeton, Trooper D.
320666	Stringer, Trooper A. J.
5573049	Such, Trooper E.
7885966	Sumnall, Corporal T.
320116	Sumner, Corporal R.
7920380	Sutcliffe, Trooper H. G.
317330	Sutton, Sergeant C.
7901636	Sutton, Trooper T.
7904078	Sutton, Corporal E.
14392518	Sutton, Trooper C.
321404	Swain, Lance-Sergeant F. M.*
5382044	Swain, Sergeant J.*
316918	Swan, Corporal G. A.*
7914803	Swan, Lance-Corporal J. J.
319550	Sweeney, Trooper R.
550491	Sykes, Corporal S.
14367724	Sykes, Trooper S.
310336	Sylvester, W.O.II (Q.M.S./T.) A.
7880500	Symes, Lance-Corporal B.
14368279	Symonds, Trooper T.
319658	Tate, Trooper J.

7934155	Tate, Trooper T. W.
322393	Tattersall, Trooper J.
317548	Taylor, Trooper B.
318808	Taylor, Lance-Sergeant E.
319743	Taylor, Lance-Corporal G.*
6140545	Taylor, Trooper G.
7899519	Taylor, Trooper P. H.*
7899925	Taylor, Trooper J.*
7901448	Taylor, Corporal M.
7920381	Taylor, Trooper H. E. D.
7934805	Taylor, Trooper T.
7937616	Taylor, Trooper P.
7940833	Taylor, Trooper F.
14524825	Taylor, Trooper A.
317363	Teate, Sergeant R.*
14396173	Telcher, Trooper G.
7916083	Thatcher, Trooper E.
319240	Theobald, Lance-Corporal G.
7917813	Theobald, Trooper E.
5113251	Thickness, Trooper R.
317150	Thomas, Lance-Corporal D.
317551	Thomas, S.Q.M.S. F.
320691	Thomas, Trooper K. R.
7902457	Thomas, Sergeant H. G., M.M.*
7914657	Thomas, Trooper E.
14342478	Thomas, Trooper J.
7937067	Thomas, Trooper C.
7937838	Thomas, Trooper F.
14342478	Thomas, Trooper J.
7893074	Thomasson, Trooper W.*
321052	Thompson, Lance-Corporal A.
550787	Thompson, Trooper.
551749	Thompson, Corporal A.
552362	Thompson, Trooper H.
3714842	Thompson, Trooper A.
7901547	Thompson, Lance-Corporal F.
315442	Thomson, Trooper J.
316229	Thomson, Trooper J.
316229	Thomson, Sergeant S.
2750661	Thomson, Trooper W.
7914398	Thornton, Trooper S.*
551687	Thursfield, Trooper.
316439	Thurston, Trooper A.
317121	Thurston, Trooper J.
7047276	Till, Trooper G.
324424	Tipper, Trooper G.
316881	Tombs, Trooper E.
321584	Tomlinson, Trooper N.
317440	Toone, Sergeant G. W.*
14230386	Towler, Trooper H.
319019	Townsend, Trooper R.
317253	Trayte, Trooper J.
317253	Treacy, Trooper R.
316503	Trenfield, Sergeant P.
320885	Tron, Trooper J. L.
3600812	Tuckerman, Trooper A.

*Wounded. †Prisoner of war.

317342	Tuczek, W./Sergeant A.
7925628	Tudor, Trooper W. J.
5182837	Turk, Corporal S.
320178	Turnbull, Trooper T.
317548	Tyler, Corporal B.
317254	Tyson, Trooper A.
7914131	Tyson, Trooper J.
7920382	Ullyart, Lance-Corporal F. J.
317320	Underwood, Lance-Corporal R.
7947736	Upton, Trooper R. N.
7899604	Vale, Lance-Corporal L.*
7938876	Vale, Trooper G.†
320218	Vallance, Trooper D.
7893616	Varney, Lance-Corporal E.
7913110	Vaughan, Trooper H.*
320011	Velvick, Trooper R.
310334	Vickers, Q.M.S./Cook E.
7927717	Vickers, Trooper G.
14732538	Vince, Trooper S.
320338	Virgo, Trooper R.
7941093	Waddell, Lance-Corporal J. W.
4534998	Waddington, Corporal T.
7920383	Wade, Trooper C.
7931143	Wade, Trooper F.
552008	Wadsworth, Sergeant C.
320129	Wager, Trooper M.
7920384	Waites, Lance-Corporal C. M.
7931217	Wakely, Trooper R.
4808945	Wakenshaw, Trooper J.
7882445	Wales, Corporal L.
4076312	Walker, Lance-Corporal V.*
4621105	Walker, Lance-Corporal W.
3455228	Walker, Trooper L.
3715535	Walker, Trooper J.
14352415	Walker, Trooper S.
7920659	Wall, Trooper F. E.
320012	Walsh, Trooper C.
7956884	Warburton, Trooper H.
319077	Ward, Lance-Corporal G.
4862032	Ward, Lance-Sergeant J.
7920385	Ward, Trooper K.
14505592	Ward, Trooper A.
14521487	Ward, Trooper, A.
14418078	Warr, Trooper R.
5931776	Warren, Trooper C.
789238	Warren, Trooper E.
7945257	Warren, Trooper D. G.
3962054	Watkins, Corporal W. H.*
2057524	Watson, Trooper G.
7907400	Watson, Trooper T.
7945512	Watson, Trooper H. C.
14517034	Watson, Trooper D.
317643	Watters, Trooper L.
7937072	Watts, Trooper R.
7920386	Waudby, Staff-Sergeant E.
320747	Webb, Boy R.

536522	Webb, W.O.I (R.S.M.) R.
7947021	Webster, Trooper A. H.
14669970	Webster, Trooper A.
317559	Wedgewood, Trooper F.
317405	Welham, Sergeant L. G., M.M.
7912292	Wellington, Trooper F.*
314644	Wells, Trooper A.
319005	Wells, Trooper F.
550754	Wells, Corporal J.
5349325	Wells, Trooper R.
7952857	Wellspring, Trooper W.
320012	Welsh, Trooper C.
321769	Welsh, Trooper A.*
550444	Wessell, Lance-Corporal E.*
320190	Westerby, Trooper M.
7920388	Wheelan, Trooper M. A.
310880	Wheeler, Trooper F.
7920387	Wheen, Trooper H.*
6144233	Whelan, Trooper J.
320192	Whetstone, Trooper A.
316321	White, Trooper.
551684	White, Trooper H.
5382255	White, Trooper H.
7914812	White, Trooper A.*
7920389	Whiteley, Trooper H.
3449850	Whitely, Trooper R.
7920662	Whitfield, Trooper H.
7963042	Whittaker, Trooper R.
548814	Whittall, Corporal W.
2821285	Wibberley, Trooper J.
321559	Widdows, Trooper G.
3853578	Wiggans, S.Q.M.S. A.
7903976	Wiglesworth, Lance-Corporal S. A.*
5508369	Wilcox, Trooper F.
7901643	Wilcox, Trooper W.
7910059	Wild, Trooper D.
3451273	Wilde, Trooper J. D.*
553689	Wilding, Trooper E.
7931146	Wildman, Trooper H. C.*
319131	Wiley, Trooper H.
551971	Wilkes, Sergeant J.
7899915	Wilkes, Trooper E.
3447916	Wilkinson, Trooper A.*
7907301	Willard, Trooper K.
7920390	Willcox, Trooper J. T.
4437708	Willett, Sergeant R.
310686	Williams, S.Q.M.S. G.
316399	Williams, W.O.II (R.Q.M.S.) F.
553825	Williams, Trooper J.
3660146	Williams, Corporal R.†
3771520	Williams, Trooper C.
7901275	Williams, Lance-Corporal V.
7913980	Williams, Lance-Corporal L.
7914813	Williams, Trooper V.
7919756	Williams, Corporal J. H.
7927792	Williams, Trooper F.

*Wounded.   †Prisoner of war.

7932542 Williams, Trooper H. H.*
7941435 Williams, Trooper F. S.
7952161 Williams, Trooper T. D. O.*
14289871 Williams, Trooper H. H.*
320550 Williamson, Boy P.
5045180 Williamson, Corporal F.
7914353 Williamson, Sergeant G. M.
316442 Wilmot, Lance-Corporal C.
5617473 Wilmot, Corporal E.
3061548 Wilson, Lance-Corporal R.
7020663 Wilson, Trooper B.
7902284 Wilson, Lance-Corporal R. P.*
7920391 Wilson, Trooper J. P.
7902284 Wilson, Trooper R.*
7936009 Wilson, Trooper A.*
14290777 Wilson, Trooper S. A.*
555617 Wilton, Trooper R.
551568 Wiltshire, Trooper K.
7912901 Winch, Lance-Sergeant E. J.
320702 Winter, Trooper T.
7893829 Winter, Lance-Corporal W.
4925577 Wisbey, Trooper D.
319650 Witt, Trooper R.
7912292 Wollington, Trooper F. W.*
319746 Wood, Trooper B.
548786 Wood, Corporal L.
552347 Wood, Corporal F.
7920392 Wood, Sergeant W. J.

7927131 Wood, Trooper A. T.
14389423 Wood, Lance-Corporal A.
317563 Woodcock, Corporal L.
7920393 Woodcock, Trooper G.*
321729 Woodford, Lance-Corporal C.
548336 Woodhouse, S.Q.M.S. A.
14520677 Wooding, Trooper L.
7870527 Woods, W.O.II (Q.M.S./M.) L.
14505592 Woodward, Trooper D.*
320736 Wooley, Corporal T.
7887073 Wooller, Trooper K.*
320736 Woolley, Trooper T.
1563838 Woolrich, Trooper F.
317126 Worswick, Sergeant E.
6722939 Worth, Lance-Sergeant G.
320157 Wortley, Trooper A.
7924818 Wrigglesworth, Lance-Corporal J.
315920 Wright, Sergeant H.
404103 Wright, Trooper R.
7918809 Wright, Trooper C.
7952056 Wright, Trooper H.
317509 Yates, Lance-Corporal.
7899442 Yates, Trooper W. H.*
7901292 Yeaman, Lance-Corporal T. C.*
320769 Young, Corporal V. G.*
552518 Young, Trooper A.
7937770 Young, Trooper P.
7958393 Zinzan, Trooper C.

*Wounded.   †Prisoner of war.

SOME OFFICERS AND OTHER RANKS OF THE REGIMENT WHO SERVED AWAY

Name and Rank.	*Service.*
Atkins, Sergeant L. J. ..	5th (Notts) Bn. Home Guard from June, 1940, to December, 1944.
Bates, F. W. (civilian) ..	No. 4 Maintenance Unit, R.A.F., Ruislip, for duration of war.
Bennett, Lieutenant-Colonel Sir Wilfred, Bt., T.D.	June, 1940, Major, Notts Yeomanry; to April, 1941, with H.Q., 1st Cavalry Division, as Major (D.A.A.G.), April to August, at Staff College, Haifa, then until September, 1942, at G.H.Q., Middle East, as Major (D.A.A.G.), and Lieutenant-Colonel (A.A.G.). September, 1942, to September, 1943, Lieutenant-Colonel (A.A.G.), G.H.Q., Persia and Iraq Force, until March, 1946, Lieutenant-Colonel (A.A.G.), War Office, when invalided out.
Bexx, Lieutenant J. C. ..	1st Bn. The Somerset Light Infantry, Home Guard, for duration of war.
Bradshaw, R.S.M. G. ..	From 1937 until end of war with Leicestershire Yeomanry (153rd Field Regiment, R.A., T.A.).
Carter, Private H.	29th City of London Home Guard from June, 1940, to March, 1944, including full-time employment as armed guard to H.M. Mails between War Office, Admiralty and G.P.O.
Chrystie, W. R.	Civil guard at British Embassy, Paris, from 1931. Remained at his post during German occupation and still serving at end of war.
Clark, Trooper T. J. E. Lance-Corporal ..	57th H.T.R., R.A.C., June, 1940, to November. 1st Northamptonshire Yeomanry from November, 1940, to May, 1942, R.A.C. Depot, Abbassia, to June, 1942; 2nd Royal Gloucestershire Hussars until January, 1943; Royal Wiltshire Yeomanry until September, 1944, when he rejoined 9th Lancers.
Collins, J.	Field Security Police, Tilbury. Was with City Police and injured in air raid.
Corbett, Corporal W. F.	46th County of London Home Guard from 1940 to 1941, then Air Raid Warden Service until end of war.
Cullen, Trooper P. G. ..	15th/19th King's Royal Hussars from June, 1940, to June, 1943. 4th Maritime R.A. until 1946.
Deedman, S.Q.M.S. E. H., M.M.	R.M.C., Sandhurst, Armoured Wing, from outbreak of war to January, 1941.
S.S.M.	"B" Squadron, R.M.C., until 1942, then on staff. On two occasions Acting R.S.M. of College. Invalided out in 1944, after having assisted in forming Headquarters Squadron.
Dobson, Orderly Room Sergeant J. ...	Ayrshire Yeomanry from 1939 until unit converted to Field Artillery in March, 1940, when transferred to R.A.
Sergeant-Clerk	A.A., London, Plymouth and South Wales until 1943.
Staff-Sergeant (Chief Clerk)	58th A.A. Brigade, Orkney and Shetland Defences, until 1945, then with 1st A.A. Fort Regiment.
Chief Clerk	28th A.A. Brigade, Chatham, until 1946.

334

Name and Rank.	*Service.*
Donovan, Police Constable J. J.	Air Ministry Police from 1940 to 1949.
Ducker, Lance-Corporal C. W.	54th Light Armoured Training Regiment, then 2nd Light Armoured Reconnaissance Brigade in 1940. Wounded in May and prisoner of war for five years. On return transferred to R.A.S.C. and discharged unfit.
Eastwick, Private A. ..	No. 3 General Hospital, R.A.M.C., with B.E.F. in France until June, 1940.
Corporal ..	No. 36 (West African) General Hospital, Nigeria, until September, 1943, then Military Hospital, Tolgarth, Wales, until 1944.
Sergeant	No. 3 Indian Base General Hospital, Poona, until June, 1945.
Edmonds, Signalman O.	44th Division, T.A., Royal Signals, from 1934 to 1941.
Emms, Corporal W. S. ..	3rd Divisional Supply Column until May, 1940, then No. 2 Ambulance Car Company until June, when evacuated from France.
Sergeant	First Army in January, 1941, to North Africa and took part in Italy landings.
Foord, Signalman W. C.	Post Office Home Guard, then Royal Corps of Signals from 1942 to 1946.
Furlong, Lieutenant-Commander (A) F. C., R.N.	Served with 9th Lancers before war. With Fleet Air Arm during war until killed 13th September, 1944.
Graham, Major A. D., M.C.	August, 1939, to September, 1940, 7th A.A. Division as Major (D.A.Q.M.G.); then "A" Battery, R.A. Training until February, 1941. Until February, 1943, Pioneer Corps (Training), then with "Pluto" (oil pipe-line project) as Major-in-command until May, 1944. May, 1944, until December with A.M.G.O.T. in Italy. Invalided out March, 1945.
Hawker, Private W. H.	Fire-fighting Squad, Central Ordnance Depot, Greenford, Mdx, until 1941, then 16th Bn. Middlesex Home Guard until disbandment.
Hodges, Corporal J. W.	Pioneer Corps, Ordnance Depot, Donnington, and various prisoner-of-war camps.
Holden, Sergeant T. ..	Warwickshire Yeomanry as Trooper in 1939. Promoted in 1941 until reached rank of Sergeant in same unit.
Holloway, Corporal W. S.	24th Bn. Hampshire Regiment Home Guard from 1940 to 1944.
Hopper, W.O.II (Chief Clerk) R. G., M.B.E.	Posted from 9th Lancers to H.Q., 29th Armoured Brigade, in 1940; to H.Q., No. 1 Army Group, in 1941.
W.O.I (Chief Clerk)	H.Q., 33rd Armoured Brigade, in 1942, until 1945, when he joined H.Q., 22nd Armoured Brigade. Discharged in 1946 after twenty-one years' service.
Judd, Sergeant E. A.	Transferred from 9th Lancers to Army Catering Corps and promoted Sergeant-Cook with 30th Workshop Control Unit, R.E.M.E., until discharged in Germany, September, 1945.
Keayes, R. W. ..	Posted to 122nd and 127th L.A.A. Batteries, R.A., as Lieutenant, October, 1940, to April, 1942. 1943 and 1946 Lieutenant (Special Branch), R.N.V.R., with Nore Command.

Name and Rank.	*Service.*
Kingstone, Brigadier J. J., C.B.E., D.S.O., M.C. ..	August, 1939, to May, 1941, in command of 4th Cavalry Brigade. May to July, 1941, in command of "Kincol," Iraq Rebellion and in Syria. June, 1942, to January, 1943, Colonel, Stirling Area, then with Leicester Sub-Area until March, 1944. March, 1944, to July, 1945, Senior Civil Affairs Officer and Chief Military Government Officer with H.Q., I Corps.
Little, Lieutenant-Colonel M. A. A. ...	Transferred to Royal Horse Guards (Blues) June, 1935. Killed in action 5th October, 1944, when Second-in-Command of 44th Reconnaissance Regiment.
Mann, Sergeant J. J.	44th Bn. London Home Guard from 1940 to 1944.
Monk, S.Q.M.S. H.	Posted to Sandhurst as Sergeant and later S.Q.M.S. (Tech.), September, 1939, to March, 1944. R.A.C. Depot, Catterick, March, 1944. In May, 1944, posted to Tilbury as S.Q.M.S. for ship's duties, ferrying troops to Egypt. Invalided, after being mined at sea, March, 1945.
Moore, Trooper T.	52nd Heavy Training Regiment from January to June, 1941, then posted to 9th Lancers.
Mountain, Lieutenant-Colonel Sir B. E. S., Bt. ..	1939 to 1940 III Corps (France) as Captain. Transferred May as Major (Lieutenant-Colonel) to Southern Command G.H.Q. until 1944. Promoted Lieutenant-Colonel and posted to S.H.A.E.F., France, 1944.
Oliver, A.C.2 F. (and Flight Sergeant)	R.A.F., Hornchurch, from 1939 until 1940.
Pilot Officer ..	R.A.F., Tangmere, until 1941.
Flight Lieutenant ..	No. 221 Group, R.A.F., Ceylon.
Squadron Leader ..	No. 224 Group, R.A.F., Burma, until 1943.
Officer Commanding	R.A.F. Station, Great Bentley, until 1945.
Pannells, Lieutenant C.	44th Bn. London Home Guard from 1940 until 1944.
Powell, Trooper I.	3rd Cavalry Training Regiment from 1940 to February, 1941, then 3rd Training Regiment, R.A.C., to August, 1941. With 9th Lancers until March, 1945.
Sergeant-Instructor	In March, 1945, to R.A. Education Corps until demobilization.
Pritchard, G.	Home Guard from 1940 to 1941.
Rawson, Captain F. A.	July to November, 1941, Officer Cadet, 164th O.C.T.U.; then posted as Lieutenant to Sherwood Foresters, 8th Battalion, until February, 1942, when he became Camp Commandant in command of Defence Platoon at H.Q., 148th Independent Brigade Group, until July, 1942. Until May, 1943, posted to 148th Pre-O.C.T.U. Training Centre. June, 1943, to January, 1944, posted to R.A.S.C., 626th Motor Boat Company, Operations Training Centre, 1944 and 1945, attached to Intelligence Corps and served at War Office, G.H.Q., India, H.Q. XV Indian Corps, Burma, "B" Force, Burma, H.Q., Advanced H.Q., ALFSEA, H.Q., Eastern Command, India (Captain). Demobilized January, 1946.
Richardson, J., M.C.	Senior Warden, Civil Defence Service, for duration of war.
Robinson, W./Sergeant W. A. (and W./W.O.II)	Transferred to Corps of Royal Military Police from 9th Lancers in 1943 and posted to No. 605 Squadron until end of war.

Name and Rank.	*Service.*
Scattergood, Corporal E.	Transferred from 9th Lancers to Corps of Royal Military Police in 1943 and posted to Base Depot.
W.S./Sergeant, W.S./W.O.II and W.S./W.O.I	No. 605 Squadron until end of war. Re-engaged in 1947 to complete twenty-two years' service.
Spickett, ex-S.S.M. J. A.	4th Cavalry Training Regiment in 1939; in July, 1940, attached to Ministry of Labour Training Centre for Administrative Training. In September formed new unit and posted to permanent staff of Hackney Technical Training Group.
Stedman, Q.M.S. H. G.	3rd Horse Cavalry Training Regiment from 1939 to 1941.
Captain and Adjutant	Commissioned in 1941 and attached to Special Training School No. 52 until August, 1945.
Symes, Sapper C. ..	Royal Engineers Post Office Reserve from 1942 to 1945.
Timms, Corporal A. J. ..	5th Bn. London Home Guard (Regent's Park H.Q. Company) from 1940 to 1945.
Todd, Brigadier C. H. N., M.C.	1939 to 1942 in command of the Greys, Palestine and Syria. February to June, 1942, Second-in-Command, 2nd Armoured Brigade, until February, 1943. Commandant, F.V.S., India, until February, 1944. In command of 50th Tank Brigade, Assam and Burma, until July, 1945.
Ward, Trooper G.	2nd Armoured Brigade H.Q. as batman to Major J. H. M. D. Scott in 1941; to H.Q., 1st Armoured Division, as batman to General Briggs in 1942. Rejoined 9th Lancers in 1943.
Warr, Private R. J.	3rd Somerset Home Guard from 1941 to 1943.
Trooper ..	55th Training Regiment, R.A.C., until 1944, when he rejoined 9th Lancers.

MADAGASCAR

SPECIAL SERVICE SQUADRON

TOWARDS the end of July, when the Regiment was under canvas at Tidworth, the 2nd Armoured Brigade was asked to form a composite squadron of Tetrarch tanks.

Major D. V. Asquith, of the Queen's Bays, was appointed Squadron Leader with, under him as Second-in-Command, Captain Peter Llewellyn Palmer, of the 10th Hussars, and Captain W. K. C. Pulteney, of the 9th Lancers, as Rear Link Captain. The Squadron was made up more or less equally by the three regiments and contained twelve tanks (three tanks in H.Q. Troop and three fighting troops of three tanks each). Two of the troops were supplied by the 9th Lancers, one from "B" Squadron commanded by Lieutenant B. M. M. Carlisle, and another from "C" Squadron commanded by Lieutenant W. R. Astles, while the third troop, which came from the 10th Hussars, was commanded by Lieutenant B. H. Malyon.

This small force assembled at Ogbourne St. George under the name of " 'C' Special Service Squadron" and there was much speculation as to its role and destiny. The 10th Hussars played host and spared no effort to complete its equipment as a front-line unit, a task which was not an easy one in England in the summer of 1941.

Early in August the Squadron was ordered to Scotland, where half of it embarked on various ships to take part in an amphibious exercise. This exercise, which was the first of its kind to take place in the war, consisted of landing an infantry brigade group on the coast near Scapa Flow. Immediately afterwards Lieutenant Malyon's and Lieutenant Astles's troops were withdrawn and shipped to Freetown, where they remained for six months.

Meanwhile the role of the Squadron was becoming clear. It would be used as armoured support for a specially trained infantry brigade in a landing on some coast held by the enemy. But there was naturally still much speculation as to where the landing would take place and, as exercise succeeded exercise during the autumn and winter of 1941, the tension gradually mounted.

Most training was done with the 1st Guards Brigade and the Squadron enjoyed working with such fine troops and good friends, but early in 1942 it moved at short notice to Melrose, where for two months it was on its own except for a short attachment of Lieutenant Carlisle's troop to the 1st Battalion Royal Marines.

In the middle of March, 1942, the Squadron was to take part in another big combined operations exercise with the 29th Independent Infantry Brigade, which contained the 1st Battalion The Royal Scots Fusiliers, 2nd Battalion The Royal Welch Fusiliers, 2nd Battalion The East Lancashire Regiment and 1st Battalion The South Lancashire Regiment, with a special battery of the Royal Horse Artillery attached. This exercise was, however, cancelled and at the same time the glad news was received that the Freetown party was returning at any moment. On the 18th of March Lieutenant Malyon and his two troops reappeared and for the first time since its formation the Squadron was together again. This state of affairs lasted for only twenty-four hours, however, for orders had already been received for the embarkation of half the Squadron for another exercise. This time there was a feeling that, at last, this might be the real thing.

On the 19th of March Lieutenant Carlisle's and Lieutenant Astles's troops were loaded on to the train at Melrose and dispatched to Glasgow. They felt sure they were going to be away for some time, but they little realized that for most of them it would be for the rest of the war. At Glasgow the six tanks were loaded into three different ships and it was learned that the party was to come under command of Major J. E. S. Simon (Royal Tank Regiment), of "B" Special Service Squadron. He already had with him six Valentine tanks divided into two troops (three tanks under Lieutenant Heywood [Royal Tank Regiment], two tanks under Lieutenant Whitaker [Royal Tank Regiment], whilst the remaining tank was the Squadron Leader's). The "C" half-squadron was similarly organized. Captain Peter Llewellyn Palmer became Second-in-Command of the Squadron, Lieutenant Carlisle had his troop of three tanks, and Lieutenant Astles had the remaining two tanks. Two Tetrarch and two Valentine tanks were embarked in each of the ships *Keren Karanja* and *Winchester Castle*, and the convoy sailed from the Clyde for an unknown destination on the 23rd of March.

The trip was a peaceful one. The main subject of conversation was the fate of the Squadron, the "cover" story that it was due to take part in the capture of Rangoon gaining little credence because the force seemed to be too small. On the 22nd of April the convoy reached Durban, where five busy days were spent getting the tanks and wireless into good order. It was at Durban that the Squadron received its orders and was issued with maps.

In short, the orders were that the 29th Independent Brigade, with No. 5 Commando and supporting arms, was to land at Courier Bay on the north corner of the island of Madagascar and to seize the important French naval base of Diego Suarez and the town of Antisarane. Intelligence as to the number of French forces which might or might not oppose the landing and the subsequent operations was scanty, and the maps turned out to be old and inaccurate. Fortunately the 17th Infantry Brigade (part of the 5th Division, which was on its way to India) had been collected at Freetown and formed the reserve which was to be landed in case of strong opposition. There was little information about the terrain through which the force would have to operate and there was none about the likely defended localities except for the coastal gun emplacements.

The naval force supporting the landing was quite considerable and was commanded by Rear-Admiral Syfret, flying his flag in the battleship *Ramillies*. Under his command were the aircraft carriers *Illustrious* and *Indomitable*, the cruisers *Devonshire* and *Gambia*, two light cruisers and various destroyers and corvettes. On board the large troopships carrying the 29th Infantry Brigade were infantry and tank landing craft which would be used for the assault.

The first landing, which was timed to take place at two hours before dawn on the 5th of May, was to be carried out by No. 5 Commando, who had the all-important task of capturing the coastal gun positions commanding the entrance to Courier Bay. But, before this, the convoy had to negotiate a narrow, rocky channel leading to the ships' anchoring positions about six miles from the shore. In the middle of this channel was a submerged rock, the successful evasion of which depended largely on a British agent working from the island whose task it was to mark this hazard with a light. As well, from the naval point of view, the height and strength of the tide and the position of the moon were important factors which had to be taken into consideration by the planning staff in the Admiralty, six thousand miles away, some months before the operation actually took place. That the ships reached their anchorages without mishap reflects great credit on those responsible for the plan.

Preceded by minesweepers and corvettes, the convoy sailed into Courier Bay in line ahead at midnight on the 5th of May. To the relief of the anxious watchers on the decks of the assault ships the all-important light marking the submerged rock could be seen twinkling ahead. Shortly after the convoy had anchored, No. 5 Commando embarked in their assault craft and made off for their beach to capture the coast defence guns. At regular intervals after this the remaining infantry battalions left for their respective beaches. At about 5 a.m., as dawn was breaking, the heartening news was received that all the guns had been captured and that all troops were ashore without incident except for a brush with some French detachments not far inland. It was learned later that the

Commandos had reached their objectives just in time; the French gunners did not man their guns at night, as they did not believe it was possible for any invaders to navigate the channel in the dark; the Commandos had arrived just as the French were marching up to the guns.

The tanks were disembarked as soon as landing craft became available and by 10 a.m. all twelve tanks of the composite Squadron were ashore. Major Simon and two other tanks, one commanded by Lieutenant Astles and the other by Lieutenant Whitaker, had been sent forward to help the infantry, and as soon as Lieutenant Carlisle's troop was assembled on the beach he was sent forward to join up with the leading party. Captain Llewellyn Palmer remained behind to assemble the rest of the Squadron and bring them on when he could.

Information about the French forces was meagre and contradictory. On the beaches there had been one or two short, sharp actions with native troops, but they had soon surrendered. But opposition was reported to be growing inland and the 1st Battalion The Royal Welch Fusiliers, who were leading the advance, were said to be pinned down by machine-gun fire from a ridge through which ran the only road towards Diego Suarez, about twelve miles away. When the tanks reached this ridge they were met by a hail of machine-gun fire, but after about half an hour's bombardment this died down. The Brigade Commander then ordered the tanks to advance to Antisarane (a town, according to their maps, about three miles farther on). It was thought that the French had no weapon capable of stopping a Valentine tank, so the advance party was made up of two Valentines from "B" Special Service Squadron and three Tetrarchs from "C" Special Service Squadron, commanded by Lieutenant Carlisle. Lieutenant Astles acted as Troop Sergeant, as Sergeant Dick was bogged down in a river farther back.

After about four miles of fast going on a good but hilly road they entered a flat plain which it was thought would surely lead into the town. The Valentine troop was about four hundred yards in front of the Tetrarchs when guns of a heavier calibre began firing from the left flank. Lieutenant Carlisle could see the Valentines halted farther down the road with their guns traversed to the left, and suddenly a platoon of Senegalese ran across the road into some huts. All guns immediately opened up. Corporal Watkins's tank was seen to catch fire, and then as Lieutenant Carlisle was moving off the road to the right his tank was hit and set on fire. It was now apparent that the French had something more than machine guns with which to hit back. When the crews of the disabled tanks collected together in some long grass at the side of the road they took stock of the position. From the two Valentines two men had been killed and one severely wounded; in the leading Tetrarch Corporal Watkins, the commander, and his gunner, Lance-Corporal Bond, had been killed, and the driver, Lance-Corporal Rickerby, severely wounded; and in Lieutenant Carlisle's tank Lance-Corporal Catt, the driver, was severely wounded and Corporal Hall, the gunner, had been hit in the leg. It was clear that they had run into a strong defensive position and that the defenders had held their fire until four tanks were in the trap. Lieutenant Astles had halted his tank in some dead ground farther back and now crawled up on hands and knees to see if he could help. Major Simon sent him back to Brigade Headquarters to report on the situation. On the way he had a brush with two lorry loads of coloured troops who were infiltrating by another road, and in this affray Corporal Gourlay, his gunner, particularly distinguished himself.

Left behind were four combatant and three wounded men. By using their automatics judiciously Major Simon, Lieutenant Carlisle, Lieutenant Whitaker and Sergeant Grime (Royal Tank Regiment), who later received the D.C.M. for his part in this stand, were able to keep the patrols off for three and a half hours until their ammunition was exhausted and they were overrun. All the time they were under heavy fire from guns of all calibres. They lay concealed in high grass and were stalked by Senegalese, who revealed their presence by low jabberings as they came to within twenty yards of the party's position.

At the end Lieutenant Whitaker was killed in a hand-to-hand fight with a Senegalese, and it was only the intervention of a fine-spirited French officer which saved the rest of them from a similar fate. He intervened and the small party was disarmed and taken prisoner.

Farther back on the Col de Bon Nouvel, the ridge over which the leading tanks had already passed, the opposition had strengthened and the infantry had a hard task getting over, only to find on the other side that they came under sustained artillery fire from hidden batteries. Captain Llewellyn Palmer was ordered to try to spot these guns; his tank was hit and in trying to carry his wounded crew to safety he was killed. For his part in this action he was awarded a posthumous Military Cross.

At the conclusion of this battle for Diego Suarez, which had lasted for nearly forty-eight hours, the composite Tank Squadron could muster crews for only three out of the original twelve tanks. Of the officers and other ranks from the 9th Lancers who took part, the following were casualties:

Killed.—Corporal W. Watkins and Lance-Corporal W. Bond.

Died of Wounds.—Lance-Corporal A. Rickerby.

Wounded.—Sergeant T. Dick, Corporal M. Hall and Lance-Corporal L. Catt.

The small party of survivors from the first action were imprisoned in the military barracks in Antisarane, where they were well treated. Their own forces, however, began to shell and bomb the town and the barracks were for the next thirty-six hours the chief objective.

The defensive position which the first party of tanks had run up against and about which there had been no previous information was later found to be a defensive line joining two heavily defended forts and built by General Joffre in 1909 when he was fortress commander of Diego Suarez. Later it held firm against two full-scale brigade attacks, so it was not surprising that the tanks had failed to pass through.

When the 29th Brigade and, later, the 17th Brigade had both failed to get through the "Joffre Line," Major-General Sturges, commanding the military operations, asked the Captain of H.M.S. *Ramillies* to lend him forty Royal Marines. They sailed in H.M.S. *Anthony* round Cape Amber (at the northern tip of the island) and entered at full speed and at night the narrow and strongly defended entrance of Diego Suarez Bay. Under heavy bombardment by coastal defence guns, H.M.S. *Anthony* steamed gallantly into the naval docks. The Royal Marines rushed ashore, throwing grenades and firing tommy-guns into the air. They made first for the naval barracks, where four hundred officers and men surrendered to them, believing them to be part of a large force attacking from the rear. Their next objective was the military barracks, where they captured the garrison and released the prisoners of "B" and "C" Special Service Squadrons. This sudden assault on the town saved the day. Diego Suarez laid down its arms and in the early morning of the 7th of May our forces poured through the "Joffre Line."

Of the rest of the campaign in Madagascar there is little to be said, for, although it took another six months before the island surrendered, Diego Suarez was the only pitched battle. The troops were prepared to fight an arduous campaign over the hilly, swampy and tropical terrain of the island that measures a thousand miles from north to south and is over four hundred miles across at its widest point. They did two more landings at Majunga on the African side and at Tamatave on the Indian Ocean side, but there was little further opposition. The French retreated on Tananarive, the capital in the centre of the island, blowing bridges and laying occasional ambushes, and when this town was captured they retreated farther south, finally to surrender on the 6th of November.

More unpleasant than the shells and the bullets were the mosquitoes of Madagascar and the many and varied tropical diseases which attacked the troops and eventually compelled the whole of the 29th Independent Brigade and its supporting arms to retire for a period of rest and recuperation in South Africa.

WIRELESS SYSTEM IN AN ARMOURED REGIMENT

This appendix has been included so that those who are not familiar with the way the wireless was organized in the Regiment can understand more easily some of the references to wireless in the History

During the early part of the war the Regiment was equipped with two types of wireless set, the No. 9 and No. 11. These were quite satisfactory in many ways, but gave only one facility: that of transmitting on one frequency. No provision was made for a system of internal communication within the tank which could be worked through the wireless set.

A month or so before the Regiment sailed to Egypt in 1941 a new set was issued, the No. 19. This proved to be the mainstay of our communication system throughout the war. It consisted of three units within one box. The first was the "A" Set, which one could pre-set on any two different frequencies within a wide range, and by turning three dials it was possible to change from one to another at will. It had a normal range of ten miles on speech, but by using Morse and special aerials it was possible to communicate at far greater distances. The second part was the I.C., or internal communication system. This enabled the commander and his crew to talk to each other. The third part was the "B" Set, which worked on a very high frequency and had only a very short range. It was used for two purposes: firstly, so that two tanks whose "A" Sets were working on different frequencies could talk to each other and, secondly, so that a troop leader could talk to his other tank commanders without monopolizing the "A" Set. The commander and wireless operator in each tank had a control box by which they could switch to any one of the three facilities that the set provided.

Each squadron had a separate frequency, and all the tanks except one in the squadron were tuned in to that frequency. This last tank was known as the squadron "rear link." Its set was tuned in to the regimental frequency through which the Colonel issued his orders to squadrons and troops of other arms who were working with the Regiment.

The officer manning the rear-link set passed the Colonel's orders to his squadron leader on his "B" Set; similarly, information was passed in this way to the Colonel. If the Colonel wanted to talk to a squadron leader he ordered the rear-link officer to tell the squadron leader to "flick" to the regimental frequency. This took a few seconds only.

Later on in the war it was found necessary to provide yet another channel of communication, this time to the infantry with whom the Regiment was working. A 38 Set was fitted into each tank and by this means the tank commanders could talk to the infantry platoons with whom they were co-operating. Certain tanks on regimental and squadron head-quarters were also fitted with two 19 Sets, so that it was possible to work on yet another wireless "group."

The diagram opposite this page shows all the wireless sets which were normally worked on the regimental and squadron groups. For simplicity only one troop is shown as being equipped with 38 Sets, and no tank is shown with more than one 19 Set.

THE ESSENTIALS OF THE REGIMENTAL WIRELESS LAYOUT

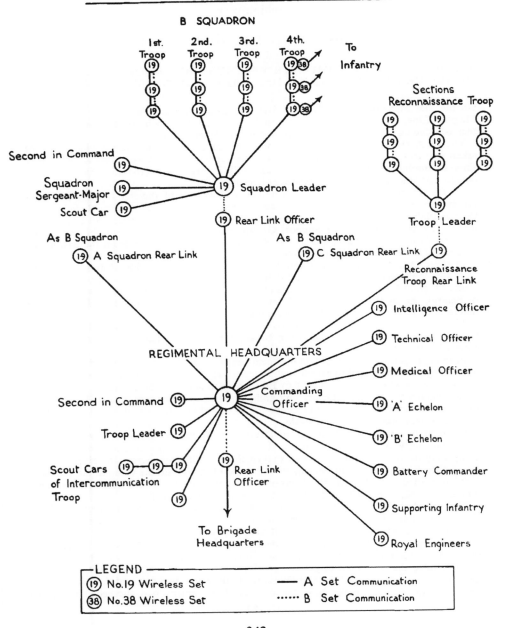

TRIBUTES TO THE 9TH LANCERS

A TRIBUTE TO THE COMPOSITE REGIMENT BY MAJOR-GENERAL H. R. SWINBURN, C.B., O.B.E., G.S.O.1, 51ST (HIGHLAND) DIVISION, FRANCE, 1940

ON the 31st May/1st June, 1940, the 51st (Highland) Division, which had been in the Maginot Line, took over the left divisional sector of the French front, which had been reconstituted on the Somme and was known as the Weygand Line.

The 1st Armoured Division, the only other British formation in France which had not taken part in the Dunkirk withdrawal, had been constantly engaged in active operations since its disembarkation in May and was badly in need of overhaul. It was therefore decided to withdraw it to the workshops at Rouen.

To strengthen the 51st Division a Composite Regiment of the 9th Lancers and 10th Hussars came under command. This force was equipped with such serviceable vehicles as were available and was under the command of Lieutenant-Colonel Peto, 9th Lancers. At first it was located behind the Support Group, which was covering the right rear of the Division from Neufchatel to Forges, to stop any enemy infiltration from the east at the junction of the British and French forces.

In the event, the situation developed very differently. On the 5th of June, when the Germans launched an offensive against the Weygand Line, they broke through the left brigade sector of the Division in the area of St. Valery-sur-Somme (which is two miles west of Belloy), and by 0500 hrs. they had penetrated the shallow forward defended area and had isolated the forward battalion headquarters.

The one reserve battalion in the Division and a squadron of the Composite Regiment were moved forward across the River Bresle, but failed to establish contact with the forward battalions.

In spite of some delay imposed on the enemy advance by the forward defended localities, one enemy party managed to get through to the River Bresle, where it destroyed a troop of anti-tank guns which had been sent to Eu to help to stabilize the situation. This enemy force, which was now behind every unit and formation headquarters of the 51st Division, then turned south towards Beauchamps—a move which directly threatened the vital Divisional crossings of the River Bresle.

Fortunately it struck the detached squadron of the Composite Regiment, which reacted most vigorously, and the enemy received a nasty setback. His movement was not only completely neutralized but he was so shaken that he withdrew across the river into the Foret d'Eu. The success of this engagement proved of immeasurable value to the Division. If it had turned out otherwise the Divisional line could not have been adjusted that night and the next day's operations would have been badly compromised.

The next day, the 6th of June, enemy pressure became general, but, to quote the Divisional War Diary, the danger spot was undoubtedly the left sector, where the enemy was attempting to reinforce his penetration of the previous day.

The Composite Regiment had now moved forward into the Dargnies area, where it was in hull-down positions. As the enemy pressed forward he was engaged by them and was so badly mauled that he failed to get any reinforcements through and lost forty prisoners, apart from other casualties. The 51st Division withdrew that night behind the River Bresle. This withdrawal could never have taken place if the enemy had succeeded in getting through to his detachment in the Foret d'Eu. His failure to do so was entirely due to the offensive-defensive action of the Composite Regiment.

With the withdrawal across the River Bresle the active work of the Composite Regiment with the 51st Division was done, and on the 8th of June it was dispatched to rejoin its own formation in the Rouen area.

To appreciate to the full the value of the vigorous offensive spirit shown throughout by the Composite Regiment—a spirit which was in the highest Cavalry tradition—it must be remembered that at this date the last British troops had left Dunkirk and that an atmosphere of dazed depression prevailed throughout France. This, combined with the streams of refugees, than which no sight in war is more pathetic, was by no means conducive to the maintenance of high morale. The 51st Division, although its eventual fate was capitulation, acknowledged a deep debt to these fine Cavalry regiments who rendered such sterling service during that short period and who throughout set such an example of high morale and offensive spirit.

A TRIBUTE TO THE 9TH LANCERS, MIDDLE EAST, 1942

H.Q., 2ND ARMOURED BRIGADE,
MIDDLE EAST FORCES.
20th July, 1942.

MY DEAR GENERAL,

I am certain that you and your Regimental Association would like to know how magnificently the 9th Lancers fought under Ronald Macdonell.

The battle started for the 2nd Armoured Brigade on the 27th of May and the 9th Lancers were in the van. From the very start the skill of their commander and the utter determination of all ranks to close with the enemy tanks were most evident.

The third day of the battle was the culminating triumph to a series of short, sharp and well-conducted actions. The 29th of May will always be a memorable date in the annals of the Regiment.

All day they, together with the remainder of the Brigade, fought and held off the combined efforts of the 15th and 21st Panzer Divisions. Over a hundred German tanks were bearing down on our already depleted numbers from one direction, whilst seventy more advanced from another: the odds were over two to one. All day the Regiment fought, using its Crusader tanks with the greatest tactical skill and hitting the Germans hard with its Grant tanks.

By the fifth day the Regiment, which had fought brilliantly and continuously, was down to four tanks and I was compelled to relieve them.

The moment they were re-equipped they were back again and the story of their action in the Sidi Rezegh area, when serving under the 4th Armoured Brigade, will find a prominent place in your regimental history. Again in the Alamein area, the first day they were in action, they accounted for eleven German tanks.

It will be a long time before the detailed story of the battle can be written, but I felt I must write to you to let you know how very proud I have been to have had the Regiment under my command for so long, and to tell you how magnificently, down to the last trooper, they acquitted themselves when the real test came.

The Regiment has suffered, but it has inflicted many more casualties on the enemy.

I mourn for many good friends among the officers and men, but the way in which they died for their country and their Regiment will be an inspiration to all for years to come.

Yours very sincerely,

(Signed) RAYMOND BRIGGS.

(Brigadier R. Briggs, Commander, 2nd Armoured Brigade.)

To MAJOR-GENERAL C. W. NORMAN,
Colonel, 9th Queen's Royal Lancers.

2A

INDEX

INDEX OF PERSONS AND PLACES

The sketch shows the advances
of the Private Army consisting of the
9th Lancers and the 2nd London Irish Rifles
carried in the Kangaroos of the 4th Hussars
during the great offensive of April 1945
between the SANTERNO and the PO.

PRESENTED TO THE 9th LANCERS by the
2nd LONDON IRISH RIFLES in memory of a
very happy and successful union.

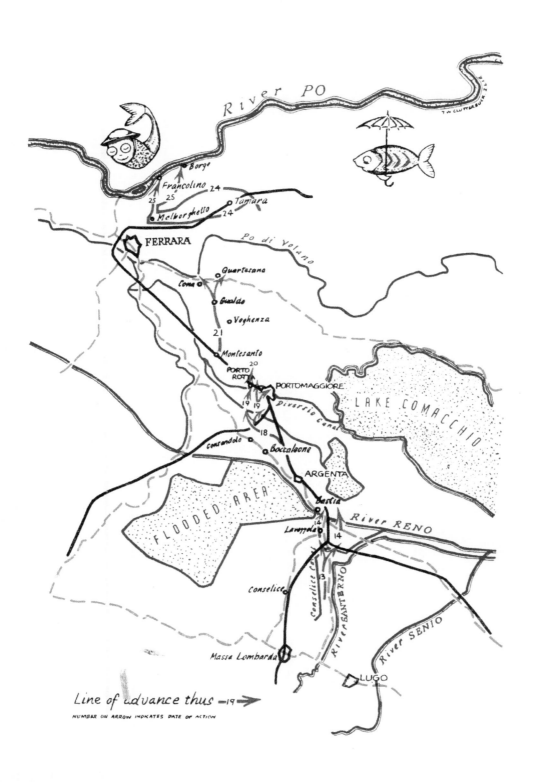

River PO

Borge
Francolino 24
25 25
Melborghetto Tamara 24

FERRARA

Po di Volano

Quartesana
Cona
Gualdo
Voghenza
21
Montesanto
20
PORTO ROTTA
PORTOMAGGIORE
19 19
Diversio Canal
LAKE COMACCHIO
18
Consandolo Boccaleone
ARGENTA
FLOODED AREA
Bastia
River RENO
14
Lavezzola
14
Conselice Canal
13
River SANTERNO
Conselice
River SENIO
Massa Lombarda
LUGO

Line of advance thus ─19→

NUMBER ON ARROW INDICATES DATE OF ACTION

9 781783 314959